ENCYCLOPEDIA OF ISLAM IN THE UNITED STATES

ENCYCLOPEDIA OF ISLAM IN THE UNITED STATES

VOLUME 2

Edited by Jocelyne Cesari

Greenwood Press
Westport, Connecticut · London

Library of Congress Cataloging-in-Publication Data

Encyclopedia of Islam in the United States / edited by Jocelyne Cesari.
    p. cm.
Includes bibliographical references and index.
ISBN-13: 978–0–313–33625–6 (set : alk. paper)
ISBN-13: 978–0–313–33626–3 (vol. 1 : alk. paper)
ISBN-13: 978–0–313–33627–0 (vol. 2 : alk. paper)
1. Islam—United States—Encyclopedias. 2. Muslims—United States—Encyclopedias. I. Cesari, Jocelyne.
BP67.U6E53 2007
297.0973'03—dc22   2007016142

British Library Cataloguing in Publication Data is available.

Library of Congress Catalog Card Number: 2007016142
ISBN-13: 978–0–313–33625–6 (set)
        978–0–313–33626–3 (vol. 1)
        978–0–313–33627–0 (vol. 2)

First published in 2007

Greenwood Press, 88 Post Road West, Westport, CT 06881
An imprint of Greenwood Publishing Group, Inc.
www.greenwood.com

Printed in the United States of America

∞™

The paper used in this book complies with the
Permanent Paper Standard issued by the National
Information Standards Organization (Z39.48–1984).

10 9 8 7 6 5 4 3 2 1

CONTENTS

PREFACE

The word *encyclopedia,* meaning a well-rounded education, comes from Classical Greek. The Center for Middle Eastern Studies at Harvard University is proud to have helped sponsor this encyclopedia, the aim of which is to provide general but also accurate and unbiased knowledge about Muslims in the Western world. It is published at a timely moment in our history. Not only is such knowledge required for a well-rounded education, it is necessary more than ever before to dispel stereotypes and correct factual errors concerning one of the world's fastest-growing religious groups. It is hoped that in a single work the scholarly as well as lay reader will be able to consult brief, concise, and clear articles on a host of topics—political, philosophical, historical, artistic, sociological—vital to understanding Muslims in the contemporary world.

To assure the highest standards of scholarship, Jocelyne Cesari, one of the leading experts on contemporary Muslim societies, was asked to be the volume's editor. She, along with a committee of expert advisors, compiled an exhaustive list of subjects to be included in the encyclopedia, commissioned articles on them by recognized scholars as well as advanced graduate student researchers, and carefully edited these to ensure accuracy of information, accessibility of writing, and consistency of form and presentation to avoid overlap or gaps. The contributors are, of course, ultimately responsible for their own opinions and interpretations, but wherever possible, the factual contents have been checked and double checked.

Acknowledgments

In addition to Jocelyne Cesari, without whose vision and hard work this encyclopedia would not have seen the light of day, I would also like to thank the following individuals whose assistance on this project was invaluable: Jon Heit, Christiaan James, Gwen McCarter, Martin Nguyen, Sam Prevatt, Aaron Spevack, and Emily Tucker.

Steven C. Caton,
Director
Center for Middle Eastern Studies
Harvard University

ALPHABETICAL LIST OF ENTRIES

LIST OF ENTRIES BY TOPIC

NOTE ON TRANSLITERATION

Transliteration of Arabic words into roman characters follows guidelines established by the *International Journal of Middle East Studies.* Where appropriate the singular or plural of the word has also been given and transliterated. Arabic technical terms commonly used in English have not been transliterated (e.g., ulema, shaykh, qadi, Sunni, suq, madrasa, etc.). Place names with accepted English spellings and personal names of prominent political leaders or cultural figures follow English norms (e.g., Gamal Abdul Nasser, Mecca).

ABOUT THE EDITOR

Jocelyne Cesari is a Research Associate in the Center for Middle Eastern Studies at Harvard University and also holds teaching positions in the Anthropology Department and the Harvard Divinity School, where she teaches on Islam in America and Global Islam. She is coordinating the Research Program on Islam in the West (www.fas.harvard.edu/~mideast/activities/islaminwest/index.html). She has published several books and articles in European and American journals. Her most recent books are *When Islam and Democracy Meet: Muslims in Europe and in the United States* (2004/2006) and *European Muslims and the Secular State* (2005). Her areas of expertise include Islam and globalization, Muslim minorities in Europe and the United States, and Islam and politics in North Africa. She has received grants to write the reports "Islam and Fundamental Rights" and "The Religious Consequences of September 11, 2001, on Muslims in Europe" for the European Commission (www.euro-islam.info).

INTRODUCTION

Even after September 11, 2001, Islam remains the fastest-growing religion in the United States. It is simultaneously the most poorly understood religion in the United States. Fundamental data and credible statistics are either missing or disputed. The study of Islam has been divided among multiple disciplines, such as politics, anthropology, and religious studies, each with its own methods and jargon. Scholarly approaches to Islam and Muslims have been further complicated by international factors, ranging from the "War on Terror" to globalized Islam itself. This encyclopedia is the first effort to synthesize the interdisciplinary study of Islam and American Muslims, drawing on sociology, anthropology, history, Islamic studies, religious studies, political science, and economics.

While the U.S. Census does not include questions on religious affiliation, the estimated size of the American Muslim population has been a contentious question in recent years, with figures ranging from two to eight million. In October 2001, a scholar at the University of Chicago concluded that only one percent of the population of the United States (that is, 1.9 to 2.8 million people) was Muslim.[1] Another 2001 study conducted by the American Religious Identification Survey yielded an estimate of 1.8 million. These findings sparked heated debate, especially after their republication by the American Jewish Committee, a group that was accused by some Muslim organizations of minimizing the importance of Islam in America. In May 2007, the Pew Research Center released polling data that estimated the number of American Muslims eighteen years old or older to be 1.4 million. This figure again generated much discussion regarding the actual size of the Muslim population in the United States.[2] The oft-cited figure of six or seven million American Muslims is based in part on immigration statistics regarding countries considered "Muslim," as well as statistics on the memberships of Islamic centers. Such methods are problematic: many immigrants from majority-Muslim countries are actually Christians, particularly those from the Arab world. Moreover, statistics acquired from Islamic centers are highly imprecise, since they commonly include not only members, but also all those associated with the centers.[3] A more reliable statistical approach is to ask questions about ancestry, which indicates a population of approximately four million American Muslims.[4]

Islam has grown through immigration and the high birthrates among immigrants, but not through these sources alone. The United States is unique among Western nations insofar as nearly half of its Muslim population (46 percent according to a 1994 estimate)[5] are converts, the majority of them African American. The remainder reflect a variety of geographic and ethnic backgrounds. Arabs are a distinct minority at just 12.45 percent of the U.S. Muslim population, and are outnumbered by groups from the Asian subcontinent (24.4 percent). Muslims from Africa, Iran, and Turkey represent, respectively, 6.2, 3.6, and 2.4 percent of the whole estimated Muslim population.[6]

The diversity of Muslim America also extends to matters of belief and practice, from the Sunni-Shi'a divide to further differences among such Shi'a groups as the Twelvers (to which most Iranians adhere) or the Nizari Isma'ilis (followers of the Aga Khan). Also present are faith groups whose Islamic identity is contested by mainstream Muslims, such as the Ahmadis and the Druzes. Sufis, whose charismatic Sunni and Shi'a leaders teach a mystical approach to Islam, are also represented. American Sufis tend to come from diverse backgrounds, and many are Euro-American converts.

The largest Muslim immigrant groups—Arab Muslims and South Asian Muslims—are quite demographically distinct from one another. Arab Americans hail from countries as diverse as Lebanon, Syria, Palestine, Egypt, Iraq, Jordan, and Morocco (and, in smaller numbers, from the other North African nations, Saudi Arabia, and the Gulf states). Arabs have immigrated to the United States since the late nineteenth century, although Christians comprised a majority of Arab immigrants until the 1960s. South Asian Americans, from India, Pakistan, Bangladesh, and Afghanistan, have primarily immigrated following the 1965 Immigration and Naturalization Act. While speakers of Arabic tend to hold positions as imams or clerics in mosques or schools, South Asians tend to have a higher socioeconomic profile and are arguably more privileged within American society.

Both converts and migrants have made the history of Muslims in America. African Americans figure prominently in the story of "indigenous" American Islam, which encompasses not only the Nation of Islam but also lesser known sects, along with artists and preachers, Sufis and mainstream Muslims, and Euro-American converts.

Voluntary Muslim immigration to the United States began in the nineteenth century. From 1875 to 1912, Muslim individuals and families fled economic hardship or political strife in the Middle East, particularly in the rural areas of what would become Syria, Jordan, Palestine, and Lebanon. Many of these immigrants settled in mid-sized American towns and found employment in mines and factories, or as merchants.

The second great wave of Muslim migration[7] occurred between 1918 and 1922, and a third followed over the course of the 1930s, as refugees fled the economic slowdown and political chaos caused by the First World War and the destruction of the Ottoman Empire. A fourth wave occurred after World War II, and included not only Muslims from the Middle East but also India, Pakistan, Turkey, and the Balkans. In contrast to previous groups of immigrants, these new arrivals were better educated and wealthier, hailing primarily from the urban centers of the Muslim world. This difference in socioeconomic status meant that they were better equipped, both culturally and in terms of education, to resist the assimilationist forces that had left preceding generations of Muslim immigrants all but invisible in American society.

The fifth wave of immigration began in 1965, during the presidency of Lyndon Johnson. The Johnson administration relaxed the quota policy that had strictly limited immigrants from many non-European countries, thereby allowing highly qualified Muslims from Africa and Asia to enter the United States in large numbers. This trend in immigration continued for decades: conservative pre–September 11th estimates put the number of immigrants arriving from the Middle East and Africa at 35,000 per year. Various political crises in the Muslim world caused spikes in migration, including the Six Day War of 1967, the Iranian Revolution of 1979, the Lebanese Civil War, unrest in Pakistan, and conflicts in Afghanistan, Bosnia, and Kosovo.

Despite the long-standing presence of Muslims in the United States, Islam's visibility in American society is a relatively recent phenomenon, a result of the religious dynamism of the two most recent waves of immigrants. The Muslim immigrants in the first part of the twentieth century were more concerned with defending secular ideologies than with promoting Islam. In this respect, Muslim immigrants reflected the dominance of such ideologies as nationalism and socialism in the public discourse of the Arab and Muslim worlds. Since the 1970s, however, the new arrivals, particularly those from the Indian subcontinent, have thrown themselves into religious activities of every kind: the construction of mosques and madrasas, the publication of religious literature, and lobbying efforts. The transnational Islamic revival has also raised the profile of Islam in America. In the 1990s, more than 2,300 Islamic institutions were counted in the United States, of which 1,500 were mosques or Islamic centers. In keeping with Islam's increasing prominence in the United States, an assessment of the status of Muslim minorities in a non-Muslim society is beginning to take shape.

The greater visibility of Islam after 1965 did not elicit hostility or surprise from American society. From the outset it was treated within the context of American inclusiveness and the framework of American civil religion. Islam did become an object of international attention as a result of the 1980 hostage crisis at the American Embassy in Tehran. In this case, however, a distinction was drawn between Muslims in the United States and Muslims abroad, a demarcation that had positive effects on the constructed identity of the American Muslim minority. Even the 1996 antiterrorism law did little to alter this state of affairs. However, the dissociation of domestic and international identities was profoundly altered by the events of September 11th. From that day, Muslims living on American soil have been the subjects of surveillance and scrutiny as part of the "Global War on Terror."

A primary result of such war measures as the USA PATRIOT Act has been the targeting of individuals defined as—or assumed to be—Muslim. In the United States, this takes the form of increased surveillance of immigrants and visitors coming from Muslim countries, racial profiling, and Department of Justice investigations of Muslims currently in the country. Such practices have heightened tensions between human rights and national security concerns, particularly in the field of immigration. The 2003 creation of the Department of Homeland Security, which combines 22 agencies and 180,000 workers from the fields of immigration, intelligence, counterterrorism, and foreign policy, has reinforced the link between immigration and international terrorism.

Tighter immigration policies are not the only consequence of September 11th for American Muslims. The designation of "foreign enemy," technically applicable only to those outside a country's borders, is beginning to be applied to certain domestic groups, such as Muslim students or religious leaders. The fight against terrorism has thus had significant consequences for Muslims living in America, as any activity related to Islam is potentially suspect and subject to surveillance. The primary reason for this generalized suspicion is the near-impossibility of differentiating between Islam as a religion and Islam as a political movement.

Understanding the conditions of Muslims in America therefore involves taking into account the political and cultural contexts in which Muslims have been living, from (at least) the civil rights movements of the 1960s to the present war, and demonstrating the effects of these contexts upon the identities, practices, and collective actions of Muslims. To this end, the influences of American culture and politics on Muslims are discussed in several entries in this work, as is the secularization of Islamic religion.

The creation of this encyclopedia presented a special challenge, for Islam in America is a young—and in some respects virtually nonexistent—field of research. This new field encounters two major issues. First, normative approaches to Islam often pervade studies on Muslims in America and lead to an essentialist bias. In this style of research, Islam appears as a set of decontextualized rules that define and constrain any Muslims at any given time. Most work on Muslims opens with a recapitulation of these rules, which include the five pillars of faith, dietary rules, and dress codes.[8] In addition to contributing to definitions of Islam as a fixed set of texts and practices through which an individual's self is denied, the normative approach exaggerates the role of Islamic doctrine in determining an individual's behavior.

Ultimately, normative approaches to Islam deemphasize the multiplicity and variability of Muslims' actual practices, and obscure ways of being Muslim that exceed the boundaries of orthodoxy. By the same token, they completely ignore the importance of the sociocultural context in which Muslims are living as they imagine and reinvent their relationships with the dogmas, rituals, and prescriptions of their traditions.

Second, some scholarly research on contemporary Islam has often fallen into the trap of presenting Muslims as exceptional because Islam itself is thought to bean an exceptional relationship to contemporary political turmoil from the Islamic Revolution of Iran to September 11th. Sociologists and political scientists who are not scholars of Islam are particularly prone to this bias. As a result, they often accept stereotypical assumptions about Islam, assuming, for example, that Islam is inseparable from politics, or that there is a necessary link between the Islamic message and violence. And yet, despite their popularity, characterizations of Islam as a religion of the sword that is necessarily in opposition against Western (i.e., Christian) civilization are not validated by serious historical analysis.[9] Nonetheless, ideologically biased assessments of Islam influence academic work, and scholars often assume that being Muslim does indeed constitute an extraordinary situation because Islam is taken to be antithetical or resistant to Western core political values.

Despite the fact that religion is not considered *a priori* to be a taboo subject in American scholarship, it is nonetheless ethnographic approaches and not religious studies that have dominated research on Muslims in the United States. Indeed, the extreme ethnic diversity of American Islam has encouraged a focus on localized ethnic communities, some of which have received more attention than others (e.g., the Arabs of Detroit or black Muslims).[10] Despite the existence of pioneering studies, there is a persistent lack of systematic comparison regarding how different ethnic groups diversify and adapt their religious practices to the American context.[11]

It should also be noted that an assimilation paradigm, which casts immigration as a process of trading one culture for another, has for some time dominated the study of Islam in America. The problem is that current debates in the sociology of immigration are now questioning this paradigm. New research advocates a pluralist approach to American society in order to account for how immigrants maintain or reinvent ethnic and clutural identities even as they adapt to their new context.[12] It is interesting to note that research in the sociology of immigration does not consider contemporary Islam and Muslims in the United States to be relevant to the discipline. Therefore, until recently, the topic of Islam in America has been the monopoly of specialists on Islam who are not well versed in the sociology of American immigration.

Finally, there are virtually no comparative studies of Islamic religiosity, and it is only recently that scholars have begun to examine religious practice.[13] Data on basic religious practices (such as prayer, fasting, dietary rules), or on cultural and political practices is not yet available. This challenge is exacerbated by the fact that Islam in America cannot be disconnected from the major trends of Islamic cultures and civilizations past and present, as indicated in numerous entries dealing with Sunnis, Shi'as, religious authorities, and fatwas, as well as with major religious, intellectual, and political figures from Ghazali to Qutb to Mawdudi to Qaradawi. It would be naïve to think that assimilation will disconnect Islam in America from the Muslim world at large. It would also be misleading to think that transnational influences are exclusively political (let alone political and radical). Multiple examples, from Sufism to the arts, demonstrate the broader cultural impact of transnational Islamic networks on Islam in the United States.

This unique and pioneering encyclopedia accordingly draws on religious, cultural, social, and political perspectives on Islam in America. It considers history, descriptions of religious practices, ideas, theories, portraits of major intellectual, religious, and political figures among American Muslims, and the influences of domestic and international politics.

The first volume examines the subject from such diverse perspectives as mentioned above. The second provides supporting primary documents, from fatwas and political declarations to excerpts from novels and songs. These reflect a wide range of positions and opinions as well as a wide range of ethnicities, cultures, and religious backgrounds. It is the hope of the editors that this encyclopedia will serve as a reference for further research, as well as a fundamental resource for educators, students, public officials, and citizens who want to learn about Islam in America.

Acknowledgments

All my gratitude goes to Steven Caton, Director of the Center for Middle Eastern Studies and Professor of Contemporary Arab Studies at Harvard University, who encouraged and supported this project from the beginning.

I would also like to thank all of my colleagues from Harvard University and other academic institutions who, as members of the advisory board, tirelessly read and reviewed all entries included in this publication.

All my thanks to Martin Nguyen (Harvard University), Aaron Spevack (Boston University), John Taylor Hebden (Harvard University), Jon Heit (Harvard University), Christiaan James (Harvard University), Gwen McCarter (Harvard University), Sam Prevatt (Harvard University), and Emily Tucker (Harvard University), whose hard work as editors was invaluable.

Notes

1. Tom W. Smith, *Estimating the Muslim Population in the United States* (New York: American Jewish Committee, October 2001).

2. Pew Research Center, "Muslim Americans: Middle Class and Mostly Mainstream" (Washington, DC: Pew Research Center, May 22, 2007).

3. Ihsan Bagby, P.M. Perl and B.T. Froehle, *The Mosque in America: A National Portrait* (Washington, DC: Council on American Islamic Relations, 2001).

4. Ilyas Ba-Yunus and M.M. Siddiqui, *A Report on the Muslim Population in the United States* (Richmond Hills: CAMRI, 1998).

5. Nick Galifianikis, "U.S. Muslim Population Grows," *Rockland Journal News,* February 10, 1994.

6. Ibid.

7. It should be noted that scholars of African American history have pointed out that the "five waves" account of Muslim presence in the United States externalizes Islam as an imported, modern phenomenon, when in fact Islam has played a continuous role in American history since before the civil war. More specifically, Islam has been a force in the African American community from the days of slavery, through the influential mid-twentieth century interpretations of Elijah Muhammad and Malcolm X, until the present day. See Sherman Jackson, *Islam and the Balckamerican: Looking Toward the Third Resurrection* (New York: Oxford University Press, 2005); Allan Austin, ed., *African Muslims in Antebellum America: A Sourcebook* (New York: Garland Publishing, 1984).

8. See, for example, Amina Mohammed-Arif, *Salaam America* (London: Anthem Press, 2002).

9. Roy Mottahedeh, "The Clash of Civilizations: An Islamicist's Critique," *Harvard Middle Eastern and Islamic Review* 2-2 (1995): 1–26.

10. For examples of this trend, see Muhammad-Arif, *Salaam America,* and Linda Walbridge, *Without Forgetting the Imam* (Detroit: Wayne State Unviersity Press, 1997), which, respectively, treat South Asian Muslims in New York City and Lebanese Muslims in Dearborn, Michigan.

11. See, for example, Yvonne Yazbeck Haddad and Adair Lummis, *Islamic Values in the United States* (New York: Oxford University Press, 1987).

12. Richard Alba, *Remaking the American Mainstream: Assimilation and Contemporary Immigration* (Cambridge, Massachusetts: Harvard University Press, 2003); Mary Waters, *The New Americans: A Guide to Immigration since 1965* (Cambridge, Massachusetts: Harvard University Press, 2007); Alejandro Portes, *Immigrant America: A Portrait* (1996; repr., Berkeley: University of California Press, 2006).

13. One recent exception is Rogaia Mustafa Abusharaf's study of Yemeni practice, "Structural Adaptations in an Immigrant Muslim Congregation in New York," which appears alongside pieces on the religious practices of other immigrant communities in Stephen Warner and Judith Wittner's edited volume, *Gatherings in Diaspora* (Philadelphia: Temple University Press, 1998).

CHRONOLOGY

1600	Slave trade begins bringing Muslims from Africa to North America.
1908	Large numbers of Muslims immigrants enter the United States from Syria, Lebanon, Jordan, Turkey, and Arab regions of the Ottoman Empire.
1913	Noble Drew founds the Moorish Science Temple of America (MSTA) in Newark, New Jersey.
1915	First Muslim place of worship in the United States is established by Albanian Muslims in Biddeford, Maine.
1919	First Islamic association is founded in Highland Park outside of Detroit, Michigan.
1920	The American Red Crescent is established in Detroit, modeling itself after the International Red Cross.
1924	Johnson-Reed Immigration Act places quotas on the number of immigrants allowed into the United States from any country.
1930	Wallace Fard Muhammad creates the Nation of Islam.
1952	Muslim members of the United States Armed Services are permitted to identify themselves as followers of Islam.
1957	Islamic Center of Washington, DC, opens.
1962	The Nation of Islam begins publishing its newspaper, *Muhammad Speaks*
1963	The Muslim Students Association (MSA) is founded at the University of Illinois in Urbana.
1964	Malcolm X makes the pilgrimage (*hajj*) to Mecca.
1965	Malcolm X is assassinated in New York.
1967	"Six Day War" in the Arab-Israel conflict takes place.
1971	The Islamic Circle of North America (ICNA) is established in New York.
1975	Elijah Muhammad dies. His son, Warith Deen Mohammed, begins to transform the Nation of Islam into a Sunni movement.
1979	Islamic Revolution begins in Iran.
1980	Louis Farrakhan reconstitutes the Nation of Islam.
1981	The Islamic Society of North America (ISNA) is created in Plainfield, Indiana. Ismail al-Faruqi, founder of American Muslim Social Scientists (AMSS) and the International Institute of Islamic Thought (IIIT), and his family are murdered near Philadelphia, Pennsylvania.
1986	The Fiqh Council of North America is established as a branch of ISNA.
1988	The Muslim Public Affairs Council (MPAC) is founded in Los Angeles.
1994	The Council on American-Islamic Relations (CAIR) is established in Washington, DC.
1995	Louis Farrakhan leads the Million Man March in Washington, DC.
1996	The first celebration of Eid al-Fitr at the White House is coordinated by First Lady Hillary Rodham Clinton.
September 11, 2001	Attacks on the World Trade Center in New York and the Pentagon in Virginia occur.

2001   The "War on Terror" begins.
                 The USA PATRIOT Act is enacted by the United States Congress.
                 Operation Enduring Freedom is launched in Afghanistan.
2003   United States leads an invasion of Iraq, deposing Saddam Hussein.
                 United States Senate passes a resolution condemning hate crimes against
                 Muslim Americans and other minorities, including Arab Americans.
2005   Amina Wadud leads the Friday prayer for a mixed-gender congregation in
                 New York.
2006   Ingrid Mattson is elected the first female President of ISNA.
                 Keith Ellison, from Minnesota's fifth district, is the first Muslim to be elected
                 to the U.S. Congress as a member of the House of Representatives.

PART I

RELIGIOUS LIFE OF MUSLIMS

This section highlights the diversity of religious practices and doctrinal positions among American Muslims. Interpretations of the Islamic tradition range from progressive approaches to traditionalism and extreme conservatism to reactionary attitudes. The range of ideas represented in this section reflects the diversity and tension in the debate about the content of the Islamic tradition across the Muslim world.

Currently, the dominant approach is to rely on the original sources, i.e., the Quran and sunna, to provide new interpretations. This emphasis on Quran and hadith can on one hand trigger very defensive positions (such as the one held by the *Salafis*) especially on culture, education, sexuality, gender, and the relationship to the West; on the other hand, this same approach can also stimulate more modernist attitudes. The integration of Muslims within Western democracies has provoked reflection on the jurisprudence of minorities (*fiqh al-aqaliyya*) as illustrated by Dr. Taha Alalwani. We are also witnessing a revival of the *madhāhib* (traditional schools of jurisprudence) through the current work of scholars like Nuh Ha Mim Keller and Hamza Yusuf. Equally diverse are the religious practices drawn from these different interpretations, from prayers to dress code to gender segregation to dietary rules. This variety represents the attempts by American Muslims to redefine Islamic religiosity in the secular American context despite an extreme politicized international context, one where Islam is often reduced—by both Muslims and non-Muslims—to a political slogan.

Section A: Doctrines and Interpretations of Islam

1. **"PMU Statement of Principles" from** *The Progressive Muslim Union of North America*

From the Progressive Muslim Union of North America web site, available online: http:// www.pmuna.org/. Accessed May 4, 2006.

In 2003, several Muslim intellectuals and activists created the Progressive Muslim Union of North America (PMU). They participated in the publication of an edited volume (Progressive Muslims: On Justice, Gender, and Pluralism) that is considered to be the movement's manifesto. While the support of the movement is difficult to gauge, it undoubtedly represents a trend among American Muslims who are born and/or educated in the United States. The following "PMU Statement of Principles" is posted on the PMU web site: http://www.pmuna.org/.

The Progressive Muslim Union of North America (PMU) is a grassroots organization that aims to provide a forum, voice, and organizing mechanism to North American Muslims who wish to pursue a progressive intellectual, social and political agenda.
Our work is guided by the following principles:

1) We affirm that a Muslim is anyone who identifies herself or himself as "Muslim," including those whose identification is based on social commitments and cultural heritage.

2) We affirm the importance of celebrating the arts, culture, and the pursuit of joy in our daily lives. We believe the restrictions imposed by some on instrumental music and the depiction of human forms in paintings and sculpture contravene the rich Muslim cultural heritage from around the globe.

3) We affirm the validity of Islamic ritual and practice as an expression of love for God, while acknowledging that specific forms of ritual and practice are individual choices and should never be imposed through coercive means.

4) We affirm the equal status and equal worth of all human beings, regardless of religion, gender, race, ethnicity, or sexual orientation. We oppose any restrictions on women's full participation in society and believe that separation and segregation of men and women is contrary to the equity among genders enshrined in the Quran. We endorse the human rights and liberties of lesbian, gay, bisexual and trans-sexual individuals. We believe that Muslim women and men, gay and straight, of all nationalities, ethnicities, and races should work together, shoulder-to-shoulder, in their effort to rejuvenate our community.

5) We affirm that justice and compassion should be the guiding principles for all aspects of human conduct. Islam holds that these qualities are characteristics of God as revealed in the holy Quran, divine qualities that are the ethical virtues to which all human beings should aspire to emulate.

6) We affirm our commitment to social and economic justice and our opposition to the culture of militarism and violence. We will support efforts for universal health care, public education, the protection of our environment, and the eradication of poverty around the world.

7) We reject the authoritarian, racist, sexist and homophobic interpretations of our faith as antithetical to the principles of justice and compassion.

8) We affirm the diversity of inspirations that motivate people to embrace a commitment to justice and compassion, including a profound faith rooted in religious traditions, ethical imperatives developed throughout the centuries, and secular and humanist values shared by many Muslims today.

9) We call for critical inquiry and dynamic engagement with Islamic scripture, early Muslim sources, the Islamic intellectual heritage, and traditional and current Muslim discourses.

10) We endorse the separation of religion and state in all matters of public policy, not only in North America, but also across the Muslim world. We believe that secular government is the only way to achieve the Islamic ideal of freedom from compulsion in matters of faith and that the separation of religion and state is a necessary pre-requisite to building democratic societies, where religious, ethnic, and racial minorities are accepted as equal citizens enjoying full dignity and human rights enunciated in the 1948 UN Declaration of Universal Human Rights.

11) We recognize the growing danger of religious extremism and view the politicization of religion and the intrusion of religion into politics as twin threats to civil society and humane civilization. We vow to resist the intrusion of religion into politics and the exploitation of religion for political ends.

12) Recognizing our participation in the broader human family, we seek to engage with and contribute to other philosophical and spiritual traditions and progressive movements.

Copyright 2004 Progressive Muslim Union of North America

2. Hussein Abdulwaheed Amin, "Mission Statement" from *IslamForToday.com*

From IslamForToday.com web site, accessed May 4, 2006. Available online: http://www.islamfortoday.com/about.htm.

Hussein Abdulwaheed Amin was born in Ireland and grew up Catholic. In October 1998, at the age of 31, he converted to Islam and subsequently created IslamForToday.com as a resource for individuals from the West who are thinking of converting to Islam or are recent converts. Consequently, it provides basic information on the Islamic tradition that may be helpful to converts and second generation immigrants.

Welcome to IslamForToday.com, an Internet home for theologically motivated Western converts to Islam and a source of information for non-Muslims seeking a knowledge and understanding of Islam.

This site was founded by a Western former Christian who converted to Islam. It began life under the name *Understanding Islam (tripod)* as a small collection of practical and theological information about Islam compiled principally for the benefit of other new Muslims. It has since expanded greatly and now comprises a considerable body of knowledge—features and links about Muslim history and civilization, Islam in the West today, the rights of women in Islam plus Muslim schools and family life. While a much wider audience will now also find many of the articles of interest, the primary purpose of this site is to be a resource for Western converts to Islam and those considering becoming Muslim.

The basis of any religion is theology—do you believe in the existence of God and if so, what do you believe about Him? The core of Islam is belief in God and, specifically, belief in the Oneness of God as opposed to polytheism (belief in Many gods) or the Christian belief of three persons in one god (trinity). But very often today the spiritual essence of Islam gets buried under the weight of "political Islam", upheavals involving Muslims in the Middle East and elsewhere, and cultural baggage brought from the "old country" by Muslim immigrants to the West. These can distract from Islamic belief and harm the spread of the religion of Islam.

I consider it essential to make a clear distinction between, on the one hand, the theology and religion of Islam and, on the other, politics and terrorism involving Muslims who sometimes swathe their local culture or regional geopolitical concerns in the cloak of Islam. Many born Muslims both overseas and among immigrant communities in the West conspicuously fail to differentiate between these.

In his introduction to the book *Four Basic Quranic Terms* by Syed Abul-Ala Maududi, the publisher explains how the writer devoted himself "mainly to the fundamentals, trying to scrub away the centuries old crusts which had dimmed the true Islamic concepts and to remove the misunderstandings that have spread gradually regarding the basic principles and purpose of Islam." This site shares that ethos and those aims. IslamForToday.com strives to focus on the *religion* of Islam.

Islam—peace through submission to God—is universal and available not just to Arabs and south Asians but to everyone regardless of race or country of origin. Islam is not an ethnic culture. It is a religion, a set of theological beliefs which have taken root across many cultures and countries from the eastern Atlantic to the South China Sea. *IslamForToday. com* aims to show how Islam can be equally relevant to life in the West today by focusing on the theological and spiritual and offering practical, daily-life guidance to converts to Islam in countries where Islam is not usually associated with the indigenous population.

In addition, since the awful events of September 11, 2001 a further dimension has been added to the work of this site, namely to tackle extremism amongst Muslims and the politicization of Islam through giving a platform to mainstream, moderate Muslims who are calling us back to what God in the Quran has commanded us to be—a "middle nation" (2:143) which does not "transgress limits" (2:190).
Please remember the *Islam For Today* team in your prayers (dua).

Wasalaam,
Hussein Abdulwaheed Amin
Founding Publisher and Editor

3. "Our Mission" from *MuslimWakeup.com*

From Muslimwakeup.com, accessed May 5, 2006. Available online: http://www.
muslimwakeup.com/info/.

Ahmed Nassef and Jawad Ali, graduates from the University of California in Los Angeles
(UCLA), created the Muslim Wakeup! web site in January 2003. Muslim WakeUp! first
appeared as a group of individuals in Los Angeles, California, in the late 1980s. The group
identified itself as uniting against all forms of oppression. Muslim WakeUp! is best known for
its central role in organizing and publicizing the first mixed-gender Friday Jum'a prayer led
by a woman, Amina Wadud, on Friday March 18, 2005.

Muslim WakeUp! seeks to bring together Muslims and non-Muslims in America and
around the globe in efforts that celebrate cultural and spiritual diversity, tolerance, and
understanding. Through online and offline media, events, and community activities,
Muslim WakeUp! champions an interpretation of Islam that celebrates the Oneness of
God and the Unity of God's creation through the encouragement of the human creative
spirit and the free exchange of ideas, in an atmosphere that is filled with compassion
and free of intimidation, authoritarianism, and dogmatism. In all its activities, Muslim
WakeUp! attempts to reflect a deep belief in justice and against all forms of oppression,
bigotry, sexism, and racism.

4. "The Assembly of Muslim Jurists in America: Mission Statement" from
The Assembly of Muslim Jurists in America

From The Assembly of Muslim Jurists in America, accessed online May 4, 2006. Available
online: http://www.amjaonline.com/English/aboutus.asp.

The Assembly of Muslim Jurists in America is an organization of specialists of traditional
Islamic Sciences (e.g., Fiqh, Hadith) who focus on Muslim life in America. AMJA is comprised
of a seven-member committee based in Folsom, California as well as an international office
in Cairo, Egypt. The members of the Permanent Committee for Fatwa are Salah Al Sawy
(Professor of Jurisprudence at Al Azhar Universities, Umm Al Qura, the Institute of Islamic
and Arabic Sciences in Washington, Vice-President of the American Open University),
Dr. Al Hussein Shuwatt (Professor of Hadith Sciences at the American Open University,
Virginia), Youssof Al Shabbily (Professor of Jurisprudence at the Institute of Islamic and Arabic
Sciences, Virginia), Farouk Al Samora'y (Head of Islamic Studies Department at the Institute
of Islamic and Arab Sciences in Virginia), Ahmad Al Sowe'y Shalbiq (Professor of Islamic
Jurisprudence at the American Open University in Virginia, Imam and orator of Al Janna
(Paradise) Mosque in Columbus, Georgia), Sahib Hassan Abd Al Ghaffar (Secretary of Islamic
Legislative Council, Chairman of the Assembly of the Holy Qur'an in Britain), and Sayed Abd
Al Aziz Al Sily (Professor of Creed at Al Azhar University and the American Open University
in Washington). AMJA jurists write opinions on specific matters of life in the United States
(e.g., using American banks and mortgages, appropriate dress, and living in a non-Muslim
society). The office in California writes and posts responses online to questions submitted
through the AMJA web site. On particularly complex issues, the California office will consult
with the AMJA office in Cairo. AMJA maintains a "fatwa bank" online that contains previous
declarations on all facets of life pertaining to Islam in the West.

The Assembly of Muslim Jurists in America (AMJA) is a non-for-profit *tax exempt*
scientific organization comprising of a select group of Muslim jurists and scholars, seeking

to manifest and clarify the rulings of *Shar'iah* (Islamic Law) concerning issues and events affecting Muslims residing in the US.

AMJA GOALS

Issuing *fatawa* (religious formal opinions or rulings) pertaining to the cases and queries submitted to the Assembly according to the rulings of *Shari'ah*.

Setting a plan for conducting lawful researches and studies on the circumstances of Muslims in the American society and the economic, social, intellectual, and educational problems Muslims recently face in such a community so as AMJA manifests their suitable juristic solutions and supervise their application.

Scrutinizing and analyzing what is published on Islam and its heritage in the media to rectify and make the best use of the authentic opinions included within it or follow up its mistakes to correct and reply.

Giving hand to Islamic financial institutions by means of conducting researches and studies, innovating forms of financing and investment contracts, and present *fatawa* and consultations these institutions ask for, in addition to training their personnel on these matters.

Holding training courses for the Imams and directors of Islamic centers in all juristic fields such as issues of family, finance, and legitimate judging, etc.

Supporting collaboration between AMJA and other juristic organizations and assemblies so as to reach what seems to be universal consensus on compulsory issues and postulates of the Islamic nation.

Handling the issue of citizenship with the rights and duties it imposes on Muslims enjoying citizenship in the West.

Supporting the activities of legitimate judging committees held by Islamic communities in Western countries, in addition to revising their decisions and recommendations, as well as setting a simplified codification on the matters of families and financial dealings so as to constitute a reference to the established judging bodies in the West.

Establishing the AMJA fund for *Zakah* (poor-due) and social joint liability, within the limits allowed by the rules and regulations in addition to getting the approval of the authorities responsible for that.

AMJA DISTINCTIVE FEATURES

Specialization: All AMJA members are holders of Ph.D. in Islamic *Shari'ah*.

Neutrality: AMJA is owned by the whole Islamic nation and is a general joint scientific forum where all activists working for Allah's religion all over the world meet away from factional coalitions or current organizational groups.

Combining between knowledge of *Shari'ah* and recognition of the reality. Like jurists, AMJA comprises an equal number of experts who enable jurists to deeply discern the reality where *fatawa* apply; "*a fatwa*" as scholars say is the knowledge of necessity in the reality. Juristic assemblies all over the world scrutinize medical issues like the transplant of body organs, human-made fertilization and human cloning, etc. However nobody says that the jurist is necessarily to be a physician so as to able to give a *fatwa* on these issues, but it is enough for him to know all details of such matters through those experts related to such assemblies; albeit those experts do not participate in the vote of deciding a juristic opinion.

Among those experts are professional experienced members like economists, lawyers, politicians, information officials, and those who are field-experienced members like

Imams and directors of Islamic centers or those who work in the Islamic financial and information institutions, etc.

The availability of a seven-*Shari'ah* Ph.D. holder-permanent committee for *fatwa*-giving, residing in the US and responsible for presenting answers to daily issues submitted to the AMJA and unanimously issuing its decision.

The availability of a committee of *fatwa*-consultants consisting of eight prominent *fatwa*-givers in the Islamic nation to which the permanent committee has recourse in need, using the highest international communication technologies including Emails and AMJA website on the internet that make contacting those in Tokyo as fast as those in Washington.

The availability of a close link between AMJA and other preceding assemblies; where the base is the coordination as well as the integration and not competition, discordance, or contradiction. Thus the membership in AMJA is available for the members of other assemblies with whom the provisions of AMJA membership correspond as shown by the main system of the Assembly. AMJA constitutes an additional power for the existing efforts; in a way of establishing coordination, combination, among them as well as enforcing the link among them on one hand and with the jurists of the Islamic nation all over the world on the other.

HOW CAN A *FATWA* BE GIVEN TO THE U.S. BY SOMEONE WHO HAS NO CONTACT WITH THE AMERICAN REALITY?

This question has been answered before; AMJA is held responsible—from the first moment—for the base that *fatwa*-givers should combine knowledge of *Shari'ah*, and recognition of the reality. "A Fatwa"—as scholars say—is the knowledge of necessity in the reality; this could be accomplished through what is previously referred to namely; the availability of a number of experts—not less than jurists at AMJA—representing the eye of AMJA by which reality is seen and several of its aspects is known. Juristic assemblies all over the world scrutinize medical issues like the transplant of body organs, human-made fertilization and human cloning, etc. However nobody says that the jurist is to be necessarily a physician so as to able to give a *fatwa* on these issues, but it is enough for him to know all details of such matters through those experts related to such assemblies;

HOW CAN AMJA—WHOSE MEMBERS ARE SPREAD ALL OVER THE WORLD—GIVE *FATWA* ON EVENTS OF THE AMERICAN SOCEITY?

Through the highest international communication technologies including Emails and AMJA website on the internet that make contacting those in Tokyo as fast as those in Washington.

5. **Salah Al-Sawy, "The Assembly of Muslim Jurists in America Fatwa Against the Danish Media and Government over the Cartoon Crisis" from** *The Assembly of Muslim Jurists in America*

From The Assembly of Muslim Jurists in America, accessed online May 4, 2006. Reprinted with permission of The Assembly of Muslim Jurists in America. Available online: http://www.amjaonline.com/English/headline.asp?Headid=98.

The Assembly of Muslim Jurists in America (AMJA; see The Assembly of Muslim Jurists in America: Mission Statement, preface to Primary document 4) issued the following fatwa in response to the Cartoon Crisis in the winter of 2005 in which Jylland-Posten, a Danish newspaper, published caricatures of the Prophet Muhammad. While representing the Prophet may be considered a sin by some Sunni Muslims, the cartoons grew into a controversy due to the negativity of the images, in particular one cartoon that depicted the Prophet's turban as a bomb. The AMJA fatwa expresses its "utmost concern, sheer resentment, and complete anger" with the Danish media for the event.

AMJA Statement on Crime of the Danish media insulting and defaming The Character of Prophet Muhammad Prayers and peace of Allah be upon him. In the name of Allah the Beneficent the Merciful

The Assembly of Muslim Jurists in America (AMJA) follows up with utmost concern, sheer resentment, and complete anger, what some of the Danish media have published of caricatures aiming at insulting and defaming the character of Prophet Muhammad, prayers and peace of Allah be upon him. This foolish conduct reflects sheer ignorance of the biography of the greatest human being that ever existed on earth for all time, and what have been followed of ignoring by the Danish authorities towards scores of official and public calls from Islamic agencies and concerned institutions for interfering with those who misbehaved, and asking them to prevent such atrocities and bring to justice those responsible, and what have happened as escalations and consequences, and what will be followed with insistence on ignoring these calls, that would be difficult to foresee!

AMJA, from its headquarters in USA, and in the name of hundreds of Islamic centers which comprise tens of thousands of immigrant Muslims, who are stunned and angered by these news, calls upon all official authorities in the Danish government to listen to the voice of reason, and realize that keeping adamant on committing such misconduct, would represent a declaration of war upon 1.3 Billions of Muslims allover the world, who worship Allah with the love of His kind Prophet Muhammad, prayers and peace of Allah be upon him, a love that surpasses the love for themselves and for their parents, their spouses, children and clans, and see in defending his honor and dignity a debt that they are ready to sacrifice for with their own lives, properties and the best of what they possess. Listening to the voice of reason and wisdom, would save the world as a whole in general, and their country in particular, tensions, woes and worries that would double its miseries and triple its ruptured concerns, and that would make it difficult to foretell its dimensions or control its consequences!

It also call upon them to learn from history, and celebrate the memory of their forefathers, the czars who honored the message of Prophet Muhammad, prayers and peace of Allah be upon him, and his messenger to them, when he came to them and confirmed their rules and affirmed their sovereignties, and that they should remember how those who insulted his message and scorned his messenger, from the emperors, were destroyed and vanished, and that they should value what all the world charters have agreed upon of respecting privacies, and protecting sanctities, on top of which is respecting the sanctity of Prophets and Messengers of Allah, who are the best of Allah's men and the noblest of His worshippers, and not to violate and insult them, on the pretext of freedom of thinking and freedom of expression, because, freedom—as conceived by the world sages—does not mean chaos and transgression on others. If freedom is stripped off its responsibility, it would become an uncontrollable tsunami that would drown all humanity in a flood of havoc and destruction. These are basic notions that must not be ignored or renounced by any judiciary or political system, whatsoever!

It also calls upon them to honor themselves with reading the biography of the Last of the Prophets, Prophet Muhammad, prayers and peace of Allah be upon him, from its genuine and neutral sources to know the extent of glory and grandeur that encompass the personality of this Noble Prophet, prayers and peace of Allah be upon him, and realize the bliss and bounty his mission have communicated to humanity, and what the world have lost with ignoring and insulting this unique character!

Is not it abominable and falsity to depict him in these drawings as a warlord of aggression and transgression, when they caricatured him in a disfigured character that his turban is transformed into a bomb, which a vile and unjust signal to that falsity?! All just and fair sages of the world have admitted that he was a mercy to mankind, as Allah says: "We sent thee not, but as a Mercy for all creatures", (Quran, 21:107). He never revenged for himself unless when sanctity of Allah is insulted, and he would sacrifice his life to revenge only for this cause. It is he that Allah has made him control his opponents at the Day of Capturing Makkah, after they have bitterly fought him and encouraged others to fight and insult him during his mission time, and he said to them: "Go! You are free!", (Reported by Bayhaqui in his Al-Sunan Al-Kubra), and it is he who declared to mankind that being fair and just is the main purpose of the missions of all messengers and prophets of Allah, as He says: "We sent aforetime Our apostles with Clear Signs and sent down with them the Book and the Balance (of Right and Wrong), that men may stand forth in justice; and we sent down Iron, in which is (material for) mighty war, as well as many benefits for mankind, that God may test who it is that will help, Unseen, Him and His apostles: for God is Full of Strength, Exalted in Might (and able to enforce His Will)", (Quran, 57:25). It is he who vowed to fight bitterly oppression and declared to the whole world Allah's saying: "And whoever among you does wrong, Him shall We cause to taste of a grievous Penalty", (Quran, 25:19). And he declared that the call of the oppressed people, Allah raises it over the clouds and says to it: "By My Might and Majesty! I will make you victorious even if after a while", (Reported by Al-Termizi). He also showed that there is not a more worthy thing than hastening the punishment in this worldly life of those who commit transgression and disconnecting family ties (Referred to a Hadith reported by Al-Termizi). It is he who, if he is given to choose between two things, he would always opt for the easiest and the simplest, unless it is a sin, and if it is so, he would be the furthest from it. It is he who used to keep his promise with his opponents in religion, and it is he who declared that he would be the opponent of those who oppressed and transgressed them on the Day of Judgment, and he made this as a permanent vow with his Muslim Ummah that still resounds at all time and in all places, where he says: "Whosoever oppresses, detracts from, overburdens, or takes by coercion from a covenanter, I am his opponent on the day of Judgment", (Reported by Abou-Dawoud and corrected by Al-Albani). It is he who tripled vowed to retaliate against those who attack the sanctity of the covenanters' blood, as when he says: "Whosoever kills a covenanter he shall never smell the perfume of Paradise whose aroma is detected from a forty years march distance", (Reported by Al-Bukhari in his Sahih). It is he who orders people to reach out for their families, even if they are non-Muslims, as Allah says: "But if they strive to make thee join in worship with Me things of which thou hast no knowledge, obey them not; yet bear them company in this life with justice (and consideration), and follow the way of those who turn to Me (in love): In the End the return of you all is to Me, and I will tell you the truth (and meaning) of all that ye did", (Quran, 31:15), and as he said to Asmaa Bent Abi-Bakr, may Allah be content with them, when her mother, who was a non-Muslim, came to reach out for her: "Reach out for your mother". It is he who kept during his lifetime on calling all people without distinction or discrimination, as well as the same people of Makkah who badly tortured him and his companions, by praying to Allah:

"O, Allah! Please, forgive my people, for they do not know", and as he called for the tribes of Dous and Thaqeef and others, he also called for the Jews who were pretending to be sneezing so that he would say to them, as a sign of good manners of Islam: "May Allah rightly guide you and give you peace of mind", (Reported by Abou-Dawoud and Al-Termizi), etc. It is he who never fought a war except to fend off aggression and transgression, and the total persons who were killed in the wars he was involved with, in both parties, did not exceed a one thousand lives, whereas the toll victims of the two world wars exceeded millions of innocent lives! As a reminder, the Crusaders killed more than 70,000 innocent Muslim lives in their aggression when they just invaded Jerusalem!

We would like to assure the Danish people and government, and the whole world as well, that Allah will make His Prophet Muhammad, prayers and peace of Allah be upon him, victorious and prevailing, and that He surely will dismember those who are hostile to him, for Allah says: "For he who hateth thee, He will be cut off (from Future Hope", (Quran, 108:3), and He said in the Divine Hadith: "Whosoever takes any of My Saints as enemies, I declare war on him", (Reported by Al-Bukhari in his Sahih), now, how about those who insult and defame the Master of Saints and the Imam of Prophets and Messengers of Allah?! History is the best teacher. Allah has disrupted and destroyed all those who ridiculed and mocked him, past and present, and made them an example for those who sympathize with them! And his life story remains clean and clear, and as a lighthouse for the whole world, that embodies purity and nobility in its highest esteem and most elevated supreme, and it renders as a lifesaver for all who wish to abandon the hellfire of libertine and luscious lust, and their souls look forward to winning the eternal bliss of Paradise in the Hereafter.

The contemporary world that mad materialism and tempting atheistic calls have made it more miserable, is in dire need to a gleam of light that shines from the sincerity and honesty of the universality of the mission of Prophet Muhammad, prayers and peace of Allah be upon him, whose light and security have reached all corners of the world, and under its shadows, humanity have enjoyed full welfare and peace. The world today, while suffering under the burdens of these contemporary catastrophes, and being distressed of woes and worries as a result of world disputes, is looking forward, from right and from left, that it may find a saver and a savior, and would predict and imagine noble characteristics and genuine features that did not and will never apply on anybody except on that savior who is this kind prophet, Muhammad, prayers and peace of Allah be upon him, who came with revelations of guidance and mercy to all creatures! So, do not submit your minds to falsehoods and lies, and do not deprive yourselves and your people the honor being acquainted to this kind prophet, prayers and peace of Allah be upon him, and consider well what he came forth with, i.e. the Noble Quran and Purified Sunnah.

And if you refuse, at least prevent your irresponsible and insolent crooks and make them stop insulting the honorable character of Prophets and Messengers of Allah, for this misconduct reflects foolishness and ignorance, and show malice and hatred towards others!!

General-Secretary Dr. Salah Al-Sawy

6. Imam Zaid Shakir, "Clash of the Uncivilized: Insights on the Cartoon Controversy" from *The Zaytuna Institute*

From The Zaytuna Institute, accessed May 9, 2006. Reprinted with permission of the Zaytuna Institute.

Imam Zaid Shakir was born in Berkeley, California in 1956. He converted to Islam in 1977 while serving in the United States Air Force. Imam Shakir was educated in classical Islamic sciences at Abu Noor University in Syria, graduating in 2001. In 2003, he moved to Hayward, California in order to lecture and teach at the Zaytuna Institute. He published the following article on February 7, 2006 on his web site in reaction to the cartoon crisis in the winter of 2005 in which a Danish newspaper, Jylland-Posten, published caricatures of the Prophet Muhammad. While Shakir understands Muslims' anger and offense at the drawings, he strongly condemns the violence and hysteria of the Muslim world's response.

As the crisis that has emerged in the aftermath of the publication of the infamous cartoons that claim to depict the Prophet Muhammad, peace and blessings of God upon him, escalates, we would do well by stepping back and attempting to analyze the situation as dispassionately as possible. By doing so, as Muslims, we can hopefully formulate a more productive and meaningful response, and avoid being exploited by either side in the ongoing conflict. Saying this, I do not mean to imply that Muslims are not justifiably angry over the caricatures. However, I would agree with those who argue that responses that involve wild outbreaks of frenzied violence are inappropriate, and they only affirm what the cartoonist is trying to imply. Namely, that Islam is a religion that encourages obscurantist violence and terrorism.

The current crisis shows the extent we Muslims are vulnerable to media manipulation, superficial shows of piety, and counterproductive one-upmanship militancy. If we start with the issue of media manipulation, it is clear that Western and Eastern media outlets played a large role in stirring up Muslim, and now Western sentiments. When the crisis initially broke in September, it was barely a blip on the media radar. Few outside of Denmark even knew of the cartoons. The Danish Muslim community, appropriately, by and large ignored the story. [1] It was only after a campaign undertaken by a delegation of Danish Muslim community activists to stimulate greater interest in the issue that the crisis reached the proportions we are currently witnessing. These activists traveled throughout the Muslim East trying to draw attention to the issue. When the issue was popularized by *Iqra* and other Arab satellite channels, and the cartoons were reprinted by several European papers, the crisis deepened. In light of that reality, it would be hard to deny the role the media has played in sparking and now perpetuating the crisis.

A question we must ask is if these cartoons, which are an example of hundreds of other anti-Islamic slights occurring daily in Europe and America, were not brought to the attention of Muslims by the media, would we be undergoing the current brouhaha?—Clearly not. That being the case, what does this say about our strategic vision? What does this say about our level of political maturity? And what does it say about our ability to engage in meaningful proactive work? The answers to these questions are obvious. We get angry about Israeli troops breaking the bones of Palestinian children, as long as it is in the media. When it disappears from our television screens, our interest vanishes with it. We raise millions of dollars for those affected by the Tsunami, as long as the images of death and destruction are beamed into our homes by the media. However, when the coverage shifts to other issues, the donations dry up. As for those crises that do not make the news in a big way, such as the ongoing famines in Mali, Niger, and the Horn of Africa, we are hardly stirred to action.

Furthermore, we go on living our lives oblivious to the ongoing abuse of Islam and our Prophet, peace and blessing of God upon him, until it becomes a major media event. At that point based on urgings issued by parties, the origins of their dubious agendas unknown to us, we are expected to drop everything and hastily rush into the fray. In many instances, our ill-conceived actions only make the situation worse.

Sometimes, those actions may constitute superficial shows of piety emanating from the mob hysteria underlying them. In the mob we are empowered, and find it easy to confront our opponents, defy the rule of law, behave with wanton abandon, or engage in other acts which under the proper circumstances we may view as supporting Islam. In terms of more constructive mass actions, such as emerging into the streets by the tens of thousands to protest the brutal, authoritarian regimes that make a mockery of the prophetic ideals of justice, mutual consultation, and service to the oppressed and downtrodden of society, we come up terribly short. Similarly, there are no credible grassroots efforts towards forming effective anti-defamation organizations to bring constructive legal action against transgressing organizations and individuals, on a fulltime, proactive basis. As individuals, we find it difficult to support the Prophet, peace and blessings of God upon him, by adorning ourselves with his lofty character traits, or reviving His Sunnah in our daily lives.

On the other hand, as mentioned above, it is all too easy to get swept up into the mob hysteria generated by the crowd, and then engage in outrageous actions that only affirm the offensive claims of the transgressing cartoonist. It is as if we are saying, "We'll show the *Kafirs* our Prophet, peace upon him was no terrorist! We'll defame the symbols of their religion [2] burn their embassies, murder their unsuspecting innocents, and behead the bloody cartoonist if we get our hands on him." [3]

This brings us to my third point, that of counterproductive, one-upmanship militancy. It is during these crises that all Muslims are supposed to drop everything and join the latest "Jihad" fad. Those of us who urge restraint are mocked as not being militant enough, or ridiculed as cowards who are afraid to "stand up to the real enemies of Islam." No differences in understanding, interpretation, or strategy are allowed, because there is only one correct approach, the one stumbled upon with the aid of modern, sensationalizing media.

Such a reactive, haphazard approach is counterproductive for a number of reasons. First of all, it destroys the basis for proactive work based on the existence of a strategic vision. As long as the enemies of Islam know that they can mobilize the Muslims to chase after an unimaginable number of distracting issues, divide our ranks by those issues, and diffuse our energies through their debate and the pursuit of their resolution, they will possess a trump card that will affect our ability to unite and work more effectively towards creating and implementing an agenda capable of effecting meaningful change in our circumstance. It also blinds us to the underlying agenda that reckless spontaneous action might be unwittingly serving.

For example, it is interesting that these events have come to a head in the immediate aftermath of the stunning landslide victory of Hamas in the Palestinian elections. That victory has rekindled, both in the East and the West, the debate around the implications of supporting democratization in the Muslim world when the biggest winners will be Islamic parties and movements. There are secularists in both the West and the Muslim world who advocate ending the democratizing experiment on that basis. However, they know that denying the democratic will of the Muslim peoples cannot be done without the support of the masses of people in Europe and America. These masses, especially in Britain and America, are increasingly wary of their governments' nefarious agenda for the Middle East. However, the frightening images of crazed crowds rampaging, looting, and burning provides a powerful justification for the extreme, repressive policies being advocated by the far right for dealing with Islam and Muslims, both domestically, and internationally.

Democracy in the Muslim world, they argue, will bring the advocates of mob rule to power.

If brutal draconian measures, such as those employed to end the democratization process in Algeria in the early 1990s, are employed elsewhere, the Western public will be psychologically prepared to accept those measures, because of the fear that has been created around the "Islamic" alternative. That fear can not only be used to justify denying the democratic will of the Muslim peoples, it can also be used to justify denying their legitimate strategic ambitions. A recent editorial in the Jerusalem Post links the fanaticism of the cartoon protests to the lawful nuclear ambitions of Iran. It states, "If anyone wants to appreciate why the West views with such suspicion the weapons programs of Muslim states such as Iran, they need look no further than the intolerance Muslim regimes exhibit to these cartoons, and what this portends."

This crisis has also occurred in the immediate aftermath of the appearance of the latest "Bin Laden" tape, intensified warnings of an imminent major terrorist attack in the West, something "on the scale of 9/11," and it coincides with the escape of the alleged mastermind of the attack on the USS Cole from a Yemeni jail. The fear associated with the latter two events, combined with the images of hysterical protesters, work to create a climate that can support unprecedented measures if another major terrorist attack were to occur in the near future—whoever the perpetrators may be.

In addition to the setbacks on the psychological front, the current crisis indicates just how bad we are losing in the Jihad of ideas. It is not without significance that the ultimate objective of Jihad is linked to ideas. The Prophet Muhammad, peace and blessings of God upon him, was asked about a man who fought to display his bravery, another who fought out of fealty to his tribe, and a third who fought to show off. Which had fought in the Way of God? He replied, peace and blessings of God upon him, "The one who fought to make the Word of God uppermost has fought in the Way of God."[4] Is the nature of the current campaign working to make the Word of God uppermost? Every Muslim needs to ask that question.

As Muslims, we are carrying the Word of God in an increasingly secular, militarized, and alienated world. What it means to carry that word is not an unknowable abstraction. We carry it by following the concrete example of our Noble Messenger Muhammad, peace and blessings of God upon him. In carrying the word, he endured unimaginable abuses and he persevered through them because he was inspired by a grand vision. That vision was to see his people saved by the life-giving, life-affirming message of Islam. No greater illustration of this can be given than the story of his expulsion from the city of Ta'if, after the arrogant leaders of that town unleashed the fools, slaves, and children against him.

In the aftermath of that onslaught, the Prophet, peace and blessings of God upon him, humbly raised his hands towards the sky and prayed:

O, God! Unto you alone do I plead my lack of strength, the paucity of my efforts, and my humiliation before the people. O, the Most Merciful of all! You are the Lord of the oppressed, you are my Lord. Unto who have you dispatched me? To a distant host who receives me repugnantly? Or to an enemy you have authorized over my affair? If you are not angry with me, I care not. It is only your goodness I seek to be covered with. I seek refuge with the Light of your Face, through which the darkness is illuminated and all the affairs of the world and hereafter are rectified, that you do not cast your anger down on me, nor cause your wrath to settle upon me. There is neither strength, nor power but with You. [5]

Two significant events are then related after this prayer was uttered by the Prophet, peace and blessing of God upon him. First of all, when presented with an offer by the Angels that God crush the city of Ta'if, the Prophet, peace and blessings of God upon him, refused saying that perhaps from the offspring of the offending hosts, there would emerge those who would worship God. This incident is well known. A lesser known incident associated with the journey to Ta'if occurred when the Prophet, peace and blessings of God upon him, was preparing to reenter Mecca, in the company of his companion Zaid bin Haritha. Zaid asked, "How can you reenter their presence when they have expelled you?" The Prophet, peace and blessings of God upon him, replied, "O, Zaid! God is bringing about through these events you have witnessed a great opening. God is most capable of assisting His religion, and manifesting the truth of His prophet."

One of the most disturbing aspects of the current campaign to "Assist the Prophet," for many converts, like this writer, is the implicit assumption that there is no da'wah work being undertaken here in the West, and no one is currently, or will in the future enter Islam in these lands. Therefore, it does not matter what transpires in the Muslim East. Muslims can behave in the most barbaric fashion, murder, plunder, pillage, brutalize and kidnap civilians, desecrate the symbols of other religions, trample on their honor, discard their values and mores, and massacre their fellow Muslims. If any of that undermines the works of Muslims in these Western lands, it does not matter. If it places a barrier between the Western people and Islam, when many of those people are in the most desperate need of Islam, it does not matter. If our Prophet, peace and blessings of God upon him, had responded to those who abused him in Ta'if with similar disregard, none of the generations of Muslims who have come from the descendants of those transgressors would have seen the light of day.

These campaigns of desperation also implicitly display a lack of confidence in God's ability to protect his religion and defend the honor of His Prophet, peace and blessings of God upon him. We should do what we can do within lawful limits, and then we depute the affair to God. When we despair of help from God and find ourselves with limited strategic resources, we sometimes press forward with the most desperate tactics imaginable, taking little time to assess the compatibility of those tactics with Islamic teachings, or their long-term implications for the cause of Islam, especially in the West.

There are certainly more constructive and productive ways to defend the honor of the Prophet, peace and blessings of God upon him. Why are we calling for a "Day of Outrage" when our Prophet has instructed us repeatedly not to become angry? There are surely times when we should become angry for the sake of God. However, under the current circumstances, are anger and outrage appropriate responses? Why not a "Day of Familiarization," where we teach people who the Prophet was and what he really represents, peace and blessings of God upon him? Why not a "Day of Sunnah," where we all vow to revive a Sunnah we have allowed to slip away from our religious life. Such a day could also include the Sunnah of showing concern for ones neighbors? We could visit them and tell them about Islam and our beloved Prophet, peace and blessings of God upon him.

Whatever we do, as Muslims in the West, we may be approaching the day when we will have to "go it alone." If our coreligionists in the East cannot respect the fact that we are trying to accomplish things here in the West, and that their oftentimes ill-considered actions undermine that work in many instances, then it will be hard for us to consider them allies. How can one be an ally when he fails to consult you concerning actions whose negative consequences you will suffer? No one from the Muslim east consults us before launching these campaigns. No one seeks to find out as to how their actions are going to affect our lives and families. The confused incompetence of the Muslim countries around the issue of moon-sighting, a situation that has painful consequences for Muslims here in America is bad enough, the added pressure generated by these reoccurring crises is becoming unbearable for many.

We have a generation of Muslim children here who have to go to schools where most of them are small minorities facing severe peer pressure. During these crises they do not have the luxury of losing themselves in a frenzied mob. Their faith is challenged and many decide to simply stop identifying with Islam. Is that what they deserve? If they are largely lost to Islam, what is the future of our religion here? We have obedient, pious Hijab wearing women, who out of necessity must work, usually in places where they are the only Muslims. Should their safety, dignity, and honor be jeopardized by the actions of Muslims halfway around the world?

I reiterate that I am not saying these cartoons, and other denigrations of our religion and our Prophet, peace and blessings of God upon him, should be totally ignored. Imam Shafi'i stated that anyone who is angered and does not respond; he is a jackass. However, our responses should be weighed on the basis of a strategic calculus we construct. Their timing should be determined by that calculus, not by media sensationalizing. They should be undertaken in consultation with those who will be directly affected by the responses they generate. And their long-range implications should be deeply considered.

In conclusion, one should not see the ongoing crisis as a clash of civilizations. Phenomena as deep and complex as civilizations cannot be thrown into conflict overnight by media-driven campaigns. A clash of civilizations would also involve the overwhelming majority of people identified by a particular civilizational nexus. The current crisis is the result of a regrettable incident that has been exploited by an uncivilized minority of provocateurs both in the West and the East to advance their conflicting agendas. As long as that exploitation continues, the crisis could aptly be called the clash of the uncivilized.

NOTES

[1] We say appropriately because the measured response of the Danish Muslim community killed the story. Certainly part of the defense of the Prophet's honor is to keep these images out of the media. The initial response of the Danish Muslims did just that.

[2] The Danish flag prominently displays a cross, the symbol of Christianity. Hence, every time a Danish flag is burned or trampled on, the symbol of Christianity is desecrated. A similar transgression against Islam would occur if the Saudi flag, which contains the Name of Allah, and the declaration of Tawhid *La ilaha illa Allah* were burned or trampled. The question here is has the entirety of Christendom transgressed against the Muslim people in a way to justify an attack on the symbol of their faith?

[3] Protestors in Britain this past Friday threatened suicide bombing attacks in European cities, and the beheading of the offending cartoonists. Insightfully, the British Muslim youth protesting wearing a mock suicide bomber's vest turned out to be a convicted heroin and crack dealer, out on parole. It is a lot easier to mobilize the Muslim youth for the anti-cartoon Jihad than to deal with the rising rates of incarceration, mental illness, failing schools, dysfunctional homes, and the drug addition and alcoholism that are ravaging the British Muslim community.

[4] Al-Bukhari, no. 7458, and Muslim, no. 1904.

[5] This prayer and the incident precipitating it are related in the various books of Prophetic biography, both ancient and modern. It is quoted here from Dr. Muhammad Sa'id Ramadan al-Buti, *Fiqh as-Sirah* (Beirut: Dar al-Fikr, 2001/1422), pp. 150–151.

7. **Yusuf Talal DeLorenzo, "Fiqh and The Fiqh Council of North America" from** *The Fiqh Council of North America*

From The Fiqh Council of North America, accessed May 11, 2006. Available online: http:// www.islamicity.com/politics/SHARIAH.HTM#S2.

Reprinted with permission of Islamicity.com.

The Fiqh Council of North America is an independent committee of Islamic scholars that seeks to advise Muslims in the United States on matters particular to the American context. The Fiqh Council is a branch of the Islamic Society of North America (ISNA) and was created in its current form in 1986. Muzzamil Siddiqi (b. 1943) has headed the council since 2004. Taha Alalwani previously led the council from 1989 to 2004. Members of the Fiqh Council are diverse; there are men and women, Sunni and Shi'a members. Consequently, the council does not ascribe to one legal school of thought (madhab), relying instead on the Quran and sunna to issue a legal ruling (fatwa), some of which have included a condemnation of terrorism, an endorsement of stem cell research, as well as yearly fatwas on moon-sighting (used to determine the beginning of major holidays like Eid al-Fitr). The council aims to develop a "fiqh for Muslims living in non-Muslim societies." It has issued fatwas on topics ranging from stem cell research (see Embryonic Stem-Cell Research, Primary document 8) to Muslim soldiers in the U.S. Army after 9/11 (see Islamic Scholars say U.S. Muslim soldiers must fight for country, Primary document 46). The Fiqh Council is located in Leesburg, Virginia. "Fiqh and The Fiqh Council of North America" is available online: http://www.islamicity.com/ politics/SHARIAH.HTM#S2

As the Muslim community in North America grows to include more ethnically and culturally diverse elements, the process of istifta' (in which consultation takes place between qualified experts on religious law and people for whom adherence to that law is an essential part of their faith) and the phenomenon of the "imported" mufti become more problematic. Immigrant and indigent American Muslims of whatever ethnic or cultural background have often been disappointed by the lack of appreciation for local conditions and circumstances on the part of such "imported" muftis. Likewise, community leaders and members alike have come to realize that the legal responum or fatawa obtained through the mail, so to speak, from muftis in Muslim majority countries often fail to address the crux of the issues presented to them for consideration. Quite often, their responses raise more problems than they settle. Certainly, this is only natural. For unless there is a clear understanding of the context of a legal question, there is little likelihood that the solution offered will be an adequate one. From here, the idea seems to have taken hold among American Muslims that the institution of istifta' or Fiqh consultation is one that is best supported by those who fully understand and appreciate the special characteristics of the North American Muslim community and the circumstances in which it strives to develop.

Over the past twenty years, the community has turned increasingly to local experts for the solutions to their Fiqh related problems. The experts consulted have not always had the sort of Fiqh qualifications traditionally required of muftis, but their understanding of local condition, coupled with backgrounds in Arabic or Islamic studies have placed them in the position of being called upon to give opinions on sensitive issues. With the rise of interest in Islamic studies in American academia, however, a number of Muslim scholars with Fiqh credentials have come to American universities for graduate studies, post graduate work, or to fill teaching posts in new or expanding departments. At the same time, American Muslims, especially converts and second generation converts (the children of converts), have sought in increasing numbers to obtain advanced Fiqh training abroad at Islamic universities and traditional Islamic institutions. All of these developments have made it possible for the community to draw upon a wider range of Fiqh expertise and experience.

In recent years, national organizations like the Islamic Society of North America, the Islamic Circle of North America and the ministry of Warith Deen Mohammed have seen the need to form committees of scholars to advise on matters related to Fiqh and the community. Out of one such committee grew the Fiqh Council of North America, an independent body of Fiqh councilors organized in view of the increasing need on the part of the growing Muslim community in North America for considered Shari'ah-based advice and counsel. Its functioning extends to the needs of individuals and organizations within the community and to those with whom they interact, Muslim and non-Muslim alike. By way of example, over the past year the Council has dealt with questions submitted by individual Muslims, by local and national Muslim organizations, by the Departments of Justice and Defense, by Muslim and non-Muslim trial lawyers, immigration lawyers, and journalists with interests as varied as biological engineering and third world politics.

The Fiqh Council of North America aims at participating, through its academic expertise, in the process of facilitating the Islamic way of life in the secular, non-Muslim environment of North America; and the way it intends to do this is by providing institutions and individuals with jointly considered legal opinions and advice that are based on the Qur'an and the Sunnah. The Council's primary objectives, as outlined in its by-laws are:

1) To consider, from a Shari'ah perspective, and offer advice on specific undertakings, transactions, contracts, projects, or proposals, guaranteeing thereby that the dealings of American Muslims fall within the parameters of what is permitted by the Shari'ah.

2) To consider issues of relevance to the community and give, from a Shari'ah perspective, advice and guidelines for policy, procedure, and practice. Such advice may take the form of position papers, fatawa, research papers, sample forms for legal agreements, or whatever else is deemed effective.

3) To consult, on issues requiring specialized knowledge and experience, with professionals or subject specialists.

4) To establish and maintain working relationships with Shari'ah experts worldwide, including muftis, university professors, researchers, Shari'ah court justices, and members of national and international Fiqh councils and academies.

5) To assist local and national organizations in the resolution of conflicts.

6) To advise in the appointment of arbiters, and review arbitration proceedings and decisions for their consistency with Islamic legal principles.

7) To commission research on relevant Islamic legal issues.

8) To maintain and develop a comprehensive Shari'ah library.

9) To anticipate and serve the particular needs of minority groups within the community; youth, women, prisoners, recent converts, etc.

10) To develop a Fiqh for Muslims living in non-Muslim societies.

In terms of its philosophy, the council's by-laws state that it will make its decisions jointly, and base them on evidence derived from the two most reliable sources of revelation: the Qur'an and the authentic Sunnah. In doing so it will employ the principles and methodologies of usul al Fiqh and consider, where relevant, the various opinions of earlier Muslim jurists. All legal schools will be considered equally as intellectual resources to be drawn from in the process of giving contemporary interpretations to the texts of revelation. In other words, the issue of madhhab or affiliation to one legal school of thought or another is one which the council considers valid only in regard to questions of worship or 'ibadat. Yet, even within that restricted area, new developments have brought about questions that the traditional imams never considered.

Among the most important approaches of the Council in its treatment of new issues and questions that apply particularly to the Muslim communities of North America is its policy of giving additional consideration, in the light of the higher purposes or maqasid of the Shari'ah, to the circumstances imposed upon Muslims by the non-Islamic environment that surrounds them.

In classical terms these circumstances are called the ahwal al mahkum 'alayki, and are mentioned only briefly, if at all, in the major works of usal. While decisions made by the council are the result of collective scholarship and consideration, members do have the right to write dissenting opinions. As a part of the process of istifta, the mustafti or questioner has the right to accept whichever opinion he feels is the more valid. And this is partly a function of his knowing better what his particular circumstances or ahwal might be.

Another matter for the consideration of the Fiqh councilor in North America is that since the tradition al Fiqh of Islam is essentially the Fiqh of the historical Muslim state and its Muslim majority, it pays little or no heed to the Fiqh of Muslim minorities except in the form of nawzil issued at times of crisis, such as during the Mongol invasions, or the crusades, or in the Moriscan period of Andalusian history. The Fiqh of these periods, however, was never developed or analyzed as it was considered to have come about under adversity and therefore fell under the category of legal exception by virtue of necessity. It is therefore essential that the councilor strive to interpret the teachings of Islam in a way that is consistent both with the higher principles of the Shari'ah and with the circumstances of Muslims living in predominantly non-Muslim societies. Such Fiqh might be known as the Fiqh of Muslims in non-Muslim environments, and its applications in today's world are probably without limit.

8. **Taha Alalwani, "Embryonic Stem-Cell Research" from** *The Fiqh Council of North America*

From the Fiqh Council of North America, accessed July 6, 2006. Available online: http:// www.fiqhcouncil.org/articles/embryo.html. Reprinted with permission of Dr. Taha Jaber Alalwani

Taha Jaber Alalwani was born in Iraq in 1935. He studied classical Islamic sciences at Al Azhar Univeristy in Cairo, Egypt. He taught in Saudi Arabia for ten years before immigrating to the United States in 1984. He is the president of Cordoba University in Ashburn, Virginia. He teaches at Cordoba's Graduate School of Islamic and Social Sciences. Alalwani is at the forefront of a reflection on the jurisprudence of minorities (fiqh al-aqalīyya) that seeks to adapt Islamic jurisprudence to the American context.

The following article was produced by a panel of Muslim scholars convened by the Fiqh Council of North America of which Alalwani was the lead author. It endorses stem cell research, considering it non-contradictory to Islamic principles. However, it stipulates several limits with regards to in-vitro procedures.

Summary:

• Whenever possible research on Stem Cells taken from adults should be encouraged.

• No in-vitro may be performed for the purpose of supplying stem cells for research.

• Whenever in-vitro is needed to deal with the problem of infertility, the sperm and ovum must be taken from an Islamically lawfully wed couple.

• As fertility clinics are forced to fertilize more than one ovum so as to increase the chances of success, unused (embryo) may be used for research instead of destroying them, provided that this is done in the first few days after fertilization and provided farther that the unused embryos are denoted without any financial return.

A majority of Muslim Americans support embryonic stem-cell research according to a new poll conducted by the Islamic Institute. The Washington-based Islamic advocacy group also announced its support for the research based on recommendations of a panel of Islamic scholars, scientists, and medical doctors (please see press release below.)

According to the Islamic Institute's poll of 629 individuals, 62% (394) stated their overall support for research on human embryos. 73% (457) stated that it is acceptable to use embryos that have already been donated from in-vitro fertilization procedures, while 61% (383) stated their support for using embryos to be donated in the future.

49% (312) of the respondents feel it is acceptable to produce embryos specifically for stem-cell research purposes, and 69% (433) believe the federal government should fund embryonic stem-cell research. However, when asked if they accept President Bush's plan to fund limited stem cell research on existing stem-cell lines, 68% (425) agreed, reflecting a national trend to accept the President's position as an acceptable middle ground.

44% (275) of the respondents stated that they have often followed the news regarding stem-cell research, while 53% (335) stated they followed the news occasionally. All figures are based on responses to a list of 10 questions submitted by the Islamic Institute to members of the community and does not necessarily constitute a scientific statistical sample.

The Islamic Institute released the following statement on its position on stem-cell research:

"Research on embryonic stem cells is one of the most promising, yet controversial issues of our time. It offers the promise of treating Parkinson's disease, Alzheimer's, spinal cord injuries, diabetes, multiple sclerosis, heart disease, and so many other fatal diseases. At the same time, due to the nature of this research, there are unprecedented areas of abuse and misuse that must be taken into consideration. Stem-cell research raises serious questions and challenges of ethics, theology, and philosophy, which the Muslim American community has to address.

In an effort to formulate a policy position on embryonic stem-cell research, and to ensure Muslim American participation in the debate of this ethical and scientific issue, the Islamic Institute convened a panel of experts, in cooperation with the Fiqh Council of North America (FCNA, North American council of Islamic jurisprudence), the Graduate School of Islamic and Social Sciences (GSISS), and the International Institute of Islamic Thought (IIIT). The panel, consisting of medical doctors, scientists, and Islamic scholars, deliberated all aspects of this topic at length, in order to develop an Islamic perspective on stem-cell research.

The panel included:

- Dr. Taha J. Al-Alawani, Chairman, Fiqh Council of North America

- Dr. Jamal Barzinji, Vice President, International Institute of Islamic Thought

- Dr. Eltigani A. Hamid, Graduate School of Islamic and Social Sciences

- Dr. Hisham Altalib, Director, International Institute of Islamic Thought

- Dr. Jamil Fayez, Professor Emeritus, Wake Forest University Medical School, infertility and reproductive endocrinology specialist.

- Mutahhar Fauzia, M.D., OB/GYN, infertility specialist

- Mohammad Jaghlit, M.D.

Though hard and extremely emotional, our opinion is based on all available scientific facts at this time, as well as full adherence to Islamic teachings.

Muslims have utterly and vehemently rejected human cloning experimentation that "contradicts Islamic legislation and is prohibited in all its forms because it contradicts with Islam." (See edict of the Mufti of Egypt on ArabicNews.com) Nevertheless, virtually all Muslim scholars see in-vitro fertilization (IVF) as a compassionate and humane scientific procedure to help infertile couples bear children. This procedure involves stimulating a woman's ovaries, removing the eggs, and fertilizing them by sperm cells from the husband in the laboratory. Days-old fertilized eggs (embryos) are implanted in the woman's uterus for normal pregnancy. IVF, Islamic scholars emphasize, has to be performed under strict guidelines, not the least of which is that the fertilization has to be of a sperm and an egg of a properly married couple.

Scientists assure us that it is inevitable and also desirable to produce several embryos to give the woman a better chance of getting pregnant. The "spare" embryos that result from IVF procedures are either frozen or destroyed. Scientists have discovered that the stem cells of these embryos have the potential to develop and differentiate into any of the 200-plus kinds of cells in the human body.

The Islamic Institute supports stem-cell research on these spare embryos from in-vitro fertilization. Under the Islamic principle of the "purposes and higher causes of the shariiah (Islamic law)", we believe it is a societal obligation to perform research on these extra embryos instead of discarding them. Thousands of embryos that would be otherwise discarded every year in fertility clinics could potentially be used for research. None of the Islamic scholars in the panel, or the ones we subsequently consulted, felt the opinion was in anyway contradictory to Islamic principles. Additionally, we strongly feel that there should be strict guidelines and proper procedures to ensure there is no potential abuse. These guidelines should include the full informed consent of the donor couple.

Finally, this opinion is based on available scientific information presented and discussed at the panel, and further consultations with specialists. It is an Islamic opinion subject to further enhancements in the case of scientific developments unknown to us at this time.

9. **"She Wants Advice for Muslims Who Live in the West" from** *Islam Questions and Answers*

From Islam Questions and Answers, accessed June 6, 2006. Available online: http://www.islamqa.com/index.php?ref=70256&ln=eng&txt=Advice%20for%20Muslims%20Who%20Live%20in%20the%20West.

Islam Questions and Answers is a web site that describes itself as dedicated to teaching Muslims and non-Muslims about Islam, providing answers to general, social, and personal questions. Shaykh Muhammad Salih al-Munajjid supervises the web site's scholastic material. The web site reflects a Wahhabi/Salafi interpretation of Islamic doctrine that is characterized by conservatism and Puritanism. It advocates separation between the Muslims and the West, which is considered to be immoral. Islam Questions and Answers also promotes strict separation of gender. The web site's materials are available in Arabic, English, French, Japanese, Indonesian, and Urdu.

This article advises Muslims to leave the West. If that is not possible, Muslims should avoid contact with Westerners as much as possible as they propagate cultures and principles contrary to Islamic values.

I am a Muslim living in a foreign country with my husband in order to earn a living. I hope that you could tell me of the obligations and duties and guidelines that a Muslim would should adhere to, because there are so many Muslim women living in foreign lands.

Answer: Praise be to Allaah

1) The first thing you should do is to leave that kaafir land, because the Prophet (peace and blessings of Allaah be upon him) disavowed himself of anyone who settles among the mushrikeen. Hence it is haraam for you to stay in the land of kufr, especially since you are there for the sake of work, and that is not one of the legitimate excuses for which you may be allowed to stay there.

2) You have to choose the Muslim land where people adhere most closely to modesty, chastity and commitment to Islam. It is well known that the Muslim lands vary in these matters, and not every country is a place where you could settle, unfortunately, rather that depends on your nationality and the laws of the land.

3) If you cannot move to that country, then you must fear Allaah, may He be exalted, and adhere to His commands in all your affairs, foremost among which must be guarding your families against disintegration and assimilation. You must pay attention to your children, both males and females, give them a good Islamic upbringing and a sense of connection to Islamic history, teach them the rulings of Islam, and teach them Arabic well.

4) The place where the Muslim family lives should be far removed from places of immorality. Conservative Muslim families should live together in one place so that they can support one another and help one another to obey Allaah, may He be exalted, and help one another to train 5 5—and teach themselves and their children.

5) It is haraam for you to give your children free rein in forming friendships with the children of the kuffaar. It is not permissible for you to allow your children to watch immoral shows and movies that destroy moral values. You must also pay attention to what they read and watch so that their thinking will not go astray and they will not lose their religious commitment.

6) Your family should have set times, even if they are short, when the entire family can get together and talk, so as to deal with problems faced by each family member before they grow worse and more complicated, or it becomes impossible to solve them.

7) You must also make good choices in the families with whom you mix, lest some of them have a negative influence on your family members and your efforts to raise them properly be wasted.

8) You should instill a hatred for this culture and its ways in the hearts of your children, and inform them that it is contrary to divine law and the sound nature of man. Give them examples and contrast it with Islamic morals, and instill a sense of connection with Islamic culture and its ways, and let them know that they will not stay in that land for long.

9) You should frequently visit the sacred land of Allaah in Makkah. Strive to perform Hajj every year and to do 'Umrah more than once a year if you can, so as to strengthen your faith and strengthen your children's bonds to Islam and the Muslims. Unfortunately we see great shortcomings in the Muslim communities who live in kaafir countries in this regard.

10) Build an Islamic library, including Islamic books, tapes and CDs, so that the family members can learn about their religion and refer easily to the rulings of Islam. Close the door to means of misguidance that may lead to their ignorance and corruption. Bring the al-Majd channel into your homes for the beneficial knowledge that it offers, and because they are trying to keep their channel free of women and music. You can also connect them to useful sites on the internet.

In fact there is a great deal of advice that we could offer, because there is so much misguidance, deviance and immorality in those kaafir lands. Every aspect of life needs its own advice and guidance. But what we said in the beginning is full of advice, which is to leave that kaafir land and move to a Muslim land. Whoever stays in the kaafir lands must realize that Allaah will ask him about his flock on the Day of Resurrection, so let him prepare an answer.

We ask Allaah to make it easy for you to leave that land and to make you steadfast in adhering to Islam and true guidance, and to make your children righteous callers to Islam.

We hope that you will also read question no. 4237, which offers more information on protecting children in the west.

And Allaah is the Source of strength.

10. "He Works in a Mixed Environment and Is Worried About His Fast" from *Islam Questions and Answers*

From Islam Questions and Answers, accessed June 6, 2006. Available online: http://www.islamqa.com/index.php?ref=50398&ln=eng&txt=Works%20in%20a%20Mixed%20Environment. For a description of the Islam Q&A see the preface to Primary document 9.

The article advises Muslims to avoid contact (e.g., eye contact, hand shaking, a man being alone with a woman in an office) between genders in the workplace. Gender relations are highly sensitive in the West for young Muslims engaging in different social activities in school, the workplace, and other events. The Salafi approach to gender relations prohibits all interactions between genders outside of the home.

Question: I work in a company where there is no other man but me. Does my mixing with women have any effect on my fast?

Answer: Praise be to Allaah. Mixing between men and women in the workplace has obvious bad effects on both men and women. These include the following:

1 — Haraam looks. Allaah has commanded the believers, men and women, to lower their gaze. Allaah, may He be exalted, says (interpretation of the meaning):

"Tell the believing men to lower their gaze (from looking at forbidden things), and protect their private parts (from illegal sexual acts). That is purer for them. Verily, Allah is All Aware of what they do. And tell the believing women to lower their gaze (from looking at forbidden things), and protect their private parts (from illegal sexual acts) and not to show off their adornment except only that which is apparent" [al-Noor 24:30, 31]

In *Saheeh Muslim* (2159) it is narrated that Jareer ibn 'Abd-Allaah (may Allaah be pleased with him) said: I asked the Messenger of Allaah (peace and blessings of Allaah be upon him) about an accidental glance and he told me to avert my gaze.

2 — There may be haraam touching, which includes shaking hands. The Prophet (peace and blessings of Allaah be upon him) said: "For one of you to be struck in the head with an iron needle would be better for him than touching a woman who is not permissible for him." Narrated by al-Tabaraani from the hadeeth of Ma'qil ibn Yasaar; classed as saheeh by al-Albaani in *Saheeh al-Jaami'*, no. 5045.

3 — Mixing may lead to a man being alone with a woman who is not his mahram, which is haraam, because the Prophet (peace and blessings of Allaah be upon him) said: "No man is alone with a woman but the Shaytaan is the third one present." Narrated by al-Tirmidhi, 2165; classed as saheeh by al-Albaani in *Saheeh al-Tirmidhi*.

According to another report: "Whoever believes in Allaah and the Last Day, let him not be alone with a woman who does not have a mahram with her, for the third one present will be the Shaytaan." Narrated by Ahmad and classed as saheeh by al-Haakim, and al-Dhahabi agreed with him. Also classed as saheeh by al-Albaani in *Ghaayat al-Maraam*, 180.

4 — Another of its evil results is that a man may become attracted to and infatuated with a woman, or vice versa, which is as a result of mixing and lengthy interaction.

5 — It also results in destruction of families. How many men have neglected their homes and families because of being attracted to a colleague at school or at work. How many women have neglected their husbands and homes, for the same reason. How many cases of divorce have occurred because of haraam relationships engaged in by the husband or wife, where mixing at work was the thing that led to it.

For these and other reasons, Islam forbids mixing that can lead to these evil consequences. We have quoted the evidence for the prohibition on mixing in detail in the answer to question no. 1200.

Based on this, our advice to you is to leave this mixed workplace and look for another job where you will be free from these haraam things. You should also be certain that whoever gives up something for the sake of Allaah, Allaah will compensate him with something better than it, and whoever fears Allaah, Allaah will grant him a way out from every difficulty.

"And whosoever fears Allaah and keeps his duty to Him, He will make a way for him to get out (from every difficulty) 3. And He will provide him from (sources) he never could imagine." [al-Talaaq 65:2–3]

If you have to stay in this job, then fear Allaah and lower your gaze and do not look at women. Avoid shaking hands with them or being alone with them, ands remember that Allaah is always watching. Remember that He knows what is secret and what is yet more hidden, and He *"knows the fraud of the eyes, and all that the hearts conceal"* [Ghaafir 40:19].

May Allaah guide us to fear Him, and to remain chaste and independent of means. And Allaah knows best.

11. "They Allow Mixing in the Mosque Because They Want People to Attend" from *Islam Questions and Answers*.

From Islam Questions and Answers, accessed June 6, 2006. Available online: http://www.islamqa.com/index.php?ref=65506&ln=eng&txt=Allow%20Mixing%20in%20the%20Mosque. For a description of Islam Questions and Answers, see the preface to Primary document 9.

The article advocates strict gender separation in the mosque for social events and celebrations, particularly dinner that break the day's fast (iftār) during the month of Ramadan.

Question: In our mosque, during ramadaan, around iftaar time, there is mixing between men and women. This has gone on for many years. The people who run the mosque use the excuse that if we do not let the people do what they want they won't come to the masjid. Also, during taraweeh they do many innovations, for example they do a tasbeeh after every four raka'aa. What advice can you give me to correct the situation?

Answer: Praise be to Allaah.

Firstly:

Free mixing between men and women is haraam, because it leads to many negative consequences and haraam things. We have quoted the evidence for the prohibitions on mixing in the answer to question no. 1200.

As mixing is forbidden at all times and in all places, then it is more emphatically forbidden if it is done in the mosques during the month of Ramadaan, because it goes against the shar'i aims for which mosques are established, such as maintaining and propagating Islam, calling people to good and forbidding them to do corrupt and evil things. It also goes against the reason for fasting, which is so that we might attain piety (taqwa) and avoid whims and desires.

All the people of the mosque should denounce this evil and strive to do away with it. Those who are in charge of the mosque are especially responsible.

No one has the right to try to justify this evil or to remain quiet about it on the grounds that not allowing mixing may cause some people to refrain from coming to the mosque. This argument is to be rejected on several fronts:

1—Remaining quiet and not denouncing evil when one is able to do so means that one is sinning. The Prophet (peace and blessings of Allaah be upon him) said: "Whoever among you sees an evil act, let him change it with his hand (by taking action); if he cannot, then with his tongue (by speaking out); and if he cannot, then with his heart (by at least hating it and regarding it as evil)—but that is the weakest of faith." Narrated by Muslim, 48. No wise person would accept for his attendance at the mosque to be a cause of his falling into sin.

2—The most important role that the mosque plays is calling people to goodness and warning them against evil. Hence those who are in charge of the mosque must explain to the people that mixing is haraam, and stop them doing it.

3—The idea that these people will never attend the mosque is merely conjecture. Even if we assume that it does happen, the established principle among the scholars is that warding off evil takes precedence over achieving good.

4—A special place for women to gather can be set up, whether it is in a particular corner of the mosque or even outside in a tent or some such, and useful programs can be offered to them, which should be supervised by women.

5—The daa'iyah is the one who should affect how things are and strive to set things right; he should not be affected by things and then look for justification.

Mixing is a problem that has arisen because we are far away from Islam. Efforts must be made to denounce it and put an end to it. If the first step is not taken in the houses of Allaah, then where shall we begin?!

You can work with some of your brothers to convince the people in charge and help them to prepare a place that is suitable for women to meet, and help them to prepare suitable programs for the women.

We ask Allaah to bless your efforts with success.

Secondly:

With regard to what you say about tasbeeh after each four rak'ahs of Taraweeh prayer, we have stated in the answer to question no. 50718 that this is an innovation which should not be done.

Shaykh Ibn Baaz (may Allaah have mercy on him) was asked: What is the ruling on raising our voices in sending blessings upon the Prophet (peace and blessings of Allaah be upon him) and praying that Allaah be pleased with the Rightly-Guided Caliphs between the rak'ahs of Taraweeh?

He replied:

There is no basis for that—as far as we know—in sharee'ah, rather it is an innovation and should not be done. The affairs of the later generations of this ummah will never corrected except by that by which the affairs of the earlier generations were corrected, which is following the Qur'aan and Sunnah and the way of the earliest generations of this ummah (the salaf), and avoiding whatever goes against that. End quote. *Majmoo' Fataawa Ibn Baaz*, 11/369.

And Allaah knows best.

©Copyright Islam Q&A 1997–2000

12. "He Is Studying in a Mixed University; How Should He Deal with Female Teachers and Students?" from *Islam Questions and Answers*

From Islam Questions and Answers, accessed June 6, 2006. Available online: http:// www.islamqa.com/index.php?ref=45883&ln=eng&txt=Studying%20in%20a%20Mixed% 20University. For a description of Islam Questions and Answers, see the preface to Primary document 9.

This article rejects co-ed educational institutions, urging young men to study in single-sex institutions outside the United States.

Question: I am a young man who is religiously committed. I am studying in a mixed university and I would like to develop my specialty further, but that requires me to interact in class, which will open channels of communication between me and other students. In addition to that there are female teachers who teach us very important subjects. How should I interact with the female students and teachers?

Answer: Praise be to Allaah.

Studying in mixed schools, institutes and universities is not permitted. The evils that exist in these institutions because of that mixing are no secret, let alone the fact that people do not learn much, if anything, in these institutions. Wise people even in kaafir countries have called for segregation between the sexes in educational institutions because of the moral damage they have noticed and the weakening of educational standards. Trustworthy have scholars have issued fatwas stating that this kind of education is not permissible.

The scholars of the Standing Committee said:

It is haraam for male and female students and teachers to mix in educational institutions, because of the fitnah and provocation of desires and immoral conduct that results from that. The gravity of the sin is compounded if the female teachers and students uncover any part of their 'awrahs or wear see-through or tight clothing, or if the students or teachers flirt or joke together, which may lead to transgression of limits and violation of honour. *Fataawa Islamiyyah*, 3/102, 103

Shaykh Ibn 'Uthaymeen (may Allaah have mercy on him) was asked:

Is it permissible for a man to study in a mixed university where men and women mix in one classroom, knowing that the student has a role to play in calling people to Allaah?

He replied:

What I think is that it is not permissible for anyone, man or woman, to study in a mixed school, because of the grave danger that it poses to his chastity, integrity and morals. No matter how great a person's integrity, morals and innocence, if a woman is sitting beside him on the seat—especially if she is beautiful and unveiled—he can hardly avoid fitnah and evil. Everything that leads to fitnah and evil is also haraam and is not permitted. We ask Allaah to keep our Muslim brothers safe from such things which will only bring evil, fitnah and corruption to their youth. If there is no other university apart from this one, he should go and study in another city or country where this mixing does not happen. I do not think that this is permissible but others may have a different opinion. *Fataawa Islamiyyah*, 3/103

This is easy those who do not have the problem of mixed schools in their country or who have access to colleges and universities that are not mixed, so they have no need to study in mixed colleges. But there remains the question of those who are faced with the problem of mixed schools in their countries. What should they do, especially if that will affect their chances of earning a living or of getting married in the future, since if they do not study in these colleges they will not be able to find a job or get married.

In this case, there is no option, and the need is great, and when the need is great, the matter may come under the heading of necessity. This necessity may be taken into consideration, provided that the following conditions are met:

1—That there be no other place where he can study, even if it is in another country

2—That he cannot obtain this certificate by means of distance learning or studying via the internet, for example

3—That he goes to study in these mixed places seeking the help of Allaah to confront fitnah.
   He should take care to lower his gaze as much as he can and not touch or shake hands with non-mahram women or be alone with them, and he should not sit right next to them.
   He should advise the girls to sit away from the boys and adhere to other Islamic guidelines as well.

4—If he notices himself slipping towards haraam things and being tempted by those of the opposite sex who are with him, then the soundness of his religious commitment is more important than any worldly aims, so he has to leave the place immediately and Allaah will make him independent of means by His bounty. And Allaah is the One Whose help we seek.

And Allaah knows best.

There follows a list of colleges and universities that are not mixed:

1—The Medical College in Dubai

2—Al-Azhar University in Egypt

3—The Imam Muhammad ibn Sa'ood Islamic University in Saudi

4—Umm al-Qura University in Makkah al-Mukarramah

5—The Islamic University in Madeenah al-Munawwarah

6—The King Sa'ood University in Saudi.

©Copyright Islam Q&A 1997–2000

13. "What Is the Age Which a Woman Should Observe Hijab from a Boy?" from *Islam Questions and Answers*

From Islam Questions and Answers, accessed June 6, 2006. Available online: http:// www.islamqa.com/index.php?ref=14259&ln=eng&txt=Woman%20Should%20Observe% 20Hijab. For a description of Islam Questions and Answers, see the preface to Primary document 9. Dress codes and rules of modesty are significant parts of Islamic religiosity among Muslim in the United States and in the Muslim world. Approaches to modesty and dress are polarized with regards to what is considered permissible or not, with the Salafi approach being the strictest, particularly with regards to the ḥijāb (veil) which the Salafi interpretation considers compulsory.

Question: What is the age at which a woman should observe hijab from a boy—is it when she reaches the age of discernment or when she reaches the age of puberty?

Answer: Praise be to Allaah.

Allaah says in the passage where He speaks of those to whom it is permissible to show one's adornments (interpretation of the meaning): *". . .or small children who have no sense of feminine sex" [al-Noor 24:31]* If a child shows some awareness of a woman's 'awrah and starts to look at her and talk to her a great deal, then it is not permissible for a woman to uncover in front of him.

This varies from one boy to another in terms of natural disposition and in terms of the company that he keeps. A boy may have a greater interest in women if he sits with people who talk about them a great deal, and if it were not for that he would not be particularly interested in them.

What matters is that Allaah has set the guidelines for this matter when He said (interpretation of the meaning): *". . .or small children who have no sense of feminine sex" [al-Noor 24:31]* i.e., these are among the ones in front of whom it is permissible for a woman to show her adornments, if they have no interest in women. *Shaykh Ibn 'Uthaymeen (may Allaah have mercy on him), Majmoo'at As'ilah tahumm al-Usrah al-Muslimah, p. 148*

Among the things which indicate that a child has started to be aware of a woman's 'awrah are the following:

- He describes women to others

- He can distinguish between a beautiful woman and an ugly one

- He compares the way women look

- He stares at women for a long time

Undoubtedly movies and soap operas, as well as social corruption, lead to children being aware of women's 'awrahs at an early age, so we have to be very careful. We ask Allaah to keep us safe and sound.

©Copyright Islam Q&A 1997–2000

14. "Celebrating Innovated Festivals" from *Islam Questions and Answers*

From Islam Questions and Answers, accessed June 6, 2006. Available online: http://www.islamqa.com/index.php?ref=10070&ln=eng&txt=Celebrating%20Innovated%20Festivals. For a description of Islam Questions and Answers, see the preface to Primary Document 9. This article argues that "innovated festivals" (e.g., the Prophet's Birthday, national holidays, or Mother's Day) are forbidden because they are not prescribed by God and they cause Muslims to imitate Christians and nonbelievers.

What is the shar'i ruling on celebrating festivals such as the birthday of the Prophet (peace and blessings of Allaah be upon him), children's birthdays, Mother's Day, Tree Week and national holidays?

Answer: Praise be to Allaah.

Firstly: 'Eid (festival) is the name given to something which returns (*ya'ood*), and is used to describe gatherings which happen repeatedly, on a yearly, monthly or weekly basis, etc. So an 'eid includes a number of things, such as a day which comes regularly, e.g., 'Eid al-Fitr and Friday; gatherings on that day; and actions such as acts of worship and customs which are done on that day.

Secondly: any of these things which are intended as rituals or acts of worship aimed at drawing closer to Allaah or glorifying Him in order to earn reward, or which involve imitating the people of Jaahiliyyah or any other groups of kaafirs, is a prohibited bid'ah, an innovation which comes under the general meaning of the hadeeth: "Whoever innovates something in this matter of ours (Islam) that is not part of it, will have it rejected." (Narrated by al-Bukhaari and Muslim).

Examples of that include Mawlid al-Nabi (the Prophet's birthday), Mother's Day and national holidays, because in the first case there are innovated acts of worship which Allaah has not prescribed, and because it involves imitation of the Christians and other kaafirs. And in the second and third cases there is imitation of the kuffaar. But in cases where the intention is to organize work to serve the interests of the ummah and to put its affairs straight, or to organize programs of study, or to bring employees together for work purposes etc., which in and of themselves do not involve acts of worship and glorification, then these are a kind of benign innovation which do not come under the meaning of the hadeeth, "Whoever innovates something in this matter of ours (Islam) that is not a part of it will have it rejected." So there is nothing wrong with such things, indeed they are allowed by sharee'ah.

And Allaah is the Source of strength. May Allaah bless our Prophet Muhammad and his family and companions, and grant them peace.

©Copyright Islam Q&A 1997–2000

15. **"Is It Permissible for Her to Listen to Music Whilst Exercising?" from** *Islam Questions and Answers*

From Islam Questions and Answers, accessed June 6, 2006. Available online: http:// www.islamqa.com/index.php?ref=78223&ln=eng&txt=Permissible%20for%20Her%20to% 20Listen%20to%20Music. For a description of Islam Questions and Answers, see the preface to Primary document 9.

This article reflects the Salafi restriction of music. While music is accepted in many trends of Islam, listening to music is considered forbidden by Salafis.

I exercise in a gym that is for women only. I have many health and psychological problems, but when I exercise, in addition to reading Qur'aan and reciting du'aa', I feel much better than I did before. My question is: Is it permissible to exercise knowing that they put on music for exercising, which has a rhythm that is suited to what the trainer is doing, or what should I do? I am confused about this as I like to exercise, and there is no gym where they do exercises without music.

Answer: Praise be to Allaah.

There is nothing wrong with a woman doing exercise if it is in a place that is only for women, where men cannot see them, so long as that is done to a limited extent and it does not distract her from something that is obligatory, and it does not lead to her missing prayers or delaying them until their time is over, or neglecting other duties.

Among the haraam things that may accompany exercise in some gyms is using music and listening to it. Al-Bukhaari narrated that Abu Maalik al-Ash'ari (may Allaah be pleased with him) said: The Prophet (peace and blessings of Allaah be upon him) said: "There will be people among my ummah who regard as permissible zina, silk, alcohol and musical instruments."

From this hadeeth the ruling on musical instruments is clear, which is that it is haraam. The fact that they are mentioned alongside other haraam things, namely silk, alcohol and zina, reinforces the fact that they are haraam.

There is no difference of opinion among the four Imams that musical instruments are haraam.

Shaykh al-Islam Ibn Taymiyah (may Allaah have mercy on him) said:
Whoever plays these instruments as a form of worship is undoubtedly misguided and ignorant. But if he does it as a form of entertainment, then the view of the four imams is that all musical instruments are haraam. It is proven in *Saheeh al-Bukhaari* and elsewhere that the Prophet (peace and blessings of Allaah be upon him) said that there would be among his ummah those who regarded zina, silk, alcohol and musical instruments as halaal, and he said that they would be transformed into monkeys and pigs. *Majmoo' al-Fataawa* (11/576, 577).

Music destroys the heart and distracts people from the truth; it generates hypocrisy in the heart. It cannot soothe the nerves or be a remedy.

Shaykh 'Abd al-'Azeez ibn Baaz (may Allaah have mercy on him) said:
Music and other kinds of entertainment are all evil, but they are things that the Shaytaan makes appear attractive and enjoyable, and he calls people to them so as to distract them from the truth by means of falsehood, and so that he can lead them away from that which Allaah loves, towards that which Allaah hates and has decreed haraam. Music, the 'ood (a kind of stringed instrument) and all musical instruments are an evil and it is not permissible to listen to them. It is narrated in a saheeh report that the Messenger of Allaah

(peace and blessings of Allaah be upon him) said: "There will be people among my ummah who regard as permissible zina, silk, alcohol and musical instruments." End quote. *Majmoo' Fataawa al-Shaykh Ibn Baaz* (3/346).

The Shaykh also said:

As for using music as a remedy, there is no basis for this, rather it is the work of fools. Music is not a remedy, but it is a disease. It is a kind of entertainment which cause sickness in the heart and leads to deviation of morals. The beneficial remedy that can calm the nerves is making the sick people listen to recitation of Qur'aan, beneficial exhortations and beneficial hadeeth. Using music as a remedy is something that gets people accustomed to falsehood and makes them even sicker. It makes listening to the Qur'aan and Sunnah and useful exhortations burdensome for them. *Laa hawla wa laa quwwata illa Billaah* (there is no power and no strength except with Allaah)." End quote. *Majmoo' Fataawa al-Shaykh Ibn Baaz* (9/429)

Based on this, you should advise these people and tell them that listening to music is forbidden in Islam and that there is no need for this haraam deed. There are many gyms which pay attention to that and they avoid playing music, which makes more people come to them. If they do not respond, then at least ask them not to use it whilst you are in the gym, so that you will not be a partner in this sin, remaining silent about an evil which you are obliged to denounce.

If you cannot do that, then you have to leave this gym: either look for another one, or look for another solution such as buying some equipment to use for exercising at home, which is better for you.

©Copyright Islam Q&A 1997–2000

16. **"Offering Gifts to Women on Christmas" from** *Islam Questions and Answers*

From Islam Questions and Answers, accessed June 6, 2006. Available online: http:// www.islamqa.com/index.php?ref=13642&ln=eng&txt=Offering%20Gifts%20to% 20Women%20on%20Christmas. For a description of Islam Questions and Answers, see the preface to Primary document 9.

This article discusses relationships between Muslims and non-Muslims. It rejects any possibility of interaction or recognition of the faith or celebrations of non-Muslims.

There is a common practice here in the West, that at Christmas time some non-Muslims, young and old, get together and gather all of their names, put them in a hat and have all of the names mixed up, then each person chooses the name of another person who they will give a gift to on Christmas day. This is called chris kringle. This basic idea was taken on by a group of sisters last year and now they want to take this practice on this year also for the end of Eid. All that the practice consists of, is each sister randomly assigned another sister for whom she must buy a gift of a set value. Some of the sisters involved believe that this practice is tashabu of the kufar, is this correct?

Answer:

Praise be to Allaah.

What some sisters have said to you, that this action is something that is not permitted, is correct, because it involves imitating the kuffaar in two ways.

Firstly it involves celebrating this festival, which is something that is haraam according to sharee'ah, including offering gifts on this festival.

Secondly, it involves imitating the kaafirs in these customs on the day of their celebration of that innovated festival.

In Islam we have only Eid al-Fitr and Eid al-Adhaa. Any other festivals that have been innovated besides these two amount to nothing, especially if they are the religious festivals of other religions or groups that are beyond the pale of Islam.

This matter opens the door to bid'ah, and it comes under the general meaning of the words of the Prophet (peace and blessings of Allaah be upon him), "Whoever innovates anything in this matter of ours that is not part of it will have it rejected." (Narrated by al-Bukhaari, *al-Sulh* 2499; Muslim, 1718). And Allaah knows best.

©Copyright Islam Q&A 1997–2000

17. Nuh Ha Mim Keller, "Who or What Is a Salafi?"

From Nuh Ha Mim Keller, "Who or What is a Salafi?" MCMXCV © nuh ha mim keller accessed May 18, 2006. Available online: http://www.masud.co.uk/ISLAM/nuh/salafi.htm. Reprinted with permission of Nuh Ha Mim Keller.

Nuh Ha Mim Keller (for a biography, see the "Keller, Shaykh Nuh" entry in Volume 1) was born in 1954 in the United States. He studied at the University of Chicago and the University of California at Los Angeles before converting to Islam in 1977. That same year, he enrolled at Al Azhar University in Cairo, Egypt to study classical Islamic sciences. He also studied and currently lives in Syria and Jordan. In the former he was named a shaykh in the Shadhili Sufi order. Keller wrote the following article in 1995. He discusses the interpretation of the Islamic tradition developed by Salafis, a term that today in the American context and beyond refers to a very conservative approach based on the imitation of the Prophet Muhammad.

The word *salafi* or "early Muslim" in traditional Islamic scholarship means someone who died within the first four hundred years after the Prophet (Allah bless him and give him peace), including scholars such as Abu Hanifa, Malik, Shafi'i, and Ahmad ibn Hanbal. Anyone who died after this is one of the *khalaf* or "latter-day Muslims".

The term "Salafi" was revived as a slogan and movement, among latter-day Muslims, by the followers of Muhammad Abduh (the student of Jamal al-Din al-Afghani) some thirteen centuries after the Prophet (Allah bless him and give him peace), approximately a hundred years ago. Like similar movements that have historically appeared in Islam, its basic claim was that the religion had not been properly understood by anyone since the Prophet (Allah bless him and give him peace) and the early Muslims—and themselves.

In terms of ideals, the movement advocated a return to a shari'a-minded orthodoxy that would purify Islam from unwarranted accretions, the criteria for judging which would be the Qur'an and hadith. Now, these ideals are noble, and I don't think anyone would disagree with their importance. The only points of disagreement are how these objectives are to be defined, and how the program is to be carried out. It is difficult in a few words to properly deal with all the aspects of the movement and the issues involved, but I hope to publish a fuller treatment later this year, insha'Allah, in a collection of essays called "*The Re-Formers of Islam*".

As for its validity, one may note that the Salafi approach is an interpretation of the texts of the Qur'an and sunna, or rather a body of interpretation, and as such, those who advance its claims are subject to the same rigorous criteria of the Islamic sciences as anyone else who makes interpretive claims about the Qur'an and sunna; namely, they must show:

1. that their interpretations are acceptable in terms of Arabic language;

2. that they have exhaustive mastery of all the primary texts that relate to each question, and

3. that they have full familiarity of the methodology of *usul al-fiqh* or "fundamentals of jurisprudence" needed to comprehensively join between all the primary texts.

Only when one has these qualifications can one legitimately produce a valid interpretive claim about the texts, which is called ijtihad or "deduction of shari'a" from the primary sources. Without these qualifications, the most one can legitimately claim is to reproduce such an interpretive claim from someone who definitely has these qualifications; namely, one of those unanimously recognized by the Umma as such since the times of the true salaf, at their forefront the mujtahid Imams of the four madhhabs or "schools of jurisprudence".

As for scholars today who do not have the qualifications of a mujtahid, it is not clear to me why they should be considered mujtahids by default, such as when it is said that someone is "the greatest living scholar of the sunna" any more than we could qualify a school-child on the playground as a physicist by saying, "He is the greatest physicist on the playground". Claims to Islamic knowledge do not come about by default. Slogans about "following the Qur'an and sunna" sound good in theory, but in practice it comes down to a question of scholarship, and who will sort out for the Muslim the thousands of shari'a questions that arise in his life. One eventually realizes that one has to choose between following the ijtihad of a real mujtahid, or the ijtihad of some or another "movement leader", whose qualifications may simply be a matter of reputation, something which is often made and circulated among people without a grasp of the issues.

What comes to many peoples minds these days when one says "Salafis" is bearded young men arguing about din. The basic hope of these youthful reformers seems to be that argument and conflict will eventually wear down any resistance or disagreement to their positions, which will thus result in purifying Islam. Here, I think education, on all sides, could do much to improve the situation.

The reality of the case is that the mujtahid Imams, those whose task it was to deduce the Islamic shari'a from the Qur'an and hadith, were in agreement about most rulings; while those they disagreed about, they had good reason to, whether because the Arabic could be understood in more than one way, or because the particular Qur'an or hadith text admitted of qualifications given in other texts (some of them acceptable for reasons of legal methodology to one mujtahid but not another), and so forth.

Because of the lack of hard information in English, the legitimacy of scholarly difference on shari'a rulings is often lost sight of among Muslims in the West. For example, the work Fiqh al-sunna by the author Sayyid Sabiq, recently translated into English, presents hadith evidences for rulings corresponding to about 95 percent of those of the Shafi'i school. Which is a welcome contribution, but by no means a "final word" about these rulings, for each of the four schools has a large literature of hadith evidences, and not just the Shafi'i school reflected by Sabiq's work. The Maliki school has the *Mudawwana* of Imam Malik, for example, and the Hanafi school has the *Sharh ma'ani al-athar* [Explanation of meanings of hadith] and *Sharh mushkil al-athar* [Explanation of problematic hadiths], both by the great hadith Imam Abu Jafar al-Tahawi, the latter work of which has recently been published in sixteen volumes by Mu'assasa al-Risala in Beirut. Whoever has not read these and does not know what is in them is condemned to be ignorant of the hadith evidence for a great many Hanafi positions.

What I am trying to say is that there is a large fictional element involved when someone comes to the Muslims and says, "No one has understood Islam properly except the Prophet (Allah bless him and give him peace) and early Muslims, and our sheikh". This is not valid, for the enduring works of first-rank Imams of hadith, jurisprudence, Qur'anic exegesis, and other shari'a disciplines impose upon Muslims the obligation to know and understand their work, in the same way that serious comprehension of any other scholarly field obliges one to have studied the works of its major scholars who have dealt with its issues and solved its questions. Without such study, one is doomed to repeat mistakes already made and rebutted in the past.

Most of us have acquaintances among this Umma who hardly acknowledge another scholar on the face of the earth besides the Imam of their madhhab, the Sheikh of their Islam, or some contemporary scholar or other. And this sort of enthusiasm is understandable, even acceptable (at a human level) in a non-scholar. But only to the degree that it does not become *ta'assub* or bigotry, meaning that one believes one may put down Muslims who follow other qualified scholars. At that point it is haram, because it is part of the sectarianism (*tafarruq*) among Muslims that Islam condemns.

When one gains Islamic knowledge and puts fiction aside, one sees that superlatives about particular scholars such as "the greatest" are untenable; that each of the four schools of classical Islamic jurisprudence has had many many luminaries. To imagine that all preceding scholarship should be evaluated in terms of this or that "Great Reformer" is to ready oneself for a big letdown, because intellectually it cannot be supported. I remember once hearing a law student at the University of Chicago say: "I'm not saying that Chicago has everything. It's just that no place else has anything." Nothing justifies transposing this kind of attitude onto our scholarly resources in Islam, whether it is called "Islamic Movement", "Salafism", or something else, and the sooner we leave it behind, the better it will be for our Islamic scholarship, our sense of reality, and for our din.

18. Asifa Quraishi, "The Muslim Family in the USA: Law in Practice" from *Women's Rights & Islamic Family Law*

Excerpt from Welchman, Lynn (Ed.), Women's Rights & Islamic Family Law (London: Zed Books, 2004), pp. 179–198. Reprinted with permission from Zed Books.

Asifa Quraishi is a professor of law at University of Wisconsin Law School where she teaches Islamic law and jurisprudence as well as Constitutional law. She was born to Pakistani parents in Santa Clara, California. She earned her B.A. from the University of California-Berkeley in 1988 and her law degree from the University of California-Davis in 1992. She has also received an LL.M. degree from Columbia Law School and an S.J.D. from Harvard Law School. Her work represents the only systematic analysis of the interactions between Islamic family law and American civil law regarding polygamy, marriage, and divorce. Quraishi highlights some of the legal and social accommodations and compromises Muslims are undertaking in the American context.

Solemnizing the union

§   THE intersection of US and Islamic law becomes important right at the formation of the family unit—the creation of the marriage itself. Each state of the USA requires a civil marriage licence for every marriage created within its borders. Details on the specific requirements for these licences vary from state to state, but generally they require an official signature of the person performing the wedding, qualified by the state to do so, and those of witnesses to the ceremony. Islamic wedding requirements, consisting of an offer and acceptance and witnesses to the event, do not conflict with this if the person offi-ciating the wedding is registered with the state as having this authority. In the United States, many Muslim leaders and lay individuals have this state authority, thus making the Muslim ceremony over which they preside simultaneously legal under the laws of the state, provided all necessary forms are filed. However, because not all Muslim marriage officiants carry such qualifications, Muslim weddings in the USA take a variety of forms. Many conduct one Muslim ceremony with a state-qualified imam, but many others have two events: a Muslim ceremony as well as a civil ceremony through state channels.[23] Still others have only a Muslim ceremony and never bother with state registration require-ments,[24] a risky practice under US law because, barring a finding of common law or putative marriage, the parties and their children have no state-enforceable legal rights upon each other, thus affecting inheritance, health insurance, taxes and even immigration issues.

Terms of the contract

As for the contents of these Muslim marriage contracts, most Muslims in the USA seem to consider only one thing really important that would not otherwise be included in a stan-dard civil marriage licence: a provision regarding the wife's bridal gift or dower (*mahr/sadaq*). The majority of classical Muslim jurists held dower to be an automatic result of the marriage contract, to the effect that even if no dower is stipulated, or it is stated that there will be no dower, the wife is entitled to claim a 'proper dower', assessed by her peers and those of her individual standing (Esposito 1982: 25; Welchman 2000: 135–6; Ali 1996: 159). Customarily the dower is divided into one part payable immediately on the marriage (the 'prompt dower', sometimes only a token amount or symbol) and another part deferred to a later date, either specified or more usually payable on the termination of the marriage by death or divorce (Rapoport 2000; Welchman 2000: 144; Moors 1995: 106–13). Written documentation of Muslim marriages thus routinely includes mention of the dower arrangements, and in the USA, many mosques and imams include a fill-in-the-blank provision in standard marriage contracts (Kadri, interview, 2000). Case law of Muslim marriage litigation in the USA reveals that Muslims do generally include *mahr/sadaq* provisions in their contracts, their nature varying with the financial status and personal preferences and aspirations of the parties.[25] Some examples of actual *mahr/sadaq* clauses in the USA and Canada are: $35,000, a Qur'an and set of *hadith*, a new car and $20,000 (Canadian), a promise to teach the wife certain sections of the Qur'an, $1 prompt and $300,000 deferred, Arabic lessons, a computer and a home gym, a trip around the world including stops in Mecca, Medina and Jerusalem, a leather coat and a pager, a wedding ring as immediate *mahr* and one year's rent for deferred *mahr*, and eight volumes of *hadith* by the end of the first year of marriage and a prayer carpet by the end of five years of marriage (al-Khateeb 1996).[26]

One case vividly illustrates the significance vested by some Muslims in their dower agreements: in *Aghili v. Saadatnejadi* (1997), the husband threatened not to record the Muslim marriage contract with state authorities unless the wife first agreed to relinquish that contract and sign a new one. The original contract included a dower of Iranian gold coins to the value of $1,400 and a provision for a payment of $10,000 as damages for any breach of contract by the husband. The husband's threat suggests that he felt bound by the *mahr* terms of the initial contract. Also, Los Angeles attorney Sermid al-Sarraf comments that he has seen, in informal divorce negotiations, a husband's recognition of the *mahr* amount, prompting the parties to include in their settlement an offset of this amount with other property (interview, 2000). Other Muslims tend not to consider the dower important at all, and include a clause about it (often only a token dower) in their contracts only because the Muslim officiating the ceremony tells them it is required (Kadri, interview, 2000).[27]

Discussions among US Muslim women include debates over the importance of the *mahr/sadaq* in the first place—some rejecting it as putting a monetary value on the bride, others advocating it as a financial protection for women in the event of death or divorce and sometimes as a deterrent against divorce (especially powerful where there is a large deferred dower).[28] There is indeed a dilemma presented by the institution: setting the *mahr* very high may provide good financial security for the wife and (where deferred) a good deterrence against husband-initiated divorce, but on the other hand, it burdens wife-initiated *khul'* divorces, which are usually negotiated with an agreement by the wife to forfeit her *mahr,* with the significant financial cost of waiving the outstanding amount and returning whatever prompt dower has already been paid. Setting the *mahr* low, or as only a token gift, has the reverse double-edged sword effect. That is, there is not as much to be lost in returning the *mahr* if the wife wants to negotiate a *khul'* divorce, but she also loses the deterrent effect on *talaq* divorce by the husband which is accomplished by a high deferred dower. Where the divorce occurs not through extra-judicial *talaq* or *khul',* but rather judicial dissolution by third-party arbiters, the impact on *mahr* payment docs not follow an absolute rule. Rather, the arbiters assess blame and harm caused by the spouses and allocate costs accordingly. Where there is no harm by the wife, she generally keeps all of the *mahr* (el-Arousi 1977: 14; Quick 190.8: 36–9; AH 1996: 125).[29]

As elsewhere in the Muslim world, additional stipulations (e.g. stipulations of monogamy, delegated right to divorce, wife's right to work outside the home, etc.) further defining the marital relationship of the new couple seem to be much less utilized than dower provisions,[30] presumably because the dower is obligatory whereas additional stipulations are not only optional but also a subject of little public awareness, and some clauses are even controversial in classical jurisprudence and local community attitudes (Kadri, interview, 2000). Nevertheless, the idea of particularizing one's Islamic marriage contract is gaining attention among the US Muslim population. Encouraged by Muslim women's organizations and activists seeing the use of additional stipulations as a tool for women's empowerment, more and more US Muslims are educating themselves about how to use the Muslim marriage contract. Says Sharifa Al-Khateeb of the North American Council for Muslim Women: 'The contract is a tool to help men and women design their future life together so there are no surprises...and so women won't be saying "I can't do this because my husband won't let me"' (Lieblich 1997).

Far from considering it a new, reformist feminist tool, many see the proactive use of the Islamic marriage contract as a way of protecting their basic Islamic rights. It is for this reason that Karamah reports it is working on a model marriage contract, grounded in classical Islamic legal principles, to be used by Muslims worldwide. One visitor to the Karamah website praises a friend for drafting her marriage contract to include clauses on monogamy and equal right to divorce (among others) and comments that many Muslim men unfortunately have a negative attitude towards drafting a marriage contract, considering it an 'insult to their ability to behave as model Muslims' and that they 'forget that in times of imminent divorce, men and women do become irrational and make demands that are hard to agree upon'.[31]

The empowering potential for women in the Islamic marriage contract has also attracted scholarly interest among academics. According to John Esposito, Islamic marriage contracts were originally intended to raise the status of women because, being party to the agreement, women could add stipulations of their own (Lieblich 2001). Carol Weisbrod (1999) notes; '[t]here is considerable interest among Islamic women in the idea of using the contractual aspects of Islamic marriage to protect women's rights.' Of course, such use of the contract stipulations presumes that the woman has the awareness and education necessary to utilize it. This is often not the case and, as Lynn Welchman has pointed out, the Islamic marriage contract system leaves 'the protection—or clarification—of rights such as education and waged employment for women out of the law per se and subject to the knowledge, ability and initiative of the individual women not only to insist on the insertion of a stipulation but to phrase it in a manner that gives it legal value' (Welchman 2000: 180). On the other hand, the marriage contract remains a very valuable tool because its grounding in classical law gives a 'clear indication of the acceptability of the changing of the more traditional parameters of the marriage relationship' (ibid., p. 180). It is for this reason that many activists take the need for education on the topic of marriage contract law so seriously, and their efforts largely focus on simply making women aware of this tool.[32]

Women's empowerment is not the only motivation, however. Those advocating the use of additional contractual stipulations focus not only on their potential to equalize gender-based advantages, but also as a way for both spouses proactively to express partnership in their new unique union. Ayesha Mustafaa of the Muslim American Society says: '[i]t forces conversation on important issues: where you are going to live, whether your wife is going to work, whether she accepts polygamy' (Lieblich 2001).[33] Similarly, Kareem Irfan, of the Council of Islamic Organizations of Greater Chicago, says: '[t]he contract forces the bride and groom to have a reality check before marriage' (ibid.). What form this reality check takes depends upon the ideologies of the individual couple. For some, it may mean a reaffirmation of traditional roles, such as that the wife won't go to college or work after the couple has children (ibid.). But for others, especially non-immigrant Muslims whose image of married life is very different from the traditional one, arrangements such as monogamy and equal access to divorce are more or less presumptions in the structure of marriage, and these men are not threatened by a woman's interest in including these (and other rights-specific terms) in the marriage contract. Indeed, in many cases it is the groom as well as the bride seeking to have such stipulations included.[34] The attitude of many of these couples is exhibited in the following statement of one Muslim bride: 'I love him…and I can't see him [taking a second wife], ever. But we put it in the contract because you never know' (ibid.). These young Muslims tend to view the contract drafting process not only as an allocation of rights and duties, but also as an exercise in learning to express their new identity as a couple, and, even more importantly, as a way to open up discussion (and determine compatibility) on important family issues (career, children, finances, residence location, etc.) that might otherwise be postponed to more stressful times (Quraishi 1999).[35] In other words, among a growing proportion of the American Muslim population, there is an interest in drafting more detailed, personalized Muslim marriage contracts—documents that are not a generic stamp of mere legal status conferred by some external authority, but rather, full, detailed expressions of the way each couple defines itself.

For those who choose to include specific stipulations in their marriage contract there are many insightful ideas from which to choose. Islamic history attests to Muslim marriage contracts including stipulations in which the husband promises not to marry additional wives (usually with the remedy that the wife may obtain a divorce, or even force a divorce of the second wife, if this promise is breached), delegates his *talaq* right to the wife, agrees not to relocate the family without the wife's consent, agrees never to prevent her from visiting her relatives, and to provide her with servants for household work as is befitting her accustomed lifestyle, among many others (Rapoport 2000: 14; Fadel 1998; 24–6; al-Hibri 2000: 57). Muslims in the United States have already taken advantage of the creativity allowed in these provisions and have included stipulations limiting visits from in-laws, that the wife will not be expected to cook or clean, protecting the wife's overseas travel required by her profession, and custody of the children upon death of either spouse (Lieblich 2001, 1997).[36] Many clauses affecting the ongoing marital relationship (such as rearing the children as Muslims, providing household services, allowing a wife to attend school, and location of the home) are included despite a realization by the couple that a US court would probably not intervene to enforce such terms (discussed further below). Other terms, such as a promise not to marry additional wives, have little effect in the USA for a different reason: the action is already prohibited by US law. Nevertheless, these couples feel it important to include such terms for religious reasons (i.e. thus preventing even a non-civil but nevertheless Muslim marriage to an additional wife), as a protection in the event they relocate to a jurisdiction that does allow such activity, and also as a mutual expression of the nature of their partnership. Finally, some marriage contracts use stipulations to provide for remedies in the event of a breach of other contractual terms (e.g. a monetary value or a wife's right to immediate divorce upon occurrence, etc.).[37]

Within the marriage

So far we have predominantly discussed areas where Islamic and US law are different, but not directly conflicting. There are, however other practices where some might regard the two laws as in direct opposition, and Muslims fall on both sides of the question of which law takes precedence. Polygyny is one of these areas. Because classical interpretations of Islamic law allow men to marry up to four wives, some Muslims believe that the US prohibition of polygamy directly violates their freedom of religion and, believing that Islam supersedes secular law, proceed to become part of a polygynous marriage. Thus, we see for example, in *N.Y. v. Benu,* a husband giving custody of his children to his wife after he married a second woman, and other reports of Muslim polygynous marriages (Little 1993; Taylor, interview, 2000). Aminah Beverly McCloud relates the dilemma faced by many US Muslim women whose husbands take a second wife—they feel religiously bound not to object to a practice God has permitted. She notes that even some Muslim leaders engage in this practice, leading to 'marriages of years of devotion fall[ing] into chaos' (McCloud 2000: 141–2). Generally the first wife in these marriages is recognized as legal under US law, but any subsequent wives and their children are not, These later wives are 'married' to the husband in Muslim ceremonies either in the USA by imams willing to do so, or in ceremonies overseas where polygyny is legal. Because of the religious dilemma, however, McCloud states that many of these women file charges not for bigamy but for some sort of fraud. She also states that 'all of the potential legal consequences of the practice of polygamy in the American context have not yet appeared, but. . . are bound to find their way into the courts as more and more women seek alimony and child support' (ibid., p. 142).

Clearly the majority of the population does not engage in polygynous marriages, but views on the practice differ, as can be seen in a book by Abu Ameenah Bilal Philips and Jameelah Jones entitled *Polygamy in Islam* (1985), providing a lengthy social and legal justification for the practice. Moreover, many Muslims themselves committed to monogamous marriages nevertheless recognize Muslim marriages involving more than one wife as Islamically valid. Thus, in an online Muslim advice column responding to a woman wondering how to marry a man already legally married in the USA, the columnist does not question the Islamic legalities of such a marriage, but nevertheless advises against it because of the woman's uneasy feelings and apparent lack of knowledge of the first wife (Hanifa 2000). Others, on the other hand, argue strongly against Muslims participating in such marriages in the United States, urging that the Qur'anic norm is monogamy and pointing to classical juristic arguments constraining the institution of polygyny (al-Hibri 1993: 66–7). For example, Azizah al-Hibri cites classical Islamic scholars stating that if marriage to a second wife causes the first wife harm, it is forbidden, and also notes Islamic schools of thought allowing the couple to include a clause in the marriage contract barring the husband from taking more wives. Similarly, Amina Wadud (1999), in addition to critiquing several traditional justifications for polygyny, undertakes her own textual interpretation of the relevant Qur'anic verses and sets forth an alternative reading of the permission for the practice, emphasizing its specific limitation to the just treatment of orphans. The Muslim Women's League makes the additional argument that because the subsequent wives are not legally recognized under the laws of the state, then by definition they cannot be treated equally, a requirement of Islamic law in polygynous marriages.[38] That is, subsequent wives in the United States not only do not have any rights to general spousal benefits (such as insurance benefits and inheritance) but they also necessarily lack any avenue of enforcing their spousal rights if a husband chooses to abuse or divorce them, since the marriage will have no validity in the US courts. There is also the possibility of a prosecution for bigamy if the authorities are so inclined. Another argument against American Muslim men marrying more than one wife relies on the simple Islamic jurisprudential principle that one must obey the laws of the land where one chooses to live, as long as they do not prevent one from performing one's religious obligations. Since polygyny is at most permitted in Islamic law, rather than being an obligation, it is held that US laws requiring monogamy should be respected.

Another area of potential conflict in types of allowable marriages lies in the question of Inter-religious marriages. Classical Islamic law allows Muslim men but not women to marry non-Muslim monotheists, those who belong to religious communities recognized as 'people of the book', whereas US law puts no religious restrictions on spousal partners (Esposito 1982: 20; Doi 1984: 36). Given the melting-pot nature of life in the USA, many Muslims, both men and women, do indeed marry non-Muslims (Haddad and Lummis 1987: 148).[39] While those who criticize Muslim women marrying non-Muslim men find a basis in standard *fiqh* positions, some object also to Muslim men marrying non-Muslims, on the basis that this constitutes an unfair double standard or results in a reduced number of Muslim men whom Muslim women may marry (Haddad and Lummis 1987: 146; Marquand 1996).[40] Others argue that the allowance is limited to those living under Muslim rule and therefore does not apply in places like the United States.[41] Azizah al-Hibri makes a *shari'a*-based argument against both Muslim men and women marrying outside the faith, arguing that the original reason (*'ilia*) for the Islamic prohibition of women marrying non-Muslim men has now changed in our context. That is, the reason classical Muslim jurists denied a woman the option of marrying a non-Muslim man was to protect her from the husband's potential denial of her free exercise of her religion (acknowledging the patriarchal nature of marriage, and the fact that Christianity and Judaism prohibited inter-faith marriages at the time). Al-Hibri concludes that this *'ilia* still exists, but argues further that additional realities of the American Muslim context (i.e. the likelihood of a Muslim man losing custody of his children and/or being unable to fulfil the Islamic obligation to raise them as Muslims if divorce from his non-Muslim wife occurs) mean that Muslim men also deserve the protective attention thus far granted to Muslim women, and, thus, the prohibition of inter-faith marriage should be extended to them (al-Hibri 2000: 68–9). Nevertheless, marriages in which the husband is Muslim and the wife Jewish or Christian are generally accepted by most US Muslims. For women marrying non-Muslim men, on the other hand, there is usually a stigma, or worse. Many Muslims follow Islamic *fiqh's* rejection of women marrying outside the faith, and most respected imams will not officiate at such ceremonies (Haddad and Lummis 1987: 145).[42] Muslim women's reactions range from disregard of the rule and consequent critical attitudes, to full support and justification of the *fiqh* position as beneficial to society and family. In between are many who reluctantly accept the rule, and perhaps seek alternative interpretations.[43]

Some inter-religious marriages involving Muslims are inter-cultural marriages between indigenous US citizens and immigrants. When the immigrant is the husband, mainstream US culture has developed the fear that the husband will ultimately abscond with his children (and perhaps the wife) to his country of origin, depriving the wife of all spousal rights recognized in the USA. The 1987 book and corresponding film titled *Not Without My Daughter*[44] arguably largely created and certainly entrenched this fear in the wider US public (Baker 2002), resulting in particular attention in the State Department information on 'International Parental Child Abduction'.[45] A piece featured on its travel website titled 'Islamic Family Law' is posted to 'make clear the basic rights and restrictions resulting from marriages sanctioned by Islamic law between Muslim and non-Muslim partners', noting that 'for Americans, the most troubling of these is the inability of wives to leave an Islamic country without permission of their husbands, the wives' inability to take children from these countries, and the fact that fathers have ultimate custody of the children'.[46] While it appears to be a sincere effort to summarize Islamic family law for those living in the United States, the State Department's narrow focus on only Muslim non-Muslim marriages skews the tone of its report and the reality of these issues. Clearly the problems addressed (inability to leave without permission of husbands, barriers to custody) are faced by all women living under Islamic law; whether Muslim or non-Muslim. The State Department's limited view perpetuates the *Not Without My Daughter* stereotype that Muslim men are a particular threat to non-Muslim American women. Moreover, stereotypes in the dominant US culture that portray Arabs and Muslims as violent fundamentalists oppressive to women further fuel distrust of inter-cultural Muslim marriages in the non-Muslim population.[47] As will be seen in the next chapter, this distrust sometimes extends to Muslims and Islamic law generally, and has a direct impact when Muslim marriages end up in divorce courts.[48]

Stereotypes also frequently confuse religion with culture, again leading to mistakes about what exactly is part of Islam and Islamic family law. For example, though arranged marriages (in various forms, ranging from complete parental control against the wishes of their children to family-arranged meetings of a potential couple) are found in many Muslim cultures (Haddad and Lummis 1987: 149–51), Islamic source texts do not require third-party intervention as a necessary or even preferred process of finding a spouse. Muslim scholars in the USA, such as the late Fazlur Rahman among others, point out that there is nothing in the Qur'an or *hadith* 'asking Muslims to have arranged marriages' (Iqbal.1987). This is true even in the face of much of classical Muslim jurisprudence requiring guardian involvement in marriage negotiations for minors and even for adult women, reasoning (among other things) that this is necessary for their protection. Some Muslim women activists emphasize the non-Qur'anic basis for these guardian rules in arguments for reform beyond patriarchal interpretations in Islamic law (al-Hibri 2000: 60; Fadel 1998). Similarly, wedding particulars, from clothing and food to where the bride and groom sit, all vary from culture to culture, none of which commands Islamic official sanction, but may often be confused as such (Chang 1990).[49] It is not just non-Muslims who confuse culture with religion. Some Muslims assume cultural practices that have been within their families for generations are actually required by Islamic law. Thus, many debates within US Muslim families, whether they are inter-generational or inter-cultural, often superficially seem to be about religion, but are really based on a mixture of cultural and religious/legal norms. These debates include, for example, arguments over the level of parental involvement in choosing one's spouse (and participation in wedding formalities themselves), the amount of pre-marital contact future spouses may have, the nature and amount of dower, allocation of household responsibilities (financial and physical), and spousal activities and work outside the home, to name just a few. Many of these issues do appear in juristic discussions (both classical and modern), but usually in the context of what role custom plays in law-making, as these issues are not specifically addressed in the Qur'an and *hadith* (see 'Intellectual Resources' in Chapter 10). As the community evolves and migrates, discussions of these topics become complicated as the line between law and culture blurs for the average Muslim.

Male superiority within the hierarchy of the family is one culturally validated but also often religiously justified ideology (Marquand 1996).[50] Many US Muslims believe in a patriarchal final authority over family matters, and look to Qur'anic verses in support of this belief. Others resist this notion as an antiquated cultural preference, and look instead to Qur'anic and Islamic concepts of partnership and equality of the sexes (Wadud 1999, 2000; al-Hibri 2000; al-Faruqi 2000; Barazangi 2000; Muslim Women's League, 'Gender Equality', n.d.). Both philosophies, and variations in between, can usually support harmonious and successful families. However, the idea of male superiority sometimes is used to justify physical and mental abuse of other family members, especially women and children, as a Muslim male's right, presented as somehow endorsed by the *shari'a* (Kadri, interview, 2000; Winton 1993).[51] In the words of Kamran Memon (1993), an attorney and one of the first in the US Muslim community to write publicly on the subject:

Tragically, some Muslim men actually use Islam to 'justify' their abusive behavior...considering themselves to be Islamically knowledgeable and disregarding the spirit of Islam, they wrongly use the Qur'anic verse that says men are the protectors and maintainers of women to demand total obedience and order their wives around...These men misinterpret a Qur'anic verse that talks about how to treat a disobedient wife and use it as a license for abuse.[52]

Even worse, as Memon and other Muslims note, is when battered Muslim women accept these religious claims and suffer the abuse, believing it to be some sort of religious duty on their part, and are unfortunately supported in this belief by Muslim community members, even leaders (Kadri, interview, 2000).[53]

This attitude, of course, disrupts the family unit with its acceptance of violence and general instability, and even more seriously if it drives the wife to flee the household or causes social workers to remove children from a dangerous family setting. Recently, members of the Muslim community have begun to recognize the problem of domestic violence, publicly speak against it,[54] and take proactive steps inspired by Islamic principles to respond to the situation (Nadir 2001: 78; al-Khateeb 1998: 17; Syed 1996; Memon 1993). For example, the Peaceful Families Project, a programme funded with a $76,000 grant from the US State Department and spearheaded by Sharifa al-Khateeb, has held conferences in several major American cities dedicated to educating and advising the American Muslim public to combat domestic violence in Muslim families (Kondo 2001). Moreover, a number of Muslim organizations have been established specifically to assist battered Muslim women, or have developed programmes targeted at this objective, through education, creation of shelters and providing legal and counselling assistance.[55]

Dissolution of American Muslim marriages

Most Muslims pursuing divorce are careful to follow local state rules in order to ensure its recognition under US law. Sometimes Islamic family law does arise in these civil divorce proceedings, usually in the form of a claim for payment of the *mahr/sadaq* amount. Family law attorney Abed Awad reports, for example, that he sees a trend of husbands resisting dower payments, sometimes using the *shari'a*-based argument that wife-initiated divorces entail the wife's forfeiture of the *mahr* (interview, 2000). Another Muslim attorney, Sermid al-Sarraf, describes one case where the spouses turned to Islamic law to assist in determining the custody of their children, each consulting different Muslim legal scholars on the question. In the end, however, other issues, such as competency and capability of support, played a stronger role in the custody decision (interview, 2000). In general, US Muslims facing divorce disputes seem to seek advice and assistance on both their Islamic and secular legal rights; and as the number of Muslim legal professionals and legal organizations in the USA grows, more and more experts become available who can assist with both simultaneously.

In a minority of cases, Islamic divorces are conducted outside the American system altogether, either by a husband's private *talaq* declaration or through a third-party determination by local Muslim arbiters, and the parties fail to file any divorce documents under state rules.[56] Such divorces would lack validity under US law, and the parties may be faced with complications in any subsequent attempts to marry in the United States (Little 1993).[57] They would also present obstacles to either spouse attempting to enforce any terms of an Islamic divorce settlement, such as the distribution of property or custody of children, in the event that the other spouse breaches the deal. Some case law discussed in the next chapter of this report, reflects efforts by the courts to deal with these extrajudicial divorces.

Deliberately opting out of US default rules

Some Muslims are proactively interested in ways to legitimately opt out of United States legal norms that potentially conflict with their Islamic preferences. For example, in community property states some Muslims are concerned that a community property distribution of half a wife's property to her husband infringes on the Muslim woman's right to full and exclusive ownership of her property.[58] Others believe that community property distributions should not be given to Muslim women in addition to their *mahr,* which they hold already to fulfil the need sought to be resolved by community property statutes.

But community property is not absolutely mandatory, even in community property states. One can opt out of community property by executing a valid pre-nuptial agreement to that effect, but few couples have the knowledge or foresight to arrange this.[59] A complicating concern is the possibility that the *mahr* agreement will be insufficient or not ultimately enforced, and therefore opting out of community property distribution will leave a Muslim woman with neither *shari'a*-based nor secular-based adequate support. Ironically, there are historically established financial compensation norms in Islamic law aimed at responding to the same problem to which community property laws are addressed. Azizah al-Hibri (2000: 57) points out in this respect that under classical Islamic law, wives who perform household chores are entitled to financial compensation from their husbands for this work or, where the woman is accustomed to it in her social circles, to have paid help to do it for them because such work is not a religious obligation. While some Muslim countries today are seeking to revive this principle in practical terms in financial distributions upon divorce,[60] the doctrine remains unknown among most lay Muslims, in the United States and worldwide, Of course, enforceability of this Islamic doctrine in the United States is dependent upon voluntary compliance by ex-spouses, as it is unlikely to be applied by United States courts without some compelling reason to do so.

19. **Asifa Quraishi, "Islamic Family Law in US Courts" from** *Women's Rights & Islamic Family Law*

Excerpt from Welchman, Lynn (Ed.), Women's Rights & Islamic Family Law (London: Zed Books, 2004), pp. 179–198. Reprinted with permission from Zed Books.

The following is a continuation of the previous entry, The Muslim Family in the USA: Law in Practice. It continues Quraishi's (for a biography, see the preface to Primary document 18). analysis of the interactions between Islamic family law and American civil law regarding polygamy, marriage, and divorce. She highlights some of the legal and social accommodations and compromises Muslims are undertaking in the American context

§   WE now turn to the question of how Muslim marriages have fared in the US courts.[61] There is fairly little awareness in the US Muslim community about this subject:, and consequently many mistaken assumptions are made. Much confusion surrounds the question of the validity of the marriage contract itself, as many assume that the Law of pre-nuptial agreements will safeguard the enforcement of Muslim marriage contract clauses.[62] As will be seen in this chapter, Muslims seeking to enforce their marriage contract as a pre-nuptial agreement have actually had varying success in the courtroom. One essential question that will be addressed is whether David Forte's prediction that there will be difficulty in 'pleading Islamic law in American courts' has been fulfilled (Forte 1983: 31), In this chapter, we will review the treatment of Muslim marriage in published US case law, and review the thoughts of Muslim attorneys working in this field.

The validity of Muslim marriages

The question begins at the beginning—whether a Muslim marriage will be recognized as valid under domestic US law in the first place. As mentioned in Chapter 11, this is only a real concern where the couple did not also follow secular state rules in registering their marriage. But even where there is only a Muslim marriage ceremony, the courts have not rejected such marriages outright, but rather undertake their own inquiry into whether the marriage was valid under the laws of the place in which it was conducted. For example, *Farah v. Farah* was a 1993 Virginia case involving the proxy marriage in England of two Pakistanis (with a subsequent wedding reception in Pakistan) who subsequently moved to the United States. Because the proxy marriage did not follow English requirements for a valid marriage, the Virginia court held that it could not recognize it as a valid marriage, stating that the fact that the proxy wedding complied with general Islamic family law rules (which would be relevant in Pakistan) was irrelevant. Conversely, in a more recent case, *Shike v. Shike* (2000), a couple married in a Muslim *nikah* (marriage) ceremony in Pakistan and subsequently documented it in Texas by having a Texas imam sign a standard Texas marriage licence. Though the couple initially believed their *nikah* to be only an engagement,[63] the court's inquiry revealed that the parties' public representations were that of a married couple and therefore the court found the marriage valid under Texas law, even though performed outside Texas. Finally, in *Aghili v. Saadatnejadi* (1997), the Tennessee Court of Appeals held that an Islamic marriage ceremony, followed by later compliance with state marriage licence law, qualified as a legal marriage, reversing the trial court's summary judgment that the Muslim marriage 'blessing' did not qualify as a solemnization ceremony.

When there is no documentation of a marriage at all, Muslim or secular, then the court is faced with the difficult question of determining whether there was a 'putative' marriage (or in some states, a 'common law' marriage). This is what happened in *Vryonis v. Vryonis,* a 1988 case in California in which a couple entered into a private *mut'a* marriage (a marriage for a temporary period of time recognized under Shi'i but not Sunni Islamic jurisprudence) with no written documentation or witnesses. The court of appeals rejected the trial court's inquiry into the wife's reasonable belief in the validity of her marriage under Islamic law, and instead inquired into whether she had a reasonable belief of a valid marriage under California law. In the end, with no evidence of public solemnization, no licence, and no public representations of the couple as a married unit, the court answered the question in the negative. In reading *Vryonis,* it is interesting to note two elements considered by the court as persuasive against the existence of a real marriage: that (1) the wife kept her own name and (2) maintained a separate bank account. Commenting on this case, Azizah al-Hibri points out that, among Muslims, these facts would carry no persuasive weight against the existence of a marriage because the changing of the wife's family name on marriage is not required by *fiqh,* and indeed has not been a characteristic of most Muslim communities. And second, Muslim women often keep separate bank accounts to protect their right under Islamic law to exclusive control over their personal property (Muslim Women's League and Karamah 1995).[64]

Finally, there have been some cases of marriages held invalid by the courts where the Muslim parties are found to have violated basic norms of justice as recognized in the USA. For example, where a Muslim parent forces a minor to marry against his or her will, the courts have brought criminal charges against the parent.[65] In such cases, parental cultural defences are unsuccessful and held simply to violate public policy and the constitutional rights of the minor.

The enforceability of specific marriage contract provisions

The question of judicial enforcement of the terms of marriage contracts is important to Muslims because, as a minority community in a secular legal system, the only authority with physical state power to which individual spouses can turn when their partner breaches a marital agreement is the domestic courts, While local Muslim authorities (scholars, imams, family elders) are widely used to assist conflicts internally, these authorities ultimately rely on voluntary compliance by the parties; they do not have the police power necessary to force compliance against a recalcitrant spouse. However, courts interpreting complex personalised Muslim marriage contracts face a dilemma because there is a judicial preference not to interfere in an ongoing marital relationship (Rasmusen and Stake 1998: 484).[66] Thus, clauses that demand compliance during the life of a marriage (such as a spouse's right to complete an education, a promise of monogamy, or the nature of raising the children), even if they do not offend public policy, are rarely the subject of judicial oversight. If the marriage is at the point of breakdown, however, the court may be willing to include breach of marital agreements in its calculation of damage remedies for the violated spouse. This is often frustrating for those who would have preferred to maintain the marital relationship as agreed, rather than receive damages for its dissolution. As American legal scholar Carol Weisbrod (1999: 51) puts it: 'In many family law cases, money is not an adequate remedy ... [but] other more direct remedies may be barred because, for example, personal services contracts are not specifically enforceable and the United States Constitution guarantees the "free exercise of religion," with all the complexities of that idea.' As will be seen, this may have serious consequences for those relying on agreements regarding the religious upbringing of the children.

Provisions regarding the *mahr/sadaq* in a Muslim marriage contract are somewhat easier for the courts to handle because they are usually already defined in terms of a monetary amount payable upon dissolution of the marriage—a secular concept understandable to US judges. In the most recent case to take up the question, *Odatalla u. Odatalla* (2002), a New Jersey court treated the Muslim marriage contract in question under standard contract law and ultimately upheld the $10,000 postponed *mahr* as binding in a US court. Said the New Jersey judge: '[W]hy should a contract for the promise to pay money be less of a contract just because it was entered into at the time of an Islamic marriage ceremony? . . . Clearly, this Court can enforce so much of a contract as is not in contravention of established law or public policy' (Odatalla 1995). What is unique about this case is that, contrary to the predominant approach of most US courts up to this point, it did not analyse the *mahr* as a pre-nuptial agreement, but rather under neutral principles of contract law.[67] Abed Awad, who litigated the case on behalf of the prevailing wife, insists that the misconstruction of *mahr* agreements as pre-nuptial agreements under US law has created a serious warping of American judicial understanding of Islamic law as well as a hindrance to providing justice to US Muslim litigants.[68] As urged by Awad in the *Odatalla* litigation, *mahr* is not consideration for the contract, but rather an effect of it— an automatic consequence whenever a Muslim couple marries (Awad 2002). This is borne out by classical jurisprudence on the subject and the fact that Muslim jurists would assign an equitable *mahr* to those wives whose contracts did not specify one (Welchman 2000: 136, 140; Rapoport 2000: 14).[69] Thus, enforcement of Muslim marriage contracts, says Awad, should be by simple contract law principles, and not by the more particularized rules of pre-nuptial agreements that vary from state to state and generally carry heightened scrutiny (Awad 2002).

The characterization of Muslim marriage contracts as pre-nuptial agreements is not exclusive to US judges. Many lay Muslims, unaware of the legal distinctions between pre-nuptial agreements and simple contracts, often refer to Muslim marriage contracts as pre-nuptial agreements, and moreover some actively advocate the employment of this legal tool by US Muslims.[70] Attorney Abed Awad points out that these Muslims are often unaware of the technical requirements attached to valid pre-nuptial agreement drafting, and also that such agreements are assumed to override all other standard laws regarding dissolution of marriage, such as inheritance, community property, alimony and so on (Awad, interview, 2001). In Islamic law, however, these are separate questions—a Muslim wife is entitled to both her *mahr* and her standard inheritance portion—and Awad points to this as another proof that the Muslim marriage contract should not be seen as a pre-nuptial agreement.

A California case illustrates what happens when pre-nuptial agreement analysis meets an incomplete understanding of Islamic law in a US court. In *Dajani v. Dajani* (1988), the California Court of Appeals interpreted the *mahr* in a Muslim marriage contracted in Jordan to be a pre-nuptial provision 'facilitating divorce' because the 5,000 Jordanian dinars became payable to the wife only upon dissolution of the marriage. In California, as in most states, a pre-marital agreement may not 'promote dissolution' and thus a promise of substantial payments upon divorce may be interpreted to invalidate that clause.[71] The court thus considered the *mahr* windfall to be potential 'profiteering by divorce' by the wife and against public policy, and held the provision unenforceable, causing Mrs Dajani to lose her expected *mahr*. Azizah al-Hibri has critiqued this court opinion, showing it to reflect a basic misunderstanding of Islamic law and the institution of deferred dower, particularly since deferred dower is also due upon the death of the husband (al-Hibri 1995: 16–17).[72] It might also be pointed out that, under Islamic law, if a woman initiates divorce extra-judicially through *khul'*, then she is likely to forfeit her *mahr*.[73] Thus, a *mahr* clause in this situation acts as a deterrent to (not a facilitator of) no-fault divorce by the wife—a result quite opposite from the 'profiteering' assumptions made by the California Court of Appeals.

The whole life of the *Dajani* case, from trial to appeal, illustrates mistakes that can be made when US judges attempt to adjudicate matters of Islamic law. At trial, for example, Muslim experts testified to the Dajani judge regarding the forfeiture of the dower upon divorce initiated by the wife, and, based on this testimony, the trial court concluded that the wife must forfeit her *mahr* because she initiated the divorce, an oversimplified understanding of Islamic law on the matter. (Unfortunately, the court did not undertake an analysis of *faskh* dissolution in Islamic law where an inquiry into harm is made, distinguishing it from extra-judicial *khul'*.) But when it got to the Court of Appeals, the inquiry into Islamic law was even more superficial: it went straight to rejecting all *mahr* provisions generally as 'facilitating divorce'.

Demographic distribution may play a role in the ability of US judges fully to understand minority religious practices affecting family law rights. For example, the *Odatalla* case originated in New Jersey, in an area with a significant Arab-American population. Similarly, New York family courts dealing with Muslim litigants have relied on their experience with the Jewish *ketuba,* a custom carrying many parallels with Muslim marriage contracting. Thus, in *Habibi-Fahnrich v. Fahnrich* (1995), the New York Supreme Court, though a bit confused in its usage of terms,[74] specifically stated: 'The *sadaq* is the Islamic marriage contract. It is a document which defines the precepts of the Moslem marriage by providing for financial compensation to a woman for the loss of her status and value in the community if tire marriage ends in a divorce. This court has previously determined that *sadaq* may be enforceable in this court.' In this case, the court ultimately ruled the *sadaq* at issue to be unenforceable, but it did so in a way that is more instructive to Muslims. In *Fahnrich* (1995), the New York court had difficulty giving effect to the *sadaq* provision in the Muslim marriage contract simply because the terms were too vague under basic contract principles. The clause '[t]he *sadaq* being a ring advanced and half of husband's possessions postponed' left too many financial calculation questions unanswered (e.g. half of which possessions calculated at what point in the marriage? Postponed until when?). Thus, it was a violation of the Statute of Frauds, not public policy, which doomed this *mahr* provision. In fact, these same criticisms would be likely to be raised under an Islamic investigation of the terms of the contract (Rapoport 2000: 5-21). In both jurisdictions, Muslims would be wise to pay more attention to writing clear terms in their marriage contracts.[75]

The need for clarity arises in another clause often included as standard in Muslim marriage contracts, stating something to the effect that the marriage is governed by Islamic law. These sorts of clauses have been found by one court to be insufficiently clear to warrant court enforcement of its terms. In *Shaban v. Shaban* (2001), the California Court of Appeals rejected a husband's attempt to enforce the *mahr* (the equivalent of $30) listed in his Egyptian Muslim marriage contract, instead awarding the wife $1.5 million in community property. The marriage contract included a clause stating that the 'marriage [was] concluded in accordance with his Almighty God's Holy Book and the Rules of his Prophet', and the husband asserted that this meant that the dissolution should be governed by 'Islamic law'. The court flatly rejected this attempt to incorporate Islamic law by reference, stating that 'Islamic law' was such a broad, abstract concept that brought too much uncertainty into the terms of the contract. Pointing out the many manifestations (schools of thought, state legislation) of Islamic law, the court concluded: 'An agreement whose only substantive term . . . is that the marriage has been made in accordance with "Islamic law" is hopelessly uncertain as to its terms and conditions.'[76]

Thus, the Statute of Frauds, requiring clear contract terms, prevented its enforcement. Interestingly, the court did not even get to the question of whether the *mahr* clause was against public policy (as they had in *Dajani,* and as the trial court had done in this case). Said the court: 'It is enough to remark that the need for parole evidence to supply the material terms of the alleged agreement readers it impossible to discuss any public policy issues. After all, how can one say that an agreement offends public policy when it is not possible even to state its terms?'

The California court's attitude in *Shaban* is significantly different from the New York Supreme Court's treatment of a similar clause in *Aziz v. Aziz* (1985), in which it found a Muslim marriage contract, with its *mahr* provision of $5,000 deferred and $35 prompt, to be judicially enforceable despite its being part of a religious ceremony, because it conformed to the requirements of New York general contract law. This is true even though the contract apparently stated that it united the parties as husband and wife 'under Islamic law'. The concerns of 'Islamic law' by incorporation so central to the California *Shaban* court apparently did not bother the New York Supreme Court. In the words of the court: 'The documental issue conforms to the requirements of [state contract law] and its secular terms are enforceable as a contractual obligation, notwithstanding that it was entered into as part of a religious ceremony.'[77]

There are two interesting aspects of *Shaban* that are relevant for our study here. First, the court's rejection of the entire contract because of a clause stating it is governed by

'Islamic law' is important to Muslims because most, if not all, Muslim marriage contracts include this type of statement. This is true even of marriage contracts drafted in the United States. Since the court appeared particularly frustrated with the lack of any other substantive terms in the contract besides this one and the *mahr* provision, it may be that, by individualizing and embellishing their marriage contracts with many substantive stipulations, Muslim couples may be able to avoid a result like the one in *Shaban,* but there is no guarantee. In addition, as will be seen in more detail later, other states have found their way to enforcing Muslim marriage contracts despite such references.

The other interesting thing about the California court's treatment of *Shaban* is its absolute lack of interest in investigating the permutations of Islamic law if it were to govern the agreement. They are justifiably concerned about the complexity and diversity of 'Islamic law' and their reluctance to engage it is understandable. Nevertheless, one is left with the impression that the court took for granted the husband's version of Islamic law—i.e. that the wife would be limited to $30 *mahr* under Islamic law, and that the obviously fairer thing to award the ex-wife of a now-wealthy American doctor after twenty-seven years of marriage is her community property entitlement of $1.5 million. But if the court had decided to make a deeper investigation of Islamic law in such a situation, they might have found that the stipulated *mahr* is not always the end of the story for a Muslim court—she might have been given an adjusted *mahr mithl* if the stipulated *mahr* was out of proportion to women of her peer group, and she might even have been awarded *muta* maintenance (equivalent to alimony) in an amount close to the community property award (Rapoport 2000). Further, Islamic legal precedent establishing that women have no obligation to do housework or even to nurse children (and thus should be compensated for it if they choose to do so),[78] points to an awareness of the very problem that community property laws in the modern West seek to remedy (al-Hibri 2000; Walter 1999). It is a mistake to assume that awards under Islamic law are necessarily going to be worse for the wife than under US law. In fact, it appears that most spouses attempting to enforce Muslim marriage contracts in US courts are wives (not husbands), attempting to enforce rather high *mahr* amounts.[79]

An interesting aspect of these cases is that they show, in general, that for those courts that do undertake the effort, they have been fairly good at understanding the relevant Islamic jurisprudence defining the nature of a Muslim marriage contract, in order to discern which elements it can enforce as a secular court. These judicial understandings are largely from their own research as well as Muslim expert witnesses presenting courtroom testimony. Though they often disagree with each other in a particular case and frequently leave out jurisprudential details, the outcome of the cases indicates that, by and large, these experts have served to give the judges a rather good idea of the important elements at work. In one case, an appellate court even corrected its trial court in understanding the nature of Muslim wedding officiants. In *Aghili v. Saadatnejadi* (1997), the Tennessee Court of Appeals, citing expert testimony, explained:

In contrast to Western religious teaching and practice (particularly in Christianity, both Catholic and Protestant, but also to some extent Judaism) Islam from its inception to the present has consistently rejected the distinction between clergy and laity. Islamic law stipulates quite precisely that anyone with the requisite knowledge of Islamic law is competent to perform religious ceremonies, including marriage. One is not required to have an official position in a religious institution such as a mosque (*masjid*) in order to be qualified to perform such ceremonies.

This understanding of Muslim wedding officials (and imams in general), though it over-states the facts in assuming there is a need for an officiant at all (Islamic law does not require one), is still instructive in accurately trying to appreciate the different structure of religious authority in Islamic law as compared to other religions, and does so in a respectful way. There is here an appreciation that a Muslim marriage does not have to look like a Christian one, and need not have an altar or a minister in order to be valid. In this case, the court's awareness resulted in its rejection of the husband's claim that his marriage was not valid because the officiant was not a real 'imam'. Said the court, his 'right to bear the title imam is irrelevant'. Of course, the education of judges is not uniform across the USA (as the *Dajani* case exemplifies), but this review of the case law indicates an overall positive picture, especially in those states that have more experience with minority religious legal traditions, such as New York.

The lesson for American Muslims from these cases is that, even though a Muslim mar-riage contract serves a religious function, if its terms are clear, an American court might find a way to enforce those terms serving a 'secular' purpose, such as the financial *mahr/sadaq* awards due upon dissolution. But a final note on secular court understandings of *mahr/sadaq* clauses: it is worth noting that Muslim jurisprudence, classical and modern, identifies a number of functions fulfilled by the institution of *mahr,* whether in its status in the contract or more broadly in the social life of the wife in particular. A number of these functions have been identified by US courts in the cases described above.[80] These include: (1) it serves the purpose of financial security for the wife in the event of a divorce;[81] (2) it may serve as a deterrent to the husband declaring a unilateral *talaq* divorce;[82] (3) it constitutes a form of compensation to a woman unjustly divorced by the husband's unilateral *talaq*; (4) it is the husband's consideration for entering the mar-riage, under basic contract law principles; or, lastly, (5) it is simply a gift from the husband to the wife.[83] Each of these functions of *mahr* might prompt a different analysis by a sec-ular court attempting to understand it in secular terms, and there is consequently the potential for inconsistencies between courts and frustration by Muslim litigants who may interpret the purpose of their *mahr* differently than that focused on by the court. For example, if the *mahr* is merely a gift, then why does Islamic law treat it as a debt owed by the husband if he chooses not to pay it? (Esposito 1982: 25; Rapoport 2000: 10). If it is compensation for unjustified unilateral divorce by the husband, then what if the divorce at issue was initiated by the wife instead? If it serves as financial support for the wife after divorce, then does the initiator of the divorce (i.e. whether it is *khul'* or *talaq*) really matter, and can secular alimony and child support payments be substituted instead? Rapoport's review of the evolution of the deferred *mahr* suggests that that institution did act as a substitute for alimony, but this does not speak to the rationale of the prompt *mahr* (Rapoport 2000). Further complicating all these analyses are the myriad variations on what *mahr* amount is payable up-front and what amount is deferred—i.e. if it is sub-stituted for alimony, then should Muslim women start asking for a large amount upfront instead of a large deferred amount, to protect themselves against the possibility that a court will award them neither alimony nor their deferred *mahr?* And then there is the question of how to treat dowers that are not specified in monetary terms at all. All of these questions remain unanswered, and perhaps there is no uniform answer that applies to the situation of every woman (i.e. while one might need financial security another might need deterrence against her husband's unilateral divorce). Nevertheless, as these cases demand more and more judicial attention, they will also draw the eye of Muslim legal experts in the USA to focus on basic Islamic jurisprudence on the subject, its appropriate interpretation in the context of modern-day USA, and then address how to present these conclusions to the judiciary.

At present, US Muslim attorneys differ over the viability of pursuing the enforcement of *mahr/sadaq* provisions in the courts. Some believe it to be generally a losing proposition, citing local cases they have seen where the *mahr* was denied (Kadri, interview, 2000). Others are optimistic about the future of *mahr* recognition in the United States and encourage those pursuing these cases (al-Sarraf, interview, 2001). Indeed, in the cases reviewed above, spouses asserting the enforceability of a Muslim marriage contract as a pre-nuptial agreement did not always succeed. In both California cases dealing with *mahr* claims as pre-nuptial agreements, *Dajani* and *Shaban,* the court ultimately refused to honour the contract. In New York and Florida, the parties fared a bit better in *Aziz* (NY) and *Akileh* (FL) the Muslim dower provisions were upheld, though the language of the Florida court indicates that they perceived the *sadaq* to be the husband's consideration for entering into the contract, an analysis with which Awad would strongly disagree.

Reviewing the history of the subject in general, it appears that interest in enforcing *mahr* provisions in the courts has taken particular hold in the Muslim community over the past five years or so. In earlier years, Muslim couples apparently tended to opt for informal recognition, voluntarily enforced through internal channels. As more and more Muslims draft formal Muslim marriage contracts in the United States, the courts will presumably see more litigation of *mahr* clauses. It remains to be seen whether there will be consistent treatment of these cases by state family law courts, and whether that treatment will be to review these cases as pre-nuptial agreements, seek to reject them as contracts with uncertain terms due to their religious references, or analyse them under straight contract law.

As for the enforceability of contractual stipulations other than the dower, there is much less case law because, as noted earlier, these sorts of stipulations are less popular in Muslim marriage contracts, and have even less frequently become the subject of full litigation ending up in published case reports. One stipulation many Muslims wonder about is a clause regarding the religious upbringing of the children, a relatively popular clause in inter-religious marriages. Specifics vary from state to state but, generally, agreements that a child will be raised in a particular religion are not enforceable in a pre-nuptial agreement, but if included in a separation agreement (when the marriage is ending) are usually recognized. For example, in *Jabri v. Jabri* (1993), a New York court held: 'Agreements between divorcing spouses with respect to the religious upbringing of their children will be upheld by the courts only when incorporated into separation agreements, court orders, or signed stipulations...In the absence of a written agreement, the custodial parent... may determine the religious training of the child.' And in *Arain v. Arain* (1994), the New York Supreme Court rejected for lack of supporting evidence a custody-change request based on a claim that the wife had violated her agreement to 'raise the child pursuant to the Muslim faith'. Muslims will note that this is in contrast to standard Islamic law rules on custody, which would hold that a non-Muslim's wife failure to raise the children as Muslims would cause her custody of the child to lapse at least once age of discrimination is reached. This US judicial policy is based on several reasons, including the unconstitutional judicial promotion of a particular religion, and avoidance of judicial interference in an ongoing marriage (*Zummo v. Zummo,* 1990). As a result, Muslim marriage contracts including a religion-of-the-child clause are unlikely to be enforced because these contracts are usually likened to pre-nuptial agreements in order to be enforced. However, upon divorce, if such an agreement is possible (either through divorce mediation, or informally between themselves), the parties may be able to accomplish this goal, if the agreement is included in their documented separation agreement. In any case, religious upbringing of the children is a complicated and risky business, and (as discussed earlier) is one of the reasons some Muslims today warn against marriage to non-Muslims' (al-Hibri 2000).

The validity of Muslim divorces

The basic rule governing the validity of divorces in US courts is *lex domicili,* that is, the validity of the divorce is dependent upon the law of the domicile of the parties (Reed 1996: 311). Thus, where it is sought to enforce Muslim divorces conducted outside the United States, the court will look to the law of the foreign state. For example, in a case as old as 1912, *Kapigian v. Minassian,* the Supreme Court of Massachusetts held as valid the Turkish law of the time which automatically nullified the marriage of a non-Muslim woman to a non-Muslim man upon the wife's conversion to Islam, and therefore upheld the divorce of a Turkish Muslim woman convert whose husband was then living (and remarried) in the United States.

Of further interest to the Muslim community is the treatment of domestic non-judicial divorces—those accomplished by verbal *talaq* or through formal approval by a local Muslim imam. These have not fared well. In *Shikoh v. Shikoh* (1958), the federal Court of Appeals for the Second Circuit held that a religious divorce granted by a local shaykh failed to constitute a 'judicial proceeding', which was required for all legitimate divorces under New York law. and held the divorce invalid. Said the court, *lex domicili* still applied: 'where the divorce is obtained within the jurisdiction of the state of New York, then it must be secured in accordance with the laws of that state'. And even where the domicile is a Muslim country, the US courts have demanded a judicial proceeding. Thus, in *Seth v. Seth* (1985), the Texas Court of Appeals refused to recognize a *talaq* divorce conducted in Kuwait as valid because there was 'no factual showing [that] any official state body in either India [where they were married] or Kuwait...had actually executed or confirmed the divorce and marriage'.

Looking over these cases as a whole, we might notice that they reflect a basic Western assumption built into the judicial reasoning—i.e. that a divorce has to be somehow officially recognized by some official body, even in a Muslim country, in order to be legitimate. However, Islamic laws of divorce do not follow this same premise, as private declarations of divorce (*talaq*) or private mutually-consented divorce agreements (*khul'*) are nevertheless given legal validity in Islamic *fiqh*. Of course, modern Muslim countries, with variations on classical Islamic law as their legislated codes, often require something more for legal recognition of a divorce, even if only a registration of an extra-judicial divorce with the authorities. The question that has apparently not yet reached a US court is whether it would recognize an extra-judicial *talaq* or *khul'* divorce if it had been registered with the state as a divorce deed, and therefore perfectly valid as a divorce in that particular country (as is the case in Egypt or Pakistan, for example) but not the subject of a 'judicial proceeding' as required by this US case precedent. If the question is ever raised and the court is willing to undertake a study of Islamic law in order to answer it, the argument might be made that the rationale behind the 'judicial proceeding' requirement is the due process principle of notice and the right to be heard,[84] and therefore *khul'* divorces (obtained extra-judicially but with mutual consent of both parties) should be recognized but *talaq* divorces (whereby a husband merely declares the divorce with no necessary consent by or even notice to the wife) should not. This level of Islamic law awareness and analysis, however, can only be hoped for, as the cases summarized thus far illustrate the serious misunderstandings of Islamic law upon which some of these cases have been adjudicated.

The divorce cases requiring 'judicial proceedings' and other cases where Islamic legal norms are rejected for violation of public policy tend to reflect the presumption that the secular rules which override religious laws are somehow better, fairer, and reflect more progressive views on women, children and human rights. Yet, US Muslim scholars might take issue with this presumption, pointing out that in some cases, Islamic law is more progressive and beneficial to women than its secular counterpart. For example, the institution of *khul'* divorces, allowing a woman to end a marriage (usually for the price of her *mahr*) without having to go through the long and often painful process of divorce litigation, might be seen as a very useful tool for women. Moreover, the right to a *mahr* is so central to Muslim consciousness that it is usually the only marital stipulation Muslim women are aware they must include in their marriage contracts. Many see the deferred *mahr* as meaningful deterrence against a hasty divorce by the husband, and the prompt *mahr* as a means of ensuring financial security and independence to women who may or may not have an outside income. When a US court strikes down a *mahr* provision (whether as too religious or against public policy), many Muslim women believe this is a step backwards, not forwards, for women. Many assert that some of these cases do a serious injustice to Muslim women and to the aspects of Islamic law that protect their interests (al-Hibri 1995). Other woman-affirming aspects of Islamic law as yet unaddressed by US courts include the recognition that a woman's household work is financially compensable, that her property is exclusively her own, and the ability personally to tailor a marriage contract. These are all illustrations of Islamic jurisprudential progressiveness, some of which have only recently been paralleled in the West. Comparing different legal systems, therefore, must be undertaken with care, and it is dangerous to assume that a comity-based recognition of an alternative norm is always a concession to the lesser law. Sometimes it may be a step forwards.

Child custody

As in every community, many Muslim divorce cases necessitate a custody determination. Islamic family law can arise in these cases when one party asserts classical *shari'a* custody rules based on the age and gender of the children (Doi 1989: 37).[85] Such claims may play a large role at the informal level (mediated divorce settlement agreements, for example) in the US Muslim community, but published case law focuses mainly on the validity of overseas custody decrees from Muslim countries. There is not a huge amount of published case law on this subject, although Henderson (1997–98: 423) notes a certain recent increase, with only three cases involving state court interpretation of custody decrees from Muslim countries being reported between 1945 and 1995, while a further three were reported in the year 1995–96 alone. These cases reveal differing treatment by states towards Islamic law's custody rules, sometimes showing deference to Muslim courts and sometimes not, but always within the context of the US standard of the 'best interests of the child'. For example, in *Malak v. Malak* (1986), the California Court of Appeals evaluated one Muslim custody decision from Abu Dhabi and one from Lebanon. The Abu Dhabi decision, awarding custody to the father because of its rule automatically granting custody to fathers when the child reaches a given age, was held inconsistent with best interest standards and was rejected. The Lebanese Muslim court decree, on the other hand, was found to comply with American courts' expectations of notice and also legitimately considered 'educational, social, psychologic[al], material, and moral factors, for the purpose of insuring the best interest of the two children and their present future and in the long run'.[86]

Some courts have recognized the child's religion as a legitimate factor to be considered in a 'best interest' analysis, for courts in a society where religion is centrally important. Thus, in *Hosain v. Malik* (1996), a Maryland court concluded that, in Pakistan, custody determination of the best interest of the child was appropriately determined according to the morals and customs of Pakistani society. Said the court:

We believe it beyond cavil that a Pakistani court could only determine the best interest of a Pakistani child by an analysis utilizing the customs, culture, religion, and mores of the community and country of which the child and—in this case—her parents were apart, i.e., Pakistan...[B]earing in mind that in the Pakistani culture, the well being of the child and the child's proper development is thought to be facilitated by adherence to Islamic teachings, one would expect that a Pakistani court would weigh heavily the removal of the child from that influence as detrimental.

Judicial consideration of the religion of the child in 'best interest' analyses is not limited to review of international decisions. Some courts have found it relevant as a positive factor in their own 'best interest' evaluation, for example, where religion has been an important part of the child's life until that point; but, again, the importance given to this criterion varies widely from state to state.[87]

Returning to *Hosain,* it is interesting to note that the court there viewed classical Islamic custody rules as not necessarily contrary to public policy. Said the court: 'We would be obliged to note that we are simply unprepared to hold that this longstanding doctrine [*hazanat*—i.e. custody] of one of the world's oldest and largest religions practiced by hundreds of millions of people around the world and in this country, as applied as one factor in the best interest of the child test, is repugnant to Maryland public policy.'

Not all American courts are so reluctant to condemn classical Islamic custody rules outright, however. In *Ali v. Ali* (1994), for example, a New Jersey court rejected a Palestinian custody decree as not in the 'best interests of the child', commenting on the law applied by Palestinian *shari'a* courts in Gaza that automatically entitles the father to gain custody of a son at age seven in the following terms: 'Such presumptions cannot be said by any stretch of the imagination to comport with the law of New Jersey whereby custody determinations are made based upon the "best interests" of the child and not some mechanical formula.' Incidentally, this attitude also finds an audience in legal academia; Henderson (1997–98), for example, devotes an entire article to warning judges to be 'circumspect of foreign custody decrees based on Islamic law' because it is 'mechanical, formulaic and should not be followed'.

One final note on American judicial treatment of Muslim marriage litigation as a whole: the fact that many of the cases reviewed in this section involve marriages either contracted or ended in a foreign country may at first seem not directly relevant to a study of Islamic family law in the United States. However, the complex international demographic of the Muslim population in the USA means that many do not live in the same place over their entire lifetime—they may, for example, emigrate to the USA early in life, move overseas later in life, or live a dual citizenship in more than one country Or, perhaps, because they have overseas relatives, an individual Muslim may live in the United States full-time, but have his/her Muslim wedding ceremony overseas with extended family. Cases where the marriage is executed or dissolved overseas could all end up being litigated in the US courts. As the population of second-generation and native US Muslims grows and more Muslim marriages end up in US courts for litigation, we may see more cases where the full law-related gamut of marital life occurs here in the USA. In these cases, comity to other nations will not be at issue, and US judges will be faced with the question of how to treat Islamic family law in the context of litigants from one of their own domestic religious minorities.

20. **Taha Jabir Alalwani, Web Summary by Omar Tarazi, "Fiqh of Minorities"** **from** *The Islamic Society of North America*

From the Islamic Society of North America, accessed May 18, 2006. Available online: http://www.isna.net/services/library/papers/fiqh/FiqhofMinorities1.html. Reprinted with permission of the Islamic Society of North America.

Taha Jabir Alalwani (for a biography see the "Alalwani, Taha" entry in Volume 1) is at the forefront of a theological work called "Fiqh of Minorities" (fiqh al-aqaliyya). The "Fiqh of Minorities" is primarily a methodological approach to applying classical Islamic jurisprudence (fiqh) to Muslim minorities living in non-Muslim countries. The United States and other Western countries are a specific focus of the "Fiqh of Minorities."

FIQH AL-GHALLIYĀT

Fiqh- (i.e. Islamic Jurisprudence) is defined by Ibn-Khaldun as the classification of actions/obligations as: obligatory, encouraged, permissible, discouraged, forbidden, based on the Qur'an, the Sunnah, and the decisions of prior jurists.

Al-'Jalliyyat- (i.e. Minorities) is a current political term signifying those groups of citizens of a state who differ in race, language, culture, or religion from the majority of the population

Fiqh Al-'Jalliyyat or Fiqh of minorities is the idea that the Muslim Jurist must relate the general Islamic jurisprudence to the specific circumstances of a specific community, living in specific circumstances where what is suitable for them may not be suitable for others. This jurist must not only have a strong background in Islamic sciences, but must also be well versed in the sociology, economics, politics, and international relations relating to that community. The purpose of Fiqh Al-'Jalliyyat is not to recreate Islam, rather it is a set of methodologies that govern how a jurist would work within the flexibility of the religion to best apply it to particular circumstances. Some of the methodologies include: *Reworking the question:*

A wrong question can lead to a wrong answer. Before answering a question the Jurist must know the problem that caused the question to be asked, and rework the question to deal with the core issue involved. When the people asked the Prophet how the moon worked, their core issue was to understand its purpose. The answer came, "They ask you concerning the new moons, Say: they are but signs to mark fixed periods of time for people and pilgrimage"(2:189). The Qur'an reworked the question and answered regarding the purpose of the cycle of new moons, not regarding the scientific mechanism that runs it.

Example #1:

A questioner asks, "Is it forbidden (haram) for a Muslim woman to be married to a non Muslim, and what should one do?"

The standard answer based on the Qur'an is that it is forbidden for a Muslim woman to be married to a non-Muslim so she should be divorced immediately. However in this particular case the circumstances are as follows:

The woman has just converted to Islam and she has a husband and two young kids

The husband is very supportive, but is not at this time interested in converting

The woman was told immediately after converting that she had to divorce her husband of 20 years

Within these circumstances the question should have been:

Is it worse for a Muslim woman to be married to a non-Muslim husband or for her to leave the religion?

The answer is that leaving the religion is much worse, so therefore it is acceptable for her to continue with her marriage and she is responsible before Allah on Judgment Day.

Example #2:

A questioner asks: "Is it forbidden to be involved in an un-Islamic/corrupt government or institution?"

The standard Fiqh answer would be yes it is forbidden, because you do not want to be corrupted by the system or be seen as supporting a corrupt system in front of other weaker Muslims who might be negatively influenced. However in this particular case the circumstances are as follows:

The government's actions can be influenced by being involved in the system.

The government has secular authority over the Muslims in that country and gives them the right to freely practice their religion.

The Muslims are awarded by the government the right to hold public office.

The government currently exerts laws and policies that are not in the best interest of the global or local Muslim community.

The Muslims have the obligation of spreading their religion.

With this information the question must be reworked to reflect the totality of the situation:

Is it permissible for Muslims to participate in the political arena of a democratic government in order to affect policy in favor of the Muslims, or is it better to not get involved for fear of being corrupted by the system?

Under these circumstances the answer is that it is permissible and an obligation on the part of the Muslim community to get involved as long as they are not forced to sacrifice their integrity. For the community it would be considered a type of jihad. If a particular member of the community feels him/her self to be too weak in religion then there is no harm if that person does not directly participate, but supports financially or in other ways instead.

Example #3:

A questioner asks: "If a Muslim sees the new moon for Ramadan should we follow him?"

The standard Islamic answer is yes. If a trustworthy Muslim sees the moon then it would be Ramadan. However in this particular case:

The questioner is part of a local community and the answer to the question will determine whether the community fasts together or is split.

The question should be reworked to say: Which is worse, being off a day one way or the other for Ramadan or splitting the local Muslim community and not following the local leadership?

Absolutely without question the unity of the community is more important, and the Prophet Mohammed commanded us to follow our leaders even if we don't like what they do.

LEARNING FROM PRIOR RULINGS:

The golden rule of Fiqh is: 'changes of Al-'Ahkam (judgments) are permissible with the change in times'. The schools of Fiqh and the past judgments were different because they were generated for different times and different people. For this reason a jurist should not apply prior historical rulings to modern situation without a careful analysis of the circumstances and reasoning that generated the prior ruling.

For example, the prophet first forbade visiting cemeteries than he allowed it later saying, "Formerly, I forbade you from visiting cemeteries. You may visit them for they remind you of Al'Akhira (i.e. the next life). The reason is that there were some bad pagan customs surrounding cemeteries, and he wanted to distance his people from that. After a time when the Muslims were stronger in their Imaan the restriction was no longer necessary so it was removed. Indeed there are many documented cases of the four enlightened caliphs making changes to the established rulings. Occasionally minor or major changes were even made to the rulings of the Prophet, because the circumstances had changed.

Some things to keep in mind regarding the early Jurists rulings:

Many early scholars did not thoroughly document how they arrived at rulings.

Many mistakes are found in historical books on Fiqh because the jurists didn't always have access to all of the relevant material. It has been only recently that jurists have been able to make computer searches to speed up research on issues.

The Muslims were not under conditions such that they had to escape to non-Islamic countries seeking lost rights or escaping from persecution.

The concept of citizen, duties of a citizen, international law, and diplomatic relations didn't exist in the form that they are today.

In ancient times, the language of military power was supreme. A country's borders were only established because the military found it difficult to move forwards.

Globalization didn't exist. People in ancient times lived on a planet of islands.

Therefore we should not fight each other over the literal rulings of the past. Rather we should study the methodology, wisdom, and intent of the prior rulings to best understand how they should apply to the modern world. The mere stress on minor issues of rulings without understanding intent will inevitably cause us to become like the people of "Al-Baqarah".

UNDERSTANDING THE PURPOSE AND INTENT:

The central theme of Fiqh is: the performance of man as inheritor of the earth particularly from the point of view of man's compliance or resistance to the divine purpose of the creation and how he falls short of that purpose. The debate regarding the realties of man's mind and our abilities to evaluate ourselves independent of revaluation has gone on for centuries. Islam recognizes the role of the human intellect as part of the decision making process. Also, we are provided with two books to help guide us in our decisions, the revelation (Qur'an) and the moving cosmos which is the sum total of all aspects of life. The study of each book leads to a better understanding of the other. Some of the criteria for the method of study that emerge to facilitate a better understanding of ultimate purposes are:

Realize the unity of message and structure within the Qur'an and studying its application by the Prophet Mohammed in specific practical everyday matters. Because the documentation of the Sunnah was not perfect and some questionable sayings have been mixed in, we should hold everything to the benchmark of the Qur'an. If a saying does not appear to be in keeping with the Qur'an, we should follow the Qur'an in such circumstances and simply acknowledge that we might not have all the information surrounding that Sunnah (i.e. the circumstances that generated it).

Be in line with the concept that the Qur'an and the Prophethood in general are a completion of the legacy of past prophets. The message and purpose have always remained the same but the form has changed as human society has matured.

Grasp the delicate differences between humanity and the individual, and how the Qur'an relates to each.

Be alert to the inherit logic of the Qur'an, and the parallel nature of that logic for both capturing the divine purpose, and the spiritual logic of the All Knowing, and yet speaking to and being logical to the unlettered human mind.

Adopt the Qur'anic concept of geography on the basis that the world is completely for Allah, and so the Qur'an is inherently a global message, and should be treated and understood as such.

Contemplate the facts of life, so that when a question is formulated it is done while taking into consideration all aspects involved.

Understand the aims and purposes of the Shari'ah as well as the resulting outcomes

Test the Fiqh verdicts to evaluate their validity by seeing if they provoke the desired outcome of bringing people closer to the pure path of Allah.

CONSEQUENCES

THE PROBLEM OF *DARU-KURER* (LAND OF INFIDELS)

Some modern scholars, and certain groups of people have thrown a significant monkey wrench in the Muslims' ability to live and interact with western countries like the United States. They pose the argument that we should all move back to Darul-Islam (land of Islam), and if we are forced to live in Daru-Kufer (land of infidels) we should consider it a temporary stay and should either not participate or fight the "Kufer" government. The answer to this argument is three fold:

THE MUSLIM *UMMAH* (NATION/MODEL)

Daru-Kufer and Daru-Islam are not concepts that existed at the time of the prophet. They were introduced later to describe the war torn oppressive world outside the borders of the Islamic state, and the peace and justice that existed within. The only group/nation concept that exists within the Qur'an and Sunnah is the concept of the Muslim Ummah. The Muslim Ummah as described in the Shari'ah is completely independent from association in any way with numbers of people or geographical locations / boundaries. Rather it is associated with the Islamic principles and the Islamic way of life as a model for people. So even a single people can represent this principle, as in fact the Qur'an does in referring to the Prophet Abraham (16:120). Abraham was indeed an Ummah, devoutly obedient to Allah, and true in faith, and he did not worship other than Allah. (3:110) You (Muslims) are the best Ummah sent out to mankind, to encourage righteousness and to forbid the harmful, and to have complete faith in Allah...

The above ayah summarizes the definition of the Muslim Ummah. The Muslim Ummah is those people who are linked no matter where they are in the world with a common love of Allah, and they stand up for justice equally even if it is against them. Both later and early Jurists understood that being the "best" for all people meant that in the past people didn't feel safe with people from other groups, but everyone feels safe and secure within and in contact with the Muslim Ummah.

FIGHTING & RELATIONSHIPS WITH OTHERS

(60:8) Allah does not forbid you from dealing kindly and justly with those who did not fight and drive you out of your homes for your religion, For Allah loves those who are just. (60:9) Allah does however forbid you from those who fought you for your religion and drove you out of your homes and supported others against you so that you will be forced to submit, and turn to them for friendship and protection, and whoever submits to them (in these circumstances) has wronged himself.

These two verses lay the legal foundation for the relations between the Muslims and Non-Muslims, and they speak for themselves. At all times justice is obligatory on the Muslim, and kindness is also until it is used as an excuse for committing treason against Allah. Other than that we should treat everyone both Muslim and non with justice, respect, and kindness so that we will get closer to Allah and attract people to Islam. Therefore, even if a government or institution is not perfect in its Islamic practices, but does not commit open and severe oppression against the Muslims, Muslims are allowed to work within the system to try to improve it. This concept is not a new one to Fiqh because all the scholars and teachers after the end of the enlightened Caliphate and the beginning of royalty continued to teach and worked within the imperfect system to serve the greater Muslim Ummah despite the problems within the government.

THE EXAMPLE OF *ABYSSINIA* (PRESENT ETHIOPIA)

The example we have of Muslims taking refuge in another country to protect themselves and their religion is the emigration in Abyssinia Like today the Muslims at that time were being persecuted in their homeland, and the Prophet Mohammed sent them to Abyssinia because their rights would be protected there.

The Quraish (the leading tribe of Makkah) sent two emissaries to make a plea before the Abyssinia king Negus to return the refugees back to Quraish. Negus however, was not about to make a judgment on people in absentia. So after hearing the arguments of the emissaries (Amr, and Abdullah) he asked to hear the defense of the Muslims. When Negus's messenger informed the Muslims of Negus's decision to hear them, they had a discussion amongst themselves and decided to stick to the truth no matter what. They also agreed upon Ja'far ibnu 'Abi Talib as a spokesperson.

When they came before the King, the Muslims didn't bow to the king, and when asked explained that they only bowed to Allah. Then Jafar said, "O King! We were a people in ignorance, we worshipped idols, rejected kin, abused our neighbors, and the strong among us oppressed the weak. We continued so until Allah sent us a prophet from among us. He invited us to worship the one God, leaving the idols of wood and stone, and to tell the truth, guard the trust, to keep good relations with both family and neighbors, to give charity...We have come to your country, chosen you and not anybody else, and desire being near you, and hope that we would not be treated unfairly in your audience, O king."

The king was impressed with the Muslims argument and granted them "political asylum". During their stay they developed very strong relations with the Negus and his people, and when his throne was challenged they prayed for him and were ready to help defend him if requested. They continued to live in Abyssinia until they were obligated to go support the new Muslim state in Madina fighting off its enemies.

SOME LESSONS TO LEARN:

Existence of Muslims in any country should be planned on the bases of being permanent, not temporary or accidental.

We should drop concepts like Darul-Islam and Darul-Kufr and consider all land to be for Allah as the Qur'an says: (7:128) Moses said to his people: "Seek support from Allah and be patient, surly the earth is Allah's to grant to the servants of his choice, and the best is for righteous."

Muslims in a foreign country should work together, within the established system to better their position as long as they do not get so carried away that they sacrifice a core pillar to their religion.

We must present Islam in our own words, in the most tactful way possible so that we gain the interest and respect of those around us.

21. **Taha Jaber Alalwani, "'Fatwa' Concerning the United States Supreme Court Frieze" from** *the Journal of Law and Religion.*

From the Journal of Law and Religion, Vol. 15, No. 1/2 (2000–2001), pp. 1–28. Reprinted with permission of Taha Jaber Alalwani and the Journal of Law and Religion.

Taha Jaber Alalwani (for a biography, see the "Alalwani, Taha" entry in Volume 1) is at the forefront of a reflection on the jurisprudence of minorities (fiqh al-aqaliyya) that seeks to adapt Islamic jurisprudence to the American context. He wrote the following fatwa in response to a question raised by Azizah al-Hibri, Professor of Law at Richmond University, regarding the permissibility of a depiction of the Prophet Muhammad in a frieze at the United States Supreme Court. In the sculpture, the Prophet is holding the Quran (as a sign of the source of Islamic legislation) and a sword (as a sign of the power of the state). Alalwani ultimately argues that the depiction of the Prophet at the Supreme Court is a positive gesture toward Muslims made by the architect and the Supreme Court. Consequently, the image "deserves nothing but appreciation and gratitude from American Muslims."

> *In the name of God, the most Gracious, the most Merciful*
> Dr. Azizah Y. al-Hibri
> Professor of Law
> University of Richmond
> Peace be upon you, with the mercy of God and His blessings.[††]

I have received your letter and the accompanying photograph, which you identified as that of a section of the frieze in the Supreme Courtroom, located in the capital, Washington, D.C. The frieze (*tunf*)[1] portrays images of eighteen of the greatest leaders in human history who played a role in either establishing or enforcing laws or *Shara'i.*[2] One of these images purports to represent the Prophet Muhammad (SAAS).[3] The artist placed the Qur'an in one hand of this image, thus symbolically recognizing it as the source of Islamic legislation. In his other hand, the figure holds a sword symbolizing the power of the state. This second symbol is in recognition of the fact that the Prophet was also a leader of his community.[4]

In your letter, you mentioned that some American Muslim organizations and individuals have expressed outrage that the Messenger of God and the final Prophet (SAAS) has been thus portrayed in visual form among those great persons in the Supreme Court frieze. You have asked for a legal opinion about the propriety of such a portrayal. My response follows (and may guidance come from God).

In embarking on this task, however, it is necessary to establish first the basic premises that undergird the Islamic juristic understanding of representations such as the one in question. This way, the opinion can be understood by everyone who reads it, and placed in its the proper perspective. Second, it is important to take into consideration the legal texts, the *usuli* principles,[5] and the sayings of the *a 'immah* (leaders of juristic schools) and early jurists with respect to this matter of representing the Prophet (SAAS) in the form of a visual image. A contemporary jurist (*faqih*) must be familiar with both the basic premises and the legal background in order to approach this issue in the correct *fiqhi* (juristic) manner. The contemporary jurist must also reach a legal opinion, which reflects acceptable juristic form and perspective, while taking into account the modern context of a current event. I hope to present an opinion in this case which is neither contested nor rendered controversial by the leaders of the Muslim community in the United States, since they already have enough juristic disagreements concerning the crescent and *hallal* meat.[6]

NECESSARY PREMISES

The following premises, which derive from recognized Islamic interpretive methods, are important in rendering a proper judgment in the case of the frieze:

1. Each culture, indeed, each civilization, has its own means of self-expression, its own methods of describing its characteristics, attitudes, and world-view. Islamic culture is no different in this regard. It has come to be known as "the culture of the Word" because its self-expression is bound to the Holy Qur'an, the explanatory *Sunnah,*[7] the Prophet's *hadith,*[8] the *al-akhbar* (narrations)[9] and the *al-athaar* (Islamic traditions).[10] Indeed, Islamic civilization is one of expression and clarity, and it is the epitome of the culture of the Word. The centrality of the Word in Islamic culture explains the fact that the art of expression and related arts, such as *tajwid* (the art of reciting the Qur'an), *qira'at* (styles of reciting the Qur'an), calligraphy, grammar, poetry, prose, and oratory, have all flourished in this civilization.

2. The Arabs, who became the first carriers of the message of Islam, valued the Word more than images and statues.[11] Although they worshipped idols, they took pride in the Word and the Poem, and not in the Statue or the Image.[12] In these ancient times, the Pharaohs embodied their vision of the afterlife in their pyramids and sunboats. The Greeks and Romans translated their genius and skills into high fortresses, huge columns, statues and images. The Arabs, however, expressed themselves in their poems and poetic *mu'allaqat*[13] in places such as 'Ukaz, Mujannah, al-Majaz, then al-Marbad and Katheemah.[14] These were the challenging arenas for the Knights of the Word, the heroes of the poems, the orators and the conveyors of beliefs, traditions and glories of days gone by. Indeed, when Islam was subsequently revealed, and the Messenger of God (SAAS) sent, his greatest miracle was the Word: the miraculous words of God in the Qur'an. In all respects, in its eloquence, fluency, purity, revelation, methodology, order, and style, the wondrous nature of the Qur'an reveals itself in its inimitability.

3. In stark contrast, Western culture is the culture of the "image," the illustration, and the statue. In Western civilization, imagery and sculpture are paramount means of expressing sacred and centrally important truths. While neither the influence of Christianity on Western civilization nor its connection to the Word is deniable, other influences were more decisive. In the view of both Islam and Christianity, Christ is the Word and spirit of God bestowed upon Mary. Yet, those nations and peoples who adopted Christianity after the time of Christ, especially the Greeks and Romans, succeeded in turning the West into a culture and civilization of imagery. Thus, in Western culture Liberty is symbolized by a statue or image; so are Beauty, Justice, Truth, Strength and Weakness, Good and Evil, and other ideas of this nature. The Greeks and the Romans have bequeathed this perspective about representation to the Western world, even to the extent of creating images of gods, prophets and abstract values.

4. Islamic culture and civilization regard the Word as the medium best capable of expressing their specificity and symbolism. The Word—in the view of Arabs and Muslims—is the medium most capable of expressing the culture's inner characteristics; for its meanings are agreed upon by linguists. Although in some sense this agreement is restrictive, the Word nevertheless encompasses a multitude of meanings. Its immense horizon ranges over various meanings and concepts, while transcending others. The Word enables intellectual faculties and human consciousness to incorporate certain meanings and exclude others, while leaving room for new interpretations, explanations and comprehension. The "culture of the Word" is thus the ultimate culture of abstraction, comprehension, transcendence, and limitless possibilities! Yet, the Word remains accessible to its students of all nations, and is abundantly available for everyone's use in a diversity of contexts. By contrast, the image can be rendered only by the talented artist. It is restricted to the elite who possesses the ability to make it powerfully symbolic of a civilization's values and ideas.

The culture of imagery regards the image as the most capable symbol for expressing ideas in a precise, physical and defined manner because the image represents an embodiment, not an abstraction. In the Western view, this embodiment of either an ideal or a material being is seen and felt, and only then realized by the intellect. Yet, by contrast to the Word, the meaning of an image is limited, and indeed, its meaning is exclusive to the maker and the individual viewer.

5. Those who support "the culture of imagery" as preferable to the "culture of the Word" partly justify their support by arguing that a child understands images even before he or she understand words. To these supporters, this fact suggests that the image is prior to the Word in the experience of human communication, comprehension, explanation and education. Consequently, it makes it preferable to the Word. Nevertheless, the image must be accompanied by a word.

6. The United States of America, where the Supreme Court occupies the highest judicial position and serves as the strongest voice in the justice system, is an open country. It embraces virtually all of the diverse cultures and civilizations on earth, which interact within the framework of equality set forth in the American Constitution. Therefore, it is only natural that Americans should attempt to express the meanings of this diversity by using the American cultural majority's means of representation: that is, the "Image." Thus, when the Supreme Courtroom displays the images of select world leaders to symbolize justice and strength in human history, and the Messenger of God and the final Prophet (SAAS) is included among them, it expresses a specific view. It is the view of those

who designed and approved the architecture of the Supreme Court building more than 60 years ago as to the diversity of cultures and civilizations that had significant impact on the legal system in the United States. Whether this expression is consistent with the Islamic juristic vision in general, or with the vision of a particular juristic school of Islam, is another matter. The juristic vision in the Islamic world diverges in some significant ways from the national visions of those countries to which Muslims have migrated. Yet, unquestionably, even Islamic judicial rulings change as the times, places, circumstances and people change.[15]

7. The Islamic vision of culture and civilization during many periods of Islamic history, especially for the non-Arab Muslim people, has also been a vision of diversity and variety. It has not been inhospitable to the forms of self-expression traditional to diverse peoples and nations who have joined the ranks of Islam, whether their means of representation had been by imagery or otherwise. However, the official expression of Islamic arts has always been guided by the requirement that it be in harmony with the *tawhidi*[16] vision and the abstract, based on the Word. Therefore, the arts of the Word, including poetry, prose, calligraphic arts, mosaic, arabesque, and similar arts, have been the fundamental means of artistic expression in Islam. Despite this clear preference for the arts of the Word, the spiritual leaders of Islam did not try to destroy the Pharaohic pyramids, the Persian throne, ancient Persian ruins, or the Greek and Roman fortresses scattered throughout its lands. Rather, Islam preserved and even maintained all of cultural expressions, including the ancient houses of worship belonging to other religions, such as synagogues, churches and monasteries and the pictures, images and other artifacts and possessions they housed. In fact, if it had not been for Islamic protection, some of these structures, artifacts and other possessions may not have survived to this day. Indeed, Muslim jurists went so far as to impose on Muslims a duty to protect from destruction places of worship of other faiths. As their justification for imposing such a duty, the jurists explained that these places of worship were among those things belonging to people of other faiths and hence should be respected. They also argued that if people did not protect each other, then each group will destroy the other's place of worship at one time or another.[17]

Is There a Text in the Holy Qur'an that Prohibits the Use of Images?

8. When we read the Holy Qur'an—the only constitutive source of legislation in Islam—we will not find within it a single text that directly addresses the question of whether making or possessing "pictures" and "images" is prohibited. Instead, we find the story that tells of the Creator's (*Subhanahu wa Ta 'ala*)[18] grant to the prophet Solomon (a king who incidentally was included in the Supreme Court frieze, the subject of this fatwa) of the power to deal with unseen creatures (*Jinn* and devils). In the story, Solomon made these *Jinn* and devils obedient to him and caused them to work to create the arches, images, and other things he desired, and Solomon was thankful to the Almighty for this power. Because the prophets are (without exception) infallible, even the slightest conception that they would make, or cause to be made, anything forbidden is unthinkable. This is just as impossible as the idea that God in His grace would give one of His messengers the ability to commit what is forbidden. The Qur'an says as much when it tells this story, reciting the deeds and words of The Almighty:

And to Solomon (We Made) the Wind (obedient): Its early morning (stride) was a month's (journey), and its evening (stride) was a month's (journey); and We made a font of molten brass to flow for him; and there were Jinn that worked in front of him, by the leave of his Lord, and if any of them turned aside from Our command, We made him taste of the chastisement of the Blazing Fire. They worked for him as he desired, (making) Arches, Images, Basins as large as wells, and (cooking) Cauldrons fixed (in their places): "Work you, Sons of David, with thanks, but few of My servants are grateful!" (S.34, A.12-13)[19]

This Qur'anic verse is a clear indication of Solomon's gratitude that the *Jinn* made things upon his command, including images of living and material things. Respected interpreters, like Ibn Kathiri and others, have confirmed that King Solomon's throne was decorated with pictures as well as statues of birds and lions, which according to interpreters, moved mechanically to inspire further awe.[20] In still another passage describing the miracles of Jesus, the messenger of God (SAAS), Jesus created replicas of birds. He said: "'In that I make for you out of clay, as it were, the figure of a bird, and breathe into it, and it becomes a bird by God's leave...'" (S.3, A.49)

In addition to the Qur'anic texts, interpreters of these texts discussed them at length to arrive at the rules regarding the making and possessing of images. None of them derived from any Qur'anic text a definitive prohibition against making and possessing images. However, these Qur'anic interpreters cited *ahadith ahad* (Prophetic sayings narrated by a single reporter),[21] upon which they based all the sayings and rulings they examined concerning the *ayah* (Qur'anic verse). These *ahadith,* studied in their totality, indicate that the Prophet Muhammad (SAAS) despised the making and dissemination of images, and the spreading use of such images among the people. There is no doubt that, in these narrations, the Messenger of God (SAAS) prohibited sculpture and drawing of images, warning strongly against such acts and holding those who engaged in them responsible for such acts until the Day of Resurrection.

Yet, we must still ask whether the *ahadith* necessarily express a prophetic Islamic view absolutely prohibiting "embodied beauties" for all places, times and peoples. We must inquire whether the *ahadith* have totally prohibited the making of images as an act of worship, or whether this prohibition is contextual. We must ask about that, which is critical in making proper Islamic rulings on this matter: the *ratio,*[22] or causal reason that determines the *manaat* (basic rationale on which the legal ruling hangs). That is, we must ask whether the meaning of the precise prohibitions, warnings, or even descriptions of the text necessarily also depend on the interpreter's knowledge of the events, circumstances and other situations about which these *ahadith* are concerned.

The Interpretive Conflict over the *Ahadith* is Ancient

9. The most intense interpretive conflict that began with the early Islamic jurists and continues among contemporary jurists arises from their differing understandings of, and attitudes toward, the Prophetic *ahadith.* This argument about what can be understood and derived from a *hadith* is one that may be found in most human approaches to interpreting texts generally. Should the *mujtahid*[23] or legislator focus on the literal words of the text and express their significance? This is the method followed by those jurists who restrict themselves to a literal reading of the text. Alternatively, should the *mujtahid* direct his or her attention to the essence of the text? This is the method followed by those who apply the analytic deductive method to the text. Finally, should the *mujtahid* use yet a third interpretive method that combines the literal reading of the text with the deductive method?

This third "holistic approach" or "comprehensive reading" of the holy text which takes into account the *ratio* and the wisdom behind the literal language might suggest that there is another reason behind the Prophet's exhortations against images. Such a reading may suggest that this strong prohibition from the Messenger of God (SAAS) is made in recognition of the realities of the early period of Islam. At that time, Muslims had just emerged from a period of infidelity and *jahiliyah* (the period of ignorance prior to Islam). There is in fact a *hadith* that says

Had your people not been close to the days of *jahiliyah,* I would have ordered that the *Bayt* [*Ka 'bah*] be demolished, brought back to it what was removed from it, made it closer to the ground, and made for it two doors, an East door and a West door, and would have thus returned it to its Abrahamic basis.[24]

This *hadith* indicates that the Messenger of God (SAAS) was striving to eradicate the making of idols and their dissemination in the Arabian Peninsula among peoples who had until recently worshipped and adored them.

However, foreseeing this idolatry, God the Almighty sent the people prophets, who are children of "'allat".[25] A great number of these prophets are named in the Holy Qur'an, while many others are merely hinted at. In interpreting the sayings of the Messenger of God (SAAS), it is critical to understand that he was ordered to follow the prophecy of prior prophets: "Those (prophets) received God's guidance. So, follow the guidance they received...." (S.6, A. 90)

Moses, one of those noble messengers, moved the children of Israel to *tawhid* (monotheism), to (the) belief in and the worship of God. However, when they came upon other peoples devoted entirely to the worship of idols, they cried, "O Moses! Fashion for us a god like the gods they have." (S.7, A. 138) It is as if humans, created of clay, have a perpetual longing for the concrete over the abstract. So, the People of Israel hastened to worship the Golden Calf as soon as the Sumarian fashioned it for them.[26] The allure of the Golden Calf is easy to see from a materialist perspective: it has a physical embodiment, whereas the God of Moses is an abstraction. The People of Israel could see the Golden Calf, could hear its lowing and its whistle; but as for the God of Moses: "No vision can grasp Him, but He grasps all visions; He is kind and has thorough knowledge (of his creatures)." (S.6, A. 103)

Knowing human nature, it was appropriate for the Messenger of God (SAAS) to take all necessary measures to prevent the Arabs from committing a mistake similar to that made earlier by their cousins, the People of Israel. This matter was of critical importance because most Arabs had worshipped idols prior to their conversion to Islam. For this reason the Prophet (SAAS) said the *ahadith* mentioned earlier. Our task in this *fatwa* is to study these *ahadith,* reflect upon them, and contemplate their meanings with the reader so that we might reach together a common understanding of their significance.

Al-Tabari, al-Qurtubi, Ibn Kathir, al-Alousi, al-Razi and other great interpreters have all compiled many of these *ahadith* and discussed them and their significance. Among these scholars, al-Hafiz Ibn Hajar was one of the most knowledgeable.[27] He was a careful student of these texts, his collection of the *ahadith* was among the most comprehensive, and his arguments were most cogent and insightful. The question of the propriety of image-making resurfaced in Islamic jurisprudence at the beginning of this century and was discussed by many scholars, among whom Sheikh Rashid Ridha was one of the most important. (For further detail on his work *see infra* p 120ff.) Thus, in this *fatwa,* we will set forth these *ahadith,* both in original text form and as they have been cited by Ibn Hajar. Then we will consider and discuss the *fatwa* pronounced by the author of al-Manar, Sheikh Rashid Ridha. Careful consideration of these sources will permit us, then, to clarify our opinion on the matter of the Supreme Court frieze in particular, in light of the wisdom derived from these sources. First, however, it may be important to those who are not students of Islam to understand the Islamic view about the importance of various sources of legislation.

10. Sources of Legislation in Islam

The Holy Qur'an is the sole constitutive source for obtaining and deriving legal rulings. What we mean by "constitutive" must be well understood: this is a precise *usuli* (foundational jurisprudence) term that distinguishes between the ruling itself and its justification or explanation. The Qur'an alone provides evidence that constitutes the legal rule that governs human responsibilities toward the Almighty. However, clarifying evidence concerning these rulings may be provided by the *Sunnah*. Explanatory evidence may be available from the *ahadith, al-akhbar, al-athaar,* and *al-ijtihaad.*[28] In Islam, there is no doubt that God (SWT) is the only One who issues and establishes legal rulings in His Book. He is the only Ruler in this sense, there is no god but Him, and therefore, it is beyond the province of human creatures to establish legal rulings over other creatures like themselves, even if the creature is a prophet, king, sultan or other type of ruler. As evidence of this, the Holy Qur'an states: "The command is for none but God." (S.12, A. 40 & 67)

Moreover, there is no doubt that the ruling of God as given in the Qur'an should be obeyed without question. He has revealed the Qur'an, and caused it to contain all of His legal rulings and laws (the *Shari'ah*):

On the day We shall raise from all peoples a witness against them, from amongst themselves. And We shall bring you as a witness against these (your people); and We have sent down to you the Book explaining all things, a Guide, a Mercy, and Glad Tidings to Muslims. (S.16, A.89)

And He said to the Prophet (SAAS) in the same *Surah* (chapter): "And We sent down the Book to you so that you should make clear to them those things in which they differ, and that it should be a guide and a mercy to a people that believe." (S.16, A. 64) He gave His Noble Prophet (SAAS) the mission of reciting the law to the people, informing them of all His legal rulings, and explaining all of these legal rulings to them, usually in a practical way: ". . . And We have sent down unto you the Message; that you may explain clearly to people what was revealed to them, and that they may reflect." (S.16, A.44)

The laws of the Almighty might also be accompanied by some of the Prophet's sayings or *ahadith* for the purpose of clarification, or even for emphasizing the binding character of that clarification. Examples are found in the Prophet's saying (SAAS): "Pray as you have seen me pray," and his saying "Take from me all of the rituals of worship" when he made the pilgrimage (*hajj*) with thousands of Muslims.[29] The Prophet then showed them the rituals of the *hajj,* by performing them himself. So that they would follow his *sunnah* (legacy and teachings), he told the people: "Take from me your rituals of worship." This saying confirmed for them the necessity of emulating him precisely in everything he did, of following in his footsteps and learning these rituals so that they could do the same. In taking him as an example and following him exactly, they could be assured of doing the right thing before God.

11. Differences Among the Jurists on the Subject of Image-Making

Islamic Jurists have differed widely on the topic of image-making. Some have taken the position that every image, whether it is a painting, photograph, sculpture, or some other representation, is prohibited if the subject of the image has a soul (for example, a human being or an animal or a bird). These jurists, however, did not prohibit images of soul-less physical objects, such as trees. As evidence of this prohibition, these jurists adopted the general proofs included in the *ahadith* of the Prophet (SAAS), which are also based on known *usuli* and juristic principles. Indeed, some jurists expanded their positions to include a general prohibition on the making, taking, selling or buying of images, based on details that could be found in the appropriate sources.

Still other jurists have taken the position that imagery is permitted, based on proofs from the texts of *ahadith* and from juristic and *usuli* principles, whether agreed upon or disputed. We will critically examine herein the arguments of two important groups of jurists who reached opposing opinions on the propriety of image-making. In so doing, we shall rely upon our earlier discussion of the *ahadith* previously cited on this issue. We shall also examine these jurists' interpretation of the *ahadith* and their use of the *ahadith* as proofs for their position.

A. The *Ahadith* of *Al-Baab*[30] and Their Discussion

Two texts are critical for a decision in this matter. In *Sahih Muslim* the Prophet (SAAS) is cited as saying: "Those who make images will be punished by God and it will be said to them: 'Breathe soul into what you have created' and they would not be able to."[31] Another version of this *hadith* has been reported as follows: "Those who try to emulate the creation of God..." (the rest of the text will follow in section B below).

The first group of Islamic jurists, who support the prohibition, argue that these *ahadith* support their *madhab* (school of thought) on the prohibition of image-making. Their *madhab* is based on the *usuli* principle that a stern warning of dire punishment on the Day of Judgment is in itself a sufficient legal indicator that the act warned against is prohibited. The vast majority of the *usuli mutakalimun* (scholars of theology who follow *usuli* jurisprudence) holds this view.

On the other hand, the juristic group that rejects the prohibition against images disagrees with the majority *madhab* because this group relies upon different versions of the same *hadith*. The group's principle of interpretation ties the legal propriety of a representation to its intention, namely, whether the image attempts to emulate the creation of God, and to the extent of resemblance between the image and the creation of God. The words of this *hadith,* as reported by Muslim, indicate that harsh judgment is imposed on: "Those who try to emulate the creation of God..." In the view of this juristic group, as long as this is the measure of the prohibition, the legal prohibition against images continues to be applicable only to the extent its *ratio* is relevant. Thus, the act of illustration that is not intended to create an exact resemblance to the creation of God is not prohibited. This view is followed by all the *usulis* who argue that analogy (*qiyas*)[22] is one of the roots of legislation; and these are the *jumhoor* (the vast majority of scholars).

B. Story About A'ishah

Another source for our understanding of the proper ruling about image-making is a story about 'A'ishah, the mother of the believers—May God be pleased with her. In this story, 'A'ishah is quoted as saying:

The Messenger of God (SAAS) entered into my chambers while I was wrapped in a piece of cloth (a curtain) with a picture on it. His face colored in anger, and he removed it saying: "Verily, the most grievously tormented people on the Day of Resurrection will be those who try to emulate the creation of God." 'A'ishah said, "So I tore it up and made two cushions out of it." (Muslim's *hadith* 1666).[33]

The first group of jurists, who adopted the prohibition, argued that the Messenger's (SAAS) anger was a strong indication of the presence of something prohibited by the *Shari'ah*. For, it was not the habit of the Messenger (SAAS) to get angry, except in cases where the prohibitions of God were being violated or His established legal rules (*hudud*) exceeded. The Messenger's (SAAS) act of removing the cloth (which had monetary value) indicated that image-making was forbidden (*haram*). Moreover, in this *hadith,* the Messenger threatened punishment for the act of making images. In the view of the first group of jurists, these striking acts by the Messenger (SAAS) were convincing proof that the prohibition against image-making was a definitive legal rule ordained by God.

The second group of jurists, by contrast, argued that the legal ruling in the case turned on the extent to which the artist attempted to emulate the creation of God. This was especially significant in a community that had just emerged from an era when both two-dimensional images and images in bas-relief were being worshipped as gods or in the belief that idol-worship would draw the people closer towards God. In such a historical environment, prohibiting image-making becomes the proper legal ruling because of the *asl*[34] principle of *"sadd al dhari 'ah"*[35] which prohibits whatever leads to infidelity or *shirk* (polytheism).

Thus, the legal ruling is dependent on the words and context of the *hadith*. The mere fact that pictures on the walls and doors in A'ishah's house—May God be pleased with her—were converted into pillows and cushions, indicates, in its context, that the fundamental rule is one of non-prohibition of images. It also indicates that the prohibition is tied to the intended use of the images. Further, this story is a testimony to Prophetic education of the people's minds and hearts, to the Prophet's (SAAS) efforts to divert people away from images and bas-reliefs. These two-and three-dimensional images impeded the people's contemplation of the abstract, and the use of their psychological and intellectual powers to understand abstract doctrinal concepts, which were the object of divine revelation.

The second group of scholars found additional benefits in this same *hadith* (Muslim's *hadith* 1666). The *hadith* also shows that the Prophet's (SAAS) natural humility and modest way of life made him loathe to see in his home what was considered in his own community an overly luxurious style of living. (In those days, the practice of hanging pictures on walls was considered a luxury.) This interpretation of the *hadith* is underscored by the Prophet's (SAAS) statement that: "Whenever...I see them [the pictures]...it brings to my mind (the pleasures) of worldly life." This *hadith* is consistent with his other *hadith,* namely that "God did not order us to cover mud and stones."

C. Another *Hadith* Supporting the "Modesty" Interpretation

The interpretation that the Prophet denounces images insofar as they represent improper luxury is also consistent with his saying in another *hadith* found in Muslim and Abu Dawoud and narrated by Zaid bin Khalid: "God has not ordered us to cover stones and clay."[36]

The *hadith* of Abu Talha which is *marfu'* (traceable all the way back to the Prophet (SAAS)) echoes the same view. According to this *hadith* 'A'ishah said,

'Angels do not enter a house in which there is a dog or a statue.' and when she was asked, 'have you heard this from the Messenger of God (SAAS)?!' she replied: '...he said: 'God has not ordered that we cover stones and clay.' Clarifying his direction to her, 'A'ishah then said: 'So I tore off [the cloth, which was hanging on the wall.] and I made two cushions from it and I filled them with fibers and [the Prophet] did not find error in this.'[37]

Scholars point out that the cushions were made of a wall-hanging that had images of horses with wings, as stated in *hadith* Muslim. Thus, the images, when transferred to the cushions, were not found to violate the rule because the cushions were useful rather than luxury items. Moreover, al-Nawawi, the most prominent jurist who has a well-known exegesis on Sahih Muslim, has commented on the Prophet's statement noting that it expressed *tanzitf* (aversion), not *tahrim* (prohibition).[39]

D. Examining *Ahadith* Cited in Favor of Prohibition

Jurists who oppose image-making, cited as proof of this prohibition the *ahadith* which mention the unwillingness of the angel Gabriel (SAAS) to enter the home of the Prophet (SAAS) because it contained images. (In some of the narrations there was also a dog in his home.) (*Hadith* No. 2104 by 'A'ishah in Sahih Muslim, al-Libas wa al-Zeenah section about a puppy entering the Prophet's home without his or 'A'ishah's knowledge and preventing Gabriel from coming to the Prophet) Among the *ahadith* on which they rely are the following:

(i) From 'A'ishah:

Gabriel promised to visit the Prophet at a specific hour but did not come...The Prophet said that neither God nor his messengers would break a promise. He looked and found a puppy under his bed and ...ordered that it be removed, and it was. Then Gabriel came...and said: The dog prevented my coming, for we do not enter a house which has a dog or an image.[40]

(ii) From Abdullah bin Omar:

Gabriel had promised to return to the Prophet (SAAS) but he stalled until the Prophet (SAAS) was distressed by this and went out to meet him, and Gabriel complained about what he had found saying: "We do not enter a house which has either an image or a dog." (Quotation compiled in abbreviated form.)[41]

(iii) From lbn 'Abbas and Abu Talha: "The Prophet (SAAS) said: 'Angels do not enter a house in which there is a dog or an image.'"[42]

In the view of these scholars, it is the existence of impure objects in the House of the Prophet (SAAS) which prevented the angels, among them Gabriel (SAAS), from entering the house. Since images were specifically listed in this category of impure objects, the legal ruling of prohibition applies to them.

On the other hand, the second group of scholars, i.e., those who permit the making and displaying of images, does not accept the view that the general unwillingness of angels to enter a place where there are impure objects or deeds implies a prohibition of image-making. This group provides two reasons in support of its position. First, not every impurity is subject to a legal ruling. This is a well-known principle, agreed upon by scholars from all of the Islamic juristic traditions. Second, the reluctance of Gabriel (SAAS) to enter a house in which there was a dog or an image is an unwillingness unique to the Prophet (SAAS), and stems from the specificity of the descent of the spirit upon him. It is unimaginable that Gabriel (SAAS) would enter any house other than the house of the Prophet (SAAS), or a house where the Prophet (SAAS) was not present. This is a matter that no one disputes. It is also undisputed among scholars that angels are unwilling to enter a house where statutes and images are displayed for the purpose of worship. Thus, scholars that permit image-making argue that the text implies only that angels do not enter homes where there is *shirk* (worshipping other gods beside God). It does not imply that angels enter no houses where images are displayed.

This group of scholars that permits images argues further that the host of *ahadith* cited in al-Baab lead to the same legal ruling about images, because each of these *ahadith* contains its own explanatory *ratio*. For example, in these *ahadith,* the Prophet (SAAS) at times forbade images out of his *zuhd* (ascetic life style). Other *ahadith* explained that Garbiel was unwilling to enter the Prophet's (SAAS) home while the dog was in it. Yet, having dogs in one's house is not legally forbidden. In fact, having a dog is clearly permitted by the text of the Qur'an and no one has spoken of it as having been prohibited at a later stage (*naskh*).[43]

Thus, if the presence of a non-prohibited dog prevented Gabriel from entering, it may be inferred that the presence of a non-prohibited image may also prevent Gabriel from doing so.

In yet another story, images were denounced because they distracted the Prophet (SAAS) during his prayers. Anas narrates: "'A'ishah had a colorful curtain which she used to cover one side of her house. So, the Prophet (SAAS) told her: 'Take it out of my sight because its designs distract me during my prayer.'"[44] Yet, that which distracts one during prayer is not prohibited in and of itself. Further, the fact that the Prophet (SAAS) did not prevent 'A'ishah from using the curtain for "design in a dress" [see the hadith],[45] or as a cushion, or some thing else, proves that images are not prohibited in and of themselves. It also clearly provides the *ratio* for the incident.

An important interpretive rule which is well known by Muslim scholars, is that *ahadith* that provide the *ratio* of the case and its applicability to other cases take precedence over those that do not. Further, explanatory texts take precedence over general ones. Moreover, the *hadith* of Abdullah bin Mas'oud and the similar *hadith* of Ibn Abbas about artists being among those who will suffer the most on the Day of Resurrection are *mawqufan* (each is *mawquf*).[46] But a *hadith* which is *mawquf* does not take precedence over the *ahadith* of 'A'ishah, the mother of the believers. Yet, the *hadith* of 'A'ishah clearly provides a *ratio* for the Prophet's (SAAS) forbiddance. For this reason, if one desires to reconcile all *ratios* on this subject, the two *ahadith* mentioned earlier must be understood in light of 'A'ishah's *hadith*.

E. Other Sources of Disagreement

Another objection to the view that images are forbidden arises from the fact that the legal ruling regarding images was one of permission for previous nations, but was later rescinded for Muslims. However, rescinding the permission was governed by the *ratio* of the *hukm.* For this reason, Solomon's (SAAS) use of images and statues was permitted simply because there was no suspicion whatsoever that he would use them for *shirk.* It is, in fact, unthinkable that a prophet upon whom the spirit has descended would worship any other gods but God. Furthermore, as a prophet, Solomon (SAAS) is considered to be infallible, just like our Prophet (SAAS). Like all other prophets, he would have also known and abided by the same doctrinal rulings, related ethical mandates, and educational methods.

Another well-known source for the dispute about images is found in a second *hadith* concerning 'A'ishah—may God be pleased with her. In this *hadith,* she said: "I used to play with *banat* (girls or dolls) in the house of God's Messenger (SAAS), and I had play-mates. When he would enter the house, my playmates would cover themselves [out of modesty]; so he would send them to me, and they would play with me."

Sheikh Rashid Ridha commented on the previous *hadith* as follows:

Some of the interpreters who take a strict view in the matter of images distorted the words of the *hadith* claiming that 'A'ishah said 'I used to play with girls' instead of 'I used to play with dolls.' Al-Hafiz said in his explanation of the hadith: 'Ibn al-Tin has narrated it [the *hadith*] from al-Dawoudi and refuted it [the distorted *hadith*]. (I said) it was also refuted by what Ibn 'Uyaynah compiled in [his book] al-Jami' from the narration of Said bin Abdul Rahman al-Makhzumi from Hisham bin 'Urwah's narration of this *hadith*: 'And they were girls that came and played with her.' In the narration of Jarir from Hisham: 'I used to play with girls and they were dolls.' 'A'ishah said, as compiled by Abu Dawoud and al-Nasa'i from another perspective: The Messenger of God (SAAS) came from a military campaign—Tabuk or Khai-bar—and the *hadith* in which he removed the cloth hanging on her door was recounted; so he drew back one side of the curtain to reveal girls (dolls) belonging to 'A'ishah, so he said: 'What's this 'A'ishah?' She answered: "*banati* ("my dolls", or "my girls"). And he saw among these dolls a winged horse. So he said: 'What's this?' She said: 'a horse.' He said: 'A horse with two wings?' She said: 'Haven't you heard that Solomon had horses with wings?' So he laughed. This is a clear indication that what was meant by 'dolls' was something other than human, contrary to the claims of the strict interpreters. Rather, it refers to dolls (toys) that are meant to be played with.[48]

This interpretation is followed by the school of thought that represents the majority of highly regarded scholars (e.g., Ibn Waddah, al-Dawoudi, al-Nawawi, al-Qurtubi, Ibn Habban, al-Mawardi, al-Khatabi, Ibn Daqiq al-Eid, and Ibn al-Sabagh). It is also the interpretation chosen by al-Hafiz bin Hajar and many others.

12. A Summary of the Proofs Used by Those Who would Prohibit Images

There are approximately thirteen (13) narrations of *ahadith* on this topic, all of which are *ahadith ahad,* and some of which are *mawquf,*[49] including the *hadith* of Ibn Mas'oud and the *hadith* of Ibn Abbas. Some *ahadith* threaten great suffering to those who try to emulate the omnipotent power of the Creator and His Divinity. But the problem of emu-lating the creation of the Almighty is not at issue in the matter of the Supreme Court frieze.

Some of these *ahadith* point out that the angel of spirit, Gabriel (SAAS), would not enter a house to bestow the divine revelation upon the Prophet (SAAS), if the house had a dog or an image. Again, these *ahadith* are not relevant to the dispute with which we are concerned, for their purpose is to clarify the nature of those places where it is proper for the revelation to descend. Some *ahadith* indicate that the *ratio* for the prohibition of images and statues lies in the fear of their use to express vanity and project an appearance of wealth and luxury in a poor society. Other *ahadith* condemn displaying images in places where they attract attention and give the impression that they deserve reverence. This impression may, in time, lead people to worship these displays as their hearts become harder. Thus, in some of the stories, the Prophet (SAAS) asked that the dis-plays be rearranged so as not to acquire an improper significance. It is not easy, therefore, to use this group of *ahadith*—as a whole or individually—to derive conclusive legal proofs supporting an absolute prohibition against image-making in general or certain images in particular, except those that have been mentioned previously.

13. The *Fatwa* of Sheikh Muhammad Rashid Ridha

In issuing his ruling on the question of image-making, Sheikh Rashid Ridha Muhammad Rashid Bin Ali Ridha Bin Muhammad Shamsuddi al-Kalamouni, was the creator of

Al-Manar Magazine and one of the religious reformers. He was one of the writers and scholars of *hadith*, literature, history and interpretation (exegeses). He grew up in al Kalamoun region, and later moved to Egypt where he studied with Muhammad Abdu. He started Al-Manar Magazine to spread his ideas of religious and social reform. He also established the school of "al-Da'wa wal Irshad." He went to Syria during the reign of King Faisal Bin al-Hussain, and was elected president for the Syrian Conference, and left when the French came. He went back to Egypt in 1920 and then traveled to India, Hijaz and Europe. He died in Cairo with the legacy of Al-Manar Magazine of which he published 34 volumes and the "Interpretation of Al Qur'an Al-Karim" in 12 volumes. He also wrote many books, including a 3-volume biography of Muhammad Abdu, a book about women in Islam, *Nida' Ila Al Jinss Allatif*[60] has usefully compiled and skillfully interpreted the *hukm* regarding image-making, as well as the display and possession of images and statues. His ruling was prepared in response to a question from Singapore regarding the propriety of oil painting, all types of sculpture, photographs, and other things made for the purpose of being worshipped[51] or revered and for other purposes. This inquirer asked whether the *hukm* regarding these matters is affected by changes in time and place as well as other factors.

Ridha held that the *ahadith* cited in the compilation of Ibn Hajar and which numbered fifteen (15) can be classified objectively into four groups:[52]

First, a number of the *ahadith* serve as a warning to the arrogant and vain who try to emulate the creation of God by showing off their own skills. In so doing, they cause worshippers to turn away from pondering the creation of God and deriving therefrom proof of His Existence, Oneness, and Providence. Instead, worshipers ponder the statues and images themselves and the genius, originality, and skill of the human creator which are embodied in them. This is a critical concern, for the most important proofs for God's existence advanced by prophets and missionaries to their followers are: (1) the proof of creation and divine invention, which has no precedent; and (2) the proof of divine providence upon living creatures.

The Second category of *ahadith* are *those* which warn of the necessity of putting aside all that may distract people from the worship of the Creator. Among the things that may be distracting are images representing virtuous people and prophets. The fear is that, though they wish to pray and remember God, people may not be able to worship only Him or remember only Him, because their hearts and minds would be occupied with other things that these images bring to mind.

In the Third category, some *ahadith* warn about the fact that having images on curtains or in houses constitutes a display of luxury and wealth which breaks the hearts of the poor who cannot afford to buy or have such images in their homes.

In my opinion, in this day and age, such extravagance has reached the extreme, as certain paintings are sold for tens or hundreds of millions at a time when millions of people are suffering hunger, sickness, ignorance, and so forth.

The Fourth category is that of *ahadith* whose purpose is to warn against promoting human capabilities for concretization while weakening human capabilities for abstraction. This trend undeniably affects the human's psychological and spiritual constitution. For this reason, religions place the greatest emphasis on addressing the human soul and spirit to guide them to the straight path. This prepares the way for guiding the human mind, acts and deeds.

Sheikh Rashid Ridha concluded from his profound discussions of these *ahadith* that making images is permitted and that there was no clear proof that they were prohibited.

He qualified his ruling, however, with the proviso that it was appropriate that there be no extravagance and that the use of images be restricted to cases of necessity.[53]

AN APPROACH THAT COULD RESOLVE THIS MATTER

We are now prepared to articulate an approach which could help resolve the question of whether the depiction of the Prophet (SAAS) in the Supreme Court frieze is prohibited or not. First, we must study the chain of narrators (*sanad*) and the text (*matn*) of the entire body of cited *ahadith,* the compilations of these *ahadith* and the *ratio* upon which the related legal ruling rests. In order to fully understand the rulings in these *ahadith,* we must also know the circumstances surrounding each ruling, the reasons the ruling occurred, and its specific characteristics. This aspect of our work, which is highly technical, has already been completed by al-Hafiz bin Hajar, al-Nawawi and other *hadith* scholars who are experts on *hadiths* that are *sahih*[54] and who have interpreted it carefully.

Second, we must describe and take into account the characteristics of each *hadith,* such as its brevity or *bayan* (expansiveness as in-depth explanation), and whether its message is absolute or restricted to its circumstances, general or specific. These steps are necessary for the *faqih* to assess the possibility of an objective reconciliation of all the *ahadith* and to reach a conclusion compatible with and common to all of them. This conclusion cannot be reached, except by patient and careful examination of the relevant *ahadith,* both individually and collectively, randomly and in a specific order. Furthermore, this examination must also be bound by other general principles, which guide the interpretation of the legal rulings of the Holy Qur'an. It must also take into account the guiding principles concerning the ranking of the *Sunnah* with respect to the Qur'an, as well as the nature of the relationship between the Holy Qur'an, the Prophetic *sunnah, al-ahadith, al-akhbar,* and *al-athaar* in the methodical and scholarly jurisprudential reasoning, as all these aspects relate to the issue at hand.

The *faqih* needs also to refer to the "science of religious sociology," and the disciplines of history and "religious anthropology," as these are among the necessary tools needed for a thorough and precise examination of various aspects of this issue.

14. Our *Fatwa* in the Matter of the Supreme Court Frieze

The subject of the "frieze" is a select group of historic figures from around the world who were lawgivers. The frieze includes images, which purport to represent our Prophet Muhammad (SAAS) and our Prophets Moses and Solomon (PBUT).

In contemplating the message conveyed by this frieze, it is important to clarify the personal attributes of the Messenger of God (SAAS) as set forth by those who wrote the *Siyar.*[55] Within the framework of the "culture of the Word," on which our civilization is built, Hind bin Abu-Halah and others have described the Messenger of God (SAAS) very precisely:

He was grandly elegant. His face (SAAS) shone like the full moon. He was taller than average, but not extremely so, and with a great stature. He used to leave his hair down, and if he parted it, it would part easily, but he did not let it grow below his earlobe. His skin was pinkish and he had a broad forehead. His eyebrows were thick, but they did not grow together in the middle. When he was angry, the vein between his brows stood out. The bridge of his nose was narrow. He had a visible aura that could be seen even at the most casual glance. His nose was well-proportioned. He had a thick beard, smooth cheeks, a sturdy mouth with a moustache. He had a small space between his front teeth. The shelf of his mouth was delicate. His neck was like that of a doll, as pure as silver. He was of moderate build, plump but firm, whether in his stomach or chest, with a wide chest, stretching between broad shoulders. If he removed his shirt, his torso was most pleasing. There was a hairline between his navel and the upper part of his chest, otherwise his breasts and stomach were bare. His arms, shoulders, and upper chest were hairy. His forearms were long and his palms were wide. There were many visible veins in his hands. His palms and feet were moist and dotted with perspiration. His feet were arched and smooth such that water flowed evenly over them. When he stood, he stood up with his full body. He walked with an even pace, gracefully but briskly, as if he were going downhill. When he turned, he turned around completely. He generally gazed down, his contemplative gaze focused more at the earth than at the sky, most of his looks being in observation. He led his Companions and initiated the greeting with everyone he met with the salutation 'Salam.'[56]

Many other *ahadith* have described the Prophet (SAAS), detailing his physical appearance and behavior so specifically that any skillful contemporary artists who had read them could have made a painting that reflects his true appearance much more closely than the photograph of the frieze which you have sent to me. There is no doubt that these detailed, precise descriptions indicate the love that those who described him and all the *sahabah* (the Prophet's companions) felt for him, almost as if one of them had kept his picture very accurately in his imagination.

An artist paints either someone he sees or someone he imagines. The Persian and Turkish Muslims have made many pictures (in miniatures) of the Prophet (SAAS) as they imagined him according to the precise descriptions they read or heard from those who described him. If it had not been for the indulgence of the scholars among these peoples with regard to representing the Prophet (SAAS), none of these pictures would have been seen or widely distributed among their people. Yet, the *sahabah* and the *tabi'oun* (the followers who met the *sahabah,* but did not meet the Prophet) did not ask any of the painters or sculptors in their times—and it seems there were many—to make a statue or an image of the Prophet (SAAS). Instead, they merely passed on his description orally or in writing because for them the Word was a better medium of expression than pictures or statues, and the oral description left the door open wide for the imagination to add to the Prophet (SAAS) the attributes of perfection that are deemed appropriate.

To think fully in the abstract requires an uncommon intellectual ability. Common people cannot engage in this process except to a very limited degree. That is why scholars sometimes used *ta'wil* (interpretations) and *tashbih* (similes) to capture the unseen in order to help all of the lay people comprehend these matters. As a human being, the Messenger of God (SAAS) is a person like us who eats food and walks through the streets. In fact, the affirmation of his humanity is, like the affirmation of his message and prophethood, an objective of the Qur'an and a necessary jurisprudential purpose. This affirmation balances the faith of the believers with their understanding of the Prophet's personality. In other words, the descriptions of the Prophet (SAAS) help believers achieve a balance between his prophethood and message, which belong to the realm of the transcendental, and his humanity and humanness, which belong to this world. This balance enables believers to take him as an ideal and an example, hence follow in his footsteps. Of course, this attitude does not require having a picture or image of the Prophet (SAAS).

When I visited the Supreme Court and saw the frieze, which is the subject of discussion, I noticed that many Prophets were missing from it. I noticed the absence of an image of the Messiah, a Prophet of Islam. The Messiah validated and amended the basic laws of Moses. So did our Prophet Muhammad (SAAS). Thus, from an Islamic point of view, the figures who represent this law are Moses, Jesus, and Muhammad.

Second, the artist who created the frieze should have referred to the Prophet's attributes mentioned in the Muslim tradition. It is no excuse that the artist had no guiding image of the Prophet (SAAS) on which to base his work; for, as indicated, the Turkish and Persian tradition are rich with images, some of which wonderfully and very accurately render the Prophet (SAAS) according to the detailed descriptions of biographers.

In our tradition, there is a story about Sultan Abdul-Hamid of the Ottoman Empire. He was reputed to have inherited a painting of the Messenger (SAAS) done by Buhayra, the Christian priest, when the Prophet was twelve years old and on a trade trip with his uncle to *al-sham,* present day Syria. Of course, this image may have been lost and destroyed by those who rebelled against Abdul-Hamid. Yet, such an image, even if it is quite old or represents the Prophet (SAAS) at a young age, could have inspired the artist and aided him in accurately rendering the delicate features of the Prophet (SAAS). By contrast, the present image in the frieze represents an Arab man who could be a leader or ruler, but it somehow does not capture the essence of a prophet. Perhaps the logic of his companions in declining to draw him becomes clear to us from this failure of the Supreme Court artist.

Still, despite these reservations, I have a great deal of gratitude and appreciation for those who insisted on including an image of our Prophet, Muhammad (SAAS), in that highly regarded site in the United States of America, in order to remind the whole world of the important contribution of the Prophet (SAAS). It is important that in a pluralistic culture like the United States he is symbolized as one of the select illustrious lawgivers who merit being honored. This is especially significant since the West has generally treated the Prophet (SAAS) and his contributions unfairly.[57]

I must be clear in saying that, for me and for every Muslim, the Messenger of God (SAAS) is the greatest and most revered personality known between the earth and heaven, not simply one lawgiver among many. Still, it was an important gesture by those who did not believe in him as a Prophet and a messenger, who did not see him as anything other than a historic personality, to include him. In a culture whose literary heritage is replete with disdainful images of the Prophet Muhammad (SAAS), it is comforting to note that those in the highest Court in the United States were able to surmount these prejudices, and display his image among those of the greatest lawgivers in human history. Isn't that effort a noble gesture that deserves from us, who believe in him as the Prophet and Messenger, every encouragement, esteem, and gratitude instead of disapproval, condemnation, and outrage?

There is no doubt that those who built the Supreme Court and placed within it all of these symbols wished to indicate that they had benefited from this diverse human heritage, directly or indirectly, and that it somehow shaped the concept of justice in the new world. They have thus espoused the message of the Prophet (SAAS) as part of their universal heritage, even though they do not believe in Islam or in the Messenger of God as we do.

In the Hudaybiyah Agreement, Imam Ali—May God be pleased with him—wrote: "This is what Muhammad, the Messenger of God, has agreed upon..." He was stopped by the Pagans' delegate, who said: "Erase it [the words: 'the Messenger of God'] for if I believed that you were the Messenger of God, I wouldn't have fought you..." But Ali did not agree to erase it himself. So the Prophet (SAAS) asked him to show him the words and he erased them himself.[58] The Prophet (SAAS) judged that others have the right to express their own position as they see it. In following the Prophet's (SAAS) example, we must remember that those who carved the frieze and placed it in the Supreme Court are not Muslims. So, it should not be expected that they would express what the Muslim believers usually express when they talk about the Prophet in his capacity as a Messenger of God (SAAS). As the Prophet (SAAS) himself respected freedom of conscience in his own dealings, so should we.

SUMMARY

Islamic jurisprudence is vast and rich and encompasses many schools of thought. If this jurisprudence is vast enough to encompass the view that prohibits paintings and sculpture representing living souls, then it should also be vast enough to encompass the view that permits them. In every age and in most unclear religious matters, people are caught between those ultra-conservatives who interpret the law strictly so as to forbid, prohibit, or restrict the scope of what is permitted, and moderates who constantly seek to enlarge the scope of what is permitted, and restrict the scope of what is prohibited. The tendency of the contemporary reformist school of Islamic jurisprudence is to take the expansive approach as to what is permitted. At the forefront of this school are esteemed jurists such as Sheikh Rashid Ridha, Sheikh Muhammad Bakheet al-Mutaiyi'i, the former Mufti of Egypt, as well as many Islamic schools of thought too numerous to describe herein.

Indeed, the famous interpreter Ibn Kathir referred to images of Prophets in his explanation of the Qur'anic verse 7:157 (al-A'raf). He repeated a narration mentioned in Mustadrak al-Hakim about the Umayyad Hisham bin al-'Aas: In the days of Khalifah (Caliph) Abu Bakr (may God be pleased with him), Hisham al-'Aas was sent with another person to Heraclius, the Emperor of Byzantium, to invite him to Islam. According to the narration, the ruler of Byzantium showed Hisham al-'Aas and his companion pictures of a number of prophets. Among these they recognized the picture of the Prophet Muhammad, Messenger of God (SAAS). When the incident was related to Abu Bakr (may God be pleased with him), he was moved to tears. He did not fault Hisham al-'Aas or his companion.[59]

The most pertinent inquiry in resolving the matter of the propriety of the frieze may not be a search of the legal rulings regarding sculpture, photography, oil painting, or other representations of living souls. Rather, it may be to ask whether the Court has the right to place among these symbols a representation of the Prophet Muhammad (SAAS), which does not reflect his true image, as described in the *sirah,* but which nevertheless accords him full respect.

My answer to this question is as follows: What I have seen in the Supreme Courtroom deserves nothing but appreciation and gratitude from American Muslims. This is a positive gesture toward Islam made by the architect and other architectural decision-makers of the highest Court in America. God willing, it will help ameliorate some of the unfortunate misinformation that has surrounded Islam and Muslims in this country.

For this reason, I would like to express my gratitude and appreciation to the early twentieth century architect and his associates who brought, in their own way, the essence of what the Prophet (SAAS) symbolized, namely, law with justice, to the attention of the American people. I hope that the Muslim leadership in the United States and around the world will join me in expressing this appreciation even though the frieze is over 60 years old.

God knows best what is right.

May God let you be successful in what He loves and in what pleases Him.

Peace be upon you with the mercy of God and His blessings.

†† [Editor's note: This fatwa (legal opinion) opens with a salutation to the person who has requested the opinion (Azizah Y. al-Hibri) from the author (Taha Jabar al-Alwani).]

1. The frieze is a band of engraved images or decoration round the top of a wall or building. In Arabic, this form of art is referred to as *tunf.*

2. *Shara'i'* (plural of *Shari'ah*) are legal systems, Islamic and otherwise.

3. Translator's Note: SAAS: *Salla Allahu 'Alayhi wa ala Allihi wa Sallam* (May the peace and blessings of God be upon him and upon his household members). This prayer is said by Muslims whenever the name of the Prophet Muhammad is mentioned or whenever he is referred to as the Prophet of God.

4. The Prophet was selected by Muslims to lead the first Muslim community, which was formed in Madinah. The symbolism of the sword was used throughout the frieze and the Supreme Court building to depict historical figures who exercised worldly authority.

5. *Usuli* Principles are basic principles employed for the interpretation of texts (the Qur'an and *Sunnah*).

6. Muslims in the United States have debated at length whether it is possible to confirm the birth of the new moon, and hence the end of Ramadan (the month of fasting) through astronomical calculations, or whether seeing the moon with the naked eye is required. They have similar debates about whether Muslims are required in the United States to eat only *hallal* meat, i.e. meat prepared in accordance with Islamic rules.

7. *Sunnah*: The sayings and example of the Prophet Muhammad (SAAS), including what he acquiesced or objected to.

8. *Hadith* (pl. *ahadith*): A saying of the Prophet Muhammad. Sometimes this word appears with the prefex "al"; this means simply "the".

9. *Khabar* (pl. *Akhbar*): Whatever is transmitted about the Prophet (SAAS), and by or about the Companions, the Successors, and their successors.

10. *Athaar.* Traditions reported by the Companions of the Prophet (SAAS).

11. Note that other Semitic cultures, such as the Hebraic one, held similar attitudes. This is clear from the Biblical passage which prohibits the making of graven images.

12. There are scholars who discussed this issue like al-Jahiz. *See* Amro bin Bahr al-Jahiz, *Al Bayan Wa Tabyeen* vol. 1 (Abdussalam Muhammad Haroun ed. & commentator, Cairo: Al-Khanjee Institute n.d.).

13. *Mu'allaqat*: Prior to Islam, Arabs used to hang poetic masterpieces on the curtains of the Ka'bahh to honor the poet. The *mu'allaqat* were the actual poems hanging on the curtains.

14. These were markets in pre-Islamic Arabia, each taking place at a certain place and specific time of year. For more detailed description of each place read Shaikh Imam Shahabuddin Bin Abduallah al-Hamawi, *Mu'jam Al-Buldan* vols. 7-8, of 10 vols. (Egypt: Assa'adah Printing House 1906).

15. *See* Imam Muhammad Ibn Idriss al-Shafi', *Risalat al-Shafi'* (10th Cent., Cairo: Matba'at Mustafa al-Baabi al-Halabi 1940); Imam Muihammad Ibn Idriss al-Shafi', *Kitab al-Um* (10th Cent. repr., Beirut: Dar al-Ma'rifah wa al'Nashr 1973).

16. *Tawhidi*: (monotheistic) the reference here is to the principle that there is no god but God.

17. *See e.g.* the discussion of Ibn Qayyim al-Jawziyyah in *Subhi al-Saleh* 666–669 (Ahkam Ahl al-Thimmah ed., 14th Cent. Damascus: Matba'at Jami'at Dimashq 1961) in which he surveys the views of various jurists on this matter.

18. *Subhanahu wa Ta'ala* (SWT): May He be praised and may His transcendence be affirmed.

19. [Editor's Note: Translation of all Qur'anic cites herein were provided by the author.]

20. Imad ad-Deen Ibn Kathir, *Tafsir al-Qur'an al-'Athim* vol. 3, 506–507 (15th Cent, repr., Riyhad: Mu'assasat al-Kutub al-Thaqafiyyah 1997); Abu Abd-Allah al-Qurtubi al-Jami', *Ahkam al-Qur'an* 271–272 (Cairo: Dar al-Kitab al-'Arabi, repr. 1967).

21. *Ahadith Ahad*: *Ahadith* for which the chain of transmission does not reach the "level of genuineness (*tawatur*)."

22. *Ratios (illah)*: The underlying cause of a *hukm* (legal ruling), its *ratio decidendi,* on the basis of which the accompanying *hukm* is extended to or applied in other cases.

23. *Mujtahid*: The scholar who makes a creative but disciplined intellectual effort to derive legal rulings from the accepted juridical sources of Islam while taking into consideration the variables imposed by the fluctuating circumstances of Muslim society.

24. *See Sahih Al-Bukhari bi Sharh al-Sindi,* at 276. "Baab Al-Hajj," the Pilgrimage Section. This *hadith* has been quoted in different ways from 'A'ishah, the mother of the believers: First among them is what Muslim and the Nasa'i compiled:

Had the people not been unbelievers in the recent past and had I funds to use to reinforce the construction of the building (Ka'bah), I would have added to it five *azera* (a specific measurement) of stone and made for it a door where people would enter and another where they would exit.

Second: "Had your people not been close to the period of *jahiliyah,* I would have demolished the Ka'bah and made for it two doors" (from *Al-Termathi* and *Al-Nasa'i*). Third: "Had your people not been close to the days of *jahiliyah,* I would have spent the treasury of the Ka'bah in the way of God, and I would have put its door by the floor and entered into it through the stones (which have been knocked down)" (from Sahih Muslim). Fourth:

Had your people not been unbelievers in the recent past (had they not quite recently accepted Islam), I would have demolished the Ka'bah and would have rebuilt it on the foundation (laid) by Abraham; for when the Quraish had built the Ka'bah, they reduced its (area), and I would also have built (a door) in the rear.

(Compiled by Ahmad in his *Musnad* (the book of *ahadith*) and in Nasa'i.) All these narrations are in the *Al-Fath Al-Kabir* (the Big Victory).

25. Children of *'allat* means that their mothers are different and their religion is one, or else that they belong to different nations, but their religion is the same in faith, purpose and goal (as explained in *Lisan al-Arab* and *al-Qamus*). Imam Abi al-fadl Jamalluddin Muhammad bin Mukrram bin Manzour al-Masri, *Lisan al-Arab* vol. 11, 470 (Beirut: Dar Sader n.d.); Majdduddin Muhammad bin Ya'quob al-Fairouzabadi, *al-Qamus Al-Muhit* 1338 (Arrissalah Inst. n.d.). Imam Mujduddin Abi Assa'addat bin, Muhammad bin al-Atheer, *Annihayahfi Gharib al-Hadith wa al-athar* vol. 3, 291 (Taher Ahmad Azzawi & Mahmoud Muhammad Attanahi revisors, Dar al-Fikr 1979).

26. Qur'an 20:85-88; 2:51. *See also* Fakhr al-Din al-Shafi', *Al-Tafsir al-Kabir* vol. 11, 87 (13th Cent. repr., Beirut: Dar al-Kutub al-'Ilmiyyah 1990) (explaining who the Sumarian was); *see also* Ibn Kathir, *Tafsir al-Qur'an al- 'Athim* vol. 3, *supra* n. 19, at 159.

27. Al-Hafiz (the "Memorizer): A title given to a person who knows most narrators of each category; and the person who occupies himself with the study of *hadith*. Among his

contributions is *Fath al-Bari* (14th Cent, repr., Riyadh: Dar al-Buhuth al-'Ilmiyyah 1982).

28. *Ijtihaad*: The effort of the jurist to derive the law on an issue by expending all available means of interpretation at his disposal and by taking into account all legal proofs related to the issue.

29. Sahih Muslim, Baab Al-Hajj Section, Hadith No. 1297.

30. *Baab* (Gate): a main chapter compiling *ahadith* around a specific topic.

31. Sahih Muslim, Hadith No. 1687.

32. *Qiyas*: Analogy, syllogism. The extension of the established *hukm* (legal ruling) of a specific case to a new case through reasoning by analogy.

33. Sahih Muslim, Hadith No. 1666. Also in Sahih Al-Bukhari, Hadith No. 5610, Baab al-Libas.

34. *Asl*: Origin; root; foundation. Source of law. The established case that forms the basis of the extension of the *hukm* in *qiyas*. A principle of law.

35. "*Sadd al dhari'ah*": means blocking a lawful justification to block an unlawful end.

36. Sahih Muslim, Hadith No. 2106 Baab Al-Libas.

37. Abu al-Hussein al-Nawawi, Sahih Muslim bi Sharh al-Nawawi vol. 7, 86 (13th Cent. repr., Beirut: Dar Ihya' al-Turath al-'Arabi n.d).

38. Sahih Muslim bi Sharh al-Nawawi v. 4, p. 818 (Cairo: Dar al-Sha'b n.d.).

39. Id.

40. Al-Nawawi, *supra* n. 37, at 81.

41. Mussnad Ahmad No. 847 in the "Baab The Ten promised with Paradise."

42. Sahih al-Bukhari, Al Maghazi Section, Hadith No. 3780, supported also by Hadith No. 4155 in Sunan Abi Dawood in "Baab Al-Libas," within the wording of: "Angels do not enter a house in which there is an image."

43. They ask you what is lawful to them (as food). Say:

Lawful unto you are (all) things good and pure: and what you have taught your trained hunting animals (to catch) in the manner directed to you by God: eat what they catch for you, but pronounce the name of God over it: and fear God; for God is swift in taking account.

Surat al-Ma'idah 5:4. There are also two other references to a dog in the story of the young men in the cave in Surat Kahf 18: 18, 22.

44. Abu al-Hassan al-Sindi, *Al-Bukhari bi Hashiat al-Sindi* vol. 4, 45 (9th Cent. repr., Beirut: Dar al-Ma'rifah n.d.).

45. Sunan Abi Dawood, ed., *Muhammad Abdul Hamid* v. 4, p. 73–4, Kitab al-Libas, Hadith No. 4155 (Beirut: al-Maktabah al-'Asriyyah n.d.).

46. *Mawquf*: a *hadith* traced back to a Companion of the Prophet (*Sahabi*) whether its chain of transmission is connected or not. *See* the *ahadiths* of Abdullah bin Mas'oud and Ibn Abbas, Sahih Muslim bi Sharh al-Nawawi, *supra* n. 37, at 92–93.

47. This *hadith* is among those compiled by al-Bukhari in the Book of Good Manners, Hadith No. 5665. (*See* 20:5 al-Manar, § 1 (n.p. 1917) (*infra* full cite in n. 48); Sahih Muslim Hadith No. (1666). Also in Sahih al-Bukhari, Hadith No. 5610, Baab al-Libas.

48. Sheikh Rashid Ridha, *The Fatawa of Al-Manar,* 20:5 Al-Manar 228 (1917).

49. For the definition of *mawqaf,* see *supra* n. 46.

50. Khairuddin Azirikli, *Al-'Alam: Qamus Trajem,* vol. 6 (Beirut: Dar Al-'ilm lil Malayeen n.d.).

51. *Supra* n. 45.

52. Ibn Hajar, *supra* n. 26.

53. *See also* the summary of his *fatwa, supra* n. 45.

54. *Sahih*: (authentic). *Hadith* whose chain of narrators is carried by truly pious persons who have been distinguished by uprightness and exactitude and whose reports and character have been free from blemish.

55. *Sirah* (pl. *Siyar*): the Arabic term for biography, and it is also used to refer to books written about the life of the Prophet (SAAS).

56. Jalal ad-Din al-Suyuti, *al-Jami' al-Saghir* vol. 2, 306–307 (Beirut: Dar al-Fikr, repr. 1981) referring to al-termadhi in *al-Shama'l,* al-Tabarani in *al-Mu'jam al-Kabir,* and al-Bayhaqi in *Shu'ab al-Imam* by Hind bin Abi-Halah.

57. Azizah al-Hibri, *Islamic Constitutionalism and the Concept of Democracy,* 24 Case W. Res. J. Intl. L. 1-27 (Winter 1992).

58. Shaikh Izuddin Abi al Hassan Ali Bin Abi al-Karam Ashibani (known as Ibn al-Athir), *Al-Kamel Fi Attarikh,* vol. 2, 204 (Beirut: Dar Sader 1965).

59. Ibn Kathir, *Tafsir al-Qur'an al-'Athim,* vol. 2, 241–243 (15th Cent, repr., Riyadh: Mu'assasat al-Kutub al-Thaqafiyyah 1997).

22. Nuh Ha Mim Keller, "Sufism and Islam"

Nuh Ha Mim Keller, "Sufism and Islam" MCMXCVIX © nuh ha mim keller accessed May 18, 2006. Available online: http://www.masud.co.uk/ISLAM/nuh/sufitlk.htm. Reprinted with permission of Nuh Ha Mim Keller.

The following treatise from Nu Ha Mim Keller (for a biography, see the "Keller, Shaykh Nuh" entry in Volume 1) addresses the status of mystical Islam within the United States vis-à-vis other traditional interpretations of Islam. It was published on his web site in 2002.

Perhaps the biggest challenge in learning Islam correctly today is the scarcity of traditional 'ulama. In this meaning, Bukhari relates the *sahih,* rigorously authenticated hadith that the Prophet (Allah bless him and give him peace) said,

"Truly, Allah does not remove Sacred Knowledge by taking it out of servants, but rather by taking back the souls of Islamic scholars [in death], until, when He has not left a single scholar, the people take the ignorant as leaders, who are asked for and who give Islamic legal opinion without knowledge, misguided and misguiding" (*Fath al-Bari,* 1.194, hadith 100).

The process described by the hadith is not yet completed, but has certainly begun, and in our times, the lack of traditional scholars—whether in Islamic law, in hadith, in *tafsir* 'Qur'anic exegesis'—has given rise to an understanding of the religion that is far from scholarly, and sometimes far from the truth. For example, in the course of my own studies in Islamic law, my first impression from orientalist and Muslim-reformer literature, was that the Imams of the *madhhab*s or 'schools of jurisprudence' had brought a set of rules from completely outside the Islamic tradition and somehow imposed them upon the Muslims. But when I sat with traditional scholars in the Middle East and asked them about the details, I came away with a different point of view, having learned the bases for deriving the law from the Qur'an and sunna.

And similarly with *Tasawwuf*—which is the word I will use tonight for the English *Sufism,* since our context is traditional Islam—quite a different picture emerged from talking with scholars of *Tasawwuf* than what I had been exposed to in the West. My talk tonight, In Sha' Allah, will present knowledge taken from the Qur'an and *sahih* hadith, and from actual teachers of Tasawwuf in Syria and Jordan, in view of the need for all of us to get beyond clichés, the need for factual information from Islamic sources, the need to answer such questions as: Where did Tasawwuf come from? What role does it play in the *din* or religion of Islam? and most importantly, What is the command of Allah about it?

As for the origin of the term Tasawwuf, like many other Islamic disciplines, its *name* was not known to the first generation of Muslims. The historian Ibn Khaldun notes in his *Muqaddima*: This knowledge is a branch of the sciences of Sacred Law that originated within the Umma. From the first, the way of such people had also been considered the path of truth and guidance by the early Muslim community and its notables, of the Companions of the Prophet (Allah bless him and give him peace), those who were taught by them, and those who came after them.

It basically consists of dedication to worship, total dedication to Allah Most High, disregard for the finery and ornament of the world, abstinence from the pleasure, wealth, and prestige sought by most men, and retiring from others to worship alone. This was the general rule among the Companions of the Prophet (Allah bless him and give him peace) and the early Muslims, but when involvement in this-worldly things became widespread from the second Islamic century onwards and people became absorbed in worldliness, those devoted to worship came to be called *Sufiyya* or *People of Tasawwuf* (Ibn Khaldun, *al-Muqaddima* [N.d. Reprint. Mecca: Dar al-Baz, 1397/1978], 467).

In Ibn Khaldun's words, the content of *Tasawwuf*, "total dedication to Allah Most High," was, "the general rule among the Companions of the Prophet (Allah bless him and give him peace) and the early Muslims." So if the *word* did not exist in earliest times, we should not forget that this is also the case with many other Islamic disciplines, such as *tafsir*, 'Qur'anic exegesis,' or *'ilm al-jarh wa ta'dil*, 'the science of the positive and negative factors that affect hadith narrators acceptability,' or *'ilm al-tawhid*, the science of belief in Islamic tenets of faith,' all of which proved to be of the utmost importance to the correct preservation and transmission of the religion.

As for the origin of the word *Tasawwuf*, it may well be from *Sufi*, the person who does Tasawwuf, which seems to be etymologically prior to it, for the earliest mention of either term was by Hasan al-Basri who died 110 years after the Hijra, and is reported to have said, "I saw a Sufi circumambulating the Kaaba, and offered him a dirham, but he would not accept it." It therefore seems better to understand Tasawwuf by first asking what a Sufi is; and perhaps the best definition of both the Sufi and his way, certainly one of the most frequently quoted by masters of the discipline, is from the sunna of the Prophet (Allah bless him and give him peace) who said:

Allah Most High says: "He who is hostile to a friend of Mine I declare war against. My slave approaches Me with nothing more beloved to Me than what I have made obligatory upon him, and My slave keeps drawing nearer to Me with voluntary works until I love him. And when I love him, I am his hearing with which he hears, his sight with which he sees, his hand with which he seizes, and his foot with which he walks. If he asks me, I will surely give to him, and if he seeks refuge in Me, I will surely protect him" (*Fath al-Bari*, 11.340–41, hadith 6502);

This hadith was related by Imam Bukhari, Ahmad ibn Hanbal, al-Bayhaqi, and others with multiple contiguous chains of transmission, and is *sahih*. It discloses the central reality of Tasawwuf, which is precisely *change*, while describing the path to this change, in conformity with a traditional definition used by masters in the Middle East, who define a Sufi as *Faqihun 'amila bi 'ilmihi fa awrathahu Llahu 'ilma ma lam ya'lam*, 'A man of religious learning who applied what he knew, so Allah bequeathed him knowledge of what he did not know.'

To clarify, a Sufi is *a man of religious learning*,because the hadith says, "My slave approaches Me with nothing more beloved to Me than what I have made obligatory upon him," and only through learning can the Sufi know the command of Allah, or what has been made obligatory for him. He has *applied what he knew*, because the hadith says he not only *approaches* Allah with the obligatory, but "keeps drawing nearer to Me with voluntary works until I love him." And in turn, *Allah bequeathed him knowledge of what he did not know*, because the hadith says, "And when I love him, I am his hearing with which he hears, his sight with which he sees, his hand with which he seizes, and his foot with which he walks," which is a metaphor for the consummate awareness of *tawhid*, or the 'unity of Allah,' which in the context of human actions such as hearing, sight, seizing, and walking, consists of realizing the words of the Qur'an about Allah that, "It is He who created you and what you do" (Qur'an 37:96).

The origin of the way of the Sufi thus lies in the prophetic sunna. The sincerity to Allah that it entails was the rule among the earliest Muslims, to whom this was simply a state of being without a name, while it only became a distinct discipline when the majority of the Community had drifted away and changed from this state. Muslims of subsequent generations required systematic effort to attain it, and it was because of the change in the Islamic environment after the earliest generations, that a discipline by the name of Tasawwuf came to exist.

But if this is true of origins, the more significant question is: How central is Tasawwuf to the religion, and: Where does it fit into Islam as a whole? Perhaps the best answer is the hadith of Muslim, that 'Umar ibn al-Khattab said:

As we sat one day with the Messenger of Allah (Allah bless him and give him peace), a man in pure white clothing and jet black hair came to us, without a trace of travelling upon him, though none of us knew him.

He sat down before the Prophet (Allah bless him and give him peace) bracing his knees against his, resting his hands on his legs, and said: "Muhammad, tell me about Islam." The Messenger of Allah (Allah bless him and give him peace) said: "Islam is to testify that there is no god but Allah and that Muhammad is the Messenger of Allah, and to perform the prayer, give zakat, fast in Ramadan, and perform the pilgrimage to the House if you can find a way."

He said: "You have spoken the truth," and we were surprised that he should ask and then confirm the answer. Then he said: "Tell me about true faith (iman)," and the Prophet (Allah bless him and give him peace) answered: "It is to believe in Allah, His angels, His inspired Books, His messengers, the Last Day, and in destiny, its good and evil."

"You have spoken the truth," he said, "Now tell me about the perfection of faith (ihsan)," and the Prophet (Allah bless him and give him peace) answered: "It is to worship Allah as if you see Him, and if you see Him not, He nevertheless sees you."

The hadith continues to where 'Umar said:

Then the visitor left. I waited a long while, and the Prophet (Allah bless him and give him peace) said to me, "Do you know, 'Umar, who was the questioner?" and I replied, "Allah and His messenger know best." He said, "It was Gabriel, who came to you to teach you your religion" (*Sahih Muslim*, 1.37: hadith 8).

This is a *sahih* hadith, described by Imam Nawawi as one of the hadiths upon which the Islamic religion turns. The use of *din* in the last words of it, *Atakum yu'allimukum dinakum*, "came to you to teach you your *religion*" entails that the *religion* of Islam is composed of the three fundamentals mentioned in the hadith: *Islam*, or external compliance with what Allah asks of us; *Iman*, or the belief in the unseen that the prophets have informed us of; and *Ihsan*, or to worship Allah as though one sees Him. The Qur'an says, in Surat Maryam,

"Surely We have revealed the Remembrance, and surely We shall preserve it" (Qur'an 15:9), and if we reflect how Allah, in His wisdom, has accomplished this, we see that it is by human beings, the traditional scholars He has sent at each level of the religion. The level of *Islam* has been preserved and conveyed to us by the Imams of *Shari'a* or 'Sacred Law' and its ancillary disciplines; the level of *Iman*, by the Imams of *'Aqida* or 'tenets of faith'; and the level of *Ihsan*, "to worship Allah as though you see Him," by the Imams of Tasawwuf.

The hadith's very words "to *worship* Allah" show us the interrelation of these three fundamentals, for the *how* of "worship" is only known through the external prescriptions of *Islam*, while the *validity* of this worship in turn presupposes *Iman* or faith in Allah and the Islamic revelation, without which *worship* would be but empty motions; while the words, "as if you see Him," show that *Ihsan* implies a human *change*, for it entails the experience of what, for most of us, is not experienced. So to understand Tasawwuf, we must look at the nature of this change in relation to both Islam and Iman, and this is the main focus of my talk tonight.

At the level of Islam, we said that Tasawwuf requires *Islam*, through 'submission to the rules of Sacred Law.' But Islam, for its part, equally requires Tasawwuf. Why? For the very good reason that the sunna which Muslims have been commanded to follow is not just the *words* and *actions* of the Prophet (Allah bless him and give him peace), but also his *states*, states of the heart such as *taqwa* 'godfearingness,' *ikhlas* 'sincerity,' *tawakkul* 'reliance on Allah,' *rahma* 'mercy,' *tawadu'* 'humility,' and so on.

Now, it is characteristic of the Islamic ethic that human actions are not simply divided into two shades of morality, right or wrong; but rather five, arranged in order of their consequences in the next world. The *obligatory* (wajib) is that whose performance is rewarded by Allah in the next life and whose nonperformance is punished. The *recommended* (mandub) is that whose performance is rewarded, but whose nonperformance is not punished. The *permissible* (mubah) is indifferent, unconnected with either reward or punishment. The *offensive* (makruh) is that whose nonperformance is rewarded but whose performance is not punished. The *unlawful* (haram) is that whose nonperformance is rewarded and whose performance is punished, if one dies unrepentant.

Human states of the heart, the Qur'an and sunna make plain to us, come under each of these headings. Yet they are not dealt with in books of *fiqh* or 'Islamic jurisprudence,' because unlike the prayer, zakat, or fasting, they are not *quantifiable* in terms of the specific amount of them that must be done. But though they are not countable, they are of the utmost importance to every Muslim. Let's look at a few examples.

(1) *Love of Allah.* In Surat al-Baqara of the Qur'an, Allah blames those who ascribe associates to Allah whom they love as much as they love Allah. Then He says, "And those who believe are greater in love for Allah" (Qur'an 2:165), making being a believer conditional upon having greater love for Allah than any other.

(2) *Mercy.* Bukhari and Muslim relate that the Prophet (Allah bless him and give him peace) said, "Whomever is not merciful to people, Allah will show no mercy" (*Sahih Muslim*, 4.1809: hadith 2319), and Tirmidhi relates the well authenticated (hasan) hadith "Mercy is not taken out of anyone except the damned" (*al-Jami' al-sahih*, 4.323: hadith 1923).

(3) *Love of each other.* Muslim relates in his *Sahih* that the Prophet (Allah bless him and give him peace) said, "By Him in whose hand is my soul, none of you shall enter paradise until you believe, and none of you shall believe until you love one another . . . ." (*Sahih Muslim*, 1.74: hadith 54).

(4) *Presence of mind in the prayer (salat).* Abu Dawud relates in his *Sunan* that 'Ammar ibn Yasir heard the Prophet (Allah bless him and give him peace) say, "Truly, a man leaves, and none of his prayer has been recorded for him except a tenth of it, a ninth of it, eighth of it, seventh of it, sixth of it, fifth of it, fourth of it, third of it, a half of it" (*Sunan Abi Dawud*, 1.211: hadith 796)—meaning that none of a person's prayer counts for him except that in which he is present in his heart with Allah.

(5) *Love of the Prophet.* Bukhari relates in his *Sahih* that the Prophet (Allah bless him and give him peace) said, "None of you believes until I am more beloved to him than his father, his son, and all people" (*Fath al-Bari*, 1.58, hadith 15).

It is plain from these texts that none of the states mentioned—whether mercy, love, or presence of heart—are quantifiable, for the Shari'a cannot specify that one must "do two units of mercy" or "have three units of presence of mind" in the way that the number of rak'as of prayer can be specified, yet each of them is personally obligatory for the Muslim. Let us complete the picture by looking at a few examples of states that are *haram* or 'strictly unlawful':

(1) *Fear of anyone besides Allah.* Allah Most High says in Surat al-Baqara of the Qur'an, "And fulfill My covenant: I will fulfill your covenant—And fear Me alone" (Qur'an 2:40), the last phrase of which, according to Imam Fakhr al-Din al-Razi, "establishes that a human being is obliged to fear no one besides Allah Most High" (*Tafsir al-Fakhr al-Razi*, 3.42).

(2) *Despair.* Allah Most High says, "None despairs of Allah's mercy except the people who disbelieve" (Qur'an 12:87), indicating the unlawfulness of this inward state by coupling it with the worst human condition possible, that of unbelief.

(3) *Arrogance.* Muslim relates in his *Sahih* that the Prophet (Allah bless him and give him peace) said, "No one shall enter paradise who has a particle of arrogance in his heart" (*Sahih Muslim*, 1.93: hadith 91).

(4) *Envy,* meaning to wish for another to lose the blessings he enjoys. Abu Dawud relates that the Prophet (Allah bless him and give him peace) said, "Beware of envy, for envy consumes good works as flames consume firewood" (*Sunan Abi Dawud*, 4.276: hadith 4903).

(5) *Showing off in acts of worship.* Al-Hakim relates with a *sahih* chain of transmission that the Prophet (Allah bless him and give him peace) said, "The slightest bit of showing off in good works is as if worshipping others with Allah . . . ." (*al-Mustadrak 'ala al-Sahihayn*, 1.4).

These and similar *haram* inward states are not found in books of *fiqh* or 'jurisprudence,' because *fiqh* can only deal with quantifiable descriptions of rulings. Rather, they are examined in their causes and remedies by the scholars of the 'inner fiqh' of Tasawwuf, men such as Imam al-Ghazali in his *Ihya' 'ulum al-din* [The reviving of the religious sciences], Imam al-Rabbani in his *Maktubat* [Letters], al-Suhrawardi in his *'Awarif al-Ma'arif* [The knowledges of the illuminates], Abu Talib al-Makki in *Qut al-qulub* [The sustenance of hearts], and similar classic works, which discuss and solve hundreds of ethical questions about the inner life. These are books of *Shari'a* and their questions are questions of Sacred Law, of how it is lawful or unlawful for a Muslim to *be*; and they preserve the part of the prophetic sunna dealing with states.

Who needs such information? All Muslims, for the Qur'anic verses and authenticated hadiths all point to the fact that a Muslim must not only do certain things and say certain things, but also must *be* something, must attain certain states of the heart and eliminate others. Do we ever fear someone besides Allah? Do we have a particle of arrogance in our hearts? Is our love for the Prophet (Allah bless him and give him peace) greater than our love for any other human being? Is there the slightest bit of showing off in our good works?

Half a minute's reflection will show the Muslim where he stands on these aspects of his *din*, and why in classical times, helping Muslims to attain these states was not left to amateurs, but rather delegated to 'ulama of the heart, the scholars of Islamic Tasawwuf. For most people, these are not easy transformations to make, because of the force of habit, because of the subtlety with which we can deceive ourselves, but most of all because each of us has an ego, the self, the Me, which is called in Arabic *al-nafs*, about which Allah testifies in Surat Yusuf: "Verily the self ever commands to do evil" (Qur'an 12:53).

If you do not believe it, consider the hadith related by Muslim in his *Sahih*, that:

The first person judged on Resurrection Day will be a man martyred in battle. He will be brought forth, Allah will reacquaint him with His blessings upon him and the man will acknowledge them, whereupon Allah will say, "What have you done with them?" to which the man will respond, "I fought to the death for You."

Allah will reply, "You lie. You fought in order to be called a hero, and it has already been said." Then he will be sentenced and dragged away on his face and flung into the fire.

Then a man will be brought forward who learned Sacred Knowledge, taught it to others, and who recited the Qur'an. Allah will remind him of His gifts to him and the man will acknowledge them, and then Allah will say, "What have you done with them?" The man will answer, "I acquired Sacred Knowledge, taught it, and recited the Qur'an, for Your sake."

Allah will say, "You lie. You learned so as to be called a scholar, and read the Qur'an so as to be called a reciter, and it has already been said." Then the man will be sentenced and dragged away on his face to be flung into the fire.

Then a man will be brought forward whom Allah generously provided for, giving him various kinds of wealth, and Allah will recall to him the benefits given, and the man will acknowledge them, to which Allah will say, "And what have you done with them?" The man will answer, "I have not left a single kind of expenditure You love to see made, except that I have spent on it for Your sake."

Allah will say, "You lie. You did it so as to be called generous, and it has already been said." Then he will be sentenced and dragged away on his face to be flung into the fire (*Sahih Muslim*, 3.1514: hadith 1905).

We should not fool ourselves about this, because our fate depends on it: in our childhood, our parents taught us how to behave through praise or blame, and for most of us, this permeated and colored our whole motivation for doing things. But when childhood ends, and we come of age in Islam, the religion makes it clear to us, both by the above hadith and by the words of the Prophet (Allah bless him and give him peace) "The slightest bit of showing off in good works is as if worshipping others with Allah" that being motivated by what others think is no longer good enough, and that we must change our motives entirely, and henceforth be motivated by nothing but desire for Allah Himself. The Islamic revelation thus tells the Muslim that it is obligatory to break his habits of thinking and motivation, but it does not tell him how. For that, he must go to the scholars of these states, in accordance with the Qur'anic imperative, "Ask those who know if you know not" (Qur'an 16:43). There is no doubt that bringing about this change, purifying the Muslims by bringing them to spiritual sincerity, was one of the central duties of the Prophet Muhammad (Allah bless him and give him peace), for Allah says in the Surat Al 'Imran of the Qur'an,

"Allah has truly blessed the believers, for He has sent them a messenger of themselves, who recites His signs to them and purifies them, and teaches them the Book and the Wisdom" (Qur'an 3:164), which explicitly lists four tasks of the prophetic mission, the second of which, *yuzakkihim* means precisely to 'purify them' and has no other lexical sense. Now, it is plain that this teaching function cannot, as part of an *eternal* revelation, have ended with the passing of the first generation, a fact that Allah explictly confirms in His injunction in Surat Luqman, "And follow the path of him who turns unto Me" (Qur'an 31:15).

These verses indicate the teaching and transformative role of those who convey the Islamic revelation to Muslims, and the choice of the word *ittiba'* in the second verse, which is more general, implies both keeping the company of and following the example of a teacher. This is why in the history of Tasawwuf, we find that though there were many methods and schools of thought, these two things never changed: keeping the company of a teacher, and following his example—in exactly the same way that the Sahaba were uplifted and purified by keeping the company of the Prophet (Allah bless him and give him peace) and following his example.

And this is why the discipline of Tasawwuf has been preserved and transmitted by *Tariqa*s or groups of students under a particular master. First, because this was the sunna of the Prophet (Allah bless him and give him peace) in his purifying function described by the Qur'an. Secondly, Islamic knowledge has never been transmitted by writings alone, but rather from 'ulama to students. Thirdly, the nature of the knowledge in question is of *hal* or *'state of being,'* not just knowing, and hence requires it be taken from a succession of living masters back to the Prophet (Allah bless him and give him peace), for the sheer range and number of the states of heart required by the revelation effectively make imitation of the personal example of a teacher the only effective means of transmission.

So far we have spoken about Tasawwuf in respect to Islam, as a Shari'a science necessary to fully realize the Sacred Law in one's life, to attain the states of the heart demanded by the Qur'an and hadith. This close connection between Shari'a and Tasawwuf is expressed by the statement of Imam Malik, founder of the Maliki school, that "he who practices Tasawwuf without learning Sacred Law corrupts his faith, while he who learns Sacred Law without practicing Tasawwuf corrupts himself. Only he who combines the two proves true." This is why Tasawwuf was taught as part of the traditional curriculum in madrasas across the Muslim world from Malaysia to Morocco, why many of the greatest Shari'a scholars of this Umma have been Sufis, and why until the end of the Islamic caliphate at the beginning of this century and the subsequent Western control and cultural dominance of Muslim lands, there were teachers of Tasawwuf in Islamic institutions of higher learning from Lucknow to Istanbul to Cairo.

But there is a second aspect of Tasawwuf that we have not yet talked about; namely, its relation to *Iman* or 'True Faith,' the second pillar of the Islamic religion, which in the context of the Islamic sciences consists of *'Aqida* or 'orthodox belief.' All Muslims believe in Allah, and that He is transcendently beyond anything conceivable to the minds of men, for the human intellect is imprisoned within its own sense impressions and the categories of thought derived from them, such as number, directionality, spatial extention, place, time, and so forth. Allah is beyond all of that; in His own words, "There is nothing whatesover like unto Him" (Qur'an 42:11).

If we reflect for a moment on this verse, in the light of the hadith of Muslim about *Ihsan* that "it is to worship Allah as though you see Him," we realize that the means of *seeing* here is not the eye, which can only behold physical things like itself; nor yet the mind, which cannot transcend its own impressions to reach the Divine, but rather certitude, the light of Iman, whose locus is not the eye or the brain, but rather the *ruh*, a subtle faculty Allah has created within each of us called the soul, whose knowledge is unobstructed by the bounds of the created universe. Allah Most High says, by way of exalting the nature of this faculty by leaving it a mystery, "Say: 'The soul is of the affair of my Lord'" (Qur'an 17:85). The food of this ruh is *dhikr* or the 'remembrance of Allah.' Why? Because acts of obedience increase the light of certainty and Iman in the soul, and dhikr is among the greatest of them, as is attested to by the *sahih* hadith related by al-Hakim that the Prophet (Allah bless him and give him peace) said, "Shall I not tell you of the best of your works, the purest of them in the eyes of your Master, the highest in raising your rank, better than giving gold and silver, and better for you than to meet your enemy and smite their necks, and they smite yours?" They said, "This—what is it, O Messenger of Allah?" and he said: *Dhikru Llahi 'azza wa jall*, "The remembrance of Allah Mighty and Majestic" (*al-Mustadrak 'ala al-Sahihayn*, 1.496).

Increasing the strength of Iman through good actions, and particularly through the medium of *dhikr* has tremendous implications for the Islamic religion and traditional spirituality. A non-Muslim once asked me, "If God exists, then why all this beating around the bush? Why doesn't He just come out and say so?"

The answer is that *taklif* or 'moral responsibility' in this life is not only concerned with outward actions, but with what we *believe*, our *'Aqida*—and the strength with which we believe it. If belief in God and other eternal truths were effortless in this world, there would be no point in Allah making us responsible for it, it would be automatic, involuntary, like our belief, say, that London is in England. There would no point in making someone responsible for something impossible *not* to believe.

But the responsibility Allah has place upon us is belief in the Unseen, as a test for us in this world to choose between kufr and Iman, to distinguish believer from unbeliever, and some believers above others.

This why strengthening Iman through dhikr is of such methodological importance for Tasawwuf: we have not only been commanded as Muslims to believe in certain things, but have been commanded to have absolute certainty in them. The world we see around us is composed of veils of light and darkness: events come that knock the Iman out of some of us, and Allah tests each of us as to the degree of certainty with which we believe the eternal truths of the religion. It was in this sense that 'Umar ibn al-Khattab said, "If the Iman of Abu Bakr were weighed against the Iman of the entire Umma, it would outweigh it."

Now, in traditional *'Aqida* one of the most important tenets is the *wahdaniyya* or 'oneness and uniqueness' of Allah Most High. This means He is without any *sharik* or associate in His being, in His attributes, or in His acts. But the ability to hold this insight in mind in the rough and tumble of daily life is a function of the strength of certainty (yaqin) in one's heart. Allah tells the Prophet (Allah bless him and give him peace) in Surat al-A'raf of the Qur'an, "Say: 'I do not possess benefit for myself or harm, except as Allah wills'" (Qur'an 7:188), yet we tend to rely on ourselves and our plans, in obliviousness to the facts of 'Aqida that ourselves and our plans have no effect, that Allah alone brings about effects.

If you want to test yourself on this, the next time you contact someone with good connections whose help is critical to you, take a look at your heart at the moment you ask him to put in a good word for you with someone, and see whom you are relying upon. If you are like most of us, Allah is not at the forefront of your thoughts, despite the fact that He alone is controlling the outcome. Isn't this a lapse in your 'Aqida, or, at the very least, in your certainty?

Tasawwuf corrects such shortcomings by step-by-step increasing the Muslim's certainty in Allah. The two central means of Tasawwuf in attaining the *conviction* demanded by 'Aqida are *mudhakara*, or learning the traditional tenets of Islamic faith, and *dhikr*, deepening one's certainty in them by remembrance of Allah. It is part of our faith that, in the words of the Qur'an in Surat al-Saffat, "Allah has created you and what you do" (Qur'an 37:96); yet for how many of us is this day to day experience? Because Tasawwuf remedies this and other shortcomings of Iman, by increasing the Muslim's certainty through a systematic way of teaching and dhikr, it has traditionally been regarded as personally obligatory to this pillar of the religion also, and from the earliest centuries of Islam, has proved its worth.

The last question we will deal with tonight is: What about the bad Sufis we read about, who contravene the teachings of Islam?

The answer is that there are two meanings of Sufi: the first is "Anyone who considers himself a Sufi," which is the rule of thumb of orientalist historians of Sufism and popular writers, who would oppose the "Sufis" to the "Ulama." I think the Qur'anic verses and hadiths we have mentioned tonight about the scope and method of true Tasawwuf show why we must insist on the primacy of the definition of a Sufi as "a man of religious learning who applied what he knew, so Allah bequeathed him knowledge of what he did not know."

The very first thing a Sufi, as *a man of religious learning* knows is that the Shari'a and 'Aqida of Islam are *above every human being*. Whoever does not know this will never be a Sufi, except in the orientalist sense of the word—like someone standing in front of the stock exchange in an expensive suit with a briefcase to convince people he is a stockbroker. A real stockbroker is something else.

Because this distinction is ignored today by otherwise well-meaning Muslims, it is often forgotten that the 'ulama who have criticized Sufis, such as Ibn al-Jawzi in his *Talbis Iblis* [The Devil's deception], or Ibn Taymiya in places in his *Fatawa*, or Ibn al-Qayyim al-Jawziyya, were not criticizing Tasawwuf as an ancillary discipline to the Shari'a. The proof of this is Ibn al-Jawzi's five-volume *Sifat al-safwa*, which contains the biographies of the very same Sufis mentioned in al-Qushayri's famous Tasawwuf manual *al-Risala al-Qushayriyya*. Ibn Taymiya considered himself a Sufi of the Qadiri order, and volumes ten and eleven of his thirty-seven-volume *Majmu' al-fatawa* are devoted to Tasawwuf. And Ibn al-Qayyim al-Jawziyya wrote his three-volume *Madarij al-salikin*, a detailed commentary on 'Abdullah al-Ansari al-Harawi's tract on the spiritual stations of the Sufi path, *Manazil al-sa'irin*. These works show that their authors' criticisms were not directed at Tasawwuf as such, but rather at specific groups of their times, and they should be understood for what they are.

As in other Islamic sciences, mistakes historically did occur in Tasawwuf, most of them stemming from not recognizing the primacy of Shari'a and 'Aqida above all else. But these mistakes were not different in principle from, for example, the *Isra'iliyyat* (baseless tales of Bani Isra'il) that crept into tafsir literature, or the *mawdu'at* (hadith forgeries) that crept into the hadith. These were not taken as proof that *tafsir* was bad, or hadith was deviance, but rather, in each discipline, the errors were identified and warned against by Imams of the field, because the Umma needed the rest. And such corrections are precisely what we find in books like Qushayri's *Risala,* Ghazali's *Ihya'* and other works of Sufism.

For all of the reasons we have mentioned, Tasawwuf was accepted as an essential part of the Islamic religion by the 'ulama of this Umma. The proof of this is all the famous scholars of Shari'a sciences who had the higher education of Tasawwuf, among them Ibn 'Abidin, al-Razi, Ahmad Sirhindi, Zakariyya al-Ansari, al-'Izz ibn 'Abd al-Salam, Ibn Daqiq al-'Eid, Ibn Hajar al-Haytami, Shah Wali Allah, Ahmad Dardir, Ibrahim al-Bajuri, 'Abd al-Ghani al-Nabulsi, Imam al-Nawawi, Taqi al-Din al-Subki, and al-Suyuti.

Among the Sufis who aided Islam with the *sword* as well as the pen, to quote *Reliance of the Traveller,* were: such men as the Naqshbandi sheikh Shamil al-Daghestani, who fought a prolonged war against the Russians in the Caucasus in the nineteenth century; Sayyid Muhammad 'Abdullah al-Somali, a sheikh of the Salihiyya order who led Muslims against the British and Italians in Somalia from 1899 to 1920; the Qadiri sheikh 'Uthman ibn Fodi, who led jihad in Northern Nigeria from 1804 to 1808 to establish Islamic rule; the Qadiri sheikh 'Abd al-Qadir al-Jaza'iri, who led the Algerians against the French from 1832 to 1847; the Darqawi faqir al-Hajj Muhammad al-Ahrash, who fought the French in Egypt in 1799; the Tijani sheikh al-Hajj 'Umar Tal, who led Islamic Jihad in Guinea, Senegal, and Mali from 1852 to 1864; and the Qadiri sheikh Ma' al-'Aynayn al-Qalqami, who helped marshal Muslim resistance to the French in northern Mauritania and southern Morocco from 1905 to 1909.

Among the Sufis whose missionary work Islamized entire regions are such men as the founder of the Sanusiyya order, Muhammad 'Ali Sanusi, whose efforts and jihad from 1807 to 1859 consolidated Islam as the religion of peoples from the Libyan Desert to sub-Saharan Africa; [and] the Shadhili sheikh Muhammad Ma'ruf and Qadiri sheikh Uways al-Barawi, whose efforts spread Islam westward and inland from the East African Coast... (*Reliance of the Traveller,* 863).

It is plain from the examples of such men what kind of Muslims have been Sufis; namely, all kinds, right across the board—and that Tasawwuf did not prevent them from serving Islam in any way they could.

To summarize everything I have said tonight: In looking first at Tasawwuf and Shari'a, we found that many Qur'anic verses and sahih hadiths oblige the Muslim to eliminate *haram* inner states as arrogance, envy, and fear of anyone besides Allah; and on the other hand, to acquire such obligatory inner states as mercy, love of one's fellow Muslims, presence of mind in prayer, and love of the Prophet (Allah bless him and give him peace). We found that these inward states could not be dealt with in books of *fiqh,* whose purpose is to specify the outward, quantifiable aspects of the Shari'a. The knowledge of these states is nevertheless of the utmost importance to every Muslim, and this is why it was studied under the 'ulama of Ihsan, the teachers of Tasawwuf, in all periods of Islamic history until the beginning of the present century.

We then turned to the level of Iman, and found that though the *'Aqida* of Muslims is that Allah alone has any effect in this world, keeping this in mind in everhday life is not a given of human consciousness, but rather a function of a Muslim's *yaqin,* his certainty. And we found that Tasawwuf, as an ancillary discipline to 'Aqida, emphasizes the systematic increase of this certainty through both *mudhakara*, 'teaching tenets of faith' and *dhikr*, 'the remembrance of Allah,' in accordance with the words of the Prophet (Allah bless him and give him peace) about Ihsan that "it is worship Allah as though you see Him."

Lastly, we found that accusations against Tasawwuf made by scholars such as Ibn al-Jawzi, and Ibn Taymiya were not directed against Tasawwuf in principle, but to specific groups and individuals in the times of these authors, the proof for which is the other books by the same authors that showed their understanding of Tasawwuf as a Shari'a science.

To return to the starting point of my talk this evening, with the disappearance of traditional Islamic scholars from the Umma, two very different pictures of Tasawwuf emerge today. If we read books written *after* the dismantling of the traditional fabric of Islam by colonial powers in the last century, we find the big hoax: Islam without spirituality and Shari'a without Tasawwuf. But if we read the classical works of Islamic scholarship, we learn that Tasawwuf has been a Shari'a science like tafsir, hadith, or any other, throughout the history of Islam. The Prophet (Allah bless him and give him peace) said, "Truly, Allah does not look at your outward forms and wealth, but rather at your hearts and your works" (Sahih Muslim, 4.1389: hadith 2564).

And this is the brightest hope that Islam can offer a modern world darkened by materialism and nihilism: Islam as it truly is; the hope of eternal salvation through a religion of brotherhood and social and economic justice outwardly, and the direct experience of divine love and illumination inwardly.

23. Muzzamil H. Siddiqi, "Basic Commitments of Muslims" from *The Islamic Society of North America*

From the Islamic Society of North America, accessed May 21, 2006. Available online: http://www.isna.net/services/library/khutbahs/BasicCommitmentsofMuslims.html. Reprinted with the permission of Muzzamil H. Siddiqi (for a biography, see the "Siddiqi, Muzzamil" entry in Volume 1) and the Islamic Society of North America.

Muzzamil H. Siddiqi was born in India in 1943. He has studied at universities in India, Saudi Arabia, England, and the United States. He received his Ph.D. from Harvard University in Comparative Religion in 1978. He lectured at universities in the United States and Pakistan, including an adjunct professorship at California State University in Fullerton. Siddiqi had held a variety of leadership roles in the including as president of the Islamic Society of North America (ISNA) (1996–2000), President of the Fiqh Council of North America, a member of the Supreme Islamic Council of Egypt, and the Supreme Council of Mosques in Mecca, Saudi Arabia. The following (Basic Commitments of Muslims, Islamic Activism, and Zakat and Charity—Our Gratitude to Allah) are khutbas (sermons) he delivered at the Islamic Society of Orange County in southern California. His interpretation represents a traditional approach to the basic tenets of Islam.

Your Lord has decreed that you worship none but Him, and that you be kind to parents. Whether one or both of them attain old age in your life, say not to them a word of contempt, nor repel them, but address them in terms of honor. 24- And, out of kindness, lower to them the wing of humility, and say: "My Lord! bestow on them Mercy even as they cherished me in childhood." 25- Your Lord knows best what is in your hearts: if you do deeds of righteousness, verily He is Most Forgiving to those who turn to Him again and again (in true penitence). 26- And render to the kindred their due rights, as (also) to those in want, and to the wayfarer: but squander not (your wealth) in the manner of a spendthrift. 27- Verily spendthrifts are brothers of the Evil Ones; and the Evil One is to his Lord (Himself) Ungrateful. 28- And even if you have to turn away from them in pursuit of the Mercy from thy Lord which you do expect, yet speak to them a word of easy kindness. 29- Make not your hand tied to your neck, nor stretch it forth to its utmost reach, so that you become blameworthy and destitute. 30- Verily your Lord does provide sustenance in abundance for whom He pleases, and He provides in a just measure: for He does know and regard all His servants. 31- Kill not your children for fear of want: We shall provide sustenance for them as well as for you. Verily the killing of them is a great sin. 32- Nor come nigh to adultery: for it is a shameful (deed) and an evil, opening the road (to other evils). 33- Nor take life—which Allah has made sacred—except for just cause. And if anyone is slain wrongfully, We have given his heir authority (to demand Qisas or to forgive): but let him not exceed bounds in the matter of taking life; for he is helped (by the law). 34- Come not nigh to the orphan's property except to improve it, until he attains the age of full strength; and fulfil (every) engagement, for (every) engagement, will be enquired into (on the Day of Reckoning). 35- Give full measure when you measure, and weigh with a balance that is straight; that is the most fitting and the most advantageous in the final determination. 36- And pursue not that of which you have no knowledge; for every act of hearing, or of seeing, or of (feeling in) the heart will be enquired into (on the Day of Reckoning). 37- Nor walk on the earth with insolence: for you cannot rend the earth asunder, nor reach the mountains in height. 38- Of all such things the evil is hateful in the sight of your Lord. 39- These are among the (precepts of) wisdom, which thy Lord has revealed to you. Take not, with Allah, another object of worship, lest you should be thrown into Hell, blameworthy and rejected. *(Al-Isra' 17:23–39)*

Surah al-Isra' was revealed to Prophet Muhammad—peace be upon him—in Makkah after his Night Journey from Makkah to Jerusalem. In this Surah Allah mentions some basic commitments of Muslims. Without fulfilling these commitments no individual or groups can succeed. Muslims have to live by these values and should invite the humanity to these principles. These principles are not limited to one race, tribe or group; they are universal in their scope and application. These are also called the *Hikmah* or the teachings of wisdom. It is wise for every one to follow them. If followed properly they are capable to increase the goodness and wisdom of all people. These principles are:

1. Worship Allah alone:

This means to recognize Allah as the ultimate reality and to recognize Allah as the Lord, to worship Him with all sincerity and to submit to Him in every aspect of life. A Muslim's life is nothing but total commitment to Allah. We are not only monotheists (people of Tawhid) but we are also theocentric people. Allah is the center of our life and He is our total and ultimate concern.

2. Be respectful and kind to the parents:

This is to acknowledge the compassion and kindness of the parents, to be grateful to them and to do one's utmost to reciprocate that love and compassion. Filial piety and devotion is the second most important commitment of Muslims. Respect and kindness to parents is not just a social duty for us; it is our religious duty and obligation.

3. Be good to your relatives, to the poor and the travelers:

This is to remember that we are interconnected in this world. Our responsibilities are not to only towards ourselves and our immediate families, but also to other relatives and to the society at large. We are all in need of each other and we are all fellow travelers in this path of life. We must see what we can do for others. Muslims must live a socially responsible life. Social responsibility begins with the family, other relatives and it includes all those who are in need.

4. Be careful with your money. Do not waste your resources:

One should be neither be too tight with one's money nor be too lose with it. Extravagance is not right, but also one should not become stingy and miserly. A Muslim is committed to the balanced life style. Money should be earned in Halal ways and it should be spent in the right manner. This principle can be applied to all resources that Allah has given us. Wise and conscientious use of resources is a very important commitment of Muslims.

5. Take good care of your children:

As we recognize the rights of the parents, we should also recognize the rights of children. Our children are our future. We must see that we raise healthy, intelligent and morally responsible children. Our commitment should be to raise them in safe and healthy environment. We must protect their life as well as their sprit and mind, their morals and manners.

6. Do not commit adultery or fornication:

Sexual perversions bring the greatest harm to individuals and societies. Observing the proper rules in this matter lead to health, happiness and good moral society. Muslims are committed to pure, clean and socially responsible life style. Islam teaches that one should not come even close to adultery or fornication. This means proper dress code for males and females, proper behavior in mixed societies and proper control on social relations and entertainments.

7. Respect every life. Do not kill anyone unless in the pursuit of justice:

This means that one should recognize the sanctity of all life and should not do anything that may jeopardize life. One should avoid aggression and violence, because these things lead to murder. Every Muslim must be committed to peaceful ways. Conflicts should be resolved by dialogue and negotiations not by killings and murders. However, justice must be maintained, because just punishment brings safety and protects life.

8. Take care of the orphans:

Orphans and all those who are vulnerable must be taken care of. Their rights must be recognized and they should be protected from all harms. A Muslim must be deeply committed to the care of young, poor, infirm and handicapped. Kindness and compassion is the basic commitment of a Muslims. It includes every one, including the animals.

9. Fulfill the promises and your commitments:

Promises and contracts are an important part of human life and human civilization. When promises are not kept people lose trust in each other and the whole society becomes weak. Muslims must be true to their words. Our commitment must be to speak the truth, to be honest and when we make a pledge we do our best to fulfill our pledges.

10. Be honest in business dealings. Do not cheat in weight or measurement:
Honest business brings progress, success and blessings. All business whether it is commercial, social or political must be done with a sense of justice and fairness. A Muslim is committed to fair dealing in everything and with every one. Dealing with a Muslim means dealing with full confidence. A Muslim businessman is the most truthful businessman. A Muslim worker is the most honest worker. A Muslim in any profession should bring honor to that profession.

11. Do things with knowledge. Do not follow the hearsay or act on half-knowledge:
The information agencies, the media have a great responsibility. A lot of injustice is done when the misinformation is given or the information is misused. Muslims should be committed to truth in information. They should promote truthful and honest reporting about everyone including their enemies. A report coming from a Muslim source should be the most trustworthy report. In a similar way Muslim should be extremely careful with their actions and reactions. They should not react without proper evidence against anyone. They should show the world how the information is ascertained.

12. Be humble and have no arrogance:
Moderation and balance is the best thing in one's behavior as well as in one's attitudes toward others. A Muslim is a dignified person, but he/she is humble. A Muslim is not boastful, arrogant or vainglorious. A Muslim thanks Allah for all His gifts. For everything the ultimate praise is for Allah and the real glory belongs to Allah.
These are the basic commitments of Muslims, as individuals and as people. These are the principles of wisdom and the universal values of Islam. When they are followed they bring justice, peace and happiness in this world and they will indeed bring success and salvation in the Hereafter. Let us all try to make these our real commitments.

24. **Muzzamil H. Siddiqi, "Islamic Activism" from** *The Islamic Society of North America*

From the Islamic Society of North America, accessed May 21, 2006. Available online: http://www.isna.net/services/library/khutbahs/IslamicActivism.html. Reprinted with the permission of Muzzamil H. Siddiqi (for a biography, see the "Siddiqi, Muzzamil" entry in Volume 1) and the Islamic Society of North America.

And say: "Work (righteousness): soon will Allah observe your work, and His Messenger, and the Believers: soon will you be brought back to the Knower of what is hidden and what is open: then will He show you the truth of all that you did." (al-Tawbah 9:105)
O Messengers! Enjoy (all) things good and pure, and work righteousness: for I am well acquainted with (all) that you do. 52- And verily this Community of yours is a single Community. And I am your Lord and Cherisher: therefore be conscious of Me. (al-Mu'minun 23:51–52)
Islam emphasizes action. Believers are those who work, work hard and continue to work until the end.

The work must be good, it should be done with the consciousness of Allah and with the conviction that everything will be shown on the Day of Judgement.

There is no dichotomy or sharp division between the secular work and religious work. All work is religious if it is done with the awareness of Allah and is done according to the rules of Allah.

The Prophet—peace be upon him—said, "If the end of the world approaches and one of you has a seedling (or plant) in his hand, if he can plant it before the end comes let him do it." (Musnad Ahmad, Hadith no. 12512)

Let us reflect on this Hadith. What do you expect from a religious teacher? An ordinary religious teacher or preacher would have said, "If the end approaches, give up everything, go to the mosque and just pray." However, the Messenger of Allah wanted to emphasize something else. These words contain another wisdom and a very important message of Islam.

First thing that is emphasized here is activism, the value of action. Action is important and it should be done under all circumstances.

Second, there is no need to make a very sharp division between the worldly actions and religious actions. All actions should be done. But keep in mind the priorities and also keep in mind what is Fard, what is Mustahabb and what is Mubah. Do not neglect a Fard for the sake of a Mustahabb or Mubah.

Do not despair or become pessimistic. Every good action is valuable whether you are able to see its fruits or not. Muslims do not work only to see the results here in this world; our ultimate goal is the success and salvation in the Hereafter.

Another important point that is given here is that no one knows when the end of the world will come. One may think that end is near, but it may not be. Only Allah knows when the end will be. So one should keep working and doing the good things.

About activism we must keep in mind the following principles of Islam:

- Deeds must be righteous. For Muslims the righteous means that which is according to the Qur'an and Sunnah. Righteous actions are actions whereby a person implements Allah's rules: a) between a person and Allah, b) between a person and other people, c) between a person and other things.

- Righteous actions include: religious actions, moral actions, social actions, economic actions, political actions, judicial actions, etc.

- Righteous actions are those that are good, and righteous actions are also those that remove evil, injustice and oppression.

- Righteous actions should be done with sincerity (ikhlas) and in an excellent manner (itqan)

- The actions should be with knowledge, wisdom, planning, and persistence.

Allah has promised those who work with faith and righteousness that He will grant them success in this world and in the Hereafter.

Allah has promised, to those among you who believe and work righteous deeds, that He will, of a surety, make them succeed in the land, as He caused those who were before them to succeed others. He will establish for them their religion, the one that He has chosen for them. He will change (their state), after the fear in which they (lived), to one of security and peace: They will worship Me (alone) and not associate aught with Me.' If any do reject Faith after this, they are rebellious and wicked.
(al-Nur 24:55)

25. **Muzzamil H. Siddiqi, "Zakat and Charity—Our Gratitude to Allah" from** *The Islamic Society of North America*

From the Islamic Society of North America, accessed May 21, 2006. Available online: http://www.isna.net/services/library/khutbahs/ZakatandCharity.html. Reprinted with the permission of Muzzamil H. Siddiqi (for a biography, see the "Siddiqi, Muzzamil" entry in Volume 1) and the Islamic Society of North America.

Speak to My servants who have believed, that they may establish regular prayers, and spend (in charity) out of the Sustenance We have given them, secretly and openly, before the coming of a Day in which there will be neither mutual bargaining nor befriending. 32-It is Allah Who hath created the heavens and the earth and sendeth down rain from the skies, and with it bringeth out fruits wherewith to feed you: it is He Who hath made the ships subject to you, that they may sail through the sea by His Command; and the rivers (also) hath He made subject to you. 33-And He hath made subject to you the sun and the moon, both diligently pursuing their courses: and the Night and the Day hath He (also) made subject to you. 34-And He giveth you of all that ye ask for. But if ye count the favors of Allah, never will ye be able to number them. Verily, man is given up to injustice and ingratitude. (Ibrahim 14:31–34)

Allah has given us many things. His blessings are countless. We should be thankful to Him all the time. We should also show our gratitude by doing good to others, by helping the poor and by spending in His cause.

A believer does good deeds recognizing Allah's goodness to him/herself. A believer's way with wealth is that he/she enjoys it with moderation and spends it to seek Allah's blessings in the Hereafter.

But seek, with the (wealth) which Allah has bestowed on you, the Home of the Hereafter, nor forget your portion in this World: but do good, as Allah has been good to you, and seek not (occasions for) mischief in the land: for Allah loves not those who do mischief. (al-Qasas 28:77)

In the Qur'an there are five words used for charity: Zakat (obligatory charity), Sadaqat (charity), Khairat (good deeds), Ihsan (kindness and consideration), Infaq fi Sabil Allah (spending in the path of Allah).

Why is there so much emphasis on charity and generosity? Because charity elevates the human personality by removing selfishness, greed and materialism. It creates compassion, care, love and kindness. It makes a person more thankful to Allah. It helps those who are in need and it provides funds for good causes and for community projects.

The Qur'an says that all prophets of Allah preached Salat and Zakat:
And We made them leaders, guiding (people) by Our Command, and We sent them inspiration to do good deeds, to establish regular prayers, and to practice regular charity; and they constantly served Us. (al-Anbiya' 21:73)

Allah—subhanahu wa ta'ala—has promised many blessings for those who help the poor and give in His cause. Allah says in the Qur'an:

The Believers must (eventually) win through, 2-Those who humble themselves in their prayers; 3-Who avoid vain talk; 4-Who are active in deeds of charity... (al-Mu'minun 22:1–4)

Those who believe, and do deeds of righteousness, and establish regular prayers and regular charity, will have their reward with their Lord: on them shall be no fear, nor shall they grieve.(al-Baqarah 2:277)

. . .Whatever ye shall spend in the Cause of Allah, shall be repaid unto you, and ye shall not be treated unjustly. (al-Anfal 8:60)

The Prophet—peace be upon him—said:

The Prophet—peace be upon him—said:

"No wealth (of a servant of Allah) is decreased because of charity." (al-Tirmidhi, Hadith no. 2247)

"Indeed Allah accepts the charity and take it by His own hand and makes it grow like one of you make grow your colt (little horse). Surely a morsal becomes like the mountain of Uhud." (al-Tirmidhi, Hadith no. 598)

There are also many warnings against those who do not spend in the way of Allah: "And there are those who collect gold and silver and spend it not in the Way of Allah: announce unto them a most grievous penalty. 35-On the Day when heat will be produced out of that (wealth) in the fire of Hell, and with it will be branded their foreheads, their flanks, and their backs, "This is the (treasure) which ye buried for yourselves: taste ye, then, the (treasures) ye buried!" (al-Tawbah 9:34–35)

And spend something (in charity) out of the substance which We have bestowed on you, before Death should come to any of you and he should say, "O my Lord! Why didst Thou not give me respite for a little while? I should then have given (largely) in charity, and I should have been one of the doers of good." 11-But to no soul will Allah grant respite when the time appointed (for it) has come; and Allah is well-acquainted with (all) that ye do.(al-Munafiqun 63:10–11)

ZAKAT IS AN OBLIGATORY CHARITY

Zakat is obligatory like Salat. There are some Muslims who do not pay Zakat and there are some who give whatever they feel like giving, without observing the rules of Zakat. Muslims must learn the rules of Zakat, just as they learn the rules of Salat. Briefly the rules are as follows:

Zakat is obligatory on those who have the Nisab (i.e. the minimum wealth owned for one year). It is about 3 ounces of gold or its cash value. Muslims should calculate carefully all their wealth. After deducting their personal and family expenses whatever is left they must give Zakat on it. The ratio of Zakat on cash, gold and silver is a minimum of 2.5%. The personal belongings such as residential home, car, clothes, furniture, computer, books etc. are exempt from Zakat. Women's jewelry is Zakatable.

Zakat is for the 1. Poor, 2. Needy, 3. Those who administer the Zakat, 4. Those whose hearts are reconciled for Islam (new Muslims etc.), 5. To free the slaves, 6. Those unable to pay their debts, 7. Travelers rendered helpless, 8. In the Way of Allah. These categories are mentioned in the Qur'an in Surah al-Tawbah 9:60. Those who have enough for their basic needs should not take Zakat. One should not give Zakat to his/her own parents, children or dependants. Zakat is also to help the needy Muslims only. Non-Muslims can be helped from Sadaqat and other charities.

SADAQATUL FITR OR ZAKATUL FITR

This is a special charity for the month of Ramadan. All those who are supposed to give the Zakat must give Sadaqatul Fitr in Ramadan for themselves as well as on behalf of their dependants. It is estimated about $8.00 per person. This charity should be given during Ramadan or before the Idul Fitr prayer. It is to be given to the poor and needy people so that they can enjoy the happiness of Idul Fitr with other Muslims.

26. **Hamza Yusuf, "BBC: Thought of the Day" from** *The Zaytuna Institute*

From The Zaytuna Institute, accessed May 9, 2006. Available online: http://www.zaytuna.
org/articleDetails.asp?articleID=65. Reprinted with permission of the Zaytuna Institute.

Hamza Yusuf (for a biography, see the "Yusuf, Hamza" entry in Volume 1) was born in
Walla Walla, Washington in 1958. He converted to Islam in 1977. In 1996, he founded the
Zaytuna Institute in Hayward, California to provide an institution of higher education in
the United States that offered instruction in classical Islamic sciences. Before founding the Zay-
tuna Institute, Yusuf spent ten years studying in the Middle East, receiving several ijāzāt
(Islamic teaching licenses). His theological position reflects a synthesis between Islamic princi-
ples and major principles of American culture (e.g., democracy, human rights).

Over two thousand years ago a wise Greek wrote, "In our sleep, pain which cannot forget falls drop by drop upon the heart until, in our own despair, against our will, comes
wisdom through the awful grace of God." As these September days return to us, they
bring with them painful memories. September 11th, etched infamously in our hearts, will
continue to serve as an unexampled testimony to the horrors man is capable of inflicting
on his fellow man. Some will say last September was a harbinger of what is to come, but
hope reminds us that our past need not be our future.

Centuries ago in Arabia, a proud and provincial people were trapped in cycles of vengeful violence. Gloriously, for a time, they were freed from those cycles when they accepted
the truth that just laws—not unruly passions—should guide men. The Quran taught
them: "If a man is slain unjustly, his heir shall be entitled to retribution. But let him not
carry his just right to excess, for his victims are sure to be assisted and avenged." Once
again, we find ourselves in cycles of excessive vengeance as our leaders plan more carnage
in their absurd dreams of eliminating evil from the world. In describing this futile pursuit,
R.D. Lange wrote: "If all of the good people kill all of the evil people none will be left to
celebrate..."

If we are to make purposeful the senseless deaths of last year due to zealous hatred, and
those that ensued in hateful retaliation, it is by hating less ourselves, by understanding
more others, by listening intently to the pain of people still suffering under the yoke of
unjust tyrannies, much like those not long removed from the West with horrible bloodshed and regicidal terror. Our leaders serve no one by arming their despots, training their
tyrants, and using them to fight wars by proxy in places like Iraq and Afghanistan. Our
leaders certainly do us no service by then punishing mercilessly entire nations for the
impudent violence of a few against their perceived malefactors. We must never punish
an entire nation for the acts of undemocratically elected tyrants or their minions, for in
doing so we insure the continuance of cycles of hatred and vengeance.

Indeed, the world has seen enough of death and destruction. Let us instead bring life
and hope to so many suffering souls, who in their hearts, in spite of so much betrayal,
look to the West with hope and expectation. Let the pain of these September days fall
on our hearts drop by drop until a growing wisdom prevails, and the despair of few fails
to infect the hopes of many. Over two hundred years ago, America declared her independence to the world by holding certain truths to be self-evident that all men are created equal
and are endowed by their Creator with certain inalienable rights, among which are life,
liberty and the pursuit of happiness.

Let us recall that these universal truths have yet to be evident for all people. In recognizing that the work of the past is incomplete, we can commit our future work to what others

so selflessly started, in the hopes that one day, liberty and justice might be realized, not for some, but for all.

2002 BBC

27. **M.R. Bawa Muhaiyadin, "Islam & World Peace: Explanations of a Sufi" from** *Islam & World Peace: Explanations of a Sufi*

Excerpt from Bawa Muhaiyadin, M.R. Islam & World Peace: Explanations of a Sufi. Philadelphia, Pennsylvania: Fellowship Press, 1987, pp. 48–53. Reprinted with permission of The Bawa Muhaiyadin Fellowship.

Muhammad Raheem Bawa Muhaiyadin was born in Sri Lanka in the early 1900s. He was a Sufi mystic who lived and taught in Sri Lanka until he traveled to the United States in 1971. In the United States, Muhaiyadin lectured and gave a variety of interviews with, for example, Time Magazine and the Harvard Divinity School Bulletin. He wrote more than twenty books on Islam and Sufism and founded the Bawa Muhaiyadin Fellowship in Philadelphia, Pennsylvania. The Bawa Muhaiyadin Fellowship is an organization that publishes and disseminates Muhaiyadin's lectures and books. Muhaiyadin died on December 8, 1986. This Order is a significant example of the hybridization of Sufism in the American context. The following is an excerpt from one of Muhaiyadin's best known works, Islam & World Peace: Explanations of a Sufi.

My brothers, the holy wars that the children of Adam are waging today are not true holy wars. Taking other lives is not true *jihad*. We will have to answer for that kind of war when we are questioned in the grave. That *jihad* is fought for the sake of men, for the sake of earth and wealth, for the sake of one's children, one's wife, and one's possessions. Selfish intentions are intermingled within it.

True *jihad* is to praise God and cut away the inner satanic enemies. When wisdom and clarity come to us, we will understand that the enemies of truth are within our own hearts. There are four hundred trillion, ten thousand spiritual opponents within the body: satan and his qualities of backbiting, deceit, jealousy, envy, treachery, the separations of I and you, mine and yours, intoxicants, theft, lust, murder, falsehood, arrogance, karma, illusion, mantras and magics, and the desire for earth, sensual pleasures, and gold. These are the enemies which separate us from Allah, from truth, from worship, from good actions and good thoughts, and from faith, certitude, and determination. These are the enemies which create divisions among the children of Adam and prevent us from attaining a state of peace.

Among the seventy-three groups of man, there are only a few who understand and fight the war against the enemy within themselves, the enemy who stands between them and Allah, the enemy who does not accept Allah and will not bow down and prostrate before Him. To cut our connection to this enemy who is leading us to hell is the true holy war.

Brothers, once we realize who is the foremost enemy of this treasure of truth which we have accepted, then we can begin our battle against that enemy. That is the holy war of faith, of the *kalimah,* and of Islam. That is the one holy war which Allah accepts.

We must not kill each other. Instead, we must wage war against the evil qualities within ourselves. When a child has bad qualities, what does the mother do? She tries to teach him and help him to develop good qualities. Does she call him an evil child? No. If he steals the belongings of another because he wants to play with them, that is a bad quality no doubt, but the child is not evil. Does the mother strike down the child just because he has some bad qualities? No, the mother explains things to him and tries to expel the bad qualities and teach him good qualities. That is her duty, is it not?

Likewise, Allah, who created us, does not strike down His creations for the evil they have committed. It would not make sense if He did that. They are all His children, the children of the Lord of all creation. As their Father and Mother, He helps them to dispel their evil ways and tries to bring them to the straight path. He seeks to make His children happy and good. That is the way God is. And just as God does not kill His children because they have evil qualities, we must not murder others or cut them down. Instead, we must try to improve them by showing wisdom, love, compassion, and God's qualities, just as a mother teaches her mischievous child to change. That is our duty.

No good can come from cutting a person down. If a mother constantly shows unity and love to her child, that will get rid of the child's bad tendencies. In the same way, we must help others to remove the evil qualities, teach them good qualities, and lead them to the state where they can become the princes of God.

My brothers, if we act with love and unity, we can dispel all our evil qualities and live as one family, as one race, as children bowing to one Lord. Once we understand this truth, we will become good children. But as long as we do not understand and do not cast off the evil, then we are bad children.

Of course, when you cut these qualities, it might hurt. It might cause difficulty and suffering. When a child is cut, the pain makes him cry. He may scream and fight or maybe even bite you. He may shout, "I will kill you!" But you must embrace him with love and patiently explain things to him, always remembering that the qualities within the child are the enemy, not the child himself.

My brothers, man has two forms, each with its own set of qualities. The war is between these two forms. One is composed of the five elements and is ruled by the mind; it lives in the kingdom of illusion, creation, and hell . The other is a pure form made of Allah's light, of His resplendence and purity. That form lives in the kingdom of heaven, in the world of pure souls. When man dwells within this good form, he speaks and acts in good ways. When he moves into the form of the elements, he speaks and acts in evil ways. One body exists within him in a formless state; the other exists outside as his form and shadow. These two bodies have opposite qualities and duties.

The heart also has two sections: one is the innermost heart and the other is the mind. The mind is connected to the fifteen worlds, which are ruled by the energies of earth, fire, water, air, and ether. Just as these five elements are mixed together in the earth and in the sky, they are also mingled within the body.

The fifteen worlds are connected to all of creation, to all forms. Seven of the worlds are above, seven are below, and the fifteenth world, which is-the center, is the mind. It is there, in the world ruled by the mind, that the holy war must be waged. The mind and the energies of the elements roam up and down throughout the fifteen worlds, manifesting as the four hundred trillion, ten thousand miracles that create differences and divisions among men. We have to fight against all these energies in all fifteen worlds. This is the major battle. Once we complete this war, then we are ready to begin our work within the innermost heart.

The innermost heart is the kingdom of Allah. That is where His essence can be found. The secret of the eighteen thousand universes and the secret of this world are contained within that heart. Allah's messengers, His representatives Es, the angels, prophets, saints, the resplendently pure souls, and His light within the soul are all to be found in a tiny point within the heart. Within that atom is contained His entire kingdom, the kingdom of truth and justice and purity, the kingdom of heaven, the kingdom of enlightened wisdom.

The eighteen thousand universes are within that kingdom of light and divine knowledge, and Allah is the ruler of all those universes. His infinite power, His three thousand gracious qualities, His ninety-nine attributes, His compassion, peace, unity, and equality are all found within those universes. That is the innermost heart, His kingdom of true faith and justice, where one can find peace.

Until we reach that kingdom, we have to wage a holy war within ourselves. To show us how to cut away this enemy within and to teach us how to establish the connection with Him, Allah sent down 124,000 prophets, twenty-five of whom are described thoroughly in the Qur'an. These prophets came to teach us how to wage holy war against the inner enemy. This battle within should be fought with faith, certitude, and determination, with the *kalimah,* and with the Qur'an. No blood is shed in this war. Holding the sword of wisdom, faith, certitude, and justice, we must cut away the evil forces that keep charging at us in different forms. This is the inner *jihad.*

My brothers in *Iman-Islam,* we must cut away the qualities which oppose Allah. There are no other enemies. Allah has no enemies. If anyone were to oppose Allah, the All-Powerful, Unique One, that person could never be victorious. You cannot raise or lower Allah. He does not accept praise or blame.

Praising Allah and then destroying others is not *jihad.* Some groups wage war against the children of Adam and call it holy war. But for man to raise his sword against man, for man to kill man, is not holy war. There is no point in that. There can be no benefit from killing a man in the name of God. Allah has no thought of killing or going to war. Why would Allah have sent His prophets if He had such thoughts? It was not to destroy men that Muhammad came; he was sent down as the wisdom that could show man how to destroy his own evil.

Once we have completely severed those qualities of satan within us, there will be no more enmity among human beings. All will live as brothers and sisters. That is true Islam, the affirmation of the unity of Allah, the oneness of Allah. Once we accept this, Allah accepts us. Once we fight and conquer these enemies of our faith, these enemies of our prayers, we will find peace within ourselves. And once we have found peace within, we will find peace everywhere. This world will be heaven, and we will have a direct connection to Allah, just as Adam had that original connection. Then we will understand the connection between ourselves and all the children of Adam.

Every child must know this and fight the enemy within. We must fight the battle between that which is permissible under God's law and that which is forbidden. If we do not do this, then the qualities of evil will kill that which is good, and the truth will be destroyed. But if we can win this huge battle, we will receive Allah's grace, and that will enable us to know His eighteen thousand universes. If we can conquer the world of the mind, we will see the kingdom of the soul, His kingdom.

May every one of us think about this and wage our own holy war. Only when we finish the battle and progress beyond will we realize that we are all children of Adam, that we are all one race, that there is only one prayer, and that there is only One who is worthy of worship, one God, one Lord. He is the Compassionate One, He is the Merciful One. He creates and sustains all lives, He does not cut them down. Once we realize this, we will stop the fighting, the spilling of blood, the murder.

We will never attain peace and equality within our hearts until we finish this war, until we conquer the armies that arise from the thoughts and differences within ourselves, until we attack these enemies with faith, certitude, and determination and with patience, contentment, trust in God, and praise of God. With divine knowledge, with justice and conscience, we must fight and win this inner *jihad*.

May the peace of God be with you. Allah is sufficient for all. Amen.

28. Cengiz Çandar, "From Chicago to Houston: Clues for 'Renaissance' in Islamic Thought..." from *Fethullahgulen.org*

From Fethullahgulen.org, written November 14, 2005. Available online: http:// www.fethullahgulen.org/content/view/2090/14/. Reprinted with permission of Cengiz Çandar.

Cengiz Çandar was born in 1948 in Ankara, Turkey. He studied at the Tarsus American College and Ankara University before becoming a journalist for the Turkish newspaper Sabah. In 1999, he was a public policy scholar at the Wilson Center and a fellow at the United States Institute of Peace. He is also a supporter of the Fethullah Gülen Movement, a movement inspired by Sufism that initially started in Turkey based on the teaching of Fethullah Gülen. Gülen was born in eastern Turkey in 1941 and began to preach and call for reform in the 1960s. Gülen's preaching and emphasis on Islam has generated a sizable following as well as characterized an unfriendly relationship with the Turkish state, which eventually caused him to move to Pennsylvania in the United States. The movement became global, spreading Islamic education and schools across continents, including the West. The following article is a reflection on the influence of the Fethullah Gülen movement in the United States.

Houston is the fourth largest city of the United States, and the capital of oil companies. Houston is also well known as a medical center with a claim to be making the most significant progress in cancer treatment.

We have not had direct contact with the Turkish agenda for the last few days. In an age of "globalization" and thanks to the Internet and other communication media, the world has become a smaller place. We are aware of what happened in şemdinli and we have already developed a conviction about its nature; but we are not breathing the air as in Turkey. We are at a distance.

First we were in the middle of the USA, in Chicago, and now we are in Houston, Texas. There is no Washington. There are no American politics.

Then, what? Why are we here?

First in Chicago, then in Houston, we have been following two conferences which are taking place consecutively. The first gathering in Chicago was entitled "Diverse Faiths, Shared Values," and the theme was "interfaith dialogue" and "harmony between civilizations," with the thought of Fethullah Gülen at its center. The title of the conference in Houston is "Islam in the Contemporary World: The Fethullah Gülen Movement in Thought and Practice."

I have witnessed and learned from my Chicago-Houston experience that Fethullah Gülen, a person who grew up in Turkey, who emerged from Turkey, can be at the center of international academic attention and a debate of international scale, as well as establishing the theme of exhaustive papers that have been submitted by prominent Western theologians and scholars of Islam—especially from American universities—to a conference which cannot be organized in Turkey, even today.

Scholars coming from various corners of the world have discussed Fethullah Gülen for two days in different venues like the Chicago Cultural Center, one of the most glorious and historical buildings of the city, the campuses of the University of Chicago, Loyola University, and DePaul University.

Chicago leads the list of the "most colorful" cities of America, each one of which is multicultural and multifaith. Just to give an example, Chicago is the city second after Warsaw to have the largest Polish population. The opening ceremony featured almost all the leading Christian personalities of the city, including the Catholic Archbishop, together with Orthodox and Protestant clergy. Theologians and scholars of Islam from the most distinguished universities of the country (Harvard, Columbia, Georgetown etc.) participated in this conference to discuss topics like "Sufi Thought and Contemporary Issues," "The Gülen Movement and Interfaith Dialogue." "Is Fethullah Gülen a Sufi? Or Can he be considered among the Ulama?" "Where does his educationalist identity fit?" "Can he be defined as neo-platonic?" "Can he be compared with al-Ghazzali, or Rumi?"

Fazlur Rahman, the great Pakistani thinker of Islam in the twentieth century, taught at the University of Chicago for many years. Fazlur Rahman left his country and came to Chicago "in exile." His thoughts, which flourished in Chicago, influenced Indonesia, the most populous Muslim country. The most significant Islamic thinkers of Indonesia were Fazlur Rahman's students in Chicago (an interesting note: Fazlur Rahman deeply influenced Professor Mehmet Aydın, a minister of state in the present government of Tayyip Erdoğan in Turkey). What I am trying to say is that Chicago already has a tradition of "studies and discussions of Islamic thought." What about Houston?

Turkey came to know this city during the series of medical operations that Turgut Özal underwent years back. Turkish journalists landed in this city numerous times in the last twenty years. I have come twice and passed through on my way to Mexico 5 years ago. But I never thought I would come back to this city for this purpose. I never thought I would be in this city to participate in this conference entitled "Islam in the Contemporary World: The Fethullah Gülen Movement in Thought and Practice," to listen to papers with highly theoretical content presented by notable American and European scholars at Rice University, the most prestigious educational institution of the city.

The topics of the papers are indeed mind-boggling and stimulating. "Fethullah Gülen's contribution to Muslim-Christian dialogue in the context of Abrahamic cooperation" compares Fethullah Gülen with Louis Massignon, the renowned French thinker and scholar of Islam. What about this one: "Dialogue: Greek foundations and the thought of Fethullah Gülen and Jürgen Habermas." And this: "Religions, globalization and dialogue in the 21st century. Fethullah Gülen and Arnold J. Toynbee."

Let me list a few more topics: "Fethullah Gülen's neo-sufism: An inventional analysis." "From Whitman to Gülen: Visions of the future of evolving democracy." "Gülen and Al-Ghazzali on Tolerance." "Progressive Islamic thought, civil society and the Gülen movement in the national context: Parallels with Indonesia."

Until today I have not heard a name that has emerged from Turkey being placed next to the names listed above.

I have always argued that Turkey, the most developed Muslim country, as it progresses towards the European Union, should also lead the "renaissance" of Islamic thought. What I saw in Houston were indications that this may actually take place.

Section B: Practices

29. **Dawud Tauhidi, "The Tarbiyah Project: A Holistic Vision of Islamic Education" from** *The Tarbiyah Project*

From The Tarbiyah Project, accessed September 1, 2006. Available online: http:// www.tarbiyah.org/Docs/Tarbiyah%20Overview.pdf. Reprinted with permission of Dawud Tauhidi.

Dawud Tauhidi is a European-American convert to Islam. He graduated from Al Azhar University in Cairo, Egypt and also received his Ph.D. in Islamic Studies from the University of Michigan. He founded the Crescent Academy International in Canton, Michigan, a suburb of Detroit, in 1991. Crescent Academy International is an Islamic school for boys and girls from kindergarten to eighth grade. Tauhidi has been at the forefront of developing what he calls a holistic and integrated approach to Islamic education. The Tarbiyah Project is the latest version of his work. It is an attempt to adapt the Islamic precepts to the American environment in order to create a harmonious socialization process for Muslim children.

Overview

The Tarbiyah Project is a vision, a framework, a set of programs and a strategic plan for the restoration and revitalization of contemporary Islamic education—for making Islamic education whole again.

Vision. The Tarbiyah Project is first a vision—a vision of what Islamic education ought to be (its principles and goals, its content and its methodology) and what it must become *in practice,* if we hope to restore a sense of wholeness, wellbeing and holiness back into education, our children and Muslim society.

Framework. Second, the Tarbiyah Project is a framework—a framework for structuring the curriculum of contemporary Islamic education, both "*what*" is taught and "*how*" it is taught. The Tarbiyah Project has a well-defined vision of the proper content, structure, process and strategies for Islamic education based on a learning system known as the Integrated Learning Model[SM].

Program. Third, the Tarbiyah Project is a set of programs—programs that focus on teaching Islamic values and encourage creative approaches to Islamic teaching and learning. Three such programs were piloted in the member schools of the Tarbiyah Consortium.

Strategic Plan. Fourth, the Tarbiyah Project is a strategic plan—a plan for developing resources for Islamic education in North America, including a plan for curriculum development, staff development and parental training, and a program of publications in the area of holistic Islamic education.

Background
THE DILEMMA
Weaving in Spiritual Learning[1]

Today we live at a critical time in the spiritual history of man. Perhaps at no other time in history has the disbelief and disregard for the Divine and the sacred been more prevalent than today. With the rise and fall of modernity, and its principles of secularism and materialism, we have ushered in an era of moral laxity, psychological malaise and ecological devastation. Furthermore, a concerted effort is underway to bring Muslim society and culture into alignment with the overall modernist project and to secularize Islam in the same way that other religious traditions have been secularized. For many, exporting secular education to the Muslim world is the best way to achieve this objective.

The Noble Quran, on the other hand, enjoins Muslims, and in fact all of humanity, to hold firmly to the *rope of God* and not be dissuaded by the glitter and clamor of modernity from living a God-centered life. However, for most people the effects of secularism and materialism have made their hold to the divine rope tenuous at best; and even then, only by the thinnest of threads. For most Muslims today, there is only tradition or habit that holds them tenuously to Islam—all the while secularism continues to spread unabated in its effort to extinguish the light of spirituality and Godwardness throughout the world.

As a result, with each passing generation, the bond of religion has become weaker and increasingly irrelevant and marginalized in modern society. Islam, in particular, has managed to remain in the news only by negative association—through protests, violence, terrorism, etc. Putting aside western political and economic involvement in that region of the world, Muslims have mostly themselves to blame for this predicament. If Muslims hope to survive as an *ummah* (global community), they will need a generation of their best minds and hearts who can solve the real problems facing Muslim society and humanity at large. Otherwise, Muslims will continue to be dismissed as irrelevant in world affairs and continue failing in their responsibility before Allah as Muslims. These are bitter but true words that we must acknowledge.

Education, of course, plays a crucial role in this dilemma. The American statesman and president, Abraham Lincoln, accurately noted that *"the philosophy of the school room in one generation will be the philosophy of government in the next."* It is no surprise, therefore, that the revamping of the educational system in the Muslim world is being pursued as a top US foreign policy objective in several Muslim countries (i.e., Iraq, Pakistan, Saudi Arabia and Indonesia).

Secular education, however, has profoundly affected the sense of balance, wholeness and wellbeing in modern man—with its emphasis on the profane and the material, and with its neglect of the spirit and character. This fact is undeniable. The statistics of drug abuse, violence, pornography, sexual promiscuity, divorce, along with a wide range of modern psychological illnesses (including depression, anxiety, alienation and loneliness) are well known and speak for themselves. The biggest victims in all of this of course are our children, as the direct product of the culture, education and family conditions under which they grow up. Whether or not the Muslim *ummah* finally lets go of *rope of God* altogether and falls into the abyss of materialism, secularism and agnosticism like most other cultures today, will depend largely on the education of the next generation of Muslim children around the world. This generation represents one of the last potential vestiges of Godwardness in the world. The situation is indeed serious.

This is the larger spiritual and cultural crisis facing Muslim educators and curriculum developers today—the ubiquitous spread and influence of secular materialism and its global reach. Muslim parents, educators and clergy, along with those of other faith-based communities, are in a serious struggle for the spiritual survival of their children and are faced with major challenges about how best to raise their children and prepare them for the challenges of the future. Some Muslims will insist the answer is simply in going back to the past; others will urge us to plunge headlong into the future. But people need both roots and branches together in order to survive and flourish. It is the divine pattern of creation that all living beings embrace the complementary principles of *continuity* and *change* together in order to develop and flourish. Spirituality helps us better understand how these matters are interconnected.

Only with the proper spiritual education can we stem the tide of secular materialism in Muslim society, re-strengthen our community's connection to spiritual and moral values, and save our children from a life of enslavement to the ideology of materialism and other ills of modern living. To achieve this, however, spiritual education cannot simply be an appendage to an otherwise secular and fragmented curriculum. Nor can it be merely a prescriptive or parochial litany of moral do's and don'ts. Instead, it must be woven skillfully and articulately throughout the curriculum and into the daily educational experiences of our children. To achieve this requires a comprehensive and holistic approach to learning and a unifying principle of education.

FACING THE CHALLENGE

The challenge of how best to educate Muslim children in the 21st century requires an honest assessment of the following questions: 1) *Where are we today?* 2) *How did we get here?* 3) *Where should we be?* 4) *How do we plan to get there?* The future of our children and community as Muslims will depend largely on how well we address these questions and to what extent we are successful in passing on to our children the sacred vision of life we have as Muslims.

The Meaning of *Tarbiyah*

For the past ten years, the Tarbiyah Project has concerned itself with these fundamental issues of contemporary Islamic education. At the center of its work has been the question of how best to integrate the sacred meaning and message of Islam into the framework of the modern curriculum. The Tarbiyah Project has developed a holistic vision and integrated approach to education that seeks to nurture the character and inner spirit of children and empower them to self-discovery, wholeness and social consciousness. The result has been a distinctive and powerful approach to contemporary Islamic education.

For those not familiar with the term *tarbiyah*, it is one of the truly beautiful words in Arabic—deeply rich in meaning. Usually it is translated as *education*. According to the classical lexicographer al-Rāghib al-Asfahānī (d. 402 A.H. /1011 C.E.) the word *tarbiyah* means *"to cause something to develop from stage to stage until reaching its completion [full potential]."*[2] This implies that something (*the fitrah*, or intrinsic nature) already exists within the child and that education is a process of unfolding and bringing out, more than a process of instilling and pouring in. This is similar to the modern-day notion of *developmental stages*.

The word *tarbiyah* is used in the Quran in verses 22:5, 26:18 and 17:24. The word *ribā'* (increase) also comes from the same linguistic root and, according to Asfahānā, even the word *rabb* (Lord) is semantically related to the word *tarbiyah*— the sense being that the *Rabb* (Lord) provides and nurtures (i.e., increases) us through each stage of development until reaching our full potential. What a beautiful notion of the word *Rabb*. The concepts of increase, elevation, growth, development, nurture and upbringing are all aspects of the word *tarbiyah*. Broadly speaking, it conveys the cosmological principle of expansion, emergence, unfoldment, becoming and fulfillment. For humankind, in particular, *tarbiyah* can be understood as the Islamic science of human growth and development. All of these concepts provide important insights into the Islamic notion of education—insights that need to be better incorporated into our modern practice of Islamic education. However, let us return to our main issue.

Where We Are Today—The Disconnection

According to Islam, a person's life should be modeled on the principles of *belief and action* together. This means that a person's *beliefs* ought to be translated into *action* and reflected in his or her conduct each day with other people. The Noble Prophet emphasized that our dealings and interactions with other people *(mu'āmalah),* in fact, are our *din* (lifeway/religion). Even though this precept is well known, the majority of Muslims today do not actually live in accordance with it nor with many of the other fundamental teachings of Islam. A person need only travel to the Muslim world today to see that the prevailing social norm gives little regard to the notion of appointments, timeliness, orderliness, equal access, due process and many of the other basic norms and etiquette of civil society, even though this violates the moral and social teachings of Islam. The day-to-day norms of Muslim society today are very much disconnected from their own spiritual, ethical and philosophical heritage. What accounts for this disconnection between *values* and *practice* in Muslim society today and what role does education play in this? This is a critical question for contemporary Muslim society and education.

How We Got There—The Reasons

The problems of Muslim society today are rooted in several social, political and educational factors. First, modernity has played a major role in the erosion of values throughout the entire world, including the Muslim world. Much of what our children learn today about values, they learn from popular culture and the mass media. This is especially true now with television satellite dishes and internet access widespread throughout the Muslim world. Second, the 19th and 20th-century experiences of colonialism, materialism and secularism have left an indelible mark on the mind-set and value system of Muslims today. Third, the lack of sufficient real freedom in Muslim society has played a subtle but important role in undermining the development of strong character in much of today's Muslim youth. True moral development cannot flourish without sufficient social, intellectual and spiritual freedom.

These factors account for much of the moral turpitude of modern-day Muslim society, particularly in the face of the globalization of secular materialism and its value system. The collective result of these factors is that Muslims today are disoriented spiritually, marginalized socially, divided politically and economically, and generally find themselves in a quandary about their role and place in modern society. This is the legacy we are passing on to our children today—and why, in turn, so many of our young people either romanticize about a return to the glorious "golden age" of Islamic civilization or effectively abandon Islam altogether in favor of modern secular materialism.

The educational system, in particular, has played a key role in the disconnection between values and practice that exists today in Muslim society. This includes the system of Islamic education as well. How so? Formal education has long been viewed primarily as a process of *transmission* rather than *transformation*. The focus has long been on teaching a fixed body of *information* that is to be memorized, rather than a set of *experiences* that is to be used as a catalyst to transform one's character. Of course, classical Islam placed great importance on spiritual, moral and personal development. Nonetheless, the drill-and-kill method of rote memorization has been the prevailing mode of instruction in Muslim education for centuries. In the quiet pace of traditional society, the teacher was the "sage on the stage" and the didactic method of instruction was the norm. However, in today's fast-paced world of multimedia, internet and global communications, the didactic method of teaching has proven insufficient and ineffective at holding our children's attention and inspiring them to adopt Islam as a system of personal and social values—especially in the face of modern, secular society. As a result, most of our young people today (except for a very small percentage) see Islam as largely irrelevant to their personal lives and, therefore, most do not adhere to it as their daily lifestyle. Put bluntly, Muslims are losing the battle for the spiritual lives of their children. In some respects, terrorism and regional violence are only perverted and desperate expressions of this failure. However, what really accounts for this failure?

The failure of education in Muslim society today is largely rooted in the way we teach children—primarily for four reasons. First, it does not focus fundamentally on character development, as it did in the time of the Noble Prophet. Instead, it focuses on facts and rote information. This is true for both secular and Islamic forms of education. Second, much of what is taught is not directly relevant to the real lives of the students themselves—their needs, concerns, challenges and aspirations. Third, the method of instruction is centered around *teaching* rather than *learning*—a subtle but important distinction. And fourth, it does not prepare students with the real-life skills needed to function successfully in today's society. Additionally, Muslim education (and much of western education as well) often lacks a solid understanding of the psychology, pedagogy and sociology of child development, including moral and spiritual development. For these reasons, much of our efforts have remained largely ineffective, resulting in little genuine education or personal development for the individual or for society.

Common Misconceptions about Education

In addition to these factors, there are several common misconceptions about education that continue to influence the thinking of most parents and even professional educators, and contribute further to the failure of education today. These misconceptions have resulted in a fragmented view of children and learning, and a mechanistic approach to education (sometimes referred to as the *factory model* of education). Because of this *assembly-line* approach on the part of educators themselves, many of our children fail in the educational process—through no fault of their own. It is time that parents and educators acknowledge and accept that each one of our children *is* unique and that one size does not fit all. This uniqueness, and the individual differences that accompany it, is exactly how God has fashioned creation. A shift in understanding is therefore needed to one that is more natural, wholesome and humane regarding children, education and the learning process. Fortunately, this change, or "paradigm shift," is now underway for many individual teachers and for some educational systems as a whole. Muslim educators need to be among those enlightened educators who are working to bring about meaningful change and improvement toward that which is good and best *(ahsan)* for children.

Listed below are some common misconceptions about education along with an alternative, holistic viewpoint.

Where We Should Be—The Vision

Muslims claim for themselves the responsibility to serve as caretakers of creation and to provide inspired leadership to the world. This is the Islamic notion of *'amānah,* or

Table 1   **Common Misconceptions of Education**

Issue	Misconception	Alternate Conception
Vision	Education seen as separate academic disciplines; disjointed view of knowledge, learning and students; the factory model.	**Tawhi-d**: A holistic and integrated view of knowledge, life, learning and the learner.
Content	Traditional subjects; information-driven; not relevant to student's life; "instruction" (ta'lem); the textbook is the curriculum.	**Tarbiyah**: Character-based; transformation-driven; "education" (tarbiyah); real-world connections; the "book of life" is the curriculum.
Structure	Vague and incoherent structure, or structured by separate academic disciplines; no unifying structure.	**Powerful Ideas**: Big ideas that can inspire and transform, the building blocks of character & personality; cross-curricular, transdisciplinary.
Process	Didactic (words & lecture); teacher as *"sage on the stage"*; factory model; one size fits all; uninteresting and uninspiring.	**Discovery Learning**: Student-centered; differentiated instruction; multiple learning styles; teacher as *"guide on the side"*; modeling & mentoring; Integrated Learning Model (ILM).
Programs	Past-focused; "about Islam"; Islam as religion; learning to perform Islamic rituals.	**Life Mastery**: Present-focused; about "being Muslim"; Islam as a lifestyle; Islam for Life Mastery (ILM).
Goals	Acquiring information, knowledge, skills mainly for the purpose of taking tests and for gaining employment.	**Beyond Schooling**: "How to learn"; lifelong and life-after learning; total human development.
Assessment	Pencil & paper; true or false; pass or fail; standardized testing.	**Authentic Assessment**: Authentic work, connected to the real life, for a real audience; multiple intelligences, modalities & formats; performance based.

stewardship. However, in order to fulfill this responsibility, Muslims need a system of education that is capable of producing young people who can identify, analyze, understand and then work cooperatively to solve the problems that face their community and humanity at large. Of course, the world will not sit by idly waiting for Muslims to assume this responsibility. In fact, Muslims have been surpassed by others more willing and able to take up the challenge. Fortunately, a sense of renewal is in the air today and enlightened Muslims are eager to find real solutions to the problems and challenges facing the Muslim community, and if necessary to re-examine traditional paradigms within Muslim society —including *how* and *what* we teach our children. To meet this challenge within education, a renewed vision of education is needed—one that is capable of producing young people with a level of understanding, commitment and social responsibility that will empower them to serve God by effectively serving society and humanity, *inshallāh*.

This vision of education of course is not a new vision, but rather a renewed vision of Islamic education. In the lifetime of the Noble Prophet education was dynamic. It was practical and relevant. It was hands-on and active. Most of all, it had the power to inspire and transform human lives. The Noble Prophet had the great ability to seamlessly connect learning to both growth *(tarbiyah)* and God *(rububīyah)* at the same time. He was the quintessential spiritual educator *(murabbī)*. He educated, inspired and empowered all within a single teachable moment. The Prophetic model of education drew its content from the everyday experiences and day-to-day problems of the early Muslim community. In fact, the entire genre of *asbāb an-nuzūl* literature (occasions of revelation), testifies to the extreme importance early Islamic education placed on the day-to-day circumstances and concerns of students and their community. It was not like Islamic education today—stagnant and unresponsive. Why? And how can we make Islamic education meaningful again to the lives of our children and their communities?

To achieve this, a concerted effort is needed. Muslim educators and parents will have to increase their efforts and cooperation to find creative solutions that will bridge the gap between values and practice in the upcoming generation of young people. Of course, schools have a primary role to play in this enterprise, especially in developing programs that foster a holistic and integrated understanding of Islamic education and that promote the role of the family in the overall process of *tarbiyah*. It is the strong belief of this writer that *tarbiyah* (i.e., transformative education) is what is needed for our youth today and should be the focus of education in the Muslim world today. Investing in "human resources" is the best and most enduring investment any society can make—and its best defense. History has shown that machines and technology cannot defend against the human spirit when it is empowered by self-determination and a higher purpose. The true goal of education is to produce such people.

This vision of Islamic education makes an important distinction between *teaching "about Islam"* (information) and *learning to "be Muslim"* (transformation). The goal of Islamic education is not to fill our children's minds with as much information about Islam as possible; rather it is to guide and assist them in *becoming Muslim,* and in the process inspiring them to transform themselves. This paradigm shift from information-driven to transformation-centered education is essential if we hope to revitalize Muslim society.

The vision of Islamic education advocated by the Tarbiyah Project is based on a *dynamic* rather than static view of Islam and Islamic education. This view is rooted in the belief that the mission of Islam is to positively affect and transform the world by first transforming ourselves, and that the purpose of Islamic education is to prepare young men and women capable of living out this mission—emotionally, morally, intellectually and collectively. To achieve this high level of education, Muslim educators, parents and other responsible adults must be serious-minded in their purpose and thoughtful in their approach. To maintain the status quo and do nothing is to condemn our children to a life of alienation from their birthright as Muslims: to understand, appreciate and practice Islam as a comprehensive way of living.

The strength of the Tarbiyah Project is in its holistic and integrated vision of education, its broad view of Islamic educational reform, and its focus on character development and human relations. The Project approaches educational improvement and reform based on two key principles. First, genuine reform will only be achievable to the extent that we transform its key stakeholders, namely, the students, staff and parents. Second, sustainable improvement will only result through a partnership that empowers the stakeholders themselves and makes them directly accountable for the learning that takes place. This is based on the Project's view of *comprehensive Islamic education:* all knowledge, all aspects of the child, all learning styles, all ages and stages of development, all times (past, present, future), all places (home, school, mosque, community at-large), and all people (student, teacher, family, community at-large).

The Tarbiyah Project therefore focuses on several areas of development, all of which are critical to the overall goal of *total human development*. Its main goal is human capacity building *(tarbiyah),* i.e., empowering students, teachers and parents towards greater efficacy in the educational process, both in their own personal growth and within the educational enterprise as a whole. The Project is built therefore around the following key areas of development: 1) human development in general, 2) curriculum development, 3) staff development (both professional and personal (including spiritual development), and 4) community development (including parent education and community service learning).

An Integrated Framework
Framework

We noted earlier that the educational system itself is a key reason for the current malaise within Muslim society. Major reform is needed in this area if Muslims hope to regain a place of respect within the world community. This reform will require rethinking and restructuring the key elements of the educational enterprise: including the conceptual framework, content and structure of the curriculum, the learning environment, and the instructional process. It should be noted, however, that this need for reform is not exclusive to Islamic education. Similar efforts at reform are of course underway in western circles of education as well. Calls for holistic education, integrated instruction, cooperative learning, character education, discovery learning and authentic assessment are major topics within contemporary education.

The Tarbiyah Project joins these efforts in calling for the reform and restoration of modern education, both western and Islamic, away from the factory model and towards a holistic model that is more natural, authentic and more effective for children. The Project's critique of modern education is an even-handed one of both secular, western education, on the one hand, and a narrow, parochial view of Islamic religious education, on the other hand. Both have failed to serve well the needs and best interest of Muslim children growing up in the 21st century.

How to Get There—The Plan

There is a critical need to restore a sense of wholeness, wholesomeness and holiness back into our vision and practice of education. *"Making education whole again"* should be the mantra of 21st-century Islamic education. The Tarbiyah Project has worked to develop such a framework or model of Islamic education that addresses and incorporates key holistic aspects in its approach to education. This framework is based on four major components:

- **Vision & System:** A unified vision and integrated system of education based on the principles of *tawhid* and *tarbiyah* (holistic education);

- **Content:** Refocusing the content and goals of education around character development and personal transformation, and around what is really worth learning: the powerful ideas, universal concepts, big questions and enduring understandings that inspire true learning and transformation;

- **Structure:** Restructuring the curriculum around a unified framework of knowledge and a related set of universal concepts that underpin all branches of knowledge and allow for true transdisciplinary integration;

- **Process:** Re-aligning the teaching and learning experience around a process of discovery learning, which is alluded to in the Quran and is developed here as the Integrated Learning Model (ILM^2).

Together, these elements provide a conceptual framework for a genuinely *tawhīdic* (holistic, integrated, spiritual) vision of Islamic education suitable for Muslim children in the 21st century. In the next section, we will consider these four components in detail.

Section 1
An Integrated Vision

The first area of education needing reform is our overall vision and conceptualization of education itself. Modern education, both western and Islamic, is based largely on a disjointed and incoherent view of life, education and the child. There is little sense of coherence or cohesion in the educational enterprise as a whole. As a result, even after 12–16 years of schooling, students seldom have a good sense of the importance of education—its real significance, value or greater purpose (other than to get a job). In large part, this is because of the fragmented view that we adults have ourselves about life and education.

Tawhīd: The Unifying Principle

Education is an integral part of the belief system of any society. A society's most cherished beliefs and ideals are embodied in its educational vision, objectives and practices. Islam offers man a simple yet profound view of life and the world, including man's role in the world and his relation to its Creator. This view is based on the Islamic principle of *tawhīd* (oneness, wholeness, integration, coherence, unity, universality and God-consciousness). This concept of *tawhīd* is the keystone of Islam and the overarching principle of the Islamic worldview and its concomitant view of education. It serves as both a philosophical and methodological construct that brings structure and coherence to our understanding of the world and all aspects of life and society, including education. All other considerations are subordinate to it.

The Tarbiyah Project is based squarely on this central principle of *tawhīd*. It serves as the starting point and basis for its unified and holistic approach to education, which includes not only the mind, but also the body and the spirit. As Islam's ultimate and highest principle, *tawhīd* obliges Muslims to adopt a holistic, integrated and comprehensive view of education. This means that Muslim educators must never lose sight of the *big picture* and greater purpose of education and life. Key elements of a *tawhīdic* view of education include: being God-centered, holistic, integrated, unified, collaborative, and systems oriented. Such ideas as the *whole child, whole language, whole-brain, whole earth, life-long learning, integrated instruction,* etc. are all fundamentally compatible with this principle of *tawhīd*.

The principle of *tawhīd* therefore should inform and shape how Muslim educators go about educating children. This includes: 1) what to teach (*content*), 2) how to organize the content (*structure*), and 3) how to go about teaching (*process*). In short, *tawhīd* should inform both our principles and practice of education. For this reason alone, Muslim educators should be the foremost proponents of a holistic and integrated approach to education, rather than the disjointed and bifurcated approach to education that is practiced, ironically, in nearly all Islamic schools and Muslim countries. In this connection, note the different approaches to the curriculum in the figure below.

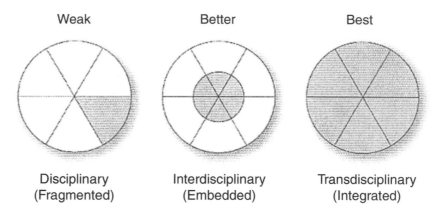

Figure 1:   **Different Approaches to the Curriculum**

The common practice among many Muslims educators of merely appending so-called "Islamic Studies" onto an otherwise secular curriculum is completely antithetical to Islam's core principle of *tawhīd* and to a holistic approach to education. The duplicitous nature of the modern Muslim psyche is what results from this type of bicentric/bifurcated system of education. Modern society, but especially Muslim society for which spirituality still resonates somewhat, must realize that this type of bifurcated and fragmented approach to education will not give our children a sense of wholeness and wellbeing that we all wish for them. Wholeness can only come from that which is itself whole, including experiences with holistic education.[3]

Implications of Tawhīd for Education

The principle of *tawhīd* has other important implications for an Islamic theory of education. Of course, first and foremost, *tawhīd* is a theological principle about the unitary nature of God. This is fundamental. In addition, it is a cosmological principle about the whole of creation, implying that creation and the laws that govern it are integrated parts of a unified system, from the smallest atoms to the largest astronomical bodies, and that the One God created and unified these elements within a single, integrated system of creation, known as the *uni-verse* (i.e., single, recurring message or purpose).

Epistemologically, the principle of *tawhīd* is reflected in the belief that real knowledge reveals the integrated nature of reality as a whole. This means that at a deep conceptual level all knowledge is unified—in its source, composition, structure and purpose. Such a view is a prerequisite for implementing an integrated model of education. Pedagogically, this principle is reflected in the notion of curriculum integration. However, curriculum integration means more here than simply making connections between topics of the curriculum, as is typically done. More significantly, it means synthesizing the content of the curriculum down to its deepest and most basic conceptual elements and structure. At this fundamental level, we find a simple and elegant match between these conceptual elements of the curriculum and the elements at work within the larger cosmos. This provides the basis for real transdisciplinary integration and deep understanding (*hikmah*). The Tarbiyah curriculum model is based on an attempt at joining these different aspects— metaphysical, cosmological, anthropological and pedagogical—into a single unified framework and views this as an important feature of a truly Islamic theory of education.

Table 2:   **Holistic Aspects of Tarbiyah Education**

Holistic Aspects	Examples
Purpose	• Life-long and life-after learning; comprehensive; <u>know</u>, <u>desire</u>, & <u>do</u> the good; God-centered perspective (whole world in His hands).
View of Children	• Whole child: mind, body, spirit; multiple intelligences and learning styles.
What to Teach	• Powerful ideas and big questions; whole world (multi-cultural); whole earth (stewardship).
How to Organize	• Transdisciplinary framework; integrated curriculum; holistic education; systems perspective.
How to Teach	• Integrated learning model; brain-compatible; differentiated instruction; total environment, whole village; whole language.

The Tarbiyah Project, then, is based on an approach to education that is truly holistic and integrated: holistic in its vision, content, structure, context and process; holistic in its view of children and how children really learn; comprehensive in its scope of mind, body and spirit; integrative in its approach to the curriculum (both *how* and *what* is taught); and integrating knowledge with application and service. It believes that these integrative aspects significantly enhance the power, relevance and effectiveness of the learning experience. The Tarbiyah Project advocates this holistic approach to education, not because it is a current trend in certain progressive circles of modern education, but rather because of its critical importance as the central principle of the Islamic worldview and its demonstrated effectiveness in more fully engaging students in their own learning. Below are certain holistic aspects of the Tarbiyah vision of education.

[1] Because of space constraints, most of the footnotes originally contained in this article have been removed here. Also note that a technical transliteration scheme has not been strictly followed in this article.

[2] Al-Rāghib al-Isfahānā, Mufradāt Alfāz al-Qur'ān, Bayrūt: al-Dār al-Shāmiyah, 1992, p. 336.

[3] It is worth noting here that the word "whole" is derived from a Germanic root word that includes the concepts of wholeness or completeness, wholesomeness or healthiness, and holiness. All three of these connotations are part of the concept of wholeness.

30. "Accomplishments" from *IQRA' International Education Foundation*

From IQRA' International Education Foundation, accessed May 29, 2006. Available on-line: http://www.iqra.org/iqraedu/home.html. Reprinted with permission of Tasneema Ghazi and IQRA'.

The IQRA' International Education Foundation was officially founded in 1983 in Chicago, Illinois with the intention of applying modern education methodologies to teaching Islamic Studies to Muslim children. IQRA' has developed curricula for students from preschool to high school grade levels. The following two entries are from the IQRA' web site.

IQRA' International Educational Foundation is committed to working in cooperation witheducators, administrators, parents, and members of the community to facilitate the acquisition of knowledge of the *Deen* of Allah (swt) and the knowledge of things created by Him. IQRA's vision was stirred by the Message of the Cave of Hira, the message to READ (with understanding) and to PROCLAIM the Truth to humanity.

The mission of IQRA' Foundation is to facilitate the acquisition of knowledge and lay the foundations of quality teaching and learning environments, primarily by: enhancing the quality of production and contents of Islamic literature, developing a comprehensive system of Islamic education and expanding the knowledge and skills of teachers through professional development programs.

IQRA' believes that Muslims in this modern pluralistic world have a duty and responsibility to:
interact with other faith communities, produce quality literature about Islam and Muslims for them to read, and demonstrate the beauty of our religion by living Islam every day.

31. **"Early Childhood Education Program in An Islamic School" from** *IQRA' International Education Foundation*

From IQRA' International Education Foundation, accessed May 29, 2006. Available online: http://www.iqra.org/iqraedu/home.html. Reprinted with permission of Tasneema Ghazi and IQRA'. For a description of IQRA', see Primary document 30.

PHILOSOPHY

Goal of the Early Childhood Program in an Islamic school is to provide opportunities for active involvement of children and their parents in a continual process of education based on the knowledge of the Qur'an and Sunnah. This includes a deep and firm belief in Allah I, His Mercy and His Guidance. Involvement of Muslim parents in the education of their children is especially important due to the many non-Islamic influences of Western American culture and environment upon them.

The Early Childhood Program in an Islamic school is to provide opportunities for active involvement of children and their parents in a continual process of education based on the knowledge of the Qur'an and Sunnah. This includes a deep and firm belief in Allah I, His Mercy and His Guidance. Involvement of Muslim parents in the education of their children is especially important due to the many non-Islamic influences of Western American culture and environment upon them.

The goal of the Early Childhood Program in an Islamic school is to provide opportunities for active involvement of children and their parents in a continual process of education based on the knowledge of the Qur'an and Sunnah. This includes a deep and firm belief in Allah I, His Mercy and His Guidance. Involvement of Muslim parents in the education of their children is especially important due to the many non-Islamic influences of Western American culture and environment upon them.

When a child enters school, both he and his parents begin a far-reaching experience. This is the time for building a sound relationship between school and home. Once established, this relationship provides solid grounds for cooperation and coordination between these two significant institutions in the child's life.

The preschool years play a unique role in the total growth and development of a child. Preschool programs are designed to help the children direct their energies to learning about and being aware of their environment. If the environment provided is Islamic, the children will be aware of their Islamic heritage and learn about their religion.

A specifically Islamic preschool program also provides the children many opportunities to interact with the Islamic environment in a positive and constructive way. The program should also help them to develop feelings of self-worth and adequacy about themselves, their families and their religion.

In order to be successful, the program needs parental cooperation and participation. Home involvement in the Islamic education and training of Muslim children cannot be overemphasized. Thus, the program should include a parent education component. The program should provide opportunities for the parents to do the following:

Realize their long-term responsibility as the primary educators and counselors of their children.

Participate in the preschool program and develop better understanding of the basic concepts of child growth and development. This participation will provide them better understanding of and deeper insight into human behavior.

Progress more comfortably in their relationships with their children and accept and enjoy them as they are.

Develop strong bonds with the Muslim community. These bonds will provide families with the needed support system, which in the past was so often provided by extended family and neighbors. To achieve these goals, the program will provide for the child, *Insha'Allah*, the following:

Opportunities for physical, social, cognitive, emotional and moral development to the extent of his capabilities and at the rate of his own growth.

An Islamic environment so that the moral and spiritual self of the child can develop under the teaching of the Qur'an and the *Sunnah*.

A secure and safe environment so that the child will not be afraid of new experiences.

Varied experiences for learning and completing developmental tasks.

Warm and supportive adults to guide and encourage both individual and group activities and to act as suitable Muslim role models for the children.

Freedom, opportunity and encouragement towards developing responsibility, self control and independence while maintaining respect for adults.

Loving, clear and intelligent beginning lessons in Qur'an and Hadith recitation and memorization, which will provide a foundation for a lifetime of study.

32. F. Thaufeer al-Deen, "Prison and the Struggle for Dignity" from *Taking Back Islam: American Muslims Reclaim Their Faith*

From Taking Back Islam: American Muslims Reclaim Their Faith, copyright Rodale Inc., Beliefnet, Inc., 2002. Reprinted with permission of F. Thaufeer al-Deen.

"Prison and the Struggle for Dignity" is a chapter in the book Taking Back Islam: American Muslims Reclaim Their Faith, edited by Michael Wolfe and published by Beliefnet in 2002. Taking Back Islam is a critical reflection by American Muslims on Islam in the United States since September 11, 2001. It won a Wilbur Award for best book on a religious theme for 2003. F. Thaufeer al-Deen had a career in law enforcement. He is currently a freelance writer and president of an educational organization, Dawahnet.

For most of their history in America, Muslims who had encounters with the criminal justice system were for the most part African-Americans. But since the 1980s, more and more immigrant Muslims have entered the country, and the nature of the crimes for which Muslims have been arrested—burglary, assault, and narcotics—have changed to more exotic offenses, such as immigration violations.

Now, in the aftermath of September 11, Muslims in America have undergone something similar to the experiences of JapaneseAmericans who were interned by the United States government during World War II. We've seen the establishment of the Office of Homeland Security and the passage of the Patriot Act—which allows for indefinite detention of noncitizens who are not terrorists on minor visa violations, allows more federal telephone and Internet surveillance by law enforcement, expands the ability of the government to conduct secret searches, gives the attorney general and the secretary of state power to designate domestic groups as terrorist organizations, and grants the FBI broad access to sensitive business records about individuals without having to show evidence of a crime. Both these developments result in policies that directly affect Muslims—invasions of privacy, ethnic profiling, and unexplained police investigations.

To understand the context of Muslims' fears about imprisonment, it's important to revisit earlier American-Muslim history. In the 1950s, American Muslims were primarily black and members of the Nation of Islam. Nation members had earlier been processed through a program of that organization called the "name assignment process." To acquire their new "name"—the famous X—the initiate had to write a letter to headquarters. Prison officials, in their mail inspection, encountered letters written in the Nation's stilted and mystical prose. Usually it was filled with anti-white hate language. While such mail reviews were normal to non-Muslims, for Nation members, the mail represented a communication link to their spiritual headquarters.

The language of these prisoners contested the right of the criminal justice system to incarcerate them. Through the 1950s and 1960s, the ability of the Nation to send proselytizing lessons through the mail to its imprisoned members was a point of legal contention.

Eventually, however, in several court cases, some of them rising to the United States Supreme Court, Nation members won rights that had been previously denied other inmates. Over time, Nation members won the right to receive religious mail, the right to visitation by their clergy, the right to a non-pork diet, and the right to wear bow ties with their prison uniforms. Eventually, they also won the right, even inside maximum-security facilities, to have visits from their "ministers," and later to hold prayer services, meetings and classes.

As a result of these victories, as well as their highly successful structured and disciplined character, members of the Nation set themselves apart from other inmates by prison officials. A love-hate relationships began to emerge over this time. Out of admiration grew a high degree of autonomy for National members, and, gradually, in a few facilities, the recognition by prison administrators that they could enhance control over inmates by enlisting Nation members as informants.

Later, in the 1970s, prisons began to encounter new types of Muslims. They tended to be orthodox Sunni and Shi'ite Muslims, and primarily immigrants. At first, members of this new group, owing to their smaller numbers, didn't participate in religious activities with earlier groups of African-American Muslims. But as the new group's numbers grew, they began to demand access to prison services and facilities. At the same time, they had no understanding of African-Americans' history in penal institutions.

One of the results of this lack of understanding is continued strained relations between African-American and immigrant Muslims. It's clear that Islam has always been "other" in the American penal system, which is rooted in a Christian view of criminal justice. For instance, crime is represented as "the fall" of an individual. The litigation process involves swearing on a religious text—the Bible. In addition, prisons tend to be located in rural areas, where encounters between visiting imams and Muslim prisoner family members and the rural prison employees have intensified Islam's "otherness".

In the post-September 11 era, conservatism grips the American government. In this new period, there have been drastic changes in United States criminal justice. Incarcerated Muslims are aware of these changes because of the degree to which they are seen as "the enemy" at the point of arrest. Nearly every "fact" and myth they have heard about Muslims confirm their status as "towel heads" and "camel jockeys." In local lockups, anecdotal evidence shows, the spiritual needs of Muslims are rarely addressed. There is no Qur'an, no clean place for prayer, no *halal* (Islamically permissible) food, and, if a family member visits, the typical screening procedure is excessively intrusive of Muslim women.

All incarcerated Muslims, it seems, are now suspected of being terrorists. Every rebellious act or word, every struggle to cling to one's dignity becomes a cause for a reaction from the guards. The isolated Muslim inmate begins an existence, far from home, family, and culture, that begins to affect him psychologically and, eventually, physically. This can lead to problems perceived by guards as non-cooperation and troublemaking. And so, pressure builds for affiliation with the prison security officers, who may be able to facilitate, say, a *halal* diet, a clean towel to pray on, or a Qur'an. For detainees, one price of these valued things can be uttering, whether truthfully or not, a whispered name.

Sometimes detainees seek to affiliate themselves with an amenable inmate group, such as Muslim gangs. In the African American Muslim groups, members are often required to make *bay'a* (a pledge of allegiance) to the group's inmate leader. That leader mayor may not be loyal to the group's external "free-world" leader. It is not a pledge to be taken lightly.

From within this safety net, Muslim inmates do their time. There is always the daily intrigue of imprisoned living—the power plays, "loves," and deaths, the pathologies of some of the correctional officers. Loyalty and the need for safety can be used as levers to press an inmate to serve and satisfy the needs and interests of others. For instance, prisoners serving life sentences without the opportunity for parole often "select" a prisoner with a shorter sentence as a "lifemate." To ensure that the selected "mate" is around longer than sentenced, the interested prisoner frames him and causes him to be convicted of some offense that adds years to his sentence.

Because of this, family visits are critical. But the visits are bittersweet because imprisonment is to everyday living as time travel would be to those left on Earth. For the prisoner, rapid changes occur in the larger society as the prisoner waits. Eventually, families snatched apart can crumble and die. And when the prisoner is released, children are older, the wife is more hardened, capable, and independent. This is anathema to many immigrant Muslim marriages and culture

The central values of Islam can mediate this effect on released Muslims, but for the majority of released offenders, the change is jarring. For those who have been detained under the War on Terrorism, incarceration often means lost positions, neighbors' suspicions, and pariah status. The question is whether these Muslim detainees will be able to return as productive and loyal citizens.

I believe we are now a nation ruled by emotion and whim, not by law. And this reality confronts the free as well as the detained and incarcerated immigrant Muslim. There is the hatred of Americans towards Muslims. There is also a war, now, that has placed ethnicity, religion, and geographic origins in question.

But there is something else. It is a Christian fundamentalism that takes literally the Bible's prophecy of a time when "every man's hands would be turned against the descendants of Ishmael, the first son of Prophet Abraham and his second 'wife' Hagar." Those descendants of Ishmael are Muslims.

For too many of their years here, the newer Muslims have lived apart from an American society that they view in conflicting ways. By faith they understand that the Islamic way of life is preferable to American hedonism-yet they need to stay within American cultural norms in order to function in America. To what example will these Muslims now turn to escape hatred, detention, imprisonment, alienation? Perhaps it will be the earlier example, an example about which they are only dimly aware—the example of African-American Muslims.

33. Zakariya Wright, "Islam and Alcohol in America: Muslim Scholars Step Forward" from *Dar al Islam*

From Dar al Islam, accessed May 19, 2006. Available online: http://www.islamamerica.org /articles.cfm/article_id/97/. Reprinted with the permission of Dar al Islam.

Dar al Islam is a nonprofit organization located in Abiquiu, New Mexico. Officially incorporated in 1979 with the goal of establishing a model Muslim village, the organization shifted focus to the education of non-Muslims in 1991. The organization defines itself as committed to the education of non-Muslims in North America by offering to teach non-Muslims (particularly in educational fields) about Islam. Its secondary objective is to aid Muslims to live in accordance with a traditional understanding of Islam (through religious retreats and training sessions) while living in the United States. Zakariya Wright is an editor and writer for Islam America, a subsidiary of Dar al Islam.

On November 23, 2005, several African American Muslims in Oakland entered an Arab-Muslim owned liquor store and, after the owner could provide no acceptable explanation for his activities, they began destroying bottles of liquor, wine and beer. The message was clear: Muslims should not be involved in selling alcohol, especially to largely Black communities victimized by economic and political isolation.

The mainstream media and even the legal system have relegated this conflict to a long-standing ethnic divide between Arab and African American communities. Some of the Muslim assailants have even been charged with hate crimes, positioning their actions in the American mind within a longstanding American tradition of White on Black racial intimidation, arson and lynching. The fact both sides of this particular incident were Muslim (not to mention both minorities) challenges the American public at large, and Muslims in particular, to take a closer look at the stakes and history involved in the issue of alcohol in Islam.

In a recent interview, the President of the Yemeni-American Grocers Association, Mohamed Saleh Mohamed, explained the supposed impasse faced by many Arab liquor store owners. "We're caught in a Catch-22. I'm not saying what we do is right, but it's within the system. The government is not going to take it away, because they need the money and taxes....America is full of opportunity, but most of the store owners come from Yemen and they are not educated, so this is the best they can do."[1]

Arab liquor store owners dominate the business in many of America's cities. In Chicago for example, there are said to be more than 3,000 Arab/Muslim owned liquor stores.[2] The vast majority of these are in poor and underprivileged Black neighborhoods, leading Imam Zaid Shakir to summarize decades of African American discontent, "Why don't you find these stores in the White or affluent neighborhoods...What has happened here, when you have a liquor store on every corner, that is an institutionalized presence."[3] Shakir has organized initiatives to put pressure on the Oakland City Hall to enforce zoning ordinances inconsistently applied between poor and affluent communities.

But it would be overly reductionist to parrot the incredulity of many American Muslims, whose rejection of alcohol consumption against the backdrop of mainstream American culture sometimes seems as distinguishing as one of Islam's five pillars. Muslim societies have had a historically more complex relationship with the sale and consumption of alcohol. A common accusation against Muslim rulers perceived as corrupt throughout Muslim history has invariably been alcohol consumption. Today, Muslim governments have found it necessary to react to enforce alcohol prohibitions.[4] Militants in Iraq have been accused of attacking and intimidating fellow Iraqi Muslims who have begun selling alcohol under American occupation.[5] Even in America, the percentage of Muslims drinking alcohol may be surprising to Muslims and non-Muslims alike. A study of American Muslims found that nearly a third had drunk alcohol in the last six months.[6]

There seems little dispute among Muslims that alcohol is indeed prohibited, and the following saying of the Prophet Muhammad (SAW) seems widely enough repeated:

Truly, Allah has cursed *khamr* (alcoholic beverages) and has cursed the one who produces it, the one for whom it is produced, the one who drinks it, the one who serves it, the one who carries it, the one for whom it is carried, the one who sells it, the one who earns from the sale of it, the one who buys it, and the one for whom it is bought.[7]

Imam Zaid Shakir thus presents the conflict between African American Muslims and Arab liquor-store owners as a disconnect over religious sincerity rather than an ethnic divide. "We must have an ethical standard that is uncompromising," he said in a recent radio interview, "Right is right and wrong is wrong." He compares the idea that Arab immigrants were forced into selling alcohol to make a living by lack of economic opportunities to terrorists killing women and children because of political oppression. "When we get into the 'but', we lose our moral consciousness."[8]

On January 27, 2006, a group of bay area Muslims marched on local Muslim-owned liquor stores to give the issue publicity and present a positive model for action beyond what Imam Zaid Shakir has called the "vigilante" behavior of the November, 2005, vandalism. Several local imams and community leaders attended the rally,[9] demonstrating a remarkable resonance with a tradition of social-conscious behavior of Islamic scholars (*ulama*).

If vice in Muslim societies has a longer history than the November incident in Oakland, so too have Muslim scholars been for centuries engaged in a struggle to make religious ideals a societal reality. A particularly interesting historical parallel emerges from the context of slavery and jihad in eighteenth and nineteenth century West Africa. The trans-Atlantic slave trade destabilized West African society from the sixteenth to nineteenth centuries not only through the extraction of huge numbers of Africans and the internal wars generated by the demand for slaves, but by the injection of large quantities of guns and alcohol European traders exchanged for slaves. Muslims and non-Muslims alike were negatively affected by the alcohol trade, and some Jolof kings (who had otherwise been Muslim since the fourteenth century) were accused to joining the non-Muslim practice of selling their own subjects to meet an insatiable appetite for alcohol.

The occasion of the slave trade was the impetus for the unification and emergence of isolated scholarly communities in an attempt to establish Islam and protect Muslims from the degenerative experience of the trans-Atlantic slave trade. Jihads were conducted by Nasr al-Din (d. 1674), Malik Dauda Sy (1690s), Karamoko Alfa (1720s), Suleyman Bal and Abdul-Qadir (1770s), Uthman Ibn Fudi (d. 1815) and al-Hajj Umar Futi Tal (d. 1864), throughout West Africa from Mauritania to Nigeria, often with the express purpose of stopping the outflow of Muslim slaves to the Americas and the inflow of alcohol.[10] It is worthy of note that all of these individuals were scholars first and foremost, who (Uthman Ibn Fudi and al-Hajj Umar in particular) composed some of the greatest works of Islamic scholarship of their day anywhere in the Islamic world. In other words, the pernicious connection between alcohol, corruption and social oppression has been identified and acted upon by Islamic scholars, particularly in a West African context. It should perhaps not be surprising that African American Muslims, whose ancestors were victims of a slave trade where alcohol played no small role, have been the first to speak out against the phenomenon of the Arab-owned liquor store.

The abuse of alcohol by either sale or consumption is nothing new in Muslim societies. But the recent march led by Bay Area Muslim leaders and scholars, such as Imam Zaid Shakir, indicates the fundamental role Muslim scholars have played and must play in Muslim societies. Scholars have historically been at the forefront of mounting protest campaigns against social injustice, campaigns which have been able affect rulers, popular sentiment and individual transgressors alike. The November incident of vandalism (also later linked to an arson attack and a kidnapping), which by all accounts reflects a lawless, irrational and violent form of Islam to the American public, is the alternative if scholars should not fulfill their role of social action.

NOTES

1. Cecily Burt, interview with Mohamed Saleh Mohamed, *The Muslim News*, December 12, 2005.

2. This reported by Imam Zaid Shakir.

3. Anas Cannon, "Interview with Imam Zaid Shakir," on *Remarkably Current Radio*, Channel 91.3 FM. For more information about the history of African American protest against the preponderance of liquor stores in Black underprivileged communities, see Adisa Banjoko, "Hip Hop predicted liquor store trashings long ago," on New American Media, December 2, 2005 (http://news.ncmonline.com/news/view_article.html?arti cle_id=de07d8311523400686599b218482867d).

4. Thus Malaysia has recently banned advertisements promoting alcohol (http://www.islamonline.net/english/news/2002-12/30/article09.shtml), while Kuwait made the news for shutting down twenty-five home breweries (http://www.islamonline.net/iol-english/dowalia/news-20-3-2000/topnews9.asp).

5. Roy McCarthy, "Iraq Violence as Puritans Ban Alcohol," in *The Observer*, 8/1/2004 (http://observer.guardian.co.uk/iraq/story/0,12239,1273782,00.html).

6. Yvonne Yazbeck Haddad and Adair Lummis, *Islamic Values in the United States: a comparative study* (New York: Oxford UP, 1987), p. 117–119. Haddad's sample group comprised 341 individuals, two-thirds of whom were immigrants. But the study found that the most likely Muslims to drink were young, American-born males.

7. Hadith found in al-Tirmidhi and Ibn Majah.

8. Anas Cannon, "Interview with Imam Zaid Shakir," on *Remarkably Current Radio*, Channel 91.3.

9. For more information, see http://www.sfbayview.com/020106/realmuslims020 106.shtml.

10. For more information on the context of the West African Jihad movements, see David Robinson, "Revolutions in the Western Sudan," in Levtzion and Pouwels (eds), *The History of Islam in Africa* (Athens, Ohio: Ohio UP, 2000), p.131–152.

34. **Hadia Mubarak, "Finding Home: The Consolidation of a Muslim American Identity" from** *Azizah Magazine*

From Azizah Magazine, August 2004, Vol. 3, Issue 3, p 92. Reprinted with permission of Azizah Magazine.

Hadia Mubarak was born in Panama City, Florida. She received a Master's degree in Contemporary Arab Studies from Georgetown University in 2005. She was the first female president of the Muslim Students Association National (MSA) and the organization's first American-born president in 2004. Azizah Magazine (for a description of Azizah Magazine, see the "Azizah Magazine" entry in Volume 1) is the only magazine publication in the United States that focuses on issues relating to women and Islam in the America. It is based in Atlanta, Georgia and ran its first publication in 2000.

Whether first generation or indigenous, Muslim Americans reach a point in their lifetime when they undergo a common struggle to define the parameters of their identity on the demographic chart of this country. They struggle to map out geographic borders for a "home" that has not yet intersected the threshold of reality. My "identity crisis" began at a really young age in this country. No one ever told me that I didn't "fit in" in America. It was enough to gather from people's uncomfortable glances and blatant glares at my mother, wearing a headscarf and long dress, as she drove my sister and me to our New Brunswick Day Care in her white Chevy station wagon.

It was enough to gather in kindergarten when I incorrectly answered a question on the infamous CAT test because I didn't know the meaning of a word in English, prompting my teacher to ask in disdain, "Don't you know what that means?" It was enough to gather from the three boys in my neighborhood, who, one day, while dangling their fishing poles in the creek by my house, asked me where I was from. The three boys scoffed "What? Cereal?" when I hastily replied that I was from Syria, a country I only knew from memories that my father passed on during Saturday breakfasts over pancakes and a Syrian dish of mamounia.

It wasn't until years later that I would find myself driving down the road to the Syrian borders for the first time in my life, searching for something different, for something that could harmonize my yearning for a second home—a home where no questions of identity were asked, where no one gawked at me or stereotyped me by glimpses of Hollywood movies showing Arab fanatics hijacking a plane, or some book they read about a Saudi Arabian princess escaping the oppression of a male-dominated society. I was searching for a place where I could belong.

My visits to my parents' native countries of Syria and Jordan only exacerbated my crisis of identity. My difficulty with communicating in the native dialect while simultaneously "appearing" like a typical Arab woman, wearing hijab, with dark eyebrows and an olive complexion, made me an object of paradox and contradiction. Not only was I perceived as an outsider, but I felt like one as well. The absence of respect for the rule of law, the bureaucratic red tape that complicated my entry to the country and the chaos that often characterized the streets and markets of the Arab world only made me feel like a greater stranger in my parents' native homeland. It was on the streets of the Arab world that I discovered the duality of my identity, which created a sense of perpetual displacement in me. I felt like a refugee whose identity lacked geographic existence—it was only my existence that gave truth to my identity.

At the age of 21, I found "home," where my sense of belonging wasn't transient or based on superficial elements like the color of my skin or the dialect with which I spoke. It was during my first week as a graduate student at Georgetown University in Washington, DC. I grabbed a friend and together, using directions we printed off MapQuest, we trekked our way to a mosque in Falls Church, Virginia. I took my place on the second floor balcony of the mosque, overlooking the men, where I was surrounded by beautiful women representing a myriad of cultures from American Caucasian, Turkish, Kashmiri to Somali, Arab, African American and Pakistani. Sitting on the forest green and tan striped carpet among hundreds of men and women I had never seen in my life, I suddenly felt this overwhelming sense of familiarity and comfort. The conglomeration of ethnicities and languages that surrounded me created a sense of belonging that settled deep within my consciousness. It reminded me of the first and only time I had visited Makkah, the holy city for Muslims, during my freshman year in college. On the streets of Makkah, I had felt this overwhelming connection with the pilgrims of Hajj that transcended any temporal quality with which I could identify. Language, race, family lineage, etc. had become not only irrelevant, but meaningless, on my scale of "identification" with the millions of people whose lives intersected mine on that tiny speck of the earth, for that fleeting moment of time in which we connected with Our Creator—at that intersection of the heavens and earth, of our beginning and end.

My humanity had been unearthed in that moment when I bowed my head to the ground with three million other heads in the Haram al-Sharif, losing all sense of "self," but gaining a complete awareness of my humanity for the first time in my life. As the rhythm of our bodily movements coincided, the bond that I felt with the unfamiliar pilgrims, whose names I never learned and nationalities I could only guess, could never be consolidated into a geographic location or national identity. It was a bond that recognized the reality of our existence: that only our souls would transcend beyond this ephemeral world...that what made us "real" was not our nationalities, our physical appearances, our financial assets, but our souls, which shared the same origin and destiny to the eternal Creator.

Sitting at that mosque in Falls Church, Virginia, I came to understand a saying I had heard from Dr. Sherman Abdul-Hakim Jackson years ago. He had said that all a Muslim needed to do to "feel at home" was join a prayer in congregation—he/she dips right into it like a fish joining a school of fish in the sea. My search for a home, a place where I could belong, came to an end.

I find myself at home in any place or gathering where God is being remembered; any place that gives testimony to my origin and ultimate end. A prophetic saying goes, "God's earth is a mosque." I am at home while praying at the Shi'aa mosque of Imam al-Hasanain in Beirut, Lebanon, at the Sufi zawiya in Amman, Jordan, at the Seven Eleven converted into a prayer area in Tallahassee, Florida, at the inter-faith chapel in Atlanta

Hartsfield Airport, at the seventh century Umayyad Mosque in Damascus, Syria and in the formal mosques of Toledo, Ann Arbor, Los Angeles, Tampa and in Panama City. My Muslim American identity, like that of many others, is one that cannot be contained within geographic borders; it does not begin nor end on a stretch of land, for an identity lives within the heart and the consciousness. I am at home in any land or place that reminds me what it means to be insan—human.

35. **Sumayya Allen, "Living and Dying in America: *Janazah* Issues for the American Muslim" from** *Azizah Magazine*

From Azizah Magazine: Fall 2002, Vol. 2, Issue 3, p 104. Reprinted with permission of Azizah Magazine.

For description of Azizah Magazine see the "Azizah Magazine" entry in Volume 1. The following article describes Muslim funeral rituals in the American context.

Concentrating intensely and sincerely, the praying Muslimah felt fear and awe of the greatness of the Creator welling up with every "Allahu akbar" pronounced. In deep communication with her Lord, she prayed as if it would be her last salah, for she did not know if it was.

Prophet Muhammad, peace be on him, urged us to approach every prayer as if it was our last. He also told us to think of death often; in preparation for the time Allah decrees our demise. Faced with considerable hardship if we fail to heed these words of prophetic wisdom, we are usually caught unprepared mentally, emotionally—even socially—to deal with death when a family member or a close friend dies. By strengthening our relationship with Allah and minding the ahadith, we can begin, in life, the process of spiritual preparation for death.

As Muslims, our first priority in preparation for death is our spiritual state as we depart this world. Just as important is the understanding of the technicalities of the funeral and burial process in accordance with Islamic law, as well as individual state laws, which may affect our family members' burial procedures. Not only should we be conscience of the approach of our own death, but we should also be prepared for the death of those close to us.

Considering the majority of Muslims here are not from an Islamic country, the issue of having non-Muslim family members unfamiliar with Islamic funeral traditions must be considered carefully. In such a case, clear communication of one's wishes are very important in preventing any family members with other beliefs from preparing the body for a Christian burial or other non-Islamic rituals. There have been many stories about Muslims who died without explicit burial instructions and were buried in accordance with other religious tenets. Having a will that explains the intentions for burial, as well as a frank discussion of the issue with all members of the family can help to alleviate such discrepancies.

A completed will for yourself, your spouse and your family members can deal with issues such as funeral arrangements, the placement of orphaned children, guidelines for inheritance according to Islamic law, and other endowments. The Islamic Society for North America (ISNA) has wills on their website that can be downloaded, and most communities periodically offer classes on drawing up the Islamic will.

Drawing up a will is but one aspect of our preparation. The janazah procedure is another. As the Muslim community in America continues to grow and flourish, more attention is being paid to the issues of janazah. With the development of Islamic legal, medical, health and social institutions, there is now a growing focus on the establishment of funeral services to fulfill these community needs. While some Muslim communities already own private cemeteries, others are in the process of purchasing land for this purpose or have secured designated sections in various graveyards and memorial parks.

Whether it is a private Muslim cemetery or a plot in a general graveyard, burial will take place according to state laws. When state laws contradict Islamic law, alternatives are looked at that are still considered acceptable by shar'iah. For instance, the Muslim burial must be performed as quickly as possible—there are no pre-funeral visitation periods such as public display and viewing of the body. Autopsies are not to be performed on the deceased, nor is the body embalmed. However, in many places, autopsies are automatic and some states require embalming if the body must cross state lines for burial. In these cases, special appeals may be made on religious grounds, but frequently these requests are not granted. You can find out more about your state laws concerning death and burials by contacting your masjid, your attorney or a local coroner.

After the body is washed and properly shrouded in white cloth, the janazah prayer is performed with the body present. Cremation and mausoleums are not allowed, so burial immediately follows. The body is placed in the grave, without a coffin, on its side facing the Kaa'bah. Since a Muslim's burial should be simple with as little money as possible spent, the use of coffins is seen as unnatural as well as unnecessary. Here again state laws may necessitate different procedures, since some states require that the body be placed in a cement vault at the bottom of the grave, while others mandate that the body be buried in a coffin. As many Muslims believe such laws conflict with Islamic law, it is beneficial to research the facts when making burial plans and to determine the need for any compromising.

One such compromise was determined by ISNA. Sayyid Syeed, the Secretary General of ISNA, points out that according to Islamic law, we must be buried touching the earth. "We come from the dust and the body must go back to the earth. If there is a legal requirement for a casket, then we place earth inside."

According to Syeed, the ISNA web site will have a link in the near future that provides information regarding Islamic laws and state laws relating to burials and funerals, as well as contact information for Islamic cemeteries and Islamic businesses that offer funeral services. Syeed points out that, in the beginning of the establishment of the Islamic community in America, the focus was on the younger generation of Muslims. Services are presently being established for the group on the other end of the spectrum. "We built and provided schools first, and now we are dealing with the issue of a rise in the number of Muslim senior citizens." As only Allah knows the hour of death, this will be a useful tool in providing information that is relevant to all ages, not only the elderly.

The web site is one example of the efforts to develop and provide funeral and burial services for the Muslim community. Currently, many communities offer body washing facilities, some have Muslim-owned cemeteries and a few have Islamic funeral homes. Still, most Muslim families have to pay to use a funeral home when there is a death and it is rare to find Muslims becoming certified morticians in the US. Even if an Islamic community does have their own facilities for washing the body and their own cemeteries, in many states, by law, a certified mortician must be called on to transport the body from one place to the next. For communities in these particular states, the need for Muslim morticians becomes a factor, whereas, in other states, like Georgia, having a certified mortician is not required.

Being informed of the laws as well as of the services offered in your local community will help you from wasting precious time after a death occurs or help avoid paying for unnecessary services, such as renting a funeral home to wash the body when there are body-washing facilities available. The funeral business is big business in America, and if you are not informed or prepared, you can face excessive charges.

In addition to exorbitant costs, those working to setting up funeral services sometimes face local opposition. A lack of organized support and budget constraints can hamper or delay the purchasing of land and buildings, the obtaining of required zoning permits, and the construction and staffing of facilities. One issue of great magnitude for Muslim funeral businesses already in operation is having an adequate staff properly trained to wash the deceased. This is particularly pressing in the case of women, since often times Islamic communities have a large number of trained men but only a few women.

Some communities provide classes for men and women that instruct on the washing of the body. When completed, the person becomes certified and is put on a list at the masjid to be on call in case of a death. One such woman, Raishma Afzal of the Dallas area, is part of the staff for washing bodies and has been volunteering for close to four years. She thinks that it is very important for masajid to hold classes so that people can learn how to wash a body. She observes that "you have to be prepared in the mind; it is difficult the first time," as most of us are not used to being in the presence of the dead. However, she affirms, "It is very rewarding from Allah to wash."

Sometimes cultural superstitions or taboos make it difficult to find a person willing to wash a body. Azita Ayyah, a part-time office manager for the Islamic Cultural Center of Northern California, said that their community has a very hard time finding volunteers willing to wash a body. The Center has a large Iranian population and Ayyah explains that tradition and superstition prevent people from volunteering. "People feel degraded to do it, their social perception prevents them." She said that at the start of the Iranian New Year, someone in the community passed away and it was extremely difficult to find a volunteer to wash the body. Everyone felt it was not good to begin their New Year in the presence of the dead, as it might bring them bad luck.

But according to Islamic tradition, and as Raishma Afzal can testify, there is much reward for the person who washes the body of the deceased. Superstitions and taboos should not prevent us from performing a religious and communal obligation. After all, we all will have to face our own deaths and we all pray that, at that time, there will be a volunteer to wash our body. The washing of the body has to be done with much respect for the deceased. There are ahadith that state the dead can still feel, so the body must be handled gently and humbly. "All of us have to go. No one can stay forever in this world," says Afzal.

One community that provides certification for people who have trained in body washing is located in the Detroit area. Dr. Judi Muhammad, Executive Vice-President of the Islamic Health and Human Services, says that communities who have difficulty finding people to assist in the washing of the deceased should "find a local legitimate scholar who is willing to give classes and have men and women take the classes who will end up being on call—being available to hospices, hospitals and other healthcare agencies." She stresses that this has to be done by people willing to volunteer their time because it is not a service that is for making money.

Likewise, the Dallas Central Mosque has a Funeral Committee that educates on washing. If their list of volunteers becomes short, they organize classes to train new volunteers. According to the Imam, Dr. Yusuf Kavakci, they try to continually have between 15 and 20 volunteers of both men and women for their body washing facilities. "Everybody must get involved and must know how to wash bodies. We must not shy away but [rather] be fearful and get ready for the next life," says Dr. Kavakci.

Getting ready for the next life begins with educating ourselves about the Islamic legalities and the local laws pertaining to this life. While more and more communities are establishing janazah facilities, it is still up to us to prepare ourselves for the inevitable. By doing so, we will be ready spiritually, emotionally and socially when it happens. Truly, we are from Allah, and to Allah we will all return.

36. Nuh Ha Mim Keller, "Becoming Muslim"

From Nuh Ha Mim Keller, "Becoming Muslim" MCMXCIII © nuh ha mim keller, accessed May 18, 2006. Available online: http://www.masud.co.uk/ISLAM/nuh/ bmuslim.htm. Reprinted with permission of Nuh Ha Mim Keller.

Nuh Ha Mim Keller (for a biography, see the "Keller, Shaykh Nuh" entry in Volume 1) wrote the following article in 1993. It is a good illustration of the conversion phenomenon in American society.

In the name of Allah, Most Merciful and Compassionate
Becoming Muslim
Born in 1954 in the farm country of the northwestern United States, I was raised in a religious family as a Roman Catholic. The Church provided a spiritual world that was unquestionable in my childhood, if anything more real than the physical world around me, but as I grew older, and especially after I entered a Catholic university and read more, my relation to the religion became increasingly called into question, in belief and practice.

One reason was the frequent changes in Catholic liturgy and ritual that occurred in the wake of the Second Vatican Council of 1963, suggesting to laymen that the Church had no firm standards. To one another, the clergy spoke about flexibility and liturgical relevance, but to ordinary Catholics they seemed to be groping in the dark. God does not change, nor the needs of the human soul, and there was no new revelation from heaven. Yet we rang in the changes, week after week, year after year; adding, subtracting, changing the language from Latin to English, finally bringing in guitars and folk music. Priests explained and explained as laymen shook their heads. The search for relevance left large numbers convinced that there had not been much in the first place.

A second reason was a number of doctrinal difficulties, such as the doctrine of the Trinity, which no one in the history of the world, neither priest nor layman, had been able to explain in a convincing way, and which resolved itself, to the common mind at least, in a sort of godhead-by-committee, shared between God the Father, who ruled the world from heaven; His son Jesus Christ, who saved humanity on earth; and the Holy Ghost, who was pictured as a white dove and appeared to have a considerably minor role. I remember wanting to make special friends with just one of them so he could handle my business with the others, and to this end, would sometimes pray earnestly to this one and sometimes to that; but the other two were always stubbornly there. I finally decided that God the Father must be in charge of the other two, and this put the most formidable obstacle in the way of my Catholicism, the divinity of Christ. Moreover, reflection made it plain that the nature of man contradicted the nature of God in every particular, the limitary and finite on the one hand, the absolute and infinite on the other. That Jesus was God was something I cannot remember having ever really believed, in childhood or later.

Another point of incredulity was the trading of the Church in stocks and bonds in the hereafter it called indulgences. Do such and such and so-and-so many years will be remitted from your sentence in purgatory that had seemed so false to Martin Luther at the outset of the Reformation.

I also remember a desire for a sacred scripture, something on the order of a book that could furnish guidance. A Bible was given to me one Christmas, a handsome edition, but on attempting to read it, I found it so rambling and devoid of a coherent thread that it was difficult to think of a way to base one's life upon it. Only later did I learn how Christians solve the difficulty in practice, Protestants by creating sectarian theologies, each emphasizing the texts of their sect and downplaying the rest; Catholics by downplaying it all, except the snippets mentioned in their liturgy. Something seemed lacking in a sacred book that could not be read as an integral whole.

Moreover, when I went to the university, I found that the authenticity of the book, especially the New Testament, had come into considerable doubt as a result of modern hermeneutical studies by Christians themselves. In a course on contemporary theology, I read the Norman Perrin translation of The Problem of the Historical Jesus by Joachim Jeremias, one of the principal New Testament scholars of this century. A textual critic who was a master of the original languages and had spent long years with the texts, he had finally agreed with the German theologian Rudolph Bultmann that without a doubt it is true to say that the dream of ever writing a biography of Jesus is over, meaning that the life of Christ as he actually lived it could not be reconstructed from the New Testament with any degree of confidence. If this were accepted from a friend of Christianity and one of its foremost textual experts, I reasoned, what was left for its enemies to say? And what then remained of the Bible except to acknowledge that it was a record of truths mixed with fictions, conjectures projected onto Christ by later followers, themselves at odds with each other as to who the master had been and what he had taught. And if theologians like Jeremias could reassure themselves that somewhere under the layers of later accretions to the New Testament there was something called the historical Jesus and his message, how could the ordinary person hope to find it, or know it, should it be found?

I studied philosophy at the university and it taught me to ask two things of whoever claimed to have the truth: What do you mean, and how do you know? When I asked these questions of my own religious tradition, I found no answers, and realized that Christianity had slipped from my hands. I then embarked on a search that is perhaps not unfamiliar to many young people in the West, a quest for meaning in a meaningless world.

I began where I had lost my previous belief, with the philosophers, yet wanting to believe, seeking not philosophy, but rather a philosophy.

I read the essays of the great pessimist Arthur Schopenhauer, which taught about the phenomenon of the ages of life, and that money, fame, physical strength, and intelligence all passed from one with the passage of years, but only moral excellence remained. I took this lesson to heart and remembered it in after years. His essays also drew attention to the fact that a person was wont to repudiate in later years what he fervently espouses in the heat of youth. With a prescient wish to find the Divine, I decided to imbue myself with the most cogent arguments of atheism that I could find, that perhaps I might find a way

out of them later. So I read the Walter Kaufmann translations of the works of the immor-
alist Friedrich Nietzsche. The many-faceted genius dissected the moral judgments and
beliefs of mankind with brilliant philological and psychological arguments that ended in
accusing human language itself, and the language of nineteenth-century science in particular, of being so inherently determined and mediated by concepts inherited from the
language of morality that in their present form they could never hope to uncover reality.
Aside from their immunological value against total skepticism, Nietzsche's works
explained why the West was post-Christian, and accurately predicted the unprecedented
savagery of the twentieth century, debunking the myth that science could function as a
moral replacement for the now dead religion.

At a personal level, his tirades against Christianity, particularly in The Genealogy of
Morals, gave me the benefit of distilling the beliefs of the monotheistic tradition into a
small number of analyzable forms. He separated unessential concepts (such as the bizarre
spectacle of an omnipotent deitys suicide on the cross) from essential ones, which I now,
though without believing in them, apprehended to be but three alone: that God existed;
that He created man in the world and defined the conduct expected of him in it; and
that He would judge man accordingly in the hereafter and send him to eternal reward
or punishment.

It was during this time that I read an early translation of the Qur'an which I grudgingly
admired, between agnostic reservations, for the purity with which it presented these fundamental concepts. Even if false, I thought, there could not be a more essential expression
of religion. As a literary work, the translation, perhaps it was Sales, was uninspired and
openly hostile to its subject matter, whereas I knew the Arabic original was widely
acknowledged for its beauty and eloquence among the religious books of mankind. I felt
a desire to learn Arabic to read the original.

On a vacation home from school, I was walking upon a dirt road between some fields
of wheat, and it happened that the sun went down. By some inspiration, I realized that
it was a time of worship, a time to bow and pray to the one God. But it was not something
one could rely on oneself to provide the details of, but rather a passing fancy, or perhaps
the beginning of an awareness that atheism was an inauthentic way of being.

I carried something of this disquiet with me when I transferred to the University of
Chicago, where I studied the epistemology of ethical theory how moral judgments were
reached reading and searching among the books of the philosophers for something to shed
light on the question of meaninglessness, which was both a personal concern and one of
the central philosophical problems of our age.

According to some, scientific observation could only yield description statements of the
form X is Y, for example, The object is red, Its weight is two kilos, Its height is ten centi-
meters, and so on, in each of which the functional was a scientifically verifiable is, whereas
in moral judgments the functional element was an ought, a description statement which
no amount of scientific observation could measure or verify. It appeared that ought was
logically meaningless, and with it all morality whatsoever, a position that reminded me
of those described by Lucian in his advice that whoever sees a moral philosopher coming
down the road should flee from him as from a mad dog. For such a person, expediency
ruled, and nothing checked his behavior but convention.

As Chicago was a more expensive school, and I had to raise tuition money, I found
summer work on the West Coast with a seining boat fishing in Alaska. The sea proved a
school in its own right, one I was to return to for a space of eight seasons, for the money.

I met many people on boats, and saw something of the power and greatness of the wind, water, storms, and rain; and the smallness of man. These things lay before us like an immense book, but my fellow fishermen and I could only discern the letters of it that were within our context: to catch as many fish as possible within the specified time to sell to the tenders. Few knew how to read the book as a whole. Sometimes, in a blow, the waves rose like great hills, and the captain would hold the wheel with white knuckles, our bow one minute plunging gigantically down into a valley of green water, the next moment reaching the bottom of the trough and soaring upwards towards the sky before topping the next crest and starting down again.

Early in my career as a deck hand, I had read the Hazel Barnes translation of Jean Paul Sartres "Being and Nothingness", in which he argued that phenomena only arose for consciousness in the existential context of human projects, a theme that recalled Marx's 1844 manuscripts, where nature was produced by man, meaning, for example, that when the mystic sees a stand of trees, his consciousness hypostatizes an entirely different phenomenal object than a poet does, for example, or a capitalist. To the mystic, it is a manifestation; to the poet, a forest; to the capitalist, lumber. According to such a perspective, a mountain only appears as tall in the context of the project of climbing it, and so on, according to the instrumental relations involved in various human interests. But the great natural events of the sea surrounding us seemed to defy, with their stubborn, irreducible facticity, our uncomprehending attempts to come to terms with them. Suddenly, we were just there, shaken by the forces around us without making sense of them, wondering if we would make it through. Some, it was true, would ask Gods help at such moments, but when we returned safely to shore, we behaved like men who knew little of Him, as if those moments had been a lapse into insanity, embarrassing to think of at happier times. It was one of the lessons of the sea that in fact, such events not only existed but perhaps even preponderated in our life. Man was small and weak, the forces around him were large, and he did not control them.

Sometimes a boat would sink and men would die. I remember a fisherman from another boat who was working near us one opening, doing the same job as I did, piling web. He smiled across the water as he pulled the net from the hydraulic block overhead, stacking it neatly on the stern to ready it for the next set. Some weeks later, his boat overturned while fishing in a storm, and he got caught in the web and drowned. I saw him only once again, in a dream, beckoning to me from the stern of his boat.

The tremendousness of the scenes we lived in, the storms, the towering sheer cliffs rising vertically out of the water for hundreds of feet, the cold and rain and fatigue, the occasional injuries and deaths of workers these made little impression on most of us. Fishermen were, after all, supposed to be tough. On one boat, the family that worked it was said to lose an occasional crew member while running at sea at the end of the season, invariably the sole non-family member who worked with them, his loss saving them the wages they would have otherwise had to pay him.

The captain of another was a twenty-seven-year-old who delivered millions of dollars worth of crab each year in the Bering Sea. When I first heard of him, we were in Kodiak, his boat at the city dock they had tied up to after a lengthy run some days before. The captain was presently indisposed in his bunk in the stateroom, where he had been vomiting up blood from having eaten a glass uptown the previous night to prove how tough he was.

He was in somewhat better condition when I later saw him in the Bering Sea at the end of a long winter king crab season. He worked in his wheelhouse up top, surrounded by radios that could pull in a signal from just about anywhere, computers, Loran, sonar, depth-finders, radar. His panels of lights and switches were set below the 180-degree sweep of shatterproof windows that overlooked the sea and the men on deck below, to whom he communicated by loudspeaker. They often worked round the clock, pulling their gear up from the icy water under watchful batteries of enormous electric lights attached to the masts that turned the perpetual night of the winter months into day. The captain had a reputation as a screamer, and had once locked his crew out on deck in the rain for eleven hours because one of them had gone inside to have a cup of coffee without permission. Few crewmen lasted longer than a season with him, though they made nearly twice the yearly income of, say, a lawyer or an advertising executive, and in only six months. Fortunes were made in the Bering Sea in those years, before overfishing wiped out the crab.

At present, he was at anchor, and was amiable enough when we tied up to him and he came aboard to sit and talk with our own captain. They spoke at length, at times gazing thoughtfully out at the sea through the door or windows, at times looking at each other sharply when something animated them, as the topic of what his competitors thought of him. "They wonder why I have a few bucks", he said. "Well I slept in my own home one night last year."

He later had his crew throw off the lines and pick the anchor, his eyes flickering warily over the water from the windows of the house as he pulled away with a blast of smoke from the stack. His watchfulness, his walrus-like physique, his endless voyages after game and markets, reminded me of other predatory hunter-animals of the sea. Such people, good at making money but heedless of any ultimate end or purpose, made an impression on me, and I increasingly began to wonder if men didn't need principles to guide them and tell them why they were there. Without such principles, nothing seemed to distinguish us above our prey except being more thorough, and technologically capable of preying longer, on a vaster scale, and with greater devastation than the animals we hunted.

These considerations were in my mind the second year I studied at Chicago, where I became aware through studies of philosophical moral systems that philosophy had not been successful in the past at significantly influencing peoples morals and preventing injustice, and I came to realize that there was little hope for it to do so in the future. I found that comparing human cultural systems and societies in their historical succession and multiplicity had led many intellectuals to moral relativism, since no moral value could be discovered which on its own merits was transculturally valid, a reflection leading to nihilism, the perspective that sees human civilizations as plants that grow out of the earth, springing from their various seeds and soils, thriving for a time, and then dying away.

Some heralded this as intellectual liberation, among them Emile Durkheim in his "Elementary Forms of the Religious Life", or Sigmund Freud in his "Totem and Taboo", which discussed mankind as if it were a patient and diagnosed its religious traditions as a form of a collective neurosis that we could now hope to cure, by applying to them a thoroughgoing scientific atheism, a sort of salvation through pure science.

On this subject, I bought the Jeremy Shapiro translation of "Knowledge and Human Interests" by Jurgen Habermas, who argued that there was no such thing as pure science that could be depended upon to forge boldly ahead in a steady improvement of itself and the world. He called such a misunderstanding scientism, not science. Science in the real world, he said, was not free of values, still less of interests. The kinds of research that obtain funding, for example, were a function of what their society deemed meaningful, expedient, profitable, or important. Habermas had been of a generation of German academics who, during the thirties and forties, knew what was happening in their country, but insisted they were simply engaged in intellectual production, that they were living in the realm of scholarship, and need not concern themselves with whatever the state might choose to do with their research. The horrible question mark that was attached to German intellectuals when the Nazi atrocities became public after the war made Habermas think deeply about the ideology of pure science. If anything was obvious, it was that the nineteenth-century optimism of thinkers like Freud and Durkheim was no longer tenable.

I began to re-assess the intellectual life around me. Like Schopenhauer, I felt that higher education must produce higher human beings. But at the university, I found lab people talking to each other about forging research data to secure funding for the coming year; luminaries who wouldn't permit tape recorders at their lectures for fear that competitors in the same field would go one step further with their research and beat them to publication; professors vying with each other in the length of their courses syllabuses. The moral qualities I was accustomed to associate with ordinary, unregenerate humanity seemed as frequently met with in sophisticated academics as they had been in fishermen. If one could laugh at fishermen who, after getting a boatload of fish in a big catch, would cruise back and forth in front of the others to let them see how laden down in the water they were, ostensibly looking for more fish; what could one say about the Ph.D.'s who behaved the same way about their books and articles? I felt that their knowledge had not developed their persons, that the secret of higher man did not lie in their sophistication.

I wondered if I hadn't gone down the road of philosophy as far as one could go. While it had debunked my Christianity and provided some genuine insights, it had not yet answered the big questions. Moreover, I felt that this was somehow connected I didn't know whether as cause or effect to the fact that our intellectual tradition no longer seemed to seriously comprehend itself. What were any of us, whether philosophers, fishermen, garbagemen, or kings, except bit players in a drama we did not understand, diligently playing out our roles until our replacements were sent, and we gave our last performance? But could one legitimately hope for more than this? I read "Kojves Introduction to the Reading of Hegel", in which he explained that for Hegel, philosophy did not culminate in the system, but rather in the Wise Man, someone able to answer any possible question on the ethical implications of human actions. This made me consider our own plight in the twentieth century, which could no longer answer a single ethical question.

It was thus as if this century's unparalleled mastery of concrete things had somehow ended by making us things. I contrasted this with Hegel's concept of the concrete in his "Phenomenology of Mind". An example of the abstract, in his terms, was the limitary physical reality of the book now held in your hands, while the concrete was its interconnection with the larger realities it presupposed, the modes of production that determined the kind of ink and paper in it, the aesthetic standards that dictated its color and design, the systems of marketing and distribution that had carried it to the reader, the historical circumstances that had brought about the readers literacy and taste; the cultural events that had mediated its style and usage; in short, the bigger picture in which it was articulated and had its being. For Hegel, the movement of philosophical investigation always led from the abstract to the concrete, to the more real. He was therefore able to say that philosophy necessarily led to theology, whose object was the ultimately real, the Deity. This seemed to me to point up an irreducible lack in our century. I began to wonder if, by materializing our culture and our past, we had not somehow abstracted ourselves from our wider humanity, from our true nature in relation to a higher reality.

At this juncture, I read a number of works on Islam, among them the books of Seyyed Hossein Nasr, who believed that many of the problems of western man, especially those of the environment, were from his having left the divine wisdom of revealed religion, which taught him his true place as a creature of God in the natural world and to understand and respect it. Without it, he burned up and consumed nature with ever more effective technological styles of commercial exploitation that ruined his world from without while leaving him increasingly empty within, because he did not know why he existed or to what end he should act.

I reflected that this might be true as far as it went, but it begged the question as to the truth of revealed religion. Everything on the face of the earth, all moral and religious systems, were on the same plane, unless one could gain certainty that one of them was from a higher source, the sole guarantee of the objectivity, the whole force, of moral law. Otherwise, one man's opinion was as good as another's, and we remained in an undifferentiated sea of conflicting individual interests, in which no valid objection could be raised to the strong eating the weak.

I read other books on Islam, and came across some passages translated by W. Montgomery Watt from "That Which Delivers from Error" by the theologian and mystic Ghazali, who, after a mid-life crises of questioning and doubt, realized that beyond the light of prophetic revelation there is no other light on the face of the earth from which illumination may be received, the very point to which my philosophical inquiries had led. Here was, in Hegel's terms, the Wise Man, in the person of a divinely inspired messenger who alone had the authority to answer questions of good and evil.

I also read A.J. Arberrys translation "The Qur'an Interpreted", and I recalled my early wish for a sacred book. Even in translation, the superiority of the Muslim scripture over the Bible was evident in every line, as if the reality of divine revelation, dimly heard of all my life, had now been placed before my eyes. In its exalted style, its power, its inexorable finality, its uncanny way of anticipating the arguments of the atheistic heart in advance and answering them; it was a clear exposition of God as God and man as man, the revelation of the awe-inspiring Divine Unity being the identical revelation of social and economic justice among men.

I began to learn Arabic at Chicago, and after studying the grammar for a year with a fair degree of success, decided to take a leave of absence to try to advance in the language in a year of private study in Cairo. Too, a desire for new horizons drew me, and after a third season of fishing, I went to the Middle East.

In Egypt, I found something I believe brings many to Islam, namely, the mark of pure monotheism upon its followers, which struck me as more profound than anything I had previously encountered. I met many Muslims in Egypt, good and bad, but all influenced by the teachings of their Book to a greater extent than I had ever seen elsewhere. It has been some fifteen years since then, and I cannot remember them all, or even most of them, but perhaps the ones I can recall will serve to illustrate the impressions made.

One was a man on the side of the Nile near the Miqyas Gardens, where I used to walk. I came upon him praying on a piece of cardboard, facing across the water. I started to pass in front of him, but suddenly checked myself and walked around behind, not wanting to disturb him. As I watched a moment before going my way, I beheld a man absorbed in his relation to God, oblivious to my presence, much less my opinions about him or his religion. To my mind, there was something magnificently detached about this, altogether strange for someone coming from the West, where praying in public was virtually the only thing that remained obscene.

Another was a young boy from secondary school who greeted me near Khan al-Khalili, and because I spoke some Arabic and he spoke some English and wanted to tell me about Islam, he walked with me several miles across town to Giza, explaining as much as he could. When we parted, I think he said a prayer that I might become Muslim.

Another was a Yemeni friend living in Cairo who brought me a copy of the Qur'an at my request to help me learn Arabic. I did not have a table beside the chair where I used to sit and read in my hotel room, and it was my custom to stack the books on the floor. When I set the Qur'an by the others there, he silently stooped and picked it up, out of respect for it. This impressed me because I knew he was not religious, but here was the effect of Islam upon him.

Another was a woman I met while walking beside a bicycle on an unpaved road on the opposite side of the Nile from Luxor. I was dusty, and somewhat shabbily clothed, and she was an old woman dressed in black from head to toe who walked up, and without a word or glance at me, pressed a coin into my hand so suddenly that in my surprise I dropped it. By the time I picked it up, she had hurried away. Because she thought I was poor, even if obviously non-Muslim, she gave me some money without any expectation for it except what was between her and her God. This act made me think a lot about Islam, because nothing seemed to have motivated her but that.

Many other things passed through my mind during the months I stayed in Egypt to learn Arabic. I found myself thinking that a man must have some sort of religion, and I was more impressed by the effect of Islam on the lives of Muslims, a certain nobility of purpose and largesse of soul, than I had ever been by any other religions or even atheisms effect on its followers. The Muslims seemed to have more than we did.

Christianity had its good points to be sure, but they seemed mixed with confusions, and I found myself more and more inclined to look to Islam for their fullest and most perfect expression. The first question we had memorized from our early catechism had been Why were you created? to which the correct answer was To know, love, and serve God. When I reflected on those around me, I realized that Islam seemed to furnish the most comprehensive and understandable way to practice this on a daily basis.

As for the inglorious political fortunes of the Muslims today, I did not feel these to be a reproach against Islam, or to relegate it to an inferior position in a natural order of world ideologies, but rather saw them as a low phase in a larger cycle of history. Foreign hegemony over Muslim lands had been witnessed before in the thorough going destruction of Islamic civilization in the thirteenth century by the Mongol horde, who razed cities and built pyramids of human heads from the steppes of Central Asia to the Muslim heartlands, after which the fullness of destiny brought forth the Ottoman Empire to raise the Word of Allah and make it a vibrant political reality that endured for centuries. It was now, I reflected, merely the turn of contemporary Muslims to strive for a new historic crystallization of Islam, something one might well aspire to share in.

When a friend in Cairo one day asked me, Why don't you become a Muslim?, I found that Allah had created within me a desire to belong to this religion, which so enriches its followers, from the simplest hearts to the most magisterial intellects. It is not through an act of the mind or will that anyone becomes a Muslim, but rather through the mercy of Allah, and this, in the final analysis, was what brought me to Islam in Cairo in 1977.

Is it not time that the hearts of those who believe should be humbled to the Remembrance of God and the Truth which He has sent down, and that they should not be as those to whom the Book was given aforetime, and the term seemed over long to them, so that their hearts have become hard, and many of them are ungodly? Know that God revives the earth after it was dead. We have indeed made clear for you the signs, that haply you will understand. (Qur'an 57:16–17)

37. **Murad Kalam, "If It Doesn't Kill You First" from** *Outside Magazine*

From Outside Magazine, reprinted with permission of Denise Shannon Literary Agency. "If It Doesn't Kill You First" by Murad Kalam (first published by Outside Magazine). Copyright © 2004.

Murad Kalam was born in Seattle, Washington in 1973 to an American mother and a Jamaican father. He entered Harvard University in 1994 and converted to Islam in his junior year. After graduating from Harvard Law School in 2002, he traveled to Cairo, Egypt on a Fulbright Scholarship. He lives in Washington, DC where he practices law as well as writing poetry and novels. The following article is from Outside Magazine in February 2004. It was also included in the second annual collection of America's Best Travel Writing in 2005 (Houghton Mifflin Company). He narrates his pilgrimage to Mecca in terms that reflect common trends among American Muslims such as sensitivity to a universal Islamic rite, concerns about security, a rejection of terrorism, and an aspiration to solve the tension between American and Islamic values.

From *Outside Magazine*

I WANDER BAREFOOT out of the Grand Mosque through a cruel blanket of Saudi heat, floating in a sea of strangers from almost every country on Earth. It's my third day in the city of Mecca, where I've come to take part in the *hajj*, the annual five-day pilgrimage to some of Islam's holiest places. This trek is required once in the lifetime of every able-bodied Muslim, and I'm one of two million people, part of the largest mass movement of humans on the planet.

The birthplace of Muhammad, the prophet of Islam, born in the sixth century, Mecca sits at the base of the Hejaz Mountains in western Saudi Arabia, forty-six miles east of the Red Sea port of Jidda. To someone watching from atop the thousand-foot peaks that surround the city, we must look like countless insects as we spill out of the high, arching gates of the 3.8-million-square-foot Grand Mosque, the most important religious site in the Islamic world.

Mecca is home to 800,000 gracious people, any of whom will tell you not to worry about your well-being when you're here. "This is Mecca," they say. "No one will harm you." Maybe not, but the less devout might steal from you—I'm barefoot because somebody ran off with my sandals this morning when I removed them, as required, before entering the Grand Mosque to pray.

Meanwhile, it's a fact of hajj life that people die all around. Earlier, I watched the Saudi religious police—the *mutawaeen*, stoic, hard-faced men with henna-dyed beards—carry green-shrouded gurneys holding the bodies of five pilgrims who died today, setting them on the marble floor of the Grand Mosque for funeral prayers.

In one twenty-four-hour period during my pilgrimage, eighty-two hajjis will die. People perish in many ways, from natural causes like heart attacks to unnatural ones like dehydration and trampling.

Trampling is what I'm concerned about at the moment, and with each frantic step I become more worried about my safety. The problem is the hajj's sheer numbers. Despite many improvements, the hajj facilities and infrastructure—which are managed by the House of Saud, the ironfisted royal family that has ruled Saudi Arabia since 1932—haven't expanded to meet the fourfold increase in attendance that has occurred over the past thirty-five years. The result is that people too often wind up in death traps.

In 1990, a stampede in the pedestrian tunnel leading from Mecca to Arafat, a rocky, arid plain twelve miles southeast of Mecca and one of the final way stations of the hajj, killed 1,426 pilgrims. Another 270 were trampled to death four years later at Jamarat, a site just east of Mecca where a ritual called the Stoning of the Devil takes place, and the most crowded of all hajj settings. In 1997, 343 pilgrims burned to death and another 1,500 were injured in a giant fire started by a gas cooker in the tent city of Mina, an encampment a few miles east of Mecca where all pilgrims gather near the end of the hajj.

It's a bizarre sensation, but I keep imagining my own demise, visualizing my shrouded body being carried into the Grand Mosque above the wheeling masses. Every Muslim knows that a believer who dies on this journey is guaranteed a place in paradise. Personally, though, I'd much rather live to tell about it.

Why take this risk? The answer starts with my spiritual beliefs. I've been a Sunni Muslim for nine years. (The Sunnis make up 90 percent of all Muslims but are the minority in Shiite-dominated nations like Iran and Iraq. Sunnis and Shiites differ on major theological matters—like who should have succeeded Muhammad after his death, in A.D. 632.) I was born in Seattle in 1973 to a Jamaican father and an American mother, grew up a lapsed Baptist turned agnostic in Phoenix, and started college in Boston, at Harvard, in 1994.

As an undergrad, I happened upon an English translation of the Koran, the written version of Muhammad's revelations from Allah. I was so floored by its persuasive power that I converted to Islam, stopped drinking, and adopted an Islamic name, Murad Kalam. Like many new converts, I was zealous and naive at first. I bought the fundamentalist line that the cause of all the Muslim world's problems—poverty, corruption, and repression—boiled down to a simple failure to apply the tenets of the religion, and nothing more.

Like every American Muslim, I've had a lot to think about in the past few years. When Al-Qaeda launched its attack on September 11, 2001, I was a third-year law student at Harvard and an aspiring novelist. I had not yet traveled to Muslim countries, but I had made friends from Egypt, Saudi Arabia, and Jordan, and they'd schooled me in the complex realities of Muslim life. While Islam is dear to the majority of Muslims, they said, Koranic law should not be taken as the cure-all for everything. In many Muslim societies, religion was a smoke screen for old-fashioned greed, tyranny, and hypocrisy, as well as numerous distortions of Muhammad's ideas for twisted political goals.

Among the worst examples of that last problem, obviously, is Al Qaeda, which has been a scourge in the United States, Afghanistan, Kenya, Yemen, and, more recently, Turkey and Saudi Arabia itself. Though Saudi Arabia, birthplace of the exiled Osama bin Laden, has been relatively safe from terror in the past, that changed after my pilgrimage, which took place in February 2003. On May 12, 2003, Al-Qaeda truck bombers hit a housing complex in the Saudi capital, Riyadh, killing twenty-six Saudis and foreigners working in the country, eight Americans among them. On November 8, terrorists, probably linked to Al-Qaeda, killed seventeen Arabs in a similar strike.

In the aftermath, Saudi officials have cracked down on terrorism with a fervor that will likely translate into heightened security measures at the 2004 hajj, which runs from

January 31 to February 4. The hajj itself has never been the target of a terror strike, but according to published reports, in a raid carried out not long after the November bombings in Riyadh, the Saudis uncovered a plot by Islamic militants to booby-trap copies of the Koran, allegedly in order to maim and kill pilgrims during the hajj.

The Saudi government has to be worried about terror occurring under its watch, since its role as keeper of the holy places is a major pillar of its legitimacy. The closest thing to such an attack occurred back in November 1979, when a radical cleric named Juhayman ibn Muhammad and hundreds of followers barricaded themselves in the Grand Mosque for two weeks to protest what they saw as political and religious corruption in the House of Saud. Before it was over, dozens of soldiers and more than a hundred of ibn Muhammad's partisans had died in gunfights.

Even though the hajj was not in progress, attacking the Grand Mosque was an incredible blasphemy, and the punishment was swift. *After* their capture, ibn Muhammad and his band were executed in cities and towns throughout Saudi Arabia—dispatched by means of public beheading.

Throughout the international turmoil following 9/11, I remained a devout Muslim, and I found myself torn between my beliefs and my country. I've worried that President George W. Bush has been too heavy-handed in his war against terror, both overseas and in the United States. At the same time, I've felt oddly insulated from any anti-Muslim backlash. Too pedigreed to lose a job, too American-looking to be assaulted, I felt alienated from my fellow Muslims in Boston, some of whom were attacked on the street by angry locals. I was drifting, missing prayers. I worried that I was failing Islam. So, in late 2001, I started thinking about trying the hajj.

To prepare for my trip, I read narratives of pilgrimages to Mecca, beginning with the hajj chapters in *The Autobiography of Malcolm X,* the 1964 book about the political and spiritual quest of the famous black Muslim activist. In older books I found tales of desert caravans, raids by Bedouin clans, near starvation, and hard-won spiritual enlightenment. For 1,500 years the hajj has been the ultimate Muslim adventure. It remains a soul-rousing journey that, I decided, could snap me in to shape.

The hajj itself predates the prophet Muhammad. According to Muslim belief Abraham established it and built the sacred Kaaba—a fifty-foot-tall windowless sanctuary made of black granite—but over time the rites in Mecca degenerated. Pagan Meccans set up 360 idols outside the Kaaba, and Mecca became a center for worshipping cult, tribal, and polytheistic gods.

Muhammad, born in A.D. 570, received his call at age forty and risked his life to establish Islamic monotheism in Mecca. Persecuted and facing imminent assassination for teaching that there is no god but Allah, he fled with his followers to Medina in A.D. 622. Later, after several battles between Muslims and nonbelievers, the Meccans converted to Islam, and the prophet returned to rule. During his final hajj, Muhammad stressed the equality of man, respect for property, and the importance of prayer, fasting, and charity.

The pilgrimage itself is a twenty-five-mile trip, made by bus and on foot that starts and ends in Mecca, with shifting dates determined from year to year by the Islamic lunar calendar. Pilgrims begin arriving two or three weeks ahead of time in Mecca, where they spend several days performing rituals and prayers inside the Grand Mosque. At this point, many hajjis take a multiday side trip to Medina, the oasis city where Muhammad established his first community of followers.

In a transition that marks the official beginning of the hajj, all pilgrims start to converge on Mina, where they camp for the night. The next day they proceed five miles farther east to Arafat, to face the Mount of Mercy, a hill where they meditate on the day of judgment. The hajjis leave Arafat at sunset and walk three miles to the valley of Muzdalifa to camp under the stars. There they pray and collect pebbles, which they'll take to Jamarat the next morning. At Jamarat, two miles northwest of Muzdalifa, hajjis throw stones at three fifty-eight-foot-tall granite pillars, symbolically warding off Satan. After completing this, pilgrims shave their heads or cut off a lock of hair, to mark the end of the hajj. Then they return to Mecca to complete their final rituals inside the Grand Mosque.

Initially, I'd wanted to do all this in the most rigorous way possible. My hope was to take a boat across the Red Sea from Cairo—where I was living for four months while researching my second novel—and then ride horseback from Jidda to Mecca, camping out in the vastness of the Arabian Peninsula.

But after checking in with the Saudi embassy in Washington, D.C., I discovered that the days of romantic pilgrimages were over. The hajj is too dangerous to allow everyone to chart his own course, and under Saudi law, to get a visa, every pilgrim who has the financial resources must make airline and hotel reservations. The embassy passed me on to the well-oiled D.C.-based hajj machine, Grand Travel, where I was informed that not only was a package tour required but also that tours were segregated by nationality.

I would be lumped in with ninety-eight other American Muslims.

Making one last stab, I asked the agent if he would book my flight and let me wing the rest. He laughed. "You want suffering, brother? You'll be suffering enough."

I set off for Saudi Arabia on January 28, 2003. Pilgrims prepare for the hajj by taking a ritual bath and putting on the symbolic robes of *ihram,* thereby entering a spiritual state in which differences of race, wealth, and nationality are erased. My robing took place in a hurry at the Cairo airport, where I followed a pimply faced Egyptian skycap into a dimly lit industrial closet.

"Get naked," he said. For ten Egyptian pounds (two bucks), the young man expertly dressed me in two white sheets, one placed horizontally around my waist, the other over my left shoulder.

Afterward, I jumped on an Egypt Air flight to Jidda. From there I traveled by bus forty-six miles to the Al Shohada Hotel, in Mecca, where I met my tour group. Once in Mecca, hajjis immediately proceed to the Grand Mosque, a massive coliseum that contains the Kaaba, the cube-shaped granite shrine toward which Muslims all over the world direct their daily prayers. Pilgrims are required to circle the Kaaba seven times, counterclockwise, praying as they go. This ritual is called *tawaf.* At the end of the hajj, when they return to Mecca, they must complete the *tawaf* again.

Two nights after I completed my initial *tawaf,* inside the airy, luxurious lobby of the Al Shohada, I got a first look at the American hajjis as we assembled to meet our tour leaders. Studying them, I felt a painful rush of our collective inadequacy. They were a collection of well-meaning people from all walks of life: taxi drivers, salesmen, mailmen, lawyers, doctors, and hotel workers. But they also seemed like a reflection of myself—slightly out of shape, self-conscious in pilgrim garb, clearly a little panicked.

We gathered in a hotel conference room, where Sheik Hussein Chowat, our spiritual adviser, paced before us, fielding questions. He's a squat, bearded, soft-spoken Arab in his forties who teaches Islam in northern Virginia. Here, it was his job to put the fear of

Allah into us, stressing the need to do everything right. "You have to do the hajj carefully," he warned. "If you don't, Allah might not accept it".

Our group leader, Nabil Hamid, a grinning, Egyptian-born chain smoker from the Washington, D.C., area, also in his forties, sat by himself at a nearby table. He was the fixer, solver of the inevitable crises: lost hajjis, broken-down buses, sickness, emotional burnout. He fiddled with his prayer beads while Hussein responded to a question posed by a middle-aged woman, also from Washington, who had completed a hajj in 2002. (Like many pilgrims, this woman had returned to the hajj on behalf of another Muslim who couldn't make the journey.) She mentioned in passing that at the end of her first hajj, she had not completed a final *tawaf* around the Kaaba.

"Sister," Hussein interrupted, "your hajj was invalid."

The woman was stunned. The sheik, with iron certainty, seemed to be telling her she had gone through great expense and weeks of pain for nothing. I wanted to find out the woman's name, but it wouldn't have done any good. I couldn't approach her or talk to her: Personal contact between unrelated women and men is forbidden here.

Now, it's my third day. With a pair of new sandals, I wander down the rolling streets to enter the Grand Mosque and pray. After ten blocks of wading through crowds, I come to the mosque's towering granite minarets, entering alongside stone-faced Turks dressed in olive-green, African women in flowery headdresses, and a gaggle of tiny Indonesians dressed in white cloaks. The whispered prayer of millions sounds like rustling water along a riverbank. The Kaaba rises above the marble floor, and I move closer, meeting the stride of the floating multitudes and chanting along with them.

I exit onto Al Masjid Al Haram, Mecca's main street, which is thick with lame and disfigured beggars. Crying children from Africa kneel on the grimy road; when they don't cry loud enough, their mothers appear from street corners and beat them. One girl has wrapped a gauze bandage around her little brother's head and smudged it with lipstick to mimic a bloody wound.

Tired and starved for a glimpse of the world beyond Mecca, I retire to a cafe in the back of my hotel to watch CNN, hoping to get the latest on the still-pending war between the United States and Iraq. Inside, I run into somebody from my tour group, Aaron Craig, a handsome African-American engineering student from San Diego. Aaron is a recent convert in his late twenties, and he's dressed like a Saudi in a full *jallabeyah* robe—a flowing anklelength gown worn by men. The robe isn't required for the hajj, but Aaron is signaling his burning desire to look 100 percent Muslim.

"You know," he tells me, sipping tea, "I've already seen lots of mistakes made by pilgrims. And the bumping and pushing and nationalism! And you wonder why we don't have Muslim unity."

This is Aaron's first visit to the Middle East. Like me when I converted, he seems convinced that pure application of Islam is the answer to everything.

"People are trying to change the religion, brother," he continues.

"What do you mean?"

"The sellout Muslims in America."

He's talking about moderates, people who live suburban lives, have non-Muslim friends, watch TV.

"Allah's religion is perfect. The sellouts want to say that jihad does not mean jihad.

Meanwhile, Muslims are being attacked in Afghanistan, Chechnya, Palestine. You have to believe in it or you are a disbeliever."

This talk startles me. *Jihad* is a loaded word, referring to both armed resistance in defense of Islam and a private struggle to bolster one's faith. I wonder if he would think I'm a sellout. My jihad has always been intensely personal, concerning prayers, family, success, and finding the peace that lately has eluded me—peace that, so far, continues to elude me during this hajj.

In the evening, when the streets are empty, I call my wife, who's in the United States, from a nearby cabin with pay phones. It's staffed by smart-alecky young Saudis dressed in Western T-shirts shirts and blue jeans. They look like they'd rather be listening to Tupac or dancing in a club—anything but herding us pilgrims around. "Why didn't you tell me the streets are filled with crooks?" I jokingly ask them in Arabic. "My sandals were stolen from the Grand Mosque."

"All Meccans are good, all Muslims are good," one replies robotically. He offers me a Marlboro, one of the few naughty pleasures tolerated in Mecca.

"No," the other declares. "Some Meccans are good. Some are bad."

It's three days later, February 3, and I'm standing in the hallway of the Dallah Hotel with Aaron. We have left Mecca, boarded a bus for Medina, and arrived at sundown, just in time to make the last prayers of the day. The ride here was soothing, with African pilgrims dressed in white walking the road beside us, chanting loudly, "*Labaik, Allah, labaik*" ("Here I am, Allah, here I am"). Medina is an oasis 2 1 0 miles north of Mecca. It's a smaller, more comfortable city, its streets cleaner and less congested.

The hotel is swarming with African-American converts and Kuwaitis. As we prepare to leave for the Prophet's Mosque, Aaron shares a big piece of news: His wife has been offered a position teaching English in Riyadh, and they're thinking of making the move.

"Murad," he says, "the Saudis—what are they like?"

There's a lot I could say about that. I spent a week in Saudi Arabia in 2002, and I was shocked by the restrictiveness of everyday life, where most pleasures, even innocent ones like G-rated movies, are banned. I've known too many American Muslims who studied in Saudi Arabia and found, alongside the unbearable dreariness, the same hypocrisies, vices, and bigotry that they thought they'd left behind.

In the end I say little to Aaron; I'm leery about interfering with his destiny. "The Saudis make loyal friends," I tell him. "But there is no social life here. I think you will miss the States."

Aaron sighs, then laughs. "I don't care," he says. "They've got Kentucky Fried Chicken and Burger King. That's all the culture I need. I just want to hear the call to prayer in the morning."

At twilight, Aaron and I wander down the windy street to the Prophet's Mosque. Set on flat land in the city center, its white granite walls are cast in beautiful greenish light. Six thirty-story minarets ascend from its corners, poking into the night sky. Inside, the shrine is huge, spanning 1.7 million square feet. At prayer time, each row of prostrate men extends nearly a mile.

Inspiring though it is, Medina does little to lift my sagging spirits during the six days we stay here. Aside from the physical discomfort—I'm suffering through my second case of flu, and my body aches from walking—something spiritual is missing. I cannot yet say that I'm feeling any different than before I arrived in Mecca, and I'm disappointed in the way the Saudis manage the whole thing, giving too little attention to safety and security. Not for the first time, I'm wondering if I'm crazy to be here.

After a week of Medina's prayer and quiet, our buses show up again on February 8, a Saturday, to take us about 210 miles to Mina, where all two million hajjis are heading to enact one of mankind's grandest mass rituals, starting tomorrow. Bounded by mountains on two sides, Mina is home to a permanent tent city that sits between the plain of Arafat and Mecca's eastern boundary. It's a small metropolis of 44,000 identical fifteen-foot-high, aluminum-framed tents, placed on a square-mile quadrant. The Jamarat overpass—a huge two-level walkway that leads pilgrims to the three granite pillars representing Satan—sits roughly a mile to the northwest, in the direction of Mecca. A string of mosques borders the tent city in every direction.

We float in to Mina, across the dirt roads between the tents, which are sectioned off by region and country. The bus stops before the entrance to what's called the Egyptian section. Nabil Hamid, our group leader, has placed us in an area called 42/2.

"Remember that number," he says sternly, pointing to a sign. "It's the only way to get back. If you are lost here, you are lost." We find our tent space, a 10,000-square-foot enclosure for fifty men.

After nightfall, Nabil leads us out to the site of Jamar at to show us the mile-long path from the tent and back. Just before we leave, Sheik Ahmed Shirbini, a forty-something Egyptian-born Muslim from Denver who's on his third hajj, issues a warning about the dangers awaiting us at the Jamarat walkway.

"If you lose your sandals, if you drop your money, your sunglasses, do not go back!" he says. "I was here four years ago, and I saw with my own eyes a man who'd dropped his wallet on the overpass trampled to death by the crowds."

Nabil carries a twelve-foot sign that reads U.S.A. We wander across the dark dirt lanes, past patches of paved road where pilgrims sleep on the ground. We turn a corner, walking down a longer road, until we come to the infamous overpass, a mile-long, three-hundred-foot-wide structure. You can get to the three granite pillars from this bridge or an underpass below it. The structure is built to hold 100,000 people, but three times that number will crowd it in the thick of Jamarat. This overload caused a collapse in 1998 that killed 118 pilgrims.

One of our group, a young doctor from Pennsylvania named Shakeel Shareef, points to the street under the bridge. "That's where all the people were killed," he says.

Hearing this, Aaron swallows and his voice goes big. "Allah is all knowing and all-powerful," he says. "If we are supposed to die at Jamarat, it is part of his will. What better place to die?"

But I can see the fear on his face. It's oddly comforting to know that he's as scared as I am.

It's eight o'clock on the morning of February 11, the day I'll perform the Stoning of the Devil ritual, and I'm lost. At the moment, I'm in Mina, walking on a street beneath the mountain valleys, surrounded by exultant pilgrims hustling toward Jamarat. On each side of me, the numberless tents sweep out beneath the mountains.

A lot has happened since this time yesterday. In the morning we left early as our bus raced toward the Mount of Mercy for the nighttime vigil. Hajjis in surgical masks streamed beside us in a fog of exhaust; young boys surfed the hoods of antiquated American school buses, their white robes flapping in the wind.

But this glorious motion didn't last long: We spent much of the day either stuck in traffic or walking around lost, and I got separated twice from my group. At sundown it looked like we might not make Muzdalifa by midnight. Sheik Hussein, our spiritual adviser, informed us that if we didn't get there by then, we would have to layout cash for the sacrifice of a sheep in Mecca, to atone for this failure in the hajj.

When a pilgrim objected to this—shouldn't our group leader, Nabil, have to pay, since he is responsible for getting us around? Sheik Hussein wagged his finger and said, "You do not understand worship! I don't care about the money! This is between you and Nabil! I am here to help you worship Allah!"

In the end we got there, but in these crowds, it's always easy to get lost again. Right now, pushing my way forward in the Mina morning, I have no idea where I am. I have a vague sense that my tent at the Egyptian camp is straight ahead, but Mina is so rambling, its hills so full of identical tents, that I can't be sure. I walk forward, pacing ahead of the crowds of half-sleeping pilgrims.

Two hours pass. When I finally get my bearings, around 10 A.M., I realize that I'm just one street removed from 42/2, but it's hard to get all the way there. Pushing through the crowds is like wading through waist-high water. I am caught on a street congested with pilgrims and tour buses, vans, and trucks on their way to Jamarat. Blocks away, pilgrims are flooding the street from both directions, coming back from Muzdalifa and racing toward Jamarat. Trapped in a hot, heaving crowd, I suffer the most terrifying claustrophobia of my life.

I force my way through the street until it is impossible to take a step forward. Suddenly there's an explosion of human pressure from all sides, and I find myself standing face to face with a small, neatly dressed Iranian hajj leader in wire-rim glasses. The Iranian's eyes go wide as pilgrims on each side of the road begin to rush toward us. Africans are shoving through. Saudi policemen stand on trucks and rooftops, doing nothing as they watch the street below them devolve into madness. Women shout "Stop!" in Farsi and wave their hands, but no one can stop the crowd from crushing in. I cannot move. I can only pray. The crowd erupts in frenzied screaming. A row of middle-aged Iranian women fall over like dominos.

Nigerian pilgrims start pushing through violently. Feeble, veiled women shout the only Arabic words understood by every pilgrim: "*Haram! Haram!*" ("Shame on you!"). Women and small old men are getting trampled in the mud. I find an opening through the maelstrom and hurry to a parked truck. I climb into the truck, my sandals left behind in the street mud, my bare feet burning on the truck bed's hot, rusty metal floor.

Nigerians crawl onto the truck from all sides. I can do little more than watch as screaming Iranian and Nigerian women are crushed on the street beneath us, a sea of white burqas, angled shoulders, crying, pleading faces, the flashing of outstretched arms. I reach down and pull a young Nigerian woman into the truck. Like me, she is crying, her face racked with fear. An old Iranian woman in her face racked with fear. An old Iranian woman in white clings to the Nigerian's waist as I pull her up, her body floating on a wave of white-cloaked women. In another language, she thanks me for saving her life.

And then, in what seems like just a moment, the street is somehow cleared behind us. Women lie moaning in the mud. The truck's engine chugs; it zips forward six or seven blocks down the now-empty street. I watch pilgrims in the distance climbing from the piled bodies to their feet on the muddy, empty road.

I jump off the truck and walk barefoot back to my camp through a cloud of diesel exhaust. The scene of the stampede is six blocks away, shockingly clear. When I return to it, the road has been swept of thirty or forty people who—I can only assume from what I saw—have been badly injured or killed. (I never find out, but the next day I read in the *Saudi Times* that fourteen people died a half-mile away in a different stampede at Jamarat.)

I am angry—angry at the Saudis for permitting such chaos. But beneath my anger, there is also exultation, something electric, happiness to have survived, the clarity that comes from facing death. Around noon, I finally reach 42/2, entering through an iron gate. Sheik Hussein is speaking with a veiled woman from the American group.

"I must talk to you," I tell him, sobbing.

He takes me by the wrist down a concrete path, and we stand in the shade of a fluttering tent. "I was almost killed, Sheik Hussein! There was a stampede in the street. I jumped into a truck. I pulled a woman up. I saved her life. I think people died there."

"It is OK," the sheik says. "It is OK if you touched the woman." "No, no. I was not asking that. I wanted to tell you that I almost died today."

"Well, it is over now," he says, without emotion. Then he leaves me at the tent.

However deadly and frantic Jamarat is, it can't be worse than what I've just seen. Though I haven't slept in thirty-six hours, nothing matters now but completing this hajj. I step inside my tent and stare at my fellow pilgrims lying on a rug. Half of them have already gone to Jamarat and returned. They eat oranges or sleep blissfully on mats in the hot, cramped tent. The rest are waiting until evening, when Jamarat is safer.

I decide to go right now. I have lost all my fear. Along with Shakeel Shareef, the Pennsylvania doctor, and a few other pilgrims, I march to Jamarat in the midday heat, collecting pebbles along the way. The streets are congested, but we weave through the crowds. We watch a pilgrim coming back from Jamarat. He is bandaged and bleeding from the head, his *ihram* robes covered in blood.

We wander into a crowd of more than a million people. A couple hundred thousand pilgrims are striding on the overpass above. "Everyone is taking the overpass," says Shakeel, pointing. "The bottom level is safer."

We follow him, making our way through the rushing crowds to the smallest pillar to throw our seven stones, but we are too far away. Shakeel is not like so many other careless pilgrims. He will not throw at the first opportunity; he waits until he is certain he will not hit another person. I watch him, banged upon by rushing hajjis, measuring his throw, stopping, moving closer. I stand behind him, my hand on his shoulder, so that we stay together.

"We have to get closer," Shakeel shouts. "If we throw from here, we'll only be hitting pilgrims. Hurry." We link arms and march into a wall of pilgrims. Hundreds of tiny pebbles pound against the sides of a granite pillar in little bursts of dust.

Right after Shakeel throws his last pebble, he is almost pushed down by a throng of Pakistanis. I grab him and pull him away from the scene. We run through the riotous crowd until we are outside again, safe, in the sun.

As we approach our camp, I turn and watch the arcing, sunwashed, overcrowded Jamarat overpass receding behind the tents. As I wander back, I realize I've made peace with the hajj and with this rough, beautiful, holy place. Everything I have suffered seems almost necessary, because I am overcome with an unutterable serenity. How is it that, by some miracle, so many people can exist in the same place at once?

We reach our camp, shave our heads, shower, change out of our *ihram* robes into *jalla-beyah* robes, roll out our matts, and sleep hard on the Mina dirt.

38. **Michael Wolfe, "Michael Wolfe, United States, 1990" from** *One Thousand Roads to Mecca: Ten Centuries of Travelers Writing about the Muslim Pilgrimage*

New York: Grover Press, 1997, pp. 523–549.

Michael Wolfe was born in 1945 to a Jewish father and a Christian mother in the United States. After spending several years in West Africa during the late 1980s, he converted to Islam. Wolfe has written travel accounts, fiction, and poetry. The following is an excerpt from One Thousand Roads to Mecca: Ten Centuries of Travelers Writing about the Muslim Pilgrimage, which is a collection of Muslim accounts of the Hajj from the eleventh to the twentieth centuries.

I [now possessed] an overview of the Hajj different from the Hajj I had imagined, and I wanted to fix it while my thoughts were fresh. I began to fill a notebook with summations. From California, I had viewed the Hajj as a journey to a physical destination. In fact, the Hajj was protean, all process. It surprised me now to see how off I'd been. In the West, the notion of pilgrimage centered on going, on reaching, on arrival. Nailing this moribund image to the Hajj was a mistake, like claiming that going home to dinner began with getting off work and ended when you reached the porch—omitting any mention of the meal.

Reaching Mecca was only a beginning. The goal of the Hajj was to perform it well. The rites were hard, sometimes unfathomable-like living. Yet they provided a counterweight to the usual view of life as a dog-and-cat fight. Elsewhere, except at the best of times, every person looked out for himself. During the Hajj, people looked out for each other. The Hajj is a shared rite of passage. I saw it through the eyes of others as much as through my own. In that way, it was like an act of love...

I especially admired the way the sweat and the symbols flowed together. By an act of imagination and exertion, a spiritual rite of some duration fulfilled a private quest. For all its public aspects, the experience was intensely personal. By giving the pilgrim a chance to choose his moment, it provided a service missing in the West since the days of the medieval palmers: it offered a climax to religious life.

39. **Shaykh Kabir Helminski, "Islam: A Broad Perspective on Other Faiths" from** *Taking Back Islam: American Muslims Reclaim Their Faith*

Copyright Rodale Inc., Beliefnet, Inc., 2002. Reprinted with permission of Kabir Helminski.
The following two entries, "Islam: A Broad Perspective on Other Faiths" and "Mom Raised Me as a Zionist," as well as "You Seem So Intelligent. Why Are You a Muslim?" are chapters in the book Taking Back Islam: American Muslims Reclaim Their Faith, edited by Michael Wolfe (for a biography, see the preface to Primary document 38) (for more information on Taking Back Islam see the preface to Primary document 32).
Kabir Helminski is an American-born Sufi shaykh in the Mevlevi Order of Muslims. He was born in Jersey City, New Jersey in 1947. He received his M.A. in psychology from Selcuk University in Konya, Turkey. He was the director of Threshold Books, which publishes primarily Sufi literature, from 1980–1999. He also toured with the Whirling Dervishes of Turkey from 1994–2000. He has written several works on the poet Rumi as well as on Sufism. His view of religious pluralism reflects the dominant opinion of American Sufis.

A SUFI POET AND SCHOLAR FINDS RELIGIOUS PLURALISM NOT ONLY ACCEPTABLE BUT INHERENT IN ISLAM

My first encounter with Islam was not in a mosque, or through a book, but by meeting a Muslim. I don't mean a nominal Muslim, but someone who was actually in the "state" of *Islam,* which literally means the peace that comes from submission to God's will. I definitely was not looking for a "religion," but I was looking for what I imagined to be Truth or Reality, and I felt that Reality in the presence of this person. In a sense, you could say that Islam is not a formulation, an ethical system, a practice, or even a revelation as much as it is a relationship to the divine.

The five pillars of Islam-bearing witness that there is one Absolute Being, worship, fasting, charity, pilgrimage-are a means to establish that relationship and are common to all sacred traditions. But that essential, conscious relationship with a spiritual dimension is the heart of the matter.

So orient yourself to the primordial religion, the innate nature upon which Allah has created humanity, without altering Allah's creation. That is *the authentic religion, but the great majority do not comprehend.*

Turn in repentance to Him and remain conscious of Him: be constant in prayer and do not be among those who worship other than God, those who split apart the Religion and create sects-each group separately rejoicing in what it has! (Qur'an 30:30–32)

This verse suggests a broad perspective, as it refers to the timeless monotheism associated with the Prophet Abraham. This primordial religion corresponds to the human nature instilled by God. The purpose of religion, therefore, is to safeguard the human soul from "altering God's creation," from being less than human. It is possible, then, to make a distinction between that primordial religion or essential Islam, the authentic core of all revealed traditions, and the Islam practiced by the community of Muhammad, which is just one possible manifestation of humanity's primordial religion.

It is from the perspective of this primordial religion that pluralism must be accepted. Muslims may believe that their faith corresponds most truly to that "first" religion, but this is not sufficient reason to deny that other religions offer an approach to God. *For each one of you (several communities) We have appointed a Law and a Way of Life. If God had so willed, He would have made all of you one community, but He has not done so that He may test you in what He has given you; so compete in goodness. To God shall you all return and He will tell you (the Truth) about what you have been disputing.*(5:48)

This suggests that God has not granted a spiritual monopoly to anyone religion. Competition in virtue reduces the chances that we will become complacent and lazy; competition in goodness increases the likelihood of humility and cooperation. *To every people have We appointed ways of worship which they observe. Therefore let them not dispute with thee, but bid them to thy Sustainer for thou art on the right way.* (22:67–69)

These ways of worship have been established by God Himself Muhammad is not asked to convert people, but to establish a harmonious relationship with them by acknowledging one Sustainer. This verse in particular seems to guide the Prophet Muhammad to a cooperative relationship with other faiths. The Islamic worldview accepts other faiths, guaranteeing the right of other religious communities to follow their own revealed tradition. As the Qur' an says, "There shall be no coercion in religion."

RIGHTING THE MISUSE OF THE QUR'AN

Now let us turn to some verses of the Qur' an that have been misused by those who try to turn Islam into a narrow, exclusive belief system.

Indeed, with God the essential religion is submission, And it was only because of envy that the People of the Book developed other views, and only after knowledge had come to them, but whoever denies the signs of God, with God the reckoning is swift. (3: 19)

Here we have one of the most important passages in the Qur' an, one that deserves careful reflection. Its context is a discussion of the essential elements of faith. The passage begins with a confirmation of the authenticity of books revealed to Moses and Jesus, referring specifically to the Torah and the Gospel. Within the context of this acknowledgement of religious pluralism, humankind is given a clear warning: "Those who reject the signs of God will suffer the severest penalty" (3:4). What does it mean to reject the signs of God? It is said that various things distract us from recognizing the signs of God: women and sons, heaps of gold and silver, fine horses (or nowadays cars), and real estate. Our *exclusive* preoccupation with the things of the world blinds us to the signs.

Submission, here, should therefore be understood as "islam" with a small "i"—a state of being, a kind of relationship with God—rather than the specific forms of religion we understand as "Islam" with a capital "I."

A friend of mine was visiting a Sufi lodge, or *tekkye,* in Bosnia. It was an enchanting location under an immense rock near a beautiful river. My friend asked a young man there how old the center was. "Two thousand years old," was the reply. "How could that be?" my friend asked. "We here in Bosnia have been practicing Islam even before the coming of the Prophet Muhammad," the boy replied.

Therefore, a verse like—And *whoso seeks a religion other than islam,* it *will not be accepted from him, and he will be at a loss* in *the Hereafter.* (3: 85)—needs to be understood in light of others such as the following: *We bestowed from* on *high the Torah,* in *which there* is *guidance and light. . . . If any fail* to *judge by what Allah has revealed, they are unbelievers* (kufar). (5:44) In other words, Jews who follow the Torah are believers.

Finally, we have what may be considered a definitive statement on the subject in this verse: *Those who believe (Muslims), the Jews, the Christians, and the Sabaeans—whosoever believe* in *God and the Last* Day *and do good deeds, they shall have their reward from their Lord, shall have nothing* to *fear, nor shall they grieve.* (2:62)

Of course there are those who claim that this verse has been "abrogated" by verses like the previous one: *And whoso seeks a religion other than islam. . .* Nevertheless, Islamic commentators say that a verse can't be abrogated if it applies to a promise. Abrogation is permissible only with legal judgments, which may be altered because of changing times.

What principles of conduct and communication are proposed by the Qur' an in relation to people of other faiths? Without a doubt, it is an approach based on courtesy and gentleness: *And do not argue with the followers of earlier revelation otherwise than* in *a* most *kindly manner* (29:46; cf 17:53; 16:125–28

Even in the most extreme cases, where it is believed that people are following beliefs that are out of accord with reality: *But do not revile those whom they invoke instead of God, lest they revile God* out *of spite, and* in *ignorance: for We have* made *the deeds of every people* seem *fair* to *them. In time, they* must *return* to *their Lord, and then* He *will make* them *understand*

When the great Sufi Jalaluddin Rumi heard of two people arguing about religion, he said, "These people are involved in a very trivial affair. Instead of arguing which of their religions is best, they could be considering how far each of them are from the teachings of their own prophets."

It should be clear that Islam is in a unique position to act as a reconciling force among different faiths because Islam has built into its very nature the tolerance and respect for all religious communities and sacred traditions.

Furthermore, we are in a position to help realign these other communities with the original spirit of revelation. I can say that from my own experience, although I was raised as a Catholic, my affection for and understanding of Jesus only deepened through my Islamic perspective; I have heard others say the same. Islam can help them to understand the extent to which man-made beliefs have led to irrational theologies and self-serving institutions. We must safeguard our own religion from the same corruption. Anyone who thinks that these reflections contribute to a weakening of faith is, in my opinion, missing the point. It is precisely because of this perspective that I can call myself a Muslim. What is faith (or *iman)* if not the widest possible perspective on our lives, and what is disbelief or denial *(kufr)* if not a contraction upon our own narrow, egoistic concerns? It is because of this sweeping panorama of faith that I can take the Divine Revelation given to Muhammad into my heart and try to walk in his footsteps.

40. Mas'ood Cajee, "Mom Raised Me as a Zionist" from *Taking Back Islam: American Muslims Reclaim Their Faith*

Copyright Rodale Inc., Beliefnet, Inc., 2002. Reprinted with permission of Mas'ood Cajee.
Mas'ood Cajee is of Indian descent but was born in 1974 in South Africa. His family moved to the United States when he was ten years old. He received a B.S. in Chemistry and a B.A. in English Literature from the University of Oklahoma in 1996. He then graduated from the University of Oklahoma College of Dentistry in 2000. He received his Master of Public Health degree from the Harvard University School of Public Health in 2003. He also is a founding board member of the Muslim Peace Fellowship and served on the National Council of the Fellowship of Reconciliation. This text illustrates the kind of dialogue between Muslims and Jews that is possible in the American context. For a description of Taking Back Islam see Primary document 32.

A WRITER WHO HAS BROKEN BARRIERS HIMSELF CALLS FOR SPIRITUAL BREAKTHROUGHS BETWEEN JEWS AND MUSLIMS.

My mom raised me as a Zionist. I'm not kidding. In fact, I made my first Muslim friend only when I went to college. Let me explain.

As a second grader, I broke the color barrier at a white private school in Apartheid-era Johannesburg, South Africa. On the first day of school, my mom gave me some motherly advice: Find the smartest kid and befriend him. That smartest kid happened to be Marc Weinberg, a Jewish bloke with brown hair and freckles whose parents were involved in the Johannesburg theatre scene.

Marc and I even collaborated on a small stage production of our own. We put on a play for our class that reenacted a battle in the Crusades. I wrote a script, and Marc made costumes with his dad's help. I think I played Salahuddin to Marc's Richard the LionHearted; we ended with a mock swordfight for Jerusalem. The gentile kids loved it, even though our acting was atrocious, and we hadn't completely memorized our badly written lines.

Soon, our mothers became friends. One day, Marc's mom gave mine a manual on raising kids compiled by a South African Zionist women's group. My mom claims she heeded the book's advice in raising me—and so I can claim that my mom raised me as a Zionist.

No, she didn't teach me to sing "Hatikvah," and I can't read Hebrew, but I do like bagels and lox, I can pronounce "Hanukkah" correctly, and I once painted stage backdrops for a *Fiddler on the Roof* production.

More important, for my mother, the Zionist women's manual embodied Jewish values that Muslims in my family and community admired: an emphasis on education and the quest for learning, strong family ties, and community networks, mutual assistance, and discipline.

Muslims respected Jews for the way they helped each other, stuck together, got educated, and were paragons of success. Indeed, Muslims yearned for the day when our community could achieve the same.

At the same time, Muslims despised both the dark side of Zionism and the cozy relationship Israel had with the Apartheid regime. The same year Marc and I staged our play, Israel invaded Lebanon, seeking to crush the PLO. Ariel Sharon, who masterminded the invasion, was responsible for the massive bloodletting at Sabra and Shatilla, the Palestinian refugee camps outside Beirut.

In South Africa, unrest was growing in the townships. Stonethrowing black kids our age were being killed in the streets or detained and tortured. The guns used to kill them included Galil assault rifles, licensed to South Africa by Israel. Just as in the Occupied Territories today, the funerals for those killed became mass protests that resulted in more killing. Funerals thus came to sustain the unrest, as a new mass movement emerged out of cemeteries, community halls, churches, and mosques. Amazingly, the white students at the school I attended were oblivious to the rising tide of struggle against Apartheid. Marc and I spoke neither about the color divide that separated us under Apartheid nor about our religious identities. He knew that I was Muslim and nonwhite, and I knew that he was Jewish and white.

My mother, for her part, continued to raise me like a good Zionist Jewish mother.

When I was ten years old, my family immigrated to the United States. Following my mom's wisdom, I befriended the smartest kid again: a Jewish boy named Elie Finegold.

Once, I spent a Shabbat with Elie and his family. At the Friday dinner, Elie recited prayers in Hebrew, and we broke challah and had some good chow. We prayed for peace in the Middle East; Leon Klinghoffer had just been killed by Palestinian hijackers on the Achille Lauro. After dinner, all the Finegold kids put on a talent show. Elie and I did a hard-rock air-guitar version of "Twinkle Twinkle Little Star."

The next morning, I accompanied the Finegolds to the Shabbat service at the Herzl Ner Tamid synagogue in an affluent suburb of Seattle.

The rabbi spoke about Abraham and his two sons, Ishmael and Isaac. I don't know if the rabbi knew that a little Muslim boy was sitting in the temple pews that day, because he laid it out. There was a simple Biblical explanation to the conflict in the Middle East. The Arabs, descendents of Ishmael, were cursed and cunning. Being labeled cursed and cunning by the Torah is big stuff; you obviously can't have peace with such a people.

I think the Finegolds pretended not to hear what their rabbi was saying because we didn't bring it up afterward. I was unsettled and scarred, of course. I had an epiphany of sorts. I had been "othered" royally.

Since Ariel Sharon ignited the al-Aqsa intifada on September 28, 2000, Muslims attending their *jum'a* congregation prayers every Friday have also been subjected to the same vitriol from our imams and *khatibs* (preachers). The Jews are cursed; the Jews are cunning. No *peace is possible when you base your very theology* against it.

The Israelis, with their Bell AH-1 Cobra and McDonnell Douglas AH-64 Apache helicopter gunships firing Hughes Towantitank missiles at Palestinians with stones and 1950s rifles, may have an overwhelming asymmetry in their weapons. But, judging their rhetoric, rabbis and imams share an eerie symmetry in their pulpit demagoguery.

Breakthroughs on the spiritual and theological fronts by Muslims and Jews need to be achieved before peace can be had and violence quelled. Political handshakes and deals in the absence of serious spiritual dialogue and an earnest quest for justice will be meaningless.

Until a mode of peace and understanding between religious Jews and religious Muslims of all stripes can be brokered, peace will be no more substantive than a mirage in the Negev desert.

I know real peace is possible because I know that Muslims and Jews have lived together in peace for centuries before and because many of my own best memories of my childhood were spent with my Jewish friends.

Today, however, real peace will be attained only through atonement, reconciliation, and—above all—through the brave leadership and scholarship of wise and sincere Jews and Muslims.

Real peace will come, then, when the recognition of the dispossession of 1948, respect for the sacred geography of Jerusalem and other sites, and the right of return of the refugees are accepted and reconciled.

Real peace will come when the arrogant, demonic dimensions of Zionism and Palestinian nationalism are forever exorcised.

Real peace will come when the Qur'an and *hadith,* and the Torah and Talmud, become the blueprints of peace and coexistence that they are.

Until then, Israeli violence, Palestinian blood, a phony peace process, and sermons about the cursed and the cunning will prevail.

I know; I was raised as a Zionist. *Allahu 'alam.* And God knows best.

41. Ingrid Mattson, "How Muslims Use Islamic Paradigms to Define America" from *Religion and Immigration: Christian, Jewish, and Muslim Experiences in the United States*

Haddad, Y., J. Smith, and J. Esposito (eds). Religion and Immigration: Christian, Jewish, and Muslim Experiences in the United States. Lanhma, Maryland: Rowman & Littlefield Publishers, 2003, pp. 199–215. Reprinted with permission of Rowland and Littlefield Publishers, Inc.

Ingrid Mattson was born in Ontario, Canada in 1963. She received her B.A. from University of Waterloo in 1987 and her Ph.D. from the University of Chicago in 1999. She converted to Islam at the end of her undergraduate studies. She teaches Islamic law and history at Hartford Seminary in Connecticut. In 2006, she became the first woman to be elected president of the Islamic Society of North America (ISNA), the largest Muslim organization in the United States. In this article, she identifies two major paradigms for Muslim interaction with American society: resistance or selective engagement.

Muslims who immigrate to the United States are a vastly diverse group. Most Muslim immigrants to the United States, however, come from the historically majority Muslim lands of Asia and Africa. Still, the cultural, linguistic, and economic diversity of this group is vast, and in these respects, many Muslims may share more with the non-Muslim American majority than with other Muslim immigrants. Some will have been educated in the English language, while others will know no English at all. Some Muslim immigrants coming from large cities will be very familiar with modern technology and business culture; others will have lived in isolated villages, subsisting mostly on local agricultural production. All Muslim immigrants, however, have in common the fact that they do not share the Christian religious tradition of the majority of Americans. Being part of a religious minority will be a new experience for most of these Muslims and will necessitate, or at least stimulate, some thoughts about the relationship between state, society, and religion. Even those generally uninterested in religious matters may be pressed to articulate a position on this subject by the questioning of non-Muslim Americans, who assume that religious identity is paramount for all Muslims. Stereotypes about Muslims being hostile to "the West" will force many Muslim immigrants to explore their religious texts and traditions to counter or, perhaps, support such assumptions.

Of course, attempts to define the relationship between Muslim and non-Muslim communities began with the birth of the first Muslim community in seventh-century Arabia. The Qur'an, the sacred text of Islam, mentions a number of different religious and political communities that were in existence at the rise of Islam. Some of these communities, such as those of the polytheists and the unbelievers, are characterized as having been irreconcilably opposed to the message of Islam and the existence of a Muslim polity. This stance necessitated a particular response from Muslims-that of resistance and opposition. Other communities, such as those of the Christians and the "People of the Book" (a broader category that also includes Christians), are characterized as sharing important beliefs and values with Muslims. With such communities, the Qur'an seems to encourage interaction and cooperation. Consequently, the Qur'an plays an important role in defining the limitations and possibilities for a shared identity between Muslims and other faith communities and political entities. Other normative sources for defining such interaction include the biography of the Prophet (sirah), independent reports about normative statements he made on this topic (hadith), the decisions of early Muslim rulers, and the legal arguments of jurists over the century.

For theologians, legal scholars, and political scientists concerned with the place of Muslims in the contemporary world, the need to understand and define the proper relationship between Muslims and other faith communities has assumed a sense of urgency. No one engaged in this process of definition and categorization is indifferent to the implications of their efforts, and each is aware that their definitions, if accepted, would yield a particular kind of society. Coming from historically predominant Muslim areas of Asia, Africa, and Eastern Europe, people such as Abdel Wahhab El-Affendi, Farid Esack, Abdullahi an-Naim, Sayyid Qutb, Rashid Ghannouchi, Prince Hasan of Jordan, and Alija Izetbegovic, as well as other politicians, activists, human rights advocates, and scholars, argue for a specific social/political order through their definitions.[1] Whatever definition these individuals offer, they know that it must at least appear to be authentically grounded in the Qur'an and Islamic tradition. Without this, the majority of Muslims will be unconvinced.

It should not be surprising, given the importance of defining communal identity in Muslim history, that this process of definition and categorization is being applied to America itself. In order to understand their role in America, Muslims need to define not only Islam but also America. Muslims need to place America in its proper theological and legal category so they can determine what kind of relationship is possible and desirable for them to have with this country. Whether or not integration initially seems like a desirable goal, this process will be affected by the immigrant's race, ethnicity, financial means, linguistic ability, and, most important for our study, what religious paradigms are available to them to interpret their particular experience with America.

Prior to categorizing and defining, however, is knowing. Even before immigration, any Muslim man or woman will know something about America. Such knowledge is dependent largely on their level of education, their facility with the English language, and their level of access to modern communication technology. Satellite dishes and the Internet permit access to American self-presentations to augment or even undermine official depictions of news events in countries where communications are state controlled. Although this is not a new phenomenon—the Voice of America has been operating for this purpose for decades—there is no doubt that new technologies are far more popular, accessible, and effective. At the same time, even the most sophisticated American self-promotion pales beside the visceral and intense firsthand encounters Muslims in many countries have had with American military might. "Smart bombs" and U.S. Marines carry powerful messages that usually outweigh the effect of CNN and Peace Corps volunteers.

So how might Muslims define America? Is it a hegemonic state with a will to power that knows no boundaries in international relations? Or is it a Judeo-Christian country, a country founded on strong religious and moral princples? Is America a secular nation-state in which religion is marginalized? Is it a hedonistic, materialistic culture that destroys family and community values? Any one of these definitions may seem accurate to certain individuals, and each definition demands a different response from the Muslims to whom it is Muslim communities are scattered across the United States, and each one is in a constant state of transition. Although we can identify different waves of immigrants into various communities and trace some continuity over generations, every day brings new Muslim immigrants to the United States. Of course, changes in attitude are found not only between generations but within individuals as well. Muslims, like all other human beings, are engaged in a continual process of positioning and defining themselves in relationship to others. People need to choose and to choose again, as long as they live, how they will be in the world. Continual self-definition is one of the distinct needs of the human condition. The definitions of America that will be reviewed in this chapter, therefore, should not be considered fixed and unchangeable for any particular Muslim community, much less for any particular Muslim individual.

I also need to stress that the paradigms I discuss may be effective at very different levels. Obviously, religious paradigms will have a minimal effect on Muslims who have had little contact with religious discourse or for those who have an explicitly secular orientation. For others, particularly those who have sustained high contact with a religious discourse, these paradigms may have great import. Further, we should not belittle the role that non-Muslim Americans and political developments play in defining America to Muslims. The way Muslims define America will necessarily depend on what aspects of this country non-Muslim Americans promote and endorse ideologically, both in public policy and in their everyday encounters with Muslims.

Given the diversity of the Muslim community and its varied experiences, it is no surprise that there is no singular understanding of its relationship to America. However, the different responses can be grouped into three general categories: paradigms of resistance, paradigms of embrace, and paradigms of selective cooperation. Although I have chosen to group the paradigms according to the position in which they place Muslims with respect to America, it must be understood that the bases for taking similar positions can vary greatly. This will depend primarily on what is considered the essence of American identity. For example, a definition of America can be based, among other things, on its Constitution, on its body of positive laws, on its leadership, or on its culture and customs. The appropriate Islamic paradigm for understanding America consequently may be historical, juridical, or theological. This is important because a historical paradigm, for example, may be more or less open to revision than a theological or juridical paradigm.

PARADIGMS OF RESISTANCE

Most traditional seminaries in the Muslim world place a great deal of emphasis on the study of the sacred law, the Shari'ah. In the Arab world, such seminaries, such as al-Azhar in Cairo, have been affected by modernist Islamic movements and teach from textbooks that, although rooted in classical thought, were written in the modern period. In other areas of the Muslim world, particularly in South Asia, many seminaries rely on "classical texts" written hundreds of years ago. In some of these texts, Muslim jurists used the term "abode of peace" to signify those geographical areas in which the sacred law of Islam was applied.[2] In opposition, the term "abode of disbelief" signified a place governed by any other system of law. According to some jurists, such a place was also an "abode of war:' that is, a state or region that must eventually be brought under Islamic sovereignty. In traditional Islamic seminaries, there has been a tendency to apply this medieval definition to modern nation-states. Since by these definitions America cannot be considered an abode of Islam or peace, the natural conclusion is that it is an abode of disbelief. Whether or not America is also an abode of war is a matter for Muslim states to decide, for warfare is the prerogative of the state. For individual Muslims, however, travel to an abode of disbelief can legally be undertaken only when it is absolutely necessary, and the individual should return to Islamic territory as soon as possible. Those Muslim immigrants to America who are influenced by these medieval juridical concepts will obviously strongly resist integration, for America can be defined only in absolute negative terms.

This medieval bifurcation of the world, however, does not have great relevance for most Muslim immigrants to America. Many are probably not even aware of these concepts, and others certainly do not consider the lands they fled to have been abodes of peace. Nevertheless, although many Muslim immigrants may not be pleased with the lands they left behind, some regret having been compelled, by political or economic circumstances, to come to America. This is because, for some of these Muslims, American culture is seen through the very negative paradigm of the *jahiliyyah*.

The term *al-jahiliyyah* occurs in the Qur'an and was used by Muslims of the Prophet's generation to designate the pre-Islamic Arabian society whose customs and practices they were rejecting in favor of a new religious and social order. Linguistically signifying both "ignorance" and "impetuosity," *al-jahiliyyah* was used in the sense of "the bad old days" of paganism, lawlessness, and the oppression of the weak by the strong. In the modern era, the term has been revived by Muslim activists who apply it both to political regimes they consider oppressive and to cultures they consider pagan and hedonistic. *Jahili* society is irreconcilably opposed to a society based on obedience to God's commands, that is, an Islamic society.

Sayyid Qutb, an Egyptian writer who was executed in 1966 by the Nasser regime for his political opposition, was particularly influential in popularizing the notion that all modern political systems are completely dominated by *jahili* concepts, practices, and institutions. He believed that any interaction with such a system will inevitably force a believer to compromise his faith and to collaborate with forces opposed to godliness. The only choice for believers, therefore, is to isolate themselves from such a system. In Qutb's words, "We must ... free ourselves from the clutches of *jahili* society, *jahili* concepts, *jahili* traditions and *jahili* leadership. Our mission is not to compromise with the practices of *jahili* society, nor can we be loyal to it. *Jahili* society, because of its *jahili* characteristics, is not worthy to be compromise with."[3] The ultimate aim of such isolation is to strengthen the Muslim so that he or she is able to change the jahili society "at its very roots." Any compromise with this type of a society will result only in superficial changes to a system that is essentially corrupt and misguided.

Qutb does not provide many details about the nature of jahili society in modern times or many details about the structure of a pious or Islamic society. His language is most powerful because it emotively evokes a cosmic struggle between good and evil and enrolls Muslims into a diverse project aimed at creating a just world order. The struggle between *jahili* society and Islam remains today a compelling paradigm for many Muslims.

When Muslims immigrate to America, this paradigm of *jahili* society, combined with the common immigrant pattern of seeking out those from one's homeland, can create a strong tendency toward isolationism. Some Muslim immigrants feel no need to even venture outside their religious communities to be convinced that they must avoid interaction with the dominant culture. Not only is it enough that they are Muslim in a country that lacks an Islamically oriented political and juridical system (many Muslims would say that most historically Muslim countries also lack this in the contemporary world), but America does not even have the ameliorating influence of a dominant Muslim culture. For Muslim immigrants with a superficial knowledge of American constitutional principles, the vulgarities of popular American political culture alone are enough to prove the truth of Qutb's words and sentiments. Other immigrants, uninterested in politics, have only to look to popular culture in general to be convinced that American society is thoroughly *jahili*. The attack on the American entertainment industry from a religious standpoint by non-Muslim Americans is further proof for Muslims who otherwise would be uninterested in the opinions of persons.

Another Islamic paradigm that is used as a basis for resistance to participation in American politics and society is the story of Pharaoh. In the Qur'an, Pharaoh is the archetypal ruler whose will to power knows no bounds. In his arrogance, Pharaoh rejects the idea that he is accountable to any morality, law, or god, and he follows only his desire. The worldly effect of his refusal to submit to God is the oppression of believers. The Qur'an states, "He was arrogant—he and his armies—on the earth without a right. Did they think that they would not have to return to Us (God)?"[4]

For asylum seekers from Iraq, forced to flee their homeland after it had been devastated by relentless American bombing, and for refugees from Palestine, who see billions of American dollars behind the might of the Israeli experience may temper such an understanding, especially when on arrival in the United States they begin new lives and start to benefit from educational and social services. They find jobs, buy homes, and even make friends with Americans. Their view of America might begin to change, or they may at least begin to distinguish between American foreign and domestic policies. At this point, the neighborhood in which they live and their economic opportunities greatly effect how their definition of America evolves.

If such Muslim immigrants come to know and understand the grievances of any African American Muslims with the history and domestic policies of the United States, they may continue to see this country as hostile toward Muslims. This is not to say that all African American Muslims see more bad than good in is country. Indeed, there are many African American Muslims who make great efforts to highlight the benefits of American constitutionalism and democracy to their immigrant brothers and sisters. However, some African American Muslims, like some non-Muslim Americans, have well-grounded and sophisticated critiques of the American political and economic system. The long history of slavery and racism under which African Americans suffered is an experience that some Muslim immigrants relate to their own history of European colonialism and imperialism. These immigrants may well understand Samory Rashid's argument that such oppression must be faced by Muslims with resistance.[5]

We should expect such arguments to be reinvigorated after the recent rapprochement between the Muslim American Society of W. D. Mohammed and the Nation of Islam under Louis Farrakhan. Farrakhan's characterization of racism, however, with its emphasis on black/white duality, seems to repel those immigrant Muslims who are more concerned with cultural and religious oppression. Nevertheless, immigrant Muslims need only look back to the early days of the Prophet Muhammad's mission to find a paradigm of black struggle against oppression in the name of righteousness. African slaves were among the earliest Muslims who suffered for their faith. The story of the African slave Bilal being tortured by the rulers of Mecca for his conversion to Islam is one that all Muslims learn in childhood.[6] Consequently, as long as many African American Muslims continue to feel that the American political system fails them, it will be difficult to convince many immigrant Muslims otherwise.

PARADIGMS OF EMBRACE

There is no doubt that many Muslim immigrants come to see the United States as their new home and their adopted country. For many, the theological and legal implications of their dual loyalties to their religion and to their country are never brought to consciousness. Muslim leaders in the United States are only beginning to seriously examine the theoretical bases for Muslim American identity. This examination has been necessitated by the claims both of some non-Muslims, such as Steve Emerson, the notorious public critic of Islam and Muslims, and of some Muslims, such as members of the caliphate revivalist group lab ut-Tahrir,[7] that a real Muslim believer can never honestly express loyalty to the American Constitution. Muslims, these critics claim, can never agree to follow any law other than Islamic law. The Qur'an states very dearly, "Whoever does not judge on the basis of what God has revealed, they are rebellious transgressors."[8]

In response to such claims, many Muslim leaders point out that the Prophet Muhammad himself not only allowed emigration but even sent some of his followers to live in a non-Muslim country and required them to obey that country's ruler. This ruler was a Christian, the negus of Ethiopia, who gave refuge to a group of early Muslim converts fleeing the persecution of the chiefs of Mecca. The story of this flight and the refuge offered to the Muslims is an important and often-told episode in the life of the Prophet Muhammad.[9] As a paradigm for cooperation between Muslims and Christians, it therefore has a strong emotive effect. Further, the fact that many Muslim immigrants to

American have taken flight from oppressive governments or situations of conflict and are welcomed by kind and tolerant Christians makes this an exceedingly suitable precedent for Muslims in America.

Nevertheless, although America can be embraced as a haven by virtue of the Ethiopian paradigm, the story also imposes limits on how deeply Muslims can assimilate to American society. The Muslim refugees to Ethiopia were guests of the ruler; they were not his loyal subjects, and there is no evidence that they participated in state institutions.

Another example cited as evidence that Muslims can participate in the ruling apparatus of a non-Muslim country is the Qur'anic story of the Prophet Joseph's experience in Egypt. Joseph himself asks the king of Egypt to place him in charge of the country's grain storehouses, and God says, "In this way we gave power to Joseph in the land."[10] This is clear evidence to some Muslims that there is no obstacle to their participation in American political and administrative institutions as long as they believe that they can effect some benefit. Others argue that this example is not normative for Muslims because the Prophet Joseph lived before the Prophet Muhammad delivered God's final message to humans. Although the theological message of all prophets was the same, their involvement in worldly affairs and the legislation they were required to enforce differed. Consequently, the Prophet Joseph remains a contested paradigm for Muslim integration to American society.

Among the most interesting efforts to permit Muslims a full embrace of American identity is the attempt to show that the constitutional democratic structure of America is almost equivalent to the political structure of an ideal Islamic state-in other words, a dialectic in which a redefinition of Islam meets a particular definition of America so that American democracy is identified with Islamic shura (consultation) and freedom of religion is identified with the Qur'anic statement "there is no compulsion in religion."[11] From a pragmatic standpoint, advocates of such a position might argue, "If the goal of an Islamic state is to allow Muslims to freely practice and propagate their religion, but not to force others to convert, and the American Constitution allows and ensures precisely these things, then is there any state more 'Islamic' in this respect than America?"

Bolstering such arguments are attempts to show not only that the American Constitution is concordant with Islamic principles but also that it may have been based on Islamic principles. Azizah al-Hibri, an American Muslim of Lebanese origin and professor of law at the University of Richmond, makes this argument in her article "American Constitutional Law: Borrowing Possibilities or a History of Borrowing."[12] Although she cautions that further research needs to be done on the historical links between Islamic and Euro-American political theory, her attempt to draw such links demonstrates her understanding that if Muslims are convinced that certain political concepts are "authentic" to their tradition, they will easily embrace those concepts.

PARADIGMS OF SELECTIVE ENGAGEMENT

Despite creative and scholarly attempts to define America in such a way that its interests can be shown to coincide with those of an Islamic state, it is unlikely that most ordinary Muslims or their religious leaders will soon be convinced by such arguments. Rather, most Muslims are striving to understand what place they should occupy, as religious minorities, in a country that they acknowledge allows great religious freedom. Many of these leaders, who are discussed later in this chapter, do not define America in much depth. Perhaps this is because they do not find any of the existing Islamic paradigms to be suitable for defining the American context and want to avoid having to rely on older models of engagement. Instead, these leaders focus on defining the character of an authentic Muslim community, emphasizing that it must make a positive societal impact whatever its size and wherever it might be.

A widely cited religious justification for the social engagement of Muslims in American society is the Qur'anic command "Let there arise out of you a group of people calling others to good, enjoining what is good and forbidding what is wrong"[13] and the frequent description of the true believers by the Qur'an as those who "enjoin the good and oppose what is wrong."[14] A widely quoted statement of the Prophet Muhammad also commands believers to take action; it is reported that he said, "Whoever sees an evil action, let him change it with his hand; and if he is not able to do so, then with his tongue; and if he is not able to do so, then with his heart—and that is the weakest of faith"[15] This statement clearly requires Muslims to change evil by whatever legal means are available to them. Although some Muslims believe that they can fulfill this by creating independent Islamic communities and institutions in the spaces that American freedom of religion permits, others believe that this duty is not fulfilled by creating ghettoes or isolated utopias within America. The dilemma for such Muslims is how to correct wrongs within American society generally without compromising their beliefs and allegiance to Islam by participating in the system without reservation. In other words, what these Muslims would like to do is to engage selectively in those organizations and institutions through which they can effect societal change but also bring an Islamic perspective to the issues and not compromise their essential religious principles.

The areas of engagement most comfortable for these Muslims to undertake, as a result, are social causes, grassroots activism, and "alternative" forms of activism: environmentalism, social justice movements, neighborhood associations, and so on. We find Muslims increasingly participating in such movements and organizations in all levels of American society. The problem is that the tolerance extended to Muslims by the non-Muslims involved in such groups is usually also extended to groups many Muslims have difficulty working with, for example, anarchists, atheists, and gay-rights activists. Consequently, a number of independent Muslim activist groups have formed across the country. In general, however, the cherished Islamic values of such groups do not prevent them from working with non-Muslim groups toward a particular shared goal.

Two such organizations, from different regions of the United States, are examples of this trend in Muslim communities. Interestingly, each of these organizations, as with many other American-Muslim groups, carries meaningful Arabic-Islamic names that are also used as acronyms for English phrase names.

The first of these organizations is named AMILA, which means "work" in Arabic and stands for "American Muslims Intent on Learning and Activism."[16] Founded in 1992 by Muslims in the San Francisco Bay Area, AMILA's membership includes both first- and second-generation young Muslim professionals and students. Reflecting the ethnic patterns of the region, a large number of members are of South Asian origin, but Arabs and Americans also have a presence in the organization. Former members of AMILA have moved on to found other organizations; among them is Asifa Quraishi, who cofounded the Muslim Women Lawyer's Human Rights Group (KARAMAH, which means "dignity" in Arabic).[17] AMILAs activities include a regular lecture series, Qur'anic memorization and religious discussion, and community activism. AMILAs projects include outreach to prisoners in local institutions, support of a local soup kitchen, and tutoring needy children. Significantly, AMILA also works with Muslim refugees who have settled in the Bay Area. The assistance given to these refugees by Muslims who are religiously motivated but at the same time deeply engaged in American society helps break down a common new immigrant impression that America is hostile to Muslims. Immigrant social services by Muslims for Muslims, a relatively new aspect of Muslim immigration to America, will no doubt change the nature and speed of the integration of Muslim immigrants to American society.

While most members of AMILA are reaching out to needy Muslims and non-Muslims from a position of affluence—that is, their activities are in the realm of charity—a very different kind of activism emerged on the south side of Chicago in the mid-1990s. A kind of solidarity of the oppressed, with Islam as the proposed solution to oppression, was formed between African American Muslims and the children of Palestinian immigrants. This solidarity was expressed in the formation of an organization called IMAN, which means "faith" in Arabic and stands for "Inner-City Muslim Action Network?" Most of the original members were students at DePaul University, where African American Muslim professor Amina McLeod helped them conceptualize the problem of racial division in Chicago generally and the Muslim community in particular. Many of the students were second- or third-generation Palestinian Muslims who had had little contact with the African Americans among whom they lived on the south side of the city. Indeed, there had been instances of explicitly hostile encounters between the two communities. Inspired by their belief in the true brotherhood of Islam, the members of IMAN decided to prove their faith through action. Their activities have expanded from an after-school tutoring program to the establishment of a mosque in a renovated liquor store owned by a former African American gang leader turned devout Muslim. Every two weeks, young Muslim men of Arab, South Asian, African, Latino, and European origin display their solidarity of faith in the "Bonds of Brotherhood" by studying and praying together all night in southside mosques. IMAN has women's and men's outreach programs geared to Muslim families and prisoners as well as a number of other programs. Significantly, IMAN has also formed multiple ties with non-Muslim grassroots activist organizations in Chicago. In the "Community Narrative" program, for example, IMAN invites members of other minority communities to share their struggles and experiences with the group. IMAN is a dynamic organization with a number of other programs and has served as a model for other Muslim communities situated in urban areas.

Community activism of the sort undertaken by the members of IMAN and AMILA does not necessitate engagement in local politics, but such a step is often inevitable, if only because of the need for project funding. Political engagement on the local level is also undertaken, often reluctantly at first, by Muslim parents trying to better their children's public school experience. At the most basic level, the accommodation of religious practices, such as prayer, dietary restrictions, and dress requirements, can bring parents to the school administration and local board. Parents may be drawn into a deeper engagement with the school system when they realize that their children are not affected only by "Muslim issues" but also by the quality of the school system as a whole.

Beyond the local level, engagement in the American political system has, until recently, been considered undesirable by many Muslims. The widespread cynicism about national politics held by Americans in general since the Nixon era has done little to reassure Muslims that they can participate politically at this level without violating their religious principles. However, the 2000 presidential election witnessed unprecedented efforts by various Islamic organizations to encourage Muslims to vote and even run for office. Increased-political engagement was to be expected, given the growth of organizations such as the Muslim Public Affairs Council and the American Muslim Council, over the past decade. However, the responsiveness of the general Muslim community to calls for political engagement by these organizations seems to have been heightened by recent political pressure felt by Muslims, both domestically and internationally. Within America, the use of secret evidence to jail more than two dozen Palestinians frightened many Muslims who may have previously felt that they would be allowed to live freely in this country without being required to engage in the political system. Internationally, the intensity of the Israeli repression of Palestinians throughout the fall of 2000 catalyzed many Muslims to demonstrate their disapproval of American foreign policy.

Now, although many immigrant groups have come to believe that the interests of their communities will be served by engaging in national politics, the Muslim community is perhaps unique in demonstrating such concern for articulating the religious justification for this participation. This is necessitated by the fact that, as was shown previously, there are a number of religious paradigms that can be used to condemn any such participation by Muslims in non-Islamic political systems. One of the common religious justifications for political participation is a statement attributed to the Prophet Muhammad in which he explicitly approves of a pact made in the pre-Islamic period (and, hence, by non-Muslims) to punish any acts of theft committed in Mecca. The group who made this pact was known as the "Confederates of Fudul" and the Prophet, who witnessed the agreement in his youth, said, "If I were invited to take part in it during Islam, I would do so."[18] This statement is taken as proof that Muslims may join with non-Muslims in political bodies to enforce a particular and limited social good.

Some who permit political participation by Muslims from a religious standpoint do so cautiously; others are more aggressive and enthusiastic. Among the prominent Muslim leaders who adopt a relatively cautious stance is Jamal Badawi, an Egyptian Canadian academic who is a widely respected Muslim speaker and leader in the Islamic Society of North America.[19] Cautious approval of political participation was also expressed at the Zaytuna Institute, a center for Islamic scholarship founded in California by American Muslim leader Hamza Yusuf. Visiting Mauritanian scholar Sheikh Abdullah Bin Bayyah, in a speech published on the Zaytuna website, urged Muslims to be guided by the principle of trying to ensure the greatest advantage for the community.[20] Interestingly, Bin Bayyah not only stressed the obligation of the Muslim community to be a positive force in society and protect its interests but also addressed the issue of the proper Islamic legal categorization of America. Correcting the notion that there were only two "abodes" in classical Islamic jurisprudence, Bin Bayyah says that beyond the abode of peace and the abode of war there is also an "abode of treaty" in which Muslims agree to respect the laws of a country if they are granted freedom and protection. America, Bin Bayyah argues, belongs to this category.

One of the strongest arguments for the participation of Muslims in national politics in 1999 came from Taha Jaber Al-Alwani, a traditionally trained Muslim jurist from Iraq who has been involved in American Islamic organizations for two decades and currently heads the North American Fiqh [Islamic Legal] Council. Al-Alwani argued in a legal verdict (fatwa) prepared for the American Muslim Council that participation in the American political system is not only permitted but also obligatory for Muslims in order to protect their interests and to correct societal evils.[21] Al-Aiwani agrees with Bin Bayyah that America is not an abode of war but argues further that such categories are outdated in the contemporary world. Indeed, rather than categorizing America, Al-Aiwani simply lists some of the "American particularities," such as religious and political freedom and legal equality for all people. The implication is that America simply does not fit any of the older Islamic paradigms for a non-Muslim political entity. If Al-Aiwani's argument is convincing to Muslims, the result could be a far more profound integration of Muslims into American society than ever before.

In many cases, those Muslims who begin from a position of "selective embrace" of America move eventually to a position of "full embrace": When their efforts to effect positive change in society bear fruit, they may come to see advantages in the American political system that they did not see before. At this point, they may abandon the former paradigm they used to define America in favor of one that is more positive and comprehensive. The shift, however, is not inevitable. In some cases, Muslim activists, like their non-Muslim counterparts, become deeply disillusioned and highly skeptical of their ability to effect anything but superficial change within the parameters of the current American political system. In such cases, a reevaluation of the appropriate Islamic paradigm for America will lead to negative results.

No matter what happens within America, the deep connections between American Muslims and their brothers and sisters overseas means that American foreign policy will always have a profound effect on the way Muslims view this country. In the 1990s alone, the Persian Gulf War and ensuing sanctions against Iraq created great animosity toward America on the part of many Muslims, while American bombing of the former Yugoslavia to protect Kosovar Muslims resulted in a fair amount of goodwill toward America.

What this means is very simple: In both foreign and domestic affairs, the way Muslims define America will always depend a great deal on what America does. Although Muslims are certainly not immune to political ideology, most are unconvinced by claims to moral and political authority that are not backed up by action. Perhaps, then, the most powerful paradigm underlying all Muslim definitions of America is the dominant Islamic theological belief that one's true convictions will inevitably be made manifest by one's actions:

They will offer their excuses to you (the Prophet) when you return to them. Say: "Offer no excuses; we will not believe you. Allah has already informed us of the true state of matters concerning you. It is your actions that Allah and His Messenger will observe. In the end will you be brought back to Him Who knows what is hidden and what is revealed. Then He will show you the truth of all that you did."[22]

NOTES

1. Farid Esack, *Qur'an Liberation and Pluralism: An Islamic Perspective of Interreligious Solidarity against Oppression* (Oxford: Oneworld, 1997); Abdullahi an-Naim, *Towards an Islamic Reformation: Civil Liberties, Human Rights and International Law* (Syracuse, N.Y.: Syracuse University Press, 1990); Sayyid Qutb, *Milestones*, translation of *Ma'alim fi'l-tariq* (Cedar Rapids, Iowa: Unity Publishing, n.d.); Rashid Ghannouchi, *Huquq al-Muwatanah: Huquq ghair al-muslim fi'-mujtama' al-Islami* (Herndon, Va.: International Institute of Islamic Thought, 1993); El Hassan Bin Talal, *Christianity in the Arab World* (New York: Continuum Publishing, 1998); Alija Izetbegovic, *Islam between East and West* (Indianapolis: American Trust Publications, 1989). For the most recent views of

El-Affendi and Ghannouchi, consult various issues of the British journal *Islam2l* or its website at http://islam2l.org.

2. For an analysis of these medieval juridical-political categories, see Majid Khadduri, *War and Peace in the Law of Islam* (Baltimore: The Johns Hopkins University Press, 1955).

3. Qutb, *Milestones*, 21.

4. *Qur'an* 28:39.

5. Samory Rashid, "Blacks and the Law of Resistance in Islam," *Journal of Islamic Law* 4, no. 2 (fall/winter 1999): 87–124.

6. A primary source for the history of the life of the Prophet Muhammad and the first Muslim community is Ibn Ishaq's *Sirat Rasul Allah*, translated as *The Life of Muhammad* by A. Guillaume (Karachi: Oxford University Press, 1955). For the story of Bilal, see pp. 143–44 therein.

7. The group's position is stated, among other places, on its website at www.khilafah.org.

8. Qur'an 5:47.

9. Guillauxne, The Lift of Muhammad, 146–53.

10. Qur'an 12:55–56.

11. Qur'an 2:256.

12. Azizah Y. al-Hibri, "Islamic and American Constitutional Law: Borrowing Possibilities or a History of Borrowing?" www.law.upenn.edu/conlawlissues/vol1/num3/alhibri.htm (accessed December 1999).

13. Qur'an 3:104.

14. Qur'an 9:71,22:41,31:17.

15. Ezzedin Ibrahim and Denys Johnson-Davies, trans., *An-Nawawi's Forty Hadith: An Anthology of the Sayings of the Prophet Muhammad* (Cambridge: Islamic Texts Society, 1997), 110.

16. For more information on AMILA, see its website at www.amila.org.

17. A further description of KARAMAH can be found on its website at www.karamah.org.

18. Guillaume, *The Life of Muhammad*, 57.

19. See his interview on the Soundvision website at www.soundvision.com/politics/badawi.html (accessed November 1999).

20. Speech found at www.zaytuna.org/sh_biri_bayyah.html (accessed November 1999).

21. *Fatwa* found at www.amconline.org/newamc/fatwa.htrnl (accessed November 1999).

22. Qur'an 9:94.

42. "Religious Belief and Practice" from *The Pew Research Center*

May 22, 2007. http://news.bbc.co.uk/2/shared/bsp/hi/pdfs/22_05_2007_muslim_americans.pdf. Reprinted with permission of The Pew Research Center. Copyright 2007 by Pew Research Center.

The Pew Research Center is a nonpartisan organization that gathers and disseminates information regarding current events, issues, and attitudes. This poll was conducted in 2006 and is the first nationwide survey to use a representative sample to measure "the demographics, attitudes, and experiences of Muslim Americans" (Foreword, p. 1). The following excerpt from the poll (pp. 21-27) highlights respondents' Islamic affiliation, converts to Islam, religious beliefs, religious practices, religious commitment, perceptions of women, and comparisons to American Christians.

Just like the larger American public of which they are a part, most U.S. Muslims say that religion is very important to them and that they accept the basic tenets of their faith.

Most pray every day and four in 10 attend a mosque at least once a week. Yet there is considerable religious diversity in American Islam, resembling the diversity of American Christianity. A large majority of Muslims accept the Koran as the word of God, but only half say that it should be taken literally, word for word. Most Muslims also say there is more than one true way to interpret the teachings of Islam.

One distinctive feature of the Muslim American population is the relatively large number of converts from outside of the tradition. Nearly one-quarter have converted to Islam, most of them from Christianity. Nearly all of the conversions to Islam are among the native-born population, and the majority of all converts to Islam are African Americans.

Islamic Affiliation

Muslims in the United States belong to diverse religious traditions within Islam. Half identify with Sunni Islam, the largest Muslim tradition worldwide. The second largest segment of the Muslim American population—about one-fifth of the total (22%)—volunteers they are just Muslim, without any particular affiliation. An additional 16% identify with Shia Islam, which is the second largest Muslim tradition worldwide. Only 5% of U.S. Muslims identify with another Muslim tradition, and 7% did not offer a response.

Sunni Muslims make up about half of both the native-born (50%) and foreign-born (53%) segments of the U.S. Muslim population, but there are bigger differences when it comes to other traditions. Among Muslim Americans who were born in the United States, just 7% identify with Shia Islam, while 30% say they are Muslim without specifying a tradition. Among Muslims who immigrated to the United States, at least as many identify themselves as Shia (21%) as say they do not have a particular affiliation (18%).

Not surprisingly, religious affiliation is strongly linked to a person's country of origin. Muslim Americans who are first- or second-generation immigrants from Arab countries are mostly Sunni (56%), with about one-fifth each either Shia (19%) or just Muslim (23%). Large majorities of Pakistanis (72%) and other South Asians (82%) are Sunni, while Iranians are overwhelmingly Shia (91%).

Overall, 20% of U.S. Muslims are native-born African Americans, nearly half of whom (48%) identify as Sunni. Another third (34%) of native-born African Americans say they are just a Muslim, and 15% have another affiliation, including Shia and the Nation of Islam.

Muslim Religious Affiliation

	Sunni %	Shia %	Nonspecific (Vol.) %	Other/DK/ Ref %
All U.S. Muslims	50	16	22	12=100
Native-born	50	7	30	13=100
African American	48	2	34	16=100
Foreign-born	53	21	18	8=100
Self/Parent from...				
Arab region	56	19	23	2=100
Pakistan	72	6	10	12=100
Other South Asia	82	4	7	7=100
Iran	6	91	3	0=100

Question: Are you Shia, Sunni, or another tradition?

Converts to Islam

More than three-quarters (77%) of Muslim Americans say they have always been a Muslim, while 23% say they converted to Islam.

Nine in 10 (91%) converts to Islam were born in the United States, and almost three-fifths (59%) of converts to Islam are African American. A 55% majority of converts identify with Sunni Islam and another quarter (24%) identify with no specific tradition. Only 6% of Muslim converts in America identify themselves as Shia.

Almost half (49%) of Muslim converts in America report that their conversion occurred when they were under 21 years of age, another third (34%) converted when they were between ages 21 and 35, and 17% when they were older than 35. The early age of most conversions to Islam resembles the typical pattern of conversion in the general public, where religious change is concentrated in adolescence and early adulthood.

Profile of Converts to Islam

Percent of Muslim converts who are . . .	%
Born in the U.S.	91
Foreign-born	9
	100
African American	59
White	34
Other race	7
	100
Tradition	
Sunni	55
Shia	6
Non-specific (Vol.)	24
Other/no response	15
	100
Age when converted to Islam	
Less than 21	49
21 to 35	34
36 and older	17
	100
Converted to Islam from	
Protestant denomination	67
Roman Catholic	10
Orthodox Christian	4
Other religion	1
No religion	15
Don't know/Refused	3
	100
Reason for converting	
Religious beliefs/practices	58
Family/marriage	18
Other	22
No answer	2
	100

Based on 179 U.S. Muslims who converted to Islam.

Two-thirds (67%) of all converts to Islam in the U.S. came from Protestant churches, 10% came from Catholicism, and just 5% from other religions. Nearly one in seven converts to Islam (15%) had no religion before their conversion.

Most converts to Islam (58%) cite aspects of the religion as the reason for their conversion. These include references to the truth or appeal of Islam's teachings, the belief that Islam is superior to Christianity, or that the religion just "made sense" to them. Just 18% of converts mentioned family reasons, such as marrying a Muslim, as the reason for their conversion.

Religious Beliefs

Overall, Muslim Americans are fairly traditional in their religious beliefs. For example, 86% say that the Koran is "the word of God" and half (50%) say that the Koran is to be read literally, word for word. Fewer than one in 10 U.S. Muslims (8%) say the Koran is a book written by men. In this regard, Muslims in this country are more likely to adopt a strict literal view of the Koran than American Christians are to adopt a strict literal view of the Bible (50% to 40%).

Views of the Koran and the Bible

Koran/Bible is...	U.S. Muslims	U.S. Christians
	%	%
The word of God	86	78
Literally, word for word	50	40
Not everything literal	25	32
Don't know	11	6
Book written by men	8	15
Other/DK/Refused	5	7
	100	100

Muslims asked about the Koran, Christians about the Bible. See topline Q.E4 and Q.E 5 for question wording. Christian comparisons from March 2007 Pew Research Center for the People & the Press nationwide survey.

Many Interpretations of Islam

	Ways to interpret Islamic teachings*		
	Only one	More than one	Other/DK
	%	%	%
All U.S. Muslims	33	60	7=100
	↓	↓	
Believe Koran is...	%	%	
The word of God	92	82	
Taken literally	66	45	
Not literally	19	28	
Other/DK/Refused	7	9	
Book written by men	5	11	
Other/DK/Refused	3	7	
	100	100	

* **Question:** Which statement comes closest to your view? There is only ONE true way to interpret the teachings of Islam, (OR) There is MORE than one true way to interpret the teachings of Islam.

Large majorities of Muslim Americans accept the basic teachings of Islam. For example, nearly all (96%) believe in "One God, Allah," and the Prophet Muhammad (94%). Belief in a future Day of Judgment (91%) and the existence of angels (87%) is nearly as common.

While U.S. Muslims hold many traditional Islamic beliefs, a 60% majority also says that "there is more than one true way to interpret the teachings of Islam.rdquo; A third says that "there is only one true way to interpret the teachings of Islam."

Views on diverse interpretations of Islam are associated with views of the Koran. Two-thirds (66%) of those who believe there is only one true way to interpret the teachings of Islam accept a literal view of the Koran. In contrast, less than half (45%) of those who believe there is more than one true way to interpret the teachings of Islam hold a literal view of the Koran.

Religious Practices

Muslims in the United States take their faith seriously. For example, 72% say religion plays a "very important" role in their life. Another 18% say it is "somewhat important," and just 9% say that religion is "not too important" or "not at all important" to them.

While religion is very important to the vast majority, not all Muslim Americans practice their faith in the same way. For instance, when asked about attending a mosque or Islamic center for salah and Jum'ah prayer, 40% say they attend either more than once a week (17%) or once a week (23%). An additional 8% say they attend once or twice a month, and 18% report attending a mosque a few times a year, especially for the Eid services. Roughly a third of Muslim Americans say they either "seldom" (16%) or "never" (18%) attend worship services.

Mosque attendance among U.S. Muslims varies by nativity and nationality. Native-born Muslims (45%), especially African Americans (54%), are more likely to attend mosque weekly than are the foreign-born (37%). Muslims of Pakistani descent (57%) are more likely to be frequent attendees compared with other South Asians (38%). Muslims of first- or second-generation Iranian descent stand out for their very low levels (7%) of weekly mosque attendance.

Overall, nearly three-quarters (74%) of Muslim Americans say they are satisfied with the quality of mosques in their area, while 15% say they are dissatisfied. Among those

Muslim Religious Attendance

	Weekly or more	Less often	Seldom/Never	DK/Ref
	%	%	%	%
All U.S. Muslims	40	26	34	*=100
Native-born	45	24	31	0=100
African American	54	20	27	0=100
Other race	34	29	37	0=100
Foreign-born	37	27	36	*=100
Self/Parents from . . .				
Arab region	45	23	31	1=100
Pakistan	57	29	14	0=100
Other South Asia	38	37	25	*=100
Iran	7	16	77	0=100

Quality of Mosques Available Where You Live

	Satisfied	Dissatisfied	(Vol.) None nearby	DK/Ref
	%	%	%	%
All U.S. Muslims	74	15	3	8=100
Attend mosque services				
More than weekly	83	16	*	1=100
Once a week for Jum'ah	83	16	*	1=100
Once or twice a month	81	17	1	1=100
Few times a year for Eid	80	15	2	3=100
Seldom	75	12	6	7=100
Never	42	14	10	34=100

who attend services weekly or more often, 83% are satisfied, while 16% are not. Satisfaction is lower among the 18% of Muslim Americans who never attend a mosque, but mostly because they don't have an opinion one way or the other. Nationwide, 3% of Muslims volunteer that there is no mosque nearby, a response that is most common among those who seldom (6%) or never (10%) attend.

Three in 10 Muslim Americans report taking part in other social and religious activities at a mosque or Islamic center outside of regular salah and Jum'ah prayers, and more than three quarters (78%) of those who are active in this regard also say they are satisfied with the quality of mosques available to them.

A solid majority of Muslim Americans (61%) say they pray every day. Roughly four in 10 (41%) report praying all five salah daily, one of the Five Pillars of Islam. Another 20% say they make some of the five salah every day; 20% make salah occasionally, while just (6%) only make Eid prayers. About one in 10 Muslim Americans (12%) say that they never pray.

Muslim Americans also assign considerable importance to other Islamic religious practices included among the Five Pillars of Islam. For example, about three-quarters of Muslim Americans say that giving charity or zakat (76%) to the poor and fasting during Ramadan (77%) are "very important" to them. A pilgrimage to Mecca is "very important" to 63% of U.S. Muslims. Small minorities of Muslim Americans say that these practices are "not too" or "not at all important," ranging from 8% for zakat to 15% for the Hajj pilgrimage.

Daily Prayer

	U.S. Muslims
	%
All five salah	41
Some of five salah	20
Occasionally make salah	20
Only make Eid Prayers	6
Never pray	12
Don't know/Refused	1
	100

Islamic Practices

How important...	Giving charity (zakat)	Fasting during Ramadan	Taking pilgrimage to Mecca	Reading Koran daily
	%	%	%	%
Very important	76	77	63	58
Somewhat important	14	11	21	23
Not too important	3	4	8	10
Not at all important	5	6	7	7
Don't know/ Refused	2	2	1	2
	100	100	100	100

Most Muslim Americans (58%) also say that it is "very important" to read or listen to the Koran daily. Another 23% say this is somewhat important, while 17% say it is not too or not at all important to read or hear the Koran every day.

Levels of Religious Commitment

Nearly one-quarter (23%) of Muslim Americans have a high level of religious commitment, which is defined as attending mosque at least once a week, praying all five salah every day, and reporting that religion is "very important" in their lives. About as many (26%) have a relatively low level of religious commitment, rarely engaging in these

Religious Commitment*

	High	Med	Low
	%	%	%
Total	23	51	26=100
18–29	26	52	22=100
30–39	24	46	30=100
40–54	20	53	27=100
55+	19	55	26=100
Men	25	48	27=100
Women	21	54	25=100
Sunni	28	54	18=100
Shia	13	44	43=100
Non-specific (Vol.)	21	51	28=100
Born Muslim	24	49	27=100
Convert	19	58	23=100
Native-born	24	56	20=100
African American	25	65	10=100
Other race	23	45	32=100
Foreign-born	22	49	29=100
Pre-1990	21	41	38=100
1990 & later	23	52	25=100

* An index based on self-reported mosque attendance, prayer and the importance of religion.

practices and generally regarding religion as less important in their lives. A majority of Muslim Americans (51%) fall somewhere in between.

Religious commitment varies by religious affiliation. Among Sunni Muslims, 28% are highly religious, compared with just 13% of Shia Muslims. Those who volunteer that they are just Muslim, without specifying an Islamic tradition, closely resemble U.S. Muslims as a whole (21% high commitment). Muslim immigrants who arrived before 1990 are more likely than native-born Muslims to report low levels of religious commitment.

Muslim men and women practice their faith in different ways. Men tend to attend services at mosques or Islamic centers more often than women (48% attend weekly or more vs. 30% of Muslim women). However, nearly half of Muslim women (48%) say that they pray all five salah every day, compared with barely a third (34%) of men.

Regular mosque attendance is particularly high among younger Muslim Americans. Fully half (51%) of Muslims under age 30 say they attend at least weekly, compared with 36% of those ages 30 to 54 and just 26% of those ages 55 and older. But daily prayer is observed somewhat more frequently by older Muslims. Nearly two-thirds (64%) of those ages 55 and older say that they pray every day, compared with 54% of Muslims under age 30.

Women and Islam

Fully 69% of Muslim Americans say that the Islamic religion treats men and women equally well. Only about a quarter of Muslims (23%) believe that Islam treats men better than women. Notably, Muslim women are about as likely as men to say that Islam treats members of both sexes equally well (71% of Muslim women vs. 66% of men).

The small group of Muslim Americans (9% overall) who say that religion is not that important in their lives stand out for their belief that Islam treats men better than women; 52% express this view. But among Muslims who say religion is very important—72% of all U.S. Muslims—an overwhelming majority (80%) says that Islam treats men and women equally well.

Muslim American women and men also express similar opinions about keeping the sexes separated when praying at mosques. About half of all U.S. Muslims (46%)—and comparable percentages of men and women—say that when praying, "Women should be separate from men, in another area of the mosque or behind a curtain."

Smaller percentages of Muslim American men and women (23% overall) say that women should pray behind men, but with no curtain. Only about one in five Muslim men and women (21% of all Muslim Americans) believe that women should pray in an area alongside men, with no curtain.

No Gender Gap in Views of Separating Men and Women at Mosques

When praying at a mosque women should pray . . .	U.S. Muslims	Men	Women
	%	%	%
Separately from men	46	48	45
Behind men, not separately	23	20	26
Alongside men	21	21	20
Other/don't know	10	11	9
	100	100	100

Similarities with American Christians

Although Muslim Americans have distinctive beliefs and practices, their religiosity is similar to American Christians in many respects. For example, U.S. Muslims are a little more likely than American Christians to say religion is "very important" in their life (72% and 60%, respectively) but a little less likely to say that they pray every day (61% vs. 70%). The two religious communities are about equally likely to attend religious services at least weekly (40% for Muslims vs. 45% for Christians). Thus in terms of the broad patterns of religiosity, American Islam resembles the mainstream of American religious life.

American Muslims & Christians

	U.S. Muslims	U.S. Christians
	%	%
Religion is "very important" in your life	72	60
Pray every day	61	70
Attend mosque/church at least once a week	40	45

Christian comparisons taken from the following Pew nationwide surveys: May 2006, Aug 2005, Jan-Apr 2007

PART II

TERRORISM AND SEPTEMBER 11, 2001

This section comprises the numerous strong condemnations of the September 11, 2001 terrorist attacks and of al Qaeda by Muslims in America. The condemnations represent various trends among the Muslim organizations and intellectuals, and use different styles of argumentation, but they are unanimous in their denunciation of the attacks, al Qaeda, and terrorism. Surprisingly, most of them were not publicized in the mainstream American media, leading to a misperception that Muslims in America condemned neither the attacks nor Osama bin Laden.

43. "A Top Urgent Statement Concerning Terrorism" from *The Assembly of Muslim Jurists in America*

Accessed online May 4, 2006. Available online: http://www.amjaonline.com/English// headline.asp?Headid=68.

The following fatwa is a statement from the Assembly of Muslim Jurists in America (AMJA; for a description, see Primary document 4) condemning all acts of terrorism. It argues that such acts are forbidden and urges perpetrators of terrorism to repent.

In The Name Of Allah The Beneficent The Merciful
The Assembly of Muslim Jurists in America (AMJA)
The Third Annual Conference
Sokoto—Nigeria
July 21–25, 2005 / Jumada (II) 15–19, 1426 A. H.

Praise be to Allah and His prayers and peace be upon His Messenger. Now that: Members of The Assembly of Muslim Jurists in America (AMJA), along with a host of Nigerian Shari'ah scholars, convening in their Third Annual Conference, "Coexistence Between Civilizations", in Sokoto—Nigeria, July 21–25, 2005 / Jumada (II) 15–19, 1426 A. H., while their ears have been tingling with the bad news of the vicious explosions that shattered the peaceful resort of Sharm El-Sheikh in Egypt, as well as the previous similar explosions in other places, they declare that Islam, which came as a mercy for all mankind, and which the Messenger of Allah, His prayers and peace be upon him, has announced in the first international declaration of human rights in his farewell pilgrim: The inviolability of blood, money, honor and dignity of man; and who used to commend his armies, marching to prevent war and aggression, not to kill a woman, a child, an elderly, a monk, nor an ailing person, or to cut down trees, or kill beasts of mount, such a religion could never find a legal, a humanitarian, or a moral justification for any of such sinful and vicious acts which are prohibited by Allah, the world religions, and condemned all over the world, and by the international declarations of human rights.

It is absolutely necessary to know the benefiting party behind these sabotage activities, so as to know the real instigator that harbor those who triggered them, rather than throwing accusations here and there without check.

The Assembly of Muslim Jurists in America (AMJA) in its third annual conference in Sokot, Nigeria, declares to the whole world the following:

• The inviolability of blood, money honor and dignity of man, are as sacred as the sanctity of Makkah in the sacred months; and any aggression on any of such inviolabilities without any right to do so, is a deadly sin that discontents and angers Allah and His Messenger.

• Combat was ordained in Islam only to prevent war and aggression, and to spread justice. Islam raised swords just for defending the religion of Islam and Muslims, and not against civilians nor non-combat men. Military actions are operated only against combating men and those who assist them in their aggression against Islam and Muslims, and against the creed of Allah.

- The Assembly prohibits acts of explosions, sabotage, and violence, and considers such operations as absolute acts of war, which actually terrify secure people, shed blood, and inflicting harm on people and lands.

- The religion that prohibits frightening and terrifying people, even by arms and without using them, would rather deserve to be worthy of prohibiting all forms of violence, terrorism, sabotage, and destruction, and demand the heaviest punishment on those who commit such vicious acts.

- The religion that rules out that a woman who imprisoned a cat and prevented it from eating and drinking until it died, will be tortured in Hellfire; and the Prophet Muhamad, prayers and peace of Allah be upon him, told us that Allah The Almighty praised a man who saved the life of a dog when he found it so much thirsty that it ate the wet dust; and it is told that Prophet Muhamad's second successor, Omar, declared his full responsibility before Allah in Madinah for a mule that stumbled in Iraq and got hurt for not paving the way for it.

A religion like this would never be imagined that it permits shedding blood, stealing money, and committing vicious acts against honor and dignity of innocent people, whether they are Muslims or non-Muslims. Allah has ordained in His Noble Quran: "If anyone killed a person not in retaliation of murder, or to spread mischief in the land—it would be as if he killed all mankind, and if anyone saved a life, it would be as if he saved the life of all mankind" (Quran, 5:32).

Finally, this is our urgent call for anyone who is involved in anything of such criminal acts in all religions and sects in the world to hasten for repentance to Allah The Almighty, and to come back to the truth which shines with its signs and its proofs, for coming back to the truth rather than being involved in mischief and disruption.

Last, we pray to Allah The Supreme to protect the whole of this Ummah and to keep it intact against acts of mischief and temptations, and to guide all humanity to His right and straight path.

Allah is the aim of our objective, Who is our Guide and Sustainer.

Prayers and peace of Allah be upon His Messenger.

44. "U.S. Muslim Religious Council Issues Fatwa Against Terrorism" from *The Fiqh Council of North America*

Accessed April 28, 2006. Available online: http://www.isna.net/index.php?id=316. Reprinted with permission of the Islamic Society of North America.

The Fiqh Council of North America (for description see Primary document 7) issued the following fatwa in response to the terrorist attacks of September 11, 2001. It condemns any terrorist act as forbidden (ḥarām) as well as cooperating with any individual or group who partakes in such acts. It also urges all Muslims to cooperate with "law enforcement authorities" in the United States to protect against other terrorist acts.

The Fiqh Council of North America wishes to reaffirm Islam's absolute condemnation of terrorism and religious extremism.

Islam strictly condemns religious extremism and the use of violence against innocent lives. There is no justification in Islam for extremism or terrorism. Targeting civilians' life and property through suicide bombings or any other method of attack is haram—or forbidden—and those who commit these barbaric acts are criminals, not "martyrs."

The Qur'an, Islam's revealed text, states: "Whoever kills a person, unless [as punishment through due process] for murder or mischief in the land, it is as though he has killed all mankind. And whoever saves a life, it is as though he had saved all mankind." Qur'an, 5:32)

Prophet Muhammad said there is no excuse for committing unjust acts: "Do not be people without minds of your own, saying that if others treat you well you will treat them well, and that if they do wrong you will do wrong to them. Instead, accustom yourselves to do good if people do good and not to do wrong (even) if they do evil." (Al- Tirmidhi)

God mandates moderation in faith and in all aspects of life when He states in the Qur'an: "We made you to be a community of the middle way, so that (with the example of your lives) you might bear witness to the truth before all mankind." (Qur'an, 2:143)

In another verse, God explains our duties as human beings when he says: "Let there arise from among you a band of people who invite to righteousness, and enjoin good and forbid evil." (Qur'an, 3:104)

Islam teaches us to act in a caring manner to all of God's creation. The Prophet Muhammad, who is described in the Qur'an as "a mercy to the worlds" said: "All creation is the family of God, and the person most beloved by God (is the one) who is kind and caring toward His family."

In the light of the teachings of the Qur'an and Sunnah we clearly and strongly state:

1. All acts of terrorism targeting civilians are haram (forbidden) in Islam.

2. It is haram for a Muslim to cooperate with any individual or group that is involved in any act of terrorism or violence.

3. It is the civic and religious duty of Muslims to cooperate with law enforcement authorities to protect the lives of all civilians.

We issue this fatwa following the guidance of our scripture, the Qur'an, and the teachings of our Prophet Muhammad—peace be upon him. We urge all people to resolve all conflicts in just and peaceful manners.

We pray for the defeat of extremism and terrorism. We pray for the safety and security of our country, the United States, and its people. We pray for the safety and security of all inhabitants of our planet. We pray that interfaith harmony and cooperation prevail both in the United States and all around the globe.

FIQH COUNCIL OF NORTH AMERICA

Members
1. Dr. Muzammil H. Siddiqi
2. Dr. Abdul Hakim Jackson
3. Dr. Ahmad Shleibak
4. Dr. Akbar Muhammad
5. Dr. Deina Abdulkadir
6. Shaikh Hassan Qazwini
7. Dr. Ihsan Bagby
8. Dr. Jamal Badawi
9. Dr. Muhammad Adam Sheikh
10. Shaikh Muhammad Al- Hanooti
11. Shaikh Muhammad Nur Abdallah
12. Dr. Salah Soltan
13. Dr. Taha Jabir Alalwani
14. Shaikh Yahya Hindi

15. Shaikhah Zainab Alwani
16. Dr. Zulfiqar Ali Shah
17. Dr. Mukhtar Maghraoui
18. Dr. Nazih Hammad

ENDORSED BY:

145 Muslim organizations, mosques and imams have endorsed the preceding fatwa as of July 28, 2005 (see p. 820). More signatory organizations are to be added in the following days. To add your American Muslim organization to the list, please use the this form.

45. "Shaykh Yusuf Al-Qaradawi Condemns Attacks Against Civilians: 44 Forbidden in Islam" from *IslamOnline.net*

Accessed April 28, 2006. Available online: http://www.islam-online.net/English/News/ 2001-09/13/article25.shtml.

Shaykh Yusuf Al-Qaradawi was born in Egypt in 1926. He was imprisoned in 1949 as a member of the Muslim Brotherhood. He received his doctorate from Al Azhar University in 1973 and is regarded as one of the most influential clerics today, especially in America and Europe. He runs a satellite television program, "Sharīʿa wa al-hayāt," (Sharia and life), from Doha, Qatar and is president of IslamOnline.net. Islamonline.net was set up in 1997. It maintains an "Ask the Scholar" section in which Internet users may submit questions on any topic and an Islamic jurist answers the question. The site also provides news, discussion on politics, economics, culture, and society. It is available in English and Arabic. In the following fatwa, Shaykh Qaradawi condemns the terrorist attacks of September 11, 2001 and violence against civilians.

DOHA, Qatar, Sept 13, 2001 (IslamOnline & News Agencies) - Renowned Muslim scholar Sheikh Yusuf al-Qaradawi denounced the attacks against civilians in the U.S. Tuesday and encouraged Muslims to donate blood to the victims of the attack.

In response to the bloody attack against civilians in the U.S., Sheikh Yusuf issued a statement Wednesday saying that:

"Our hearts bleed for the attacks that has targeted the World Trade Center [WTC], as well as other institutions in the United States despite our strong oppositions to the American biased policy towards Israel on the military, political and economic fronts.

"Islam, the religion of tolerance, holds the human soul in high esteem, and considers the attack against innocent human beings a grave sin, this is backed by the Qur'anic verse which reads:

"Who so ever kills a human being for other than manslaughter or corruption in the earth, it shall be as if he has killed all mankind, and who so ever saves the life of one, it shall be as if he had saved the life of all mankind," (Al-Ma'dah:32).

"The Prophet, peace and blessings be upon him, is reported to have said, 'A believer remains within the scope of his religion as long as he doesn't kill another person illegally'," the prominent scholar said.

He added that haphazard killing where the rough is taken with the smooth and where innocents are killed along with wrongdoers is totally forbidden in Islam. No one, as far as Islam is concerned, is held responsible for another's actions. Upon seeing a woman killed in the battlefield, the Prophet, peace and blessings be upon him, denied the act and said: "That woman shouldn't have been killed anyway!".

Even in times of war, Muslims are not allowed to kill anybody save the one who is indulged in face-to-face confrontation with them. They are not allowed to kill women, old persons, children, or even a monk in his religious seclusion.

Council on American-Islamic Relations (CAIR)
Muslim Public Affairs Council (MPAC)

Canadian Council on American-Islamic Relations
Council of Shia Muslim Scholars of North America
Muslim Student Association of the US & Canada

Islamic Sharia Advisory Institute of North America
Kashmiri American Council
United Muslims of America
Islamic Center of Northeast Florida
Islamic Movement of Florida
The Council of Islamic Organizations of Greater Chicago
Islamic Society of Washington Area
Islamic Foundation of Central Ohio
Islamic Center of Little Rock
Al Nur Islamic Center
Dar As-Salaam, Islamic Society of San Francisco
Indian Muslim Relief & Charities
Islamic Center Of Reseda
Islamic Society of Orange County
Masjid Al- Taqwa

Muslim Community Center of San Francisco
South Valley Islamic Center

Assadiq Islamic Educational Foundation
Islamic Center of Tampa
Masjid Al- Ansar
Masjid Al- Ihnsan
Masjid Jama Al Mumineen

Islamic Society of North America (ISNA)
Muslim American Society (MAS)

American Federation of Muslims of Indian Origin
Islamic Networks Group & Affiliates
USA Halal Chamber of Commerce, Inc & The
Islamic Center for Halal Certification

Islamic Resource Group
Minaret of Freedom Institute
Muslim Ummah of North America
Islamic Center of South Florida
Islamic Society of Central Florida
Islamic Center of New England
Muslim Federation of New Jersey
Virginia Muslim Political Action Committee
Greenway Islamic Center
American Muslim Voice
Elmhurst Islamic Center
Islamic Center Of Fremont
Islamic Education Center
Long Beach Islamic Center
Muslim Community Association of the Peninsula

Muslim Community Services, Inc.
Yaseen Foundation and the Muslim Community Center

Bay County Islamic Society Inc
Islamic Jaffaria Association
Masjid Al- Faizal
Masjid Al- Nahl
Masjid Miami

Islamic Circle of North America (ICNA)
Muslim Student Association of the US & Canada (MSA)

American Muslim Alliance
Muslim Public Affairs Council
Islamic Center of America

Islamic Schools League of America
Project Islamic HOPE
Islamic Shura Council of Southern California
Islamic Foundation of South Florida
Islamic Society of Tampa Bay Area
Islamic Center of Maryland
Islamic Council of Ohio
Islamic Association of West Virginia
Afghan Cultural Center
Blossom Valley Muslim Community Center
Hidaya Foundation
Islamic Center of Pleasanton/Dublin
Islamic Learning and Practicing
Masjid Al- Rasul
Muslim Community Association of the San Francisco Bay Area
South Bay Islamic Association
Masjid Al- Kauthar

Islamic Center of Boca Raton
Islamic Society of Pinellas County
Masjid Al- Hijrah
Masjid An- Noor
Masjid Muttaqeen

Masjid Sahmsuddin
Nur Ul Islam
Islamic Center of Marietta
Masjid Dar- ul-Argum
The Mosque Foundation
Islamic Center of Somerset
Islamic Society of Boston
Islamic Society of Baltimore
Islamic House of Wisdom
Daar-ul-Islam Masjid
Masjid Al Heyder
Islamic Association of Raleigh
Islamic Center Passaic County
Islamic Society Essex County
Umar Mosque
Islamic Center of Cleveland
Uqbah Mosque Foundation
Muslim Community of Knoxville
Islamic Society of Greater Houston
All Dulles Area Muslim Society (ADAMS)
Masjid Darul Huda
Islamic Center of Blacksburg VA
Islam Mossaad
Souleiman Ghani
Ali Shakoor
Muzammil Siddiqi
Tarek Mohamed
M. Rezar Rahman
Ziyad Dahbour
Hashem Mubrak
Hassan Sabri
Mohamed Banglori

Miami Gardens Masjid
Palm Beach Mosque
Masjid Al Muminun
Belleville Mosque and Islamic Education Center
The Muslim Community Center
Islamic Association of Greater Shreveport
Howard County Muslim Council
Mecca Learning Center
Kalamazoo Islamic Center
Islamic Center of Cape Girardeau
Masjid Mohammed
Islamic Center of Raleigh
Islamic Center Old Bridge
Muslim Center of Middlesex County
Islamic Center of New Mexico
Islamic Society of Greater Columbus
Islamic Center of Portland , Masjid As-Saber
Muslim Community of North East Tennessee
Muslim Children Education & Civic Center
Darassalam
Muslim Association of Virginia
Rashid Lamptey
Didmar Faja
Riaz Ahmad
Ahmad Sakr
Shakeel Syed
Mujahid Abdul-Karim
Tahir Anwar
Rudolph Ali
Jalal Khan
Ziad Taha
Moneer Khan

Muslim Community of Palm Beach County
Dalton Islamic Center
Islamic Center of Des Moines
Masjid Centralia
Islamic Society of Michiana
Masjid Abu Bakr Al Siddique
Islamic Society of Annapolis
Muslim Community Center
Al- Mu'minun Islamic Center
Islamic Society of Greater Kansas City
Islamic Association of Cary
American Islamic Academy
Islamic Educational Center North Hudson
Siddiquia Jamia Masjid
First Cleveland Mosque
Masjid Saad Foundation
Foundation for Islamic Education
Masjid Al- Noor
Islamic Society of Salt Lake City
Islamic Center of Virginia
Mustafa Center
Rizwan Jaka
Rashid Ahmed
Mubashir Ahmed
Misbah Eldereiny
Ismail Majoo
Abdul Karim Salih
Ilyas Anwar
Sayed Mohammad Jawad Qazwini
Zaid Malik
Rashid Ahmad
Ziah Sheikh

Muhammad Sultan
Kamruz Hosein
Mohamed Zakaria Badat
Usman Rahaman
Murtaza Kakli
Hammad El- Ameen
Ibrahim Dremali
Abdul Malik Mujahid
Mohammed Sirajuddin
Abdur Rahman Bashir
Anwer Hasan
Abid Husain
Habib Diab Ghanim
Tariq Jameel
Shafiq Malik
Said Mohammed
Mohammed Sheibani
Shaykh Al- Tayyab
Mohamed Alhayek
Saif Ul-Nabi
Isam Rajab
Zahid Siddiqi
Siraj Haji
Ramez Islambouli
Mohammad Islam
Abdul Wahid
Mohammed M. Safa
Rafi Uddin Ahmed
Syed Samee
Anwar N Haddam
Ghulam Nabi Fai
Zain Ali

Mohammed al Masri
Nasir Ahmed
Tarik Chebbi
Khalil Hussain
Foad Farahi
Roshan Ali
Amjad Taufique
Abdul W. Kazi
Kifah Mustapha
Husein Turki
Talal Eid
Amin Ezzeddine
Faizul Khan
Hasan Al- Qazwini
Samuel Ansari
Shahir Safi
Maha El- Genaidi
Shakil Ahmed
Mohammad Qatanani
Ismail Elshikh
Tariq Khawaja
Abu Nuruzzaman
Fawaz Damra
M.N. Tarazi
Samir Horani
Taneem Aziz
Ali Mohammed
Shaheed Coovadia
Mohammad Zia
Agha Saeed
Zafar Siddiqui
Imad-ad-Dean Ahmad

Haitham Barazangi
Roshan Ali
Rashad Mujahid
Hamid Samra
Abdul Hamid Samra
Osman Chowdhury
Furqan Muhammad
Zahir Ansari
Elkheir Elkheir
Sayed Jumaa Salam
Shaykh Besyouni
Mohammad Arrafa
Azad Ejaz
Mohammad Ali Elahi
Muhammad Nur Abdallah
Hafiz Inayadullah
Salam Al- Marayti
Mohammed Bainonie
Alvi Fakhruddin
Abubakr Nadwi
Nimer Judeh
Abbas Ahmad
Sohail Khan
Ziad Abu Hummos
Sheikh Mustafa Ahmad
Danish Siddiqui
Mohamed Magid
Abdul Hameed
Mohamad Jamal Daoudi
Sayed Moustafa Al- Qazwini
Karen Keyworth
Najee Ali

Islamic Society of East Bay
Imam Olivar Mohammed
(EACH) Education for Afghan Children
Muhammad Quadir
Basym Hasan
Mr. Mikal Akhtab
Br. Waseem Abdul Baari
Hamid Ahmed
Olive Tree Foundation
Dr. Fauzia Khan
Mohammed Joz
Imam Ahmed Elkhaldy
Waqar Qureshi
Ayah Nuriddin
Islamic Center of Marietta/Masjid Al-Hedaya
Sr. Rafia Syeed
Al-Fatih Academy
Khalid Rashied
Rasidah Zan
Abdul Rahman and Ra'ufa Clark

Basit Qari
Mohamed Elsanousi
Zubair Alam
Discover Islam
Muhammad 'Abdur-Razzaq Miller
Al Islam In Focus Productions, Inc.
Sr. Jumaana Salma Amatullah
Batavia Islamic Center
Shahid Hashmi
Ahmed Nezar
Salaam Muhammad
Islamic Center of Cedar Rapids
Adam Abu Bakar
Mr. Sulman Yousuf
The Ummah Project
Bridging the Gap, INC
Dr. Firoj Khan
Imam Rabbil Ramjohn
Muslim Womens Education and Advocacy Network
Heart of the Rose (Tariqa Shadhuliyyah)

As Salaam Islamic Center of Raleigh
Abdullah Akbar
Hazem Galal
Dr. Adel Elsaie
Dr. Abdu Moheet
Jumaana Amatullah
Br. Waa'il Abdul Salaam
Muneeb Nasir
Nur Azlina Abdul Aziz
Islamic Center of the Capital District
Mr. Abdul Wahab
Mr. Masum Azizi
Roxie France-Nuriddin
Br. Amjad Taufique
Cherine Abdalla - Smith
Afeefa Syeed
Council of Pakistan American Affairs
Al-Huda Islamic Center
Muslim Community Center of Greater Pittsburgh

Qaradawi then asserted that is why killing hundreds of helpless civilians who have nothing to do with the decision-making process and are striving hard to earn their daily bread, such as the victims of the latest explosions in America, is a heinous crime in Islam. The Prophet, peace and blessings be upon him, is reported to have stated that a woman was qualified to enter Hell because of the cat she locked up to death.

"If such is the ruling applied in protecting animals, no doubt, aggression against human beings, a fortiori, deserves greater protection, for human beings are honored by Allah Almighty and are His vicegerents on earth," he added.

Al Qaradawi said, "we Arab Muslims are the most affected by the grave consequences of hostile attack on man and life. We share the suffering experienced by innocent Palestinians at the hands of the tyrannical Jewish entity who raze the Palestinian homes to the ground, set fire to their tilth, kill them cold-bloodedly, and leave innocent orphans wailing behind.

"With this in mind, the daily life in Palestine has become a permanent memorial gathering. When Palestinians face such unjust aggression, they tend to stem bloodletting and destruction and not to claim the lives of innocent civilians."

"I categorically go against a committed Muslim's embarking on such attacks. Islam never allows a Muslim to kill the innocent and the helpless.

"If such attacks were carried out by a Muslim—as some biased groups claim—then we, in the name of our religion, deny the act and incriminate the perpetrator. We do confirm that the aggressor deserves the deterrent punishment irrespective of his religion, race or gender," he added.

"What we warn against, even if becomes a reality, is to hold a whole nation accountable for a crime carried out by a limited number of people or to characterize a certain religion as a faith giving support to violence and terrorism," Qaradawi said.

Qaradawi clarified that when the well-known Oklahoma incident was carried out by a Christian American, who was driven by a personal interests, Christianity, America or even the Christian world, were not accused of the attack because a Christian master-minded it.

"I have been asked several questions on TV programs and on public lectures about the martyr operations outside the Palestinian territories, and I always answer that I do agree with those who do not allow such martyr operations to be carried out outside the Palestinian territories.

"Instead we should concentrate on facing the occupying enemy directly. It is not permissible, as far as Islam is concerned, to shift confrontation outside the Palestinian territories. This is backed by the Qur'anic verse that reads: "Fight in the way of Allah against those who fight against you, but begin not hostilities. Lo! Allah loves not, aggressors," the renowned Muslim scholar concluded.

46. Caryle Murphy, "Islamic Scholars Say U.S. Muslim Soldiers Must Fight for Country" from *The Washington Post*

Caryle Murphy, A section p. A22 October 11, 2001 (Thursday). Reprinted with permission of The Washington Post.

The following is a fatwa from Shaykh Yusuf al-Qaradawi (Grand Islamic Scholar and Chairman of the Sunna and Sira Council, Qatar), Judge Tariq al-Bishri (First Deputy President of the Council d'etat, Ret., Egypt), Muhammad S. al-Awa (Professor of Comparative Law and Sharia, Egypt), Haytham al-Khayyat (Islamic Scholar, Syria), Mr. Fahmi Houaydi (Islamic Author and Columnist, Egypt), Shaykh Taha Jabir Alalwani (Chairman of the North

America Fiqh Council, Sterling, Virginia). It was neither much discussed nor publicized. Muhammad Abdur-Rashid was the senior Muslim chaplain in the United States Army prior to the U.S. invasion of Afghanistan in October 2001. He asked the above clerics whether it would be permissible for American Muslims enlisted in the U.S. Armed Forces to participate in a war waged against a Muslim country. The Muslim scholars agreed that such action would be permissible.

Sheikh Yusuf al-Qaradawi [Grand Islamic Scholar and Chairman of the Sunna and Sira Council, Qatar]
Judge Tariq al-Bishri [First Deputy President of the Council d'etat, Ret., Egypt]
Dr. Muhammad S. al-Awa [Professor of Comparative Law and Shari'a, Egypt]
Dr. Haytham al-Khayyat [Islamic Scholar, Syria]
Mr. Fahmi Houaydi [Islamic Author and Columnist, Egypt]
Sheikh Taha Jabir al-Alwani [Chairman of the North America Fiqh Council, Sterling, Va.]

This English version was translated from the original Arabic, authorized and approved by authors of the statement.

Following is the fatwa text:
In The Name of God, The Compassionate, The Merciful
Legal Fatwa

This is the reply to the (religious) inquiry presented by Mr. Muhammad Abdur-Rashid, the most senior Muslim chaplain in the American Armed forces. It concerns the permissibility of the Muslim military personnel within the US armed forces to participate in the war operations and its related efforts in Afghanistan and elsewhere in other Muslim countries.

In his question he states that the goals of the (war) operations are:

1) Retaliation against those "who are thought to have participated" in planning and financing the suicide operations on September 11th, against civilian and military targets in New York and Washington (he then detailed the consequences of these operations.)

2) Eliminating the elements that use Afghanistan and elsewhere as safe haven, as well as deterring the governments which harbor them, sanction them, or allow them the opportunity for military training in order to achieve their goals around the world.

3) Restoring the veneration and respect to the US as a sole superpower in the world.

Furthermore, he concludes his inquiry by mentioning that the number of the Muslim military personnel, in the three branches of the American armed forces, exceeds fifteen thousand soldiers. Hence, if they refuse to participate in fighting, they will have no choice but to resign, which might also entail other consequences. Finally, he asks if it is permissible, to those who can transfer, to serve in different capacities other than direct fighting.

The reply:
Praise be to God and peace and blessing be upon the messengers of God. We say: This question presents a very complicated issue and a highly sensitive situation for our Muslim brothers and sisters serving in the American army as well as other armies that face similar situations. All Muslims ought to be united against all those who terrorize the innocents, and those who permit the killing of non-combatants without a justifiable reason. Islam has declared the spilling of blood and the destruction of property as absolute prohibitions until the Day of Judgment. God (glory be to He) said: "Because of that We ordained

unto the Children of Israel that if anyone killed a human being—unless it be in punishment for murder or for spreading mischief on earth—it would be as though he killed all of humanity; whereas, if anyone saved a life, it would be as though he saved the life of all humanity. And indeed, there came to them Our messengers with clear signs (proofs and evidences), even then after that, many of them continued to commit mischief on earth." 5:32

Hence, whoever violates these pointed Islamic texts is an offender deserving of the appropriate punishment according to their offence and according to its consequences for destruction and mischief.

It's incumbent upon our military brothers in the American armed forces to make this stand and its religious reasoning well known to all their superiors, as well as to their peers, and to voice it and not to be silent. Conveying this is part of the true nature of the Islamic teachings that have often been distorted or smeared by the media.

If the terrorist acts that took place in the US were considered by the Islamic Law (Shar'-iah) or the rules of Islamic jurisprudence (Fiqh), the ruling for the crime of "Hirabah" (waging war against society) would be applied to their doers. God (Glory be to He) said: "The recompense of those who wage war against God and His Messenger and do mischief on earth is only that they shall be killed or crucified or their hands and their feet be cut off from opposite sides, or be exiled from the land. That is their disgrace in this world, and a great torment is theirs in the Hereafter. Except for those who (having fled away and then) came back with repentance before they fall into your power; (in that case) know that God is Oft-Forgiving, Most Merciful." 5: 33–34.

Therefore, we find it necessary to apprehend the true perpetrators of these crimes, as well as those who aid and abet them through incitement, financing or other support. They must be brought to justice in an impartial court of law and punish them appropriately, so that it could act as deterrent to them and to others like them who easily slay the lives of innocents, destroy properties and terrorize people. Hence, it's a duty on Muslims to participate in this effort with all possible means, in accordance with God's (Most High) saying: "And help one another in virtue and righteousness, but do not help one another in sin and transgression." 5:2.

On the other hand, the source of the uneasiness that American Muslim military men and women may have in fighting other Muslims, is because it's often difficult—if not impossible—to differentiate between the real perpetrators who are being pursued, and the innocents who have committed no crime at all. The authentic saying by the prophet states: "When two Muslims face each other in fighting and one kills the other, then both the killer and the killed are in the hell-fire. Someone said: we understand that the killer is in hell, why then the one who's being killed? The prophet said: because he wanted to kill the other person." (Narrated by Bukhari and Muslim.)

The noble Hadith mentioned above only refers to the situation where the Muslim is in charge of his affairs. He is capable of fighting as well as capable of not fighting. This Hadith does not address the situation where a Muslim is a citizen of a state and a member of a regular army. In this case, he has no choice but to follow orders, otherwise his allegiance and loyalty to his country could be in doubt. This would subject him to much harm since he would not enjoy the privileges of citizenship without performing its obligations.

The Muslim (soldier) must perform his duty in this fight despite the feeling of uneasiness of "fighting without discriminating." His intention (niyya) must be to fight for enjoining of the truth and defeating falsehood. It's to prevent aggression on the innocents, or to apprehend the perpetrators and bring them to justice. It's not his concern what other consequences of the fighting that might result in his personal discomfort, since he alone can neither control it nor prevent it. Furthermore, all deeds are accounted (by God) according to the intentions. God (the Most High) does not burden any soul except what it can bear. In addition, Muslim jurists have ruled that what a Muslim cannot control he cannot be held accountable for, as God (the Most High) says: "And keep your duty to God as much as you can." 64:16. The prophet (prayer and peace be upon him) said: "when I ask of you to do something, do it as much as you can." The Muslim here is a part of a whole, if he absconds, his departure will result in a greater harm, not only for him but also for the Muslim community in his country—and here there are many millions of them. Moreover, even if fighting causes him discomfort spiritually or psychologically, this personal hardship must be endured for the greater public good, as the jurisprudence (fiqhi) rule states.

Furthermore, the questioner inquires about the possibility of the Muslim military personnel in the American armed forces to serve in the back lines—such as in the relief services' sector and similar works. If such requests are granted by the authorities, without reservation or harm to the soldiers, or to the other American Muslim citizens, then they should request that. Otherwise, if such request raises doubts about their allegiance or loyalty, cast suspicions, present them with false accusations, harm their future careers, shed misgivings on their patriotism, or similar sentiments, then it's not permissible to ask for that.

To sum up, it's acceptable—God willing—for the Muslim American military personnel to partake in the fighting in the upcoming battles, against whomever, their country decides, has perpetrated terrorism against them. Keeping in mind to have the proper intention as explained earlier, so no doubts would be cast about their loyalty to their country, or to prevent harm to befall them as might be expected. This is in accordance with the Islamic jurisprudence rules which state that necessities dictate exceptions, as well as the rule that says one may endure a small harm to avoid a much greater harm.

And God the Most High is Most Knowledgeable and Most Wise.

47. Shaykh Muhammad Hisham Kabbani, "Islamic Extremism: A Viable Threat to U.S. National Security" from *the Islamic Supreme Council of America*

From presentation by Shaykh Muhammad Hisham Kabbani at an Open Forum at the U.S. Department of State, January 7, 1999. Available online: http://www.islamicsupremecouncil. org/bin/site/wrappers/extremism_inamerica_unveiling010799.html. Reprinted with permission of the Islamic Supreme Council of America.

Shaykh Muhammad Hisham Kabbani was born in 1945 in Beirut, Lebanon. He received his undergraduate degree in chemistry from the American University of Beirut and studied medicine at the University of Louvain in Belgium. He also received a degree in Islamic Law from the University of Damascus. He is a Sufi shaykh of the Naqshbandi Order and was sent to the United States in 1991 to set up Islamic study centers. In 1997, he established the Islamic Supreme Council of America in Fenton, Michigan. The Islamic Supreme Council uses traditional Islamic jurisprudence (fiqh) to provide fatwas for Muslims in America. The following is a transcript from an open forum at the U.S. Department of State at which Shaykh Kabbani discussed his perspective on Islamic extremism and its relationship to the

United States. His remarks created a huge controversy among American Muslim organizations, which protested that his presentation was biased and dangerous for the future of Islam in the United States.

As salaamu alaykum wa rahmatullahi wa barakatuh. It is a greeting in the Arabic language which means peace be upon you all. I was very happy to see that my name was written double "shaykh." Because you know that shaykh might mean oil shaykh, or a fundamentalist, extremist. So two opposites make a positive—two negatives multiplied by each other become a positive. So those who wrote that were very clever...thank you very much.

It was a delightful opportunity to hear from Dr. Fairbanks and the honorable Congressman Dana Rohrabacher because I think such kinds of events will lead to more understanding about Islam, what Islam believes and what Islam rejects. I think that many, many people in the United States and in western countries, in Europe, are afraid of a monster called Islam. And as the honorable Congressman Dana Rohrabacher said, it is an insult to consider the whole of Muslims, to take them into one side, and make them extremists. Really it is not correct. It is a little bit insulting.

I don't want to say too much, in order to make it easy on our children. Our children are living here, they are American, and they are born here. All these American Muslims, from parents who migrated here from Europe in the 18th century or the 19th century or the 20th century, are really good Muslims, and they have a friendship with all different faiths. So really they feel shy when Islam is being focused on as a religion of terrorism and extremism—which is completely wrong.

On behalf of the Islamic Supreme Council of America, and many, many Muslims—because I cannot speak on behalf of *all* Muslims, as many non-profit organizations in America do. Immediately when something happens in the Middle East or that region they send media alerts saying they are speaking on behalf of the whole Muslim community, which is completely incorrect. So on behalf of many Muslims, I will say that it is an opportunity to address you and to give you the authentic, traditional voice of Islam. It is a voice of traditional Islam, which is moderation and tolerance and love—loving and to be loved—and living in peace with all other faiths and religions.

As in the time of Prophet Muhammad, peace be upon him, when he established his first state after having received the message for 13 years. He established a state in a city called Medina, located in Saudi Arabia now. First it had Jews, it had Christians, it had people of all kinds of different faiths, and never he fought with anyone. He never killed anyone, but was always educating and giving the message of God, as Moses, as Jesus. We do not go into all these details because people, I think, like to hear more about comparative Islam nowadays, and what is going on in the Muslim ideas, and in the world today.

I would like to emphasize that even a thief who steals something, cannot have his hand cut for stealing—as is practiced in some countries nowadays—under the name of Islam, when the rest of what that country is doing is against the name of Islam. The leaders of some of these countries try to label themselves as pioneers of Islam when they practice extremist ideology and in fact do not observe Islamic practices in their homes. In their homes you will find all kinds of un-Islamic materials or un-Islamic works. Islam never cuts anyone's hand unless certain principles have been followed. Not only that: in the whole history of Prophet's time, only one or two people had their hands cut. Before that time they were killing people; they were killing the thief. It was a cultural matter supported by a message that reduced the penalty from killing to cutting the hand. And it was not practiced too much in the time of the Prophet unless it was a very severe case. Even throwing stones; never in the Qur'an, never in the Holy Qur'an can you find one verse that says that you have to throw stones at someone who committed adultery and stone them until death. Anyone can read the Qur'an and we will not find one verse that sentenced anyone who committed adultery to death.

These things have to be clarified before we begin, because extremists are using these kinds of ideology in order to benefit their own positions, to successfully brainwash the minds of Muslims and other people who will then support them.

What is the definition of extremism? We can see in all of history: even when the first settlers came to the United States they were from different countries; Spain, England, France, European Countries. They were fighting on this land and fighting with the Indians. Do we call this extremism? A fight for a better living, which you understand you are doing not for a religious motive, is not extremism. Extremism in Islam, or in religion, is when you use religion to label intolerance, to turn from religion and take ideas that you can extract for yourself, or deduce for yourself, and use to make a militant movement and disturb the peace in your country or around the world. That is called "extremism," and "Islamic Extremism." But a movement for better living, that is not extremism.

For example, they are fighting in Ireland and in Poland, as Dr. Fairbanks mentioned. They were fighting the Soviet Union, communism. Can you say this is extremism? It is not extremism. They are trying to escape from the oppression they have suffered for many, many years. Even in Israel, we see that there are peace treaties that have been accepted by not all of the Muslim countries, but the majority of the Muslim countries —including Egypt, Syria, Jordan, including the PLO, including Lebanon, including Saudi Arabia, including Qatar, including Morocco. Many Muslim countries have agreed on the peace treaties. Now we see that fighting is no longer a legitimate action that people can commit since they oppose the peace treaty that has been signed by the democratic leadership that they have elected.

In Palestine, we see what happened with Yasser Arafat. He was elected. I am not saying if Yasser Arafat is good or bad, we are not going to discuss that subject, but since democracy plays a big role in the Muslim world now, we have to trust in the fact that he has been elected. He signed a treaty, it means they have to go along with it. If they don't go along, it means they have the right to complain and criticize like any opposition, but without using the name of Islam and creating confusion in the West and in other countries. [It is confusing] to say that it is under the name of Islam that we are conducting a militant movement against a certain country or against anywhere in the world. So that is one of the main problems that we are facing nowadays.

When we come back to what is threatening the security of Russia and the security of the United States, here at home, we see a threat that will grow if the leadership of this country does not quickly stop the kind of extremist ideology that is filtering in—the same extremist ideology that it is being spread all over, in many places around the United States. I will come soon to that.

But I would like to say that Prophet (sall' allahu alayhi wa sallam) Prophet Muhammad (peace be upon him) gave us many examples in his holy traditions. For 18 months God asked Prophet, in Holy Qur'an, to direct his face when he prayed—when we pray we direct our face to Mecca which is the Ka'aba of the Muslims, the House of God in Mecca, so God asked him to face that. After some time Prophet directed himself toward al-Aqsa, Jerusalem, which we know as the Bayt ul-Maqdis, Jerusalem of today. For 18 months he directed his faith to worship God toward the place of Jesus and the place of Moses, where they were born and where they brought their message, in order to show that there is a completion, and a connection between Judaism, Christianity and Islam. This was also to earn the respect of the Jews and the Christians in order to educate them about the message of Islam and show them that it is not hostile to Judaism and Christianity. It was one of the main themes in Islamic history that Prophet tried many times to make peace treaties and to extend his hand to the Jews and to the Christians in his area, wherever he was living. Later, when he the religion was well established, he turned his face towards Mecca while Jews and Christians were living in the same town.

Islam, in general, is a religion that calls for respecting everyone and living together with everyone. Now we are seeing that something is going astray from Islam, as has happened in every religion, as Dr. Fairbanks said. Between Catholicism and Protestantism you can see there is a difference. Modernity came, and new thinkers came into Islam. In their countries, where they didn't have any relationship with the outside world, they began to think that they could bring something new into the Islamic way, in their own tribes. They made sure the way Islam had traditional evolved over 1200 years could be modified and changed to a way that suits the Bedouins and tribes in the desert, because that's where it evolved, this kind of mentality and ideology.

It began in the 17th and 18th century, when this ideology was supported by the tribes. The man who brought it to the tribes was a Muslim scholar by the name of Muhammad ibn Abd-al Wahhab. This was in the Eastern part of what we call Saudi Arabia during the 17th and 18th century. These ideas were going forth and back, forth and back. Sometimes they were put down and other times they were supported. There was a struggle with the Muslims trying to keep them down with the support of the Ottoman Empire. They were successful until the Ottoman Empire dissolved and finished in the middle of 1920 and the new regime came—it was the secular regime of Mustafa Kemal [Ataturk]. They then found an opportunity in the tribes, which no longer had the support of the Ottoman Empire in that area. They had freedom to go and change the ideas and brainwash the minds of Muslims in this area. Slowly, slowly in the many years from 1920 until today they were very successful in establishing a new ideology in Islam that is very extremist in its point of view. It was not so militant, however; it didn't take the form of militancy, but it took the form of revival or renewal of Islamic tradition.

They were completely against Sufism because they think that you can go directly to God without the intercession of any saint, friend of God, or any person who can help you. The traditional Muslim believed, over 1300 or 1400 years of Islam—until today— that there can be an intermediary between you and God. This ideology prevented and prohibited that, but it was not militant until recently, when it took a militant standpoint and enforced itself in many regions around the world. Unfortunately, it has evolved in many Muslim countries like Lebanon, Syria a little bit, Egypt too much, Saudi Arabia, Jordan, and many countries like Algeria, Tunisia, Morocco a little bit, now in Pakistan, India, Indonesia, Malaysia too much now, China a little bit, and now it is coming to the Caucasus. Their way of thinking is that Islam has to be reformed, and with a sword. They think they cannot reform Islam except with the mentality of a sword and the mentality of a gun. Unfortunately, extremism appeared in Islam, but not because of Islam. Islam always presented—and I say it many times that Prophet Muhammad used to act this way with his neighbors or his friends that are not Muslims—gifts, flowers, and love, not ever holding a sword against them, or ever starting a struggle or a fight against them.

There are many events in Muslim history where the Prophet made peace treaties with non-Muslims.

These people nowadays are developing two ways of understanding the situation of Islam. From one side they think that they have to reform it; it is a duty on them, they have been brainwashed to think that they have to cleanse the world of devils and demons and of countries that suppress them, oppress them, and try to shut them down. We always see that. I am speaking openly to give advice to the government and the US officials in order to open their minds because this is a big danger that may result in a struggle within the United States.

Recently there was an article in a Saudi gazette called *al-Majalla*. They interviewed me and they asked me how I think Muslims should be involved in the political system. And I said Muslims have to be involved in the political system because they are part of this nation, they are part of this culture, and they are part of this country. So they quoted me and then they have on the other page another man who they asked the same question, and he said no. He said that we must tell America that before speaking with us they must govern in their country under the Islamic Shariah, under the Islamic law; before we will be part of the system, they have to be part of our Islamic law.

We know in Islam Prophet Muhammad, sall' allahu alayhi wa sallam, mentioned in many places in Holy Qur'an things like there is no compulsion in religion, that people are free to take any religion they like. These extremists are not thinking with the Holy verses of Qur'an. Instead they are trying to impose their extremist ideas upon everyone, Muslim and non-Muslim. It has become a struggle for governments to reconcile or compromise. There is no way; you might compromise with a moderate Muslim, with a Muslim that is living happily around the world, but you cannot compromise, you cannot build a bridge with an extremist. He's never going to agree with you, because he thinks—this is their thinking, there is nothing else—that they have a duty and they have to deliver the message that either you follow us or you are under our attack. They are declaring war against anyone who will not go with them. This is why they are against their government, for example, in Saudi Arabia, they are against their government in Egypt, they are against their government in Jordan, they are against their government Syria, they are against their government in Pakistan, they are against their government in the Caucasus, and in Chechnya, and in all these countries, because they are infiltrating inside and indoctrinating people with their new ideas and new method.

As we see it from inside, from within—because I don't want to go into too much definition and explanation of Islam—what we are seeing as Muslims is that extremism became more of a business than a message because it involves drugs, and drugs are not allowed in Islam. Planting Opium and Cocaine and Hashish, Hash, is not allowed in Islam. Womanizing is not allowed in Islam, drinking is not allowed in Islam. We see these extremists are planting Opium, are planting Cocaine, and are selling this, justifying their acts as Muslims to reestablish and reform Islam around the world but they are committing all kinds of un-Islamic acts and un-Islamic behavior.

Recently they found in London, between London and France and all that area in Western Europe, that there is a big network of women that one of the very famous Arabic newspapers—either *al Wasat* or *al Watan al Arabi*—revealed in a big report two or three months ago. They found a network run by Muslim women who, during the day, are covered from top to bottom and, during the night, have dates. They are dating high officials in many countries around the world to take the information from them and to give it to the extremists. We have to ask ourselves: is this Islamic or un-Islamic? If it is Islamic we cannot see it in any verse of Holy Qur'an or any narration of Prophet. It is un-Islamic. So on what basis are they saying they are working under the name of Islam? So we see that now it is more a business and more a struggle, a fight, openly between extremism and America.

It is completely obvious to anyone who considers the matter and the situation. You will find that it is an open fight between the West and the Extremists. In the last report that we printed in our Muslim Magazine—which is going to come in January, after one week (it went to print)—we show how extremism evolved and how many extremist groups have formed a coalition among themselves although they differ in ideology. They differ in belief but because a coalition benefits everyone, they formed an alliance. We mention in the Magazine, and according to our sources, that bin Laden has asked Hezbollah, Hamas, and Jihad al-Islami, and Ga'amat al Islamiyyi, to form a coalition and he was able to bring them together under one network in order to work together, although each one differs from the other in his point of view.

So that's what is going on under the name of Islam, but Islam itself is innocent of such kinds of actions. As we represent Muslims, and we have on our board 157 international scholars from around the world—they are on our advisory committee, our board of advisors—we condemn all kinds of extremism wherever it is. We want to tell people to be careful, that something major might hit quickly because they were able to buy more than 20 atomic nuclear heads from some of the mafia in the ex-Soviet Union, in the republics of the ex-Soviet Union, and they traded it for $30 million dollars and 2 tons of Opium that has been shipped to the Caucasus and now is being distributed through all the Caucasus and the ex-Soviet republics.

They were able to get more than 20 nuclear warheads and now they are hiring thousands of scientists from the ex-Soviet Union who have no jobs. They are giving them salaries of $2000 a month, in order to try to build an atomic reactor in Khost, underground, and in order to break these atomic warheads into smaller partitions, like small chips, to be put in any suitcase, even in a handbag, and be shipped anywhere in the world. This might affect the whole stability of peace around the world. This has to be very well monitored, and very well looked upon, because it is a danger for all humanity.

Moreover, what we are interested in in the United States. I'd like to say that there have been many non-profit organizations established in the United States whose job is only to collect money and to send it, as you know—most of you know—to send it to extremists outside the United States. This is a big dilemma that is facing us here, because you don't know where the money is going, and it is more than hundreds of millions of dollars that have been sent to extremist parties in the Middle East and the Far East, as well as Afghanistan and the Caucasus now. Our sources say that many, many millions of dollars have been collected and sent. They send it under humanitarian aid, but it doesn't go to humanitarian aid. They say that it is to help the people of this country or that country, and they show on television and on their flyers that they are delivering it to help homeless people or poor people. Yes, some of it will go to homeless people and poor people but the majority, 90 per cent of it, will go into the black markets in these countries and buying weapon arsenals.

I know this from my home country of Lebanon where we used to receive a lot of aid from the United States and United Nations. As soon as the aid arrived in Lebanon, you could see a little bit go to the public and the rest would be sold in the black market. For a box that costs more than $100, you can go and buy it in the black market for less than $20. All this money, that came under humanitarian aid, they resell so you cannot trace it, they go back and buy weapons with it to fight and to spread extremism under the name of Islam.

The second issue that United States has to look on within, for security, is the fact that there are many Muslim organizations that claim to speak on behalf of the Muslim community but that in reality are not moderate, but extremist. They hijacked the mike, or they were elected because they are good speakers, but they give a wrong idea about Islam. Always we see them in the media criticizing and complaining and sending action alerts and media alerts and showing people that we do not accept this or we reject that.

Like, for example, with the recent issue of Iraq. The Islamic Supreme Council sent a statement that there are victims in Iraq and there is bloodshed in Iraq, but it is a matter of national security to stop Saddam Hussein from running the country, and it is not a Muslim issue. When everyone was saying from the Muslim community that it is a Muslim issue, we stood fast and we stood alone to say that it is not a Muslim issue but that it is a political issue. Saddam Hussein is a communist in his background. He is of the socialist Ba'ath party, which does not believe in religion. It is secular and does not believe in religion. Anyone who has a beard or anyone wears a turban will be put in prison within a day. This is the mentality of this kind of regime. So it is not a Muslim issue, it's a political issue. It's a Muslim issue when you are hurting the people, and you are hurting a whole community as if we were to say that we are fighting the Iraqi people. But the policy was not to fight the Iraqi people. The policy was to fight a tyranny that was running Iraq. That's a big difference. So we stood up and we said this and we have received a lot of criticism from the Muslim community. But we want to advise the American community and we want to advise our government, our congressmen, that there is something big going on and people are not understanding it.

The third major problem that is now going on is that you have many mosques around the United States and there is not an organized government or policy to look over the mosques like in Muslim countries where you cannot open a mosque by yourself, and you cannot open a charity by yourself. It has to be done according to the structure of the Islamic religion. That's why in the Muslim countries, you cannot find extremist ideology. As soon as you find the extremist ideology they kick them out and bring in traditional Islamic scholars. The extremist ideology comes from the street so the extremists don't know what they are talking about. So they form small circles in different homes or different basements or in different areas and they begin to brainwash the people. That's why we find this kind of movement is becoming big now, especially when the idea is that we have a struggle between us and the United States. "United States is not supporting us," "United States is supporting someone else," they find that United States is not supporting Afghanistan, as Congressman Rohrabacher said. The United States supported Pakistan, the United States supported Egypt, the United States supported PLO and the peace treaty, the United States supported Saudi Arabia, the United States supported Kuwait. The United States is supporting whomever they can, but sometimes it is out of reach that they can support everyone. So they cannot be blamed. The United States cannot be blamed for something that they cannot control.

The most dangerous thing that is going on now in these mosques, that has been sent upon these mosques around the United States—like churches they were established by different organizations and that is ok—but the problem with our communities is the extremist ideology. Because they are very active they took over the mosques; and we can say that they took over more than 80% of the mosques that have been established in the US. And there are more than 3000 mosques in the US.

So it means that the methodology or ideology of extremist has been spread to 80% of the Muslim population, but not all of them agree with it. But mostly the youth and the new generation do because they are students and they don't think except with their emotions and they are rebellious against their own leaders and government. This is the nature and psychology of human beings. When we are students in university or college we always fight the government, whether they are right or wrong, we have to attack the government. This is how they have been raised.

In this way we see that the extremist ideology, and this is the fourth danger, is beginning to spread very quickly into the universities through the national organizations, associations and clubs that they are establishing around the universities. Most of these clubs—they are Muslim clubs and the biggest is the national one—are being run mostly by the extremist ideology that they do not understand other than to say that America is wrong and they are right. You can find this on the Internet; you can find it everywhere on homepages and websites that they are against the United States. This is where we don't know how far it goes, and how far it is out of hand. This might affect the whole university system in the United States. Through the universities there will be the most danger. If the nuclear atomic warheads reach these universities, you don't know what these students are going to do, because their way of thinking is brainwashed, limited and narrow-minded.

This is what I want to say to you, to present to you from within the Muslim community. We want to tell you that the Muslim community as a whole is innocent from whatever extremism and extremist ideology is being spread around the world. I don't know if there is time or not, but I know that to go in detail on how extremism evolved would take a lot of time, so I've tried to summarize as much as possible. I'd like to tell you that extremism, when a person has been brainwashed, demands that a person doesn't think, even if his father or his mother or his brother tells him to stop, he has to go to do what he has been asked to do. That's why there are 5000 suicide bombers being trained by bin Laden in Afghanistan who are ready to move to any part of the world and explode themselves. They are very sophisticated, they can buy anything they need locally and then put it on and explode themselves.

The problem of extremism is a big danger, and it can be solved if the West better understands Islam and builds bridges with the moderate Muslims, the traditional Muslims. This way, the Muslim community will eliminate the extremist threat from within. Otherwise, media, television, newspapers, and the leadership will not understand that there is a difference between extremists and Muslims. They have to begin a dialogue with Muslims from around the United States, and they have to have good advisors. What I am seeing, unfortunately, are those that are advising the media, or advising the government are not the moderate Muslims. Those whose opinion the government asks are the extremists themselves. Those that have been quoted in the newspapers, in the magazines, in the television, in the media are the extremists themselves. You are not hearing the authentic voice of Muslims, of moderate Muslims, but you are hearing the extremist voice of Muslims. That's why they are getting a wrong idea, because the extremists are very well supported, are very well affiliated with outside regimes that have sponsored them with billions of dollars to be active in the United States. They have been successful in doing that so the media does not listen except to them. I am even hearing that there are advisors to many congressmen, to many senators, to many organizations that are supporters of extremism and not moderate Muslims.

Thank you very much, may God bless you.

Moderator: We'll take questions from the mike, and while you're making your way, you need to come to the mike so we can pick you up.

Questioner (unidentified): Shaykh Kabbani, extremism is always found near ignorance. Dr. Fairbanks had alluded that there were sales of information on how to practice the faith in its traditional way. But what I thought you said was that this information was for sale. Is there any endeavor, since most are impoverished and cannot afford this, to give them fundamental, correct beliefs of your faith.

Shaykh Kabbani: I think that there are ways to give that literature to the people, to educate them. But it is not cheap to do that, it is very expensive. The moderate Muslims never have financial support to do that. If they can find grants, and find money, then they can have leaders of these organizations, then we can easily [sell information] and educate people about traditional Islam. The extremists have already printed out the ideology of extremism, and distributed it all over the world. You'll find it in any mosque in America.

Moderator: Maybe that would be a good way for NGOs to spend their money instead of on something that can be sold for arms.

Questioner (unidentified): I have two questions for the Shaykh. First, you were talking about specific information, a specific number of warheads and a specific amount of money paid for these warheads. Have you informed our government about this information...

Shaykh Kabbani: When they ask me I will inform them.

Questioner (continued): Is our government doing something about this? This is really dangerous information that you are providing us and it is very serious. I am concerned, personally, for my safety and the safety of my family and the safety of the American people.

Shaykh Kabbani: I am also concerned, that is why I am speaking. For the reason I am concerned I am putting it to our government. But whether they will now take my advice or not, I cannot say.

Questioner (continued): My second question is: I represent one of the non-profit Muslim organizations and it strikes me that basically you are making yourself the only legitimate Muslim organization here. I am personally not an extremist but how could you deny me the right to protest my government's actions? Since we live in a democracy—we're preaching about democracy—so I disagree with my government's action in Iraq, how could you deny me that, and because of that call me an extremist or anything else? And you say that in your action alert that the Iraqi issue is not a Muslim issue; according to UN statistics about one million Iraqis have died from the sanctions, and about 80% of the Iraqi population is Muslim, and about 800,000 Muslims have died, is it a Muslim issue? And why can I not say that it is a Muslim issue, and what is wrong with me saying that it is a Muslim issue? As an American who is Muslim, practicing his right in a democracy, that is America.

Shaykh Kabbani: Thank you for clarifying this issue. First, I'll say I don't represent the whole Muslim issue, I represent our organization and some of the Muslim community. It is on videotape and you can go back and hear what I said. The second question when you say that you don't have the right, of course you have a right, anyone has the right, to say anything and to complain and to make your voice heard. But I am saying that there is no right for militancy, when we have the right in democracy to speak up and say what we want to say, and you are free. Don't use militancy in order to support your idea, and if they don't agree with your opinion, you are going to fight with them. That's where I am specifying about extremism in general. And about Iraq, you consider it a Muslim issue, I don't consider it a Muslim issue. When Iraq attacked Kuwait, what it a Muslim issue or not? They killed Muslims in Kuwait. Is this a Muslim issue or not? When Iraq killed 5,619 Egyptians in Iraq, is this a Muslim issue or not a Muslim issue? When Iraq attacked Iran and killed hundreds of thousands of Iranians with chemical weapons, is this a Muslim issue or is it not a Muslim issue? So, how can I consider that one is a Muslim issue, though we never heard anyone speaking about Iranians being killed by the Iraqi chemical weapons, or Kuwaitis being assassinated by the Iraqi fighting, and Egyptian being killed by the Iraqis. Why don't we say this is a Muslim issue, and be fair for both sides.

This is what I like to express and you have a free right to consider it Muslim or not. But for me, it is a Muslim issue to take out the sanctions, that is a Muslim issue, we have to take the sanctions out, we have to relieve the victims of Iraq. But the tyranny of the leadership, that is the problem, you know that he killed hundreds of thousands of Turks, he attacked many Muslims inside the country. So why do we say to America or to the West that you are killing the Muslims, but we cannot say to Saddam Hussein he is killing the Muslims? So I don't see that it is fair to be a Muslim issue, but I do see that it is fair to see it more as a political issue against Saddam Hussein, and to relieve sanctions and to relieve the people from being victims under the oppression of Saddam Hussein.

(Inaudible question from the same audience member)

Shaykh Kabbani: Some Muslim non-profit organizations are working with extremists. And if you want to name them we can name them, privately.

Questioner (unidentified): I'm just interested in knowing more about the sale of these warheads, who, what, when, why and where?

Shaykh Kabbani: Everyone is going to be worried about these nuclear heads. I am also worried about all the information we got from that region of the world. First I want to say that bin Laden is married to the leader of the Taliban movement, to Mullah Omar, he is married to his daughter. So bin Laden is the son-in-law of Mullah Muhammad Omar, who is the leader of Taliban. I am also worried; we get the information, from reasonable sources and from very respected sources, and through friends we have around the world, that this has happened recently. The opium was shipped through the Caucasus from Afghanistan reaching a state adjacent to Russia. And they have made a deal that Taliban will move [bin Laden] to that state and to leave Afghanistan, because the pressure that the United States is putting on Afghanistan is that they want Taliban is that they want them to move [bin Laden] out or to be assassinated. There is now some kind of networking being made in order to move bin Laden to one of the Caucasus republics and through this Caucasus republics' mafia, he was able to get these 20 plus atomic warheads, according to these sources. And not only that, they are worried also that there is now around 36,000 atomic warheads under the control of some political regime in the area and some of the mafia, and they believe some of these atomic warheads are in the hands of the extremist groups.

Questioner (continued): So the warheads actually belong to bin Laden?

Shaykh Kabbani: Yes, the 20 plus warheads actually belong to his organization. According to the sources we get our information from, and we have a good article in our magazine explaining this in our coming issue.

Questioner (continued): One other question that is about the mosques in this country. You say that 80% of them are run by the extremists, I wonder what you mean by that.

Shaykh Kabbani: 80% of them have been being run by the extremist ideology, but not acting as a militant movement. We don't know if this will lead in the future to be more in the hands of militant extremism or not. There are two kinds of extremism: there is the extremism ideology and there is the extremist militant movement. In the future some of them might be working or affiliating themselves with such kinds of militant extremism.

Questioner (continued): You said, on the other hand, that most American Muslims are peace loving, yet their mosques are being run by these extremists?

Shaykh Kabbani: Muslims, in general, are peace loving and tolerant. And a Muslim likes to go and find a place to go and make his service, make his worship and go and doesn't interfere. So the board of trustees of these mosques is being run by these extremists.

Questioner (unidentified): I have a request for a clarification of something you said and then a question. You mentioned earlier in your talk that because there now is a treaty between the Israelis and the Palestinians, that fighting against the Israelis is no longer justified. But if the treaty is not carried out, and of course the present government of Israel is not carrying out the treaty, at some point would you agree that fighting is justified again?

Shaykh Kabbani: As long as we can make peace we must not fight. As long as we can negotiate and come into good terms, we must not fight. And this is what we are seeing in many of the Arab countries and Muslim countries that are involved in these extremist acts.

Questioner (continued): My question is this: if the present Israeli government is succeeded by another one like it, do think it would help the United States to disarm the Islamic fundamentalists around the world? To come out very frankly, I'm saying that the U.S. will not support Israeli extremism and denounce this as not keeping treaties that were signed in the White House. Would this help disarm the Muslim Fundamentalists in their campaign against the United States?

Shaykh Kabbani: Can you repeat the question?

Questioner (continued): Ok. I'll repeat it more briefly. If the present Israeli government is succeeded by another similar extremist Israeli government in the elections that are coming up, would it help the United States to disarm the Muslim fundamentalists, that is, would it help us with the Muslim masses in the world, to come out very clearly I'm saying and denounce Israeli Extremism? Would this be a useful thing for the United States to do for our own protection?

Shaykh Kabbani: We have first to define if the assumption is correct that there will be an extremist government coming or not. Or, who can define what is extremist and what is not extremist according to the Israeli people. I cannot define what is extremist or not. It is a Israeli opinion to say if their government is extremist or not. And then we can go with our assumption if they are extremist or not. But since the Arabs and the Muslims are trying to make a peaceful relationship, as it happened with Egypt, as it happened with Jordan, as it happened now with PLO, if it will go along now or not, or it will be abided by or not, we don't know yet. Also what will happen now with Syria and with Lebanon, for what is there to fight and what need to have people with arms and weapons? Because we saw this problem happening with our people in Lebanon, we saw that when people have weapons, and not government – because these people are not government movements, these movements are personal movement organizations, they are coming from ordinary people – they come together and make an opposition movement. It's not a government fighting another government; it's not Egypt fighting Israel, or Jordan fighting Israel. It's a movement within the country that they are opposing. So they can oppose with word of mouth. If Hamas for example, let's say Hamas, since you are referring to Israel, if Hamas is going to fight and explode everywhere in Israel, is it going to change anything? With whom is the power, is it with Hamas, or is it with the Israelis? So they can disturb the peace, but they cannot implement anything if Israel does not want to come and make peace and make a conference with the Arabs and say that they want to live in peace and live together. That's why I think that weapons must not be in the hand of movements that are not government movements, but militant movements. We saw this in Lebanon, they were killing each other from door to door, Muslim killing Muslim, Shi'ite killing Shi'ite, Christian killing Christian, Christian killing Muslim, when they had weapons in their hands. But when weapons are not in the hands, everyone can come and make peace treaties.

Questioner (unidentified): My question is in regard to the influence of bin Laden and these new Extremist strains and other so-called fundamentalist groups. You spoke about a recent conference where bin Laden had a number of extremist groups come together under some kind of umbrella organization. As far as I understand, in the past, groups like Islamic Jihad or Islamic Organization or Muslim Brotherhood have focused on reforming their own states, whether it be from the top, attacking the government, or from below with the people. Are we seeing a change within these organizations as well as their debate within, that you know of, Muslim Brotherhood or Islamic Jihad or Ga'amat al Islami, that you know of, that's contesting this idea of attacking these external enemies like the United States? Could you comment on this?

Shaykh Kabbani: What we saw recently that this umbrella organization and this network of these different organizations coming with bin Laden under one organization, with ideologies, it doesn't mean that they are like Muslim Brotherhood, that they are any more militant, like at the time of Jamal Abdul Nasser. They are a group that is trying to promote their own ideology in the country and trying to fool the government in the way they work things and what they believe. So it is not a militant movement anymore, but it is an economic movement. But, we see the other groups like al Jihad al Islami and Jama'at al Islami and the other groups in Lebanon, they are more of a militant movement because they carry weapons. Muslim Brotherhood doesn't carry weapons, they are not as the others that carry weapons. We see the others that carry weapons are coming together to network because they found they would be more powerful and support for themselves if they work together as a network. This might make a threat not only to the United States, but to the whole world. We have heard that they have come to South America, to build up a big network there, in South America, with the mafia that is existing there in order to smuggle into the United States or to smuggle more through the Caucasus.

Questioner (unidentified): Shaykh, I was wondering if you would talk about whether you're at all concerned that with the dismal understanding that exists in the United States of Islam and Islamic groups, are you not at all concerned that as you send out these alarm bells about extremists and militants that moderate and peace-loving Muslims will be caught up in this net of reaction?

Shaykh Kabbani: Can you repeat the question?

Questioner (continued): Are you concerned that in warning Americans, who know very little about Islam, in warning them so strongly as you have, about the militancy, that they will also turn against the moderates?

Shaykh Kabbani: From my point of view it is better to say something than to keep quiet. If I kept quiet, a danger might suddenly come that you are not looking for, so in preventing that danger from coming I am trying to sacrifice and give something to the Americans in order that they understand that there is something coming up slowly, we don't know where it is going to hit, it might be here, might be outside, might be any country, and might affect the interest of the United States. So that's why I said in the presentation that the United States, the media must work with the Muslims, must work with the Muslims that are everywhere and they are very moderate, and they are very well known to be moderate and traditional and denouncing extremism. How do you know a moderate Muslim from non-moderate? One who denounces extremism. So it is better to build bridges in this way you can understand Islam and the media will eliminate extremist Muslims from Islam. As I heard in a meeting yesterday, that United States government is expressing its policy; President Clinton asked to separate extremism from Islam, to show they are completely separate entities, and that Islam as a religion has nothing to do with extremism. That's how the media has to look at it. It is the duty of the media not to jump quickly and fire accusations against the whole of Muslims, to provoke the Muslims. They have to go and work with the Muslims to separate theirs from the extremist ideology.

Moderator: Are there any other questions? Thank you very much for joining us, it was a great pleasure to have you.

48. Nuh Ha Mim Keller, "The Woman: A Parable"

MCMXCVIII © nuh ha mim keller, accessed May 18, 2006. Available online: http://www. masud.co.uk/ISLAM/nuh/parable.htm. Reprinted with permission of Nuh Ha Mim Keller.

Nuh Ha Mim Keller (for a biography see the "Keller, Shaykh Nuh" entry in Volume 1) wrote the following parable in response to the terrorist attacks of September 11, 2001. Imitating the Oriental narrative style, Keller's story seeks to demonstrate that the pursuit of worldly pleasures will bring only death and spiritual loss to Muslims. It can also be read as a moral condemnation of the political use of Islam. That is, using Islam to pursue material goals like the September 11th hijackers did.

A man was walking through the marketplace one afternoon when, just as the muezzin began the call to prayer, his eye fell on a woman's back. She was strangely attractive, though dressed in fulsome black, a veil over head and face, and she now turned to him as if somehow conscious of his over-lingering regard, and gave him a slight but meaningful nod before she rounded the corner into the lane of silk sellers. As if struck by a bolt from heaven, the man was at once drawn, his heart a prisoner of that look, forever. In vain he struggled with his heart, offering it one sound reason after another to go his way— wasn't it time to pray?—but it was finished: there was nothing but to follow.

He hastened after her, turning into the market of silks, breathing from the exertion of catching up with the woman, who had unexpectedly outpaced him and even now lingered for an instant at the far end of the market, many shops ahead. She turned toward him, and he thought he could see a flash of a mischievious smile from beneath the black muslin of her veil, as she—was it his imagination?—beckoned to him again.

The poor man was beside himself. Who was she? The daughter of a wealthy family? What did she want? He requickened his steps and turned into the lane where she had disappeared. And so she led him, always beyond reach, always tantalizingly ahead, now through the weapons market, now the oil merchants', now the leather sellers'; farther and farther from where they began. The feeling within him grew rather than decreased. Was she mad? On and on she led, to the very edge of town.

The sun declined and set, and there she was, before him as ever. Now they were come, of all places, to the City of Tombs. Had he been in his normal senses, he would have been afraid, but indeed, he now reflected, stranger places than this had seen a lovers' tryst.

There were scarcely twenty cubits between them when he saw her look back, and, giving a little start, she skipped down the steps and through the great bronze door of what seemed to be a very old sepulcher. A soberer moment might have seen the man pause, but in his present state, there was no turning back, and he went down the steps and slid in after her.

Inside, as his eyes saw after a moment, there were two flights of steps that led down to a second door, from whence a light shone, and which he equally passed through. He found himself in a large room, somehow unsuspected by the outside world, lit with candles upon its walls. There sat the woman, opposite the door on a pallet of rich stuff in her full black dress, still veiled, reclining on a pillow against the far wall. To the right of the pallet, the man noticed a well set in the floor.

"Lock the door behind you," she said in a low, husky voice that was almost a whisper, "and bring the key."

He did as he was told.

She gestured carelessly at the well. "Throw it in."

A ray of sense seemed to penetrate for a moment the clouds over his understanding, and a bystander, had there been one, might have detected the slightest of pauses.

"Go on," she said laughingly, "You didn't hesitate to miss the prayer as you followed me here, did you?"

He said nothing.

"The time for sunset prayer has almost finished as well," she said with gentle mockery. "Why worry? Go on, throw it in. You want to please me, don't you?"

He extended his hand over the mouth of the well, and watched as he let the key drop. An uncanny feeling rose from the pit of his stomach as moments passed but no sound came. He felt wonder, then horror, then comprehension.

"It is time to see me," she said, and she lifted her veil to reveal not the face of a fresh young girl, but of a hideous old crone, all darkness and vice, not a particle of light anywhere in its eldritch lines.

"See me well," she said. "My name is Dunya, This World. I am your beloved. You spent your time running after me, and now you have caught up with me. In your grave. Welcome, welcome."

At this she laughed and laughed, until she shook herself into a small mound of fine dust, whose fitful shadows, as the candles went out, returned to the darkness one by one.

49. **Hamza Yusuf, "America's Tragedy" from** *the Zaytuna Institute*

Accessed July 6, 2006. Available online: http://www.muslimsforjesus.org/Current% 20Affairs/America's%20Tragedy-An%20Islamic%20Perspective%20by%20Shayk% 20Hamza%20Yusuf%20at%20the%20Zaytuna%20Institute.htm.

The following is an excerpt from a talk Hamza Yusuf (for a biography see the "Yusuf, Hamza" entry in Volume 1) gave on Sunday, September 30, 2001 at the Zaytuna Institute in which he discussed the terrorist attacks of September 11, 2001 and their effects on American Muslims. In this excerpt, he says that if a woman is in danger or threatened due to the anti-Islamic climate caused by the attacks, she need not wear the ḥijāb (veil).

Q: How should women wear the hijab?

Shaykh Hamza: I think that the area that we are in is probably one of the safest areas in America, but there are other areas where it is dangerous. Shaykh Abdullah Bin Bayyah gave a fatwa, and it was a very good, sound fatwa. His point was that if Muslim women were in danger of being harmed or accosted, they should not go out, and if they have to go out, he said that they are not obliged to wear the hijab. That is what he said. He gave all his usuli proofs for it, so I would stipulate with that that if there are dire circumstances, then that is a dire rukhsa from a person with a valid license in Islamic law because Islam is an intelligent religion. The laws are there to serve human beings; we are not there to serve the law. We are there to serve Allah, and that is why whenever the law does not serve you, you are permitted to abandon it, and that is actually following the law.

That is where the confusion lies because people do not realize that. The law is for our benefit, not for our harm. Therefore, if the law harms us, we no longer have to abide by it. For example, pig is prohibited because it harms us, but if we are going to die without eating pig, we do not follow the law anymore because now the law says eat the pig. If you are worshipping the law, then you cannot understand that. You cannot worship the sacred law because the law is there to serve you; it is for your maslaha, your benefit, and that is our fiqh.

At night, especially, people have to be careful. It is always better to be in groups. Generally in most places, people will come to your defense. There is a lot of sensitivity in this area. There are non-Muslim women all over the country who have been wearing scarves in solidarity with the Muslim women. It has been shown all over. I would recommend having a PR campaign.

Show pictures of Mary Magdalene or the Virgin Mary since they are basically wearing the hijab, and explain that this is a sign of purity as it always has been, so people should not desecrate it. Do this to remind them that it is from their own tradition. Also, have a picture of a nun next to a Muslim woman, and ask why is one pure and the other impure? By what criteria are you judging? You can do things like that just to take things home to people.

50. **Muqtedar Khan, "Memo to Mr. Bin Laden: Go to Hell!" from** *Ijtihad.org*

February 6, 2003. Available online: http://www.ijtihad.org/BinladenII.htm. Reprinted with permission of Muqtedar Khan.

Muqtedar Khan was born in India. He received his Bachelor's degree from Osmania University in 1987, his M.B.A. from Bombay University in 1989, his M.A. from Florida International University in 1995, and his Ph.D. from Georgetown University in International Relations in 2000. He is an Assistant Professor of Political Science at the University of Delaware and a nonresident Senior Fellow at the Brookings Institution in Washington, DC. In the following article, he condemns Osama Bin Laden for the terrorist attacks of September 11, 2001 while affirming support of the American political system, a position that is shared by many American Muslims.

Mr. Bin laden,

In the name of Allah, The Most Merciful, the Most Benevolent.

I begin by reciting some important principles of Islam to remind you that there is more to Islam than just a call to arms.

1. Islam was sent as mercy to humanity (Quran 4:79).

2. Do not make mischief on the earth (Quran 29:36).

3. People, We have created you from a male and a female, and made you into nations and tribes that you might know one another. The noblest of you before God is the most righteous of you. (49:13)

4. There are among the People of the Book (Jews and Christians) upstanding nations that recite the message of God and worship throughout the night, who believe in God, who order honor and forbid dishonor and race in good works. These are the righteous. (3:113–114).

I am writing this to make it clear that there are Muslims in America and in the world who despise and condemn extremists and have nothing to do with Binladen and those like him for whom killing constitutes worship.

Islam was sent as mercy to humanity and not as an ideology of terror or hatred. It advocates plurality and moral equality of all faiths (Quran 2:62, 5:69). To use Islam, as a justification to declare an Armageddon against all non-Muslims is inherently unIslamic—it is a despicable distortion of a faith of peace. One of Allah's 99 names in the Quran is "*Al Salam*" which means Peace. Thus in a way Muslims are the only people who actually worship peace. Today this claim sounds so empty, thanks to people like you, Mr. Bin Laden. You and those like you are dedicated to killing and bringing misery to people wherever they are. God blessed you with the capacity to lead and also endowed you with enormous resources. You could have used your influence in Afghanistan to develop it, to bring it out of poverty and underdevelopment and show the world what Islam can do for those who believe in it. You chose to provoke and bring war to a people who had already been devastated by wars.

Yes many innocent people lost their lives in America's war on Afghanistan and many more might lose their lives in Iraq. This is indeed regrettable. But we must never forget as to how the West is divided over this and how nations and people within nations are agonizing in Europe and in America over this decision to go to war in Iraq. While many Americans and Europeans oppose the war, Muslim nations have already agreed to cooperate in this war. No Muslim leader has tried to play the role of a statesman on this issue. It is a tragedy that there is not a single Ted Kennedy, Jimmy Carter or Nelson Mandela in the entire Muslim world who would stand up and speak for justice!

Before we rush to condemn America we must remember that even today millions of poor and miserable people all across the world are lining up outside US embassies eager to come to America, not just to live here but to *become an American.* No Muslim country today, can claim that people of other nations and other faiths see it as a promise of hope, equality, dignity and prosperity.

Yes, we American Muslims will continue to challenge the Bush administrations' proposal to wage war against Iraq. We think a regime change in Washington is as necessary as a regime change in Baghdad, but that is an intramural affair. Once the war is declared, make no mistake Mr. Saddam Hussain and Mr. Bin Laden, We are with America. We will fight with America and we will fight for America. We have a covenant with this nation, we see it as a divine commitment and we will not disobey the Quran (9:4)—we will fulfill our obligations as citizens to the land that opened its doors to us and promised us equality and dignity even though we have a different faith. I am sure Mr. Bin Laden, you can neither understand nor appreciate this willingness to accept and welcome the other.

Sure at this moment out of anger, frustration and fear, some in America have momentarily forgotten their own values. I am confident that, God willing, this moment of shock and insecurity will pass and America will once again become the beacon of freedom, tolerance and acceptance that it was before September 11th. On that day Mr. Binladen, you not only killed 3000 innocent Americans, many of whom were also Muslims, but you signed the death warrants of many innocent people who will die in this war on terror and many more who will live but will suffer the consequences, the pain and the misery of war. Before September 11th, the US was giving aid to Afghanistan and was content to wait for the Iraqi people to free themselves and the rest of the world from their dictator. On that day you changed the rules of the game and Muslims in many places are suffering as a direct consequence.

When the Prophet Muhammad (saw) and his companions fought in the name of Islam, Allah made them victorious and glorified them in this world. They made Islam the currency of human civilization for over a millennium. You and your men on the other hand face nothing but defeat, global ridicule and contempt and run and hide like rats in caves and dungeons. You live in the dark. Your faith neither enlightens you nor enables you to live in the light and you have made Islam the currency of hate and violence.

Let me tell you that I would rather live in America under Ashcroft and Bush at their worst, than in any "Islamic state" established by ignorant, intolerant and murderous punks like you and Mullah Omar at their best. The US, patriot act not withstanding is still a more Islamic (just and tolerant) state than Afghanistan ever was under the Taliban.

Remember this: Muslims from all over the world who *wished to live better lives* migrated to America and Muslims who only *wished to take lives* migrated to Afghanistan to join you.

We will not follow the desires of people (like you) who went astray and led many astray from the Straight Path. (Quran 5:77)

I conclude by calling upon you Mr. Bin Laden and your Al Qaeda colleagues and Mr. Saddam Hussain to surrender to International Courts and take responsibility for your actions and protect thousands of other innocent Muslims from becoming the victims of the wars you bring upon them.

51. **Andrea Elliot, "Reject Call for Holy War, Florida Muslim Leader Says" from** *The Miami Herald*

October 13, 2001, 1B.
Maulana Shafayat Mohammed was born in Trinidad and graduated from Daarul Uloom Deobandi, an Islamic University in India before coming to the United States. He is the Imam at the Darul Uloom in Pembroke Pines, Florida. Friday, October 12, 2001 Mohammed called on American Muslims to support the United States' military campaign in Afghanistan and reject statements from Osama Bin Laden calling for jihad against the United States. This represents one among many local initiatives taken by Muslim leaders across the United States to condemn terrorism, al Qaeda, and the attacks of September 11, 2001.

REJECT JIHAD LOCAL MUSLIM LEADER SAYS

A prominent local Muslim leader called for Muslims in America to "jump off the fence" Friday and support U.S. military action in Afghanistan, while rejecting the Taliban's declared holy war. Cultural ties to the Middle East and fear of retaliation by anti-American Muslims have stopped local Muslims from publicly denouncing

Osama bin Laden's jihad, or holy war, said Shafayet Mohamed, the religious leader of Darul Uloom in Pembroke Pines, South Florida's largest mosque.

"This is not a holy war. This is not justified and does not include all Muslims," said Mohamed, who delivered the *khutbah,* or sermon, to more than 700 congregants and crews from three television stations.

Osama bin Laden's video taped statement, released Sunday, prompted Mohamed's sermon, he said. Bin Laden called for Muslims every where to unite, further escalating anti-U.S. protests in the Middle East.

In the video, bin Laden said: "These events have divided the whole world into two sides. The side of believers and the side of infidels, may God keep you away from them. Every Muslim has to rush to make his religion victorious. The winds of faith have come."

In response, Mohamed and other local imams, or religious leaders, have assured their followers that bin Laden and the Taliban are not qualified to call for a jihad, and that his cause is political and anti-Muslim by nature. A true jihad, said Mohamed, is dying "in the path of God, by doing good, without killing anyone."

Mohamed said he felt compelled to summon the media to his mosque Friday and announce support for U.S. military action in Afghanistan, even though he believes his sermon will invite criticism.

"I am going to be very much criticized for this. I do not support the pack," said Mohamed, of Trinidad. "Coming from the West and being a Caribbean [man], I do not have the cultural background to have emotions get in the way of my judgment."

Local Muslims with family members in the Middle East—including many who attend Darul Uloom—are more likely to struggle over whether to support U.S. military action, he and other leaders said.

"Over there are our relatives, our friends. It might happen to them. If they die you think we're gonna be happy? We're not gonna be happy," said Palestinian-American Sofian Zakkout, director of the Muslim Association of America, AMANA in Miami. Zakkout said he is resolutely opposed to military activity by the United States in Afghanistan. He said America should try to bring those responsible for the Sept. 11 terror attacks before a court of law.

"I am supporting our government but not by the war. No religious Muslim, Jew or Christian would ever support a war in this earth," he said.

"We have to work in a more intelligent way against the terrorists but not by killing. We can't go an eye for an eye."

Mohamed, 42, told his congregants the opposite, reading chapter five, verse 45 of the Koran, "an eye for an eye, a tooth for a tooth."

"I am quoting the Koran," Mohamed said. "How could the Muslim leaders in the U.S. denounce armed forces against the Taliban when you've got Afghanis against the Taliban? I see some strong hypocrisy here."

Munir Khan, the imam of the Islamic Movement of Florida in Hollywood, offered a view that fell somewhere between those of Zakkout and Mohamed.

"I don't think anybody would be comfortable with any kind of bombing," he said, "but if that's what it takes to bring about justice then that's what we will have to do." After hearing Mohamed speak, 56-year-old Abdul Omar Ali agreed that the United States' military strategy is appropriate.

"What is a holy war?" asked Ali, a Trinidadian who lives in Hollywood. "Are we going to use our knowledge to determine what is a holy war or are we going to be led by other people who have their agenda?"

52. "The Case of the Taliban American" from *CNN.com*

Accessed May 20, 2006. Available online: http://www.cnn.com/CNN/Programs/people/ shows/walker/profile.html. Reprinted with permission of CNN.com

John Walker Lindh, "the Taliban American," was born in Washingon, DC in 1981. He moved with his family to San Anselmo in northern California. After seeing the film "Malcolm X," he became interested in Islam, eventually converting from Catholicism to Islam in 1997 at the age of 16. Lindh traveled to Yemen in 1998 to study Arabic. After studying in a madrasa in Pakistan, he went to Afghanistan where he joined the Taliban government and then al Qaeda. He attended an al Qaeda military training camp and fought against the American supported Afghan Northern Alliance. Lindh was captured by the Northern Alliance in November 2001. After a trial in the United States, he was sentenced to 20 years in prison for his activities. Lindh is one of the rare American Muslims to have participated in the Taliban and al Qaeda movements. Until this, involvement of American Muslims within radical and violent Islamist movements has been uncommon.

(CNN)—John Walker Lindh spent his formative years in an affluent Northern California community known for its tolerance and open-mindedness. So how did he end up training in al Qaeda camps and fighting on the Taliban front lines in Afghanistan?

In interviews conducted with CNN and U.S. military and intelligence sources, the once seemingly typical Marin County, California, teen revealed a journey of spiritual zeal, linguistic and cultural education and battlefield training that ended with Walker Lindh bloodied and dazed after a prison uprising last November near Mazar-e Sharif.

"He's not someone that would, that I would have ever imagined, could pick up a gun at all," said his father Frank Lindh, who separated from Marilyn Walker about two years ago.

An emotional Walker Lindh addressed a Virginia court at his sentencing hearing October 4, more than 10 months after U.S. military forces detained him in northern Afghanistan.

He apologized for fighting alongside the Taliban, saying, "had I realized then what I know now...I would never would have joined them." The 21-year-old said Osama bin Laden is against Islam and that he "never understood jihad to mean anti-American or terrorism."

"I understand why so many Americans were angry when I was first discovered in Afghanistan. I realize many still are, but I hope in time that feeling will change," he said in a 14-minute statement, according to The Associated Press.

Walker Lindh was sentenced to 20 years in prison as part of an agreement reached in July under which he pled guilty to one count of supplying services to the Taliban and a criminal information charge that he carried a rifle and two hand grenades while fighting against the U.S.-backed Northern Alliance.

As part of the plea deal, the government dropped all other counts in a lengthy criminal indictment, including one of the most serious charges—conspiracy to kill U.S. nationals. CIA officer Johnny Michael Spann was killed in the Mazar-e Sharif uprising.

"He was a soldier in the Taliban. He did it for religious reasons. He did it as a Muslim, and history overcame him," his attorney, James Brosnahan, said in July.

"John loves America," his father said. "And we love America. God bless America."

"ALLEGIANCE TO JIHAD"

Most Americans didn't believe Walker Lindh's father when the public first was introduced to Walker Lindh, or the "Taliban American" as he became known.

When found in Afghanistan by U.S. military forces in November 2001, Walker Lindh was shoeless, covered in dirt and lying in a hospital bed, where he was recovering from wounds received in the prison battle. Initially, Walker Lindh expressed reluctance to be taped, but with the camera rolling and lights on, he told his story to CNN.

Bearded, his face coated in grime, he appeared exhausted as he described his battlefield experiences and his reasons for becoming a Taliban soldier.

"I was a student in Pakistan, studying Islam," Walker-Lindh told CNN in a non-American accent, which he attributed to the fact he been speaking Arabic exclusively for months. "I came into contact with many people who were connected with the Taliban.

"I was in [Pakistan's] Northwest Frontier Province. The people there in general have a great love for the Taliban. So I started to read some of the literature of the scholars and my heart became attached to it. I wanted to help them one way or another."

In secret documents summarizing his interrogations by U.S. troops and FBI officials, Walker Lindh said that he studied Arabic and Islam in Yemen starting in July 1998 and, after a brief return home to California, he returned to Yemen.

He went to Pakistan in October 2000 and joined a radical Islamic group, getting military training to fight against Indian forces in Kashmir. After becoming disillusioned with the cause, according to interrogation reports, Walker Lindh asked to join the Taliban.

Because he was not native to Afghanistan and did not speak the local languages, Walker Lindh said he joined the "Arab group"—or al Qaeda, headed by bin Laden. Aware of al Qaeda's anti-U.S. position, he agreed to attend their camp, the documents said.

Walker Lindh told interrogators that he declined to take part in operations against Israel and the United States, but continued with his training and even met bin Laden.

"At some point during the training, Lindh said he had been offered to swear allegiance to . . . al Qaeda," an FBI document said. "Lindh stated that he declined, however he swore allegiance to Jihad" . . . or holy war against enemies of Islam, as defined by al Qaeda.

INSPIRED BY 'MALCOLM X' MOVIE

Afghanistan was a long way from the Washington, D.C., suburb of Takoma Park, Maryland, where John Walker Lindh spent his earliest years. His father was a Catholic who worked as a government lawyer, and his mother was a health care aide who became a follower of Buddhism. He was the middle of three children.

"I remember playing football, basketball, soccer, catch, stuff like that," Andrew Cleverdon, his best childhood friend, told CNN.

When his son was 10, Frank Lindh accepted a job as a lawyer for Pacific Gas & Electric, and the family moved to Marin County, just north of San Francisco.

Walker Lindh attended Tamiscal High, an alternative school for self-directed students in Lakespur, California. Frank Lindh described his son as "very musical, very adept at languages and very studious."

He was also very interested in spiritual matters. Walker Lindh told FBI interrogators that he became interested in Islam at age 12 after watching the movie, "Malcolm X," which discussed Mecca, Saudi Arabia and the religious pilgrimage Hajj.

In early 1997, as he turned 16, he became a Muslim and regularly attended a mosque in Mill Valley, California. He used the names Suleyman al-Lindh and Suleyman al-Faris.

Despite Walker Lindh's independent spirit, he was eager to absorb the teachings of Islam, said Abdullah Nana, who prayed with him at the mosque.

"It's my observation that new Muslims are influenced by the people around them. Whoever they lean on for their Islamic advice and for their Islamic questions, they will be influenced by these people," Nana said.

A "VERY SPIRITUAL YOUNG MAN"

Frank Lindh called his son "a sweet kid" who was devoted and committed to his conversion to Islam. He said he was proud of his son's dedication to study the Koran and thought his conversion had been good for him.

Walker Lindh's quest for knowledge about Islam carried him to Yemen for nine months in July 1998, according to interrogation reports. After going home to California, he returned to continue his studies in Yemen on February 1, 2000, and then left for Pakistan that October.

In Pakistan, Walker Lindh enrolled in an Islamic fundamentalist school, known as a madrasah, where he became interested in the Muslim fight in Kashmir. Encouraged not to tell others he was American, he joined the Harakat-ul Mujahedeen-Al Almi (HUM), an organization blamed by Pakistan for terrorist attacks and failed assassination attempts on President Pervez Musharaff.

Soon Walker Lindh became disillusioned with the HUM's cause and, after undergoing 24 days of military training, he instead chose to join the Taliban, according to interrogation reports.

He told the FBI that he spent seven weeks at an al Qaeda camp—al Farooq—about a two-hour bus ride from Kandahar, beginning June 1, 2001. Three weeks were devoted to weapons familiarization, one week to studying maps/topography, one to battlefield training and one to explosives. Walker Lindh said he did not undergo any WMD training, although he said he believed al Qaeda offered such training in Kandahar.

Walker Lindh told interrogators that bin Laden visited the camp several times, usually with one of his sons. Walker Lindh and four others met bin Laden on one occasion, and the al Qaeda leader "made small talk and thanked them all for taking part in the Jihad," according to the FBI report.

REMORSE AND SIGNS OF REGRET

Shortly before Walker Lindh left for Afghanistan, he sent his parents an e-mail message saying he was heading to a cooler climate. Frank Lindh said he did not know that his son was in Afghanistan until he saw him on CNN.

"I had no indication or reason to be concerned that he would put himself in danger like this by going to Afghanistan," Frank Lindh told CNN's "Larry King Live."

Bill Jones, a family friend in San Rafael, California, described Walker Lindh as "very sweet, unassuming, very spiritual young man—rather frail, not an all-American football player or anything like that, certainly not a fighter."

Walker Lindh's parents "were very, very upset and very confused because what they saw on CNN was frightening," Jones said. "They hadn't seen or heard from him in seven months, and they were desperate....They tried to get a hold of him. They couldn't, and so to see him lying on the hospital floor with his blackened face and his eyes rolling into his skull really frightened them."

Walker Lindh had ended up in Mazar-e Sharif after being deployed to the Taliban front lines, where he was on September 11. His military questioners wrote that Walker Lindh "showed remorse and signs of regret" when asked about the terrorist attacks. Walker Lindh said one of his instructors had said the attacks were the first in three waves of attacks against U.S. interests.

When the U.S. bombardment began, Walker Lindh told CNN that he fled 100 miles on foot to Konduz, where he was one of more than 3,000 Taliban soldiers taken prisoner in the garrison. He was disarmed and boarded a truck to Mazar-e Sharif.

DUNGEON OF DEATH

Walker Lindh was one of about 80 Taliban fighters who survived the prison revolt in late November near Mazar-e Sharif, in northwest Afghanistan.

Northern Alliance troops put down the uprising with the aid of U.S. warplanes, but hundreds of prisoners, as well as Spann, were killed.

The uprising was "all a mistake of a handful of people," Walker Lindh told CNN. "This is against what we had agreed upon, and this is against Islam. It is a major sin to break a contract, especially in military situations."

He said he intended to surrender but was drawn into battle when one of his comrades threw a grenade. After taking a bullet in his upper-right thigh, he fled to the basement bunker, where he and dozens of other Taliban remained for seven days. During that time, gasoline was poured into the basement and ignited, and grenades were exploded.

Walker Lindh, a thin man of about 5 feet 10 inches, described the basement as a dungeon and said it was full of the stench of dead bodies.

He and the other survivors did not emerge until Northern Alliance forces diverted an irrigation stream into the bunker, flushing them out.

"We were standing in water, freezing water, in the basement for maybe 20 hours," Walker Lindh said. "If we surrender, the worst that can happen is they torture us or kill us, right? Right here in the basement they're torturing us and killing us. We might as well surrender, at least we have a chance."

"I DON'T THINK HIS MIND WAS WORKING"

Walker Lindh was among three truckloads of prisoners—most of them wounded or dead—who emerged or were taken from the basement on November 29.

Walker Lindh spent weeks on the USS Bataan, a Navy warship in the North Arabian Sea, being interrogated by U.S. investigators before he was transferred from the ship to a U.S. military post at Kandahar International Airport in Afghanistan. From there, he flew to the United States on January 23, a U.S. military source said.

His return to the United States was an emotional one for his parents, who spoke with reporters outside a federal courthouse in Alexandria, Virginia, shortly after the January hearing.

"My love for him is unconditional and absolute, and I am grateful to God that he has been brought home to his family," Marilyn Walker said.

Under terms of his plea agreement, Walker Lindh cannot benefit financially from any telling of his story. He will also work with U.S. intelligence officials, telling them what he knows concerning the Taliban and al Qaeda.

Should he again associate with terrorists, he could be brought back into court, where he would be considered an enemy combatant, said U.S. Attorney Paul McNulty. In addition, Walker Lindh withdrew any claims he was mistreated while in U.S. military custody.

Brosnahan said his client would continue to study Arabic, the history of Islam and the Koran while in prison, and that he expected he would be able to serve out his term in a facility closer to his family, in Northern California.

Federal prosecutors have told the judge they have no objections to Walker Lindh's request to serve his prison time near his family.

53. "Free Muslim Coalition: Mission Statement" from *The Free Muslims Coalition*

Accessed May 4, 2006. Available online: http://www.freemuslims.org/about/. Reprinted with permission of Kamal Nawash and The Free Muslims Coalition.

The Free Muslim Coalition is a nonprofit organization that was founded by Kamal Nawash after the terrorist attacks of September 11, 2001. Nawash is a Palestinian-American born in Bethlehem in 1970. He entered the United States in 1979. He received his J.D. from Thomas Cooley Law School in Michigan and a LL.M. in International Legal Studies from American University in Washington, DC. He also ran unsuccessfully for a United States Senate seat in Virginia in 2003. He founded the Free Muslim Coalition to give greater visibility to American Muslims' denunciation of September 11th and terrorism in general.

ABOUT FMC

The Free Muslims Coalition is a nonprofit organization made up of American Muslims and Arabs of all backgrounds who feel that religious violence and terrorism have not been fully rejected by the Muslim community in the post 9-11 era.

The Free Muslims was created to eliminate broad base support for Islamic extremism and terrorism and to strengthen secular democratic institutions in the Middle East and the Muslim World by supporting Islamic reformation efforts.

The Free Muslims promotes a modern secular interpretation of Islam which is peace-loving, democracy-loving and compatible with other faiths and beliefs. The Free Muslims' efforts are unique; it is the only mainstream American-Muslim organization willing to attack extremism and terrorism unambiguously. Unfortunately most other Muslim leaders believe that in terrorist organizations, the end justifies the means.

As written recently by Khaled Kishtainy, columnist at Al-Sharq Al-Awsat Newspaper, "place on the Islamic intellectuals and leaders of Islamic organizations part of the responsibility for [this phenomenon] of Islamic terrorism, as nearly all of them advocate violence, and repress anyone who casts doubts upon this. Naturally, every so often they have written about the love and peace of Islam but they did so, at best, for purposes of propaganda and defense of Islam. Their basic position is that this religion was established by the sword, acts by the sword, and will triumph by the sword, and that any doubt regarding this constitutes a conspiracy against the Muslims."

The Free Muslims finds this sympathetic support for terrorists by Muslim leaders and intellectuals to be a dangerous trend and the Free Muslims will challenge these beliefs and target the sympathetic support given to terrorists by Muslims.

The Free Muslims encourages Muslims and Arabs to be proud of their faith and at the same time critical. The community of the faithful must now take steps to bring Islam into the 21st century. As the Free Muslims's founder recently said, "The only way that we as a people can make a profound difference and improve the quality of life for all Muslims is if all of us make a difference individually."

Other Americans have spoken up against terrorism, but never before has this message come with such clarity from Muslims or Arabs. Muslims are the only ones who can resolve the problem of terror in Islam, and sadly until the founding of this Free Muslims, they were the only group who had not definitively spoken up against the use of terror.

Free Muslim Coalition Against Terrorism, © Copyright 2006

54. "Mission Statement: Muslims Against Terrorism (M-A-T): The First Anti-Terrorism NGO in the World for Global Peace and Justice" from *Muslims Against Terrorism*

From Muslims Against Terrorism, accessed May 5, 2006. Available online: www.m-a-t.org. Reprinted with permission of Syed B. Soharwardy and Muslims Against Terrorism.

Muslims Against Terrorism (MAT) was founded on January 11, 1998 in Calgary, Canada by Imam Syed B. Soharwardy. Soharwardy was born in Pakistan where he received his early education in Islamic Studies from his father. He received his B.A. in Islamic Studies from the University of Karachi. He also received his Bachelor of Engineering from the N.E.D. University of Engineering & Technology in Karachi, his Master of Sciences in Management Engineering from the New Jersey Institute of Technology in Newark, New Jersey, and his Master of Engineering from the University of Calgary. The MAT web site provides articles, courses, and information about Islam for non-Muslims.

To be the leading Muslim organization in the world for creating awareness about the dangers of terrorism and it's various causes such as oppression, exploitation and injustice, and unite people to stop terrorism.

MAT OBJECTIVES

1. To work with the western media in providing Muslim perspectives on issues related to Terrorism.

2. To establish and strengthen the working relationships with the non-Muslim communities especially Christian community, and help them in understanding the issues and problems of Muslim community.

3. To work with other Muslim organizations in order to stop terrorism.

4. To provide assistance to the victims of terrorism.

5. To help young Muslims in social, economical and educational matters.

55. "Recommendations" from *The Muslim Public Affairs Council*

Excerpt from "The Muslim Public Affairs Council, Counterterrorism Policy Paper," September 2003. Reprinted with permission of The Muslim Public Affairs Council.

The Muslim Public Affairs Council (MPAC) was founded in 1988 by Maher Hathout and Salam Al-Marayati. Hathout was born in Egypt and came to the United States in 1971. A retired physician, he has written and lectured extensively on Islam, Muslims, and their relation to the United States. In 2000, he delivered the invocation at the Democratic National Convention in Los Angeles, California. A-Marayati was born in Iraq in 1960 and came to the United States in 1964. He attended the University of California, Los Angeles for his bachelor's degree and the University of California, Irvine for his M.B.A. MPAC is a nonprofit organization that advocates Muslim participation in the U.S. political system, the development of Muslim grassroots organizations, and is a watchdog group for Muslim portrayals in the media. MPAC also seeks to provide information on Islam and Muslims for U.S. policy makers. It has offices in Washington, DC. and Los Angeles. The Counterterrorism Policy Paper addresses terrorism and national security issues from an American Muslim perspective. In addition to making counterterrorism recommendations, the report highlights the necessity to protect American Muslims' civil liberties.

RECOMMENDATIONS FOR U.S. POLICYMAKERS
GENERAL POLICIES

Defining Terrorism:

• The U.S. Government should adopt a single definition of terrorism to be used by all agencies of the federal government. This definition should not place arbitrary restrictions on either the perpetrators (state or non-state actors) or targets (governments or civilians) of the act.[278] Similarly, the U.S. Government should adopt a single set of criteria for the designation of individuals, groups, states and other entities as "terrorist" for use by the Departments of State, Justice, Defense, Treasury and other federal agencies.

• MPAC offers the following definition of terrorism: "any violent or threat of violent action targeting non-combatants in order to achieve political or military goals."

Inclusion of American Muslims:

To date, American Muslims have been *de facto* excluded from participating in the development of U.S. counterterrorism policies and from nearly all efforts, both official and unofficial, to develop effective responses to terrorism. Currently, there are no Muslims working on counterterrorism matters in the Departments of Defense, Justice, Homeland Security, State or Treasury.

Various government agencies should intensify their efforts to hire qualified individuals of credible standing from within the American Muslim community. Such individuals, with their understanding of the complex sentiments in the Middle East and their cultural and political sensitivity toward the Muslim world, should be part of substantive policymaking decisions in our government. American Muslims can also serve the crucial role as cultural interpreters between law enforcement and the American Muslim community.

Counterterrorism Strategy:

In order to garner public support, increase grassroots participation in government efforts and clarify our nation's counterterrorism strategy, the House and Senate should conduct oversight hearings on the White House's *National Strategy for Combating Terrorism*. Again, the inclusion of members of the American Muslim in such hearings would provide a valuable perspective to the policy makers. Providing a platform for the "usual suspects" of self-appointed terrorism experts with their own political agenda has proven, time and again, to be a fatal mistake.

ECONOMIC & FINANCIAL

Terrorist Designations/Asset Forfeiture:

Individuals and entities labeled by the President as "specially designated nationals" (SDNs) and "specially designated global terrorists" (SDGTs) currently have no legal means of challenging those classifications. Those so designated are subject to a blocking order that may only be appealed through the designating entity itself, the Department of Treasury. It is worth noting here that Muslim charities have experienced a major drop in their income over the last two years as American Muslims are worried about "guilt by donation," which is interfering with the Muslim rite of charity giving. Some charities have reported an increase in cash donations, making it more untraceable for government agencies.

- Terrorist designations by the U.S. Government should be made subject to judicial review before a permanent blocking order is rendered. Individuals, groups, and other entities so designated should be afforded the opportunity to appeal the designation before a magistrate (or other independent tribunal).

- The Treasury Department should establish an accreditation agency whose job it is to certify that U.S. charities are in compliance with the guidelines outlined in its recently released "Voluntary Best Practices for US-Based Charities."

- The Office of Foreign Assets Control (OFAC) should provide simplified lists to community-based organizations, and provide outreach and training that can help community members detect problems. OFAC should also more vigorously market these services to the general public through an establishment of a community outreach office.

- Funds seized by the U.S. Government from Muslim charities as "terrorist assets" should either be returned to the donors or re-directed to their intended recipients abroad through legitimate non-governmental channels. The Government should publicly and repeatedly reassure Muslim donors that they will not be targeted on the basis of good faith donations made to organizations that may be made suspect in the future.

FOREIGN POLICY

America has experienced different forms of domestic terrorism such as acts conducted by the unibomber, Timothy McVeigh and others whose main motivation is the resentment of one or more of the US's domestic policies, whether it is abortion rights, environmental policies, or what they consider the government's abuse of power. Foreign terrorists, on the other hand, are motivated mostly by what they perceive as a fault in US foreign policy and using that to recruit their members and operatives. The following recommendations may be extremely helpful to US foreign policy makers in developing effective policies that can also undermine the spread of terrorists' ideologies and their recruitment efforts.

- United States policymakers and diplomats should pursue a foreign policy that is rooted in the American values of freedom and justice for all. Being perceived as serving the agendas of special-interest groups will only increase anti-American sentiment and create a breeding ground for recruiting terrorists. Countries with citizens who have a high degree of anti-American sentiment will hesitate to help the United States carry out its counterterrorism policies.

- Consensus-based diplomacy is essential to maintaining a broad, inclusive, and effective international coalition against terrorism. The United States should work with UN member states to establish a consensus definition of terrorism.

- The State Department should establish standard criteria for "Foreign Terrorist Organization" (FTO) and "State Sponsors of Terrorism" designations based on U.S. law, existing definitions of terrorism, and international standards, rather than on political considerations.

- To enhance the credibility of the War on Terrorism internationally, The U.S. Government should consistently condemn and take actions against perpetrators of acts of terrorism, whether by state or non-state actors.

Arab-Israeli Conflict:

A just resolution to the Arab/Israeli conflict brokered by the United States will dramatically reduce anti-American sentiment in the Arab and Muslim world. The United States should serve as an even-handed peace broker between Israelis and Palestinians by redoubling its commitment to secure a just, equitable, and lasting resolution to the conflict, that is based on international law. It should be highlighted here that the major points of the conflict: the Israeli occupation, the right of return of the Palestinian refugees, and the status of Jerusalem can adequately be addressed by international law.

Democracy-Building/Economic Reform/Foreign Aid:

Nations plagued by authoritarianism, civil strife, poverty, humanitarian disasters, and other crises are fertile breeding grounds for radicalism and terrorism. Conversely, increased respect for human rights, socioeconomic development, and civic empowerment can help mitigate some of the root causes of extremism and terrorism. American Muslim institutions, including educational and charitable institutions, can play a significant role in this regard by helping to provide intellectual and financial resources to support economic and political development in Muslim countries.

- Given both the prominence and diversity of "revivalist" trends in most Muslim nations, as well as Secretary Powell's affirmation that Islam and democracy are not necessarily incompatible, the State Department should develop dialogues and cultivate relationships with those within the Islamic movement who subscribe to democratic principles. In doing so, the United States should promote democracy without direct involvement or interference on behalf of (or against) one or another individual, group, or philosophical/ideological trend.

- The United States should place greater priority on promoting economic reform, democratic development, and human rights in countries most affected by international terrorism by reapportioning foreign aid in favor of countries, programs, and issues that have greatest need.

- In the past, U.S. policymakers have encouraged American businesses to invest in economic and infrastructure development overseas, with less emphasis on human development projects. The U.S. Government should encourage private investment in developing social, civic, and political institutions in host countries.

- The US Agency for International Development (USAID) and other agencies of the US Government should work constructively with Muslim charitable institutions to meet the urgent development and subsistence needs of many of the Muslim world's poor and dispossessed.

Human Rights:

The US has had a great political capital as a champion of human rights, which goes back to the Wilson Principles. It is unfortunate that a lot of that capital has eroded over the years and the US needs to reestablish that credibility worldwide. In doing so, some of the most recent violations of human rights in this country and abroad must come to an end, such as:

- The United States should refrain from abusing its power in utilizing the material witness statute.

- The United States should abandon the "enemy combatant" designation in the War on Terrorism, as this designation violates constitutional rights.

- The United States should extend "enemy combatants" held in Guantanamo Bay the rights entitled to them under the Geneva Conventions.

Public Diplomacy

- The United States should regularly consult Arab-American and American Muslim educational, civic, and political institutions in devising and implementing public diplomacy initiatives aimed at Arab and Muslim audiences.

- The United States should inform foreign students from the Muslim world on compliance with new immigration standards as they pursue higher education in the United States.

- In addition to having the US Information Agency, which is supposed to educate the world about America, the US government should increase its efforts to educate its citizens about other countries. This may be accomplished either through the Department of Education or a separate agency set up specifically for that purpose as long as it is able to effectively disseminate information to the American public about other nations and cultures. America is no longer separated from the rest of the world by ocean wide seas but by a few clicks on a keyboard.

Law Enforcement:

- Law enforcement should hold forums on how members of faith and ethnic communities can enhance dialogue with the FBI, Department of Justice and Homeland Security agencies in the local areas. As an example, the Washington Field Office (WFO) of the Federal Bureau of Investigation has formed an Advisory Committee of representatives of Muslim and Arab organizations which meets regularly on monthly basis. The Committee has also organized a forum for the local community to meet the officials from the FBI's WFO to discuss issues of concern to the community and law enforcement, which is a very effective communication and confidence building measure.

- Publicly acknowledge positive role models within the community for their efforts to help in forming a partnership between law enforcement and the local community.

- Present clear, unambiguous suggestions to citizens who want to assist in law enforcement efforts. The public needs to understand more clearly what it means to be 'vigilant,' and it needs clear directives on how to report suspicious behavior. Federal and local agencies must provide specific tips on recognizing criminal behavior while discouraging hoaxes and vigilantism. These guidelines must be easily accessible on hard copy as well as on the web.

- Work with schools, both public and private, to educate students about the White House strategy on combating terrorism.

- Develop a phone and email contact list of the local representatives of law enforcement for community-based organizations so members of the community can reach out to report a problem they are having or a lead on a crime. The FBI, US Attorney's Office, Department of Justice, State Attorney General, County District Attorney, County Sheriff, Mayor, and City Attorney must be on the list.

Politicization/Secrecy/PublicConfidenc

- The Attorney General should work to regain the confidence of the Muslim community by assuring members of the community that he rejects the notion of "Islamic terrorism"[279] and by instructing federal agents, prosecutors, and other law enforcement officials to use Islamic terminology properly.

- The Justice Department should terminate its use of secret evidence and/or secret courts.

- The Department of Justice should abandon the so-called "PATRIOT II" and cease trying to pass "PATRIOT II" piecemeal though Congress.

Immigration Policies:

- Changes to immigration policy should be applied uniformly to all immigrants in the United States regardless of their religion, ethnicity, and national origin. For example, the Immigration and Naturalization Services (INS) Special Registration program, which was initiated in late 2002 and abandoned in mid 2003, was applied primarily to males from Arab and predominantly Muslim countries and was a complete failure that wasted scarce resources and was counterproductive to America's image overseas.

RECOMMENDATIONS FOR THE AMERICAN-MUSLIM COMMUNITY AND ORGANIZATIONS

While some individual Muslims, motivated by political agenda rather than religious guidance, have sought (and may still seek) to inflict harm on American citizens and interests, the American Muslim community, along with its political, religious, educational, and charitable institutions, are integral components of American civic and political life, and can have a positive impact on American civil society. In this spirit, MPAC offers the following recommendations that focus on how the American Muslim community can contribute to discerning the name of Islam and Muslims from the acts of a misguided few as well as fulfill their role as partners in making America and the world safer:

- National Muslim organizations should develop educational materials and other initiatives designed to educate law enforcement officials, particularly at the Departments of Justice, Treasury, and Homeland Security about Islamic culture, the proper use and meanings of religious terms (such as jihad), and the histories behind the growth and ideologies of Islamic movements.

- The nation's leading Muslim organizations should work in concert with other civil liberties groups to protect America's constitutional freedoms. Issues American Muslim organizations can work on with other groups include:

(1) "enemy combatant" and material witness statutes

(2) the use of secret evidence in cases the government brings against defendants

(3) the granting of the rights accorded by the Geneva conventions to the prisoners at Guantanamo Bay, and

(4) working to repeal unconstitutional measures of the USA-PATRIOT Act.

- National and local Muslim institutions, including mosques and Islamic schools, should work towards fostering an American Muslim identity by becoming financially free of foreign influences. They should also check their membership databases with the lists of suspected individuals and institutions provided by the Office of Foreign Assets Control (OFAC).

- Muslim religious institutions should take steps to mitigate extremism and angry rhetoric by establishing educational and training programs that:

(1) emphasize the importance of tolerance, citizenship, and social/civic responsibility as Islamic values; and

(2) educate mosque officials about their responsibilities regarding irresponsible speech and/or activity on their premises.

- National and local Muslim institutions should take steps to understand the new guidelines of the Department of the Treasury for all non-profit organizations. They should also engage the authorities in a constructive dialogue to develop mutual understanding and to find fair, practical means for compliance with guidelines.

- National and local Muslim organizations should work with interfaith leaders, human relations commission representatives, and civic leaders, along with law enforcement officials at the local, state, and federal levels to establish community-based task forces to discuss measures for protecting the nation from terrorism and hate crime and civil rights violations.

APPENDIX A
STATEMENTS BY LEADING ARAB AND ISLAMIC AUTHORITIES ON THE SEPTEMBER 11TH TERRORIST ATTACKS ON THE UNITED STATES

"American Muslims utterly condemn what are apparently vicious and cowardly acts of terrorism against innocent civilians. We join with all Americans in calling for the swift apprehension and punishment of the perpetrators. No political cause could ever be assisted by such immoral acts."
—*American Muslim Political Coordinating Council (AMPCC), September 11, 2001*

"The Conference strongly condemned the brutal terror acts that befell the United States, caused huge losses in human lives from various nationalities and wreaked tremendous destruction and damage in New York and Washington. It further reaffirmed that these terror acts ran counter to the teachings of the divine religions as well as ethical and human values, stressed the necessity of tracking down the perpetrators of these acts in the light of the results of investigations and bringing them to justice to inflict on them the penalty they deserve, and underscored its support of this effort. In this respect, the Conference expressed its condolences to and sympathy with the people and government of the United States and the families of the victims in these mournful and tragic circumstances."
—*Organization of the Islamic Conference, October 10, 2001*

"The General-Secretariat of the League of Arab States shares with the people and government of the United States of America the feelings of revulsion, horror and shock over the terrorist attacks that ripped through the World Trade Centre and Pentagon, inflicting heavy damage and killing and wounding thousands of many nationalities. These terrorist crimes have been viewed by the League as inadmissible and deserving all condemnation."
—*League of Arab States, September 17, 2001*

"The undersigned, leaders of Islamic movements, are horrified by the events of Tuesday 11 September 2001 in the United States which resulted in massive killing, destruction and attack on innocent lives. We express our deepest sympathies and sorrow. We condemn, in the strongest terms, the incidents, which are against all human and Islamic norms. This is grounded in the Noble Laws of Islam which forbid all forms of attacks on innocents. God Almighty says in the Holy Qur'an: 'No bearer of burdens can bear the burden of another' (Surah al-Isra 17:15)."

—Mustafa Mashhur, Muslim Brotherhood (Egypt); Qazi Hussain Ahmed, Ameer, Jamaat-e-Islami (Pakistan); Muti Rahman Nizami, Ameer, Jamaat-e-Islami (Bangladesh); Shaykh Ahmad Yassin, Islamic Resistance Movement (Palestine); Rashid Ghannoushi, Nahda Renaissance Movement (Tunisia); Fazil Nour, Parti Islam SeMalaysia (Malaysia); and 40 other Muslim scholars and politicians, September 14, 2001.[280]

"The terrorists acts, from the perspective of Islamic law, constitute the crime of hirabah [war against society]."
—Religious edict (fatwa) signed by: Shaykh Yusuf Al-Qaradawi, Grand Islamic Scholar and Chairman of the Sunna and Sira Countil (Qatar); Judge Tariq al-Bishri, First Deputy President of the Council d'etat (Egypt), Dr. Muhammad s. al-Awa, Professor of Islamic Law and Sharia (Egypt); Dr. Haytham al-.Khayyat, Islamic scholar, (Syria); Fahmi Houaydi, Islamic scholar (Syria); Shaykh Taha Jabir al-Alwani, Chairman, North America High Council (USA), September 27, 2001.

"Hijacking Planes, terrorizing innocent people and shedding blood constitute a form of injustice that can not be tolerated by Islam, which views them as gross crimes and sinful acts."
—Shaykh Abdul Aziz al-Ashaikh, Grand Mufti of Saudi Arabia, Chairman of Senior 'Ulama, September 15, 2001

"Attacking innocent people is not courageous, it is stupid and will be punished on the day of judgement. . . . It's not courageous to attack innocent children, women and civilians. It is courageous to protect freedom, it is courageous to defend oneself and not to attack."
—Shaykh Muhammed Sayyid Al-Tantawai, Rector of Al-Azhar University (AFP, Sept. 14, 2001)

"Killing of people, in any place and with any kind of weapons, including atomic bombs, long-range missiles, biological or chemical weapons, passenger or war planes, carried out by any organization, country or individuals is condemned. . . . It makes no difference whether such massacres happen in Hiroshima, Nagasaki, Qana, Sabra, Shatila, Deir Yassin, Bosnia, Kosovo, Iraq or in New York and Washington."
—Ayatollah Ali Khamene'i, Supreme Jurist-Ruler of Iran (Islamic Republic News Agency, Sept. 16, 2001)

"It is wrong to kill innocent people. It is also wrong to Praise those who kill innocent people."
—Mufti Nizamuddin Shamzai, Pakistan (New York Times, Sept. 28, 2001)

"Neither the law of Islam nor its ethical system justify such a crime."
—Zaki Badawi, Principal of the Muslim College in London (Arab News, Sept. 28, 2001)

"Our hearts bleed for the attacks that has targeted the World Trade Center, as well as other institutions in the United States. . . . I categorically go against a committed Muslim's embarking on such attacks. Islam never allows a Muslim to kill the innocent and the helpless."
—Shaykh Yusuf Al-Qaradawi, Grand Islamic Scholar and Chairman of the Sunna and Sira Countil, Qatar (IslamOnline.com, Sept. 13, 2001)

"Beside the fact that they are forbidden by Islam, these acts do not serve those who carried them out but their victims, who will reap the sympathy of the whole world. . . . Islamists who live according to the human values of Islam could not commit such crimes."
—Shaykh Muhammad Hussein Fadlallah, spiritual guide of Hizbullah (Lebanon) (AFP, Sept. 14, 2002)

"The horrific terrorist attacks of Sept. 11, 2001, in the United States were perpetrated by cult of fanatics who had self-mutilated their ears and tongues, and could only communicate with perceived opponents through carnage and devastation."
—Muhammad Khatami, President of Iran, in address before United Nations General Assembly, November 9, 2001

APPENDIX B
STATEMENTS BY AMERICAN OFFICIALS OPPOSING ANTI-MUSLIM INCITEMENT AND VIOLENCE

"The spirit behind this holiday is a reminder that Islam brings hope and comfort to more than a billion people worldwide. Islam affirms God's justice and insists on man's moral responsibility. This holiday is also an occasion to remember that Islam gave birth to a rich civilization of learning that has benefited mankind."
—President George W. Bush, December 5, 2002 (during visit to Islamic Center of Washington, DC)

"Some of the comments that have been uttered about Islam do not reflect the sentiments of my government or the sentiments of most Americans. Islam, as practiced by the vast majority of people, is a peaceful religion, a religion that respects others. . . . By far, the vast majority of American citizens respect the Islamic people and the Muslim faith. After all, there are millions of peaceful-loving Muslim Americans. . . . Ours is a country based upon tolerance. . . And we're not going to let the war on terror or terrorists cause us to change our values."
—*President George W. Bush, November 13, 2002 (following anti-Islam slurs by Evangelical Christian leaders)*

"I assured [President Obasanjo], and assure those Muslims who live in his country, that our war that we now fight is against terror and evil. It's not against Muslims. We both understand that the Islamic faith teaches peace, respects human life, is nonviolent. And I want to thank the President's leadership in sending a—not only a message of tolerance and respect, but also his vision, which I share, that our struggle is going to be long and difficult. But we will prevail. We will win. Good will overcome evil."
—*President George W. Bush, November 2, 2001 (after meeting with Nigerian President Olusegun Obasanjo)*

"These acts of violence against innocents violate the fundamental tenets of the Islamic faith, and it's important for my fellow Americans to understand that. . . . The face of terrorist is not the true faith of Islam. That's not what Islam is all about. Islam is peace. These terrorists don't represent peace, they represent evil and war. . . . America counts millions of Muslims amongst our citizens, and Muslims make an incredibly valuable contribution to our country. . . . In our anger and emotion, our fellow Americans must treat each other with respect. . . . Those who feel like they can intimidate our fellow citizens to take out their anger don't represent the best of America. They represent the worst of humankind. And they should be ashamed of that kind of behavior. . . . And it is my honor to be meeting with leaders who feel just the same way I do. They are outraged; they're sad. They love America just as much as I do."
—*President George W. Bush, September 17, 2001 (after meeting American Muslim leaders in Washington, DC)*

". . .our nation must be mindful that there are thousands of Arab-Americans who live in New York City who love their flag just as much as the three of us do. And we must be mindful that as we seek to win the war that we treat Arab-Americans and Muslims with the respect they deserve. I know that is your attitudes as well. Certainly the attitude of this government, that we should not hold one who is a Muslim responsible for an act of terror. We will hold those who are responsible for the terrorist acts accountable and those who harbor them."
—*President George W. Bush, September 13, 2001*

"Since Tuesday the Justice Department has received reports of violence and threats of violence against Arab-Americans and other Americans of Middle Eastern and South Asian descents. We must not descend to the level of those who perpetrated Tuesday's violence by targeting individuals based on their race, their religion, or their national origin. Such reports of violence and threats are in direct opposition to the very principles and laws of the United States and will not be tolerated."
—*Attorney General John Ashcroft, September 13, 2001*

". . .Americans of Arab or South Asian decent [sic] and people of the Muslim faith were also injured and killed in Tuesday's attacks. In addition, they also are—along with other Americans—involved in relief operations, and other efforts to alleviate suffering. Any threats of violence or discrimination against Arab or Muslim Americans or Americans of South Asian descents are not just wrong and un-American, but also are unlawful and will be treated as such. As the Attorney General reminded us today, we must not descend to the level of those who perpetrated Tuesday's violence by targeting individuals for threats of violence based on their race, religion, and national origin. To do so would be to grant terrorists a victory they cannot- and would not – otherwise achieve."
—*Assistant Attorney General for Civil Rights, Ralph F. Boyd Jr., September 13, 2001*

"Nobody should blame any group of people or any nationality or any ethnic group. The particular individuals responsible or the groups responsible, that's up to law enforcement and it's up to the United States government to figure out. And citizens of New York should, even if they have anger, which is understandable, and very, very strong emotions about this, it isn't their place to get involved in this. Then they're just participating in the kind of activity we just witnessed. And New Yorkers are not like that."
—*New York Mayor Rudolph Giuliani, September 11, 2001*

"Whereas vengeful threats and incidents of violence directed at law-abiding, patriotic Americans of Arab or South Asian descent, particularly the Sikh community, and adherents of the Islamic faith have already occurred: Now, therefore, be it Resolved by the House of Representatives (the Senate concurring), That the Congress—(1) declares that in the quest to identify, bring to justice, and punish the perpetrators and sponsors of the terrorist attacks on the United States on September 11, 2001, that the civil rights and civil liberties of all American, including Arab-Americans, American Muslims, and Americans from South Asia, should be protected; and (2) condemns any acts of violence or discrimination against any Americans, including Arab-Americans, American Muslims, and Americans from South Asia."
—*Joint resolution by the Senate and House of Representatives (H.Con.Res. 227), September 26, 2001*

"We will also do all we can to protect the rights that make America such a special place. We will not adopt the characteristics of those who attack us. If we begin to compromise the civil liberties of our citizens, the terrorists will have won. In light of these traumatic events, I've heard reports of Americans who have attacked other Americans simply because of their race, ethnicity, religion or clothes. These attacks must stop. This is not a war against Islam. It is against terror. Those who did this are murderers, not martyrs. They cannot get to heaven by unleashing hell. The American Muslim community has said this loudly and repeatedly. Just as terror is not Islam, we must say to anyone who would lash out against Muslims this is not America..."
—*House Democratic Leader Rep. Dick Gephardt (D-MO)*

"No religious or ethnic group in our diverse society—including Arab Americans and Muslim Americans should be made to suffer because of fanatics half a world away. Americans should channel their anger into good works for others, not to acts of prejudice and hatred directed at other Americans."
—*Rep. Jim Moran (D-VA)*

"Anyone who resorts to acts of violence against Arab-Americans and/or American Muslims is giving the perpetrators of these heinous acts exactly what they wanted. Now more than ever, Americans of all ethnic and religious backgrounds must stand tall together in defense of our rich diversity and in defiance of those who seek to tear apart the American fabric."
—*Rep. Tom Davis (R-VA)*

"The terrorists who attacked the World Trade Center and the Pentagon are not representative of the vast majority or [sic] Arabs or Moslems in the United States. . . . We cannot allow anger at this horrible act to lead us to hate or discriminate against innocent individuals who happen to be of Middle Eastern descent. Terror has no regard for religion or ethnicity. If we attack the innocent simply because of their ethnic status, we are no better than the terrorists who attacked us."
—*Rep. Mike Pence (R-IN)*

". . . it is wrong and irresponsible to jump to conclusions and make false accusations against Arabs and Muslims in our communities. Above all, we must guard against any acts of violence based on such bigotry. Please do your part in defending America's rich religious and ethnic diversity."
—*Sen. Edward Kennedy (D-MA)*

"During this period of appalling pain for the American people, for the people of the entire world, as we absorb the shock and injustice of these acts—the Pentagon and the ashes of the World Trade Center now crime scenes—we resolve to apply our values as Americans as we seek justice. Even as national authorities focus on suspected individuals and organizations, we must not hurt or terrorize Americans of Arab Descent or Islamic faith. We, as Americans, proudly enshrine and practice justice and not vengeance, liberty and not racism and stereotyping."
—*Washington Gov. Gary Locke*

APPENDIX C
CONTEMPORARY DEFINITIONS OF TERRORISM
U.S. Government

"'terrorism' means an activity that (i) involves a violent act or an act dangerous to human life, property, or infrastructure; and (ii) appears to be intended (A) to intimidate or coerce a civilian population; (B) to

influence the policy of a government by intimidation or coercion; or (C) to affect the conduct of a government by mass destruction, assassination, kidnapping, or hostage-taking."
—*Executive Order on Terrorist Financing, George W. Bush, President, United States, September 2001*

"the term 'international terrorism' means activities that (A) involve violent acts or acts dangerous to human life that are a violation of the criminal laws of the United States or of any State, or that would be a criminal violation if committed within the jurisdiction of the United States or of any State; (B) appear to be intended—(i) to intimidate or coerce a civilian population; (ii) to influence the policy of a government by intimidation or coercion; or (III) to affect the conduct of a government by mass destruction, assassination, or kidnapping; and (C) occur primarily outside the territorial jurisdiction of the United States, or transcend national boundaries in terms of the means by which they are accomplished, the persons they appear intended to intimidate or coerce, or the locale in which their perpetrators operate or seek asylum;"
—*Section 2331 of Title 18, United States Code (as amended by the USA PATRIOT Act)*

"'domestic terrorism' means activities that (A) involve acts dangerous to human life that are a violation of the criminal laws of the United States or of any State; (B) appear to be intended (i) to intimidate or coerce a civilian population; (ii) to influence the policy of a government by intimidation or coercion; or (iii) to affect the conduct of a government by mass destruction, assassination, or kidnapping; and (C) occur primarily within the territorial jurisdiction of the United States."
—*Section 2331 of Title 18, United States Code (as amended by the USA PATRIOT Act)*

"Terrorism means premeditated, politically motivated violence perpetrated against noncombatant targets by subnational groups or clandestine agents, usually intended to influence an audience."
—*U.S. Department of State (Section 2656f(d) of Title 22, United States Code)*

"Terrorism is the calculated use of violence or threat of violence to inculcate fear; intended to coerce or to intimidate governments or societies in the pursuit of goals that are generally political, religious or ideological."
—*U.S. Department of Defense (DoD Instruction 2000.16, DoD Antiterrorism Standards, June 14, 2001.)*

"Terrorism is the unlawful use of force and violence against persons or property to intimidate or coerce a government, the civilian population, or any segment thereof, in furtherance of political or social objectives."
—*Code of Federal Regulations (28 C.F.R. Section 0.85)*

"Domestic terrorism is the unlawful use, or threatened use, of force or violence by a group or individual based and operating entirely within the United States or Puerto Rico without foreign direction committed against persons or property to intimidate or coerce a government, the civilian population, or any segment thereof in furtherance of political or social objectives."
—*Federal Bureau of Investigation (Terrorism in the United States: 1999, p. ii)*

"International terrorism involves violent acts or acts dangerous to human life that are a violation of the criminal laws of the United States or any state, or that would be a criminal violation if committed within the jurisdiction of the United States or any state. These acts appear to be intended to intimidate or coerce a civilian population, influence the policy of a government by intimidation or coercion, or affect the conduct of a government by assassination or kidnapping. International terrorist acts occur outside the United States, or transcend national boundaries in terms of the means by which they are accomplished, the persons they appear intended to coerce or intimidate, or the locale in which their perpetrators operate or seek asylum."
—*Federal Bureau of Investigation (Terrorism in the United States: 1999, p. ii)*

". . .the unlawful use or threat of violence against persons or property to further political or social objectives. It is generally intended to intimidate or coerce a government, individual s or groups to modify their behavior or policies."
—*Public Report of the Vice President's Task Force on Combating Terrorism (Washington, DC: Government Printing Office, February 1986), p. 1.*

"Terrorism is the illegitimate, premeditated violence or the threat of violence by subnational groups against persons of property with the intent to coerce a government by instilling fear amongst the populace."
—*House Permanent Select Committee on Intelligence, Subcom. on Terrorism and Homeland Security, July 2002.*

International Bodies

"...criminal acts intended or calculated to provoke a state of terror in the general public, a group of persons or particular persons for political purposes..."
—*United Nations General Assembly, UNGA Res. 51/210, December 17, 1996.*

"act intended to cause death or serious bodily injury to a civilian, or to any other person not taking an active part in the hostilities in a situation of armed conflict, when the purpose of such act, by its nature or context, is to intimidate a population, or to compel a government or an international organization to do or to abstain from doing any act."
—*United Nations General Assembly, International Convention for the Suppression of the Financing of Terrorism, adopted December 9, 1999.*

"'Terrorism' means any act of violence or threat thereof notwithstanding its motives or intentions perpetrated to carry out an individual or collective criminal plan with the aim of terrorizing people or threatening to harm them or imperiling their lives, honour, freedoms, security or rights or exposing the environment or any facility or public or private property to hazards or occupying or seizing them, or endangering a national resource, or international facilities, or threatening the stability, territorial integrity, political unity or sovereignty of independent States."
—*Organization of the Islamic Conference (OIC), Convention on the Combating of International Terrorism, adopted at Ouagadougou, July 1, 1999.*

Academia

"the threat or use of violence for political purposes when such when such action is intended to influence the attitudes and behavior of a group wider than its immediate victims; its ramifications transcend national boundaries."
—*Anthony C.E. Quainton (1990)*

"the systematic use of unorthodox political violence by small conspiratorial groups with the purpose of manipulating political attitudes rather than physically defeating an enemy."
—*Martha Crenshaw (1983)*

"Terrorism constitutes the illegitimate use of force to achieve a political objective when innocent people are targeted."
—*Walter Laqueur (1999)*

"Terrorism [is]...any type of political violence that lacks an adequate moral or legal justification, regardless of whether the actor is a revolutionary group or a government."
—*Richard A. Falk*

"Terrorism is the use or threatened use of force designed to bring about political change."
—*Brian Jenkins (1985)*

"the deliberate creation and exploitation of fear through violence or the threat of violence in the pursuit of political change."
—*Bruce Hoffman (1998)*

"peacetime equivalents of war crimes."
—*Alex Schmid (1992)*

"Terrorism is the systematic use of intimidation for political ends."
—*David Moss (1971)*

"Terrorism involves the intentional use of violence or the threat of violence by the precipitator against an instrumental target in order to communicate to a primary target a threat of future violence."
—*Jordan Paust (1977)*

"Terrorism may be defined as systematic and organized violence against non-resisting persons to create fear in them for the purpose of retaining or gaining governmental authority."
—*Milenko Karanovic (1978)*

"terrorism is seen as the resort to violence for political ends by unauthorised, non-governmental actors in breach of accepted codes of behavior..."
—*Juliet Lodge (1982)*

"Terrorism may be described as a strategy of violence designed to inspire terror within a particular segment of a given society."
—*M. Cherif Bassiouni (1981)*

APPENDIX D
INTERNATIONAL TREATIES AND CONVENTIONS ON TERRORISM

International Conventions

Convention on Offences and Certain Other Acts Committed on Board Aircraft, signed at Tokyo on 14 September 1963. (Deposited with the Secretary-General of the International Civil Aviation Organization)

Convention for the Suppression of Unlawful Seizure of Aircraft, signed at the Hague on 16 December 1970. (Deposited with the Governments of the Russian Federation, the United Kingdom and the United States of America)

Convention for the Suppression of Unlawful Acts against the Safety of Civil Aviation, signed at Montreal on 23 September 1971. (Deposited with the Governments of the Russian Federation, the United Kingdom and the United States of America)

Convention on the Prevention and Punishment of Crimes against Internationally Protected Persons, including Diplomatic Agents, adopted by the General Assembly of the United Nations on 14 December 1973. (Deposited with the UN Secretary General). International Convention against the Taking of Hostages, adopted by the General Assembly of the United Nations on 17 December 1979. (Deposited with the UN Secretary General)

Convention on the Physical Protection of Nuclear Material, signed at Vienna on 3 March 1980. (Deposited with the Director-General of the International Atomic Energy Agency)

Protocol on the Suppression of Unlawful Acts of Violence at Airports Serving International Civil Aviation, supplementary to the Convention for the Suppression of Unlawful Acts against the Safety of Civil Aviation, signed at Montreal on 24 February 1988. (Deposited with the Governments of the Russian Federation, the United Kingdom and the United States of America and with the Secretary-General of the International Civil Aviation Organization)

Convention for the Suppression of Unlawful Acts against the Safety of Maritime Navigation, done at Rome on 10 March 1988. (Deposited with the Secretary-General of the International Maritime Organization)

Protocol for the Suppression of Unlawful Acts against the Safety of Fixed Platforms Located on the Continental Shelf, done at Rome on 10 March 1988. (Deposited with the Secretary-General of the International Maritime Organization)

Convention on the Marking of Plastic Explosives for the Purpose of Detection, signed at Montreal on 1 March 1991. (Deposited with the Secretary-General of the International Civil Aviation Organization International Convention for the Suppression of Terrorist Bombings, adopted by the General Assembly of the United Nations on 15 December 1997. (Deposited with the UN Secretary General)

International Convention for the Suppression of the Financing of Terrorism, adopted by the General Assembly of the United Nations on 9 December 1999. (Deposited with the UN Secretary General)

Regional Conventions

European Convention on the Suppression of Terrorism, concluded at Strasbourg on 27 January 1977. (Deposited with the Secretary-General of the Council of Europe)

OAS Convention to Prevent and Punish Acts of Terrorism Taking the Form of Crimes against Persons and Related Extortion that are of International Significance, concluded at Washington, D.C. on 2 February 1971. (Deposited with the Secretary-General of the Organization of American States)

SAARC Regional Convention on Suppression of Terrorism, signed at Kathmandu on 4 November 1987. (Deposited with the Secretary-General of the South Asian Association for Regional Cooperation)

Arab Convention on the Suppression of Terrorism, signed at a meeting held at the General Secretariat of the League of Arab States in Cairo on 22 April 1998. (Deposited with the Secretary-General of the League of Arab States)

Treaty on Cooperation among States Members of the Commonwealth of Independent States in Combating Terrorism, done at Minsk on 4 June 1999. (Deposited with the Secretariat of the Commonwealth of Independent States)

Convention of the Organization of the Islamic Conference on Combating International Terrorism, adopted at Ouagadougou on 1 July 1999. (Deposited with the Secretary-General of the Organization of the Islamic Conference)

OAU Convention on the Prevention and Combating of Terrorism, adopted at Algiers on 14 July 1999. (Deposited with the General Secretariat of the Organization of African Unity)

SOURCES: U.S. Department of State

   United Nations (http://untreaty.un.org/English/Terrorism.asp)

[278] See also U.S. House of Representatives. Permanent Select Committee on Intelligence. Subcommittee on Terrorism and Homeland Security, *Counterterrorism Intelligence Capabilities and Performance Prior to 9-11: A Report to the Speaker of the House of Representatives and the Minority Leader,* July 2002.

[279] Similar to statements articulated by the State Department and Secretary Powell.

[280] Originally published in Arabic in al-Quds al-Arabi (London), September 14, 2001, p.2 (http://www.alquds.co.uk/Alquds/2001/09Sep/14%20Sep%20Fri/Quds02.pdf, accessed on DATE). English cited in MSANews, http://msanews.mynet.net/MSA-NEWS/200109/20010917.15.html, accessed on DATE).

56. Statements from American Government Officials

The following is a short list of statements regarding Islam and Muslims made by President George W. Bush after September 11, 2001, by former President Bill Clinton, and statements from other press briefings. President Bush referred to the U.S. "War on Terror" as a crusade in a press briefing on September 16, 2001, provoking a negative reaction from the Muslim world. In his State of the Union Address of 2002, he referred to Iraq, Iran, and North Korea as constituting an "axis of evil." In the other excerpts listed, President Bush, former presidents, and other U.S. government officials iterate respect and tolerance toward Islam and Muslims.

These statements highlight a continuous feature of American policy: condemn and fight terrorism while avoiding confusing such efforts with a war against Islam.

"Our nation must be mindful that there are thousands of Arab-Americans who live in New York City, who love their flag just as much as [we] do. And we must be mindful that as we seek to win the war, that we treat Arab-Americans and Muslims with the respect they deserve. I know that is your attitudes as well. Certainly the attitude of this government, that we should not hold one who is a Muslim responsible for an act of terror. We will hold those who are responsible for the terrorist acts accountable and those who harbor them."

President George W. Bush, September 13, 2001

PRESIDENT MEETS WITH MUSLIM LEADERS

September 26, 2001
Remarks by the President in Meeting with Muslim Community Leaders
The Roosevelt Room

THE PRESIDENT: It's my honor to welcome to the White House my fellow Americans, Arab Americans, Americans who are Muslim by faith, to discuss about the current issues that took place, the aftermath of the incident, and what our country is going to do to make sure that everybody who is an American is respected.

I have told the nation more than once that ours is a war against evil, against extremists, that the teachings of Islam are the teachings of peace and good, and the al Qaeda organization is not an organization of good, an organization of peace. It's an organization based upon hate and evil.

I also want to assure my fellow Americans that when you pledge allegiance to the flag, with your hand on your heart, you pledge just as hard to the flag as I do; that the outpouring of support for our country has come from all corners of the country, including many members of the Muslim faith. And for that I am grateful.

I appreciate the contributions of time, the contributions of blood to help our fellow Americans who have been injured. And I'm proud of the Muslim leaders across America who have risen up and who have not only insisted that America be strong, but that America keep the values intact that have made us so unique and different—the values of respect, the values of freedom to worship the way we see fit. And I also appreciate the prayers to the universal God.

And so, thank you all for coming. I don't know if you all remember the Imam led the service at the National Cathedral—he did a heck of a good job, and we were proud to have him there. And I want to thank you very much for the gift you gave me, Imam, the Koran. It's a very thoughtful gift. I said thank you very much for the gift. He said, it's the best gift I could give you, Mr. President. I appreciate that very much.

EXCERPT FROM THE STATE OF THE UNION, JANUARY 29, 2002

My hope is that all nations will heed our call, and eliminate the terrorist parasites who threaten their countries and our own. Many nations are acting forcefully. Pakistan is now cracking down on terror, and I admire the strong leadership of President Musharraf. (Applause.)

But some governments will be timid in the face of terror. And make no mistake about it: If they do not act, America will. (Applause.)

Our second goal is to prevent regimes that sponsor terror from threatening America or our friends and allies with weapons of mass destruction. Some of these regimes have been pretty quiet since September the 11th. But we know their true nature. North Korea is a regime arming with missiles and weapons of mass destruction, while starving its citizens.

Iran aggressively pursues these weapons and exports terror, while an unelected few repress the Iranian people's hope for freedom.

Iraq continues to flaunt its hostility toward America and to support terror. The Iraqi regime has plotted to develop anthrax, and nerve gas, and nuclear weapons for over a decade. This is a regime that has already used poison gas to murder thousands of its own citizens—leaving the bodies of mothers huddled over their dead children. This is a regime that agreed to international inspections—then kicked out the inspectors. This is a regime that has something to hide from the civilized world.

States like these, and their terrorist allies, constitute an axis of evil, arming to threaten the peace of the world. By seeking weapons of mass destruction, these regimes pose a grave and growing danger. They could provide these arms to terrorists, giving them the means to match their hatred. They could attack our allies or attempt to blackmail the United States. In any of these cases, the price of indifference would be catastrophic.

We will work closely with our coalition to deny terrorists and their state sponsors the materials, technology, and expertise to make and deliver weapons of mass destruction. We will develop and deploy effective missile defenses to protect America and our allies from sudden attack. (Applause.) And all nations should know: America will do what is necessary to ensure our nation's security.

We'll be deliberate, yet time is not on our side. I will not wait on events, while dangers gather. I will not stand by, as peril draws closer and closer. The United States of America will not permit the world's most dangerous regimes to threaten us with the world's most destructive weapons. (Applause.)

Our war on terror is well begun, but it is only begun. This campaign may not be finished on our watch—yet it must be and it will be waged on our watch.

We can't stop short. If we stop now—leaving terror camps intact and terror states unchecked—our sense of security would be false and temporary. History has called America and our allies to action, and it is both our responsibility and our privilege to fight freedom's fight. (Applause.)

PRESIDENT BUSH PRESS CONFERENCE

September 16, 2001

THE PRESIDENT: Today, millions of Americans mourned and prayed, and tomorrow we go back to work. Today, people from all walks of life gave thanks for the heroes; they mourn the dead; they ask for God's good graces on the families who mourn, and tomorrow the good people of America go back to their shops, their fields, American factories, and go back to work.

Our nation was horrified, but it's not going to be terrorized. We're a great nation. We're a nation of resolve. We're a nation that can't be cowed by evil-doers. I've got great faith in the American people. If the American people had seen what I had seen in New York City, you'd have great faith, too. You'd have faith in the hard work of the rescuers; you'd have great faith because of the desire for people to do what's right for America; you'd have great faith because of the compassion and love that our fellow Americans are showing each other in times of need.

I also have faith in our military. And we have got a job to do—just like the farmers and ranchers and business owners and factory workers have a job to do. My administration has a job to do, and we're going to do it. We will rid the world of the evil-doers. We will call together freedom loving people to fight terrorism.

And on this day of—on the Lord's Day, I say to my fellow Americans, thank you for your prayers, thank you for your compassion, thank you for your love for one another. And tomorrow when you get back to work, work hard like you always have. But we've been warned. We've been warned there are evil people in this world. We've been warned so vividly—and we'll be alert. Your government is alert. The governors and mayors are alert that evil folks still lurk out there.

As I said yesterday, people have declared war on America, and they have made a terrible mistake, because this is a fabulous country. Our economy will come back. We'll still be the best farmers and ranchers in the world. We're still the most innovative entrepreneurs in the world. On this day of faith, I've never had more faith in America than I have right now.

Q: Mr. President, are you worried this crisis might send us into a recession?

THE PRESIDENT: David, I understand that there are some businesses that hurt as a result of this crisis. Obviously, New York City hurts. Congress acted quickly. We worked together, the White House and the Congress, to pass a significant supplemental. A lot of that money was dedicated to New York, New Jersey and Connecticut, as it should be. People will be amazed at how quickly we rebuild New York; how quickly people come together to really wipe away the rubble and show the world that we're still the strongest nation in the world.

But I have great faith in the resiliency of the economy. And no question about it, this incident affected our economy, but the markets open tomorrow, people go back to work and we'll show the world.

Q: Mr. President, do you believe Osama bin Laden's denial that he had anything to do with this?

THE PRESIDENT: No question he is the prime suspect. No question about that.

Q: Mr. President, can you describe your conversation with the President of Pakistan and the specific comments he made to you? And, in addition to that, do you see other —you've asked Saudi Arabia to help out, other countries?

THE PRESIDENT: John, I will—obviously, I made a call to the leader of Pakistan. We had a very good, open conversation. And there is no question that he wants to cooperate with the United States. I'm not at liberty to detail specifically what we have asked him to do. In the course of this conduct of this war against terrorism, I'll be asked a lot, and members of my administration will be asked a lot of questions about our strategies and tactics. And in order to protect the lives of people that will be involved in different operations, I'm not at liberty to talk about it and I won't talk about it.

But I can tell you that the response from Pakistan; Prime Minister Vajpayee today, of India, Saudi Arabia, has been very positive and very straightforward. They know what my intentions are. They know my intentions are to find those who did this, find those who encouraged them, find them who house them, find those who comfort them, and bring them to justice.

I made that very clear. There is no doubt in anybody's mind with whom I've had a conversation about the intent of the United States. I gave them ample opportunity to say they were uncomfortable with our goal. And the leaders you've asked about have said they were comfortable. They said, we understand, Mr. President, and we're with you.

Q: Mr. President, the Attorney General is going to ask for enhanced law enforcement authority to surveil and—things to disrupt terrorism that might be planned here in the United States. What will that mean for the rights of Americans? What will that mean—

THE PRESIDENT: Terry, I ask you to talk to the Attorney General about that subject. He'll be prepared to talk about it publicly at some point in time. But what he is doing is, he's reflecting what I said earlier in my statement, that we're facing a new kind of enemy, somebody so barbaric that they would fly airplanes into buildings full of innocent people. And, therefore, we have to be on alert in America. We're a nation of law, a nation of civil rights. We're also a nation under attack. And the Attorney General will address that in a way that I think the American people will understand.

We need to go back to work tomorrow and we will. But we need to be alert to the fact that these evil-doers still exist. We haven't seen this kind of barbarism in a long period of time. No one could have conceivably imagined suicide bombers burrowing into our society and then emerging all in the same day to fly their aircraft—fly U.S. aircraft into buildings full of innocent people—and show no remorse. This is a new kind of—a new kind of evil. And we understand. And the American people are beginning to understand. This crusade, this war on terrorism is going to take a while. And the American people must be patient. I'm going to be patient.

But I can assure the American people I am determined, I'm not going to be distracted, I will keep my focus to make sure that not only are these brought to justice, but anybody who's been associated will be brought to justice. Those who harbor terrorists will be brought to justice. It is time for us to win the first war of the 21st century decisively, so that our children and our grandchildren can live peacefully into the 21st century.

Q: Mr. President, you've declared we're at war and asked those who wear the uniform to get ready. Should the American public also be ready for the possibility of casualties in this war?

THE PRESIDENT: Patsy, the American people should know that my administration is determined to find, to get them running and to hunt them down, those who did this to America. Now, I want to remind the American people that the prime suspect's organization is in a lot of countries—it's a widespread organization based upon one thing: terrorizing. They can't stand freedom; they hate what America stands for. So this will be a long campaign, a determined campaign—a campaign that will use the resources of the United States to win.

They have roused a mighty giant. And make no mistake about it: we're determined. Oh, there will be times when people don't have this incident on their minds, I understand that. There will be times down the road where citizens will be concerned about other matters, and I completely understand that. But this administration, along with those friends of ours who are willing to stand with us all the way through will do what it takes to rout terrorism out of the world.

Q: Mr. President, in your conversation with Pakistan's leader, was there any request or demand you made of him that he failed to satisfy?

THE PRESIDENT: The leader of Pakistan has been very cooperative. He has agreed with our requests to aid our nation to hunt down, to find, to smoke out of their holes the terrorist organization that is the prime suspect. And I am pleased with his response. We will continue to work with Pakistan and India. We will work with Russia. We will work with the nations that one would have thought a couple of years ago would have been impossible to work with—to bring people to justice. But more than that, to win the war against terrorist activity.

The American people are used to a conflict where there was a beachhead or a desert to cross or known military targets. That may occur. But right now we're facing people who hit and run. They hide in caves. We'll get them out.

The other day I said, not only will we find those who have affected America, or who might affect America in the future, we'll also deal with those who harbor them.

Q: Mr. President, would you confirm what the Vice President said this morning, that at one point during this crisis you gave an order to shoot down any civilian airliner that approached the Capitol? Was that a difficult decision to make?

THE PRESIDENT: I gave our military the orders necessary to protect Americans, do whatever it would take to protect Americans. And of course that's difficult. Never did anybody's thought process about how to protect America did we ever think that the evil-doers would fly not one, but four commercial aircraft into precious U.S. targets—never. And so, obviously, when I was told what was taking place, when I was informed that an unidentified aircraft was headed to the heart of the capital, I was concerned. I wasn't concerned about my decision; I was more concerned about the lives of innocent Americans. I had realized there on the ground in Florida we were under attack. But never did I dream we would have been under attack this way.

That's why I say to the American people we've never seen this kind of evil before. But the evil-doers have never seen the American people in action before, either—and they're about to find out.

Thank you all very much.

GEORGE W. BUSH:

"The face of terror is not the true faith of Islam. That's not what Islam is all about. Islam is peace. These terrorists don't represent peace. They represent evil and war."
Remarks by the President at Islamic Center of Washington, D.C.
Washington, D.C.
September 17, 2001

"All of us here today understand this: We do not fight Islam, we fight against evil."
Remarks by President George W. Bush to the Warsaw Conference on Combating Terrorism
November 6, 2001

"The teachings of many faiths share much in common. And people of many faiths are united in our commitments to love our families, to protect our children, and to build a more peaceful world. In the coming year, let us resolve to seize opportunities to work together in a spirit of friendship and cooperation. Through our combined efforts, we can end terrorism and rid our civilization of the damaging effects of hatred and intolerance, ultimately achieving a brighter future for all."
President's Message for Eid al-Fitr
December 13, 2001

BILL CLINTON:

"We have had problems with terrorism coming out of the Middle East. . . this is not inherently related to Islam, not to the religion, not to the culture."

The President's News Conference, U.S. Government Printing Office, Jakarta, November 15,
1994; http://www.gpo.gov

PRESS BRIEFING BY ARI FLEISCHER

Q: *The President's visit to the Islamic center you mentioned has an important domestic purpose.* Does it have an international purpose, as well? How concerned is the President that in defending ourselves we could ignite, not among the government of the region, but among the people of the region, a kind of religious conflict, a holy war?

MR. FLEISCHER: Well, I think it's fair to say that any actions the President takes domestically have international repercussions. The world is looking to us to see how we react to the fight against terrorism. The world will follow America's lead in many cases. And we will continue to work directly with many of those other nations.

But I remind you, also, Terry, that many of those nations have their own threats from within and they have to ask themselves if they fail to act against terrorism, will that further embolden the terrorists and send a signal that they can get away with more?

Q: But is there a concern that this could degenerate into a conflict, not between terrorism and civilization, but between Islam and Christianity?

MR. FLEISCHER: This attack had nothing to do with Islam. This attack was a perversion of Islam.

"Press Briefing by Ari Fleischer," September 17, 2001; http://www.whitehouse.gov/news/releases/2001/09/20010917-8.html

57. President Jimmy Carter, "State of the Union Address, 1980: 'The Carter Doctrine'"

The following is an excerpt from former President Jimmy Carter's State of the Union Address in 1980 in which he laid out what became known as the "Carter Doctrine." According to this doctrine, "An attempt by any outside force to gain control of the Persian Gulf region will be regarded as an assault on the vital interests of the United States of America, and such an assault will be repelled by any means necessary, including military force."

The region which is now threatened by Soviet troops in Afghanistan is of great strategic importance: It contains more than two-thirds of the world's exportable oil. The Soviet effort to dominate Afghanistan has brought Soviet military forces to within 300 miles of the Indian Ocean and close to the Straits of Hormuz, a waterway through which most of the world's oil must flow. The Soviet Union is now attempting to consolidate a strategic position, therefore, that poses a grave threat to the free movement of Middle East oil.

This situation demands careful thought, steady nerves, and resolute action, not only for this year but for many years to come. It demands collective efforts to meet this new threat to security in the Persian Gulf and in Southwest Asia. It demands the participation of all those who rely on oil from the Middle East and who are concerned with global peace and stability. And it demands consultation and close cooperation with countries in the area which might be threatened.

Meeting this challenge will take national will, diplomatic and political wisdom, economic sacrifice, and, of course, military capability. We must call on the best that is in us to preserve the security of this crucial region.

Let our position be absolutely clear: An attempt by any outside force to gain control of the Persian Gulf region will be regarded as an assault on the vital interests of the United States of America, and such an assault will be repelled by any means necessary, including military force.

During the past 3 years, you have joined with me to improve our own security and the prospects for peace, not only in the vital oil-producing area of the Persian Gulf region but around the world. We've increased annually our real commitment for defense, and we will sustain this increase of effort throughout the Five Year Defense Program. It's imperative that Congress approve this strong defense budget for 1981, encompassing a 5-percent real growth in authorizations, without any reduction.

We are also improving our capability to deploy U.S. military forces rapidly to distant areas. We've helped to strengthen NATO and our other alliances, and recently we and other NATO members have decided to develop and to deploy modernized, intermediate-range nuclear forces to meet an unwarranted and increased threat from the nuclear weapons of the Soviet Union.

We are working with our allies to prevent conflict in the Middle East. The peace treaty between Egypt and Israel is a notable achievement which represents a strategic asset for America and which also enhances prospects for regional and world peace. We are now engaged in further negotiations to provide full autonomy for the people of the West Bank and Gaza, to resolve the Palestinian issue in all its aspects, and to preserve the peace and security of Israel. Let no one doubt our commitment to the security of Israel. In a few days we will observe an historic event when Israel makes another major withdrawal from the Sinai and when Ambassadors will be exchanged between Israel and Egypt.

58. "Foreign Policy, Terrorism, and Concerns about Extremism" from *the Pew Research Center*

May 22, 2007. http://news.bbc.co.uk/2/shared/bsp/hi/pdfs/22_05_2007_muslim_ americans.pdf. Reprinted with permission of The Pew Research Center. Copyright 2007 by Pew Research Center.

The Pew Research Center is a nonpartisan organization that gathers and disseminates information regarding current events, issues, and attitudes. This poll was conducted in 2006 and is the first nationwide survey to use a representative sample to measure "the demographics, attitudes, and experiences of Muslim Americans" (Foreword, p. 1). The following excerpt from the poll (pp. 49–56) highlights respondents' perceptions of the wars in Iraq and Afghanistan, the War on Terror, responsibility for the September 11th attacks, concerns about Islamic extremism, suicide bombing, al Qaeda, and the Israeli-Palestinian conflict.

Muslim Americans express broad dissatisfaction with the direction of U.S. foreign policy. Most say that the U.S. made the wrong decision in using force against Iraq, and while there is greater support for the decision to use force in Afghanistan, more say it was the wrong thing to do than say it was right. A majority of Muslim Americans say that the U.S.-led war on terror is not a sincere effort to reduce international terrorism, and fewer than half say they believe the attacks of 9/11 were carried out by groups of Arabs.

At the same time, Muslims in the United States are widely concerned about Islamic extremism, and express strong disapproval of terrorists and their tactics. In fact, about three-quarters (76%) say they are very or somewhat concerned about the rise of Islamic extremism around the world, and 61% say they are concerned about the possible rise of Islamic extremism in the U.S. Similarly, more than three-in-four say that suicide bombing in defense of Islam is never justified, and just 5% express favorable views of al Qaeda. On the question of the Israeli-Palestinian conflict, most Muslims in the U.S say that a way can be found for Israel to exist so that the rights and needs of Palestinians are met, a view that is not shared by Muslims in predominantly Muslim countries.

Iraq, Afghanistan and the War on Terror

By an overwhelming margin, most Muslim Americans say that the U.S. made the wrong decision in using military force against Iraq (75% wrong decision vs. 12% right

Views of U.S. Military Force in Iraq and Afghanistan

| | Iraq | | Afghanistan | |
	Right	Wrong	Right	Wrong
	%	%	%	%
All U.S. Muslims	12	75	35	48
Men	14	79	42	46
Women	9	71	27	50
Rep/lean Rep	40	54	60	32
Dem/lean Dem	8	86	34	57
Ind, no leaning	8	57	26	32
Native-born	11	85	26	65
Foreign-born	13	70	40	40
U.S. general public*	45	47	61	29

* April 2007 Pew Research Center for the People & the Press national survey.

decision). Even with the gradual erosion in overall public support for the war, Muslims are much more likely than Americans in general (47% in April 2007) to say that invading Iraq was the wrong decision.

Broad opposition to the use of force in Iraq is found across all groups of Muslims in the U.S., although native-born Muslims are more likely than the foreign-born to say that using force in Iraq was the wrong decision (85% vs. 70%). About two-thirds of Muslim Americans are Democrats or lean Democratic and, not surprisingly, opposition to the war is strongest among them. But even among the small minority of Muslims who describe themselves as Republicans or lean toward the Republican Party, most (54%) say that using force in Iraq was the wrong decision. By contrast, among Republicans and Republican leaners in the public as a whole, a large majority (76%) says that using force in Iraq was the right decision.

While more Muslim Americans (35%) express support for the use of force in Afghanistan, nearly half (48%) say it was the wrong decision. This is in contrast to the views of the

Sincere Effort to Reduce Terrorism?

	Yes	No	(Vol.) Both	DK/Ref
	%	%	%	%
All U.S. Muslims	26	55	2	17=100
Native-born	20	71	1	8=100
Foreign-born	30	49	2	19=100
*Muslims in...**				
Turkey	20	63	7	10=100
Morocco	17	66	4	13=100
Jordan	11	52	23	14=100
Pakistan	6	59	5	30=100

Question: Do you believe the US led war on terrorism is a sincere effort to reduce international terrorism, or don't you believe that?

* Pew Global Attitudes Project, March 2004.

general public, which says that taking military action in Afghanistan was the right decision by a margin of about two-to-one (61% to 29%).

When it comes to America's military action in Afghanistan, Muslims born in the United States express far more opposition than those who immigrated to the U.S. About two-thirds of all native-born Muslims (65%) say that using force in Afghanistan was the wrong decision, compared with 40% of foreign-born Muslims. A majority of Republicans and Republican leaners (60%) say using force in Afghanistan was the right decision, while a majority of Democrats and Democratic leaners (57%) take the opposite point of view.

The relatively low levels of support among U.S. Muslims for using force in Iraq and Afghanistan are consistent with their doubts about the U.S.-led war on terrorism. A majority of Muslims in America (55%) say that they do not believe the war on terrorism is a sincere attempt to reduce international terrorism, while half as many (26%) say the U.S. effort is genuine. Native-born Muslims are even more likely than the foreign-born to express skepticism about U.S. intentions in the war on terrorism (71% vs. 49%, respectively).

Muslim Americans' views on the war on terrorism are similar to levels of skepticism about U.S. intentions among Muslims in other parts of the world. A majority of Muslims in Morocco (66%), Turkey (63%), Pakistan (59%) and Jordan (52%) doubt the sincerity of the U.S.-led war on terrorism, according to the 2004 Pew Global Attitudes study.

Responsibility for 9/11 Attacks

Asked whether they believe groups of Arabs carried out the attacks against the United States on Sept. 11, 2001, 40% of Muslim Americans say yes, while 28% say they do not believe this, and about a third (32%) say they do not know or decline to answer the question.

When those who say Arabs were not involved in the 9/11 attacks are asked who they believe was responsible, most say they do not know or declined to answer. Seven percent of Muslims overall say that the attacks were the result of a conspiracy involving the United States government or the Bush administration. Very small proportions hold others responsible, including individuals other than Muslims (1%), Israel or Jewish interests (1%), and crazy or misguided people (1%).

Despite widespread doubts about the official accounts of 9/11, Muslims in the U.S. are more likely than Muslims living in a number of European and majority-Muslim countries

Who Was Responsible for 9/11?

	US Muslims
	%
Believe groups of Arabs responsible	40
Don't believe Arabs responsible	28
Bush/U.S. conspiracy responsible	7
Israel/Jews responsible	1
Insane/misguided people	1
Other/non-Muslims responsible	1
Don't know/Refused	18
Don't know/Refused	32
	100

Do You Believe Groups of Arabs Carried Out the 9/11 Attacks?

	Yes	No	DK/Ref
	%	%	%
All U.S. Muslims	40	28	32=100
18–29	38	38	24=100
30–39	37	30	33=100
40–54	45	24	31=100
55+	49	16	35=100
College grad	55	24	22=100
Some college	43	30	27=100
HS or less	34	30	36=100
Religious commitment			
High	29	46	25=100
Medium	38	24	38=100
Low	53	22	25=100
*Muslims in...**			
France	48	46	6=100
Germany	35	44	21=100
Spain	33	35	32=100
Great Britain	17	56	27=100
Nigeria	42	47	11=100
Jordan	39	53	8=100
Egypt	32	59	9=100
Turkey	16	59	25=100
Indonesia	16	65	20=101
Pakistan	15	41	44=100

Question: Do you believe that groups of Arabs carried out the attacks against the United States on Sept. 11, 2001, or don't you believe this?

* Pew Global Attitudes Project, May 2006.

to believe that groups of Arabs carried out the attacks. For instance, Muslims in the U.S. are more than twice as likely as Muslims in Great Britain (17%), Turkey (16%), Indonesia (16%) and Pakistan (15%) to say that groups of Arabs carried out the 9/11 attacks. In all of these countries, clear majorities or pluralities reject the official account of the attacks.

In the U.S., younger Muslims are more likely than older Muslims to say they do not believe that groups of Arabs carried out the 9/11 attacks. Indeed, among Muslims under the age of 30, 38% reject the fact that groups of Arabs were responsible for 9/11. By comparison, among Muslims 55 and older, just 16% say that Arabs were not responsible for the attacks.

Views on this question also are linked to education and religious commitment. A majority (55%) of Muslims with college degrees attribute the attacks to the activities of Arab groups. This drops to 43% among those with some college and 34% among those who have not attended college. Muslims who are most committed to their religion are approximately twice as likely as those who express relatively low religious commitment to say they do not believe groups of Arabs were responsible for 9/11 (46% vs. 22%).

How Concerned Are You about the Rise of Islamic Extremism Around the World?

	Very	Somewhat	Not too/not at all	DK/Ref
	%	%	%	%
All U.S. Muslims	51	25	19	5=100
18–29	42	39	16	3=100
30–39	63	18	17	2=100
40–54	51	21	23	5=100
55+	54	18	18	10=100
Native-born	54	25	19	2=100
Foreign-born	50	26	19	5=100
Arrived pre-1990	65	20	12	3=100
1990 or later	43	31	21	5=100
Muslims in...*				
Great Britain	52	25	20	4=101
France	35	38	27	0=100
Spain	29	31	38	3=101
Germany	29	29	37	5=100
Pakistan	43	29	9	19=100
Indonesia	30	38	32	*=100
Jordan	31	30	38	1=100
Nigeria	24	33	41	2=100
Egypt	22	31	45	2=100
Turkey	15	24	43	18=100

* Pew Global Attitudes Project, May 2006

Concern about Islamic Extremism

Though Muslims in the U.S. have doubts about the war on terrorism and the official account of 9/11, they are nonetheless concerned about Islamic extremism and express high levels of opposition to both terrorists and their tactics. Indeed, the vast majority of Muslims say that they are either very concerned (51%) or somewhat concerned (25%) about the rise of Islamic extremism around the world.

By this measure, Muslims in the U.S. are more concerned about Islamic extremism around the world than are Muslims in many European and majority-Muslim countries. In France, Germany and Spain, for example, only about a third of Muslims say they are very concerned about the rise of Islamic extremism around the world, compared with 51% in the United States. And with the exception of Pakistan (where 43% are very concerned about Islamic extremism), less than a third of the Muslims in predominantly Muslim countries surveyed by Pew last year say they are very concerned about Islamic extremism.

While native-born and foreign-born Muslims express similar levels of concern over global Islamic extremism, there is a sizable difference between immigrants who arrived in the U.S. long ago and those who immigrated more recently. About two-thirds (65%) of Muslims who immigrated to the U.S. prior to 1990 say they are very concerned about Islamic extremism around the world, a view shared by 43% of those who have arrived more recently.

Fewer U.S. Muslims express concern about the potential for Islamic extremism to arise in the United States. Slightly more than a third (36%) say they are very concerned about

How Concerned Are You about the Rise of Islamic Extremism in the United States?

	U.S. Muslims	U.S. general public
	%	%
Very concerned	36	46
Somewhat concerned	25	32
Not too concerned	14	13
Not at all concerned	20	5
Don't know/Refused	5̲100	4̲
		100

this possibility. Still, 61% of Muslims in the U.S. say they are at least somewhat concerned about the possible rise of extremism in the U.S. The American population as a whole is somewhat more concerned about Islamic extremism in the U.S. than are Muslim Americans: 78% of the public say they are very or somewhat concerned about Islamic extremism at home.

Can Suicide Bombing be Justified?

In addition to being more concerned about the rise of Islamic extremism, Muslims in the U.S. are far less likely than Muslims in other parts of the world to accept suicide bombing as a justifiable tactic. The overwhelming majority of Muslims in the U.S. (78%) say that the use of suicide bombing against civilian targets to defend Islam from its enemies is never justified. In this regard, American Muslims are more opposed to suicide bombing than are Muslims in nine of the 10 other countries surveyed in 2006; opposition is somewhat greater among Muslims in Germany (83%).

Overall, 8% of Muslim Americans say suicide bombings against civilian targets tactics are often (1%) or sometimes (7%) justified in the defense of Islam. Muslims in France, Spain and Great Britain were twice as likely as Muslims in the U.S. to say suicide

Can Suicide Bombing of Civilian Targets to Defend Islam be Justified?

	How often justified...			
	Often/sometimes	Rarely	Never	DK/Ref
	%	%	%	%
All U.S. Muslims	8	5	78	9=100
Muslims in... *				
France	16	19	64	1=100
Spain	16	9	69	7=101
Great Britain	15	9	70	6=100
Germany	7	6	83	3=99
Nigeria	46	23	28	3=100
Jordan	29	28	43	*=100
Egypt	28	25	45	3=101
Turkey	17	9	61	14=101
Pakistan	14	8	69	8=99
Indonesia	10	18	71	1=100

See topline Q.H1 for full question wording.
* Pew Global Attitudes Project, May 2006.

More Support for Suicide Bombing Among Younger Muslims

	(NET) Ever justified	Often/ sometimes	Rarely	Never justified	DK/Ref
	%	%	%	%	%
All U.S. Muslims	**13**	*8*	*5*	78	**9=100**
18–29	26	*15*	*11*	69	5=100
30 or older	9	*6*	*3*	82	9=100
*Muslims in…**					
Great Britain	**24**	*15*	*9*	70	**6=100**
18–29	35	*19*	*16*	59	6=100
30 or older	17	*13*	*4*	77	6=100
France	**35**	*16*	*19*	64	**1=100**
18–29	42	*19*	*23*	57	1=100
30 or older	31	*15*	*16*	69	*=100
Germany	**13**	*7*	*6*	83	**3=99**
18–29	22	*13*	*9*	77	1=100
30 or older	10	*5*	*5*	86	4=100
Spain	**25**	*16*	*9*	69	**7=101**
18–29	29	*17*	*12*	65	6=100
30 or older	22	*14*	*8*	71	7=100

*   Pew Global Attitudes Project, May 2006.

Views of al Qaeda

	Favorable*	Somewhat unfav	Very unfav	DK/Ref
	%	%	%	%
All U.S. Muslims	5	10	58	27=100
18–29	7	16	58	19=100
30–39	4	8	59	29=100
40–54	4	7	60	29=100
55+	2	7	62	29=100
College graduate	1	7	78	14=100
Some college	1	14	68	17=100
HS or less	7	10	48	35=100
Native-born	7	16	51	26=100
African American	9	25	36	30=100
Other race	4	6	69	21=100
Foreign-born	3	7	63	27=100
Arrived pre-1990	1	5	75	19=100
1990 or later	5	8	57	30=100
Religious commitment				
High	5	13	51	31=100
Medium	6	11	58	25=100
Low	*	5	66	29=100
Always a Muslim	3	7	60	30=100
Convert to Islam	7	19	54	20=100

*   Combined "very" and "somewhat" favorable.

bombing can be often or sometimes justified, and acceptance of the tactic is far more widespread among Muslims in Nigeria, Jordan and Egypt.

There are few differences on this question in the United States across Muslim ethnic groups, but age is an important factor. Younger Muslims in the U.S. are more willing to accept suicide bombing in the defense of Islam than are their older counterparts. Among Muslims younger than 30, for example, 15% say that suicide bombing can often or sometimes be justified (2% often, 13% sometimes), while about two-thirds (69%) say that such tactics are never justified. Among Muslims who are 30 or older, by contrast, just 6% say suicide bombings can be often or sometimes justified, while 82% say such attacks are never warranted.

The higher levels of support for suicide bombing seen among young American Muslims resembles patterns found among Muslims in Europe, where Muslims also constitute a minority population. In Great Britain, France and Germany, Muslims under the age of 30 are consistently the least likely to say that suicide bombing is never justified. In other words, the share who think suicide bombing against civilians can *ever* be justified, even if rarely, is higher among those younger than 30 compared with those who are older. About a quarter (26%) of younger U.S. Muslims say suicide bombing can at least rarely be justified, 17 percentage points higher than the proportion of Muslims ages 30 and older (9%) who share that view. The age gap is about as wide in Great Britain (18 percentage points) but somewhat narrower in Germany (12 points), France (11 points) and Spain (7 points).

Views of al Qaeda

Overall, 68% of Muslim Americans view al Qaeda either very unfavorably (58%) or somewhat unfavorably (10%). Of the rest, a large proportion (27%) declined to express an opinion on the terrorist group, while just 5% of Muslims in the U.S. have a very (1%) or somewhat (4%) favorable view of al Qaeda. While no group of Muslim Americans expresses high levels of support for al Qaeda, there are notable differences in the degree to which certain groups express disapproval of the organization. For instance, fewer than half (36%) of native-born African American Muslims express a *very*unfavorable view of al Qaeda. By contrast, roughly two-thirds of other native-born Muslims (69%), as well as foreign-born Muslims (63%), hold very unfavorable views of al Qaeda.

The Israeli-Palestinian Conflict

Most Muslims in the U.S. express optimism that a balanced solution to the Israeli-Palestinian conflict can be found. Indeed, 61% of Muslim Americans say that "a way can be found for Israel to exist so that the rights and needs of the Palestinian people can be taken care of," compared with 16% who say that the rights and needs of Palestinians cannot be taken care of as long as Israel exists.

In this regard, the opinions of U.S. Muslims closely resemble those expressed by the U.S. public as a whole, and are starkly in contrast to the views of Muslims in other parts of the world. In eight predominantly-Muslim populations surveyed by Pew in 2003, roughly half or more of the Muslims interviewed said that: "The rights and needs of the Palestinian people cannot be taken care of as long as the state of Israel exists." This view was particularly strong in Morocco (90%), as well as among Muslims in Jordan (85%), the Palestinian Authority (80%), Lebanon (75%) and Kuwait (73%).

Can a Way be Found for Israel and Palestinian Rights to Coexist?

	Yes	No	DK/Ref
	%	%	%
All U.S. Muslims	61	16	23=100
College grad	74	10	16=100
Some college	74	12	14=100
HS or less	51	22	27=100
Native-born	64	18	18=100
Foreign-born	61	17	22=100
Arrived pre-1990	71	13	16=100
1990 or later	57	20	23=100
Self/Parents from...			
Arab region	49	32	19=100
Pakistan	67	6	27=100
Other South Asia	59	11	30=100
*General public in...**			
United States	67	15	18=100
Israel	67	29	5=101
*Muslims in...**			
Morocco	5	90	5=100
Jordan	14	85	1=100
Palestinian Auth.	17	80	3=100
Lebanon	17	75	8=100
Kuwait	22	73	5=100
Pakistan	23	58	19=100
Indonesia	26	60	14=100
Turkey	33	49	18=100

See topline Q.H4 for question wording.
* Pew Global Attitudes Project, May 2003.

By contrast, the 2003 study found two-thirds (67%) of Americans and an equal proportion of Israelis expressing confidence that a way can be found for the needs of both Israel and the Palestinian people to be met.

The view that Israel can exist in a way that addresses Palestinians' rights is more common among well-educated Muslims in the United States: Nearly three-in-four college graduates express this view, compared with 51% of those with only a high school education or less.

Native-born and foreign-born Muslims hold similar opinions on this issue, but recently arrived Muslim immigrants are somewhat less optimistic about finding a way for Palestine and Israel to coexist peacefully than are immigrants who have been in the U.S. for a longer period of time (57% vs. 71%). Muslims who came from Arab countries are significantly more skeptical about the Israel/Palestinian situation than are immigrants from elsewhere: Nearly a third (32%) of Muslim Americans who are first- or second-generation immigrants from the Arab region say that the rights of Palestinians cannot be taken care of as long as Israel exists.

PART III

CHALLENGES OF CITIZENSHIP

This section highlights how American Muslims are conciliating their Islamic affiliation with the American political context. The majority insist on the compatibility between Islam and American citizenship as well as the special responsibility of American Muslims to defend fundamental rights after September 11, 2001 in both the United States and the Muslim world. Certain polls from 2001 and 2004, as well as the data from a study released by the Pew Research Center in 2007 (Pew Research Center: *Muslim Americans: Middle Class and Mostly Mainstream.* May 22, 2007. http://pewresearch.org/pubs/483/ muslim-americans), show the interest Muslims take in mainstream American politics. More work needs to be done on the impact of Setpember 11th on this political mobilization of American Muslims.

59. Ingrid Mattson, "American Muslims' 'Special Obligation'" from *Taking Back Islam: American Muslims Reclaim Their Faith*

An excerpt from Taking Back Islam: American Muslims Reclaim Their Faith, copyright Rodale Inc., Beliefnet, Inc., 2002. Reprinted with permission of Ingrid Mattson.

In this article, Mattson (for a biography see the "Mattson, Ingrid" entry in Volume 1) argues that due to their location and context American Muslims have a "special obligation" to work against injustice. This article was first written in September 2001. For a description of Taking Back Islam: American Muslims Reclaim Their Faith see the preface to Primary document 32.

The terrorist attack on Sept. 11th exacerbated a double-bind American Muslims have been feeling for some time. So often, it seems, we have to apologize for reprehensible actions committed by Muslims in the name of Islam. We tell other Americans, "People who do these things (oppression of women, persecution of religious minorities, terrorism) have distorted the 'true' Islam."

And so often we have to tell other Muslims throughout the world that America is not as bad as it appears. We say, "These policies (support for oppressive governments, enforcement of sanctions responsible for the deaths almost 1 million Iraqi children, vetoing any criticism of Israel at the United Nations) contradict the 'true' values of America."

But frankly, American Muslims have generally been more critical of injustices committed by the American government than of injustices committed by Muslims. This has to change.

For the last few years, I have been speaking publicly in Muslim forums against the injustice of the Taliban. This criticism of a self-styled Muslim regime has not always been well-received. Some Muslims have felt that public criticism of the Taliban harms Muslim solidarity. Others have questioned my motives, suggesting that I am more interested in serving a feminist agenda than an Islamic one. My answer to the apologists has always been—who has the greatest duty to stop the oppression of Muslims committed by other Muslims in the name of Islam? The answer, obviously, is Muslims.

I have not previously spoken about suicide attacks committed by Muslims in the name of Islam. I did not avoid the subject—it simply did not cross my mind as a priority among the many issues I felt needed to be addressed. This was a gross oversight. I should have asked myself, Who has the greatest duty to stop violence committed by Muslims against innocent non-Muslims in the name of Islam? The answer, obviously, is Muslims.

American Muslims, in particular, have a great responsibility to speak out. The freedom, stability, and strong moral foundation of the United States are great blessings for all Americans, particularly for Muslims.

Moreover, we do not have cultural restrictions that Muslims in some other countries have. In America, Muslim women have found the support and freedom to reclaim their proper place in the life of their religious community. And Muslims have pushed and been allowed to democratize their governing bodies. Important decisions, even relating to theological and legal matters, are increasingly made in mosques and Islamic organizations by elected boards or the collective membership.

But God has not blessed us with these things because we are better than the billions of humans who do not live in America. We do not deserve good health, stable families, safety and freedom more than the millions of Muslims and non-Muslims throughout the world who are suffering from disease, poverty, and oppression.

MAKING SENSE OF THE CRISIS

Muslims who live in America are being tested by God to see if we will be satisfied with a self-contained, self-serving Muslim community that resembles an Islamic town in the Epcot global village, or if we will use the many opportunities available to us to change the world for the better—beginning with an honest critical evaluation of our own flaws.

Because we have freedom and wealth, we have a special obligation to help those Muslims who do not—by speaking out against the abuses of Muslim "leaders" in other countries.

In his speech to the nation, President Bush argued that American Muslim leaders and other moderates represent the true voice of Islam. This is true, and we therefore need to raise our voices louder.

So let me state it clearly: I, as an American Muslim leader, denounce not only suicide bombers and the Taliban, but those leaders of other Muslim states who thwart democracy, repress women, use the Qur'an to justify un-Islamic behavior and encourage violence. Alas, these views are not only the province of a small group of terrorists or dictators. Too many rank-and-file Muslims, in their isolation and pessimism, have come to hold these self-destructive views as well.

The problem is that other Muslims may not listen to us, no matter how loud our voices. Surely President Bush wants the moderate voices not only to be raised, but to be heard. American Muslim leaders will be heard only if they are recognized as authentic interpreters of Islam among the global community. This will be very difficult to achieve, because our legitimacy in the Muslim world is intimately linked with American foreign policy. An understanding of some important developments in Islamic history and theology will clarify this apparently odd dependence.

According to Islamic doctrine, after the death of the Prophet Muhammad, no Muslim has the right to claim infallibility in interpreting the faith. There is no ordination, no clergy, no unquestioned authority. This does not mean that all opinions are equal, nor that everyone has the ability to interpret religious and legal doctrine. Solid scholarship and a deep understanding of the tradition are essential. But not all scholars are considered authoritative. Most Muslims will accept the opinions only of scholars who demonstrate that they are truly concerned about the welfare of ordinary people. People simply will not listen to scholars who seem to be mostly interested in serving the interests of the government.

Throughout Muslim history, religious leaders who advocated aggression against the state were usually marginalized. After all, most Muslims did not want to be led into revolution—they simply wanted their lives to be better. The most successful religious leaders were those who, in addition to serving the spiritual needs of the community, acted as intermediaries between the people and state. There have been times, however, when hostile forces attacked or occupied Muslim lands—for example, the Mongol invasions, (Christian) Crusades, European colonialism, and the Soviet invasion of Afghanistan. At those times, people needed revolutionary leaders; those who were unable to unite the people against aggression were irrelevant.

The question we need to ask is, at this point in history, what do Muslims need to hear from their leaders? What voices will they listen to?

In the midst of a global crisis, it seems that American Muslims are being asked to choose between uncritical support for rebels acting in the name of Islam, and uncritical support for any actions taken by the American government. Osama bin Laden has divided the world into two camps: those who oppose the oppression of the Muslim people, and those who aid in that oppression. President Bush has divided the world into two camps: those who support terrorism, and those who fight terrorism.

Where does this leave American Muslim leaders who oppose the oppression of the Muslim people and who want to fight terrorism? In the increasingly strident rhetoric of this war, we may be considered traitors by both sides.

Nevertheless, we must continue to speak. We have to speak against oppressive interpretations of Islam and against emotional, superficial, and violent apocalyptic depictions of a world divided. And in our desire to show ourselves to be patriotic Americans, we cannot suppress our criticisms of the United States when we have them.

We have to do this, not only because it is the right thing to do, but also because if we do not, the Muslim world will remain deaf to our arguments that peaceful change is possible, and that revolt and ensuing lawlessness almost always cause the greatest harm to the people.

It is in the best interest of the United States that we be permitted to continue to speak. In many parts of the world, those who speak out against corruption and unfair government policies are jailed, tortured, and killed. In such circumstances, very few people—only those who are willing to risk losing their property, their families, their security, and their lives—will continue to speak out. Only the radicals will remain.

60. Muqtedar Khan, "A Memo to American Muslims" from *Ijtihad.org*

October 5, 2001. Available online: //www.ijtihad.org/memo.htm. Reprinted with permission of Muqtedar Khan.

In the following article, Muqtedar Khan (for a biography, see the preface to Primary document 50) condemns those responsible for the terrorist attacks of September 11, 2001, as well as Muslims who have not publicly condemned the attacks themselves. Khan accuses Muslims of hypocrisy in not condemning abuses committed by Muslim states. He also urges American Muslims to speak publicly "to ensure that Islam is not misrepresented."

In the name of Allah, the most Benevolent and the Most Merciful. May this memo find you in the shade of Islam enjoying the mercy, the protection and the grace of Allah

I am writing this memo to you all with the explicit purpose of inviting you to lead the American Muslim community in soul searching, reflection and reassessment.

What happened on September 11th in New York and Washington DC will forever remain a horrible scar on the history of Islam and humanity. No matter how much we condemn it, and point to the Quran and the Sunnah to argue that Islam forbids the killing of innocent people, the fact remains that the perpetrators of this crime against humanity have indicated that their actions are sanctioned by Islamic values.

The fact that even now several Muslim scholars and thousands of Muslims defend the accused is indicative that not all Muslims believe that the attacks are unIslamic. This is truly sad.

Even if it were true that Israel and the US are enemies of the Muslim World, wonder what is preventing them from unleashing their nuclear arsenal against Muslims, a response that mercilessly murders thousands of innocent people, including hundreds of Muslims is absolutely indefensible. If anywhere in your hearts there is any sympathy or understanding with those who committed this act, I invite you to ask yourself this question, would Muhammad (pbuh) sanction such an act?

While encouraging Muslims to struggle against injustice (Al Quran 4:135), Allah also imposes strict rules of engagement. He says in unequivocal terms that to kill an innocent being is like killing entire humanity (Al Quran 5:32). He also encourages Muslims to forgive Jews and Christians if they have committed injustices against us (Al Quran 2:109, 3:159, 5:85).

Muslims, including American Muslims have been practicing hypocrisy on a grand scale. They protest against the discriminatory practices of Israel but are silent against the discriminatory practices in Muslim states. In the Gulf one can see how laws and even salaries are based on ethnic origin. This is racism, but we never hear of Muslims protesting against them at International fora.

The Israeli occupation of Palestine is perhaps central to Muslim grievance against the West. While acknowledging that, I must remind you that Israel treats its one million Arab citizens with greater respect and dignity than most Arab nations treat their citizens. Today Palestinian refugees can settle and become citizens of the United States but in spite of all the tall rhetoric of the Arab world and Quranic injunctions (24:22) no Muslim country except Jordan extends this support to them.

While we loudly and consistently condemn Israel for its ill treatment of Palestinians we are silent when Muslim regimes abuse the rights of Muslims and slaughter thousands of them. Remember Saddam and his use of chemical weapons against Muslims (Kurds)? Remember Pakistani army's excesses against Muslims (Bengalis)? Remember the Mujahideen of Afghanistan and their mutual slaughter? Have we ever condemned them for their excesses? Have we demanded international intervention or retribution against them? Do you know how the Saudis treat their minority Shiis? Have we protested the violation of their rights? But we all are eager to condemn Israel; not because we care for rights and lives of the Palestinians, we don't. We condemn Israel because we hate "them".

Muslims love to live in the US but also love to hate it. Many openly claim that the US is a terrorist state but they continue to live in it. Their decision to live here is testimony that they would rather live here than anywhere else. As an Indian Muslim, I know for sure that nowhere on earth, including India, will I get the same sense of dignity and respect that I have received in the US. No Muslim country will treat me as well as the US has. If what happened on September 11th had happened in India, the biggest democracy, thousands of Muslims would have been slaughtered in riots on mere suspicion and there would be another slaughter after confirmation. But in the US, bigotry and xenophobia has been kept in check by media and leaders. In many places hundreds of Americans have gathered around Islamic centers in symbolic gestures of protection and embrace of American Muslims. In many cities Christian congregations have started wearing *hijab* to identify with fellow Muslim women. In patience and in tolerance ordinary Americans have demonstrated their extraordinary virtues.

It is time that we acknowledge that the freedoms we enjoy in the US are more desirable to us than superficial solidarity with the Muslim World. If you disagree than prove it by packing your bags and going to whichever Muslim country you identify with. If you do not leave and do not acknowledge that you would rather live here than anywhere else, know that you are being hypocritical.

It is time that we faced these hypocritical practices and struggled to transcend them. It is time that American Muslim leaders fought to purify their own lot.

For over a decade we have watched as Muslims in the name of Islam have committed violence against other Muslims and other peoples. We have always found a way to reconcile the vast distance between Islamic values and Muslim practices by pointing out to the injustices committed upon Muslims by others. The point however is this—our belief in Islam and commitment to Islamic values is not contingent on the moral conduct of the US or Israel. And as Muslims can we condone such inhuman and senseless waste of life in the name of Islam?

The biggest victims of hate filled politics as embodied in the actions of several Muslim militias all over the world are Muslims themselves. Hate is the extreme form of intolerance and when individuals and groups succumb to it they can do nothing constructive. Militias like the Taliban have allowed their hate for the West to override their obligation to pursue the welfare of their people and as a result of their actions not only have thousands of innocent people died in America, but thousands of people will die in the Muslim World.

Already, half a million Afghans have had to leave their homes and their country. The war has not yet begun. It will only get worst. Hamas and Islamic Jihad may kill a few Jews, women and children included, with their suicide bombs and temporarily satisfy their lust for Jewish blood, but thousands of Palestinians then pay the price for their actions.

The culture of hate and killing is tearing away at the moral fabric of the Muslim society. We are more focused on "the other" and have completely forgotten our duty to Allah. In pursuit of the inferior jihad we have sacrificed the superior jihad.

Islamic resurgence, the cherished ideals of which pursued the ultimate goal of a universally just and moral society has been hijacked by hate and call for murder and mayhem. If Binladen were an individual then we would have no problem. But unfortunately Binladen has become a phenomenon—a cancer eating away at the morality of our youth, and undermining the spiritual health of our future.

Today the century old Islamic revival is in jeopardy because we have allowed insanity to prevail over our better judgment. Yes, the US has played a hand in the creation of Binladen and the Taliban, but it is we who have allowed them to grow and gain such a foothold. It is our duty to police our world. It is our responsibility to prevent people from abusing Islam. It is our job to ensure that Islam is not misrepresented. We should have made sure that what happened on Sept. 11th should never have happened.

It is time the leaders of the American Muslim community woke up and realized that there is more to life than competing with the American Jewish lobby for power over US foreign policy. Islam is not about defeating Jews or conquering Jerusalem. It is about mercy, about virtue, about sacrifice and about duty. Above all it is the pursuit of moral perfection. Nothing can be further away from moral perfection than the wanton slaughter of thousands of unsuspecting innocent people.

I hope that we will now rededicate our lives and our institutions to the search for harmony, peace and tolerance. Let us be prepared to suffer injustice rather than commit injustices. After all it is we who carry the divine burden of Islam and not others. We have to be morally better, more forgiving, more sacrificing than others, if we wish to convince the world about the truth of our message. We cannot even be equal to others in virtue, we must excel.

It is time for soul searching. How can the message of Muhammad (pbuh) who was sent as mercy to mankind become a source of horror and fear? How can Islam inspire thousands of youth to dedicate their lives to killing others? We are supposed to invite people to Islam not murder them.

The worst exhibition of Islam happened on our turf. We must take first responsibility to undo the evil it has manifest. This is our mandate, our burden and also our opportunity.

61.   Imam Zaid Shakir, "American Muslims, Human Rights, and the Challenge of September 11, 2001" from *The Zaytuna Institute*

Accessed May 9, 2006. Available online: http://www.zaytuna.org/articleDetails.asp? articleID=23. Reprinted with permission of the Zaytuna Institute.

In the following article, Imam Zaid Shakir (for a biography see the "Shakir, Zaid" entry in Volume 1) argues that the growth of Islam in the United States has provided conditions for "an understanding of Islam which creates a strong human rights imperative."

Human rights regimes constitute one of the critical aspects of modern international political life. Like many other contemporary political phenomena, the idea of human rights originated in the secular political milieu of the modern West. Although Islam has historically been characterized by viable teachings, which have helped to insure the protection of basic human rights, it has yet to produce a human rights regime, which mirrors that of the modern West.

With the growth of Islam in America, certain conditions have combined to produce an understanding of Islam which creates a strong human rights imperative. Foremost amongst these conditions is the minority composition of the Muslim community. Traditional concerns of ethnic and religious minorities, especially strong among African American Muslims, lead to many Muslims viewing Islam as a system that will provide relief from the harsh realities of political under-representation, discrimination, race-based prejudice, economic stagnation, and other real or perceived maladies.

These concerns, combined with the strong human rights imperative of Islamic movements based in the Muslim world, movements which are combating in many instances brutally repressive states, create a very strong human rights discourse among those advancing the Islamic call in America. That call, beginning in earnest with the missionaries of the Ahmadiyya movement in the 1920s, focused on contrasting the worst failings of American societies, such as racism and racial discrimination, with an idealized and simplistic view of the Islamic Shari'ah. Malcolm X was able to synthesize the many currents informing that discourse into a fully developed human rights agenda.

With the tragic events of September 11, 2001, the prevailing Muslim human rights discourse has been called into question, as the idealized view of Islam has been undermined by acts of wanton, inhumane violence, allegedly committed in its name. Critics point to those tragic events and similar acts as indicators of Islam's inability to accommodate a system of modern human rights. To effectively respond to the challenges presented by these allegations, Muslims will have to radically reform the way that we understand and conceptualize human rights.

The philosophical basis on which we build any proposed human rights regime will have to be clearly and rigorously articulated. Vague, ambiguous, or meaningless generalities will have to be clarified by appropriate legal and technical language. We will have to cease avoiding the discussion of critical issues by hiding behind our cultural and religious uniqueness. Existing declarations will have to be accompanied by firm, well-defined legal and constitutional guarantees which allow us to extend, in meaningful ways, existing theoretical guarantees to those groups which most frequently experience human rights abuses in our lands, specifically: women, and ethnic, racial, as well as religious minorities.

While acknowledging the shortcomings in contemporary Islamic human rights schemes, we must also recognize that Islam contains the necessary foundation for the construction of a viable, modern system of human rights. If we are able to discover and build on that foundation, we will be able to meaningfully discuss human rights, even in the changed post September 11, 2001 political climate.

INTRODUCTION

The tragic events of September 11, 2001, have called into question many fundamental Islamic principles, values, and beliefs. The ensuing discourse in many critical areas reveals the weakness of Muslims in making meaningful and substantive contributions towards a clear understanding of the Islamic position on a number of critical issues. The purpose of this paper is to examine one of those issues, human rights, in an effort to identify:

1. How human rights are defined in the Western and Islamic intellectual traditions;

2. Why human rights issues are of central importance to Islamic propagation efforts in North America;

3. What are the implications of the tragic events of September 11, 2001 for prevailing Muslim views of human rights.

This paper is not designed to respond to the attacks of those authors who assail the philosophy, conceptualization, formulation, and application of human rights policy among Muslims. Such a response would be quite lengthy, and owing to the complexity of the project, would probably raise as many questions as it resolved. Nor is it an attempt to call attention to the increasingly problematic indifference of the United States government towards respecting the civil liberties and other basic rights of its Muslim and Arab citizens. We do hope that this paper will help American Muslims identify and better understand some of the relevant issues shaping our thought and action in the critical area of human rights. Hopefully, that enhanced understanding will help lead to the creation of a vibrant, sober, relevant Islamic call in this country.

PART ONE: DEFINING HUMAN RIGHTS

A review of the relevant literature reveals a wealth of definitions for human rights. Some of these definitions are quite brief, others quite elaborate. [1] However, few of these definitions deviate far from the principles delineated by the Universal Declaration of Human Rights (UDHR), issued by the UN General Assembly in 1948. That landmark document emphasizes, among other things:

The right to life, liberty, and security of person; the right to freedom of thought, speech, and communication of information and ideas; freedom of assembly and religion; the right to government through free elections; the right to free movement within the state and free exit from it; the right to asylum in another state; the right to nationality; freedom from arbitrary arrest and interference with the privacy of home and family; and the prohibition of slavery and torture.

This declaration was followed by the International Covenant on Economic, Social, and Cultural Rights (ICESCR), in 1966. In the same year, the International Covenant of Civil and Political Rights (ICCPR), was also drafted. These arrangements, collectively known as the International Bill of Human Rights, were reaffirmed in the Helsinki Accords of 1975, and buttressed by the threat of international sanctions against offending nations. When we examine these and other international agreements governing human rights, we find a closely related set of ideas, which collectively delineate a system of fundamental or inalienable, universally accepted rights.

These rights are not strictly political, as the UDHR mentions:

The right to work, to protection against unemployment, and to join trade unions; the right to a standard of living adequate for health and well-being; the right to education; and the right to rest and leisure

In summary, we can say that human rights are the inalienable social, economic and political rights, which accrue to human beings by virtue of their belonging to the human family.

Defining human rights from an Islamic perspective is a bit more problematic. The reason for this is that there is no exact equivalent for the English term, human rights, in the traditional Islamic lexicon. The frequently used Arabic term, *al-Huquq al-Insaniyya,* is simply a literal Arabic translation for the modern term. However, our understanding of the modern term, when looked at from the abstract particulars which comprise its definition, gives us insight into what Islam says in this critical area. For example, if we consider the word right (*Haqq*), we find an array of concepts in Islam, which cover the range of rights mentioned in the UDHR.

If we begin with the right to life, Islam clearly and unequivocally guarantees that right. The Qur'an states, *Do not unjustly take the life which Allah has sanctified.* [Qur'an 6:151] Similarly, in the context of discussing the consequences of the first murder in human history, *For that reason [Cain murdering Abel], we ordained for the Children of Israel that whoever kills a human being for other than murder, or spreading corruption on Earth, it is as if he has killed all of humanity. And whoever saves a life, it is as if he has saved all of humanity.* [Qur'an 5:32]

It should be noted in this regard, as the first verse points out, Islam doesn't view humanity as a mere biological advancement of lower life forms. Were this the case, there would be little fundamental distinction between human and animal rights, other than those arising from the advancement and complexity of the human mind. However, Islam views human life as a biological reality, which has been sanctified by a special quality that has been instilled into the human being the spirit (Ruh). [2] The Qur'an relates, *then He fashioned him [the human being] and breathed into him of His spirit.* [Qur'an 32:9]

It is interesting to note that this spiritual quality is shared by all human beings, and precedes our division into nations, tribes, and religious collectivities. An illustration of this unifying spiritual bond can be gained from considering a brief exchange, which occurred between the Prophet Muhammad (Peace and Blessings of Allah be upon him), and a group of his companions (May Allah be pleased with them). Once a funeral procession passed in front of the Prophet (Peace and Blessings of Allah be upon him) and a group of his companions. The Prophet (Peace and Blessings of Allah be upon him) reverently stood up. One of his companions mentioned that the deceased was a Jew, to which the Prophet (Peace and Blessings of Allah be upon him) responded, "Is he not a human soul?" [3]

Possession of this shared spiritual quality is one of the ways our Creator has ennobled the human being. Allah says in this regard, *We have truly ennobled the human being?* [Qur'an 17:70] This ennoblement articulates itself in many different ways, all of which serve to highlight the ascendancy of the spiritual and intellectual faculties in man. It provides one of the basis for forbidding anything, which would belittle, debase, or demean the human being, and its implications extend far beyond the mere preservation of his life. [4] It guarantees his rights before birth, by forbidding abortion, except in certain well-defined instances; and after death, it guarantees the right of the body to be properly washed, shrouded, and buried. It also forbids the intentional mutilation of a cadaver, [5] even in times of war, and forbids insulting or verbally abusing the dead, even deceased non-Muslims. While these latter points may be deemed trivial to some, they help create a healthy attitude towards humanity, an attitude that must be present if acknowledged rights are to be actually extended to their possessors.

If we examine other critical areas identified by the UDHR for protection as inalienable rights, we can see that Islam presents a very positive framework for the safeguarding of those rights. In the controversial area of religious freedom, where Islam is identified by many in the West as a religion which was spread by forced conversion, we find that Islam has never advocated the forced acceptance of its creed, in fact, the Qur'an unequivocally rejects this idea, *Let there be no compulsion in [accepting] Religion, truth clearly distinguishes itself from error.* [Qur'an 2:256] Allah further warns His Prophet (Peace and Blessings of Allah be upon Him) against forced conversions, *If your Lord had willed, everyone on Earth would have believed [in this message]; will you then compel people to believe?* [Qur'an 10:99]

In this context, every human being is free to participate in the unrestricted worship of his Lord. As for those who refuse to do so according to the standards established by Islam, they are free to worship as they please. During the Ottoman epoch, this freedom evolved into sophisticated system of minority rights known as the Millet System. Bernard Lewis comments on that system:

Surely, the Ottomans did not offer equal rights to their subjects, a meaningless anachronism in the context of that time and place. They did however offer a degree of tolerance without precedence or parallel in Christian Europe. Each community—the Ottoman term was Millet—was allowed the free practice of its religion. More remarkably, they had their own communal organizations, subject to the authority of their own religious chiefs, controlling their own education and social life, and enforcing their own laws, to the extent that they did not conflict with the basic laws of the Empire. [6]

Similarly positive Islamic positions can be found in the areas of personal liberties, within the parameters provided by the Islamic legal code. We will return to a brief discussion of those parameters, and their implications for an Islamic human rights regime. However, it isn't the purpose of this paper to engage in an exhaustive treatment of this particular subject.

Stating that, we don't propose that Islamic formulations in this regard are an exact replica of contemporary Western constitutional guarantees governing human rights policy. Muslims and non-Muslims alike, when examining the issue of human rights within an Islamic legal or philosophical framework, should realize that human rights regimes, as we know them, are a contemporary political phenomenon, which have no ancient parallel. However, we are prepared to defend the thesis that Islam has historically presented a framework for protecting basic human rights, and that it presents a system of jurisprudential principles that allow for the creation of a viable modern human rights regime, totally consistent with the letter and spirit of Islam.

PART TWO: THE RELEVANCE OF HUMAN RIGHTS FOR ISLAM IN AMERICA

Islam in America has historically been characterized by a strong advocacy of human rights and social justice issues. This is so because it has been associated with people who would be identified as ethnic minorities. The first significant Muslim population in this country, the enslaved believers of African origin, would certainly fit that description. [7] The various Islamic movements, which arose amongst their descendents, appeared in a social and political context characterized by severe oppression. That socio-political context shaped the way Islam was understood by the people embracing it. It was a religion, in of all its variant understandings, which was seen as a source of liberation, justice, and redemption. [8]

When the ethnic composition of the Muslim community began to change due to immigration in the 1970s, 1980s, and into the 1990s, the minority composition of the Muslim community remained. These newly arriving non-European immigrant Muslims were generally upwardly mobile, however, their brown and olive complexions, along with their accents, and the vestiges of their original cultures, served to reinforce the reality of their minority status. This fact, combined with the fact that the most religiously active among them were affiliated with Islamic movements in the Muslim World, movements whose agenda were dominated by strong human rights and social justice concerns, affected the nature of the Islamic call in this country, keeping human rights concerns to the fore.

Illustrative of this human rights imperative is the stated mission of the Ahmadiyya Movement when it began active propagation in America. Mufti Muhammad Sadiq, the first significant Ahmadi missionary to America, consciously called to a multicultural view of Islam, which challenged the entrenched racism prevalent in early 20th Century American society. [9] This message presented Islam as a just social force, capable of extending to the racial minorities of this country their full human rights. However, there were strong anti-white overtones of the Ahmadi message, shaped by Mufti Muhammad Sadiq's personal experience, and the widespread persecution of people of Indian descent (so-called Hindoos) in America, which dampened the broader appeal of the Ahmadi message. Those overtones were subsequently replaced by the overtly racist proclamations of the Nation of Islam, which declared whites to be devils. In the formulation of the Nation of Islam, Islam came to be viewed as a means for the restoration of the lost preeminence of the "Asiatic" Blackman. This restoration would be effected by a just religion, Islam, which addressed the social, economic and psychological vestiges of American race-based slavery. In other words, Islam was the agent that would grant the Muslims their usurped human rights. [10]

The pivotal figure who was able to synthesize these various formulations into a tangible, well-defined human rights agenda was Malcolm X. [11] By continuing to emphasize the failure of American society to effectively work to eliminate the vestiges of slavery, he was an implicit advocate of the justice-driven agenda of the Nation of Islam, even after departing from that movement. His brutal criticism of the racist nature of American society, which he often contrasted with the perceived racial harmony of Islam, highlighted by his famous letter from Mecca [12] in which he envisioned Islam as a possible cure for this country's inherent racism, was the continuation of the original multi-cultural message of the Ahmadiyya Movement. Finally, his evolving thinking on the true nature of the struggle of the African American people, and his situating that struggle in the context of the Third World human rights struggle, reflected the human rights imperative which figured so prominently in the call of Middle Eastern groups such as Egypt's Muslim Brotherhood, and the Indian Subcontinent's Jamaati Islami, groups which had a strong influence on the founders of this country's Muslim Students Association (MSA) in 1963. [13]

These various groupings, along with the Dar al-Islam Movement, the Islamic Party of North America, and Sheikh Tawfiq's Mosque of Islamic Brotherhood, [14] which would develop in many urban centers during the 1960s and 1970s as the purveyors of an emerging African American "Sunni" tradition, a tradition consolidated by the conversion of Malcolm X to the orthodox faith, represented in their various agendas, the crystallization of the sort of human rights agenda which Malcolm was hammering out during the last phase of his life. These groups all saw Islam as the key to liberation from the stultifying weight of racial, social, and economic inequality in America.

The Iranian Revolution of 1979 further strengthened this human rights imperative. The revolution was presented by its advocates in America, who were quite influential at the time, as an uprising of the oppressed Muslim masses, the "*Mustadafin*," to secure their usurped rights from the Shah, an oppressive "*Taghut*." This message, conveyed strongly and forcefully through the call of the Muslim Students Association: Persian Speaking Group (MSA-PSG), was extremely influential in shaping the human rights imperative in American Islam, not only because of its direct influence, but also because of the vernacular of struggle it introduced into the conceptual universe of many America Muslims, and the way it shaped the message of contending "Sunni" groups. The combined influence of these forces worked to insure that human rights issues were prominent in the call of Islamic organizations and individuals prior to the tragic events of September 11, 2001.

PART THREE: THE CHALLENGE OF SEPTEMBER 11, 2001

The tragic events of September 11, 2001 present a clear challenge to the human rights/ social justice imperative of Muslims in North America. The reasons for this are many and complex. The apocalyptic nature of the attacks of September 11, 2001, particularly the assault on, and subsequent collapse of the World Trade Center towers, led many observers to question the humaneness of a religion which could encourage such senseless, barbaric slaughter. Islam, the religion identified as providing the motivation for those horrific attacks, was brought into the public spotlight as being, in the view of many of its harshest critics, an anti-intellectual, nihilistic, violent, chauvinistic atavism. [15]

The atavistic nature of Islam, in their view, leads to its inability to realistically accommodate the basic elements of modern human rights philosophy. [16] This inability was highlighted by the September 11, 2001 attacks in a number of ways. First of all, the massive and indiscriminant slaughter of civilians belied, in the view of many critics, any claims that Islam respects the right to life. If so, how could so many innocent, unsuspecting souls be so wantonly sacrificed? Secondly, "Islam's" refusal to allow for the peaceful existence of even remote populations of "infidels," the faceless dehumanized "other," calls into question its respect for the rights of non-Muslims within its socio-political framework. It also highlights its inability to define that "other" in human terms.

As a link between the accused perpetrators of the attacks, Usama bin Laden, and the Taliban rulers of Afghanistan was developed by both the United States government and news media, the human rights position of Islam was called into further question. The Taliban, by any standards of assessment, presided over a regime that showed little consideration for the norms governing international human rights. Much evidence exists which implicates the Taliban in violating the basic rights of women, ethnic minorities (non-Pashtun), the Shi'ite religious minority, detainees, artists, and others, using in some instances, extremely draconian measures. Many of these violations occurred under the rubric of applying what the regime identified as Islamic law. The news of Taliban excesses, coupled with the shock of the events of September 11, 2001, combined to create tremendous apprehension towards the ability and willingness of Islam to accommodate a meaningful human rights regime. [17]

The political climate existing in America in the aftermath of September 11, 2001 has been exploited by certain elements in American society to call into question any humanitarian tendencies being associated with Islam. For example, in the aftermath of the brutal murder of Daniel Pearle, an act whose implications are as chilling as the attacks of September 11, 2001, Mr. Pearle's bosses at the Wall Street Journal, Peter Kann and Paul Steiger remarked, "His murder is an act of barbarism that makes a mockery of everything that Danny's kidnappers claimed to believe in." Responding to those comments, Leon Wieseltier, of the New Republic, stated, "The murder of Daniel Pearle did not make a mockery of what his slaughterers believe. It was the perfect expression, the inevitable consequence, of what his slaughterers believe" [18] This, and similar indictments of Islam, challenge the ability of American Muslims to effectively speak on human rights issues in obvious ways.

If we examine the actual nature American Muslim human rights discourse prior to September 11, 2001, we find that it was based in large part on Muslims contrasting the generalities of the Shari'ah, with the specific shortcomings American society and history in relevant areas of domestic and international policy and practice. [19] This discourse ignored the positive human rights strictures contained in sections of the American constitution, the Bill of Rights, and the UDHR, to which the United States is a signatory.

As in other areas, this inadequate approach produced a false sense of moral superiority among Muslims in America. This sense was shattered by the attacks of September 11, 2001, in that many Americans were suddenly pointing to what they viewed as the inadequacy of Islamic human rights regimes, their inadequate philosophical basis, and their failure to guarantee basic human rights protection, especially for women, religious, racial, and ethnic minorities living in Muslim lands.

Responding adequately to these charges will require a radical restructuring of current Islamic human rights discourse, and the regimes that discourse informs. The generalities, which formerly sufficed in that discourse will have to be replaced by concrete, developed policy prescriptions, which stipulate in well-defined, legal terms, how viable human rights protections will be extended to groups identified as systematically suffering from human rights abuses in Muslim realms.

An example of the dangerous and inadequate generalities alluded to above, can be glimpsed from a brief examination of the Cairo Declaration on Human Rights in Islam (CDHRI). Article 24 of that document states, "All the rights and freedoms stipulated in this Declaration are subject to the Islamic Shari'ah." [20] Such a statement is meaningless, considering the vast corpus of subjectively understood literature that could be identified as comprising the Shari'ah, unless the relevant rulings and principles of the Shari'ah are spelled out in exacting detail.

While this paper has consciously avoided mention of those features of Islam which would be antithetical to the Western concept of personal liberty, such as the lack of freedom to choose one's "sexual orientation," there are major civil liberties issue which must be addressed, in clear and unequivocal terms, if Islam's human rights discourse is to have any credence. Hiding behind Islam's cultural, or religious specificity to avoid providing answers to difficult questions will not advance a deeper understanding of our faith amongst enlightened circles in the West. Islam indeed has much to say in the area of human rights. However, much foundational work has to be done before we can speak clearly and authoritatively, especially in the changed post September 11, 2001 political climate.

In *Islam and Human Rights,* Ann Elizabeth Mayer, whose work has been previously cited, [21] acknowledges,

the Islamic heritage comprises rationalist and humanistic currents and that it is replete with values that complement modern human rights such as concern for human welfare, justice, tolerance, and equalitarianism. These could provide the basis for constructing a viable synthesis of Islamic principles and international human right [22]

Perhaps the greatest challenge before us in this regard is successfully identifying those rationalist and humanitarian "currents" and riding them to a new, more enlightened shore. Doing this will require, among other things, a bold, but mature assessment of the proper relationship between creed and action in the social and political realms. A serious attempt to engage in a rational application of legal principles to contemporary social and political problems in no way implies adopting the methodology of the *Mu'tazila*, medieval Muslim legal and theological rationalists. Using rationalization as the standard to assess the veracity of revelation, and using ration as the basis for discovering meaningful Islamic solutions to pressing social or political problems, in areas where revelation provides no articulated guidance, constitute two entirely different projects.

That being said, our attempts at solving novel contemporary socio-political problems must be guided by well-defined methodologies. Applicable methodologies have been expounded on by Muslim scholars of jurisprudential principles, and those who have assessed those methodologies, and the rulings they inform in light of the great overarching objectives of Islamic law. These scholars include the likes of Imam al-Shatibi, author of the groundbreaking work, *al-Muwafaqat,* [23] and Imam 'Izz al-Din bin 'Abd al-Salam, author of *Qawa'id al-Ahkam,* [24] and many others. These writings are part of a rich heritage of scholarship and thought, which allowed Muslims to adequately respond to a succession of civilizational challenges throughout our long and illustrious past. If we are able to master that rich heritage, and use the best of it to address the burning issues of our day, we will be able to meaningfully discuss human rights, and the full array of issues that currently vex and perplex us. By so doing, we will be able to step confidently into the future.

NOTES

[1] One such concise definition of human rights is mentioned in Paul E. McGhee, "Human Rights," in *The Social Science Encyclopedia*, ed. Adam and Jessica Kuper (London, New York: Routledge, 1985), p. 369. He states, "Human rights are the rights and freedoms of all human beings." Cyrus Vance presents a much more elaborate definition in which he envisions human rights encompassing the security of the person, meeting his vital needs, civil and political liberties, and freedom from discrimination. Abridged from Cyrus Vance, "The Human Rights Imperative," in *Taking Sides: Clashing Views on Controversial Issues in World Politics*, ed. John T. Rourke (Guilford, CT: The Dushkin Publishing Group, Inc., 1992), pp. 254–255.

[2] Islamic scholars have defined the spirit (*Ruh*) in various ways. Perhaps the best translation would be "life-spirit." Its true nature is unknown to any human being, although there has been much speculation as to what exactly it is. It is created before the creation of the bodies, which will house it. Worldly life begins with its entrance into the body, and ends with its extraction from the body.

[3] This incident is based on a rigorously authenticated tradition, which has been conveyed by Al-Bukhari, no. 1312; Muslim, no. 2222; and al-Nasa'i, no. 1920.

[4] A beautiful discussion of the ways the human being has been ennobled by God can be found in Imam Fakr al-Din al-Razi's commentary of the relevant Qur'anic verse, 17:70. See, Fakhr al-Din al-Razi, *al-Tafsir al-Kabir* (Beirut: Dar Ihya al-Turath al-'Arabi, 1997), vol. 7, pp. 372–374.

[5] This practice is condemned based on a tradition related by Imam Ahmad, Abu Dawud, and Ibn Majah.

[6] Bernard Lewis, *What Went Wrong: Western Impact and Middle Eastern Response* (Oxford, New York: Oxford University Press, 2002), pp. 33–34

[7] For a moving, well-document description of the history, lives, institutions, struggles, and legacy of the Africans enslaved in the America, see, Sylviaane A. Diouf, *Servants of Allah: African Muslims Enslaved in the Americas* (New York, London: SUNY Press, 1998).

[8] See, Robert Dannin, *Black Pilgrimage to Islam* (Oxford, New York: Oxford University Press, 2002). Dannin presents a good summary of the evolution of Islam among African-Americans. His book is especially valuable for its detailed treatment of the evolution of the African-American Sunni Muslim community. See, also Richard Brent Turner, *Islam in the African American Experience* (Bloomington: Indiana University Press, 1997).

[9] Turner, pp. 121–131.

[10] For a detailed introduction to the racist ideology of the Nation of Islam, see, Elijah Muhammad, *Message to the Black Man* (Chicago: Muhammad's Temple No. 2, 1965). Especially insightful in this regard is a chapter entitled, "The Devil," pp. 100–122.

[11] The theme of human rights figured prominently in the political oratory of Malcolm X during the last two years of his life. At the time of his assassination, he was in final stages of a campaign to charge the United States in the United Nations- with violating the human rights of the then 20,000,000 African Americans in this country. Many observers feel that campaign, a source of great embarrassment for the United States, may have resulted in his death. His views on this subject are presented, among other places, in a speech entitled, "The Ballot or the Bullet?" in George Breitman, ed., *By Any Means Necessary* (New York: Pathfinder Press, 1970), pp. 21–22. See, also, "Interview with Harry Ring Over Station WBAI, January 28, 1965," in *Two Speeches by Malcolm X* (New York: Pathfinder Press, 1965), pp. 28–29.

[12] Alex Haley with Malcolm X, *The Autobiography of Malcolm X* (New York: Ballentine Books, 1964) pp. 338–342.

[13] The Muslim Students Association (MSA) was formed in 1963 among immigrant Muslims. It would eventually evolve into the Islamic Society of North America (ISNA). Formed in 1982, ISNA is the largest Islamic organization in North America. See, Dannin, p. 73; and Turner, p. 236.

[14] For a summary of the inter-group dynamics between the Islamic Party of North America, Dar al-Islam, and Sheikh Tawfiq's Muslim Islamic Brotherhood, see Dannin, pp. 65–73.

[15] For example, The New Republic's Jonah Goldberg refers to Islam as, "anti-capitalist, alien, sometimes medieval, and often corrupt theocratic fascism." Jonah Goldberg, "The Goldberg File," *The New Republic*, 1 October 2001.

[16] Perhaps the most thorough assessment of Islam and human rights is Ann Elizabeth Mayer, *Islam and Human Rights: Tradition and Politics* (Boulder: Westview Press, 1999). Although simplistically lauded by many critics of Islam as "an understated and powerful repudiation of the notion of 'Islamic Human Rights,'" Mayer's argument is far more involved. While identifying many of the problems plaguing contemporary Islamic human rights regimes, Mayer sees Islam's rich tradition as being capable of producing an effective, modern human rights movement.

[17] For an indication of the extent of the reported human rights abuses of the Taliban, see Ahmad Rashid, *Taliban* (London, New York: I.B. Tauris Publishers, 2000), chs. 4,5,8. Also, see Michael Griffin, *Reaping the Whirlwinds: The Taliban Movement in Afghanistan* (London: Pluto Press, 2001), ch. 12.

[18] Leon Wiesiltier, "The Murder of Daniel Pearl," *The New Republic*, 25 February 2002

[19] A widely circulated pamphlet, among Muslims, which illustrates this approach is, Mawlana Abu'l 'Ala Mawdudi, *Human Rights in Islam* (Leicester, England: Islamic Foundation, 1980).

[20] This declaration was submitted to the World Conference on Human Rights, Preparatory Committee, Fourth Session. Geneva, April 19, May 7, 1993.

[21] See note 16.

[22] Mayer, p. 192.

[23] Imam Ibrahim bin Musa Abi Ishaq al-Shatibi, *al-Muwafaqat* (Beirut: Dar al-Ma'rifa, 1997).

[24] 'Izz al-Din 'Abd al-'Aziz bin 'Abd al-Salam, *Qawa'id al-Ahkam* (Damascus: Dar al-Tiba'a, 1996).

62.   **Imam Zaid Shakir, "On the Passing of Rosa Parks (1913–2005)" from** *The Zaytuna Institute*

Accessed May 9, 2006. Available online: http://www.zaytuna.org/articleDetails.asp?articleID=84. Reprinted with permission of the Zaytuna Institute.

In the following article, Imam Zaid Shakir (for a biography see the "Shakir, Zaid" entry in Volume 1) relates the Muslim experience in the United States since September 11, 2001 to the African American struggle during the Civil Rights Movement in the 1960s, in particular in the person of Rosa Parks. Such a comparison seeks to Americanize the discourse on Islam, focusing on the domestic experience of American Muslims and thereby countering the dominant narrative of Islam as a foreign policy issue.

As I was leaving my neighborhood en route to *Tarawih* prayers last night, a car ran through a stop sign and nearly crashed into my vehicle. Fortunately, I was able to swerve and avoid any contact. Reverting back to some pre-Islamic ghetto instincts, I immediately reversed, and sped up the street behind the reckless perpetrator. I caught up with the car about half a mile up the road and shouted at the driver, "Why don't you learn how to drive!" The driver, a female, shouted back, "f____ you! Terrorist!" Apparently my Kufi, and my wife's Hijab were sufficient evidence to indicate that we were Muslim. The word "terrorist," dripping with deep contempt and hatred, based on a prejudiced view of two total strangers, sounded eerily like another word that symbolizes the worst sort of prejudicial hatred this country has known, namely, "nigger."

Something foul is happening in this country as we move deeper into this post 9-11 world. The growing racist hatred and denigration currently directed at Muslims is indicative of a deep sickness. The most disturbing aspect of this malady is that it is being deliberately induced. The strategists behind the campaign may be motivated by their selfish service to a foreign power, they may be motivated by an attempt to justify massive security budgets, they may be motivated by a deep hatred of Islam. Whatever their motivation, they know that the climate they are creating is one that is often characterized by pogroms, and sometimes by genocidal slaughter.

This climate is fueled by fictitious e-mails speaking of fictitious diatribes uttered by fictitious Imams urging the Muslim faithful to indiscriminately kill the "infidels." It is fueled by the reckless jingoism of hatemongering radio personalities. It is fueled by government misinformation campaigns that create a public perception of imminent danger to the people of this country from a technologically backwards, politically divided, socially truncated Middle East. It is also fueled by the ill-conceived, strategically counterproductive actions of a handful of misguided Muslims who call themselves *Mujahideen*.

If the current climate deepens and manifests in concerted campaigns of violence against the Muslims of this country it will not be an anomalous situation. The genocide that destroyed the Indian nations that once occupied this land took place in a similar climate. In the 1880s Chinese immigrants were shot in the streets of some western cities and hamlets like stray, rabid dogs. Those pogroms could only take place because a climate of hatred and bigotry had been created. The internment of the Japanese during World War Two took place in a climate of hate that was cultivated throughout the 1930s. Finally, it was in a climate of bigotry and hatred that dehumanizing violence was visited upon successive generations of African Americans.

During such times, it takes a tremendous amount of courage to resist and demand that the country live up to the meaning of those lofty words that accompanied her inception, "We hold these words to be self evident, that all men are created equal, that they are endowed by their Creator with certain unalienable rights, that among these are Life, Liberty, and the pursuit of Happiness."

This week one of the giants who dared to make such a demand has passed on. On December 1, 1955, Rosa Parks made the fateful decision refusing to stand to surrender her seat to a white passenger on a Montgomery, Alabama bus. For that decision, she will forever stand in our memories. Many Muslims, especially those who are new to this country may ask, "What do we find to honor in this non-Muslim lady? She did not do anything big." Let us be explicit in answering that query. In the climate of hatred that provided the context for Rosa Parks' simple act of defiance, many people were being brutally murdered for far less. In that climate, what she did was monumental, and she suffered because of it. She and her family were harassed relentlessly in the aftermath of her arrest. The pressure became so great that in 1957 her husband, Raymond Parks, suffered a nervous breakdown. That same year she left the south to reside in Detroit, Michigan.

That said, her act of defiance in and of itself could be considered small. It was not even the first incident of its kind in Montgomery. However, God decreed that on that day, Rosa Parks would sit. And because she sat Dr. Martin Luther King, Jr. stood up; because she sat the city of Montgomery, Alabama stood up; because she sat the South stood up; because she sat a nation's conscience was roused.

In the ensuing agitation, civil and voting rights legislation was passed, affirmative action legislation was passed, a black man ascended to the bench of the Supreme Court, and most significantly, for most of those reading this message, immigration laws were amended allowing a flood of Muslim immigrants to enter this land. Now the political winds are changing and the current mood is a harbinger of a struggle ahead for American Muslims. We may well face the kind of climate faced by Rosa Parks deep down in Dixie. That climate will challenge us in ways that it challenged Mrs. Parks.

History remembers Rosa Parks favorably, just as it remembers the legions that preceded her in demanding a dignified existence for African Americans in this country. As we embark on our struggle to maintain our dignified existence here, we should ask ourselves, "How will history remember us?" The answer to that question lies in how we respond to another question, the simple question that was presented to Rosa Parks, "Will we stand or will we sit?"

63. Hamza Yusuf, "Education and the Inner City" from *IMAN Central*

Accessed May 9, 2006. Available online: http://www.imancentral.org/modules.php? op=modload&name=News&file=article&sid=16.

The Inner-City Muslim Action Network (IMAN) is a non-profit organization in Chicago, Illinois that provides social services, networking, and outreach activities to Muslims in largely working class neighborhoods in South and Southwest Chicago. For a biography of Hamza Yusuf see the "Yusuf, Hamza" entry in Volume 1. In this interview, he argues for the utility and importance of Islamic injunctions to become educated and active citizens who address the issues of poverty and social inequality within American society.

1. EDUCATION AND THE INNER CITY

One of the broad, common threads that runs through Zaytuna Institute, the Inner-City Muslim Action Network (IMAN) and a host of other Muslim organizations in the United States is that of education. Organically grown organizations will necessarily have differences, one from the next, in substantive focus, instructional method and academic intensity of educational programs. Despite these organizational differences, what are the core elements of a successful curriculum that will (a) sustain and (b) empower contemporary Muslims?

SHAYKH HAMZA: The key element of any sound curriculum is to ensure that basic humanistic tools are imparted to help a student become a better human being and a critical element in the human process. By critical here, it is implied that someone is able to see what's wrong, identify it as a wrong and then able to evaluate the steps needed to redress the wrong.

For instance, a major wrong in contemporary America is consumerism (i.e. the goal of life is to accumulate wealth and material goods). This disenfranchises the poor from a societal project and builds resentment, which leads to anger and envy, which are two of the seven deadly sins, ... and one alone is enough to kill you! When we assess the project of consumerism, we realize that as an increasing venture it becomes clearly untenable for large numbers of people. It is a selfish path and ignores the very reality that if resources continue to be exploited at present rates, we will exhaust the earth's plentitude. An example: the monitoring of areas in which have ocean fishing takes place has shown that in the last twenty years, over ninety percent of the fish have been decimated. The root problem is that fish are not allowed to replenish their numbers due to over-fishing of areas that once had seemingly inexhaustible resources. Much of the fishing is processed into cat food. In most cultures, cats live off the leftover food of families, but here, they are spoiled into tasty treats that devastate our ocean's supplies further upsetting the delicate balance of the natural food chains in the oceans. Due to the critical nature of this type of information, it may surface from time to time; however it isn't news that one finds in daily corporate owned newspapers.

A student must also be able to think critically about the world he or she finds himself or herself in. So teaching students to think is of the essence of any serious training. For Muslims this includes an ability to access divine or sacred tradition in his or her daily life—in other words, to make the message real through implementation. This can only be done in an environment in which people are helped to live the message of submission to God.

2. LEADERSHIP, ADVERSITY, AND GLOBAL CONSCIOUSNESS

IMAN's Taking it to the Streets is held in Chicago's Marquette Park, where Martin Luther King, Jr. marched, and was stoned, only decades ago. Many Muslims today have drawn analogies between the current state of Muslims in America and the state of the broader African-American population during the era of MLK, Malcolm X, Thurgood Marshall and others. To what extent are these analogies on point? How can a focus on the history of race relations in this country enhance or detract from a contemporary Muslim's consciousness?

SHAYKH HAMZA YUSUF: Enfranchisement is a process that has been present in this country since the start. Many communities who have been here for hundreds of years, in the case of native people, millennia, are still struggling for full inclusion into America. However, we must not despair due to clear signs of improvement. To deny advancement in many areas is ingratitude. Minority communities are in fact majorities in many communities now and they are running entire cities in America for the first time in over two hundred years. There is an immense opportunity to realize the dreams of philosophers of the past today in this country. The idea of equality before the law has rarely been conceived in human history, let alone achieved, and yet it is an ideal that is accepted now by the majority of people in this country. It still has a long way to go before it is indeed a reality experienced by all peoples in all cases. The Muslims are at the end in a long line of people that have come to these shores or were already here, attempting to realize their rights as equal before the law.

Many people before the Muslims have struggled and many have died in order that we as offspring or migrants might enjoy the rights that we do today. Those people must never be forgotten; it is incumbent upon Muslims in America to know their stories. The stories have people of all colors as protagonists. There have always been people of color who have opposed the injustices of racism, sexism and intolerance but we should not forget that there have been numerous good white people who have opposed injustice and they should not be forgotten. The issue cannot be black and white but rather wrong and right. It is as simple as that. We stand not with our tribe but with our principles and should they be against our tribe then we must act as witnesses "unto God even against yourselves."

3. "PROGRESS" IN THE INNER CITY AND THE WORLD

You have previously discussed the "myth of progress" and asserted that the highest level of spiritual progress was achieved over a millennium ago in the desert and oasis of Arabia during the time of God's Emissary, may He grant him His peace and blessings. While "spiritual entropy" may be a regrettable reality facing humanity (at least en masse), today's Muslims in and out of the inner city, and abroad, hold conflicting views about the extent to which achieving material comfort necessarily involves dealing with, or is equated with, embracing "capitalism" with all of its arguably negative aspects (exploitation of labor, riba, corruption of big business, environmental neglect, etc.) and thereby losing religion. Is there a confluence or a contradiction in attempting to achieve both spiritual and material success in the contemporary globalizing economy?

SHAYKHA HAMZA YUSUF: The problem with poverty in America is that it deprives the poor of their dignity. This is so for a number of reasons: one, the Calvinist view, which affects many Americans, states that wealth is a sign of God's blessings upon the person. In that way, poverty is seen almost as a punishment. In essence, this perspective states that in this land of plenty, there must be something wrong with you if you don't have anything. This way of viewing the world permeates our culture and does untold damage to countless souls.

Islam teaches us that wealth is inner wealth. The Prophet Muhammad, peace be upon him, said, "Contentment is an inexhaustible treasure." He also said, "Wealth is not a lot of goods but it is being satisfied with what one has." The endless pursuit of more is a disease, and as the hadith (prophetic tradition) states, "Nothing will fill the mouth of the child of Adam except the dirt of the grave. If someone had a mountain of gold, they would only desire another."

What we need to learn in this country is how to be poor with dignity. We need to learn to keep clean houses, clothes and bodies, to eat pure food, and to do this with money earned untarnished by illegal transactions. This is available to anyone willing to turn to God for support.

We must also free ourselves of resentment and envy of others and what they have. The Prophet, peace be upon him said, "Look to those better than you in your spirituality but look to those with less than you in your material reality. For indeed that will help you to aspire to be better and to be grateful for what you have."

Finally, poverty is "all my glory" according to the richest man that ever lived, the Prophet Muhammad, peace be upon him. He chose to lower his standard of living in order that others might have more. That is his way.

64. Tariq Ramadan, "An International Call for Moratorium on Corporal Punishment, Stoning, and the Death Penalty in the Islamic World"

*March 30, 2005. Available online: http://www.tariqramadan.com/article.php3?id_
article=264 Reprinted with permission of Tariq Ramadan.*

Tariq Ramadan (for a biography, see the "Ramadan, Tariq" entry in Volume 1) was born in Switzerland in 1962. He is a professor and prominent public intellectual. He is an outspoken advocate of Muslim rights in Europe, the United States, and the Middle East as well as a critic of Israeli policies in Palestine and the French ban of the ḥijāb in public. He is also the grandson of Hassan Al-Banna (1906–1949), the Egyptian founder of the Muslim Brotherhood who was executed by the Egyptian government in 1949. In 2004, Ramadan was scheduled to teach at The University of Notre Dame when his visa was revoked by the U.S. State Department, causing protest from American Muslims and academics.

Ramadan wrote the following article in April 2005. It was published in many newspapers and journals in the United States, Europe, and the Muslim world. Ramadan calls for an immediate moratorium on ḥudūd penalties (ḥudūd refers to the most serious crimes, e.g., murder, and their corresponding corporal punishments as outlined in classical Islamic jurisprudence) that some Muslim countries apply. He advocates for an examination and critique of the legal texts dealing with ḥudūd in order to void these prescriptions.

Muslim majority societies and Muslims around the world are constantly confronted with the fundamental question of how to implement the penalties prescribed in the Islamic penal code.

Evoking the notion of *sharî'a,* or more precisely *hudûd* [1], the terms of the debate are defined by central questions emerging from thought provoking discussions taking place between *ulamâ'* (scholars) and/or Muslim masses: How to be faithful to the message of Islam in the contemporary era? How can a society truly define itself as "Islamic" beyond what is required in the daily practices of individual private life? But a critical and fruitful debate has not yet materialized.

Several currents of thought exist in the Islamic world today and disagreements are numerous, deep and recurring. Among these, a small minority demands the immediate and strict application of *hudûd,* assessing this as an essential prerequisite to truly defining a "Muslim majority society" as *"Islamic".* Others, while accepting the fact that the *hudûd* are indeed found in the textual references (the *Qur'an* and the *Sunna* [2]), consider the application of *hudûd* to be conditional upon the state of the society which must be just and, for some, has to be *"ideal"* before these injunctions could be applied. Thus, the priority is the promotion of social justice, fighting against poverty and illiteracy etc. Finally, there are others, also a minority, who consider the texts relating to *hudûd* as obsolete and argue that these references have no place in contemporary Muslim societies.

One can see the opinions on this subject are so divergent and entrenched that it becomes difficult to discern what the respective arguments are. At the very moment we are writing these lines- while serious debate is virtually non-existent, while positions remain vague and even nebulous, and consensus among Muslims is lacking- women and men are being subjected to the application of these penalties.

For Muslims, Islam is a message of equality and justice. It is our faithfulness to the message of Islam that leads us to recognize that it impossible to remain silent in the face of unjust applications of our religious references. The debate must liberate itself and refuse to be satisfied by general, timid and convoluted responses. These silences and intellectual contortions are unworthy of the clarity and just message of Islam.

In the name of the scriptural sources, the Islamic teachings, and the contemporary Muslim conscience, statements must be made and decisions need to be taken.

WHAT DOES THE MAJORITY OF THE *ULAMĀ* SAY?

All the *ulamâ'* (scholars) of the Muslim world, of yesterday and of today and in all the currents of thought, recognize the existence of scriptural sources that refer to corporal punishment (*Qur'an* and *Sunna*), stoning of adulterous men and women (*Sunna*) and the penal code (*Qur'an and Sunna*). The divergences between the *ulamâ'* and the various

trends of thought (literalist, reformist, rationalist, etc.) are primarily rooted in the interpretation of a certain number of these texts, the conditions of application of the Islamic
penal code, as well as its degree of relevance to the contemporary era (nature of the
committed infractions, testimonials, social and political contexts, etc.).

The majority of the *ulamâ'*, historically and today, are of the opinion that these
penalties are on the whole Islamic but that the conditions under which they should be
implemented are nearly impossible to reestablish. These penalties, therefore, are *"almost
never applicable"*. The *hudûd* would, therefore, serve as a "deterrent," the objective of
which would be to stir the conscience of the believer to the gravity of an action warranting
such a punishment.

Anyone who reads the books of the *ulamâ'*, listens to their lectures and sermons, travels
inside the Islamic world or interacts with the Muslim communities of the West will inevitably and invariably hear the following pronouncement from religious authorities: *"almost
never applicable"*. Such pronouncements give the majority of *ulamâ* and Muslim masses a
way out of dealing with the fundamental issues and questions without risking appearing
to be have betrayed the Islamic scriptural sources. The alternative posture is to avoid the
issue of *hudûd* altogether and/or to remain silent.

WHAT IS HAPPENING ON THE GROUND?

One would have hoped that this pronouncement, *"almost never,"* would be understood
as an assurance that women and men would be protected from repressive and unjust treatment; one would have wished that the stipulated conditions would be seen, by legislators
and government who claim Islam, as an imperative to promote equality before the law
and justice among humans. Nothing could be further from the reality.

Behind an Islamic discourse that minimizes the reality and rounds off the angles, and
within the shadows of this *"almost never"*, lurks a somber reality where women and men
are punished, beaten, stoned and executed in the name of *hudûd* while Muslim conscience
the world over remains untouched.

It is as if one does not know, as though a minor violation is being done to the Islamic
teachings. A still more grave injustice is that these penalties are applied almost exclusively
to women and the poor, the doubly victimized, never to the wealthy, the powerful, or
the oppressors. Furthermore, hundreds of prisoners have no access to anything that
could even remotely be called defense counsel. Death sentences are decided and carried
out against women, men and even minors (political prisoners, traffickers, delinquents,
etc.) without ever given a chance to obtain legal counsel. In resigning ourselves to having
a superficial relationship to the scriptural sources, we betray the message of justice
of Islam.

The international community has an equally major and obvious responsibility to
be involved in addressing the question of *hudûd* in the Muslim world. Thus far, the
denunciations have been selective and calculated for the protection of geostrategic and
economic interests. A poor country, in Africa or Asia, trying to apply the *hudûd* or the
sharî'a will face the mobilization of international campaigns as we have seen recently. This
is not the case with rich countries, the petromonarchies and those considered "allies".
Towards the latter, denunciations are made reluctantly, or not at all, despite ongoing
and acknowledged applications of these penalties typically carried out against the poorest
or weakest segments of society. The intensity of the denunciations is inversely propor-
tional to the interests at stake. A further injustice!

THE PASSION OF THE PEOPLE, THE FEAR OF THE *ULAMĀ'*

For those who travel within the Islamic world and interact with Muslims, an analysis imposes itself: everywhere, populations are demonstrating an increasing devotion to Islam and its teachings. This reality, although interesting in itself, could be troubling, and even dangerous when the nature of this devotion is so fervent, where there is no real knowledge or comprehension of the texts, where there is so little if any critical distance vis-à-vis the different scholarly interpretations, the necessary contextualization, the nature of the required conditions or, indeed the protection of the rights of the individual and the promotion of justice.

On the question of *hudûd,* one sometimes sees popular support hoping or exacting a literal and immediate application because the latter would guarantee henceforth the *"Islamic"* character of a society. In fact, it is not rare to hear Muslim women and men (educated or not, and more often of modest means) calling for a formal and strict application of the penal code (in their mind, the *sharî'a*) of which they themselves will often be the first victims. When one studies this phenomenon, two types of reasoning generally motivate these claims:

1. The literal and immediate application of the *hudûd* legally and socially provides a visible reference to Islam. The legislation, by its harshness, gives the feeling of fidelity to the *Qur'anic* injunctions that demands rigorous respect of the text. At the popular level, one can infer in the African, Arabic, Asian as well as Western countries, that the very nature of this harshness and intransigence of the application, gives an Islamic dimension to the popular psyche.

2. The opposition and condemnations by the West supplies, paradoxically, the popular feeling of fidelity to the Islamic teachings; a reasoning that is antithetical, simple and simplistic. The intense opposition of the West is sufficient proof of the authentic Islamic character of the literal application of *hudûd.* Some will persuade themselves by asserting that the West has long since lost its moral references and became so permissive that the harshness of the Islamic penal code which punishes behaviors judged immoral, is by antithesis, the true and only alternative *"to Western decadence".*

These formalistic and binary reasoning are fundamentally dangerous for they claim and grant an Islamic quality to a legislation, not in what it promotes, protects and applies justice to, but more so because it sanctions harsh and visible punishment to certain behaviors and in stark contrast and opposition to the Western laws, which are perceived as morally permissive and without a reference to religion [3]. One sees today that communities or Muslim people satisfy themselves with this type of legitimacy to back a government or a party that calls for an application of the *sharî'a* narrowly understood as a literal and immediate application of corporal punishment, stoning and the death penalty.

When this type of popular passion takes hold, it is the first sign of a will to respond to various forms of frustration and humiliation by asserting an identity that perceives itself as Islamic (and anti-Western). Such an identity is not based on the comprehension of the objectives of the Islamic teachings (*al maqâsid*) or the different interpretations and conditions relating to the application of the *hudûd.*

Faced with this passion, many *ulamâ'* remain prudent for the fear of losing their credibility with the masses. One can observe a psychological pressure exercised by this popular sentiment towards the judicial process of the *ulamâ',* which normally should be independent so as to educate the population and propose alternatives. Today, an inverse phenomenon is revealing itself. The majority of the *ulamâ'* are afraid to confront these popular and simplistic claims which lack knowledge, are passionate and binary, for fear of losing their status and being defined as having compromised too much, not been strict enough, too westernized or not Islamic enough.

The *ulamâ*, who should be the guarantors of a deep reading of the texts, the guardians of fidelity to the objectives of justice and equality and of the critical analysis of conditions and social contexts, find themselves having to accept either a formalistic application (an immediate non-contextualized application), or a binary reasoning (less West is more Islam), or hide behind *"almost never applicable"* pronouncements which protects them but which does not provide real solutions to the daily injustices experienced by women and the poor.

AN IMPOSSIBLE *STATUS QUO*: OUR RESPONSIBILITY

The Islamic world is experiencing a very deep crisis the causes of which are multiple and sometimes contradictory. The political system of the Arab world is becoming more and more entrenched, references to Islam frequently instrumentalized, and public opinion is often muzzled or blindly passionate (to such a point as to accept, indeed even to call for, the most repressive interpretations and least just application of the *"Islamic sharî'a"* and *hudûd*).

In terms of the more circumscribed religious question, we can observe a crisis of authority accompanied by an absence of internal debate among the *ulamâ* in the diverse schools of thought and within Muslim societies. It becomes apparent that a variety of opinions, accepted in Islam, are whirling today within a chaotic framework leading to the coexistence of disparate and contradictory Islamic legal opinions each claiming to have more *"Islamic character"* than the other.

Faced with this legal chaos, the ordinary Muslim public is more appeased by *"an appearance of fidelity"*, then it is persuaded by opinions based on real knowledge and understanding of the governing Islamic principles and rules (*ahkâm*).

Let us look at the reality, as it exists. There is a today a quadruple crisis of closed and repressive political systems, religious authorities upholding contradictory juristic positions and unknowledgeable populations swept up in remaining faithful to the teachings of Islam through religious fervor than through true reflection. The crisis cannot legitimize our silence. We are accomplices and guilty when women and men are punished, stoned or executed in the name of a formal application of the scriptural sources.

It leaves the responsibility to the Muslims of the entire world. It is for them to rise to the challenge of remaining faithful to the message of Islam in the contemporary era; it is for them to denounce the failures and the betrayals being carried out by whatever authorities or any Muslim individual. A prophetic tradition reports: "Support your brother, whether he be unjust or victim of an injustice." One of the Companions asked: "Messenger of God, I understand how to support someone that is a victim of injustice, but how can I support him who is unjust?" The Prophet (peace be upon him) responded: "Prevent him from being unjust, that is you support to him."[4]

It thus becomes the responsibility of each *'âlim* (scholar), of each conscience, every woman and man, wherever they may be to speak up. Western Muslims either hide behind the argument that they are exempt from the application of the *sharî'a* or *hudûd* since they are "in a minority position" [5]. Their avoidance of the questions leaves a heavy and troubling silence. Or they express condemnation from afar without attempting to change the situation and influence the mentalities. These Muslim women and men who live in spaces of political freedom, who have access to education and knowledge, shoulder—in the very name of the Islamic teachings—have a major responsibility to attempt to reform the situation, open a relevant debate, condemn and put a end to injustices perpetrated in their name.

A CALL, SOME QUESTIONS:

Taking into account all these considerations, we launch today a call for *an immediate international moratorium on corporal punishment, stoning and the death penalty* in all Muslim majority countries. Considering that the opinions of most scholars, regarding the comprehension of the texts and the application of *hudûd,* are neither explicit nor unanimous (indeed there is not even a clear majority), and bearing in mind that political systems and the state of the majority Muslim societies do not guarantee a just and equal treatment of individuals before the law, it is our moral obligation and religious responsibility to demand for the immediate suspension of the application of the *hudûd* which is inaccurately accepted as an application of "Islamic *sharî'a*".

This call doubles itself with a series of basic questions addressed to the body of Islamic religious authorities of the world, whatever their tradition (*sunnî or shî'î*), their school of thought (*hanâfî, mâlikî, ja'farî,* etc.) or their tendencies (literalist, *salafî,* reformist, etc.):

1. What are the texts (and what are their respective degrees of recognized authenticity), that make reference to corporal punishment, stoning and to the death penalty in the corpus of the Islamic scriptural sources circumscribed to what the specialists call the *hudûd*? Where are the margins of possible interpretations and on which points are there clear divergences (*al ikhtilâf*) in the history of the Islamic law and in the contemporary era?

2. What are the conditions (*shurût*) stipulated for each of the penalties by the sources themselves, the consensus of the scholars (*al ijmâ'*) or by individual scholars through Islamic law history and jurisprudence (*fiqh*)? Where are the divergences on the stipulations and what "extenuating circumstances" were sometimes elaborated by religious authorities throughout history or within the different schools of thought?

3. The socio-political context (*al wâqi'*) was always considered by the *ulamâ'* as one of the conditions needed for the application of *hudûd.* The importance of this question is such that it demands special treatment (and participation within the debate from intellectuals, notably those who are specialized in the social sciences). In which context today is it possible to apply *hudûd*? What would be the required conditions in terms of political systems and the application of the general legislation: freedom of expression, equality before the law, public education, eradication of poverty and social exclusion? Which are, in this domain, the areas of divergence between the legal schools and the *ulamâ'* and on what are these disagreements based?

Studying these questions are meant to clarify the terms of the debate with regards to the interpretative latitudes offered by the texts, while simultaneously taking into account the determining state of contemporary societies and their evolution. This intra-community reflection requires from the start a double understanding of the texts and contexts, in keeping solemnly with the objectives of the Islamic message. On the whole, this must allow us to respond to the questions of what is applicable (and according to which methods) and what is no longer applicable (considering the required conditions are impossible to reestablish as well as the fact that societal evolution is clearly moving away from the required ideal).

This undertaking requires, from within, rigour, time and establishing spaces of dialogue and debate, nationally and internationally, between the *ulamâ'*, Muslim intellectuals and inside the Muslim communities since this matter is not only about a relationship to the texts, but equally, to the context. In the interval, there can be no justification for applying penalties that sanction legal approximations and injustices such as is the case today[6]. A moratorium would impose and allow a basic debate to unfold in serenity, without using it as an excuse to manipulate Islam. All injustices made legal in the name of Islam must stop immediately.

BETWEEN THE LETTER AND OBJECTIVES: FIDELITY

Some will understand this call as an instigation to disrespect the scriptural sources of Islam, thinking that to ask for a moratorium goes against the explicit texts of the *Qu'ran* and *Sunna*. Precisely the opposite is true: all the legal texts demand to be read in light of the objective intended to justify them (*Al-maqâsid*). Foremost among these objectives, we find stipulated that the protection of the integrity of the person (*an- nafs*) and the promotion of justice (*al-'adl*) are primordial. Therefore, a literal and non-contextualized application of *hudûd*, with no regard for strict and numerous stipulated conditions, and one which would present itself as being faithful to the teachings of Islam, is in fact a betrayal if according to the context, for it produces an injustice.

The caliph 'Umar ibn al-Khattab established a moratorium towards thieves when he suspended the application of the punishment during a famine. Despite the *Qur'anic* text being very explicit on this, the state of the society meant it would have been an unjust literal application: they would have castigated poor people whose potential theft would have been for the sole purpose of surviving in a state of absolute poverty. Therefore, in the name of absolute justice demanded by the global message of Islam, 'Umar ibn al-Khattab decided to suspend the application of a text: keeping with the literalist interpretation would have meant disloyalty and betrayal of the superior value of Islam that is justice. It is in the name of Islam and in the understanding of texts that he suspended the application of one of these injunctions. The moratorium finds here a precedent of the utmost importance.

Reflection and necessary reform within Muslim majority societies will not occur but from within. It is for Muslims to take up their responsibilities and set in motion a debate that opens an intra-community dialogue, while refusing the continued legalized injustices in the name of Islam, i.e. in their name. An endogenous dynamic is imperative

This does not mean that the questions put forward by non-Muslim intellectuals or citizens should be dismissed. On the contrary, all parties must learn to decentre themselves and move towards listening to the other, to the other's points of reference, logic and their aspiration. For Muslims, all queries, from their co-religionists or women and men who do share their religious conviction, are welcome. It is for us to make use of these questions as a spark of dynamism to our thoughts. This is how we can remain faithful to the justice demanded by Islam while taking into account also the demands of the contemporary era.

CONCLUSION

This call for *an immediate moratorium on corporal punishment, stoning and the death penalty* is demanding on many fronts. We are defining it as a call to consciousness of each individual so that she/he realizes that Islam is being used to degrade and subjugate women and men in certain Muslim majority societies in the midst of collusive silence and chaotic judicial opinions on the ground. This realization implies:

— A mobilization of ordinary Muslims throughout the world to call on their governments to place an immediate moratorium on the application of *hudûd* and for the opening of a vast intra-community debate (critical, reasonable and reasoned) between the *ulamâ,* the intellectuals, the leaders and the general population.

— Taking the *ulamâ* to account so that they at last dare to report the injustices and instrumentalization of Islam in the field of *hudûd* and, in the name of fidelity to the Islamic texts, to put out a call for an immediate moratorium emulating the example of 'Umar ibn al-Khattab.

— Promoting education of Muslim populations so that they go beyond the mirage of the formalism and appearances. The application of the repressive interpretations, measures and punishment does not make a society more faithful to the Islamic teachings. It is more the capacity to promote social justice and the protection the integrity of every individual, woman or man, rich or poor, that determines a truly authentic fidelity. The priority, according to the norms of Islam, is given to the protection of rights not to administering punishments which are meant to be implemented under strict and conditioned exceptions.

— This movement for reform from within, by the Muslims and in the name of the message and reference texts of Islam, should never neglect listening to the surrounding world as well as to the inquiries that Islam raises in non-Muslim minds. Not to concede to responses from "the other", from "the West", but, in order to remain, in its mirror, more constructively faithful to oneself.

We urge all of those that take heed to this call to join us and make their voices heard for the immediate suspension of the application of *hudûd* in the Muslim world so that a real debate establishes itself on the question. We say that in the name of Islam, of its texts and of the message of justice, we can no longer accept that women and men undergo punishment and death while we remain utterly silent, as accomplices, through a process which is ultimately cowardly.

It is urgent that Muslim throughout the world refuse the formalist legitimization of the teachings of their religion and reconcile themselves with the deep message that invites towards spirituality, demands education, justice and the respect of pluralism. Societies will never reform themselves by repressive measures and punishment but more so by the engagement of each to establish civil society and the respect of popular will as well as a just legislation guaranteeing the equality of women and men, poor and rich before the law. It is urgent to set in motion a democratization movement that moves populations from the obsession of what the law is sanctioning to the claim of what it should protect: their conscience, their integrity, their liberty and their rights.

NOTES

[1] A concept which literally means "limits". In the specialized language of Muslim jurists, (*fuqahâ*), this term is inclusive of the punishment which is revealed in the application of the Islamic Penal code. *Sharî'a, literally "the way to the source" and a path to faithfulness, is a corpus of Islamic jurisprudence the in-depth definition of which is beyond the scope of this paper. Sharî'a has sadly been reduced to legalistic formulae of a penal code in the minds of many, Muslims and non-Muslim alike*

[2] Prophetic tradition: texts which report what the Prophet of Islam (peace be upon him) did, said or approved of during his lifetime.

[3] In Muslim countries, laws that we see as being "borrowed from the west" are often interpreted as tools by dictatorial governments to mislead and legitimize their autocratic character, and more importantly, to promote a westernized culture and morals.

[4] *Hadîth* reported by al-Bukhârî and Muslim.

[5] The argument is weak and dangerous as it tacitly accepts the application of *hudûd* within today's societal context as "Islamic"

[6] If ever in doubt, all circumstances require the benefit of the doubt towards the accused according to a legal universal principle (acknowledged from the start by the tradition of Islamic jurisprudence)

65.   "Every Act Is Political: Samina Ali, An Email Interview with Shauna Singh Baldwin" from *Shauna Singh Baldwin*

Accessed May 28, 2006. Available online: http://www.sawnet.org/books/writing/ samina_ali_interview.html. Reprinted with permission of Shauna Singh Baldwin.

Samina Ali was born in Hyderabad, India and immigrated to the United States with her family when she was six months old. Growing up, she spent half the year in Minnesota and the other in India. Ali received her B.A. from the University of Minnesota, Twin Cities in 1993. She then graduated from the University of Oregon with her M.F.A. Her first novel, Madras on Rainy Days, is an autobiographical novel in which the lead character, Layla, struggles with being a part of society in the United States and a conservative Muslim society in India. Madras on Rainy Days earned the Prix Premier Roman Etranger 2005 Award (France) and was a finalist for the PEN/Hemingway Award and California Book Reviewers Award. The following interview was conducted with Ali after the publication of Madras on Rainy Days. It highlights important dimensions shared by the majority of second generation immigrant Muslims, namely a loyalty to the American political system and society, an emotional link to the culture and country of the parents, and the challenges of conciliating both in the post–September 11th context.

Which country/countries do you belong to legally/spiritually?

I am an American citizen, naturalized when I was about eight. I was born in Hyderabad, India and immigrated with my parents to the US when I was close to 6 months old. I grew up in both places; it was important to my father that his family not forget our heritage, meaning our Indian culture and Urdu language and religion of Islam, so he sent my two brothers, mother and me back to India every year. In India, I went to a Catholic school and I learned Urdu and Arabic and Indian English, and while here, I studied French and English. I grew up very confused and never knew what was my home. When I was in India, I wanted to be in the U.S., when in the States, I wanted to be in India. It was in India that I felt American and in America that I felt Indian—how is that for split identity! I remember Western travelers used to tell me how "at home" they felt in India, that it was their "spiritual home", but my own confusion really prevented me from understanding what they meant. It wasn't until I went to Italy in 2003 and spent some time there that I got it. Italy did feel like home to me, strangely, I did feel connected to the history, the people, the place. Spiritual home to me, then, implies a place where one journeys and feels roots that are imperceptible, indefinable. That's how I felt in Italy (and I've traveled to many places and not felt that).

India is my birthplace and home, my heart, my core. My first book, MADRAS ON RAINY DAYS, is entirely set in Hyderabad because I wanted to start at the roots and then branch out. Now I feel comfortable writing about America in my second novel. Strangely, after the publication of my novel, I also finally feel at home in both America and India. It's almost as though the two places were dueling inside me, each trying to express itself, each with a distinct identity, and only when I gave a full voice to one and am about to give a full voice to the other that both are satisfied. Writing has brought me home.

Do you believe a writer can ever be apolitical? Should we?

I think there are many writers out there who are apolitical, who write simply to tell a story or who write simply to get published. Writing for writing's sake. I was at the LA Book Festival in 2004 and had this same question asked of me. There were four other panelists with me and all of them insisted that they were simply telling a story, nothing more. Three of those other writers are white males. When I finally spoke up, I seemed to have started a huge debate! What I said there is what I still believe: some of us simply do not have a choice but to be political in our writing. For instance, I am a Muslim woman. For many years now, there have been many other people telling the story of Muslim women.

Today, when Muslim women are the hot topic, the voices speaking out for them are still not Muslim. I am aware of what is being being about Muslim women and, more importantly, who is saying it. As such, it's very important to me to give a voice to my own experience and to have that one experience be expansive enough to include a general human experience even as I am dispelling stereotypes.

When I was trying to sell my book, I had editors ask me forthrightly to change parts of it: set half in the U.S. and half in India; have the American lover, Nate, storm Layla's wedding and "save" her, like a literary Rambo figure; show how Muslim women are repressed in India, denied their freedoms, asexual, while showing how America affords them freedoms they never dreamed up. Again, a perpetuation of stereotypes—worse, it would have been coming from a Muslim woman!

The act of writing for me is political. But for me, as a Muslim woman in post-9/11 America, almost every act is political: the way I dress, speak, present myself, raise my child, write!

At 19, I read that you experienced an attack by Hindus in Hyderabad. Have you drawn on that incident in your writing, yet? Was it in any way responsible for your becoming a writer?

I grew up half in India so I grew up with military curfews and riots. This is simply part of life there, unfortunately, the civil unrest that results from tremendous political ambitions. The incident you're speaking about happened after I had gotten in my arranged marriage to a man back in India when I was 19. I had been married to him for close to six months by then and living with his family in a neighborhood that was predominantly Hindu. It was election season, which is when these old wounds get stirred, and a Hindu man came to our home one night and told us that our house was targeted. He said a gang of Hindu men was coming that same evening. We thanked him for informing us, but then there was nothing to do. It was dark so we weren't safe in trying to run away.

Our neighbors suddenly seemed like strangers or, worse, enemies. We had no phone, and even if we did, no police to call. Usually the police are involved in these crimes— remember, these are political crimes that manifest as religious ones. My mother-in-law, a conservative Muslim woman who only liked me to dress in loose shalwar-kameezes told me to put on jeans under my clothes—to further deter rape. She and I stayed in my bedroom all night, locked inside the house and then the room, while the men of the house went to the roofs. It was the worst night of my life. I thought I was going to die—with strangers!

My parents and brothers had already returned to the States and I believed I would never see them again. Then it occurred to me: here I am, having fulfilled each of my parents' dreams for me: I was the dutiful daughter who was doing a business major at university, who had gotten into an arranged marriage against her will to a Muslim Indian man, who had spent all her life traveling between two countries and two languages, and all for this! In all my parents' efforts in trying to keep me protected and safe, they had landed me at death's doorstep. Worse, I had allowed it to happen because I believed I didn't have a choice. I had handed over my life to them. I resolved that night that if I did ever make it back to the U.S., I was going to begin my life, lead it the way I wanted, and not be confined to my parents' and culture's and religion's expectations of me.

And that is what I did. The gang never did make it to our house. As in the novel, they did stop and murder a Muslim couple before they got to our house, and somehow this deterred them or they used up too much time, who knows, but we were saved. I will never forget though that I was saved at the price of a fellow Muslim sister's life. She was raped and murdered. I've written this exactly in the novel. I gave her a voice. I gave my story a voice. Elie Weisel says that writing is a way of saying, "this happened to me, this is the way it was, a way of saying 'Ameen.'" Well, this did happen to me and this is the way it was, and now I say Amen!

In an article in Rediff you say: "In the post-9/11 environment, Muslims are overtly discriminated against, stereotyped, demonized. Muslim men are seen as terrorists and 'evil,' controlling and dominating women. Muslim women are seen as sexually repressed and uneducated, their bodies and movements controlled. I hope the novel exposes Western readers to ordinary Muslims and thereby humanizes them. I also hope Layla can prove that a woman, even a Muslim woman, can come out from under the weight of tremendous familial and cultural expectations to become her own person." *Post 9/11/01, has there been any change in your editor/publisher's perception of your work? Did the Attack on the World Trade Center affect the willingness of US editors to publish your work?*

Most people think that selling a book after 9/11 must have been easy for a Muslim woman. It really wasn't. I was writing about Muslims, yes, but certainly not writing about what others wanted to hear. In hindsight, it makes sense to me that FSG published my book without changes to my message. The publishing house does a marvelous job of publishing writers from places like South Africa and other politically charged areas of the world, places that cannot be excused or lied about, and neither, unfortunately, can the story I've written. Not only did the publishing become more difficult, but the audience is also more reluctant to see the message. I'm working against many stereotypes and machines of power and Muslims have no power right now. So any change I make will be slow yet valuable.

Did the Attack on the World Trade Center on 9/11/01 and the threat of terrorism/being labelled a terrorist affect your writing life in any way?

I've not written a new work since 9/11 so I'm not sure how it will affect my characters. However, I am working on a novel right now, just at the beginning of one, and I am working through this very issue. I'm not sure how to touch the topic because it is so loaded.

Interestingly, there are young American writers I know of out there who have already published on the subject, even moving their characters into Iraq and telling the story from the Iraqi point of view, but I cannot write something without fully digesting it in all its nuances. I wouldn't feel responsible as a writer or thinker or human. Since my characters are Muslim, it's especially important that I understand and present this accurately. The larger Muslim community in America has really been supportive of my work and my message, and the weight of their faith does give me courage to proceed.

Have you experienced racism or have you been targeted as a visible minority in your home town or while travelling? Has there been an increase since 9/11/01?

Fortunately, I haven't, but I know it's because of the way I look and people's ignorance: no one knows how to place me; even other Indians sometimes ask me where I come from! I've traveled with my two brothers, however, and both are men who are over 6 feet tall with black hair and dark eyes, Muslim names and faces, and it's a hassle. They get stopped at least three times even before they reach the line for the security check. Then they get pulled over again.

A few times I've been stopped at the airport while trying to check in. I was told my name was on the "terrorist list" and it would take 45 minutes to clear up. God knows what they then do to "clear this up," but in those 45 minutes to an hour, I sit and fume! Yet it always come down to this: we are all doing this to each other. Muslims and nonMuslims alike. There is no one to blame.

Salman Rushdie, writing in the Virginia Quarterly, says: "Even the literature of other countries is failing to make its way into the United States. The Treasury Department's Office of Foreign Assets Control (OFAC) regulations now restrict the editing of work from what are called enemy countries. If a text arrives from, let's say, Iran or North Korea and is subjected to editing in the United States, that can be dubbed trading with the enemy and possibly lead to criminal prosecution. This is an amazing upside-down piece of insanity. If it were applied backwards to the period of the Soviet Union, it would mean that people editing samizdat texts in the West could be subject to prosecution. The madness in this is that if you publish the text unedited, as a mess, that's all right, but if you try to perform the normal publishing function of editing so that you can present it to the public in a clean form, that's a crime."

Has your work been affected by the new rules, and if so how?

This is crazy! No, fortunately, I've not experienced anything outright. Again, the pressures I feel are unspoken. The message I want to deliver about Muslims is one that many people in this country, at this point in history, are simply not yet ready to hear. I was at a Yale conference recently, and when I brought this up during my symposium, all of us in the room said simultaneously, without even planning it: "Oh yes, the subaltern CAN speak, but will anyone listen?"

66.   Muhammad Ali Hasan, Seeme Gull Hasan, "Mission Statement" from *Muslims for Bush*

July 4, 2004. Available online: http://www.muslimsforbush.com/. Reprinted with permission of Muhammad Ali Hasan.

Muslims for Bush was founded by Muhammad Ali Hasan and his mother, Seeme Gull Hasan, in Pueblo, Colorado. Prior to the presidential elections of 2004, Muslims for Bush provided information to encourage American Muslims to support President Bush in his presidential campaign for reelection. After the elections, the organization was renamed "Muslims for America." Muhammad Ali Hasan was born in the United States in 1980. He received his bachelor's degree from Occidental College in Los Angeles, California. At the time of writing (2006), he is pursuing his Masters in Film Directing at Chapman University. Seeme Gull Hasan was born in Pakistan and became a U.S. citizen in 1979 and is an active member of the Republican Party and fundraiser for the party in Colorado. Although this movement does not reflect a majority political position among American Muslims, it is important to mention as a sign of the diversity of their political perspectives.

On behalf of everyone at Muslims For Bush, I, Muhammad Ali Hasan, would personally like to welcome you to our website and thank you for taking the interest to check us out. In reading the points we have listed within our mission webpage, we feel that it will become easy for every American, Muslim or not, to realize that we are all concerned about the same issues. While the Patriot Act, War on Terror, and the Liberations of Iraq & Afghanistan heavily affect Muslims, they have equal impact among all Americans, as well.

In making this page, we hope to bring about greater attention to these issues. While we are saddened that wars and conflict are occurring, we are extremely supportive of the steps that President Bush is taking to not only make this world better for Muslims, but more importantly, better and more peaceful for everyone, regardless of religion, culture, gender, and race

As American Muslims, many of us know what it is like to be racially profiled, questioned by the FBI, or asked off of an airplane. As a matter of fact, I, Muhammad Ali Hasan, was asked off of a United Airlines flight in April of 2002, and more recently, detained and surrounded by four LAPD officers for around one hour in the American Airlines terminal of Los Angeles International Airport. It should be noted that in each case, I was treated with respect by all officers and FBI agents, and despite delay, was eventually allowed to board my airplane. Despite my frustrations over such searches that I often found to be unnecessary, I, along with many other American Muslims, still felt that President Bush is leading our country, and the world, to the right direction of peace.

Yes, the risks and consequences have sometimes been devastating. However, should President Bush's vision of the world become a reality, for the first time in centuries, we would live in a world of complete peacefulness! Palestinians and Israelis would both be free of conflict. Baghdad, and the rest of Iraq, would once again be a capital of commerce and intellect. Afghani cities like Kabul and Kandahar would boast flourishing populations of educated women! The effects that take place in Palestine, Iraq, and Afghanistan, would certainly spill over to the rest of the world, creating a shockwave of open economies, free markets, more educational opportunities, governments of democracy, and thus, more freedom!

We here at Muslims For Bush, greatly admire anyone whose visions and aspirations for the world are one of peace, education, and prosperity for all!

In starting Muslims For Bush, we hope to amass a large membership, enabling us to hopefully influence policies within Washington. The War on Terror could most certainly use further input, as well as domestic policies dealing with security. In reading our main points upon this page though, we are confident that all readers will see that President Bush is a man who listens and takes serious problems into strong consideration, for the purposes of brainstorming solutions.

We are deeply concerned about the history of Senator Kerry and the plans that he has for Muslims, both of the world and America. Yet, these are not problems that only concern Muslims—Senator Kerry's policies will impact everyone, which is why we hope you read our mission points, to see the difference that Senator Kerry could possibly have upon all of us!

Most importantly though, Muslims For Bush is not just about getting President Bush re-elected. This is about getting Americans, and Muslims, more involved and excited about the American political process!

We live in times of trying to liberate countries, help others, and having to take strong approaches towards completing these goals. As Americans, we have a proud history of accomplishing similar tasks in Japan and Germany, as well as within our own country, right after our Civil War. It should be noted though that, as of today, America has never been as large, diverse, prosperous, and educated as it is right now! And we are only getting better!

Not only have our best days arrived, our better ones will always be within the future! Never should we underestimate the things we can do to help this world, as Americans. We here at Muslims For Bush certainly do not underestimate it. As proud Muslims and Americans, we embrace President Bush's vision! And like true Americans, we are only inclusive! We invite all Americans, regardless of religion or belief, to help us in re-electing President Bush, share his vision with the rest of the world, and do our best to bring about world peace.

And we can do this, not just because some of us are Muslim, but more so, because we are Americans!

May Allah Bless this world and America!

Muhammad Ali Hasan
Co-Founder & President of Muslims For Bush
Seeme Gull Hasan
Co-Founder

67. The American Muslim Taskforce on Civil Rights and Elections—Political Action Committee (AMT-PAC), "Muslim Coalition Offers Qualified Kerry Endorsement" from *The Council on American-Islamic Relations*

October 21, 2004. Available online: www.cair.com/default.asp?Page=articleView& id=1275&theType=NR. Reprinted with the permission of The Council on American-Islamic Relations. The American Muslim Taskforce on Civil Rights and Elections—Political Action Committee (AMT-PAC) is a political action committee that represents the following different American Muslim organizations: American Muslim Alliance (AMA), Council on American-Islamic Relations (CAIR), Islamic Circle of North America (ICNA), Islamic Society of North America (ISNA), Muslim Alliance in North America (MANA), Muslim American Society (MAS), Muslim Ummah of North America (MUNA), Muslim Student Association-National (MSA-N), Project Islamic Hope (PIH), and United Muslims of America (UMA). AMT-PAC produces "Election Plans" for each national election in attempts to organize American Muslims' electoral impact. In the following statement, AMT-PAC encourages American Muslims to vote for Senator John Kerry in the 2004 presidential election as a protest of the Bush Administration.

October 21, 2004

WASHINGTON, D.C.—Following careful consideration of overall U.S. interests, interaction with presidential campaign officials and extensive input from the Islamic community, the American Muslim Taskforce on Civil Rights and Elections–Political Action Committee (AMT-PAC) is calling on Muslims nationwide to cast a protest vote for Sen. John Kerry. AMT-PAC is an affiliated political action committee of the American Muslim Taskforce on Civil Rights and Elections (AMT). AMT is an umbrella organization representing American Muslim Alliance (AMA), Council on American-Islamic Relations (CAIR), Islamic Circle of North America (ICNA), Islamic Society of North America (ISNA), Muslim Alliance in North America (MANA), Muslim American Society (MAS), Muslim Ummah of North America (MUNA), Muslim Student Association-National (MSA-N), Project Islamic Hope (PIH), and United Muslims of America (UMA). SEE:

http://www.americanmuslimvoter.net/ Muslims are a potential swing-voting bloc in key battleground states such as Florida, Michigan, Ohio, Pennsylvania, and Wisconsin. There are an estimated seven million Muslims in the United States. In its statement, AMT-PAC said: "We believe that our vote is the best guarantee of our civil rights and the best expression of our citizenship. Unfortunately, the Bush administration has been insensitive to the civil liberties and human rights of American Muslims, Arab-Americans and South Asians. Today, American Muslims are being treated like second-class citizens. American Muslims are also disappointed with a number of domestic and foreign policies instituted by the Bush administration since the 9/11 terror attacks. AMT-PAC appreciates the outstanding role of Ralph Nader in highlighting the denial of civil liberties to religious and ethnic minorities. We acknowledge the considerable outreach to our community by Sen. Kerry's campaign, particularly by his campaign co-chair Sen. Edward Kennedy. We also appreciate the ongoing dialogue with Muslim leaders about problems posed by the USA PATRIOT Act. While the Kerry campaign has critiqued a number of Bush administration polices, it has so far failed to explicitly affirm support for due process, equal justice and other constitutional norms. We are also disappointed that his campaign has shied away from expressing unambiguous support for principles enshrined in the U.S. Constitution that prohibit use of ex post facto laws, secret proceedings and secret evidence. Because pluralism is based on partial agreements, support for Sen. Kerry is premised on our overall effort to help restore liberty and justice for all. Mindful of disagreements with Sen. Kerry on some domestic and international issues, including the war in Iraq, we are willing to work with him to help restore due process and equal justice in accordance with the U.S. Constitution. AMT-PAC therefore urges American Muslim voters and their allies in the struggle for civil rights to focus on the real issues: civil liberties, human rights, international peace and justice, jobs, education, health care, economic development of inner cities, and sound foreign policy. It is vital for the protection of our liberties to vote together, in high numbers, and for a common purpose."

68. Zahid Bukhari, Sulayman Nyang, and John Zogby, "American Muslim Poll 2004: Shifting Political Winds & Fallout from 9/11, Afghanistan, and Iraq" from *Project MAPS*

Published October 19, 2004. Available online: http://www.projectmaps.com/AMP2004 report.pdf. Reprinted with permission of Project MAPS. Copyright 2006 by Zogby International.

Project MAPS is based at the Center for Muslim-Christian Understanding at Georgetown University. Project MAPS conducts research on Muslim participation and contribution to American public life. It has produced two major reports and surveys of American Muslims (2001 and 2004) that provide the most comprehensive picture of American Muslim demographics, religious practices, social and political opinions, and media relations that is currently available. The second survey is presented below. It highlights the majority of American Muslims' upper class status, their attachments to fundamental American values, and their interest in politics. The polling was conducted by Zogby International, a polling agency with offices in Washington, DC, and Utica, New York.

I. Introduction:

Project MAPS: Muslims in American Public Square is presenting the results of the second American Muslims Poll. The first poll was conducted through the Zogby International in the months of November and December 2001. The 2004 Poll covers the following areas:

1) Demographics: gender, generation and ethnicity, U.S. born and immigrants, income and education levels, age and occupation.

2) Religious practices: relationship with the mosque, ethnic composition of congregations, conversion to Islam, importance of religion in their life and interaction between the mosque and politics.

3) Opinion and behavior on social and political issues: party affiliation, voting in the presidential election, impact of the American Muslim Taskforce, foreign policy and other domestic issues relating to religion and public life.

4) Fallout from 9/11, Afghanistan and Iraq: reaction, backlash, racial profiling, war against terrorism, and wars in Afghanistan and Iraq.

5) Media and financial habits: sources of news, exposure to ethnic media, portrayal of Muslims and Islam in the mainstream media as well as in Hollywood, stocks ownership and being in the investor club.

The project commissioned Zogby International to conduct the Poll through phone interviews of a nationwide representative sample of the American Muslim population during the months of August and September 2004. The questionnaire was developed with by the Project MAPS team and staff of Zogby International. Several questions of 2001 poll are repeated in 2004 to have a comparative picture of the American Muslim community. Project MAPS seeks to document the role and contribution of the Muslim community in the American public life. It is a research project that began in 1999 with the support of The Pew Charitable Trusts. The Pew Charitable Trusts are supporting the MAPS project as part of a larger examination of seven major religious groups in the United States and their place in public life. The Project is housed at Georgetown University's Center for Muslim-Christian Understanding (CMCU).

The project website, www.projectmaps.com, has all information of the activities and development of the project.

II. Methodology and Sample Characteristics:

Zogby International conducted interviews of 1,846 persons, 18 years and older, nationwide who identify themselves as Muslim. From Thursday, August 5 to Wednesday, September 15, 2004, phone interviews were conducted. All calls were made from Zogby International headquarters in Utica, N.Y. The telephone list was created by matching the zip codes of 300 randomly selected Islamic centers, against their respective local telephone exchanges. Listings of common Muslim surnames were then identified from the local telephone exchanges and called.

An additional sample of Afro-American Muslims was interviewed in-person September 1-15, 2004, at locations in New York, Washington, D.C., Atlanta, GA, and Detroit, MI. The additional surveys were required to account for Afro- American Muslims with Anglo-American or non-Muslim surnames who were not called on in the telephone survey. A slight weight was added to ethnicity to more accurately reflect the Muslim population.

The margin of error is +/– 2.3 percentage points. Margins of error are higher in sub-groups.

II. Executive Summary:

American Muslims are at a political and social crossroads at the end of 2004. In a few short years, they have undergone massive political shifts, and have become a relevant part of the political landscape. If one looks at American Muslims ca. 2000, and then ca. 2004, without an understanding of the events that have occurred in that four-year span, such a sea change has occurred for this group that any political observer would be stunned.

We recommend considering all results of this report in conjunction with the results of the Project MAPS/Zogby study conducted in 2001, immediately following the September 11 attacks.

Sample Characteristics

Sample Characteristics	Frequency	Valid Percent*
Sample size	1846	100
Region		
East	672	36
South	423	23
Central/Great Lakes	482	26
West	269	15
Registered to vote		
Registered to vote	1521	82
Not registered to vote	320	17
Not sure if registered	5	0
Likely to vote		
Very likely to vote	1338	88
Somewhat likely to vote	107	7
Not likely to vote	55	4
Not sure of voting likelihood	20	1
Party ID		
Democrat	721	50
Republican	171	12
Independent/Minor party	445	31
Libertarian	12	1
Not sure of party	97	7
Ideology		
Progressive/very liberal	204	11
Liberal	340	19
Moderate	729	40
Conservative	287	16
Very conservative	37	2
Libertarian	37	2
Not sure of ideology	192	11
Did not answer ideology	21	—

Country of Birth		
Born in U.S.	665	36
Not born in U.S.	1177	64
Not sure if born in U.S.	4	0
Ethnicity		
South Asian	619	34
Pakistani	(347)	(19)
Indian	(159)	(9)
Bangladeshi	(76)	(4)
Afghan	(37)	(2)
Arab	485	26
African American	371	20
African	137	7
Other ethnicity	216	12
Not sure of ethnicity	18	1
Age I		
18–29	382	21
30–49	759	42
50–64	496	28
65+	153	9
Age II		
18–24	225	13
25–34	305	17
35–54	821	46
55–69	364	20
70+	76	4
Did not answer age	56	—
Education		
Less than high school	89	5
High school graduate	236	13
Some college	424	23
College graduate+	1081	59
Did not answer education	16	—
Occupation		
Managerial	184	10
Medical	165	9
Professional/Technical	419	23
Sales	90	5
Clerical	30	2
Service	74	4

Blue-Collar/Production	53	3
Student	155	8
Homemaker	187	10
Teacher/education	158	9
Retired	115	6
Other occupation	191	10
Not sure of occupation	13	1
Did not answer occupation	12	—
Marital Status		
Married	1283	70
Single, never married	337	18
Divorced/widowed/separated	205	11
Civil union/domestic partnership	5	0
Spouse Religion		
Spouse is Muslim	1137	89
Spouse not Muslim	132	10
Not sure if spouse is Muslim	—	—
# of Person in Household		
1 in household	179	10
2 in household	336	19
3 in household	301	17
4 in household	392	22
5 in household	328	18
6 in household	150	8
7+ in household	133	7
Did not answer household	27	—
1 adult	226	12
2 adults	912	50
3 adults	331	18
4 adults	191	11
5 adults	82	5
6+ adults	38	2
Not sure of adults	34	2
Did not answer adults	32	—
1 child	303	17
2 children	338	19
3 children	233	13
4 children	73	4
5 children	34	2
6+ children	19	1

Not sure of children	32	2
Did not answer children	50	—
Stocks/Investor Class		
Own stock personally	505	21
Own stock through 401 (k)	505	21
Other pension plan	327	14
No stocks	999	41
Not sure of stocks	81	3
Did not answer stocks	—	—
Stocks in Islamic financial institutions	73	4
No stocks in Islamic financial institutions	1710	94
Not sure of stocks in Islamic financial institutions	44	2
Did not answer stocks in Islamic financial institutions	19	—
Investor class	394	22
Not investor class	1356	74
Not sure if investor class	76	4
Did not answer investor class	20	—
Income		
Less than $15,000	172	11
$15,000–$24,999	147	9
$25,000–$34,999	160	10
$35,000–$49,999	276	17
$50,000–$74,999	308	19
$75,000 or more	529	33
Did not answer income	255	—
Gender		
Male	1074	58
Female	772	42

*   Numbers have been rounded to the nearest percent and might not equal 100.

Muslims are a politically active group. A high proportion of registered Muslim voters (95%) plan to vote in national elections, and of that group, 88% are very likely to vote. In light of that, political horserace questions are particularly interesting, especially when one views the dramatic shift away from the Republican Party and President Bush versus the 2000 election.

Comparison with the 2001 Project MAPS/Zogby poll shows a massive migration away from the Republican Party by Muslim voters. It also shows a huge movement away from President Bush's re-election effort, favoring Senator Kerry over President Bush by a lopsided 76% to 7% margin. The overwhelming support for the Kerry/Edwards team and the near lack of support for the Bush/Cheney team is mirrored across all demographic strata. Even among Republicans, Kerry/Edwards lead by a near two-to-one margin, 50% to 28%.

In the post-9/11 world, Muslim identity is key in voting decisions. Nearly sevenin- ten Muslim voters say being a Muslim is important in their voting decision. Yet Muslims are not yet fully engaged, politically. By a three-to-one margin, Muslims are not active member of their political party. In a troubling sign for Republicans, however, this is less pronounced among Democrats, where the margin drops to two-to-one. Additionally, Muslims are more likely to have volunteered time for a political candidate than to be active party members.

And Muslims clearly intend to be a part of the political system long-term: 86% of Muslims say it is important for them to participate in politics. By similar numbers, Muslims say it is important to them for their children to participate in politics. Nearly two-thirds of Muslims say they follow what's going on in government and public affairs most of the time.

Add to this desire to be a part of the political system the fact that three-in-five American Muslims are dissatisfied with the way things are going in American society today, and Muslims become a clearly-potent political entity. And, despite their negative view of the direction of the country, a majority of American Muslims say this is a good time to be a Muslim in America.

Muslims also have a strong desire for political unity within their religion. Eight-in-ten American Muslims agree with following the agenda of the American Muslim Taskforce on Civil Rights and Elections (AMT), a US-wide coalition of the ten largest Muslim organizations. A majority of American Muslims say that American Muslims should vote as a bloc for president this year. Seven-in-ten American Muslims say the endorsement of a presidential candidate by the AMT would be important. Muslims overwhelmingly back changing U.S. policy in the Mideast as the best way to way wage the war on terror. Muslims would prefer the government backed a Palestinian state and was less supportive of Israel.

The survey also finds mixed news on American Muslims' relations with other Americans. Slightly more than a third of Muslims say that in their own experience, Americans have been respectful of Muslims, but that American society overall is disrespectful and intolerant of their culture. Another third take the unqualified position that Americans have been tolerant and respectful of Muslims. A majority of Muslims say a friend or family member has suffered discrimination since the September 11 attacks. The 2004 Project MAPS/Zogby shows a group gaining political self-identity and flexing political muscles, and stands in stark contrast with some of the results in the 2001 survey.

III. Narrative Analysis:

2. Are you registered to vote in the United States?

Yes	82%
No	17
Not sure	—

990. Why are you not registered to vote?

Not a citizen	59%
Not interested/never thought about it/never got around to it	13
Too difficult to register	3

My vote doesn't make a difference	1
Considers it un-Islamic	2
*Other	17
Not sure	6

* **Other:** (Number in parentheses denotes frequency of similar response.) Eligibility (16); disillusioned with politics (6); too busy (5); in process of registering (1).

3. Do you intend to register to vote?

Yes	72%
No	21
Not sure	8

Nearly three-quarters (72%) of American Muslims who are not currently registered to vote say they plan to do so, while one-in-five (21%) does not.

A high proportion of South Asians are both not registered to vote and intend to become registered.

(Asked only of registered voters)

4. How likely are you to vote in national elections?

Very likely	88%
Somewhat likely	7
Not likely	4
Not sure	1

A high proportion of registered voters (95%) plan to vote in national elections, and of that group, 88% are very likely to vote

The likelihood of voting is uniform across all party identifiers, and varies no more than 5% along ideological lines.

991. Why are you not likely to vote in national elections?

Never enough time	5%
Generally not interested	20
Usually don't like the choice of candidates	20
My vote doesn't make a difference	7
Other	29
Not sure	19

* **Other:** (Number in parentheses denotes frequency of similar response.) Too busy (4); in disillusioned with politics (2); health reasons (2); deciding (1).

5. In the 2000 presidential election, the candidates were Democrat Al Gore, Republican George W. Bush, Reform Party's Pat Buchanan, and the Green Party's Ralph Nader. For whom did you vote?

Gore	38%
Bush	27
Buchanan	—
Nader	11
Someone else	1
Did not vote	18
Not sure	5

Note: While these numbers are useful for identifying that a drift has occurred among voters, Zogby International recommends using the results of the 2001 Project MAPS/ Zogby poll to determine more accurate representation of 2000 candidate support.

6. In which party are you either registered to vote or do you consider yourself to be a member of—Democrat, Republican, Independent/minor party, or Libertarian?

Democrat	50%
Republican	12
Independent/minor party	31
Libertarian	.9
Not sure	7

Comparison with the 2001 Project MAPS/Zogby poll shows a migration away from the Republican Party by Muslim voters. In 2001, 23% of Muslims identified themselves as Republicans while 40% called themselves Democrats and 28% independents. Now, only 12% call themselves Republicans while 50% of Muslims are Democrats and 31% are independents.

7. If the election for president and vice president were held today and the candidates were Republicans George W. Bush and Dick Cheney, and Democrats John Kerry and John Edwards, for whom would you vote?

Bush/Cheney	7%
Kerry/Edwards	76
Someone else	5
Not sure	12

The overwhelming support for Kerry/Edwards and the near lack of support for Bush/ Cheney is mirrored across all demographic strata. Even among Republicans, Kerry/ Edwards lead by a near two-to-one margin, 50% to 28%. Support for Bush/Cheney is strongest among very conservative Muslims, at 27% versus 52% for Kerry/Edwards, and drops as voters move to the left politically. Among moderates, Bush/Cheney only garner 5% of the vote versus 77% for Kerry/Edwards, and among liberals and progressives, they net 4% of the vote versus 83% for Kerry/Edwards.

Support for Kerry/Edwards is stronger among African-Americans, at 82% versus 5% for Bush/Cheney.

Kerry/Edwards also performs very well among converts to Islam, where all converts support them at a rate ranging from 80% to 87%. Bush/Cheney never get above 9% with this group, and only break 10% among Muslim immigrants who came to the United States in the 1990s.

8. If the election for president were held today and the candidates were Republican George W. Bush, Democrat John Kerry, Independent Ralph Nader, Libertarian Michael Badnarik, and Constitution Party's Michael Peroutka, for whom would you vote?

Bush	7%
Kerry	68
Nader	11
Badnarik	—
Peroutka	—
Someone else	1
Not sure	12

The addition of independent Ralph Nader saps away a substantial part of Muslim support for Mr. Kerry. While Mr. Kerry manages 76% support in a hypothetical two-way match-up, he only receives 68% support when Mr. Nader is added. Mr. Bush maintains his 7% support.

Mr. Bush fares no better among conservative voters in this scenario, but Mr. Kerry's support fades among liberals and progressives. Mr. Kerry drops 10% from the previous question among independents, 7% among Democrats, and 6% among Republicans, when voters are given other choices.

9. Why are you voting for Bush?
*Question was open-ended: (Number in parentheses denotes frequency of similar response.)
Agree with his policies/views/agenda (32);
Like him as a man (14);
Best choice/leadership qualities (14);
Always votes Republican (9); Bush should finish what he started (9); dislikes Kerry (5); truthful (3); lesser of two evils (2).

10. Why are you voting for Kerry?
*Question was open-ended: (Number in parentheses denotes frequency of similar response.)
Opposed to George Bush, his policies/agenda/views/decisions (296);
Support Kerry, his policies/agenda/views/decisions (249);
Always votes Democratic (92); better choice (70); time for a change (66); War in Iraq (44); disappointed with Bush (43); return fairness/legitimacy to government (24); commitment to civil liberties/civil rights (20); lesser of two evils (18).

11. Why are you voting for Nader?
*Question was open-ended: (Number in parentheses denotes frequency of similar response.)
Agrees with his policies/agenda/views (3); dislikes other candidates (3); his commitment to the Constitution (1).

12. Why are you voting for that candidate (Badnarik or Peroutka)?
*Question was open-ended: (Number in parentheses denotes frequency of similar response.)
Supports his policies/agenda/views (72);
Opposed to Democrats/Republicans/Need third party (39);
Trust (12); best choice (9); time for a change (8); ethnicity (7); commitment to civil liberties (7); Israeli/Palestinian conflict (6); return fairness/legitimacy to government (4).

13. How important is being Muslim in your decision for whom to vote?

Very important	51%
Somewhat important	18
Not important	29
Not sure	2

Nearly seven-in-ten Muslim voters say being a Muslim is important in their voting decision. This sentiment is higher among Democrats, at 72%, and independents, at 69%, than it is among Republicans, who say it is important at a rate of 57%.

African-Americans are the racial demographic most likely to say being a Muslim is important in their voting decision, at a rate of 83%.

The higher a Muslim's education level, the less importance they place on being a Muslim when they vote.

Among the various occupations, homemakers and people in service professions are more likely to rate being a Muslim as very important in their voting decision, while

Other groups are generally uniform on this question.

14. Which of the following is the most important factor when deciding your vote?

Domestic policy	44%
Foreign policy	34
Other	14
None/Not sure	8

All geographic areas are similar to the overall numbers except for the Western U.S., where foreign policy bests domestic policy as the most important factor for Muslim voters by a 42% to 36% margin.

Republicans are more likely than Democrats (40% versus 34%) to select foreign policy as the most important factor when they vote, although both groups select domestic policy with equal frequency (44% versus 44%). This does not reflect along ideological lines, however, where all groups are within the margin of error.

African-Americans are much more likely than other racial groups to select domestic policy (63% versus a range of 35% to 44%). They are also less likely than other races to select foreign policy (19% versus a range of 34% to 39%).

Single Muslims are more likely than married Muslims to select foreign policy (42% versus 34%), though the two groups are equally likely to select domestic policy (41% versus 43%).

Women are only slightly more likely than men (46% versus 42%) to select domestic policy, and slightly less likely than men (42% versus 35%) to select foreign policy.

Domestic policy resonates more heavily with immigrants who arrived during the 1980s (45%) and less-so the longer an immigrant has been in-country. Conversely, foreign policy resonates more heavily with those immigrants who arrived before 1970, and generally is of less concern to more-recent immigrants, although those who have immigrated since 1990 defy both trends, and split fairly evenly on the choice (35% say domestic policy and 39% say foreign policy).

906. Which description best represents your political ideology?

Moderate	40%
Liberal	19
Conservative	16
Progressive/very liberal	11
Very conservative	2
Libertarian	2
Not sure	11

The greatest strength for conservatives is seen in the West, where 20% of Muslims apply that label to themselves. A slightly higher percentage of residents of the South and Great Lakes region call themselves moderates (42% for both) than do residents of the East and West (37% and 39%).

The oldest respondents, those aged 65+, are the most likely to call themselves liberals or progressives (31%), while they are also slightly more likely than other groups to call themselves conservative or very conservative (20%).

As education level increases, so does the percentage of respondents calling themselves moderate, from 22% of those with less than a high school diploma to 44% of those who have graduated from college.

Ideology does not vary much by gender, nor is there a large amount of variation based on year of immigration or conversion.

Teachers and educators are more likely than other groups to call themselves liberal or progressive (36%) while managers and students are more likely to call themselves conservative or very conservative (23% of managers and 22% of students).

15–20. Questions pertaining to political activity

Table 1.   **Political Activities by American Muslims**

	Yes	No	Not sure
Called or written the media or politician on a given issue, or have you signed a petition	54	45	1
Attended a rally in support of a politician or a cause	46	54	—
Visited a political website	41	59	1
Participated in a boycott of a product or a business	36	63	1
Given a contribution or volunteered your time or services to a political candidate	35	64	1
Consider yourself to be an active member in your political party	24	73	3

By a three-to-one margin (73% versus 24%), Muslims do not consider themselves an active member of their political party. This is less pronounced among Democrats, where the margin drops to two-to-one (65% versus 33%). Republicans mirror the overall trend, while among self-described independents, the margin is 80% to 17%. Africans and African-Americans are more active in their parties (37% and 31%) while South Asians are less active (18%) than other races. Members of the investor class are more likely than non-investors to be involved in their party (30% versus 23%). Retirees and members of the medical profession are more likely to be involved as well.

Muslims are more likely to have volunteered time for a political candidate than to be active party members. More than one-in-three Muslims (35% say they have volunteered time for a political candidate, while nearly two-thirds (64%) have not. Those living in the West are more likely to volunteer time for a candidate (42% versus a range of 32% to 38% elsewhere). Half of Republicans (52%) say they have volunteered time for a candidate, while two-fifths (41%) of Democrats say they have. More than one-in-three independents (36%) say they have volunteered time for a candidate as well. The likelihood of volunteering for a candidate increases with both age and education, as well as time in-country for immigrants. More than half of those in the investor class (53%) say they have volunteered politically. Retirees, teachers and professional/technical workers are more likely (47%, 44% and 43%) to volunteer time for a candidate, while people in the service industry and homemakers are less likely (12% and 20%).

Two-in-five Muslims (41%) say they have visited a political website, while the remaining three-fifths (59%) say they have not. Those living in the West are more likely to have done so (47%) while those living in the East are less likely (35%). Progressives are more likely (57%) than conservative and very conservative Muslims (39% and 36%) to say they have done so. The youngest Muslims (18-29 year-olds) are more likely to view political websites (53%) while the eldest Muslims (age 65+) are less likely (29%). Men are more likely than women to view political websites (44% versus 37%). Half (51%) of professional/technical workers say they have visited political websites, while 80% of retirees and 77% of blue-collar workers say they have not. The response to this question is even across party lines.

A majority of Muslims (54%) have written the media or a politician on a given issue. This is true among all political parties and ideologies. Those in the West are more likely (60%) while those in the South are less likely (51%). African-Americans are more likely than other races, with 73% saying they have written such a letter, while Africans are less likely, with 31% saying the same. Members of the investor class are more likely than non-investors (67% versus 50%) to have written the media or a politician.

21–22. How important is it for you...for your children...to participate in politics?

Table 2. **Muslims Seek a Seat at the Political Table**

	Very important	Somewhat important	Not important	Not sure
For you	53	33	13	1
For your children	58	24	10	7

Eighty-six percent of Muslims say it is important for them to participate in politics. This is nearly seven times as many as who say it is not important. This holds across all geographic regions.

Men are more likely than women to rate this very important (57% versus 48%) though both groups rate it as important in roughly equal percentages.

Democrats are more intense on this issue, with 59% saying that it is very important, while 49% of Republicans said the same. A higher number of Republicans are lukewarm on this issue, with 40% saying it is somewhat important, versus 29% of Democrats who say the same. On ideological grounds, progressive are far more likely than other groups to say it is very important (72% versus a range of 51% to 59%).

Africans are more likely to say this is very important (63%) and South Asians are less likely (49%). As both education and age increase, respondents are more likely to say this is very important.

By similar numbers, Muslims say it is important to them for their children to participate in politics. This is important for 82% of Muslims, and not important for one-in-ten (10%).

Muslims in the Eastern U.S. are the least intense on this question, with 55% saying it is very important, while all other regions are at 59% to 60%.

A smaller gender gap exists on this question than the previous one, with 56% of women and 60% of men rating this very important. A marriage gap is present, however, as 85% of married Muslims call it important, versus 75% of single Muslims.

Republicans are a bit more likely than Democrats to say it is important for their children to participate in politics: 87% of Republicans say it is important, versus 83% of

Democrats. This is reflected on ideological lines, where those who call themselves very conservative are as likely as progressives (70% and 69%, respectively) to say it is very important.

As in the previous question, the number calling this very important increases with both age and education.

23. How often do you discuss politics with family and friends?

Always	42%
Sometimes	48
Hardly ever	8
Never	3
Not sure	—

Few demographic areas differ substantially with the overall numbers in this question.

The more extreme the ideological viewpoint of a Muslim, the more likely they are to discuss politics with family and friends—those who call themselves very conservative or progressive are much more likely than moderates, liberals and conservatives to say they always discuss politics.

Teachers and professionals are more likely to always discuss politics with family and friends (55% and 51%, respectively) while students and homemakers are more likely to only do so sometimes (63% and 59%, respectively).

24. How often would you say you follow what's going on in government and public affairs?

Most of the time	64%
Some of the time	26
Only now and then	7
Hardly at all	3
Not sure	1

Nearly two-thirds (64%) of Muslims say they follow what's going on in government and public affairs most of the time. This varies little on geographic or partisan lines, though those who call themselves progressive are more likely than other groups (81% versus a range of 59% to 67%) to say they do so most of the time.

Men are more likely than women to say they follow government and public affairs most of the time (67% versus 59%), though a higher percentage of women than men are likely to say they follow this some of the time.

African Americans are more likely (71%) and Africans are less likely (45%) to say they follow what's going on most of the time.

As their age and education increase, more Muslims say they follow government and public affairs. The same is generally true of income and the amount of time an immigrant has been in the United States.

Teachers, professionals/technical workers, and managerial workers are more likely than other groups of workers to say they follow government's happenings most of the time (71%, 70%, and 73%, respectively).

American Muslim Taskforce:

The American Muslim Taskforce on Civil Rights and Elections (AMT) is a US-wide coalition of the ten largest Muslim organizations. The AMT has identified "A Civil Rights Plus Agenda" pertaining to the Presidential Election. This agenda consists of Civil and human rights for all,

Domestic issues of public good and general welfare, Global peace with justice, prevention of war, and US relations with the Muslim world.

881. How strongly do you agree in following this agenda during the presidential elections?

Strongly agree	57%		
Somewhat agree	24	Agree	81%
Somewhat disagree	3		
Strongly disagree	3	Disagree	6
Not sure	14		

Eight-in-ten (81%) American Muslims agree with following the agenda of the American Muslim Taskforce, while only 6% disagree. Of those in agreement, a solid majority of respondents strongly agree with following the AMT's agenda.

The support for the AMT agenda fluctuates somewhat by geographic region. Muslims in the South and West are more likely to strongly agree (61% and 60%, respectively) than those in the East and Central/Great Lakes (54% each).

Democrats are more likely than Republicans to support the agenda of the AMT—85% of Democrats support it, versus 76% of Republicans. Democrats are also more intense in their support, with 62% saying they strongly support the AMT's agenda, versus 53% of Republicans.

Support for the AMT agenda does not clearly follow ideological lines, though a majority of all ideological persuasions say they support it. Progressives are the most likely to strongly agree, with 70% saying they do.

882. Do you agree or disagree that US Muslims should vote in a bloc for one of the presidential candidates in 2004?

Agree	53%
Disagree	36
Not sure	11

A majority (53%) of American Muslims say that American Muslims should vote as a bloc for president this year. Slightly more than one-in-three (36%) disagree. Support for this idea is strongest in the South and East, where 54% and 55%, respectively, agree.

While Democrats back voting as a bloc by a margin of 55% to 36%, Republicans are much more divided, with 47% agreeing that Muslims should vote as a bloc, and 43% disagreeing—just outside the poll's margin of error. Independents agree by margins similar to the Democrats. Ideologically, however, progressive, liberal, conservative and very conservative Muslims all agree with voting as a bloc, with a range of 56% to 58% saying they agree.

Men are a bit more likely than women to agree with voting as a bloc, by a 56% to 50% margin. A majority of all ethnicities, however, say they agree.

Support for group voting also is stronger among the youngest American Muslims (56% of 18–29 year-olds say they agree with voting as a bloc) but declines steadily, receiving the support of 46% of those aged 65+. Likewise, American Muslim immigrants who have been in the country longer are less likely to agree than those whose arrival is more recent.

A majority of most professions say they agree with voting in a bloc, however, home-makers and those in sales are less likely (41% and 48%, respectively) than others to say they agree.

883. If the American Muslim Taskforce (AMT) endorses one of the Presidential candidates, how important would it be in your decision for whom to vote?

Very important	40%
Somewhat important	29
Not important	26
Not sure	5

For seven-in-ten (69%) American Muslims, the endorsement of a candidate by the AMT would be important. For a quarter of American Muslims (26%), this would not be important.

Muslims in the South are more likely than elsewhere to say this is important (73%) while Muslims in the East are less likely (67%). Men and women call an AMT endorsement important in similar numbers.

African-Americans are more likely (49%) than other ethnic groups to call an AMT endorsement very important, while South Asians are less likely (39%). South Asians are also more likely to call it not important (27%).

Recent immigrants and those who converted the longest ago are more likely than others in their groups to say an AMT endorsement is very important to them.

25. What do you consider to be the most important issue facing American society today?

Jobs/economy	24%
War on Terror/Iraq	19
Constitutional issues	136
Morality	

*Question was open-ended: (Number in parentheses denotes frequency of similar response.)
Politics/government (98); racism/discrimination/bias (90); education (56); healthcare (51); drugs/crime/violence (12)

26. What do you consider to be the most important issue facing the Muslim American community today?

Constitutional issues	28%
Bias/racism	24
Becoming mainstream	11
Foreign policy	8

*Question was open-ended: (Number in parentheses denotes frequency of similar response.)
Unity (96); domestic issues (85); security/safety (60); Israeli-Palestinian conflict (29); politics/government (24); morality (17).

27–36. I am now going to read a list of community activities, please tell me if you have ever donated time, money or been an officer of any.

Table 3.   **Muslim Involvement in the Community: Time, Money, and Leadership**

	Donated time	Donated money	Served as an officer	A combination of these	None of these	Not sure
School or youth programs	22	9	1	31	35	1
Any arts or cultural organization	10	17	1	14	57	1

Any neighborhood, civic or community group	22	6	1	18	53	1
Any organization to help the poor, sick, elderly or homeless	13	30	1	31	24	1
Any professional organization	12	11	2	21	53	2
Any mosque or other religious organizations	11	18	1	41	28	1
Any trade or labor unions	4	5	—	8	83	1
Any veteran's or military service organizations	4	13	1	7	75	1
Any ethnic organizations	8	8	—	19	64	1
Any Muslim political action or public affairs organization	7	8	—	14	69	1

A majority (63%) of American Muslims are active in school or youth programs.

Of these, 22% say they have donated time, 9% say they have donated money, 1% say they have served as an officer, and three-in-ten (31%) say they have performed a combination. A third (35%) say they have done none of these things. Women are more likely than men (24% to 21%) to donate time, but men are more likely to donate money (10% to 8%). Recent converts (1990-present) are more likely to donate time (36% versus a range of 16% to 22%), while those who converted the longest ago (pre-1970) are more likely to donate money (14% versus a range of 2% to 6%).

Muslim Americans are more likely to donate money than time to arts or cultural organizations (17% versus 10%). Those in the West are more likely to donate money (21%) while those in the South are less likely to donate money (15%). Democrats are more likely to donate money than time (19% versus 10%) while Republicans pick money over time by a smaller 15% to 12% margin. African-Americans are more likely to donate money (22%) and time (11%) while Africans are less likely to donate money (10%) and Arabs and Africans are less likely to donate time (8% each). Homemakers are less likely to donate time (5%) while students are less likely to donate money (9%).

More Muslims (53%) say they have not donated money or time, or served as an officer, of a community or civil group than say they have. One-in-five (22%) have donated time, 6% have donated money, 1% have served as an officer, and another one-in-five (18%) say they have done a combination of those things. Men are slightly more likely than women (49% versus 43%) to involve themselves in a community or civic group. African Americans are more likely (65%) to have involved themselves in a civic or community group, while South Asians are less likely (41%).

Three-quarters (75%) of American Muslims say they have donated time or money, or served as an officer, of an organization to help the poor, sick, elderly or homeless. One-in-four (24%) say they have not. Those in the South are more likely than elsewhere to do a combination of these things (35%) or donate time (18%) while those in the East and West are more likely to donate money (33% and 32%, respectively. Those in the South are less likely to donate money (23%). Women are more likely than men to contribute to charitable organizations (79% versus 72%). African Americans are more likely to contribute (83%) while Africans are less likely (57%).

Forty-five percent of American Muslims say they have donated time or money, or served as an officer of a professional organization. This is fairly uniform across geographic regions. Those with the strongest ideological beliefs, progressive and very conservative Muslims, are more likely to contribute to a professional organization, 57% and 58%, respectively. Men are slightly more likely than women (47% versus 42%). African Americans (67%) are more likely to do so, while Africans are less likely to do so (31%).

Seven-in-ten (71%) say they have donated time or money, or served as an officer of their mosque. Those in the South and Central/Great Lakes regions are more likely (43%) to do a combination of those things; those in the West are more likely to donate money (20%). Democrats are more likely than Republicans to donate time (11% versus 7%) while Republicans are more likely than Democrats to donate money (23% versus 18%). One-in-three (32%) Republicans are likely to not be involved at all in the running of their mosque, higher than the 28% of Democrats who do not donate time, money or leadership. African Americans are more likely to be involved in one of those ways (85%) while Africans are less likely (63%).

The vast majority (83%) of Muslims have not donated time or money, or served as an officer of a labor union. Those living in the Central/Great Lakes region are a bit more likely to have done so than their contemporaries elsewhere in the country. Democrats are more likely to do so than Republicans (19% versus 13%). Progressives are more likely to do so (23%) than other ideologies. Men are more likely than women to do so (18% versus 13%). African Americans are more likely to do so (36%) and Africans are less likely to do so (6%). Those over the age of 65 are more likely to say they have done so.

A quarter (25%) say they have donated time or money, or served as an officer of a veteran's or military service organization. This climbs to 29% in the South and shrinks to 21% in the West. African Americans are more likely to do so (36%) while Africans and Arabs are less likely to do so (16% and 19%, respectively). Seniors (those over the age of 65) are more likely to do so (39%) while the youngest demographic (18-29 year-olds) are less likely to do so (15%).

More than one-in-three (35%) say they have donated time or money, or served as an officer of an ethnic organization. For those living in the West and Central/Great Lakes region, this climbs to 39%, while it drops to 31% in the East. African Americans are more likely to do so (58%) while Africans are less likely to do so (18%).

Three-in-ten (30%) say they have donated time or money, or served as an officer of a Muslim political action committee or public affairs organization. Those in the West are more likely to do so (36%) while those in the South are less likely to do so (26%).

Democrats are more likely than Republicans to do so (32% versus 28%). Progressives are the ideology most likely to do so (46%) while conservatives and liberals are less likely to do so (25% and 23%, respectively). African Americans are more likely to do so (46%) while Africans are less likely to do so (12%).

37–41. Do you strongly agree, somewhat agree, somewhat disagree, or strongly disagree with each of the following statements?

Table 4. **Muslim Values in a Secular Society**

	Agree*	Disagree*	Not sure
Muslims should donate to non-Muslim social service programs like aid for the homeless	97	2	1
Muslims should participate in the political process	95	3	2

Muslims should participate in interfaith activities	90	4	5
Muslims should financially support worthy non-Muslim political candidates	87	9	4
The influence of religion and moral values in American public life should increase	85	12	4

(* Agree and disagree each combines strongly and somewhat.)

American Muslims say with near-universality that Muslims should donate to non-Muslim service programs like aid for the homeless (97%). Those living in the West are a bit less intense in their support of this notion than elsewhere, with 80% strongly agreeing, versus a range of 84% to 86% in other regions. Democrats agree by a slightly larger percentage than Republicans. Men are slightly more intense, but women agree overall by a slightly higher percentage. Agreement also declines slightly with age.

With near-unanimity, American Muslims agree that Muslims should participate in the political process (95%). Agreement with this notion is weakest in the West, where it drops to 92%, and strong disagreement jumps to 4%—the highest of any region. Democrats and Republicans agree in similar percentages, but Democrats are more intense in their agreement. Moderates are more likely to agree than those at the ideological extremes. Men and women agree in similar percentages, but men are more intense on this than women.

Nine-in-ten (90%) American Muslims say Muslims should participate in interfaith activities. This holds across all geographic regions, but intensity is lower in the West. Democrats are a bit more likely to agree than Republicans (92% versus 87%). Intensity of agreement increases with age.

Eight-in-nine (87%) American Muslims agree Muslims should support worthy non-Muslim political candidates. Agreement is most intense in the South, where 71% of Muslims strongly agree, and least intense in the West, where 60% of Muslims strongly agree. Democrats are slightly more likely than Republicans (89% versus 86%) to agree. Men and women agree in equal numbers, but men are more intense in their agreement. Africans are more likely to disagree (14%) while Arabs are less likely to disagree (5%).

Eighty-five percent of American Muslims say that the influence of religion and spiritual values in American life should increase. As ideological viewpoint shifts to the right, support for this notion increases; 76% of progressives agree, while 91% of conservatives do as well. Among immigrants, those most-recently arrived agree in a higher percent than do those who have been here longer.

42. How satisfied are you overall with the way things are going in American society today?

Very satisfied	7%		
Somewhat satisfied	28	Satisfied	35%
Somewhat dissatisfied	31		
Very dissatisfied	32	Dissatisfied	63
Not sure	2		

Three-in-five (63%) American Muslims are dissatisfied with the way things are going in American society today. A third are satisfied with the way things are going.

These percentages hold, generally, across geographic lines, though those in the West have a more negative outlook (67% dissatisfied).

Republicans are more satisfied than Democrats, with 48% saying they are satisfied versus 32% of Democrats.

Along ideological lines, progressives are far more likely to be dissatisfied, with 77% responding that way. This contrasts with liberals, who are more likely to be satisfied, with 42% responding positively.

Women are slightly more negative than men, with 66% of women saying they are dissatisfied versus 62% of men.

African Americans are more likely to be dissatisfied (82%) while South Asians are less likely (54%).

43. Do you feel the U.S. is fighting a war on terrorism or a war against Islam?

Terrorism	33%
Islam	38
Not sure	29

A plurality of American Muslims say the U.S. is fighting a war on Islam (38%) rather than terror (33%). However, one-in-three (29%)is not sure. The end result is a fairly even split.

Geographic lines impact response. All regions reflect the overall numbers except the South, where 38% of Muslims say the U.S. is fighting a war on terror, versus 32% who say the war is on Islam. Westerners are more likely to say the U.S. is fighting a war on Islam, with 43% taking that position.

Party impacts response as well. Democrats say "war on Islam" over "war on terror" by a 41% to 31% margin. Republicans, conversely, say the U.S. is fighting a war on terror, and not on Islam, by a 47% to 31% margin. Independents say "war on Islam" by a 39% to 33% margin.

Progressives and conservatives say the U.S. is fighting a war on Islam (46% and 40%, respectively), while moderates and liberals split evenly.

Men choose "war on terror" over "war on Islam" by a 38% to 36% margin, while women say "war on Islam" over "war on terror" by a 42% to 27% margin. The oldest respondents (65+) say the U.S. is fighting a war on terror by a margin of 44% to 38%, while middle-aged respondents (30–64) see a war on Islam.

44. Is this a good time or a bad time to be Muslim in America?

Good time	51%
Bad time	36
Not sure	13

A majority (51%) of American Muslims say this is a good time to be a Muslim in America. Slightly more than a third (36%) say it is a bad time.

This holds across all geographic regions, although "good time" wins out by a plurality (47%) in the South, where a higher percentage of Muslims than elsewhere call it a bad time to be a Muslim (39%).

This opinion does not vary greatly by party, though slightly more Republicans say it is a bad time to be a Muslim than do Democrats (40% versus 37%). Independents are more positive than partisans on this issue, with 51% saying it is a good time, and 35% saying it is a bad time. As political ideology shifts left, there is a greater likelihood the respondent will say it is a bad time to be a Muslim, and among progressives more say it is a bad time than good (46% versus 41%).

Arabs are more likely than other ethnicities to say it is a bad time, with 40% selecting that option. African Americans are more likely to say it is a good time, with 57% taking that position.

46–47. . Do you strongly support, somewhat support, somewhat oppose or strongly oppose the U.S. military action against Afghanistan...the war in Iraq?

Table 5.   **Muslims on Post-9/11 U.S. Military Action**

	Support*	Oppose*	Not sure
U.S. military action against Afghanistan	35	5381	11
War in Iraq	13		6

(* Support and oppose each combines strongly and somewhat.)

Muslim Americans are more likely to support the war in Afghanistan than the war in Iraq, with 35% supporting the former and 13% supporting the latter. In both cases, opposition outweighs support.

On Afghanistan, support is fairly uniform across geographic regions. Opposition is heaviest in the West, where 57% oppose the military actions against the Taliban.

In all categories, Muslims have strong convictions—more Muslims strongly oppose the war in Afghanistan than somewhat oppose it, and more Muslims strongly support the war than somewhat support it. Men are much more likely to support the war than women, 43% versus 24%, while women are more likely to oppose the war than men, 60% versus 48%. African Americans are more likely than other ethnic groups to oppose the war (71%) while Africans are less likely to oppose it (35%)—the only ethnic group where support outweighs opposition (43% versus 35%).

The war in Iraq is less popular still. Four-in-five (81%) Muslim Americans oppose that conflict, while one-in-eight (13%) supports it. The most intense opposition is in the West, where 86% are opposed. Republicans are more likely than Democrats to support the war (28% versus 9%). Every ethnic group is opposed to the war by lopsided numbers, though Africans and South Asians are split 73% to 14% and 74% to 15%, making them the least anti-war ethnic groups.

48. Thinking about the current status of the war in Iraq, do you strongly agree, somewhat agree, somewhat disagree, or strongly disagree that it has been worth it?

Strongly agree	8%		
Somewhat agree	7	Agree	15%
Somewhat disagree	10		
Strongly disagree	69	Disagree	79
Not sure	6		

The results to this question mirror those of the previous question, where respondents indicate they oppose the war in Iraq by an overwhelming margin. Here, four-in-five American Muslims (79%) say they disagree that the war has been worth its costs, versus the 15% who say it was worth it. Also, those who say the war was not worth the cost are more intense than those who say it was worth it.

As in the previous question, Republicans are more likely to say the war was worth its costs than Democrats, 26% versus 12%. Independents track with Democrats on this question. This question also tracks on ideological lines: the further left the respondent, the most likely they are to say the war has not been worth the costs.

Men are more likely than women to rate the war worth its costs, with 18% agreeing it has been worth it versus 12% of women.

African Americans are more likely to say the war has not been worth its costs, with 84% responding this way; Africans are more likely than other groups to say it has been worth the costs, with 20% agreeing.

No clear pattern emerges along occupational lines.

49. Which of the following do you think was the most important reason why the U.S. went to war with Iraq?

Controlling oil	39%
Desire to dominate the region	16
Protecting Israel	16
Freeing the Iraqi people of oppression	5
Weakening the Muslim world	5
Promoting peace and stability in the Middle East	4
Preventing spread of weapons of mass destruction	3
Spreading democracy	2
None/Not sure	10

Two-in-five (39%) American Muslims say the U.S. went to war in Iraq to control Mideastern oil. One-in-six (16%) say the war was launched by a U.S. desire to dominate the Mideast, while another one-in-six (16%) believe the war was an effort by the U.S. to protect Israel, and 5% say it was an effort to weaken the Muslim world. Only one-in-twenty (5%) believe the primary aim of the war was to liberate the Iraqi people, 4% say it was to promote peace and stability in the Mideast, and 3% say it was to prevent the spread of WMD.

The belief that oil drove the war is strongest in the South (43%) and weakest in the Central/Great Lakes region (34%). Those in the West are more likely than others to say the aim of the Iraq war was to dominate the region (20%), and those in the West and Central/Great Lakes regions are more likely than others to credit a desire to protect Israel (18% each).

Ideologically, similar percentages of respondents say that oil drove the Iraq war. However, as ideology shifts to the left, there is a greater likelihood a respondent will say the war was driven by a U.S. desire to dominate the region—only 12% of conservatives choose this option, while 23% of progressives do. Progressives are also the ideological group most likely to support the argument that the war was launched to prevent the spread of WMD (5%).

All ethnicities are most likely to say oil was the driving force behind the Iraq war. A majority of African Americans (54%) say the war was an effort by the U.S. to control oil, while Africans are less likely to support this position than any other ethnic group (27%). Arabs are more likely than other groups to say the war was driven by a desire to protect Israel (25%).

50. Do you agree or disagree that the military effort in Iraq could lead to more terrorism aimed at the U.S.?

Agree	78%
Disagree	12
Not sure	10

Nearly four-in-five (78%) American Muslims believe that the war in Iraq could lead to more terrorism aimed at the United States. One-in-eight (12%) disagree.

These numbers hold steady across geographic regions.

Republicans are more likely than Democrats to disagree with this idea (17% versus 8%) while independents fall between the two parties. The response is generally consistent with the overall numbers for the ideological demographic.

Men are slightly more likely than women to disagree with this statement: 14% of men and 10% of women disagree.

Investors are more likely to agree than non-investors (85% versus 77%).

Arabs are more likely than other ethnicities to agree with the statement (82%) while Africans are less likely (65%).

51–52. Do you strongly agree, somewhat agree, somewhat disagree, or strongly disagree that the war in Iraq could lead to more instability in the Middle East and across the Muslim world... that the war in Iraq will result in more Democracy in the Arab world?

Table 6.   **Muslims on Possible Outcomes of the War in Iraq**

The war in Iraq...	Agree*	Disagree*	Not sure
Could lead to more instability in the Middle East and across the Muslim world	82	12	7
Will result in more Democracy in the Arab world	28	63	9

(* Agree and disagree each combines strongly and somewhat.)

American Muslims overwhelmingly believe that the Iraq war could lead to more instability in the Mideast (82% versus 12% who disagree). But three-in-ten (28%) also believe the war could lead to more democracy in the Arab world.

On the first question, responses are consistent with the overall response geographically. Democrats are somewhat more likely to agree with the notion than Republicans (85% versus 80%), and independents mirrored Democrats. Gender has minimal impact on response. On racial lines, however, Arabs are more likely—and with higher intensity— to agree with the premise (86%) than are other racial groups. Africans are less likely (71%) than others to agree.

On the second question, responses varied somewhat geographically. Westerners are less likely than others (22%) to believe more democracy in the Arab world will result from the Iraq war, while those in the Central/Great Lakes region are more optimistic in their assessment: 31% say greater democracy in the Arab world will result. Republicans are more likely to agree with the premise than Democrats, 34% versus 26%. Men are more likely than women to agree (30% versus 26%). Africans are more likely than other ethnicities to say the war will lead to democracy (37%), while Arabs are less likely (25%). Blue collar/production workers are more likely than other professions to believe the war will lead to democracy in the Arab world (43%), while professional/technical workers, homemakers, and retirees are less likely (24% each).

53. If you had to choose ONE of the following ways to wage the war against terrorism, which would you choose?

Changing America's Middle East policy	76%
Using U.S. Military Covert/Special Forces	2
Use of strategic nuclear weapons	1
Attacking Iran	1
Contracting with mercenaries	1

U.S. Air Force bombing	1
Biological warfare	1
None of the above/Other	11
Not sure	8

Respondents overwhelmingly say they would fight the war on terror by changing U.S. policy in the Mideast (76%). No other answer gained more than 2%, and most were less than 1%.

These numbers remain generally consistent across all demographics, although some cross sections have a higher number selecting none of the above and not sure.

531, 54–56. Do you agree or disagree that. . .?

Table 7.   **Muslims on U.S. Foreign Policy in the Mideast**

	Agree	Disagree	Not sure
The U.S. should support a Palestinian state	87	5	7
One of the most effective ways to fight terrorism is to deal with the social, economic, and political inequalities that affect the majority of people in the world	87	7	6
The U.S. should reduce financial support to Israel	80	9	11
The U.S. should reduce its support of undemocratic regimes in the Muslim world	66	20	14

There is widespread support for the U.S. backing a Palestinian state, with eight-in-nine (87%) agreeing with that premise. Support mirrors the overall number in all geographic regions. There is slightly higher support for the U.S. backing a Palestinian state among political independents (92% versus 90% of Republicans and 88% of Democrats). Moderates and progressives are more likely to back this policy (92% and 90%, respectively), while support is lower among conservatives (86%). Men agree in a slightly higher percentage than women (89% versus 85%) with more women undecided. Arabs are more likely to agree than other ethnic groups (94%) while Africans are less likely (78%).

Muslims also overwhelmingly support the notion that the U.S. must deal with social, economic and political inequalities around the world to defeat terrorism (87%), though 7% disagree. Support for this stance rises to 90% in the South. Independents are more likely than either party to agree as well, with 91% agreeing versus 88% of Democrats and 84% of Republicans. Moderates and progressives are more likely to agree than other ideologies (90% and 93%, respectively). The response is fairly consistent across ethnic lines.

A reduction in U.S. support for Israel is supported by four-in-five American Muslims (80%). Support for this stance is strongest in the South, at 82%, while it is weaker in the East, at 78%. Democrats agree with this approach more than Republicans, 83% to 75%, but independents are even more likely to agree (87%). Response is consistent regardless of gender. Arabs are more likely than other ethnicities to support this position (87%) and Africans are less likely (67%).

Two-thirds (66%) of American Muslims agree that the U.S. should reduce its support of undemocratic regimes in the Muslim world. One-in-five (20%) disagree, and 14% are unsure. This idea resonates more strongly in the West, where support climbs to

72%, and less in the East, where it drops to 63%. Republicans are more likely than Democrats to support this policy, 70% versus 65% of Democrats (and 69% of independents). Men are more likely to agree than women, 70% versus 61%. Those age 30-49 are more likely than other age groups to agree (73%) while the youngest Muslims (18-29 year-olds) are less likely to agree (55%). Investors are more likely to agree than non-investors, 74% versus 65%. Arabs are more likely than other ethnic groups to agree (76%), while African Americans are less likely (51%). Blue collar/production workers are less likely than other professions to agree (45%) and more likely to disagree (30%). Students hold similar numbers.

57. Secretary of State Colin Powell has described the Kashmir issue as the central issue between India and Pakistan. Do you agree or disagree with this assessment?

Agree	64%
Disagree	18
Not sure	17

Two-thirds (64%) of Muslims agree with Secretary Powell: Kashmir is the central issue between India and Pakistan. One-in-five (18%) disagree, and one-in-six (17%) are not sure.

Agreement is strongest in the South, where 70% of Muslims agree.

Independents agree in a higher percentage than Democrats or Republicans (72% versus 68% of Republicans and 63% of Democrats). This dovetails with the ideological response, where moderates are more likely to agree than those with stronger ideological identities: 70% of moderates agree, versus a range of 62% to 65% among other ideologies.

Men are far more likely than women to agree with Secretary Powell's assessment, 71% versus 55%.

South Asians are more likely than other ethnic groups to agree, with 82% taking that position. African Americans are less likely to agree (45%).

58. I will now read you several statements about American's attitudes toward Muslims that you have experienced in your own personal experience and the attitudes of Americans toward Muslims overall—in the society as a whole. Please tell me which statement best reflects Americans' attitudes toward Muslims since the September 11 attacks:

Table 8.   **Muslims Contrast Their Neighbors & American Society**

	%
B: In my experience, Americans have been respectful and tolerant of Muslims, but American society overall is disrespectful and intolerant of Muslims	35
A: In my experience and overall, Americans have been respectful and tolerant of Muslims	32
D: In my experience, Americans have been disrespectful and intolerant of Muslims, but American society overall is respectful and tolerant of Muslims	16
C: In my experience and overall, Americans have been disrespectful and intolerant of Muslims	12
Not sure	5

Slightly more than a third of Muslims (35%) say that in their own experience, Americans have been respectful of Muslims, but that American society overall is disrespectful and intolerant of their culture. Another third (32%) take the unqualified position that Americans have been tolerant and respectful of Muslims. One-in-six (16%) say they have encountered Americans who are disrespectful and intolerant of Muslims, but that American society, overall, has been respectful and tolerant. One-in-eight (12%) say that in both their personal experience and the overall context, Americans have been disrespectful and intolerant of Muslims.

Republicans are more likely than other partisans to say that in both their experience and overall, Americans have been respectful and tolerant (37%). This is the most popular position among Republicans. Democrats, meanwhile, are more likely to say that in their personal experience, Americans have been tolerant and respectful, but that American society is not (37%). Independents split evenly between these options.

Men are more likely than women to say that Americans are respectful and tolerant (36% versus 27%). Women are more likely than men to say that, in their experience, Americans are tolerant and respectful, but that, overall, American society is not (40% versus 31%).

Africans and South Asians are more likely to take the unqualified position that Americans have been respectful and tolerant (39% and 40%, respectively). African Americans and Arabs are more likely to say that in their own experiences, they've found Americans tolerant and respectful, but that American society is neither (34% and 37%, respectively). African Americans are also far more likely than other ethnicities to select the blanket statement that Americans are disrespectful and intolerant (28%).

59–60. Have you . . . your friends or family . . . personally experienced anti-Muslim discrimination since the September 11 attacks?

Table 9. **Muslims on Discrimination Post-9/11**

	Yes	No	Not sure
You	40	59	1
Your friends or family	57	41	2

While a majority (59%) of Muslims have not directly experienced anti-Muslim discrimination since the 9/11 attacks, most (57%) know someone who has.

More Democrats than Republicans say they have personally experienced anti-Muslim discrimination (43% versus 39%, and 38% of independents). The number is also higher on the edges of the ideological spectrum, and lower for moderates. The younger the respondent, the more likely they are to say they have experienced such discrimination— while a quarter (23%) of seniors (age 65+) say they have, half (50%) of 18-29 year-olds say the same. African Americans are more likely than other groups to say they have been discriminated against, with 46% saying they have. South Asians are less likely than other ethnicities to say they have experienced anti-Muslim discrimination (37%).

Slightly more Westerners say their friends or family have experienced anti- Muslim discrimination than those from other geographic regions (60%, versus a range of 56% to 57% elsewhere). Democrats are more likely than Republicans to say someone they know has been the victim of post-9/11 anti-Muslim discrimination, by a 60% to 53% margin. Women are far more likely than men to say their friends or family have experienced anti-Muslim discrimination, by a 64% to 52% margin. Members of the investor class are more likely than non-investors to say the same, 63% versus 56%. The young are far more likely than the elderly to say their friends or relatives have been discriminated against: 70% of 18-29 year-olds say they know someone who has been the victim of anti-Muslim discrimination, while half as many seniors, 35%, say the same.

Arabs and African Americans are more likely than other racial groups to respond in the affirmative to this question (58% each).

61. Where have you, your family, or your friends experienced such discrimination? ***(Choose all that apply)***

At work	32%
With friends, acquaintances, neighbors	27
At school	21
Other	19
Not sure	2

A third (32%) of American Muslims who have either experienced discrimination, or know someone who has, say the discrimination occurred in the workplace. Slightly more than a quarter (27%) say the discrimination occurred among friends, acquaintances, and neighbors. One-in-five (21%) say the discrimination occurred at school.

62. Have you been a victim of profiling since the September 11 attacks?

Yes	26%
No	70
Not sure	4

Seven-in-ten (70%) American Muslims say they have not been victims of profiling since 9/11. A quarter (26%) say they have.

Democrats are more likely than Republicans to say they have been profiled, 25% versus 20%. Among independents, however, that percentage jumps to 31%—nearly a third. There is also a clear increase in those who say they were profiled as their ideological identity shifts to the left.

Men are more likely than women to say they have been a victim of profiling (28% versus 23%). Investors are more likely than non-investors, as well, 31% versus 24%. The younger the respondent, the more likely they are to say they have been profiled, with 30% of the youngest demographic saying they have, versus 12% of the oldest.

African Americans are much more likely than other groups to say they have been profiled (36%) while Africans are less likely (20%).

63. Which of the following describes anti-Muslim discrimination you have experienced personally or that has been experienced in your community? ***(Choose all that apply.)***

I am not aware of any discrimination	20%
Verbal abuse	25
Racial profiling by police resulting in a stop, search or arrest	14
Destruction of property	10
Denial of employment	10
Physical abuse or assault	7
Boycott of Muslim- or Arab-operated businesses	6
*Other	5
Not sure	3

* **Other:** (Number in parentheses denotes frequency of similar response.)

Hostility/distrust (41); racial profiling at airport (32); government/legal harassment (16); cultural/religious profiling (6); denial of goods/services (5); civil rights violations (5); immigration issues (3); denial of housing (2).

64–88. Now I am going to read you a list of issues that are being discussed in this country today. Please tell me if you strongly favor, somewhat favor, somewhat oppose, or strongly oppose each issue.

Table 10.   **Muslims on Law, Priorities, and Use of the Public Treasury**

	Favor*	Oppose*	Not sure
Providing universal health care for citizens	96	3	1
Eliminating all forms of racial discrimination	95	4	2
Increase in funding for after school programs	94	4	2
Stricter laws and regulations to protect the environment	94	5	2
Providing more generous government assistance to the poor	92	6	2
Debt relief for poorer countries	88	8	4
Increasing foreign aid for poorer countries	88	9	3
Making it more difficult for people to buy guns	81	17	2
Banning the public sale and display of pornography	76	21	3
Allowing religious institutions to apply for government funding to provide social services	70	25	6
Stronger laws to fight terrorism	69	24	7
Providing vouchers to families for tuition in private schools, including religious schools	66	28	6
More cuts in the income tax	65	29	6
The death penalty for persons convicted of murder	61	35	4
Allowing more research using stem cells	60	25	15
Making abortions more difficult to obtain	55	38	8
Forcing every American Citizen to speak English fluently	52	46	2
Allowing public schools to display the 10 Commandments	51	41	8
Allowing non-denominational prayers to be read in the classroom	48	44	8
Eliminating affirmative action programs that give some consideration to minorities in hiring and entrance into college	37	56	7
Making the exchange of non-prescription drugs legal	33	42	25
Making it legal for doctors to give terminally ill patients the means to end their lives	31	61	8
Allowing research related to human cloning	28	62	10
Allowing gays and lesbians to marry legally	15	79	6
Sending more United States troops to Iraq	11	83	6

(* Favor and oppose each combines strongly and somewhat.)

Nineteen-out-of-twenty American Muslims favor providing universal healthcare for citizens. Support for this policy is stronger among Democrats than Republicans, by a 98% to 90% margin, and Democrats are much more intensely in favor. Support drops steadily as a Muslim's ideology shifts to the right, going from 99% among progressives to 95% among conservatives, who are also less intense on this issue. While fluctuations occur elsewhere, nearly every other demographic is at 95% support.

By a near-unanimous 95%, American Muslims favor eliminating all forms of racial discrimination. This holds across all demographic lines, although support drops to 91% in the Western states.

Ninety-four percent of American Muslims favor increasing funding for afterschool programs. This support cuts across all geographic lines, though it is more intense in the Eastern and Western states. Democrats are far more likely than Republicans to strongly support this, by a 81% to 69% margin, though their overall favorabilities are similar. Support—and especially intense support—for after-school programs increases the further left the respondent is ideologically. This issue is similarly popular with both genders. African Americans are more supportive of increasing this funding than any other race, with 98% favoring an increase. Younger Muslims are also more intense in their support than older Muslims.

Muslims overwhelmingly support stricter environmental laws (94% in favor, versus 5% opposed). Support is stronger among Democrats than Republicans (97% of Democrats favor stricter laws; 92% of Republicans favor stricter laws). While support is near-universal, support is more intense among progressives and liberals than among conservatives and moderates. Given the high support for stricter laws, there is little discernible difference among other demographic criteria.

American Muslims strongly favor increasing government assistance to the poor, by a 92% to 6% margin. Support is higher among Democrats than Republicans, by a 95% to 83% margin. Support increases the further left a respondent is ideologically, and the lower a respondent's income. Younger Muslims are more likely than their elders to favor increasing government aid to the poor.

Debt relief for poorer countries is a policy favored by eight-in-nine (88%) Muslims. Support is higher in the East and lower in the Western states. Democrats are more likely than Republicans to strongly favor this approach, 65% to 55%, though the groups support it overall in similar percentages. Independents are even more likely to favor this stance. Debt relief is favored by all ethnic groups, but more intensely by Africans, where 71% strongly favor it. Men are more likely than women to favor debt relief, 90% versus 86%, and they do so with greater intensity.

Increasing foreign aid for poorer countries is favored by 88% of Muslim Americans, and opposed by one-in-eleven (9%). Democrats favor this more than Republicans, by a 89% to 81% margin, and Democrats are more intense in their support. Men and women are at parity on this issue. Africans are more likely than other ethnic groups to support an increase in foreign aid (96%).

Four-fifths (81%) of Muslims favor making it more difficult for people to buy guns. A much smaller one-in-six (17%) oppose more restrictions on gun ownership. Support is slightly higher in the Central/Great Lakes region (82%) and lower in the Western states (79%). Democrats are more likely than Republicans to favor gun restrictions, 86% versus 76%, with independents falling between the parties. Support increases somewhat as the respondent's ideology shifts left. Women are more likely than men to favor gun restrictions, by a 85% to 78% margin. African Americans are less likely to support this stance than other ethnicities (74%).

Three-quarters (76%) of Muslims favor banning the public sale and display of pornography. A fifth (21%) oppose this policy. Support for a ban is slightly weaker in the Western states, at 72%. Republicans are slightly more likely to favor a ban than Democrats, 78% versus 75%. Women are more likely than men to favor a ban, by a 79% to 74% margin. Married Muslims are more likely to favor banning pornography than single Muslims, by a margin of 77% to 69%. Support for a ban increases somewhat with age, as well.

Seven-in-ten (70%) Muslims support allowing religious institutions to apply for government money to provide social services. Support is uniform across all geographic regions, although it is more intense in the South. Support does not vary significantly based on party identity or gender. African Americans are more likely than other groups to support this policy (80%). Support for this policy decreases as age increases.

Seven-in-ten (69%) Muslims favor stronger anti-terror laws, while 24% are opposed. Republicans are more likely than Democrats to support this, by a 78% to 69% margin. Men are more likely to favor stronger anti-terror laws than women, by a margin of 71% to 66%. Married Muslims are also somewhat more in favor of stronger laws to fight terrorism, by a 71% to 65% margin. African Americans are much less likely than other groups to support stronger anti-terror laws (48% versus a range of 74% to 86% for other ethnicities).

Vouchers to attend private schools are supported by two-thirds (66%) of Muslims, and opposed by one-in-three (28%). These levels hold across geographic lines, as well as party—though a slightly higher percentage of independents oppose vouchers than do either Democrats or Republicans. The vouchers gain support as a respondent's ideology shifts to the right. Vouchers are also more heavily supported by younger Muslims, and support steadily decreases with age, as well as income. Women are somewhat more intense in their support than are men, with 49% of women strongly favoring the vouchers versus 43% of men. Support is higher among African Americans than other ethnicities (80%).

A majority (65%) of Muslim Americans favor more income tax cuts, while three-in-ten (29%) are opposed. Support is slightly higher in the West (67%). Republicans are more likely than Democrats to favor this, 74% versus 63%. Income tax cuts resonate more with Arabs than other ethnicities (73% in favor). No ready correlation can be made to income level.

Three-fifths (61%) of Muslims favor the death penalty for convicted murderers. Support is weakest in the East, where 58% of Muslims support the death penalty, and more uniform elsewhere. Republicans are far more likely to support the death penalty than Democrats, 72% versus 54%. Independents fall between the two parties. Support increases as a respondent's ideology shifts to the right. Men are more likely than women to support the death penalty, by a 66% to 54% margin. Support is higher among Arabs than other ethnicities, at 68%, and lower among African Americans, at 41%. A majority (54%) of this latter group opposes the death penalty.

Three-in-five (60%) Muslims favor allowing more stem-cell research. Men are more likely than women to favor stem-cell research, 63% versus 55%. Support is stronger among South Asians (65%) than other ethnic groups. Support generally increases with income levels. Muslims in the medical profession are far more likely than other classifications of workers to favor increasing stem-cell research (76%).

A majority (55%) of Muslims favor making it more difficult to obtain an abortion, while 38% oppose this. The strongest support for this position is found in the Central/ Great Lakes region, where support increases to 58%, and weakest in the East, where support is at 53%. Republicans are more likely than Democrats to favor abortion restrictions, 62% versus 53%. Independents are less likely to favor this, at 51% in favor. As respondents shift to the political right, they are more likely to be in favor of this. Men are more likely than women to favor abortion restrictions, by a 57% to 53% margin. Arabs are more likely than other groups to support this position as well (58%) though Africans are more intensely in favor of this issue.

Half (52%) of American Muslims favor forcing every American citizen to speak English, while 46% oppose this stance. Easterners are more likely (57%) than those living elsewhere in the country to favor this. Republicans are more likely than Democrats to favor mandatory English, by a 69% to 51% margin. Support generally increases as a respondent's political ideology shifts to the right, and as their age increases. Men are somewhat more likely than women to favor mandatory English, 53% versus 51%, though men are much more intense on this issue. South Asians are more likely to favor this (61%) while African Americans are more likely to be opposed (30%).

American Muslims are divided on allowing public schools to display the Ten Commandments. A slight majority, 51% are in favor, and 41% are opposed. Support for the Ten Commandments is strongest in the Central/Great Lakes area, where 54% are in favor. This issue gains support as a respondent's ideological identity shifts to the right. Women are slightly more likely than men to support displaying the Commandments, 54% versus 49%. Africans and Arabs are more likely than other racial groups to support the display of the Commandments (57% and 55%, respectively). Support for displaying the commandments grows, and grows in intensity, the lower a Muslim's income.

A slight plurality (48%) of Muslims favor allowing non-denominational prayers to be read in the classroom, while nearly as many are opposed (44%). Half (50%) of Republicans support the prayer, while 47% of Democrats and 49% of independents do so. Support is higher and more intense among Muslims who call themselves conservative or very conservative, and weakest among progressives, who are split, 45% in favor and 49% opposed. Men and women support school prayer in roughly equal percentages. African Americans are more likely than other ethnicities to support school prayer (53%). Support increases with age, but decreases as income level increases.

More Muslims oppose eliminating affirmative action than support curtailing the programs that give consideration to minorities entering college or applying for jobs (56% opposed versus 37% in favor). Republicans are more likely than Democrats to favor eliminating affirmative action, by a 44% to 34% margin. Progressives are much more likely to oppose eliminating affirmative action than other groups (70%). Men and women have rough parity on this issue. African Americans are more likely than other groups to oppose the elimination of affirmative action (73% opposed), while Arabs are more likely to favor eliminating affirmative action than others, with 44% in favor.

A third (33%) of Muslims favor making the exchange of non-prescription drugs legal. A plurality, 42%, oppose this. In the Southern states, the numbers achieve nearparity, with 36% supporting legalization and 39% opposing it. While Democrats and Republicans support legalization in somewhat equal numbers, Democrats oppose it by higher percentages than Republicans, 43% versus 35%. Independents are slightly more likely than either party to support legalization. Africans and South Asians are more likely than other groups to favor legalization (37% and 36%, respectively).

A majority of American Muslims oppose legalizing physician-assisted suicide (61%). Those in the Eastern and Western states are more likely to favor allowing doctors to help their terminally-ill patients end their lives, 33% and 34%, respectively, than are Muslims living elsewhere. Republicans are more likely to support giving doctors this ability than Democrats or independents, by a margin of 36% to 33% to 32%. Africans are more likely than other ethnic groups, and with more intensity, to support this (35%). While the overall level of support for physician-assisted suicide is fairly level across all age groups, intensity increases among the oldest respondents. Muslims in the medical profession are slightly more likely than other work demographics to support this.

More than three-fifths (62%) of Muslims oppose research into human cloning, and they do so with high intensity. A quarter (27%) favor further cloning research. Republicans are more likely than Democrats to favor cloning research, 32% versus 26%, and support grows to 34% among independents. Men are more likely than women to support cloning research, 34% versus 21%. South Asians are more likely than other ethnic groups to support this research (36%) while African Americans are far more likely to oppose it (84%).

American Muslims strongly oppose gay marriage. Eight-in-ten (79%) Muslims are opposed, and of that group, the vast majority are strongly opposed. Support for gay marriage is higher among Westerners, where 23% favor it. Support is low across party lines, though the strongest support, ideologically, is among progressives, with 32% favoring allowing gays and lesbians to marry. Support remains consistent across gender lines as well. Young Muslims are a bit more likely to support gay marriage than their elders.

A solid majority (83%) of American Muslims oppose sending more troops to Iraq, while one-in-nine (11%) favor it. This holds across all geographic regions. Republicans are more likely than Democrats or independents to favor sending more troops to Iraq (23% versus 6% of Democrats and 9% of independents). This does not reflect as strongly in ideology. Women are slightly more likely than men (82% versus 79%) to oppose sending more troops. African Americans are more likely than other ethnicities to oppose deploying more troops (91%).

Religious Practices:

Finally, I am going to ask you some questions about religion and how it impacts your daily life.

89. On average, how often do you attend the mosque for salah and Jum'ah Prayer

More than once a week	29%
Once a week for Jum'ah	25
A few times a year especially for the Eid	16
Once or twice a month	10
Never	10
Seldom	9
Not sure	1

Three-in-ten (29%) Muslims attend mosque for salah and Jum'ah prayer more than once a week, and another quarter (25%) attend once a week. The remaining 56% are less devout.

Mosque attendance is stronger in the South, where one-in-three (32%) Muslims attend mosque more than once a week, and a quarter (24%) attend weekly; attendance is weaker in the Central/Great Lakes region, where a quarter (26%) attend more than once a week, and 27% attend weekly.

Democrats are more likely than Republicans to attend mosque at least weekly, with 54% of Democrats doing so versus 41% of Republicans. More independents attend at least weekly than either party (58%).

Men are more likely than women to attend at least once a week, 63% versus 42%. Women are most likely to attend a few times a year, especially for the Eid (23%).

African Americans are more likely to attend at least weekly than other ethnicities, with 72% doing so. Arabs are less likely than others to attend at least weekly (41%).
(Asked of those who attend seldom or never)

90. Why do you not attend mosque more often?
*Question was open-ended: (Number in parentheses denotes frequency of similar response.)
Too busy/no time (110); religion allows prayer at home (74); not practicing (68); disagrees with agenda/views of mosque (51); gender restrictions (32); security reason post-9/11 (12); fanaticism (5); does not trust leadership (3); agnostic (3).

91. Which one of the following statements is true about the participants of the mosque you generally attend?

There is no clear-cut majority; participants belong to several ethnic groups	49%
The majority of the participants belong to two or three ethnic groups	21
The majority of the participants belong to one ethnic group	19
Not sure	10

Half (49%) of American Muslims attend a mosque with a multi-ethnic makeup and no clearly-dominant group. Another one-in-five (21%) attend a mosque where the majority of the participants belong to two or three ethnic groups, and another fifth (19%) attend a mosque where the majority or worshippers belong to one ethnic group.

Progressives are more likely than other political ideologies to belong to a one-ethnicity mosque (25%) while conservatives are more likely to belong to a multi-ethnic mosque (52%).

Among ethnic groups, African Americans are more likely than others to attend a one-ethnic-group mosque (44%), while Africans are more likely to belong to a multiethnic mosque (69%).

92. How would you rate the Muslim religious leadership in your mosque?

Excellent	32%		
Good	29	Positive	61%
Fair	20		
Poor	7	Negative	27
Not sure	12		

Three-fifths of Muslims rate the religious leadership of their mosque positively, and a third (32%) rate it excellent. Slightly more than a quarter (27%) rate the religious leadership of their mosque negatively.

The most positive assessment of religious leadership comes from the Central/Great Lakes region (66% positive). Those in the Western states are less likely to rate their religious leadership positively (57%) than others elsewhere.

Democrats are more likely to rate their religious leadership positively than are Republicans and independents, 65% versus 55% for Republicans and 57% for Democrats. (Here, Republicans and independents are virtually identical.) This does not immediately translate on ideological lines, however, as conservatives rate their religious leadership more highly than other ideological groups (66%).

Women are more likely than men (66% versus 58%) to rate their religious leadership positively.

African Americans are more likely than other ethnicities to rate their religious leadership positively (76%), and with higher intensity.

93. Excluding salah and Jum'ah prayer, how involved are you in the activities at the mosque. Would you say that you are...?

Very involved	18%		
Somewhat involved	25	Involved	43%
Not very involved	24		
Not at all involved	31	Not involved	55
Not sure	3		

More Muslims say they are not involved in the activities of their mosque than are, 55% to 43%.

Republicans are less likely to be involved in their mosque than are Democrats: 34% of Republicans and 45% of Democrats say they are involved. Two-fifths (40%) of Republicans are not at all involved in running their mosque.

Men and women are involved in running their mosques in roughly equivalent numbers.

More African Americans than other ethnic groups are involved in the running of their mosques (74%). Arabs are less involved than other groups (31%).

(Asked of those who are very, somewhat, or not very involved)

94. Which of the following describes how you have volunteered for your mosque?
   (Choose all that apply)

Charity work	27%
Fund raising efforts	24
Sunday school activities	18
Prayer arrangements	14
Other	11
Not sure	6

*Other: (Number in parentheses denotes frequency of similar response.) Programs/activities (33); financial (23); operations (14); donated services (12); donated facilities (11); public relations (9); donated time/support (7); provided food service (4).

95. Did you happen to attend a mosque for Jum'ah prayers or salah in the last seven days?

Yes	50%
No	49
Not sure	1

Muslims split evenly on recent mosque attendance, with half (50%) saying they attended mosque for Jum'ah prayers and salah, and half (49%) not having done so.

Muslims in the South are more likely to say they attended (55%) than elsewhere.

Democrats are more likely to say they attended than Republicans, 51% versus 39%.

Men are more likely to say they attended than women, 59% versus 37%.

African Americans are more likely to say they attended than other groups, 74% versus a range from 35% to 63% for other ethnicities.

People in sales, service, and blue collar occupations are more likely to say they attended in the last week (60%, 62%, and 60%, respectively); homemakers are less likely than other professions to say they attended in the last week (34%).

96. Concerning daily salah or prayer, do you in general, pray all five salah daily, make some of the five salah daily, occasionally make salah, only make Eid Prayers, or do you never pray?

Pray all five salah daily	49%
Make some of the five salah daily	22
Occasionally make salah	15
Only make Eid Prayers	5
Never pray	7
Not sure	3

Half (49%) of American Muslims pray all five salah daily, while another fifth (22%) make some of the salah daily. Only 7% say they never pray.

Westerners are less likely than those in other geographic regions to pray all five salah (41%); they are also more likely to say they only occasionally pray the salah than those in other regions (19%).

As a Muslim's political identity shifts to the right, they are more likely to pray all five salah daily; among progressives, 43% choose this response, but among conservatives, it is 53%.

Women are more likely than men to say they pray all five salah daily, 54% versus 45%. Men are more likely than women to only occasionally make salah (16% to 13%), only make Eid prayers (6% versus 4%) or never pray (9% versus 6%).

Africans are more likely than other ethnic groups to pray all five salah daily (63%). South Asians are more likely to say they only pray some of the five salah (29%). Arabs are more likely to say they never pray (13%).

The younger a respondent, the more likely they are to say they pray all five salah daily; the older a respondent, the more likely they are to say they never pray.

97. How important is religion or spirituality in your daily life? Is it very important, somewhat important or not very important?

98. Would you say the role of Islam in your life is very important, somewhat important, or not very important?

Table 11.   **The Role of Religion and Islam in Daily Life**

	Very important	Somewhat important	Not very important	Not sure
Religion or spirituality in your daily life	82	14	4	—
The role of Islam in your life	82	14	4	—

By equal percentages, American Muslims rank both the role of religion, and of Islam itself, as very important in their lives: 82% say each is very important, 14% say somewhat important, and 4% say not very important.

Those living in the West are less likely to rate either very important (77% for religion, 79% for Islam).

As a respondent's political ideology shifts right, so does the likelihood they consider both religion/spirituality and Islam very important; as it shifts left, there is an increasing likelihood they will select somewhat important.

Women are more likely than men to rank religion and Islam as very important (87% versus 78% for religion, 85% versus 79% for Islam).

Arabs are less likely than other ethnicities to rate either religion or Islam as very important (77% for each category).

99. Were you raised as a Muslim or did you convert?

Raised	79%
Convert	20
Not sure	1

Four-fifths (79%) of American Muslims were raised Muslim, but one-fifth (20%) are converts.

More Central/Great Lakes residents say they were raised Muslim (84%) than elsewhere. More Easterners say they are converts (23%).

No obvious correlation occurs with political ideology. However, Republicans are more likely than either Democrats or independents to have been raised Muslim, 87% versus 74% of Democrats and 76% of independents.

More women than men are converts (25% versus 17%).

A higher proportion of married Muslims are converts than are single Muslims (18% versus 11%). Among those divorced/widowed/separated, the proportion jumps to half (49%).

African Americans are distinct from other ethnicities on this question. While all other ethnicities are nearly unanimous as Muslim-raised, among African Americans, 68% are converts.

100. What was the main reason you converted to Islam?

Read about the religion and was inspired to convert	38%
Was influenced by a fellow Muslim	32
Married someone who was a Muslim	12
*Other	14
Not sure	4

* **Other:** (Number in parentheses denotes frequency of similar response.) Spiritual indoctrination (8); philosophical influence (5); answer to personal quest (4); community outreach (3); organizational influence (3); Divine intervention (3); spiritual/intellectual/social inspiration (2); parental/family influence (2); mainstream religious hypocrisy (1).

The two prime causes of conversion are reading about Islam and being inspired to convert, or being influenced by a fellow Muslim. In most geographic regions, reading about Islam is the top reason for conversion, except in the Central/Great Lakes region, where a plurality, 39%, were influenced to convert by a fellow Muslim.

For liberals and progressives, being influenced by a fellow Muslim is the main reason for conversion. For conservatives and moderates, reading about the religion and being inspired to convert is the more common cause of conversion.

Among African Americans, the largest convert community, 39% became Muslims after being influenced by a fellow Muslim, 34% converted after reading about Islam and being inspired, and 7% converted due to marriage.

500. If you were not raised a Muslim, what year did you convert?

101. In your opinion, should mosques keep out of political matters or should they express their views on day-to-day social and political questions?

Should keep out of politics	37%
Should express their views	57
Not sure	6

A majority (57%) of American Muslims say mosques should express their views on social and political questions. More than a third (37%) say mosques should keep out of politics.

Republicans are more likely than Democrats to say mosques should keep out of politics, 44% to 37%, while independents overwhelmingly say they should express their views (62%).

Men and women see nearly eye-to-eye on this question. However, single and divorced/widowed/separated Muslims are much more likely than married Muslims to say mosques should express their views (69% and 67%, respectively, versus 53% of married Muslims).

African Americans are more likely than other ethnic groups to say mosques should express their views (84%). Half (50%) of South Asians say mosques should stay out of politics, more than other ethnic groups.

102. Do you think it is right for khatibs to discuss political candidates or issues in the khutbah?

Yes	39%
No	51
Not sure	10

Half (51%) of Muslims say it is not right for khatibs to discuss political candidates or issues while delivering their khutbah. Two-in-five (39%) say it is appropriate.

Republicans are more likely than Democrats to say this is inappropriate, by a 61% to 49% margin.

Men are slightly more likely than women to say this is appropriate behavior, by a 40% to 38% margin. A higher percentage of women are unsure than men.

African Americans are more likely to say this is acceptable than other ethnicities (57% versus a range of 30% to 41%).

Media Habits:

103. Which of the following best describes how you get most of your information about international affairs or foreign policy?

Television	53%
Online	17
Newspaper	13
Radio	5
Family and friends	2
Books	1
Magazines	1

School	—
*Other	5
Not sure	2

* **Other:** (Number in parentheses denotes frequency of similar response.) Verbal/written media (59); travel-related (2); organizational outreach (1); life experience (1).

More than half (53%) of Muslims turn to television for their international affairs and foreign policy news. Of the remainder, one-in-six (17%) turn to the internet, and one-in-eight (13%) get their news from a newspaper.

Among progressives, the number getting their news online jumps to 24%, significantly higher than any other ideological subgroup.

As respondent age decreases, or education increases, the likelihood of them using the internet for their news steadily increases.

Women are more likely than men to get their news from television, by a 55% to 52% margin. Men are more likely to get their news from the internet than women, by a 18% to 14% margin.

Africans are more likely to use television for their news (63%) than other ethnic groups. African Americans are more likely to use newspapers than other groups (18%). One-in-five (20%) South Asians get their news online.

104. Which of the following best describes how often you watch, read or listen to information about international affairs?

Daily	72%
A few times a week	22
Rarely	3
Once a month	2
Never	1
Not sure	1

Seven-in-ten (72%) Muslims follows international news on a daily basis. Two-in-five (22%) get international news a few times a week.

Southerners are more likely than others to get their international news daily (74%). Those in the Central/Great Lakes region are less likely than others to do this on a daily basis (69%).

Republicans are more likely than Democrats to follow international news on a daily basis, by a 80% to 76% margin.

Men are more likely than women to get their news on a daily basis, 76% versus 66%. Women are more likely than men to get their international news a few times per week, 25% versus 20%.

Arabs and African Americans are more likely than other ethnic groups to get their news on a daily basis (76% and 75%, respectively). Africans are less likely than others to do so (51%).

As age increases, so does the likelihood of obtaining international news on a daily basis: 57% of 18-29 year-olds do so, but 86% of those above the age of 65 do so.

105. When watching television for information about international affairs, which of the following stations do you turn to most often?

CNN	38%
ABC News	14
Local news	6

NBC News	5
CBS News	4
Fox News	4
C-Span	4
MSNBC	4
*Other	15
Do not watch TV/Not sure	5

* **Other:** (Number in parentheses denotes frequency of similar response.) Domestic news channels (98); ethnic/Arab satellite television (69); international stations (69); internet (4).

CNN is the choice of nearly four-in-ten (38%) American Muslims. ABC places second, at 14%. Viewership of other channels is much lower.

CNN is more popular among Muslims in the South, where 46% choose it over its competition. ABC is less popular in this same region than elsewhere.

CNN is less popular among African Americans than among other groups (31%) and is more popular among Africans (49%).

106. Do you regularly watch any media targeted towards specific ethnic groups?

Yes	25%
No	74
Not sure	2

A quarter (25%) of Muslims watch media targeted to ethnic groups, which three-quarters (74%) do not.

African Americans are more likely to watch media targeted to ethnicity than other ethnic groups (40%). Africans are less likely to do so (12%).

Muslim converts are more likely to watch ethnically-targeted media, and do so more frequently as the length of time since conversion increases.

107–108. Do you think the mainstream American media...Hollywood...is fair in its portrayal of Muslims and Islam?

Table 12. **The Portrayal of Muslims On-Screen**

	Yes	No	Not sure
The mainstream American media	17	76	7
Hollywood	10	77	12

American Muslims overwhelmingly say both mainstream American media and Hollywood are not fair in their portrayal of Muslims.

The responses to these questions vary little based on political party or ideology.

African Americans are more likely than other ethnicities to say both mainstream media and Hollywood are not fair to Muslims (88% on media, and 91% on Hollywood).

69. **"Results of Poll of American Muslims Released"** from *Zogby International*

Published January 08, 2002. Available online: http://www.zogby.com/search/ ReadNews.dbm?ID=527. Reprinted with permission of John Zogby and Zogby International.

The following is a press release from Zogby International, a polling agency with offices in Washington, DC, and Utica, New York, regarding the results of a Zogby poll of American Muslim opinions in 2002. According to Zogby, a majority of American Muslims approved of President Bush's handling of the terrorist attacks of September 11, 2001. A majority also believed that the United States' war on terror was not being fought against Islam.

Washington, DC—The first ever systematic poll of American Muslims finds a 58% approval rating of President Bush for his handling of the terrorist attacks on September 11 and two-thirds agree with the Bush Administration's assertion that the war is being fought against terrorism, not Islam. Two-thirds also responded that a change in America's policy in the Middle East is the best way to wage the war against terrorism. "The Poll clearly shows the determination of the Muslim community," said Project MAPS Co-Director Zahid Bukhari of Georgetown University's Center for Muslim Christian Understanding. "Although it took the heat after September 11, more than 50% experienced incidents of backlash, the community is yet very much eager to fully participate in the American Public life. The American Muslims have great potential to become a moral voice in the society. "The poll results were released today by Project MAPS: Muslims in the American Public Square at the National Press Club. Zogby International interviewed 1,781 persons nationwide who identify themselves as Muslim from November 8 through November 19, 2001. John Esposito, University Professor and Director of the Center for Muslim-Christian Understanding, said "This opinion poll, part of a major project sponsored by the Center for Muslim-Christian Understanding and the PEW Charitable Trust, provides important new insights into the demographics, voting habits, and participation of Muslims in American public life. "The poll results also suggest that American Muslims favor big government solutions to issues like health care and poverty but are conservative on other social issues like the death penalty, gay marriage, abortion, and pornography. American Muslims report significant involvement in the broader community through donations to non-Muslim social service programs and participation in the American political process.

70. Mohamed Elshinnawi, "Is Islam Misunderstood in America?" from *Voice of America News*

Published May 24, 2006. Available online:http://www.voanews.com/english/2006-05-24-voa33.cfm.

The following is an article from Voice of America (VOA), an international multimedia broadcasting company founded in 1942 and funded by the United States government. The article summarizes the findings of a 2006 opinion survey of Americans' attitudes toward American Muslims and Islam. According to the poll, approximately 55 percent of Americans have a favorable opinion of American Muslims and one in three Americans thinks Islam encourages violence. The article argues that negative media portrayals of Islam and frequent media focus on extremists like al Qaeda are the root cause of the negative view of Islam among Americans.

Washington, DC
24 May 2006

A new survey of U.S. public attitudes toward Muslim-Americans and Islam finds that a majority of Americans—5 percent—regard Muslim-Americans favorably, but that smaller numbers—only 41 percent—have favorable impressions of Islam as a religion. The study by the Washington, DC–based Pew Research Center indicates that many Americans perceive a link between Islam and violence, with more than one in three saying Islam is more likely than other religions to encourage violence among its believers. Experts on Islamic-American relations believe such negative views stem from American ignorance of Islamic culture.

Muslims and Islamic culture have long been an integral part of American society. But today, almost years after the 9/11 attacks by radical Islamists and the start of America's war on terror, many Americans associate Islam with violence and extremism.

We asked a random sample of people in downtown Washington, DC, what immediately comes to mind when they hear the word "Islam". "Unfortunately, the first thought that I have is something maybe a little charged with aggression and negativity," said one woman. A man remarked, "The fact that I work in Washington, DC, makes me especially fearful of Islamic terrorism, especially in the time after September 11." Another woman shared her thoughts: "I know it is a religion founded by Muhammad, and that he was a General, a warrior." Another man talked about his fears: "It brings a little bit of fear to me after being here on September 11th and watching the planes go in."

The Washington, DC-based Pew Research Center did a more scientific survey. Gregory Smith, who co-authored the study say, "Only about four in 10 say they have favorable views of Islam, and there is also a minority of the public—but a substantial minority, about one third in our survey last summer—who say that they are concerned that Islam encourages violence among its believers."

American Muslim leaders blame the US news media for generating what Nihad Awad, Executive Director of the Council for American Islamic Relations calls "Islamophobia".

"The kind of coverage that the American audience has been receiving about Islam and Muslims leads one to just one conclusion, that Islam is bad and Muslims are violent," he said. "The media has failed to capture the reality of the Muslim world and only focused on the actions of the few."

One of the problems with the media's portrayal of Islam, experts say, is that violent acts committed by Islamic terrorists aligned with al-Qaida make the news far more often than the peaceful aspects of Islamic culture.

Dr. Yvonne Haddad is Professor of Islamic History at the Center for Muslim-Christian Understanding at Georgetown University in Washington, DC. "It is very difficult for Americans to distinguish between al-Qaida and *not* al-Qaida," she said. "It is very difficult for them to distinguish between the few people who are terrorists and the rest of Muslims who are just people trying to make their living, trying to raise their kids and have a peaceful life."

According to the Pew Research Center study, public perceptions depend heavily on a few key factors. Gregory Smith explained. "One of the most powerful factors shaping views of Islam is education," he said. "Those Americans who have more education tend to be more favorable toward Muslim Americans and Islam than Americans with less education. Interestingly, age was also a good predictor of views of Muslim Americans and Islam, with young people tend to be more favorable than were older people."

Betsy McCormick, a working professional, says she gained a more positive view of Islam by traveling and having direct contact with Islamic culture in the Middle East: "I guess there are a lot of distorted views, because I have traveled to Egypt and I sort of witnessed the practice of the religion and I found it very enriching and very interesting," she said.

Some Americans, including Patricia Hagen, believe a dialogue among the people of the three monotheistic faiths—Christianity, Islam and Judaism—is the best approach to overcome misunderstandings. "Better understanding—and I think it is got to come from within all of the three major religions, to work together," she said. "Coming from a Christian background, Abraham is the founder of Judaism [and] Christianity as well as Islam, so we came from the same foundation, now we have to build upon that foundation."

But building that trust will be a challenge. The Pew study suggests many Americans believe the terrorist attacks of recent years are just the first salvoes of an intensifying conflict between Islam and the West.

71. "Political and Social Values" from *The Pew Research Center*

May 22, 2007. http://news.bbc.co.uk/2/shared/bsp/hi/pdfs/22_05_2007_muslim_ americans.pdf. Reprinted with permission of Pew Research Center. Copyright 2007 by Pew Research Center.

The Pew Research Center is a nonpartisan organization that gathers and disseminates information regarding current events, issues, and attitudes. This poll was conducted in 2006 and is the first nationwide survey to use a representative sample to measure "the demographics, attitudes, and experiences of Muslim Americans" (Foreword, p. 1). This excerpt from the poll (pp. 41–48) highlights respondents' political party affiliations, opinions of American political parties, the role of government, social values and conservatism, and voting participation.

Muslim Americans show a decided preference for the Democratic Party, a preference that is reflected in their voting patterns and many of their political attitudes. Most U.S. Muslims identify as Democrats or lean to the Democratic Party. By a lopsided margin (71%–14%), more Muslims say they voted for John Kerry than George Bush in the 2004 presidential election.

Muslim Americans' views of President Bush's job performance also are highly negative. Indeed, while the president's overall job approval rating is low nationwide (35% in April 2007), Muslims are less than half as likely as the general public to say they approve of the way Bush is handling his job as president (15%).

Muslim Americans' Political Views

	U.S. Muslims
Party Identification	%
Dem/lean Democratic	63
Rep/lean Republican	11
Ind/other/no preference	26
	100
Ideology	
Conservative	19
Moderate	38
Liberal	24
Don't know	19
	100
2004 Vote*	
Kerry	71
Bush	14
Other/don't know	15
	100
Bush approval	
Approve	15
Disapprove	69

Don't know	<u>16</u>
	100
Prefer...	
Big govt/more services	70
Small govt/few services	21
Depends/Don't know	9
	100
Government...	
Should do more for needy	73
Can't afford to do more	17
Neither/Both/DK	<u>10</u>
	100

* Among those who report having voted in the 2004 election.

On balance, more Muslims in the United States characterize their political views as moderate (38%) rather than liberal (24%); just 19% describe themselves as conservatives. In the general public, self-described conservatives outnumber liberals by a margin of 34% to 19%.

Muslims' attitudes regarding both the size and scope of government are quite liberal. By a wide margin, more Muslim Americans say they prefer a bigger government, providing more services, than a smaller government with fewer services. A large majority also favors greater government aid for the poor, even if it adds to the national debt.

But the political attitudes of U.S. Muslims are not uniformly liberal. On key social issues, Muslims in the U.S. are much more conservative than the general public. Most say that homosexuality is a way of life that should be discouraged, rather than accepted, by society. A large majority of Muslims (59%) also say that government should do more to protect morality in society.

On the question of mixing religion with politics, Muslims in the United States are divided, much like the general public. About four-in-ten (43%) say that mosques should express their views on social and political matters, while a slightly larger share (49%) say that mosques should keep out of political matters. On this question, there are substantial differences between native-born and foreign-born Muslims. Native-born Muslims express overwhelming support for the notion that mosques should express their views on social and political matters. By contrast, a large majority of foreign-born Muslims – many of whom come from countries where religion and politics are often closely intertwined – say that mosques should keep out of political matters.

Compared with the general public, Muslims are somewhat less engaged in political matters. In part, this is because many Muslim immigrants are not citizens of the United States, and thus are not eligible to participate in elections. But even among those eligible to register and vote, Muslims are somewhat less likely than the public as a whole to do so.

Party Affiliation and Views of Bush

When asked about their general outlook on politics, 38% of Muslim Americans describe their political views as moderate; a quarter describe themselves as liberal, while 19% describe themselves as conservative. U.S. Muslims, considered as a whole, are much less likely than the general population to describe themselves as political conservatives.

Overall, 63% of Muslims are Democrats (37%) or say that they lean toward the Democratic Party (26%). Only about one-in-ten (11%), by contrast, are Republicans or Republican leaners, with the remainder (26%) unaffiliated with either political party.

Democratic affiliation is much higher among Muslims than it is among the public as a whole: about half of Americans (51%) identify themselves as Democrats or lean Democratic. Republican affiliation is much lower among Muslims than among the general public (11% vs. 36%).

Party Affiliation

	Rep/lean R	Dem/lean D	Ind, no leaning
	%	%	%
All U.S. Muslims	11	63	26=100
Conservative	25	60	15=100
Moderate	9	72	19=100
Liberal	10	81	9=100
Native-born	7	78	15=100
African American	4	78	18=100
Other	10	78	12=100
Foreign-born	15	57	28=100
Arrived pre-1990	12	73	15=100
1990 or later	17	51	32=100
U.S. general public*	36	51	13=100
Conservative	61	31	8=100
Moderate	31	56	13=100
Liberal	11	818=100	

* Based on national surveys January-March 2007 by the Pew Research Center for the People & the Press.

Political ideology, which is closely linked to partisanship among the public as a whole, seems to have less of an impact on Muslim Americans. Even among those Muslims who describe their political views as conservative, a large majority (60%) aligns with the Democratic Party while only 25% identify with the Republican Party. Among the general public, by contrast, most conservatives are Republicans or Republican leaners (61%), while most liberals are Democrats or lean Democratic (81%).

Muslim immigrants who have arrived in the U.S. since 1990 are less likely to identify with the Democratic Party than are Muslims who were born in the United States, or earlier waves of immigrants. This is largely due to the fact that recent arrivals are less likely than others to identify with either of the major parties.

Muslim Americans' preference for the Democrats over the Republicans carries over into the ballot box. Overall, Muslim voters supported Kerry over Bush by about five-to-one. These figures roughly correspond with estimates from the 2004 exit polls, which found that 85% of Muslim Americans voted for Kerry, while 13% supported Bush. Self-described liberal Muslim Americans report voting for Kerry at higher rates than do conservative Muslims. But even among conservatives, a sizable majority (63%) chose Kerry, while only about one-in-five (21%) voted for Bush.

Bush's Job Performance

	Approve	Disapprove	DK/Ref
	%	%	%
All U.S. Muslims	15	69	16=100
Conservative	21	70	9=100

Moderate	12	74	14=100
Liberal	12	83	5=100
Native-born	6	85	9=100
Foreign-born	20	61	19=100
Arrived pre-1990	12	81	7=100
1990 or later	24	51	25=100
Religious Commitment			
High	11	76	13=100
Medium	15	67	18=100
Low	18	68	14=100
U.S. general public*	35	57	8=100

*   April, 2007 Pew Research Center for the People & the Press national survey.

Majorities of both native-born and foreign-born Muslims voted for Kerry. But foreign-born Muslim voters are more than twice as likely as Muslims born in this country to say they voted for Bush (21% vs. 8%).

Negative evaluations of Bush among Muslim Americans continue to the present. Only 15% of Muslims in the U.S. say that they approve of Bush's performance in office; more than four times as many (69%) say that they disapprove of Bush's job performance. Again, there are few demographic or ideological differences in views of Bush; even self-described conservatives disapprove rather than approve of Bush's job performance by 70%–21%.

Role of Government

By more than three-to-one, Muslim Americans say they prefer a bigger government that provides more services (70%) over a smaller government providing fewer services (21%). In contrast with the general public, there are only small ideological differences among Muslims in views of the size and scope of government.

Most Muslims Favor Activist Government...

	Smaller	*Prefer government that is...* Bigger	Depends/DK/Ref
	%	%	%
All U.S. Muslims	21	70	9=100
Conservative	19	70	11=100
Moderate	26	66	8=100
Liberal	19	77	4=100
Native-born	26	66	8=100
Foreign-born	19	72	9=100
U.S. general public*	45	43	12=100

Question: Would you rather have a smaller government providing fewer services, or a bigger government providing more services?

*   January 2007 Pew Research Center for the People & the Press national survey.

Large majorities of Muslim American liberals (77%), moderates (66%) and conservatives (70%) express support for a bigger government that delivers more services. Among the general public, by contrast, there are sharp ideological divisions: 57% of liberals support bigger government, while 58% of conservatives support smaller government.

Consistent with their preference for a larger government providing more services, most Muslims (73%) say that government should do more to help the needy even if it means going deeper into debt. Just 17% believe that the government cannot afford to do much more to help the needy. Support for greater government aid to the poor also cuts across ideological and demographic groups, though native-born Muslims express even more support for this position than do immigrants (84% vs. 69%).

...And More Help for the Needy

| | The federal government... | | |
	Should do more to help the needy	Can't afford to do more for needy	Neither/ Both/DK
	%	%	%
All U.S. Muslims	73	17	10=100
Conservative	71	20	9=100
Moderate	72	22	6=100
Liberal	84	13	3=100
Native-born	84	13	3=100
Foreign-born	69	19	12=100
U.S. general public*	63	28	9=100

Question: Which comes closer to your view? The government should do more to help needy Americans, even if it means going deeper into debt (OR) The government today can't afford to do much more to help the needy.

* January 2007 Pew Research Center for the People & the Press national survey.

Social Conservatives

Despite their support for the Democratic Party and liberal views on the role of government, Muslim Americans tend to be more conservative when it comes to social and moral issues. By more than two-to-one (61% vs. 27%), U.S. Muslims say that homosexuality is a way of life that should be discouraged by society, not accepted. By contrast, 51% of the general public says homosexuality is a way of life that should be accepted by society, while 38% believe it should be discouraged.

As is the case with the general public, religious commitment is strongly related to views about homosexuality. The most highly religious U.S. Muslims—the 23% of Muslims who attend mosque at least weekly, pray all five salah a day, and say religion is very important to them personally—overwhelmingly oppose homosexuality, with 73% saying it should be discouraged by society. Muslim Americans with a medium level of religious commitment, who constitute about half of all Muslims, also generally believe homosexuality should be discouraged (66% vs. 21%). By comparison, Muslim Americans with relatively low religious commitment (about a quarter of the total) are divided: 43% say homosexuality should be discouraged while 47% say it should be accepted.

Homosexuality Should Be...

	Discouraged	Accepted	Neither/Both/DK
	%	%	%
All U.S. Muslims	61	27	12=100
18–29	57	32	11=100
30–39	58	26	16=100

40–54	69	26	5=100
55+	59	22	19=100
Conservative	69	23	8=100
Moderate	60	27	13=100
Liberal	54	38	8=100
Religious commitment			
High	73	16	11=100
Medium	66	21	13=100
Low	43	47	10=100
Native-born	61	30	9=100
African American	75	20	5=100
Other	44	42	14=100
Foreign-born	60	26	14=100
Self/Parents from			
Arab region	67	21	12=100
Pakistan	65	28	7=100
Other South Asia	70	25	5=100
U.S. general public*	38	51	11=100

Question: Which comes closer to your view? Homosexuality is a way of life that should be accepted by society (OR) homosexuality is a way of life that should be discouraged by society.

* September, 2006 Pew Research Center for the People & the Press national survey.

Both native-born Muslims and foreign-born Muslims express similar levels of disapproval of homosexuality. But native-born African American Muslims stand out for their particularly high levels of opposition to homosexuality (75% say homosexuality should be discouraged).

Muslim Americans strongly believe that government should be involved in promoting and protecting morality in society. Overall, 59% say that government should do more to protect morality in society—about half as many say they worry that the government is becoming too involved in the issue of morality (29%). Here again, Muslims differ from the overall population. Overall, 51% of the public worries that the government is becoming too involved in the issue of morality.

The view that government should be involved in protecting morality is widely shared among Muslim Americans. Young (61% of those under 30), old (56% of those over 55), native-born (54%), and foreign-born (63%) all agree about government's role in regulating morality. The view that government should work to protect morality is especially common among recently arrived immigrants (69%).

Government Involvement in Protecting Morality

	Should do more	Too involved	Neither/Both/DK
	%	%	%
All U.S. Muslims	59	29	12=100
18–29	61	28	11=100
30–39	58	32	10=100
40–54	59	29	12=100
55+	56	31	13=100
Native-born	54	38	8=100

Foreign-born	63	25	12=100
Arrived pre-1990	56	35	9=100
1990 or later	69	19	12=100
Self/Parents from			
Arab region	72	20	8=100
Pakistan	61	27	12=100
Other South Asia	56	28	16=100
U.S. general public*	37	51	12=100

Question: Which comes closer to your view? The government should do more to protect morality in society (OR) I worry the government is getting too involved in the issue of morality.

* September 2006 Pew Research Center for the People & the Press national survey.

Even though most agree that government should be involved in protecting morality, U.S. Muslims are divided on the question of whether mosques should be involved in politics. Slightly more than four-in-ten Muslims (43%) say that mosques should express their views on day-to-day social and political matters, while slightly less than half (49%) believe that mosques should keep out of political matters. Among the public as a whole, 51% support churches and other houses of worship expressing their views on social and political questions, while 46% say they should keep out of politics.

Should Mosques Express Political Views?

	Express views	Keep out	DK/Ref
	%	%	%
All U.S. Muslims	43	49	8=100
Native-born	68	28	4=100
African American	79	19	2=100
Other race	54	39	7=100
Foreign-born	30	60	10=100
Self/Parents from			
Arab region	42	43	15=100
Pakistan	32	67	1=100
Other South Asia	25	61	14=100
Iran	10	82	8=100
U.S. general public*	51	46	3=100
White	50	47	3=100
African American	62	35	3=100

Question: Should mosques keep out of political matters, or should they express their views on day-to-day social and political questions?

* July 2006 Pew Research Center for the People & the Press national survey. General public asked same question about "churches and other houses of worship."

The roughly even division on this question among all U.S. Muslims reflects the deep disagreement on this issue between native-born Muslims and foreign-born Muslim Americans. Native-born Muslims, especially African Americans, express overwhelming support for the notion that mosques should express their views on social and political matters (68% among all native-born Muslims and 79% among native-born African American

Muslims). U.S. Muslims who were born abroad take the opposite view, with six-in-10 saying that mosques should keep out of political matters.

Voting Participation

On several measures of political engagement, Muslim Americans demonstrate less active involvement in politics than the general public. In part, this reflects the large number of immigrants and the fact that as many as 23% of Muslims in America are not U.S. citizens. But even among the 77% of U.S. Muslims who are citizens, fewer report being registered to vote than in the public at large. While 76% of Americans nationwide say that they are absolutely certain they are registered to vote, 63% of Muslim citizens say the same.

Voter Registration and Turnout

	U.S. Muslim citizens	General public
Registered to vote?	%	%
Yes	63	76
No	30	20
Don't know/Refused	<u>7</u>	<u>4</u>
	100	100
Vote in 2004 election?		
Yes	58	74
No	39	22
Don't know/Refused	<u>3</u>	<u>4</u>
	100	100

Young Muslim Americans, like young people in the general population, are much less likely than older people to be registered to vote. Less than half of eligible U.S. Muslims (48%) under 30 are registered to vote, at least 20 points lower than among Muslims who are older than 30. There is little difference in registration rates between native-born Muslims and immigrants who have gained citizenship.

Voter Registration Lags among U.S. Muslims

	Registered to vote
	%
U.S. Muslim citizens	63
18–29	48
30–39	68
40–54	73
55+	69
Household income	
$75,000+	67
$50-$74,999	74
$30-$49,999	64
Less than $30,000	67
Native-born	65
Foreign-born	62
Self/Parent from	
Arab region	50

Pakistan	83
Other South Asia	65

In addition, Muslim Americans with higher annual incomes are no more likely than poorer Muslims to say they are registered to vote. Among the general public, annual income traditionally is correlated with political engagement in general and voter registration in particular. But income is not related to registration rates among Muslim Americans.

Consistent with patterns in voter registration, eligible Muslim voters are less likely to say they voted in the 2004 general election compared with the population as a whole. Fewer than six-in-ten Muslim American citizens who were age 18 or older in 2004 (58%) say they voted in the presidential election, compared with 74% of all registered voters.

PART IV

GENDER AND ISLAM

The status of women has emerged as a major topic in the discussion and renegotiation of the Islamic tradition in the context of secular America. Topics such as gender equality, sexuality, and social and political rights are discussed in the United States as they are in the Muslim world. However, the question of female religious leadership has been debated in a more specifically American manner, particularly after Dr. Amina Wadud led Jum'a prayer for a mixed congregation and delivered the Friday *khutba* (sermon) on March 18, 2005. Organized by *Muslim WakeUp!*, the prayer was highly publicized in the American media and in the Muslim world. It received a wide variety of responses, ranging from support to critique to condemnation. Responses to this event ranged from traditional to progressive, with a variety of opinions being expressed on the status of women in Islam. Consequently, it serves here as an efficient lens through which to consider the entire debate on Muslim women in the United States.

Another topic more specific to the American context and an object of controversy is the right to homosexuality. Largely taboo in the Muslim world, the debate on homosexuality has become increasingly public in the U.S. as more Muslims are arguing for and defending their identity as Muslims and homosexuals.

72. **Amina Wadud, "March 18, 2005: A Woman Leads Congregational Prayer in New York" from** *Inside the Gender Jihad: Women's Reform in Islam*

Oxford: Oneworld Publications, 2006, pp. 246–252.
Amina Wadud was born Mary Teasley in Washington, DC, in 1953. She attended the University of Pennsylvania, where she converted to Islam in the early 1970s, taking the name Amina Wadud. She received her Ph.D. from the University of Michigan in Islamic Studies and is currently a professor in the Department of Philosophy and Religious Studies at Virginia Commonwealth University. An activist for women's rights, Wadud is a controversial figure in the Muslim world, particularly for leading a Friday congregational prayer of both men and women in New York City on March 18, 2005. Here, she recounts her experience of that Friday prayer.

My theoretical reconstruction of historical male hegemony in public ritual leadership in Islam need not be duplicated in order for me to address the particulars of the prayer service on March 18, 2005. That it was sensationalized in the media, and therefore open to a frenzy of global responses, reiterates the point I just raised above. Therefore, it has already been given extensive public attention and anyone interested in the twists and turns of the debates has more than ample access through these various publications.

The completion of this book with its discussions on multiple aspects and experiences inside the gender *jihad* is a clear indication that the roles I have played in this struggle are neither limited to this one symbolic act nor concluded by performing this act. To many people, worldwide, I am only known through sensationalized controversies. That is understandable. I hope they will eventually come to understand that sensationalist responses to certain public actions are not the basis of, and never can be the goal of, my identity quest as a female in Islam. For this reason, I rejected all invitations to do further interviews relating to the congregational prayer in New York City when those invitations were clearly expecting to gain more attention by publishing articles and presenting news programs focused on the event *just because* it had gained such attention. That is an unfortunate consequence of addressing issues of gender within today's climate of sensationalism. There are, however, a few points about this particular event that only I can tell.

These are offered here, as a matter of public record, in order that my participation is reconfigured along the lines of my lifetime experience within the struggles for justice and Islam.

In the fall of 2004, I was one of several invitees, recognized for participation in progressing Islam from its various aspects of stasis and stagnation, to join the advisory committee to a newly forming group who chose the name "Progressive Muslim Union." Despite the existence of a plethora of organizations worldwide who use the word "progressive" in their name, and despite the number of self-identified progressive Muslims who were among the invitees,[21] lengthy discussion over ownership of the word progressive," including the exclusion of some members of the existing P.M.U. governing board, managed to consume a great deal of time. The organization has been established, the name has been retained (with "in North America" added), but a number of the invitees, myself included, are not affiliated with P.M.U.

Until the prayer, I tried to remain with the group as an advisory board member. The organizers expressed their hope to organize a conference through the Harvard University Diversity Project during the March 18-20 weekend. I was invited to lead congregational prayer the Friday of that conference. I accepted. The conference was not successfully organized, but several months later I received a new invitation to lead congregational prayer on the same date as previously scheduled. After looking into the logistics (I had committed myself to do a presentation at Auburn University Seminary in New York the Thursday evening before), I asked the University organizers if they would arrange the return flight to Richmond in order to allow me to stay in New York throughout the day on Friday. This is the simple logistical background for my participation in this particular event. The organizing committee would occasionally contact me about the developments in planning. One of the organizers, Asra Nomani, who was on tour for her recent book publication, was able to secure needed funds from her publishers, in order to actually assist the plan to come to fruition. I gave most of my energy to considering both the content of my Thursday evening lecture, and the substance of the *khutbah*. I had not forgotten the extent of the controversy that had followed the previous public announcement and participation in a similar invitation in South Africa more than a decade before. Thus, I was especially keen that I concentrate on the nature of public ritual as a performance directed toward Allah, rather than an act of defiance against those who have created the necessity for a gender *jihad* by simply denying women the full human dignity with which Allah has created us. My conclusion was to keep the prayer service as close to the normative male privileged procedure, while contributing from my own female perspective, and encouraging greater gender parity in public ritual leadership.

When the organizers began to publicize the intention to have "the first" female-led Friday congregational prayer service with me as its leader, the climate also began to heat up. This increased the tension for me between potentially competing intentions. I deliberately chose to turn away any media attention focused my way. I agreed to participate in a press conference before the prayer as requested by the organizers. My comments included the comment that "The only thing different about this for me was that I do not do press conferences before prayer." I followed that by saying, "After this, I would not be giving any more interviews." For several months, I did not. However, in the first two weeks following the prayer, the requests flowed in with other responses to the prayer at a rate of about fifty a day.

When I left the press conference to observe the quiet time I needed before the actual prayer, the organizers fielded questions from the media and tried to get the prayer space set up. I had reminded them of a few details about the ritual format even as a break from the male exclusive format would occur simultaneously. I explicitly mentioned that the second call to prayer should be given *after* I had walked to the front of the congregation, faced and pronounced the greeting: "*As-Salaamu Alaykum,* Peace be Upon You." The young woman giving the call to prayer started to make that second call while I was on my way to the podium. To cover up this break, I had no recourse but to sit on my prayer rug facing the congregation with my head bowed until she finished. I then stood up to take the podium, facing the congregation using only handwritten notes. I will give a brief overview here, noting that between the large portions given in Arabic then translated into English, and the portions only in English, it would be cumbersome to attempt a whole reconstruction for inclusion here, as requested. All those parts recited in Arabic were followed by English translation, nearly doubling the delivery time (while here I refer to their having beenn recited in Arabic). The text provided below is a nearly all English reconstruction for general readership.

ANOTHER STAND AT THE PODIUM, *KHUTBA* TO THE *SALAT AL-JUMU'AH* ON MARCH 18, 2005

(The beginning was recited in Arabic and translated into English.)

Praise be to Allah, Lord of all Worlds (or all alternative universal possibilities). I begin in the name and praise of Allah *ta'ala.* I bear witness that there is no god but Allah, One, with no partners; and I bear witness that Muhammad, Ibn-'Abd Allah, is the Prophet (and Messenger) of Allah. May Allah's praise be upon him, and upon his *ahl* (people), and his (immediate) companions, and his wives, and upon all who follow the guidance, (all of them) together until the day of reckoning; Amin.[22]

Allah, *ta'ala* says in the Qur'an, "Oh you who securely believe! If you hear the call to the *salah* on the day of the communal gathering (*al-jumu'ah*), hurry to the remembrance of Allah and leave aside your selling. That is better for you if you but knew" (62:9).[23]

"Allah, there is no god but the God, (and) He/She/It is," the Ever-Living, the Self-Subsistent Fount of All Being. Neither slumber over takes Him, nor sleep. His is all that is in the heavens and all that is on earth. Who is there that could intercede with Him, unless it be by His leave? He knows all the lies open before [human beings] and all that is hidden from them, whereas they cannot attain to aught of His knowledge save that which He wills [them to attain]. His eternal power overspreads the heavens and the earth, and their upholding wearies Him not. And He alone is truly Exalted, Tremendous[24] (*ayat al-kursi*, 2:255).

Surely the men who surrender and the women who surrender, and the men who believe and the women who believe, and the men who obey and the women who obey, and the men who speak the truth and the women who speak the truth, and the men and the women who are patiently steadfast, and the men who are humble and the women who are humble, and the men who give in alms and the women who give in alms, and the men who fast and the women who fast, and the men who guard their private parts and the women who guard their private parts, and the men who guard their private parts and the women who [guard their private parts], and the men who remember Allah abundantly and the women who remember—Allah has prepared for them forgiveness and a vast reward (33:35).[25]

I stand before you in all my imperfections and weaknesses confessing that I bear sincere love of Allah and love for all of Her *ayat*/signs. These signs are everywhere. The buds of many colors, including green, are now being born in my yard from trees and bushes; and early flowers like crocuses and daffodils follow the birth of the buds. These are part of Allah's infinite mercy and their beauty reflects Allah's Self-Disclosure.

Allah pre-existed the creation of this world and as Creator, according to the Qur'an, promised that guidance would come in countless forms for humankind—if we but think and reflect.

The greatest mercy and guidance in the form of Allah's Self-Disclosure is, without a doubt, the gift of revelation. Revelation or *wahy,* to actual human beings, some of whom were chosen as messengers, holding the responsibility to convey those messages to all of humanity. There is no one chosen people, exclusive members of one of the world's many religions-some no longer in existence—some so widespread by numbers and powers that they look upon themselves as exclusively "the chosen." The "chosen" are all of humanity. Anyone (and everyone)—whether existing before the lifetime of the Prophet Muhammad (saw) or existing now, with no (direct or immediate) access to the special mission of the Prophet (as) as *khitmat-ul-anbiya,* seal of the prophets—is also chosen by the very gift of life that Allah has granted from three pronouns for God are indeed intentional of Its mercy and wisdom.

As Muslims we are fortunate to have Allah's generosity in the form of the last known effort of revelation as Self-Disclosure (in words), the Qur'an al-Karim. So let us build upon that gift today. (Read in Arabic first (Among His signs is that He)) has created you from a single *nafs* and created from it, its mate: and spread from the two, countless men and women (4:1). This unity of origin, I would say, reflects two important implications, both extensions of the fundamental principle, *tawhid*: (1) of course Allah is One, Allah is Unique, Allah is united and Allah unifies (all things in creation); (2) no human being is ever the same as Allah, able to know or understand all of Allah's intention for the creation of humans, or the entire cosmos. Yet all human beings have been granted the potential to experience at-one-ment with Allah for fleeting moments in the creation, and eternally *fi-l-akhirah* (in the Ultimate and Permanent End)

Since humans, created from a single soul, by a single Lord of love, mercy and power, one dimension of experiencing that one-ness is by living before, in surrender to, Allah *ta'ala,* to practice the unity of human beings. *Tawhid* is the foundation of Muslim unity. Let us look at this *tawhidic* paradigm, as it relates to all human actions and interactions as well as to, our gathering here today.

(Here I provided a succinct explanation of the *tawhidic* paradigm and horizontal reciprocity between any two humans, especially emphasizing between male and female humans, as detailed in chapter 1. The remainder of the *khutbah* was in Arabic, with the following English translations.[26])

Unto such of them as may [yet] attain faith and do righteous deeds, Allah has promised forgiveness and a reward supreme. We seek forgiveness from Allah and we ask of Her special blessing and mercy and forgiveness. Oh you who believe, seek forgiveness from Him, the Forgiver, the Bounteous. Our Lord, indeed I have wronged my soul a grave wrong and none forgives except You, so forgive me in this and in all things.

(Here, I sat sideways on the prayer mat and continued some personal remembrance, seeking more forgiveness and asking for guidance.)

The second and last part of the *khuthah* continued in Arabic and was delivered with the following translations:

Ya sin is our roof and ceiling. *Kaf Ha Ya 'Ayn Sad* are sufficient for us; *Ha Mim 'Ayn Sin Qaf* are our supporters or advocates. Allah will make you sufficient unto them all, and He is the All-Hearer, the All-Knower. The covering of the Divine Throne has come down upon us, and the Eye of Allah is watching us. With the Power of Allah, no one has power against us or over us.

Allah is enough for me! There is no deity save Him. In Him have I placed my trust, for He is the Sustainer, in awesome almightiness enthroned. In the Name of Allah, with Whose Name nothing on the earth and in the heaven can harm: and He is All-Hearing and All-Knowing. And there is no strength nor power save in Allah, the Sublime, the Tremendous. Limitless in His glory is the Sustainer, the Lord of Almightiness, [exalted] above anything that [human beings] may devise by way definition. And Peace be upon all His message-bearers! And all praise due to Allah alone, the Sustainer of all the worlds. And May Allah send blessings on our master, Muhammad, and on his family and people and companions and also peace.

In the name of Allah, the Most Gracious, the Dispenser of Grace. O Allah, O Light, O Truth, O Obvious Manifest, shower me with Thy Light and teach me of Thy Knowledge, and make me understand of Thee, and make me hear Thee, and make me see Thee. Thou art Powerful over everything.

O Existent One, O Thou who art Present in all difficulties, O Thou of Hidden Kindness, of Subtle Making, O Gentle one, Who does not hasten, fulfill my need, with Thy Mercy, O Most Merciful of the Mercifuls. Glory be to Thee on Thy Grace, after Thy Knowledge. Glory be to Thee on Thy Forgiveness, after Thy Power. But if those [who are bent on denying the truth] turn away, say: Allah is enough for me! There is no deity save Her. In Him have I placed my trust for It is the Sustainer, in awesome almightiness enthroned. There is none like Him, and He is the Hearer, the Knower.

Amin.

Please join me in reciting al-Fatihah, the Opening chapter of the Qur'an.

Then I asked for the *iqamah,* immediate call preceding the prayer itself. I turned for the first time to face the *qiblah,* direction for prayer, toward the Ka'abah in Makkah, and I made my silent prayer of intention and raised my head with my hands at the sides of my face to recite *"Allahu Akbar,"* God is greatest. I was shocked to find cameras and journalists directly in front of me! This was *not* where I wanted to direct my prayer. This was not something I had given consent to. As I struggled with this surprising distraction while continuing with the long-ago-memorized portions of the prayer, I finally stumbled over the last few lines of the *surah* I had selected for the first unit of the prayer. This was the same *surah* I used for leading large congregations approximately 90% of the time I would accept this role as prayer leader. This *surah* was also part the sermon I had given in Cape more than a decade before. *Surah Inshirah,* the 94th chapter, is my reminder that difficulty in life comes with ease in life. A few members from the congregation offered the requisite reminder of the portions over which I lost my flow of thoughts and memory. It reminded me of the difficulty before me: I was not facing the media, they were inappropriately located in the direction of prayer, as the organizers later told me, because they could not be controlled.

I was facing the reality that Allah is present in all ways, at all times, and in all places, and all I needed to do was to look with the eyes of my heart and turn my prayer back on track:

an act of worship toward Allah. When those who claim a tradition of authority to prevent women from standing in front of men because the men might get distracted, it is the responsibility of the men, prior to the prayer, to consent and then to respond through consciousness of the act of worship and not the incidents of form. So, despite my lack of consent, I took self-responsibility at that moment to remember what the prayer represents: an act of devotion to That which is beyond our eyes' vision, as could be disturbed by the weakness of our hearts. If we settle our hearts back to Allah, then and only then can we hope to complete the worship as intended. That is what I did. The cameras and the media disappeared before my heart and no longer presented a distraction to my eyes.

Finally, I must acknowledge with gratitude those about whom I had the most knowledge of in organizing this event: Ahmad Naseef, Asra Normani, and Saleemah Abdul-Ghafur. Many others were involved but I never spoke with them directly. May Allah bless us all in this one moment in the timelessness of the cosmic order and important events in the gender jihad for justice and reform in Islam.

73. "A Statement from the Organizers of the March 18th Woman-Led Jum'ah Prayer" from *Muslim WakeUp!*

March 13, 2005. Available online: http://www.muslimwakeup.com/main/archives/2005/ 03/a_statement_fro_1.php#more.

Muslim WakeUp! (for a description of Muslim WakeUp! see the preface to Primary document 3) is best known for its central role in organizing and publicizing the first mixed-gender Friday Jum'a prayer led by a woman, Amina Wadud, on Friday March 18, 2005. The event was schedule to occur at the Sundaram Tagore Gallery in New York City, but following bomb threats the organizers moved it to an Anglican Church in a different part of the city. Approximately one hundred people attended and participated in the prayer. In the following entry, Muslim WakeUp! outlines its motivations and objective for Wadud's prayer, namely "Muslim women reclaiming their rightful place in Islam." The statement also addresses security concerns for the event after the original location received bomb threats.

As word has spread in our community and around the world about our intentions to hold a mixed-gender Friday congregational prayer led by a woman imam, we want to re-assert our motivations and objectives in organizing this event.

Fundamentally, this event is about Muslim women reclaiming their rightful place in Islam. It is not about any specific person or personality. Our sole agenda is to help create Muslim communities that reflect the egalitarian nature of Islam.

This event is not a protest, and the Muslims who will be gathering on March 18th will come together in worship of God. This is a spiritual convening—nothing more, nothing less.

Those who will gather for the prayer later this week will do so as a result of deeply held convictions that are rooted in our faith. Our understanding of the Qur'an and of the Prophetic tradition has led us to the same conclusions about the admissibility of female-led prayer that led the great Muslim jurist, historian, and Qur'anic scholar Al-Tabari to hold the same view 1,100 years ago.

We love and care deeply for our community, and we understand that good people will arrive at varying conclusions regarding the Islamic basis for female-led prayer. This is not an attempt to "change" Islam, nor to condemn others who interpret our religion differently than we do.

If Muslims are to rise to the many challenges that face us, we must create safe spaces for dialogue among ourselves—silencing opposing views accomplishes nothing except the growth of resentment and driving more people away who feel marginalized. As a community, we need to acknowledge the richness of our faith and the multiplicities of interpretation that have existed within our tradition.

Unfortunately, instead of engaging in thoughtful discussion, a small minority within our community continues to favor intimidation and threats over conversing with, to use the words of our Qur'an, "that which is more beautiful," billati hiya ahsan (Qur'an 16:125).

As a result, due to security concerns, the owner of the space that had originally offered to host the Jum'ah can no longer do so.

We are committed to holding a congregational prayer that ensures the safety of all the women, men, and children in attendance. For this reason, after consulting with concerned members of our community as well as law enforcement authorities, we have decided not to publicly announce the new location for the prayer. Those who are interested in attending must fill out the form below, and we will contact them directly with more information.

We are also looking to make arrangements for an Internet broadcast of this historic event, and more information will be published on the details of the broadcast as soon as we have them.

Finally, we want to thank all our supporters in the Muslim community who have sent us messages from around the world expressing their solidarity with us and our intentions.

God willing, the day will come when Muslims anywhere in the world will be able to stand in worship of the One God without fear or intimidation.

74. "A Statement from the Assembly of Muslim Jurists in America about the Issue of Women Leading the Friday Prayer and Delivering the Ceremony" from *The Assembly of Muslim Jurists in America*

AMJA; accessed May 2006. Available online: http://www.amjaonline.com/English// headline.asp?Headid=58. Reprinted with permission of The Assembly of Muslim Jurists in America.

The following is a fatwa from the Assembly of Muslim Jurists in America (for a description see The Assembly of Muslim Jurists in America: Mission Statement, Primary document 4). The fatwa argues that it is impermissible for a woman to lead the Friday prayer and deliver the khutba. This fatwa was issued in response to Amina Wadud's leading the first public female-led Friday prayer in New York City on March 18, 2005. The fatwa expresses a traditional and classical opinion that is likely shared by many American Muslims, both male and female.

In the name of ALLAH most Merciful, most Beneficent

All praise is due to ALLAH and may the peace and the blessing of ALLAH be upon our Prophet Mohamed.

A question was raised to AMJA about the permissibility of a woman leading the Friday prayer and delivering the ceremony. The question was raised as it was announced in a Masjid in the New York area that a woman plans to lead the Friday prayer and deliver the Khutbah.

AMJA totally denounces such action, which is a complete heresy, and affirms the following facts:

- The ultimate reference and the supreme source of legislation of Islam is the Book of ALLAH (SWT) (i.e. the Glorious Qur'an) and the purified *Sunnah* of the Prophet (PBUH). The Prophet said : "*I left amongst you that which if you hold on to, you will never go astray after me: the Book of ALLAH (SWT) and my Sunnah.*" Consensus and unanimity on the interpretation of a certain text in these two sources is an irrefutable proof for its meaning and a clear unambiguous sign and evidence that any other later interpretation is nullified, void and rejected. ALLAH (SWT) said in Surat Al-Nisaa what can be translated as: "*If anyone contends with the Messenger even after guidance has been plainly conveyed to him, and follows a path other than that becoming to men of Faith, We shall leave him in the path he has chosen, and land him in Hell, what an evil refuge*" And the Prophet (PBUH) described the successful group among the ones that went astray as being "*who follow and behave as what I and my companions follow and behave.*"

- Secondly: A unanimous consensus for the entire *Ummah*, in the east and west that women can not lead the Friday prayer nor can they deliver the ceremony. Whoever takes part in such a prayer, then his prayer is nullified, whether he was and Imam or a follower. It is never found in any jurisprudential text, from *Sunnah* Scholars of *Fiqh* (Hanafi, Maliki, Shafi nor Hanbali) or even of the *Shiite* scholars, that a woman can lead the Friday prayer nor deliver the ceremony. This opinion is an innovation and a heresy on any account, nullified by all scholars.

- Some of the evidence that led to the above mentioned consensus is what came in the purified *Sunnah* that the rows of the women should be behind the rows of the men in the prayer. In the *Hadeeth* narrated by Anas (in Bukhari) said, "*the Prophet (PBUH) prayed as Imam for Anas, his mother and his Aunt, he made Anas stand on his right side and Anas's mother and his aunt behind them*". Same arrangement was followed in the Masjid of the Prophet (PBUH) and across the entire *Ummah* for centuries. Imam Muslim narrated that the Prophet (PBUH) said, "*The best rows for the men are the front ones and the least good are the ones towards the back, and the best rows for the women are the ones towards the back the least good are the ones towards the front.*" This was for no other reason but to protect them from any embarrassment and to close the door on any evil thoughts or temptations that might come into the hearts of whomever might be looking at them otherwise. How could it be possible then that a woman can be in front of all rows leading the Friday prayer?!

- Another evidence is that is well established in Islamic jurisprudence that ALLAH (SWT) has not made prayer in congregation mandatory for women, neither is it obligatory that women pray Friday prayers. The Prophet (PBUH) mentioned in the authentic narration through Abu Dawood: "*Friday prayer is mandatory upon each Muslim (to be performed) in a congregation, the only types of people who are exempedt: a slave, a woman, a young boy or a sick person (i.e. it is not mandatory for these people to attend the congregation).*" In addition, the Prophet (PBUH) informed Muslim women that their prayer at home is better for them than attending the congregation, out of mercy upon them that they face the hassles of going out and to shield them from temptations. The Prophet (PBUH) said "*Do not prevent the women from going to the Masjid, however, it is better for them to pray at home*" [narrated by Imam Ahmed and Abu Dawood]. Given that it is not mandatory for a woman to pray in the Masjid to achieve the intent of the legislator (ALLAH (SWT)) of making it easy upon women by praying at home as well as shielding them from temptations, how can it be reasonable and acceptable that a woman goes up on the pulpit to deliver the ceremony, and stand in front of the rows as Imam!!

- It was never recorded that a single woman, across Islamic history, has performed such an act, nor even demanded to do it. It has never happened at the lifetime of the Prophet (PBUH), nor during the time of the companions, or their followers, not even in later generations and centuries. This is by itself constitutes a clear proof on the invalidity of this opinion, and that anyone who calls for it or help to implement it is a heretic.

If any of this has a shade or legitimacy, the most qualified women to actually do it were the mothers of the believers; most of them were knowledgeable brilliant scholars who transmitted to us a lot of the knowledge disseminated by the Prophet (PBUH). A good example of them is the eloquent, articulate, bright and knowledgeable Ai'sha, daughter of Abu Bakr, wife of the Prophet (PBUH), mother of the believers. If there was any shred of evidence that this act is good and permissible, these shining examples among Muslim women would have taken the lead to it. There were numerous women scholars across Islamic history, jurisprudential references and narration experts; they were honest, trustworthy and experts in what they accomplished. Imam Hafiz Athahabi said: "It was never recorded that a woman propagated a false *Hadeeth* attributed to the Prophet (PBUH)", he also mentioned that "I am not aware of any woman that was accused of propagating falsehoods or ones that their narrations disregarded". Among the teachers of Imam Hafiz bin Asaker were eighty something women. Similarly for Imam Abu Muslim al-Farahidi, who reported the narration of seventy women. Imam Shafii, Bukhari, Ibn Khalakan and Ibn Haian all had women among their teachers. None of these noble women scholars ever attempted to lead the Friday prayer nor deliver the ceremony, even that they were superior in knowledge over many of their contemporary men in Jurisprudence, Religious knowledge and narrations from the Prophet (PBUH).

Muslim women participated in all aspects of Islamic work throughout Islamic history: as a scholar and jurisprudential reference, as participating in all kinds of worship, as helpers in the field of relief and emergency aid and in the enjoining of good and forbidding of evil. But never were they Imams for Friday prayers or have ever delivered Friday ceremonies.

It is a logical, fundamental conclusion that only men are allowed to perform such a function as leading the Friday prayer and delivering the ceremony. Whoever disputes this fact can take as much time as he/she wants to dig out one single example form the volumes of Islamic Jurisprudence across the centuries, and he/she will miserably fail.

• Lastly: Those who are calling for such acts, are taking as an excuse a narration that Um Waraqah was given the permission by the Prophet (PBUH) to lead her household members in the prayer. This narration, even assuming that it is authentic, has nothing to do whatsoever with the Friday prayer. It is talking about some very specific circumstances where a woman can lead the prayer inside her home, and has no relation to Friday prayer and general congregations.

AMJA delivers this somber warning message to the entire *Ummah,* not to give any credit to such false initiatives that contradicts with the basics and fundamentals of the religion, and is a totally heretic innovation. AMJA reminds Muslims that we are to follow only the Book of ALLAH and the purified *Sunnah* of the Prophet (PBUH). Muslims should pay careful attention to whom they are seeking the guidance from, indeed he who strives to cling on to his religion nowadays is suffering as much as a person who is trying to keep a tight fist on a piece of flaming charcoal in the palm of his hand. AMJA extends a sincere supplication to non but ALLAH (SWT) to save us from all trials and tribulations, and to guide us all to that which is closest to the mercy and pleasure of ALALH (SWT), as He is the only One Capable of that.

It is ALLAH (SWT) alone that we seek in all of our actions, and it is he alone that can guide to the straight path.

Fatwa-issuing Permanent Committee

75. **Hina Azam, "A Critique of the Argument for Woman-Led Friday Prayers"**
from *Alt.Muslim.com,*

*Published March 18, 2006. Available online: http://www.altmuslim.com/perm.php?
id=1416_0_25_0_C2. Reprinted with permission of Alt.Muslim.com.*

*Hina Azam is an American citizen and a professor at the University of Texas at Austin. She
teaches in both the Department of Middle Eastern Studies and at the Center for Women's and
Gender Studies, focusing on Islamic studies and specifically on Islamic law and gender issues.
Azam received her Ph.D. from Duke University in 2005. She wrote the following article in
response to Amina Wadud's leading the first public female-led Friday prayer in New York City
on March 18, 2005. While she supports the goal of the mixed-gender prayer, she contends that
the arguments presented in support of this practice are not methodologically sound. Instead,
Azam believes more in-depth work on the interpretation of Islamic sources is necessary. Some
American Muslim feminists, keen to remain within the framework of the Islamic tradition,
also express this position.*

Heaven knows I have wished for women to be able to lead salat al-jumu'ah. But wishful
thinking is not a sound methodology.

All Muslim eyes today are turned toward New York, where *Muslim WakeUp!* and the
Muslim Women's Freedom Tour have organized the first public woman-led Friday prayer
service in ... well, perhaps ever. Needless to say, this event has stirred up quite a bit of controversy. In order to justify the event, MWU has posted an article by Nevin Reda arguing
for the religious validity of female imams for mixed-sex Friday prayers. A few other such
pieces, though not having the depth of Nevin Reda's, also exist on the internet. On the
other side of the court, one can find articles opposing female imams for jumu'ah services.
My contention here is that the argument in favor of woman-led jumu'ah salat is not
persuasive, for reasons that have been only partially explained in some of the existing critiques.

As a starting thought, let me say that PMU/MWU! serves an important function in the
Muslim community in its role as gadfly. Many of the issues they raise, pertaining to
women, sexuality, the use of violence, interfaith relations and the like, are ones that need
to be raised in an open way. They have thrown down the gauntlet to the rest of the
ummah, and that is to be lauded. I agree with their overall goal of improving women's
position within Islamic law, and of seeking gender equity. I also support a critique of
classical Islamic legal methodology, and revision where appropriate. As for the issue of
women leading salat al-jumu'ah, I have no personal objection to it. However, it is the
divine will that I believe we are charged with discerning, not our personal sensibilities.
Thus, my disagreement with the progressive position is not over the content of the
rulings, but with the legal methodology by which the rulings are being argued, which does
not appear to me to be sound.

In order to arrive at any new legal doctrine, or hukm, one must employ a systematic
methodology by which to extract meaning from the sources. Traditionally, this methodology has been categorized under the rules of ijtihad. If the classical principles of ijtihad are
not viewed by progressive Muslims as being adequate, either in whole or in part, for
discerning the will of God, then they must present an alternative.

The centerpiece of a proper juristic methodology is a sound system of legal reasoning
which is consistent with the texts of the Qur'an and the most-likely-authentic Sunna,
and which emerges from a spirit of piety and submission to Allah (or khushu'). By sound

reasoning, I mean that any argument that is proffered should progress along logical lines that are internally consistent. The classical jurists of Islam developed such a methodology. They devised ways of both grading the reliability of, and extracting meaning from, the texts, ways that by and large are very sound. For example, the fuqaha' isolated different degrees of textual clarity: Does a text reasonably permit of only one meaning? Two? More? Are there other texts that help us decide between two possible meanings in the first text? They also came up with principles for determining when a strict application of the law might be set aside for reasons of individual or social necessity. The important point for our purposes is that while jurists might have disagreed about specific rulings, they followed a well-elucidated methodology that was highly rational, that was consistent with the Qur'an and Sunna/hadith, and that appears, from my readings, to have emerged from a very real spirit of humility before God. The classical methodology of discerning the divine intent is truly awe-inspiring, and a formidable challenge to anyone who seeks to arrive at wholly new hukms, in large part because—as a method—it remains highly persuasive.

I do not say that the classical juridical methods were flawless. There were clearly differences of opinion between the jurists over specific rulings, and these differences arose from methodological disagreements. However, despite these differences in methodology and content, there were broad swaths of moral action that were treated in nearly identical fashion by most expounders of the law. Any attempt to come to fiqh positions that are not given somewhere within the existing corpus must:

a) explain why the existing methodology is unacceptable (that is, why it necessarily leads to conclusions that are makruh or haram), and

b) provide an alternate methodology that is more capable than the existing one at discerning the divine intent.

The proposed ruling—that women may lead men in salat al-jumu'ah—violates several basic texts and classical interpretive principles, and its proponents provide neither a sound critique of the traditional legal methodology or nor an improved one to replace it. The impression one gets is that there is no consistent methodology, that in fact, the desired ruling (the permissibility of women leading mixed-sex congregations for salat al-jumu'ah) dictates their use of texts and of interpretive method. Heaven knows I have wished for women to be able to lead salat al-jumu'ah. But wishful thinking is not a sound methodology.

Because the arguments in favor of women leading jumu'ah, and mixed congregations generally, is being made using traditional sources and methodology, let me explain why I think their argument is flawed.

1. SALAT AL-JUMU'AH AND THE REQUIREMENTS OF THE IMAMAH ARE ISSUES OF WORSHIP ('IBADAT), AND THUS SHOULD NOT BE MODIFIED

Some might ask, is the issue of women leading salat one of social norms or religious law?

Answer: In a nutshell, the laws of Islam have been divided by the scholars into two broad categories, those that have to do with the rights of God, and those that have to do with the rights of human beings. Certain acts are purely in fulfillment of one, and some the other, and some fulfill both. Prayer, as one of the 'ibadat (forms of worship) has been considered to be almost purely in the category of rights of God. This is in distinction to social, economic and political activities, which are seen as having to do with the rights of human beings.

The jurists gave human interpretation very little scope in modifying the rules regarding the forms of worship. They reasoned as follows: The elements of salat—its physical format, the formulae read within it, the specifics of the surahs that may be read, the rules regarding special types of salat (such as jumu'ah, eid, janaza), the rules regarding what constitutes tahara (ritual purification), the number of raka'at in each type, the times of day, the alignment of men and women, the khutab—all of these were established during the life of the Prophet under divine guidance. We simply do not know the reasons for their form. Furthermore, because salat is so critical to proper practice of Islam, it is not an area that one may tamper with.

Thus, the scholars operated according to the principle that the rule (asl) in social laws (mu'amalat) is permissibility (ibahah), and the rule in religious observance ('ibadat) is prohibition (tahrim). In ordinary language, this means that in the area of ordinary life (social and individual), we may assume that a lack of evidences (dala'il) regarding an activity indicates that we can do it. In the area of the ibadat, however, we are to take the opposite approach: Unless there is a dala'il indicating that something is permissible, we are to assume it is prohibited. It is a very conservative approach to the ibadat, undoubtedly, and I believe for good reason.

The consensus among the scholars on the issue of leadership of salat (imamah), both in terms of leading the actual salat and of delivering the khutba, falls under the laws of 'ibadah, and is not simply a question of social norm. We submit to the form of the salat that the Prophet did, and pray as he did. Just as we cannot decide that the ritual aspect is old-fashioned and we now want to pray sitting in pews, we cannot modify the rules of imamah. A hard pill to swallow for some, perhaps, but the goal is jannah, in the end.

2. WOMEN LEADING MIXED CONGREGATIONS IN FARD SALAT DOES NOT CONSTITUTE A GRAVE NEED, FOR WHICH ORDINARY RULES OF SALAT AND IMAMAH MAY BE SET ASIDE

According to the traditional methodology, the selection of a weaker hukm over a stronger hukm can only be done when there is a dire social or individual need, or a threat of injustice or loss of life. For example, when Umar b. al-Khattab suspended the law of cutting off the hand for theft in a period of hunger, that was a dire need. When one is permitted to consume alcohol or pork when on the verge of death, that is a dire need.

Women leading salat simply does not qualify as a dire need, either individually or socially. Nor does a woman delivering the khutba (which is part of the salat). Nor does bringing the women up to the front or having a mixed congregation. Furthermore, non-engagement in any of these actions does not result in a loss of life or well-being, intellect, property, lineage, or religion. Non-engagement does not constitute injustice. On the level of necessity, then, this proposed hukm does not pass the muster.

This is not to say that there are not grave problems concerning gender equity in our community. Women in the Muslim community generally, and in the mosque in particular, are seen as being "good Muslims" when they are most silent, most unobtrusive, most compliant with male-driven policies. Walls and curtains, crowded and substandard prayer areas, prohibitions from entering the "main" area or going through the "main" door, lack of comfortable and direct access to imams/scholars, gender separation of couples and families upon entrance into the mosque—all of these contribute to a feeling of alienation among Muslim women. All of these problems, however, should be rectified without violating the sanctity of our 'ibadat.

3. TARAWIH AND LEADING ONE'S SLAVES AND KIN IS FUNDAMENTALLY DISTINCT FROM JUMU'AH, AND THE RULES FROM ONE CANNOT BE TRANSLATED TO THE OTHER

Although the majority of scholars said that women cannot ever lead men in jama'ah (congregation) for any prayer, there were a few (such as al-Tabari, al-Muzani, Abu Thawr and Ibn Taymiyya) who made exceptions. The exceptions were based not on any one hadith, such as that of Umm Waraqa, but on all the textual and rational evidences taken together. These exceptions were of two sorts:

1) That a woman may lead salat al-tarawih if there is no male who has memorized the Qur'an, as long as segregation and the rows are maintained, and

2) That a woman may lead her own male kin (her husband, her children, her slaves) in her own household, if she is the most knowledgeable of them.

Each of these exceptions has its particular logic, a logic that cannot be extended to Friday prayer within the existing interpretive methodology.

Tarawih is distinct from jumu'ah in several key respects: Tarawih is a nafl salat, while jumu'ah is a fard salat. Tarawih is ideally offered in one's own home, while jumu'ah is the most public of congregations. Tarawih becomes the grounds for an exception, according to the Hanbali jurists, because of the importance of reciting and hearing Qur'an during the month of Ramadan. So important is it, they reasoned, that if a woman were the only one who had memorized or could read and recite Qur'an, it warranted an exception to the rule of male-led salat. It is very difficult to argue that in an entire locality, there is no man who is capable of leading jumu'ah, while for the much smaller tarawih, it is more likely that a woman may be the one who has memorized most Qur'an.

Leading salat al-fard in one's own household is distinct from jumu'ah in several key respects, which all stem from the fact that in one's own home, the assumption is that one is leading maharim (blood-relatives) only, while the assumption is that in jumu'ah, one is leading mostly ghayr maharim (strangers). The rules for relationship between maharim are well-known: A woman need not cover herself or be as concerned for modesty around her husband, parents, siblings, children. She can touch them, relax, etc.

In short, the jurists who were open to women's imamah still limited their exceptions to tarawih and household salat. They took the hadith of Umm Waraqa seriously, but did not run with it to the point of trampling all the other dala'il, as does the progressive approach to this issue.

4. THE HADITH OF UMM WARAQA DOES NOT PROVIDE A SUFFICIENTLY PERSUASIVE BASIS FOR WOMEN LEADING MIXED CONGREGATIONS IN SALAT AL-JUMA'A

At most, one might reasonable argue that a woman can lead her own household, as have a minority of jurists. The progressives' argument on the general permissibility of women's imamah hinges in part on the idea that in the hadith of Umm Waraqa, "dar" means area or locality. While this is one of the possible meanings of "dar," it is highly unlikely in this context. For example, no one ever suggests that when the early Muslims prayed at the "dar" of al-Arqam, they were praying in al-Arqam's locality rather than within the confines of his private residence. Perhaps the strongest evidence that "dar" literally means her home is the fact that there are multiple variants of this hadith. While in Tabaqat Ibn Sa'd, the word used is "dar," the version given by Abu Dawud in his Sunan uses the word "bayt," which not only means "home" but even "room within a home."

Nevin Reda's argument (on the MWU site) is particularly inconsistent on the meaning of "dar" in Umm Waraqa's hadith. On one hand, she says that "dar" likely means "area," and that Umm Waraqa was thus designated to be imam of her locality. On the other hand, she says that "dar" means "home," and that Umm Waraqa's home functioned as the jami' masjid of her area. Both readings are speculative, and cannot be used as a basis upon which to construct a general permissibility of women's imamah, especially when there are no other supporting texts for that idea, and when there are several texts indicating that in all other known circumstances, men served as imams over other men.

In the same way, the argument that Umm Waraqa's congregation must have included more than just her 2 slaves and perhaps the elderly man who served as her muezzin can hardly pass as strong evidence for women leading jumu'ah or mixed jama'ah. Likewise, the contention that there must have been more than 3-4 people in order for there to have been a designated muezzin is not strong. There can be a muezzin even for such a small group, and most jurists held that even a lone man doing salat should call adhan for himself. Numbers have nothing to do with the need for a muezzin.

In general, the arguments that are given in support of the upcoming female-led jumu'ah, in combination with the extent of the modifications being made to traditional laws of salat, reflect an ends-justify-the-means approach. It appears that it has already been decided that it is permissible for women to lead a mixed congregation in jumu'ah. Any textual or rational indicants that these rulings might be invalid are conveniently rejected. At the same time, texts that are seen as supporting the pre-determined ruling are championed in a way that is highly selective and methodologically inconsistent.

Furthermore, the claims being made are far more sweeping than the evidence warrants. For example, Nevin Reda writes, "From the above evidence it is abundantly clear that Qur'anic and hadith evidence is overwhelmingly in favor of woman imams." Can it really be that the same scholars who preserved for us the hadith of Umm Waraqa could have been so dimwitted as to have missed "abundantly clear" rulings? That we are the first to realize that the Prophet had actually established a second mosque in Madina and designated Umm Waraqa as its imam? While it may be fashionable to ignore or undermine the classical legal tradition, I have a hard time understanding how one could reasonably think that those interpretive methods were all flawed, that the jurists were all wrong, and that we have arrived at the true Islam—which happily enough, matches our own cultural sensibilities.

My recommendation is that we study and critique the tradition, and work on developing a legal interpretive methodology that leads to more equitable rulings, yes. But I would also recommend a much greater dose of caution and of humility, in light of the gravity of the task. I would seek to remind us all that our first priority is to seek the good pleasure of Allah, whose guidance for humanity may not always be scrutable.

Given both a recognition of the marginalization of women from public religious life and the need to preserve the sanctity of the 'ibadat, there are other ways for women to become integrally involved in jumu'ah in a public teaching capacity, and I would encourage masajid to implement these. I realize that my recommendations will not satisfy those who favor women leading mixed congregations, and this is fine. I think it is also clear by now that I am not willing, at this point, to concede the legitimacy of that route, wallahu a'lam. I suggest these avenues for those who remain unconvinced of the progressive position, who seek to preserve the integrity of the 'ibadat, but who also would feel that women must have greater visibility within the religious life of the community:

1) Women may write the Friday khutbas to be delivered by the khatib with proper attribution to the author. In my experience, imams are more than happy to have someone else do the work of putting together the khutba, and the practice of khatibs reading sermons written by others is well-known.

2) Women may deliver public lectures just prior to the khutba. The practice of a public talk between the adhan and the beginning of the khutba is found in much of the Muslim world and is an even more direct way than the above for women to communicate their ideas directly to the congregation. One idea for dual-language communities is that the talk delivered by the woman can be the basis for the khutba, which would essentially be a translation of it.

3) Women may be the translators of the khutba, as the translation is not technically part of the khutba. This is clearly not a function in which her own ideas will be disseminated, but in many communities, even hearing a woman's voice, either through one's headset or after the khutba, would be a significant improvement over the status quo.

Some might regard these suggestions, particularly #2, as being so close to women giving the khutba that I am just hairsplitting. Others may feel that these suggestions do not go far enough, since they stop shy of restructuring the jumu'ah rules. My hope, however, is that for those who seek a middle course, these will provide a sound basis for action while remaining within the parameters of the tradition.

76. Adam Wild Aba, "Muslim Women Can Lead Some Prayers: Scholars" from *IslamOnline.net*

Published March 12, 2005. Available online: http://www.islam-online.net/English/News/ 2005-03/12/article06.shtml. Reprinted with permission of IslamOnline.net.

The following entry is a news article describing reactions to Amina Wadud's being the first woman to lead Friday prayer in New York City on March 18, 2005. It focuses on the responses of Massoud Sabri (an Egyptian researcher for Islamonline.net's fatwa department), Shaykh Yusuf Al-Qaradawi (a prominent shaykh in Qatar; for a biography see the "al-Qaradawi, Yusuf" entry in Volume 1), and the Assembly of Muslim Jurists in America (AMJA). All the responses presented condemn prayer led by women, which is representative of the mainstream position among American Muslims and in the broader Muslim world. Adam Wild Aba is a correspondent for IslamOnline.net.

CAIRO/WASHINGTON, March 12, 2005—Muslim women can lead women in prayers, and children in supererogatory prayers, but they are not allowed to lead the Friday prayer, which is not obligatory on women, said a member of IslamOnline.net's Fatwa team.

It is neither a discriminatory nor a derogatory measure not to allow women to lead the worshipers in the Friday prayer, said Massoud Sabri.

"Attending the Friday prayer is not a *fard* (obligatory) on women at the first place," he added.

The London-based Arabic-language *Al-Sharq Al-Awsat* newspaper reported on Friday, March 11, that Amina Wadud, professor of Islamic studies at Virginia Commonwealth University, will be the first woman to lead a public, mixed-gender Friday prayer on March 18 in New York City.

Wadud, the author of the book *Qur'an and Woman: Rereading the Sacred Text from a Woman's Perspective,* will also deliver the Friday sermon, according to the paper.

Sabri said women can lead each other and children in all prayers.

He added that some Hanbali jurists said women can lead men in supererogatory and Tarawih prayers and others said it is permissible for them to lead men in funeral prayers.

"In addition, other jurists said women can lead their family members, including men, in prayers" Sabri said.

He added that the majority of scholars agree it is impermissible for women to lead men in the five obligatory daily prayers.

Sabri noted, however, that in his book *Al-Muhalla bil Athar* Imam Ibn Hazm quotes Imam Abu Hanifah as allowing, though not favoring, women to lead men in prayers.

Imam an-Nawawi, in his book *al-Majmu',* quotes other scholars as allowing women to lead men in prayers.

UNIQUE STATUS

Sabri underlined that Islam does in no way take over women's rights to play a leading role in society; but rather has granted them with wide-ranging freedoms.

Women used to be in charge of the market place during the time of Caliph 'Umar Ibn Al-Khattab. Women have recently become doctors, scholars, muftis, ministers and judges.

"Jurist said women can assume high-level posts and some said a woman can even assume the presidency if she is more qualified than men," added Sabri.

Islam honors women and regards them as equal and vital to life as man. Their rights are meant to preserve her identity, honor, and chastity.

In one of his Hadiths (sayings), Prophet Muhammad (PBUH) said: "Women are men's counterparts."

Sabri cited the story of Prophet Muhammad (PBUH) as a case in point.

"Khadija (Prophet's Muhammad's wife may God be pleased with her) helped the Prophet in his uphill struggle to spread the Islamic faith and his eternal message. She also used to be a tradeswoman."

OPPOSITION

The Assembly of Muslim Jurists in America has reiterated opposition to Wadud's decision.

In a fatwa seen by IOL on Saturday, March 12, the Assembly said that Muslim women cannot take the pulpit or lead Friday prayer; otherwise the prayer is invalid.

It said that throughout Muslim history it has never been heard of a woman leading Friday's prayer.

Wadud's camp cites in online statements Prophet Muhammad's (PBUH) permission to a woman called Um Waraka to lead her family in prayers.

But the Assembly maintained that the story, if proved correct, has to do with inside-home prayers involving women or family male members in the extreme, but has nothing to do with Friday's prayers.

Established in 2002, the Assembly is a not-for-profit organization of Muslim jurists and scholars, seeking to issue and clarify rulings of Shar'iah (Islamic Law) concerning issues affecting Muslims in America.

77. Asma Barlas, "The Patriarchal Imaginary of Father/s: Divine Ontology and the Prophets" from *Believing Women in Islam: Unreading Patriarchal Interpretations of the Qur'an*

Austin: University of Texas Press, 2002, pp. 93–127.
Asma Barlas (b. 1950) is Professor of Political Science and International Relations at Ithaca College. Adopting the feminist approach of the social sciences and cultural studies fields, her work demonstrates how Islamic law has up to now been formulated by men for men. She maintains that the Quran itself is solidly egalitarian in its positions and that male religious authorities have interpreted it in a patriarchal manner. Her book is considered a staple of the feminist approach, deconstructing the patriarchal assumptions of the Islamic tradition and rereading the Quran through a woman's lens.

Invent not similitudes
For God: for God knoweth,
And ye know not.
   The Qur'ān (16:74)[1]
God has said: "Take not
(For worship) two gods:
For [God] is just One God
Then fear Me (and Me alone)."
   The Qur'ān (16:51)[2]

Islam, I began this work by saying, need not be read as a religion of the Father/fathers, that is, as a patriarchal religion, if by patriarchy we mean father-rule and/or a politics of male privilege based in theories of sexual differentiation. Both forms of patriarchy associate the male/masculine with the Self, knowledge, truth, and sovereignty, while representing the woman as different, unequal, or the "Other."[3] In monotheistic religions these representations draw on a patriarchalized view of God, whereas in secular contexts they are based in specific claims about biology and culture. I thus visualize patriarchy as a continuum and move between its different poles in interpreting the Qur'ān. I hope to show that the Qur'an challenges the constitutive myths of patriarchy and that it does not inherently or symbolically (biologically or culturally) privilege males, masculinity, fathers, or father-right/rule. Beyond that, I will show that the teachings of the Qur'ān are radically egalitarian and even antipatriarchal.

I substantiate this claim by examining the nature of Divine Self-Disclosure and the Qur'ānic narratives of the prophets Abraham and Muhammad. Specifically, I focus on the Qur'ān's repudiation of the patriarchal imaginary of God-the-Father and the irreconcilable conflict between Islamic monotheism (*Tawhīd*) and theories of father-right/male privilege. In this context, I examine the Qur'ān's refusal to sacralize the prophets as real or symbolic fathers, as well as its sustained critique of the historical practice of fathers' rule. In Chapters 5 and 6, I explain why we cannot derive theories of male privilege or sexual inequality and differentiation from the Qur'ān's position on sex/gender, sexuality, the family, and marriage. Together, these chapters aim to clarify the scriptural basis of sexual equality in Islam and to challenge feminist claims that patriarchy has God on its side and conservative ones that "the Islamic family was to be essentially male-worshipping" (Bouhdiba 1985,11).

I. (Re)presenting God

Since "a culture's idea of divinity is central not only to that culture's religious life but also to its social, political, familial institutions and relationships,"[4] how we define God has implications not only for patriarchies but also for a theology and hermeneutics of liberation. In other words, "sacred knowledge [as] master knowledge"[5] has the power to shape our views not only of God but also of our own moral, social, and sexual self-worth and relationships. As such, when sacred knowledge is used to engender or sexualize God (humanize or anthropomorphize God) as male, it also underwrites male privilege since men acquire power from "the fact that the source of ultimate value is often described in anthropomorphic images as Father or King."[6] Indeed, feminists believe that it is the "exclusively masculine symbolism for God, for the notion of divine 'incarnation' in human nature, and for the human relationship to God" that reinforces sexual oppression (Daly 1973, 4).

Since the use of sacred knowledge to engender God or, rather, to represent God as male impedes a theology of liberation, attempts to depatri-archalize theology and to evolve a liberatory hermeneutics start by engaging the sexual/textual politics of sacred misrepresentation. In this context, some theorists favor degendering "the word *God*" (Ramshaw 1995, 19), while others want to reengender God by recovering God's "female guises" (Raschke and Raschke 1995). Yet others have sought to revive the ancient goddess cults as a counterpoint to masculinist constructions of God. In spite of the differences between them, however, all three approaches reveal that the problem as scholars see it ultimately is not so much that a specific *sex* has been ascribed to God, but that a specific *meaning* has been ascribed to this sex historically, one that has served to legitimize sexual hierarchy and inequalities. Arguably, then, it is not God's representation as male that is problematic but our own definitions of male/ness; that is, sexed representations of God are problematic only to the extent that specific constructions of gender are. Nonetheless, as long as our views of gender remain questionable, so does God's depiction as Father/male. That is why, in my own analysis, I begin by examining the nature of Divine Self-Disclosure in the Qur'ān—before discussing the various "Creator models"[7] Muslims have formulated.

Divine Self-Disclosure

The single most essential aspect of God's Self-Disclosure in the Qur'ān is that God is One, hence Indivisible; this principle of Divine Unity (Tawhīd) extends to the idea that God is Incomparable, hence Unrepresentable. Both separately and together, these doctrines preclude associating forebears, partners, or progeny with God, or misrepresenting God as father, son, husband, or male. I will, therefore, consider each proposition in turn. Monotheism would not be monotheism if it were not based in the idea of God's Indivisible Unity. As the Qur'ān repeatedly warns and confirms, "Your God is One God" (16:22; in Ali, 661). In fact, one entire Surah is dedicated to the theologeme of Divine Unity:

> Say: [God] is God,
> The One and Only;
> God, the Eternal, Absolute;
> [God] begetteth not,
> Nor is [God] begotten;
> And there is none
> Like unto [God].
>   The Qur'ān (Surah 112; in Ali, 1806)

God is Absolute and God's nature is Unity. *Tawhīd,* as Merryl Wyn Davies (1988, 58) points out, is the foundation of "the Islamic conceptual fabric," and, as a concept, it rules out the notion of "dichotomy, of mutually opposed difference. Any reduction to mutually opposed difference would be false opposition, a reductive destruction of balance." Thus, the very manner in which the Qur'ān describes God's Unity rules out binary modes of thinking that structure patriarchal thought.[8]

Since God is Indivisible, God's Sovereignty also is indivisible. No one—other deities, or divine consorts and offspring, or humans —can partake in it; *shirk,* the symbolic extension of God's Sovereignty to others, is the only unpardonable sin mentioned in the Qur'ān. In explaining why God and God's Sovereignty are Indivisible, the Qur'ān states that, had there been multiple gods and many sources of Divine Sovereignty, "behold, each god Would have taken away What [each] had created, And some would have Lorded it over others!" (33191; in Ali, 889). In contrast to the existential and moral chaos unleashed by polytheism, monotheism makes for a just and coherent moral universe, since God—as Toshihiko Izutsu (1964, 129) reminds us—never does any wrong (*Zulm*) to anybody; rather, God in the Qur'ān is an ethical construct associated with the concepts of truth and justice. Indeed, the idea of God's Justness is integral to God's Unity (monotheism). As L. E. Goodman (1996,16) says, "God here is universal, not local or parochial," an "Absolute [Who] brooks no evil" (22). In fact, it is the

goodness of God, integrating all affirmative values, that renders the God of Abraham[9] universal. Had evil remained, conflict would be ineradicable—one deity or tribe of deities for one value or farrago of values and another deity or swarm of deities for another. Moral coherence would be lost and, with it, the very possibility of an idea of God. (Goodman, 28)

God's Unity thus is foundational to "the intellectual advance [that represents the] purgation of evil from the idea of the divine," since it is only "when dualism finally yields to monotheism and acknowledges the insubstantiality of evil and the pure reality of the Good" that evil is nullified (Goodman 1996, ix, 29).

God's Unity means not only that God has no partners but also that God is neither Son (Christ) nor Father (of Christ or of other deities). Allegations to the contrary by the Jews, Christians, and polydieists during the Prophet's lifetime, led the Qur'ān to admonish them unendingly. Says the Qur'ān,

> In blasphemy indeed,
> Are those that say
> That God is Christ
> The son of Mary.
> Say: "Who then
> Hath the least power
> Against God, if [God's] Will
> Were to destroy Christ
> The son of Mary, his mother,
> And all—every one
> That is on the earth?"
>   The Qur'ān (5:19; in Ali, 246-47)

Christ, the Qur'ān repeatedly clarifies, was a prophet who forbade his own deification and sacralizing God as his Father:

> Christ Jesus the son of Mary
> Was (no more than)
> An apostle of God,
> Say not "Trinity": desist:
> It will be better for you:
> For God is One God:
> Glory be to [God]:
> (Far Exalted is [God]) above
> Having a son.
>   The Qur'ān (4:171; in Ali, 234)

The Qur'ān also condemns Jewish sacralizations of God as father; as it says:

> The Jews call 'Uzair a son
> Of God, and the Christians
> Call Christ the Son of God.
> That is a saying from their mouth;
> (In this) they but imitate
> What the Unbelievers of old
> Used to say: God's curse
> Be on them: how they are deluded
> Away from the Truth!
>   The Qur'ān (9:30; in Ali, 448)

The Qur'ān is equally severe in castigating the polytheists who, it says, "falsely, Having no knowledge, Attribute to [God] Sons and daughters. Praise and glory be To [God Who is] above What they attribute to [God]!" How, asks the Qur'ān, "can [God] have a son When [God] hath no consort?" (6:100–101; in Ali, 319). When another Ayah condemns the polytheists for ascribing only daughters to God, it is not because God deems them less worthy than sons; it is because the polytheists assign to God "what they hate (for themselves)" (16:62; in Ali, 672). Not only did the Arabs of the Prophet's time regard the birth of girls as a calamity, but they buried many alive, a practice God condemns as utterly heinous and promises to punish.[10] That it is no better to ascribe sons to God than it is daughters is clear from numerous Āyāt, including those quoted above.

Not only does God not stand in the *literal* relationship of son, father, husband, or partner to a divine pantheon, then, but God also does not stand in the *symbolic* relationship of a father (or jealous wife)[11] to human beings, either. Thus, the Qur'ān also rejects designations of God as a figurative father:

> (Both) the Jews and the Christians
> Say: "We are sons
> Of God, and His beloved."
> Say: "Why then doth [God]
> Punish you for your sins?
> Nay, ye are but men,—
> Of the men [God] hath created:"
>   The Qur'ān (5:20; in Ali, 247)

Given the Qur'ān's unrelenting rejection of God's sacralization as Father, it seems unconscionable to read Islam as a theological patriarchy. If God can only be a *patriarch* or, rather, God can only be *patriarchalized,* to the extent that God can in fact be sacralized as *Father,* how can God's Self-Disclosure in the Qur'ān be interpreted as providing the basis either for patriarchalized views of God or for theories of father-right/rule based in such views? If God is not Father in Heaven in either a literal or a symbolic sense, how can fathers represent their rule on earth as replicating the model of divine patriarchy? And if—as the Qur'ān makes clear—we cannot, in what sense is God "on the side" of fathers or of patriarchy? Indeed, if God is not father, son, or husband, in what sense can God be male ("He")?

Ironically, while Muslims reject misrepresentations of God as father/ male, most see no problem in continuing to masculinize God linguistically and to propagate, on the basis of this view, theories of male rule/privilege over women. One needs therefore to inquire into the paradox of masculinist conceptions of God and the idea of a symbolic continuum between God's Rule and man's in the absence of the Qur'ānic view of God as Father/male. This paradox, I believe, is a function of the Creator models in Ian Netton's (1989) words and of a semiotic collapse in Muslim theology between the signifier (the word "God") and the Signified (God), and I examine each in turn.

Creator Models: (Re)theorizing the Divine

As the four Creator models—the Qur'ānic, the mystical, the allegorical, and the neo-Platonic—attest, Muslims have conceived of "their one God in several widely different ways" (Netton 1989, 2). Nonetheless, all "Islamic thinking about God, centers upon the divine names or attributes revealed in the [Qur'ān]" (Murata 1992, 9). Drawing on such Āyāt as "there is nothing Whatever like unto [God]" (42:11; in Ali, 1307) and "Glory be to God, the Lord of Inaccessibility, Above everything [ascribed to God]" (37M80),[12] the classical position (*tanzīh*) in dogmatic theology (*kalām*) began by declaring God Incomparable, hence Unrepresentable, especially in terms of "human form or human attributes" (Sherif 1985,16). However, since this position stressed God's Transcendence to the exclusion of God's Immanence, it also ended up conveying the sense of a God whom (argued scholars such as ibn al-Arabi) "no one could possibly love since He was too remote and incomprehensible" (Murata, 8). The theological cost of rendering God incomparable, then, was also to render God remote, hence dissimilar to humans. This is why the sapiential tradition has concentrated on God's Immanence, interpreting it as nearness to, and similarity with, humans by way of *tashbīh.* However, even those Muslims who stress similarity, notes Murata (53), "give priority to incomparability" so as to remain within Islamic norms. As she says, *tashbīh* and *tanzīh* represent the two poles between which Muslims have tended to think about God, and both, I will argue, anthropomorphize God.

Thus, readings of Islam as a "theological patriarchy" emerge from within *kalām,* which "is locked into an approach that places God the King and the Commander (a close associate of God the Father) at the top of its concerns" (Murata 1992, 3). It seems God's very transcendence creates the desire to render God intimate in uniquely human terms. Hence, it is *kalām* (and the *Sharī'ah* that derives from it), says Murata, that establishes God's primacy as King/Lord/Ruler, and in one case, even as Father; however, the solitary reference, by ibn al-Arabi, to God as Father is anomalous both because of its Christian[13] connotations (Murata, 145), and because in Islam God's relationship to humans is ontological and ethical in nature, not consanguinal or contractual (Asad 1993).

It is not just *kalām* that anthropomorphizes God; so, too, does the sapiential tradition that, maintains Murata (1992, 79), seeks to establish a spiritual, as distinct from a social, matriarchy—by "affirming the primacy of God as Merciful, Beautiful, Gentle, Loving"—even though Muslim theologians "refuse to apply the word father (or mother) to God."

If both *kalām* and sufism misrepresent God (by engendering God), so too do neo-Platonic models that represent God in terms of essences and attributes. According to Izutsu (1964,48), the idea of God understood "as a transcendental 'essence' opposed to its 'attributes' is no longer a [Qur'ānic] concept in its original form." Indeed, even the word "Allah," he (51) says, does not "denote in philosophy simply the same thing as that living God of Creation and Revelation...so vividly depicted in the [Qur'ān]." God in the Qur'ān, insists Izutsu (49), can "epistemologically...only be an object of *Urn* [knowledge]. In other words, God can only be known to [humans] indirectly." Even when the Qur'ān assigns an "immanent aspect" to God, the "Quranic Creator Paradigm,"[14] as Ian Netton (1989,22) calls it, conveys the idea of "a God Who (1) creates *ex-nihilo*; (2) acts definitively in historical time; (3) guides His people in such time; and (4) can in some ways be known *indirectly* by His Creation" (my emphasis).

Although all Creator models (except the allegorical, which represents God in purely symbolic terms) anthropomorphize God, there is nothing in the doctrines of Divine Transcendence or of Divine Immanence that should lead us to do so. Thus, in its avowal that "there is none Like unto [God]" (112:4; in Ali, 1806), the Qur'ān establishes that God is Unique, hence beyond representation, and also beyond gender since gender is nothing but a representation of sex. In the ideas of Divine Transcendence and Incomparability, then, we have compelling theological reasons to reject God's engenderment. In fact, inasmuch as the doctrine of Divine Immanence also recognizes Divine Incomparability, it provides equally compelling reasons to reject God's engenderment. Even the sufis, who emphasize God's Immanence (hence similarity to humans) do not reject the idea of God's Incomparability; rather, they arrive at similarity after bringing out incomparability, says Murata (52). What they dispute is not the idea of incomparability, but that it is "the only valid point of view." However, even if we do not take Incomparability as the only valid viewpoint, it is not necessary, even though it is difficult, to think and speak of divine similarity in sexed or gendered terms since there is nothing in the idea of Divine Immanence itself that should lead us to engender God.

To understand this point, it is necessary to recall that God's engenderment results both from using gendered languages to speak about God and from labeling God's attributes masculine or feminine. The sufis, for example, emphasize attributes they feel reflect "'feminine' qualities like love, beauty, and compassion" (Murata, 56), even though the Qur'ān itself does not define God, or these qualities, in such terms. Similarly, the Qur'ān speaks of God's love for humans; it is theology that, in translating this theme, declares God "'similar' (*tashbih*) in some fashion to His Creation," and it justifies this move by referring to such Āyāt as "Wherever you turn, there is the face of God" (2:115, in Murata, 9). However, references to God's face, or hands, or even to God's attributes, are insufficient in themselves to allow us to depict God as a "distant, dominating, and powerful ruler" or as "a strict and authoritarian father" or as "a warm and loving mother" (9). Rather, such portrayals stem from imposing onto Divine Ontology a system of gender dualisms and binary thought in which men are defined as stern, distant, and authoritarian and women as close, loving, and gentle. Yet nothing in the ideas of distance and sternness renders them (or God) male (*kalām*), or love and nearness that renders them (or God) female (sufism). Nonetheless, such ideas of the masculine and feminine principles infuse

Muslim conceptualizations of God, even as their own views of *Tawhid* (Divine Unity) suggest that God incorporates, but also transcends, all (gender) dualisms and oppositions.

God and the Masculine and Feminine Principles

Muslim mystics and scholars, says Seyyed Hossein Nasr (1987, 185), interpret "the Quranic statement that God reveals Himself in the Universe through His Names" to mean that "Being manifests itself through its Qualities." Humans see these qualities as manifesting the masculine and feminine principles and, since we view these principles as being opposed to each other, as also manifesting opposites. Thus, God is "the all-comprehensive reality, the coincidence of opposites, in whom all characteristics are found" (Murata 1992, 95). God is the First and the Last, the Evident and the Immanent, the Subduer and the Bestower, the Expediter and the Delayer, the Exalter and the Abaser, the Creator of Death and the Alive, and on, as the ninety-nine beautiful Names of God reveal. According to Murata (93), these opposing attributes have led sufis and scholars to search for the "deepest roots of polarity in the Real." Since God's Reality as manifest in the cosmos "can be described by opposite and conflicting attributes," she says, the cosmos too can be viewed "as a vast collection of opposites." However, not only does this collection "display the activity of the single Principle," but "opposing forces [are not] absolutely opposed," rather, they are "complementary or polar" (10–12). Polarity, as Roger Ames defines it, is to be understood as a "holographic" view of the world, not as duality. The difference, he says, is that the separateness implicit in dualistic explanations yields a view of "a world of 'things' characterized by discreteness, finality, closedness, determinateness, independence, a world in which one thing is related to the 'other' extrinsically." In contrast, polar explanations give rise to

a world of "foci" characterized by interconnectedness, interdependence, openness, mutuality, indeterminateness, complementarity, correlativity, coextensiveness, a world in which continuous foci are intrinsically related to each other. (Murata, 10)

Polarity thus manifests not the exclusion implied by duality, but the relationship of opposites within an internally differentiated organic unity. (However, as Murata says, the distinctiveness of polarity emerges only through a critique of duality, hence the latter's usefulness for defining certain theological positions.)

As theorists observe, there is in polar explanations a sense of a "higher order unity [that] supersedes contradictions," much like the "unifying function of the dialectic" (Grosz 1990, 65). And it is such a view of unity that underpins Islamic conceptions of God. Inasmuch as it does, it also challenges both "orthodox" and feminist Muslim assertions that there is a strict separation of masculine and feminine principles in Islam (Bouhdiba 1985; Sabbah 1984). Such views ignore that Muslims throughout the ages have understood Tawhīd to signify multiplicity-in-unity, meaning that all principles (masculine or feminine) are interconnected in the totality of God's Being. Thus, among Gods attributes are ones we label "feminine," like loving, creating, nourishing, forgiving, being patient, compassionate,[15] and so forth. At the same time, however, God also is stern in justice, powerful, and a ruler, attributes we think of as masculine. However, the Qur'ān itself does not engender (masculinize or feminize) God's attributes, and even though femininity and masculinity "have figured very strongly in interpretation of the Qur'ān," they have done so without explicit Qur'ānic sanction, argues Wadud (1999, 22).

Polarity—or the interconnectedness of opposite principles—defines not only God's Reality but the reality of humans as well who, says Murata (43), being "made in the form of God [also] manifest the whole."[16] This means, in effect, that women and men do not embody mutually exclusive or opposite attributes; rather, they incorporate both masculine and feminine attributes.[17] In a polar conception, women are not women because they manifest a lack (defined in terms of feminine traits) and men are not men because they possess what women lack (masculine traits). Rather, *each* manifests *the whole*.

Indeed, if Islam were to designate women and men as opposites (man as the Self and woman as the Other, man as having and woman as lacking something), it could not reasonably hold them to identical standards of moral praxis; lacking knowledge, rationality, the ability to reason (attributes associated with the masculine/Self), women would be unable to understand, or act upon, Divine Truth. The Qur'ān does not, therefore, define women and men in terms of sex or gender attributes; rather, it teaches that humans were created from a single Self (*nafs*), possess the same attributes, and have the same capacity for moral choice, reasoning, and individuality (see Chapters 5 and 6). As such, there is nothing in the concept of divine incarnation in humans, or in monotheism itself, as feminists allege, that is anti-women. In fact, inasmuch as the idea of *Tawhīd* allows for a holistic view of human identity, it is liberatory not only for women but also for men.[18]

Language and the Semiotic Collapse

It is not only social constructions of gender, including our ideas of masculinity and femininity, that have led Muslims to anthropomorphize God; so have the discursive strategies they have employed to read the Qur'ān. In particular, masculinist representations of God result from the tendency to collapse the signifier (the word "God") with the Signified (God); that is, to confuse gendered languages with God's Reality. On the other hand, the tendency to represent men as sovereign/rulers over women arises not only in masculinized representations of God, but also in misreading the Quran's position on human subjectivity (vice-regency) which is interpreted as establishing men's superiority over women.[19] It is thus through a double movement, a semiotic one and an analogical one, that God is masculinized and men deified.

The semiotic collapse of the Signified with the signifier dates from medieval times, but few scholars have studied it or its implications for Muslim masculinizations of God. In fact, Netton (1989, 3), who uses modern linguistic and semiotic theories to analyze medieval Muslim theology, locates the opposite tendency in it: toward a semiotic *disjuncture* resulting from its adherence to the theme of Divine Transcendence. This adherence, he says, grew out of a desire to *rid* formulations about God of "grosser anthropomorphisms [by] stripping God...of all human attributes." As Netton (331) explains it, however, the problem is that once we

accept a theory of God's utter transcendence after the frequent manner of so many of the medieval philosophers, and then say that "God knows," or "God has knowledge," the theologeme "divine knowledge" is basically meaningless in deconstructive terms, since what does it really mean to predicate knowledge of a transcendent divinity?

According to Netton, then, it was theology's attempt to deanthropomorphize God that occasioned a "radical break between the...signifier and the signified," leading logically to the "prospect of an endless semiosis" and semiotically to a "paradigm of imperfect signification." In such a context, he argues (1989, 331), even the term "God" becomes "almost equally meaningless."

To me, however, Netton's example shows that far from emptying out the term "God" and thereby making it meaning-less, Muslim theology *invested* it with a specific, patriarchal/ized meaning by continuing to assume that God's Transcendent Reality was male ("He"). The semiotic disjuncture thus is also a semiotic *collapse* since God has been masculinized in the midst of efforts to rid our ideas of God of human attributes! Indeed, efforts to deanthropomorphize ideas of God have never involved finding a suitable theological *language* to speak about God. Not only do Muslims collapse gendered terms with God's Reality (masculinizing God by a mere use of words rather than by means of a sound theological argument), but they also fail to consider the ways in which gendered meanings subvert the Qur'ān's purposes. For example, rendering the word *insān* as "man" even where such a usage runs counter to the Qur'ān's intent gives a totally different meaning to its Āyāt for, if *insān* did refer only to man, then women would be "exempted from almost all the Islamic injunctions" (Shahab 1993, 403).

The androcentric nature of language is, of course, likely to create persistent problems in signification. It may therefore be that "because all our words fall short of His reality, a huge range of more or less unsatisfactory ways of talking about God is positively desirable" (Tugwell in Netton 1989, 134). However, when some modes of God-Talk[20] are always undesirable to the same group of believers (women), and for the same reasons (their paternalism or sexism), it is time to say that some unsatisfactory ways of talking about God are, in fact, worse than others. The Qur'ān itself offers us better ways to talk about God by using terms like *Rabb* and Allah, that have no human counterpart or equivalent. It is thus all the more troubling when we translate such terms as "King" or "Lord," which not only are androcentric but which also fail to convey the sense of creatorship and sovereignty implicit in terms like *Rabb* and Allah. In fact, words like king and lord encourage false analogies between God's Sovereignty and man's, even though the two are wholly different, as I will argue below. Similarly, confusing words like "He" or "Himself" with God's Reality—which the Qur'ān also conveys in sex/gender-neutral terms as "We, Us, I"—subverts the rich pluralism of scriptural language, reducing God's Reality to one term or attribute.

Even when the Qur'ān refers to God as "He," it does not mean that God is male, or like one. As the Qur'ān says, God cannot be explained by way of similitude (by comparison with another). In that God's representation as "He" or as "King/Lord" is, in fact, premised on our idea of males and what we take to be definitive about their social or sexual roles, it is a similitude, and thus contrary to the Qur'ān's injunctions. As the Qur'ān's teachings suggest, humans (hence our languages) cannot comprehend, much less define, God; moreover, God's recourse to human language is meant only to communicate with us in words we can understand, not to delimit God's Reality. However, instead of recognizing the limitations of language, Muslim theology confuses it *with* Divine Reality, ignoring how this confusion results in humanizing God. And, of course, when "anthropomorphisms succeed in containing God, we have no God; we have instead a glorified image of ourselves" (Ramshaw 1995, 21).

It may be that the only way we know how to think or talk is from within our own sexed/engendered bodies and experiences; moreover, as Gail Ramshaw (1995, 20) says, in "a century obsessed with sexuality, it is difficult to image a being beyond sexuality." However, what we need is an anamnestic practice,[21] a working toward an unrepresentable something that allows us to think and speak differently than we otherwise could. Unfortunately, however, there is much at stake for most Muslims in *not* learning to think or speak differently, given the real and symbolic value of masculinist images and language in sustaining male privilege. Masculinizing God is the first step in positing a hierarchy in which males situate themselves beneath God and above women, implying that there is a symbolic (and sometimes literal) continuum between God's Rule over humans and male rule over women. However, the assumption, no matter how indirect, that God's Sovereignty and man's are coextensive fundamentally misreads the nature both of Divine Sovereignty (hence the doctrine of *Tawhīd*) and of human vice-regency. (As my discussion in later chapters shows, it also misreads the Qur'ān's definitions of faith and human e quality.)

Divine Sovereignty, Human Vice-Regency

I noted above that God's Sovereignty is a function of God's Unity, which is absolute and extends over all living and nonliving worlds and is not contingent on human approval or acceptance of it, though faith hinges on our voluntarily accepting it. (This is why the "master-slave" metaphor[22] cannot convey the sense of willed submission to Divine Truth that defines Muslim praxis.) In contrast, human vice-regency is finite and a trust from God and not meant to further one's own personal power or glory; as the Qur'ān says, "If any do seek For glory and power,—To God belong All glory and power" (35:10; in Ali, 1155). The concept of vice-regency derives from the term *khilāfah*, a word the Qur'ān uses twice for humans, not just for men. As a verb, *khilāfah* signifies succession, and Muslim scholars believe it has a dual meaning:

that of [hu]mankind in general succeeding, according to God's will, to the inheritance of the earth; as well as the implication that each generation of [hu] mankind succeeds the other in assuming the obligations of the status of *khilāfah*. (Davies 1988,92)

In other words, the idea of vice-regency is not contingent on sex, and while it is a relational term (Davies, 92), it does not mean that humans are vice-regents *over one another*. Rather, they are vice-regents *on earth*, on which they nonetheless have been warned not to walk "with insolence" (17:37; in Ali, 704).

That humans are vice-regents over the earth and that their vice-regency is a trust from God emerges from Ayah 33:72: "Verily, We did offer the trust [of reason and volition] to the heavens and the earth, and the mountains: but they refused to bear it because they were afraid of it. Yet [humans] took it up" (in Davies 1988,92). The concept of trust, or *ammanah*, says Davies,

entails responsibility and the notion of rights and duties implicit in the terms of the trust. The *khilafah* has been entrusted to inherit the earth, to have the use of all the bounties for the sustenance and enrichment of [hu]mankind's life on it. The capacities of *fitrah* [human nature] are the means to be employed so that the status and role of the *khilafah* can be enjoyed....Since all men and women are *khilafah* there is a basic equality in their rights of access to and enjoyment of the bounties of earthly existence. (93)

There is thus no reason to assume that only males are vice-regents on earth, much less vice-regents over women.

The finite nature of human vice-regency and its trust-like nature are clear also from God's admonishment to David:

O David! We did indeed
Make thee a [vice-regent]

On earth: so judge thou
Between [humans] in truth
(and justice):
Nor follow thou the lusts
(Of thy heart), for they will
Mislead thee from the Path
Of God: for those who
Wander astray from the Path
Of God, is a Penalty Grievous,
For that they forget
The Day of [Account].
    The Qur'ān (38:26; in Ali, 1223)

Even a prophet and a king like David is not infallible inasmuch as he is capable of "follow-ing the lusts" of his heart, and even the vice-regency of a prophet and a king like David is a trust from God, not a function of his own sovereignty over humans. Significantly, even the vice-regency of a prophet and king like David is meant to establish God's Rule on earth, not his own.

To establish that humans are not rulers/sovereign in the same way that God is would be to belabor an obvious point to believers. But, if we concede that, how can we then extrapolate from God's Rule/Sovereignty over humans to man's over woman? Yet, exegetes customarily draw on both views of man as vice-regent (and ruler) and of God as King, Lord, and Ruler, to advocate men's dominion over women, in some cases even ordering wives to prostrate themselves before their husbands (Tabrisi in Murata 1992, 176), a form of worship Muslims reserve solely for God. Similarly, following a *hadith,* most Muslims hold that ingratitude to a husband is like ingratitude to God (Thanawi in Metcalf 1990, 23), explicitly equating God and husbands. In much the same vein, Muslims who reject ibn al-Arabi's depiction of God as Father nonetheless accept the typology deriving from his portrayal that represents fathers as the high, spiritual aspects of existence, and mothers as the low, corporeal ones. This is so in spite of the fact that the Qur'ān elevates mothers over fathers (see Chapter 6), as does tradition. However, not only is it rank hubris to asso-ciate males with God in this way, but the misassociation also violates the concept of Tawhīd that places God above such correspondences and also establishes the principle of the indivisibility of God's Sovereignty.

Misrepresentations of God as male, and of male sovereignty as being coextensive with that of God, derive not from the Qur'ān, then, but from the tendency to anthropo-morphize God on the one hand, and to misconstrue the theme of vice-regency on the other. Such misrepresentations are common not only among "orthodoxies," but also among many Muslim feminists who routinely assail Islam's "paternalistic" and "uncom-promising monotheism" (Hussain 1994), drawing on representations of monotheism itself as unremittingly misogynistic. As I have argued, however, monotheism as embodied in the doctrine of *Tawhīd* is vital not only to a purification of our idea of God but also to our being able to *reject* patriarchalized misrepresentations of God and, along with these, theories of father-right or male privilege. The idea of *Tawhīd* also is essential to our idea of humans as inherently good and as manifesting *"the whole"* (Murata 1992, 43; her emphasis). By rejecting gender dualisms and binaries, we open up a space to theorize human subjectivity in terms that respect the complete equality and humanity of women and men.

II. Desacralizing Prophets as Fathers

we worship
None but God;
. . . we associate
No partners with [God];
. . . we erect not,
From among ourselves,
Lords and patrons
Other than God
    The Qur'ān (3:64)[23]

The Qur'ān challenges misrepresentations of fathers as surrogates of a divine patriarch by rejecting the mythos of God-the-Father. Likewise, the Qur'ān challenges the concept of father-right by refusing to sacralize the prophets as real or symbolic fathers. I illustrate this now by (re)reading the Qur'ānic narratives of the prophets Abraham and Muhammad. To understand the point of my reading, it is necessary to recall that patriarchy has ranged from traditional modes in which the father was symbolically the "common father of all those. . .under his authority,"[24] to classical ones based in theories of political obedience and rights, to modern and contractual forms. Here I concentrate on the first definition of patriarchy because I wish to examine the Qur'ān's position on father-right. In later chapters, I will interpret its teachings with the definition of modern patriarchy in mind.
God, Abraham, and Abraham's Father
Usually exegetes in all three monotheistic religions read Abraham's narrative as confirming his status as a patriarch[25] rather than as *displacing* father-right and thereby subverting the imaginary of the prophet-as-father. The latter reading, though, is con/textually plausible and is actually more congruent with the idea of *Tawhīd* (the indivisibility of God's Sovereignty).

    The Qur'ānic story of Abraham opens with his search for God, which begins when God shows him "the power And the laws of the heavens And the earth" so that he might discern God's Reality (6:75; in Ali, 309). At the outset, however, Abraham confuses the manifestations of God's Power ("signs of God") with God's Reality:

when the night
covered him over,
He saw a star:
He said: "This is my [Rabb]."
But when it set,
He said: "I love not
Those that set."
When he saw the moon
Rising in splendour,
He said: "This is my [Rabb]."
But when the moon set,
He said: "Unless my [Rabb]
Guide me, I shall surely
Be among those
Who go astray."
When he saw the sun

Rising in splendour
He said: "This is my [*Rabb*];
This is the greatest (of all)."
But when the sun set,
He said: "O my people!
I am indeed free
From your (guilt)
Of giving partners to God.
"For me, I have set
My face, firmly and truly,
Towards [God] Who created
The heavens and the earth,
And never shall I give
Partners to God."
   The Qur'ān (6:76–79; in Ali, 309–10)

In the Qur'ān's narration, Abraham arrives at Divine Truth through a dual process of reasoning and spiritual submission (*islam*), and it is this process that brings him to an awareness of his father's sin of *shirk* (extending God's Sovereignty to others, in this case to false gods) and ultimately to a break with him. Incidentally, false gods are not just idols; there is he who takes "for his god His own passion (or impulse)," says the Qur'ān (25:43; on Aloi, 935). The break between father and son occurs when Abraham having come to recognize God's Reality, confronts his father in an exchange that truly is instructive for determining the Qur'ān's position on father-right:

Behold, he said to his father:
"O my father! why
Worship that which heareth not
And seeth not, and can
Profit thee nothing?
"O my father! to me
Hath come knowledge which
Hath not reached thee:
So *follow me: I will guide*
Thee to a Way that
Is even and straight."
   The Qur'ān (19:42-43; in Ali, 776; my emphasis)

Thus Abraham begins by rejecting his father's *gods,* and then his father's *authority,* calling on his father to follow him instead, challenging the very core of father-right as it is structured in patriarchies (where the father derives his authority from his assumed association with God, knowledge, and truth). This inversion is not meant, however, to establish Abraham's authority over his father, as the Qur'ān makes clear, but that of Abraham's God; and only after his father rejects God does Abraham reject his *father.* In effect, what leads Abraham into the conflict with his father is his "uncompromising monotheism"; as such, the conflict between his (belief in) God and (obedience to) his father is necessarily a conflict between monotheism and patriarchy (in its traditional sense). Indeed, Abraham's break with his father is embedded in a larger discourse that seeks to uncover the tensions that have existed historically between God's Rule and fathers' rule. As the

Qur'ān details it in the Abrahamic narrative and in others, the struggle to establish God's Rule constantly has run up against the ways of the fathers who were "void of wisdom and guidance" (2:170; in Ali, 67). This theme is palpable in Abraham's address to his community:

> Behold! he said
> To his father and his people,
> "What are these images,
> which ye are
> (So assiduously) devoted?"
> They said: "We found
> Our fathers worshipping them."
> He said, "Indeed ye
> Have been in manifest
> Error—ye and your fathers."
> They said, "Have you
> Brought us the Truth,
> Or are you one
> Of those who jest?"
> He said, "Nay, your [*Rabb*]
> Is the [*Rabb*] of the heavens
> And the earth...Who
> Created them (from nothing):
> And I am a witness
> To this (truth)."
>   The Qur'ān (21:51–56; in Ali, 834)

The basis of the polytheists' faith as they themselves declare it is adherence to patriarchal traditions, and it is this practice that Abraham attacks, with God's full approval, as the Qur'ānic narrative makes clear. In fact, Abraham attacks not only this practice but its material culture as well by breaking the polytheists' idols and then challenging them to get the biggest idol to identify him as the culprit. On their ensuing confusion, he asks why they take for "Worship, besides God, Things that can neither Be of any good to you Nor do you harm?" (21:66; in Ali, 836). Unable to persuade him of their logic and evidently at a loss for inventiveness, the polytheists—his father among them—determine to consign Abraham to a fire, from which he is saved by God's Mercy. As a righteous man, Abraham prays to God on his father's behalf and is told that God's Mercy is not for those who persist in espousing falsehoods after the truth has reached them.

Central to Abraham's embrace of God, and *the condition* for the embrace, then, is his break with his father. The conflict between God's Rule and father's rule at the heart of Abraham's story also finds exposition in the Qur'ān's warnings to believers to "fear (The coming of) a Day When no father can avail Aught for his son, nor A son avail aught For his father" (31:33; in Ali, 1089). For believers, then, the Rule of God (monotheism) must take precedence over the rule of fathers (patriarchy) and the pursuit of worldly success, which, the Qur'ān reminds us, is transitory.

One could perhaps argue that Abraham's story, as well as the Qur'ān's disapproval of misguided fathers, applies only to unbelievers; that God's bestowal of prophethood on Abraham and his line is meant to replace the rule of unbelieving fathers with that of believing fathers. In other words, it is possible that the Qur'ān disapproves of fathers' rule only when it conflicts with God's Rule, which is to say it is opposed to a specific *content* of father-right and not to its *form*. However, the Qur'ān itself offers evidence against such a reading. Three themes in particular are relevant here: First, the Qur'ān seeks to establish the rule not of believing fathers but of their God (God's Rule takes precedence over the institutions of prophethood, fatherhood, and motherhood); second, while the Qur'ān extols Abraham and his line, including the Prophet Muhammad, it does not do so by valorizing them as fathers; finally, the Qur'ān does specify parental, as against paternal, rights, but never in terms of sovereignty or rule over children (I consider this last point in Chapter 6).

When the Qur'ān extols Abraham and his line, it does so in order to establish their moral certitude as *believers* and not their real or symbolic status or rights as *fathers;* thus, when Abraham's progeny testify that they are following their fathers, they actually are attesting to following the *God* of their fathers:

> Were ye witnesses
> When Death appeared before Jacob?
> Behold, he said to his sons:
> "What will ye worship after me?"
> They said: "We shall worship
> *Thy God and the God of thy fathers,*—
> Of Abraham, Isma'il, and Isaac—
> The One (True) God:
> To [God] we bow (in Islam)"
>   The Qur'ān (2:133; in Ali, 54–55; my emphasis)

Incidentally, in Islam, references to the "God of our fathers" never devolve into viewing God-as-father, unlike in the Hebrew Bible in which, says Paul Ricoeur (1974, 484), "Yahweh is 'God of our fathers' before being father." However, according to Ricoeur (486), even in the Bible, "Yahweh's 'I am that I am'" dissolves "all anthropomorphisms, of all figures and figurations, including that of father."

As the Qur'ān makes clear, then, believers are expected to submit to the God of believing fathers, not to the fathers themselves. Indeed, a central motif of the Abrahamic narrative is establishing Abraham's own submission to God's Will:

> Behold! [Abraham's *Rabb*] said
> To him: "Bow (thy will to Me):"
> He said: "I bow (my will)
> To [my *Rabb*]."
> And *this was the legacy*
> That Abraham left to his sons,
> And so did Jacob;
> "Oh my sons! God hath chosen
> The Faith for you: then die not
> Except in the Faith of Islam."
>   The Qur'ān (2:131–32; in Ali, 54; my emphasis)

What makes Abraham a believer is his willingness to yield up his will/ sovereignty to God; he is thus not sovereign in the sense in which fathers are sovereign in traditional patriarchies where the legitimacy of their rule derives from its association with God's Rule/Sovereignty. Submission to God's Will, however, does not make one an associate in God's Sovereignty, but *subject* to it.

Second, when God rewards Abraham and his line with the mantle of prophethood, God does so by designating Abraham an imām and not by anointing him as a symbolic patriarch/ruler:

> And remember that Abraham
> Was tried by his [*Rabb*]
> With certain Commands,
> Which he fulfilled:
> [God] said: "I will make thee
> An Imām to the Nations."
> [Abraham] pleaded: "And also
> (Imāms) from my offspring!"
> [God] answered: "But My Promise
> Is not within the reach
> Of evil-doers."
> The Qur'ān (2:124; in Ali, 52)

Etymologically, *imām* is related to *ummah* or community, and *umm*, or mother. In this Āyah, its primary meaning, says Yusuf Ali (1988, 52 n. 124), is to be

foremost: hence it may mean: (1) leader in religion; (2) leader in congregational prayer; (3) model, pattern, example; (4) a book of guidance and instruction…; (5) a book of evidence or record….Here meanings 1 and 3 are implied.

In effect, the term *imām* is sex/gender-neutral[26] and is applicable to both humans and nonhuman things. Thus, God's favors to Abraham do not entail sacralizing him as a symbolic father; rather, God designates Abraham an *imām*. Indeed, as the episode of his near-sacrifice of his son reveals, it is Abraham's willingness to yield up his rights as father in favor of the Rule/Rights of God (his de-sacralization as father) that establishes him as a true believer in the Qur'ān's account.

In the Qur'ānic account, the idea of the sacrifice appears to Abraham in a vision,[27] which he shares with his adolescent son, whom the Qur'ān does not name:

> when (the son)
> Reached (the age of)
> (Serious) work with him,
> [Abraham] said: "O my son!
> I see in vision
> That I offer thee in sacrifice:
> *Now see what is*
> *Thy view!"* (The son) said:
> "O my father! Do
> As thou art commanded:
> thou will find me,
> If God so wills one
> Practising Patience and Constancy!"
> So when they had *both*

Submitted their wills (to God),
And he had laid him
Prostrate on his forehead
(For sacrifice),
We called out to him,
"O Abraham!
Thou hast already fulfilled
The vision!"
    The Qur'ān (37:102–5; in Ali, 1204–05; my emphasis)

Thus, it is only after Abraham's son freely, and in his own voice, consents to the sacrifice that they proceed further. The fact that Abraham does not assume his son's consent illustrates that, without it, the sacrifice would not carry moral weight in view of the Qur'ān's teachings about the voluntary nature of faith. It also shows that Abraham does not have the right of life and death over his son, as fathers did in traditional patriarchies (Abraham does not "rule over" his son). As the Qur'ānic account makes clear, it is the son's *expressed will*, not just the father's vision, that clears the way for the sacrifice, a fate from which God saves both; as the Qur'ān says tersely, this was "obviously A trial—" (37:106; Ali, 1205). Abraham, the dearly beloved prophet of God, cannot dispose of his own son as he wishes, even in the name of God, until his son, at his own discretion, agrees to it! And, once again, it is God Who saves a (believing) son from a (believing) father.

Traditionally, as noted, exegetes have read this account as establishing the primacy of father-right since, after all, it is Abraham who sets out to sacrifice his son and not the other way around. But such a reading transforms into a tale of patriarchal tyranny what clearly is a moral allegory about the consensual and purposive nature of faith, its primacy over kinship and blood, the existential dilemmas that can result from submitting to God's Will (especially where it comes into conflict with one's own life), and, not least, the insignificance of the father's will in comparison to God's Will. These themes infuse all of the Qur'ān's teachings, not just the Abrahamic parable. Indeed, the Abrahamic parable is one way to illustrate these themes in intimately personal terms. Thus, they emerge also from God's counsel to the Prophet Muhammad and to all believers,

Take not
For protectors your fathers
And your brothers if they love
Infidelity above Faith:
If any of you do so,
They do wrong.
Say: If it be that your fathers,
Your sons, your brothers,
Your mates, or your kindred;
The wealth that ye have gained;
The commerce in which ye fear
A decline: or the dwellings
In which ye delight—
Are dearer to you than God,
Or his Apostle, or the striving
In [God's] cause—then wait

Until God brings about
[God's] Decision: and God
Guides not the rebellious.
    The Qur'ān (9:23–24; in Ali, 444–45)

The Qur'ān does not mention daughters here, but then it is giving examples of what the Arabs of those times held dear. Those Arabs were practicing female infanticide and were unlikely to have found any references to daughters meaningful. Nonetheless, the Qur'ān's command applies equally to daughters. It instructs women, no less than men, not to take the males in their families (the heads of the family) as their protectors if doing so interferes with their practice of faith. Clearly, the Āyāt here were encouraging the pagans and polytheists of the Prophet's time to choose belief in God even if doing so led them to break with their families (as Abraham did with his father). However, what is significant is that the Qur'ān expressly legitimizes the principle of disobedience to males in their capacity as fathers, brothers, and so on. (It also mandates disobedience to parents on similar grounds; see Chapter 6.) To say that faith should take priority over social or material attachments and accoutrements—a teaching that finds a powerful allegorical expression in Abraham's story—is not to say anything about the legitimacy of father's rule, or even to say anything out of the ordinary, at least to believers. But to suggest that for God's Rule to exist, the father's rule must either be broken (Abraham's father) or subordinated symbolically to God's Rule (Abraham as father) is indeed to say something revolutionary. Thus, it is not just that the Qur'ān seeks to establish the primacy of God's Rule over father-right/rule; rather, in delineating the relationship between God's Rule and father's rule, the Qur'ān *dislocates* the latter. God comes to dis-place (not re-place) fathers. In fact, one Ayah expressly bids people to "Celebrate the praises of God, As ye used to celebrate The praises of your fathers" (2:200; in Ali, 80). (This does not mean that God wishes to *be* a Father, as the Qur'ān makes clear.) It is in light of this moral that the Qur'ān's refusal to sacralize Muhammad, the Seal of Prophets, as a symbolic father also becomes so significant, as I argue below.

There is one additional way in which Abraham's story can be read as illustrating the Qur'ān's opposition to father-right, and this has to do with how the Qur'ān—through the Abrahamic story—defines faith itself. Thus, when God accepts Abraham's prayer to make his line *imāms,* God does not promise them all freedom from evildoing; as the Qur'ān says, God "blessed [Abraham] and Isaac: But of their progeny Are (some) that do right, And (some) that obviously Do wrong, to their own souls" (37:113; in Ali, 1206; see also Ayah 2:124 above). In other words, faith is not a function of kinship or sex but remains transcendently personal, that is, in the reach of the moral personality alone. This theme finds an illustration not only in Abraham's story, in which the son of a disbelieving father embraces Divine Truth, but also in Noah's story, in which the son of a prophet breaks with this truth and becomes one of the lost. Similarly, the wife[28] of the prophet Lot is of those who disbelieve and is punished by God, whereas the wife of the unbelieving pharaoh is of those who believe and is saved by God. In all instances, the prophets pray on behalf of their kin to God but, as the Qur'ān tells us, no "bearer of burdens [can] Bear another's burden.... Even though he be nearly Related" (35:18; in Ali, 1158). Rather, says the Qur'ān, each soul must account for "herself," and warns us to "guard yourselves against a Day When one soul shall not avail another, Nor shall compensation be accepted from her Nor shall intercession profit her Nor shall anyone be helped (from outside)" (2:123; in Ali, 51–52). In place of intercession the Qur'ān privileges the idea of individuals as free moral agents and as witnesses to their own deeds,[29] and in place of bloodlines, the idea of a morally defined community, the *ummah*. That is why the Qur'ān describes the "nearest of kin to Abraham," as "those who follow him...And those who believe" (3–68; in Ali, 140). Such a view of faith, says Arkoun (1994, 57) opens up

an infinite space for the promotion of the individual beyond the constraints of fathers and brothers, clans and tribes, riches and tributes; the individual becomes an autonomous and free person, enjoying a liberty guaranteed by obedience and love lived within the community.

The very structure of faith in Islam, then, is at odds with (traditional) patriarchy. Faith privileges the Rights and Rule of God (freedom) over the rule of even believing fathers (necessity, tradition). Since moral freedom "is achieved only by moving towards God" (Murata 1992, 79), the rule of the father, which sets up man as a parallel node of authority over women and children, becomes an impediment to faith. It therefore matters little whether or not the father is a believer (the content of father-rule is immaterial); it is the very form of father-rule (its assumed parallelism to God's Rule) that is unacceptable.

Prophet Muhammad and Symbolic Father/hood

The Qur'ān's opposition to father-right continues to surface in its account of the Prophet Muhammad's life. The opposition is discernible in its narration, for the benefit of the Prophet and of believers, of the history of unbelief against which God's messengers[30] had to contend. It also is discernible from God's refusal to anoint the Prophet as a symbolic father. The Qur'ān's opposition to the idea of male rule and sovereignty, on the other hand, emerges from its delineation of the relationship between God and prophets on the one hand, and from the nature of the Prophet Muhammad's marital relationships (which we can deduce from the Qur'ān and Tradition) on the other.

In the Qur'ān's telling, the conflict between belief and un-belief has manifested itself historically as a struggle between God's Rule and fathers' rule (following the ways of the fathers, or ancestors). As God tells the Prophet, whenever God

sent a Warner
Before thee to any people,
The wealthy ones among them
Said: "We found our fathers
Following a certain religion,
and we will certainly
Follow in their footsteps."
He [the Warner] said; "What!
Even if I brought you
Better guidance than that
Which ye found
Your fathers following?"
They said: "For us,
We deny that ye (prophets)
Are sent (on a mission
At all)."
So We exacted retribution
From them: now see

What was the end
Of those who rejected (Truth).
    The Qur'ān (43:23–25; in Ali, 1328–29)

Plainly, then, following their fathers has led people to reject God, and their rejection has been the cause of their destruction. This antagonism between monotheism and traditional patriarchy is evident from a number of narratives in the Qur'ān, including that of Moses. When Moses takes God's message to Pharaoh, his people ask him if he has "Come to us to turn us Away from the ways We found our fathers following" (10:78; in Ah, 504). Similarly, it is the Arabs' adherence to their fathers' ways that keeps them from embracing Islam and the Prophet Muhammad. As the Qur'ān says:

When it is said to them:
"Come to what God
Hath revealed; come
To the Apostle":
They say: "Enough for us
Are the ways we found
Our fathers following."
What! even though their fathers
Were void of knowledge
And guidance?
    The Qur'ān (5:107; in Ali, 275)

Adherence to patriarchal traditions has kept not only unbelievers from the path of God but also many believers (People of the Book, i.e., Christians and Jews), who, says the Qur'ān, "take their priests And their anchorites to be Their lords in derogation of God.... Yet they were commanded To worship but One God" (9131; in Ali, 448). The very persons entrusted with interpreting sacred knowledge have misled people, both because of perversity in their hearts (2:7; in Ali, 123) and their cupidity, which drives them to "Devour [in falsehood] the substance of [*insān*] And hinder (them) from the Way of God" (9:34; in Ali, 449). (This scathing criticism of professional interpreters of sacred knowledge, who claim to be intermediaries between God and believers, may be why Islam did not ordain a clergy.)

It is in the context of the history of this conflict between monotheism and patriarchy that we need to interpret the Qur'ān's categorical assertion that even though he is "closer To the Believers than Their own selves" (33:6; in Ali, 1104), "Muhammad is not The father of any Of your men, but (he is) The Apostle of God, And the seal of the Prophets" (33:40; in Ali, 1119). While this Āyah meant to clarify the Prophet's relationship to his adopted son, its assertion that he does not stand in the symbolic relationship of father to his own community returns us once again to the role of fathers, and it does so by *refusing* to consecrate them! From the denial of symbolic fatherhood to the Prophet, which exegetes pass over in silence, I derive the lesson that, in Islam, God's Rule displaces *rule* by the father, whether or not the father is a believer. At the same time, the concept of *imām* (which does not give the sense of rule/sovereignty and is not sex/gender specific) displaces the *imaginary* of the father altogether. In other words, the Qur'ān views fathers in a fundamentally different way than patriarchies do (see Chapter 6 as well).

Given that the Prophet is not sacralized as father, is it also a mere coincidence that he loses his father, Abdullah, in his own infancy, and all his sons in theirs; that only his daughters survive, at a time and in a place when people viewed girls as a curse? Or, do these events in his life illustrate the superficial nature of many of our priorities and the Qur'ān's moral that neither fathers, nor progeny, nor spouses, nor wealth, nor false gods will stand people in better stead than God's Mercy? Is that not why the Qur'ān reassures the Prophet, when he stands alienated from his entire tribe, that he will not find those

> who believe
> In God and the Last Day,
> Loving those who resist
> God and [God's] Apostle,
> Be though they were
> Their fathers or their sons,
> Or their brothers, or
> Their kindred. For such
> [God] has written Faith
> In their hearts, and strengthened
> Them with a spirit
> From [God's Self].
>   The Qur'ān (58:22; in Ali, 1518)

In other words, believers are expected to define social ties and relationships through faith, hence the Islamic perception of a community united by a shared *moral* worldview rather than by blood, sex/gender, race, or age. (Significantly, the first to join the new *ummah* were a woman—Khadijah, the Prophet's first wife, twice widowed, some fifteen years older than he, and a merchant[31]—and Ali, his cousin, a preteen youth.)

In the absence of valorizations of Muhammad as a symbolic father, there remains the complex issue of how best to interpret the Qur'ānic injunctions to obey and follow him while also not taking one another "for lords." Clearly, the Prophet is a role model for Muslim women and men,[32] both in his capacity as prophet and as a moral individual whose character embodies the best of the masculine and feminine traits as we describe them. Thus, he is said to have been unyielding and stern in justice and yet also "a man of kindness, gentleness, integrity, and humility"[33] who had "a mild and forgiving disposition, and disliked unpleasantness and cruelty."[34] Indeed, his nature and habits are "those we may think of as particularly feminine: he is humble, gentle, given to few words, eager to serve others, always ready to work with his own hands, pious beyond measure. He keeps his gaze lowered"[35] In other words, the Prophet was unconventional by the hyper-masculinist standards not only of traditional Arab culture,[36] but also by modern ones, that disparage tenderness, gentleness, and humility in men. In Muhammad, therefore, all Muslims have an exemplary model for emulation. The problem, however, is that in their desire to live by his standards and ethics, most Muslims have ended up canonizing his *Sunnah* (praxis) and even elevating it over the Qur'ān itself, which—for reasons I explained in Chapter 3—is inappropriate. How, then, do we find the balance between following the Prophet and not idolizing him? The Qur'ān itself makes clear that following and obeying the Prophet means obeying and following *God*, not idolizing the *Prophet* himself. (This is why Muslims are offended by the old European way of referring to them as Muhammadans.) It is on the basis of this distinction between God and prophets that Islam also denies divinity to Christ. To those who sacralize prophets, the Qur'ān says that

It is not conceivable that a human being unto whom God had granted revelation, and sound judgment, and prophet-hood, should thereafter have said unto people, "Worship *me* beside God"; but rather [did he exhort them], "become [*Rabbani*] by spreading the knowledge of the divine writ, and by your own deep study [thereof]." And neither did he bid you to take the angels and the prophets for your lords: [for] would he bid you to deny the truth after you have surrendered yourselves unto God? (3:79-80; in Asad, 79; emphasis in original)

(*Rabbani*, says Asad (79 n. 62), is someone devoted "to the endeavour to know the Sustainer (*ar-rabb*) and to obey Him.") The Āyāt not only make a clear distinction between God and prophets, but they also can be read as establishing the primacy of the Qur'ān (Divine Writ) over the narratives of the Prophet's life and praxis (*Ahadith*). This may seem obvious, but, as I noted earlier, Muslims interpret the Qur'ān by way of the *Ahadith* (and thus by way of the Prophet's assumed *Sunnah*), rather than the other way around (using the Qur'ān to determine the accuracy of both as recorded by Muslims). They also take the Prophet's *Sunnah* (as textualized in the *Ahadith*) to abrogate the Qur'ān, practices that, from the Qur'ān's perspective, seem inadmissible. To be sure, one cannot obey the God of the prophets without obeying the prophets and, in order to obey the latter, we need knowledge of their life and practices (*sunnahs*). However, the Qur'ān clarifies that the *sunnahs* of the prophets cannot outweigh Divine Writ, nor, indeed, do we need to emulate the prophets themselves inasmuch as that can result in glorifying them. As the Qur'ān says, "Muhammad is only an apostle; all the [other] apostles have passed away before him: if, then, he dies or is slain, will you turn about on your heels?" (3:144; in Asad, 89). The point, evidently, is to contrast Muhammad's mortality with God's Immortality, and the absence of prophetic sovereignty with the Reality of Divine Sovereignty. God is Ruler, Sovereign, Savior, not Muhammad. The Qur'ān, argue scholars, makes clear that "Muhammad was a human being, and therefore fallible; the Prophet himself urged the first Muslim community to discriminate between his opinions as a human being and his teachings as a prophet" (Davies 1988, 59). Consequently, reversing the relationship between the Qur'ān and his *Sunnah* or sacralizing his *Sunnah* (thus encouraging its ritualized imitativeness) contravene both the Qur'ān's and his own teachings.

If the Qur'ān does not sacralize the Prophet as father, it also does not sacralize him as husband by designating him ruler, guardian, or manager over his wife's affairs, or those of his people. As it says, "thou art One to admonish. Thou art not one To manage [people's] affairs" (88:2i-22; in AH, 1729). Although these Āyāt, which exemplify the principle of the uncoerced nature of faith and of moral responsibility, are not directed at the Prophet's relationships with his own wives, there are others that are, and none of them suggest that he forced compliance on his wives to God's injunctions. Thus, according to Ahmed (1992, 56), after the Āyāt on veiling were revealed, the Prophet gave his wives the choice of remaining married to him or getting a divorce. Nor did the Qur'ān force the Prophet's wives to obey God (or the Prophet). Instead, it held out to those who were righteous the promise of a doubled reward, and to those who were guilty of "manifest lewdness" a double punishment (33:30-31). The Qur'ān suggests that this exception is a function of the fact that his wives "are not like any Of the (other) women"[37] (33:32; in Ali, 1115). Presumably, as the Prophet's consorts, they were required to be role models for the entire community and therefore carried a greater moral responsibility. As such, the Qur'ān holds them to standards of behavior it does not require of others. For instance, it asks them to speak to men not of their household from behind a curtain, not to remarry after their husband's death, and to remain in their homes and not to go into public arenas to make a wanton display of themselves. However, there is controversy regarding the last injunction contained in Ayah 33:30. Arberry (1955,124) renders it as "Remain in your houses; and display not your finery, as did the pagans of old." According to some scholars, the Qur'ān placed this restriction on the Prophet's wives because they were not permitted to remarry after his death. Others, however, argue that the word *qarna* (translated as "stay quietly in your homes") was rendered as *qirna* (in Basra), meaning "have dignity and serenity."[38] As Kaukab Siddique (1990) points out, the Qur'ān could not have required the Prophet's wives to be sequestered in this way since it commands them to *udhkurna*: to mention, teach, spread God's Words which required their presence in the public arena; nor did the Prophet himself confine his wives to their home. (Two of his wives, the daughters of Omar and Abu Bakr—the first two caliphs of Islam—are said to have rebuffed attempts by their fathers to restrict them, saying that if the Prophet did not do so, their fathers had no right to demand it of them either.)

By all indications, the Prophet did not behave like a traditional head of household in other matters, either. He is said to have done his own household chores including preparing his own food. Not only did his wives not wait upon him, but his status as God's Messenger did not deter them from sometimes quarreling with him, and one of them divorced him by saying that she sought refuge in God from him.[39] There is no record that he ever abused them physically or verbally. Indeed, "for most of his life Muhammad himself respected and trusted women, was strongly influenced by a number of forceful females, and attempted to provide for equal participation of women in the religious life of the new community" (Smith 1985, 20). He also was far more progressive than his peers on the issue of children's position in the community (Levy 1962, 91).

Yet, it is usually not these egalitarian aspects of the Prophet's *Sunnah* that many Muslim men want to emulate today; rather, they place a great deal more emphasis on the fact of his multiple marriages, as also on the age of one of his wives, 'Ayesha, which they use to legitimize marriages to little girls. In this context, it is important to be aware, first, that the Qur'ān permitted the Prophet to contract specific types of marriages as "a privilege for thee only, not for the (rest of) believers" (33:50; in Pickthall, 305). The privilege given to the Prophet seems to have been in his capacity as God's Messenger and not as a man, otherwise, why would God have denied it to other men? Moreover, the Qur'ān also circumscribed the Prophet's polygyny by forbidding him to "to take (other) women henceforth, nor that thou shouldst change them for other wives even though their beauty pleased thee" (33:52; in Pickthall, 305). However, as M.M. Pickthall (406) points out, the Prophet was allowed to marry more wives than were others "because, as head of the State, he was responsible for the support of women who had no other protector. With the one exception of Ayeshah, all his wives had been widows." Similarly, Wiebke Walther (1981,34) notes that in "most of his marriages, if not in all of them [the Prophet] is said to have also had the solidarity of his community in mind." As I will argue in Chapter 6, these standards do not apply to all men, and the Qur'ān does not, in fact, favor generalized polygyny. (It also is important to recall that the Prophet is said to have discouraged his son-in-law, Ali, from taking a second wife.)

As far as 'Ayesha's age at the time of her marriage to the Prophet is concerned, it is a matter of ongoing controversy among Muslims. Conservatives (and *Western* Orientalists) put her age as low as nine years, based on *Ahadith* that claim that she was playing with dolls when she got married. This could well be true since the concept of childhood is a relatively recent one, and the age of consent for women in most cultures in those days was quite low. (Even in the United States, the age of consent for women was between seven and ten as late as 1889 and was raised to eighteen only as the result of feminist campaigns.)[40] As such, there was nothing aberrant in the practice of marrying young girls fourteen centuries ago (though it is today, given that we now recognize children as children). On the other hand, however, Muslims who calculate 'Ayesha's age based on details of her sister Asma's age, about whom more is known, as well as on details of the Hijra (the Prophet's migration from Mecca to Madina), maintain that she was over thirteen and perhaps between seventeen and nineteen when she got married. Such views cohere with those *Ahadith* that claim that at her marriage 'Ayesha had "good knowledge of Ancient Arabic poetry and genealogy" and "pronounced the fundamental rules of Arabic-Islamic ethics" (Walther 1981, 75). However, most of what we know about 'Ayesha, including the details of her marriage, are reconstructions that remain susceptible to interpretive controversy and manipulation in view of the very different meaning of her life for Sunni and Shii Muslims. (After the Prophet's death, 'Ayesha led an unsuccessful revolt against Ali, the Prophet's cousin and son-in-law, the fourth caliph of Islam whom the Shii follow as *Imām*.) Not only are Muslims thus particularly invested in specific reconstructions of her life, but the most definitive work on it was begun a century and a half after her death. This work drew for its details on "oral reports transmitted over three to four generations" (Spellberg 1994, 2); thus, "even the earliest Arabic written sources on Aisha's life already capture that life as a legacy, an interpretation." As D. A. Spellberg puts it (191), in studying 'Ayesha, one therefore is studying "male intellectual history, not a woman's history, but reflections about the place of a woman, and by extension, all women, in exclusively male assertions about Muslim society." To what extent estimates of 'Ayesha's age or the details of her marriage also embody displaced male desires must then permanently remain open to question. However, it is safe to say that men who wish to marry children today in order to indulge their sexual lusts under the guise of adhering to the Prophet's *Sunnah* seem to have forgotten another crucial aspect of it: that the Qur'ān unequivocally rules against lechery in a marriage, as my discussion of its position on sexuality will show in Chapter 5. Given that the Prophet's life was meant to exemplify the Qur'ān's teachings, it is safe to assume that his marriages were not, in fact, based in lust notwithstanding attempts to portray them as such. This is more than can be said for those who—on the pretext of following his *Sunnah*—are engaging in lecherous behavior that the Qur'ān repeatedly warns against.

In Conclusion

The Qur'ān's teachings about God and prophets, I have argued, clearly undermine the imaginary of "the Father/fathers" inasmuch as they do not allow us either to engender God (represent God as Father/male) or to condone theories of father-right/rule and male privilege. This is because if Qur'ānic monotheism is intolerant, as its feminist critics allege, it is intolerant of men/fathers arrogating to themselves rights that belong only to God.

It is true, of course, that the Qurān's teachings recognize that, in patriarchies, men are the locus of authority, which may be why so many Āyāt are addressed to men. Here I refer not just to the use of the words *an-nas* or *bashar* (incorrectly translated as man), but also to Āyāt that explicitly address men (fathers and sons). There are those who read these Āyāt as, in fact, being inclusive of women; in other words, they believe that references to fathers actually are references to both male and female ancestors. If this is so, then my argument becomes moot (and the arguments of those who read such Āyāt as sexist become redundant). If, on the other hand, one takes many of the Qur'ān's references as in fact addressing men, then my argument may serve to establish that the Qur'ān does not privilege fathers or males and that it takes the notion of father-rule and male privilege to task in a number of ways.

In this context, what seems to be worthy of comment in the Qur'ān is not that patriarchies exist, but that historically they have provided the core of resistance to Divine Truth. This is partly why the Qur'ān objects to the idea of father-right whether or not the father is a believer; that is, it opposes not only the content but also the form of father's rule. At least, this is how I understand the Qur'ān's delineation of the Rule of God vis-a-vis the lives of both prophets and ordinary humans. If my reading is correct, then it becomes possible to say that the Qur'ān is an antiparriarchal text, or at the very least, it can be read as one. Nonetheless, Muslims have not done so, both because of their own investment in patriarchy and because of their belief that the Prophet's community is above interpretive error.[41]

78. **Robert F. Worth, "Gay Muslims Face a Growing Challenge" from** *The New York Times*

Robert F. Worth, "Gay Muslims Face a Growing Challenge" Metro Section, Sunday January 13, 2002.

Homosexuality is considered to be forbidden in orthodox Islam and the topic remains taboo in most Muslim societies. As a result, homosexual activity and homosexual individuals face severe punishments throughout the Muslim world, such as when 23 Egyptian men were sentenced to prison for terms of one to five years for alleged sexual immorality (i.e., homosexuality) in November 2001. However, claiming both Muslim and homosexual identities has become increasingly public in the United States, especially with the creation of the organization Al-Fatiha, which began in 1997 as an e-mail listserv for gay Muslims. The organization, based in Washington, DC, seeks to provide community, support, and awareness for lesbian, gay, bisexual, transgender, intersex, and questioning (i.e., those questioning their sexual orientation) Muslims. Even as Al-Fatiha is challenging the orthodox position on homosexuality and having effects in the Muslim world, it remains controversial and its members continue to face challenges to their identities, faiths, and physical safety even in the pluralistic American context. The following article highlights the difficulties homosexual American Muslims face as they navigate between hostility from orthodox Islam and anti-Muslim sentiments in the United States following the terrorist attacks of September 11, 2001.

In late September, two F.B.I. agents visited the home of Ramzi Zakharia, a Palestinian Muslim who lives in Jersey City. He said they told him they had heard that he had posted subversive comments on a Web site, including some that were critical of United States foreign policy.

The interview had barely begun when Mr. Zakharia offered what he saw as a defense: he is gay. He could hardly be an Islamic terrorist, he said, when he lives in a way that fundamentalists view as the height of Western corruption.

"If the Taliban knew about me, I'd be on their top 10 list," he joked.

The agents laughed with him. But for Mr. Zakharia and other gay Muslims living in the United States, the joke is a bitter one. Viewed as potential terrorists by some Americans since Sept. 11 because of their religion, they are reviled even by mainstream Muslims because of their sexual orientation.

"We really felt caught in between," said Faisal Alam, the executive director of Al-Fatiha, a group for gay Muslims founded in 1997 in Washington. "The last thing you could do was call the mosque for help."

In most Islamic societies, homosexual behavior is a crime, punishable in some cases by death. Even in the United States, many Muslims say they cannot be openly gay for fear that they would be rejected by other Muslims or attacked by extremists.

Members of Al-Fatiha and the Gay and Lesbian Arab Society of New York say they have been threatened and harassed by people accusing them of debasing Islam. Many Islamic religious authorities refuse to even discuss homosexuality; while one imam at a New York City mosque with a reputation for liberalism said he did not consider it a sin, he would not say so on the record for fear of becoming a target.

Although reconciling their sexual and spiritual life has always been difficult, several gay Muslims said the Sept. 11 attacks and their aftermath have driven them more deeply than ever into a double life.

"I have one friend who goes through phases when he is ultrareligious—he won't return calls from us, he goes to the mosque every day," Mr. Zakharia said. "Then suddenly he goes back to a gay lifestyle. There is no in between."

Some are resigned to the belief that their impulses are evil, and regard the holy month of Ramadan as an opportunity to redeem themselves, several gay Muslims said.

"They stop having sex or drinking, and these are men who would ordinarily be out at the clubs every night," said Tarek, a gay Muslim in New York who, like others, asked that his last name not be used. "They live with an internalized rejection, and they think that if they are good enough during Ramadan, God will be easier on them for the sins they commit the rest of the year."

Muslim clerics are far from the only people who are hostile toward homosexuality. In October, an Associated Press photograph that appeared in newspapers showed a Navy crewman on an aircraft carrier standing next to a bomb on which the words "Hijack this" and a crude antigay slur had been scrawled.

Yet to be both Muslim and gay may be particularly challenging, because unlike Christianity and Judaism, Islam is still inseparable from culture and politics in many countries where it is practiced. "It's a whole way of life, dictating everything from your politics to what you wear to how much dowry you give your wife," Mr. Alam said. "To say you're going to change one part of it is to shake the whole foundation, for many orthodox Muslims."

That perceived threat is reflected in harsh penalties in many Arab and Islamic countries. Under the Taliban, people found to have engaged in homosexual behavior had a brick wall collapsed onto them. This was done several times in the last several years, according to international news reports and Taliban radio and newspaper sources. Other countries are similarly severe.

Yet if the United States represents freedom and safety to gay Muslims, many of them also say they have been shocked and upset, since Sept. 11, by their fellow Americans' ignorance and disrespect toward Islam, even among other gays.

"There was an explosion of anti-Muslim and anti-Arab sentiment in the gay community after 9/11," said Abdullah, who runs an e-mail service for gay Muslim men in Washington that has about 350 active members. "You heard people saying, 'We've just got to kill those Arabs,' that kind of thing."

Several said they had been offended by articles in the gay and mainstream press suggesting that Mohamed Atta and other hijackers may have been motivated by repressed homosexual rage.

For the most part, gay Muslims say they have resigned themselves to keeping their sexuality secret. But a few are following in the steps of the Western gay liberation movement, defending the notion that Islam and homosexuality can be reconciled.

Perhaps the most well known of those is Mr. Alam, whose Al-Fatiha is the only organization specifically representing gay Muslims in this country. He said he conceived of the group five years ago, shortly after suffering a nervous breakdown that he attributed to his realization that he was gay. As a teenager, he had worked as a volunteer with Muslim youth groups, and he refused to abandon the religion. After an Internet search for other gay Muslims, which met with resounding silence, he created his own e-mail list, sending it to Muslim student groups. He said people began joining instantly, though it took months for others to find the courage to post their own messages. Since then, the group has grown quickly, with nine chapters in three countries and about 200 active members.

"Our mission is to try to help Muslims to reconcile two identities they cannot keep together," Mr. Alam said.

One key to doing that is challenging the notion that Islam absolutely forbids homosexuality. There are seven references in the Koran to the "people of Lot," or the Sodomites, whose destruction is explicitly associated with their sexual behavior. There is also one passage that has been taken to suggest a legal prohibition against homosexuality, and it is relatively mild: "And as for the two of you who are guilty thereof, punish them both. And if they repent and improve, then let them be. Lo! Allah is relenting, merciful."

Some other Koranic verses prescribe much harsher punishments for other sins, like fornication, which merits 100 lashes.

There are other, harsher sayings attributed to the prophet Muhammad about homosexuality. Yet Mr. Alam said that in Islam, as in Christianity, homosexuality's status is ultimately a matter of interpretation.

He added that homosexuality is woven into many features of Islamic history and culture, perhaps in part because of stricter gender segregation than is common in the West. It is mentioned in "The Thousand and One Nights" and other literary works of the Arab world. And Western writers from André Gide to William S. Burroughs have described the Muslim countries of North Africa as places where gay travelers could indulge their passions more freely than they could where they lived. Still, homosexual behavior has always been clandestine.

That may have more to do with Islam's general insistence on discretion in sexual matters than any specific animosity toward homosexuality, said Feisal Rauf, the imam of the Al-Farah mosque in TriBeCa.

Others are less open-minded. Last year, a London-based extremist group called Al-Muhajiroun issued a fatwa, or religious ruling, declaring that any member of Al-Fatiha was an apostate, and that the punishment for apostasy is death, Mr. Alam said. Because of such threats, he said, Al-Fatiha has kept all details of its meetings secret until shortly beforehand, and has asked for and been given police protection in some cases. "We're challenging 1,400 years of dogma," Mr. Alam said. "There's bound to be a battle."

79. **Ayesha Akram, "Gay, Lesbian Muslims Seek Out 'Marriages of Convenience'"**
from *Religion News Service*

Copyright 2007 Religion News Service. Used by permission.
For a description of homosexuality, Islam, and Al-Fatiha (a gay Muslim advocacy organiza-
tion) in the United States, see Primary document 78. The following article highlights the chal-
lenges homosexual Muslims face when confronted with familial and societal pressures to marry.

NEW YORK—On a Web site for gay South Asians, 27-year-old Syed Mansoor uploaded
the following message last summer:

"Hi, I am looking for a lesbian girl for marriage. I am gay but I would like to get married because of pressure from parents and society. I would like this marriage to be a 'normal' marriage except for the sex part, please don't expect any sexual relationship from me.

"Being an Indian gay person, I believe it is so much worth it to give up sex and have a
nice otherwise normal family. We can be good friends and don't have to repent all our life
for being gay/lesbian."

Across the globe and especially in America, hundreds of other gay Muslims have started
to pursue marriages of convenience—or MOC, as they are known—in which gay
Muslims seek out lesbian Muslims, and vice versa, for appearances sake.

Mansoor works as an accountant and is a devout Muslim. He strictly abstains from
drinking alcohol or eating pork and is particular about offering early-morning prayers.

To his friends on Wall Street, he is a financial whiz; to his parents, a devoted son. But
Mansoor is also part of a burgeoning trend of gay Muslims adopting marriages of convenience.

Hard statistics on the trend are hard to come by, but on a single Web site for South
Asian gays and lesbians seeking such marriages, almost 400 requests had been uploaded.

They ranged from a desperate plea from Atlanta—"I just finished medical school, and
the pressure for me to get married is becoming ridiculous. I can't have a conversation with
my parents without them pressuring me"—to a straightforward one from Texas: "I will
not object to her having sex with other women."

Mansoor credits the Internet for making these marriages a real possibility for gay
Muslims. Gay activists agree, and say that in recent years, they have seen a rise in such
marriages among Muslims.

Jack Fertig, a co-coordinator for Al Fatiha, a national advocacy group for gay Muslims,
says he comes across at least one such e-mail request every month.

"It's obvious that this is becoming a viable option," he said. "People are seeking, looking and trying to make connections that could develop into such marriages."

Other activists say gay Muslims are resorting to these unions for reasons of self-
preservation.

"Marriages of convenience are the result of gay Muslims wanting to avoid emotional
and physical harm to themselves," says Muhammed Ali, a board member of Homan, a
Los Angeles-based support group for gay Iranians.

Homosexuality is a crime punishable by death in much of the Islamic world. In Iran
last year, two gay teenagers were publicly executed, while in Afghanistan, the Taliban
government would torture homosexuals by collapsing walls on them.

Though gay Muslims in America don't have such fears, they still seek out marriages of
convenience as a way of staying in the closet. Many of them worry about being ostracized
from their families if their secret is revealed.

An marriage of convenience is the perfect solution, Mansoor said.

"It's a great option," he said. "I get married to a lesbian, we sleep in different rooms and remain friends. Meanwhile I can have a boyfriend."

Mansoor is also willing to throw a financial incentive into the deal. A year has passed since he posted his request on an online discussion board and as yet he has received no replies. But Mansoor continues to hope.

"Now that I have a good job and earn handsomely, my family keeps asking, 'Why don't you find a wife?'" he said. "I plan to have a marriage of convenience just to satisfy the world."

***

Muslim authorities around the world have repeatedly emphasized that homosexuality is not permissible. Muzammil Siddiqi of the Islamic Society of North America said there is no flexibility on this topic.

"Homosexuality is a moral disorder. It is a moral disease, a sin and corruption...No person is born homosexual, just like no one is born a thief, a liar or murderer," he said. "People acquire these evil habits due to a lack of proper guidance and education."

Mainstream Islamic scholars also take an unfavorable view of MOCs. The face of Imam Omar, a scholar at the Islamic Cultural Center of Manhattan, crinkled with laughter when he was asked about this phenomenon. "These people are Muslims?" he asked.

Omar receives all sorts of inquiries and is now rarely taken aback. But a query about marriages of convenience stunned him. "What kind of marriage is this?" he asked. "A nikah (marriage) in Islam needs to be consummated. There is no concept of marriage in Islam without sexual relations."

Running his hand through his salt and pepper beard, he continued: "Homosexuality is strictly forbidden in Islam. I say to these people do not circumvent marriage. Do not change the rules of religion."

Mansoor shook his head when the Imam's proclamation was repeated to him. With a shrug of his thin shoulders, he said: "I don't care about what people say," he said. "I can't change myself. I just can't."

Though some gay men feel a union of convenience is the best option, Rachel Sussman, a marriage counselor in New York, said they may not know what they are getting into.

"It's opening up a Pandora's box," she said. "What happens if his partner falls in love with someone? What happens if he falls in love with someone who is not OK with him being married?"

Sussman says that arrangements can potentially lead to depression, anxiety and severe marital distress.

But Ali, of Los Angeles, disagrees. He doesn't think MOCs are any unhealthier than other arrangements. "It is such a complicated notion about what is a healthy marriage and what is a marriage of convenience," he said.

"If you look at our traditional culture, marriages were usually marriages of consensus and convenience and not necessarily emotional marriages. If two people care enough about each other to help each other out, whose to say they won't have a good marriage?"

PART V

RACE AND ISLAM

Since the time of slavery, African Americans have played a significant role in the shaping of American Islam. Numerous African American groups have claimed their connection to Islam as a way to assert their collective identity in American society, the foremost being the National of Islam. More recently, Malcolm X (1925–1964) and Warith Deen Mohammed (b. 1933), son of Elijah Muhammad, emerged as fundamental actors of the inclusion of African American Islam in the global Muslim world. A new generation of African American Muslims and descendents of immigrants is rising, trying to bridge the gap between African American Muslims and the rest of the Muslim groups in the United States, at least at the elite level. However, Islam is still used as a way to reinforce or strengthen racial identity, as shown by Louis Farrakhan of the Nation of Islam.

80. **Nicholas Said, "In London, Paris, and the West Indies" from** *The Autobiography of Nicholas Said; a Native of Bornou, Eastern Soudan, Central Africa*

Memphis: Shotwell & Co., Publishers, 1873. Reprinted with permission of Documenting the American South, The University of North Carolina at Chapel Hill Libraries.

In 1836, Nicholas Said was born in Kouka in the eastern Sudan. Captured in tribal warfare, Said became a slave. With various owners, he traveled widely, from Tripoli to St. Petersburg to New York City. Eventually he reached the American South where he set up a school for American children. The following is an excerpt from his autobiography, which is testimony to the Islamic component of the slavery period in the United States.

While in Rome, I one day saw in the *Giornale di Roma* an article respecting the invasion of Soudan by Said, Pacha of Egypt.

The article said that the subjugation of Soudan had been very difficult. I never have heard anything about that matter since, and moreover doubt its veracity.

May it never happen that my dear country should ever be under Egyptian despotism.

On the 25th of May, 1857, we got our passports to Visa, and forthwith left Rome for Civita Vecchia, where we took a steamer belonging to the French *Messagerie Imperiale* for Marsailles, which we reached in forty-eight hours.

Remaining here only a few hours, we left this city for Paris, stopping a little while in Lyons.

Shortly after our arrival in Paris, a grand ball was given at the *Palais du Corps Legislatif,* in honor of the Due de Morney's marriage with one of my master's nieces, a daughter of his brother Sergius, of whom mention has already been made.

His Excellency took lodgings at the Hotel Mirabeau, in the Rue de la Paix.

The Prince was now very anxious to visit England, and leaving the greater portion of his effects at the Hotel Mirabeau, we left Paris, in June, for Boulogne sur Mer.

I did not rest a moment during our stay in Paris, but was here, and there and everywhere, seeing everything, and learning everything.

I believe there is more wealth and more wretchedness, more learning and more vice, more gayety and less virtue in Paris than in any other city in the world.

It would be pleasant to me to describe the magnificent edifices, *boulevards,* and parks of the great city, its monuments of sculpture and its galleries of paintings, its churches, colleges, libraries and its world-renowned scientific associations, its operas, theatres and other places of gayety and fashion; but I must forbear.

On reaching Boulogne, we immediately embarked on board an English steamer for Folkestone, the birthplace of Harvey, of the "Circulation of the blood" celebrity.

Remaining here only a day, we took the rail for London, which we reached late at night.

As some said it was unaristocratic to live at the hotels, the Prince had before-hand engaged a private house on Prince street, Hanover square, whither we immediately repaired.

During the sojourn of three months in London, the Prince was repeatedly invited to the residences and country seats of the nobility, and on these occasions, was always permitted to accompany him

He was also on several occasions invited to the court, both at Buckingham palace and Windsor castle, and was always accepted cordially and cheerfully by Her Brittanic Majesty.

At these places, I had excellent opportunities of seeing many of the prominent men of England, among them Lords Palmerston, John Russell, Barrington, Westmoreland, and many others, besides numbers of ambassadors, etc. etc.

During my stay in England, I worked hard to learn the English language; so by the time I left there I had laid a very good foundation upon which to build afterwards.

Of all the people I have ever seen in my life, the English nobility are the highest livers, and the most fastidious in their surroundings. Indeed I disgraced myself at the country residence of Lady Waldegrave's by *associating with her footmen,* and I was forced much to my regret to give over my hitherto pleasant visits to her under-household because, being a *valet de chambre,* and having degraded myself by mixing with my inferiors, I would have been compelled to remain with them in all future visits.

At the expiration of the time above stated we returned to Paris, by the way of Dover and Calais. The succeeding seasons from 1858, to 1866, were passed alternately in Italy, Germany, France, and England.

In the spring of 1867 while in Ryde, (Isle of Wight) I had an irresistible desire to visit my native country. I at first tried to overcome that feeling but all in vain.

When I communicated my wishes to the Prince he tried to ridicule me, stating that I was no longer an African but a citizen of Europe. He said I could not reconcile myself to the manners and customs of my countrymen. He moreover told me if I would stay with him twenty years he would give me a pension the rest of my days. All this, however, did not deter me from returning to Soudan.

All the Prince could do was to draw a promise from me to return to him after spending a year in Central Africa.

Accordingly having furnished me three hundred pounds sterling; this kind and best of men left London for Geneva *via* Paris, and I removed quarters to the "Strangers' Home, for Asiatics, Africans, and South Sea Islanders," located on the West India Dock; superintended by Mr. Marshall Hughes, a model christian and gentleman.

This gentleman, I learned, had formerly been, for upwards of twenty years, an officer in the British East India army.

While waiting here for a steamer to convey me to Malta, from which point I expected to get passage for Tripoli, and then with a caravan to Fezzan, and then across the Desert to Bornou, I was sent for to see "a gentleman."

Answering the summons, I soon found myself in the presence of a well dressed and genteel looking man, with long, flowing, sandy whiskers, who informed me that I had been recommended to him by a gentleman, the name of whom he declined to reveal, and said he desired my services as a valet.

The gentleman said he contemplated marriage and a bridal tour through the West Indies, the British North American Provinces, and the United States; that he would not be absent more than twelve months; that he would take good care of me, and show me many new things to tell my people of on my return, and that he would bring me back to England.

He gave me twenty-four hours for consideration and reflection, during which time my fondness for travel asserted its supremacy, I concluded to go with him, and we arranged that I should have £3.11s. for my services per month, besides which he was to pay my travelling, board and clothing expenses, and physician fees, in the event of sickness.

The name of my new employer was De Sanddrost I. J. Rochussen, then lately from Paramaribo, (Dutch Guinea), and at the time that I engaged service with him, was staying at the Marlborough Hotel in Fleet street, and in the immediate vicinity of St. Paul's Cathedral.

As soon as he was married we removed to the Paddington Hotel, and shortly afterwards, took the rails for Wells City, Sommerset. We remained only a few days here, and went to Liverpool, stopping a few days in Bristol, Exeter, Manchester; and at the former place took passage on board the "Bohemian," commanded by captain Granger, for Portland, Maine, United States.

We landed in Portland in December 1867, and on the morn of our arrival, we left for Boston, Mass.

We stayed here two days, and then left for New York.

As it was Mr. Rochussen's intention to pass the winter in the West Indies, he made no delay in the Northern States, but what was absolutely necessary. Accordingly, after staying only three days at the Metropolitan Hotel, we took the English Screw Steamship "Karnak," for Nassau, N. P. We made this port in five days.

Here I was perfectly beside myself with joy, on finding a great many liberated Africans, but all of them came from the coast of Guinea, Mandigoes, Nangoes, Kissi, Dahomey, Amatifous, and Kromantis. Consequently, I could not converse with them.

The English government of the West Indies had most of the young men in the army. They wore similar uniforms to the French "Turcos," and performed their evolutions, or tactics, with remarkable precision. The military brass band is also very much admired by all who have ever heard it play.

About eleven miles west of Nassau, there is a village called Adelaide, where the freshly rescued Africans used to go, and remain until properly trained to the usages and modes of the civilized world. This place is now perfectly deserted, and nothing can be seen but the ruins of huts built in the African style.

There were still remaining, however, two or three hovels, and as hunger pressed Mr. and Mrs. Rochussen and myself, we managed to buy a couple of pullets, a pot was procured, and I was called upon to display my culinary ability. After partaking of my cooking, which both Mr. and Madame Rochussen pronounced excellent, we returned to Nassau.

After remaining here one month and a week, Mr. Rochussen concluded to visit Hayti, and accordingly we took passage on board the brig Victoria, for Cape Haïtien, and touching at Inagua, Long Key, and Long Island, (Bahamas). After nineteen days of the most wretched sailing, we reach Cape Haïtien.

I found myself exceedingly delighted at finding myself in the country where the heroes of the "Haytien Independence" contended with the armies of Napoleon the Great.

I had always admired the exploits of Toussaint, L'Ouverture, Dessalines, Christophe, and other negro leaders, whose heroism and military talent are an honor to the African race.

Hayti, or Hispaniola, certainly deserves the appellation of the "Queen of the Antilles."

Nothing can excel it in picturesque beauty. It is very mountainous, and viewing it from the sea, it has a grand and magnificent appearance.

Cape Haïtien, in the time of the French occupation, must have been a place of considerable importance.

It is situated at the terminus of a small bay, and the foot of a mount, which totally hides it from view on all sides. It is defended by several forts and redoubts the greater portion of which are in a dilapidated condition.

The language spoken here is French, but only the educated can speak perfectly. They have, however, among them a *patois* which they call *Créole*. It is an admixture of French and several African languages, and is quite unintelligible to a Frenchman.

Notwithstanding all the natural advantages which this country possesses, no sign of industry is to be seen in it.

This country, when it was a French colony, produced wheat, rice, corn, cotton, indigo, etc. etc. It is now grown up in thick forests of mahogany and other valuable timber, which, with gold and the tropical fruits that grow there spontaneously, constitute the chief articles of export.

I understood while there, that the policy of that government is to keep things in that condition, lest England France, the United States or Spain might envy and take possession of it.

The government of Hayti, I am sorry to say, is most shamefully managed. It is a perfect image of anarchy; and goes to prove that the pure negro and the mulatto, who considers himself, (by virtue of his caucassian half-bloodedness,) the superior of the former, and who always wants to rule him, cannot possibly live in harmony and prosperity.

The fault is, (in nine cases out of ten,) the mulattoes', who, unduly and arrogantly, are presumptuous.

The prejudice of color in the West Indies between the negro and the hybrid mulatto is much greater than exists in the United States.

I shall truly and fearlessly say that the Southern white has ten-fold more humane feeling towards the black man than the West India mulatto, I shall also include the Northern mulatto, though there are noble exceptions in both cases.

It is a burning shame that instead of making that country prosperous and its people industrious and happy, the *soidisant,* aristocrats and educated people of Hayti should pay attention to mean and low party dissensions.

No wonder the whites of different countries maintain that the negro is incapable of self-government. How is it possible for a community to be prosperous when its population entertain inveterate animosities among themselves?

I would prefer that Hayti were one of the English or French colonies rather than in its present condition.

The President of the Republic at the time I was there was Giffrard, a truly intelligent, able and excellent man, who introduced reform, created a navy, and did a host of other good things for his country, which he loved with genuine patriotism, notwithstanding which the mulattoes undermined and eventually revolted and overthrew him.

I have since learned that they have executed Salnave–in short, should an angel come from heaven to rule that country they would not be pleased with him.

We remained at Cape Haïtien seven weeks, after which we left for Gonaïves by land.

On our route lay several insignificant but most picturesque villages, the principal among which is Plaisance, where we passed a night. There are several dangerous passes on this route, but we made that port in three days without any remarkable event.

From appearance Gonaïve boasts more commerce than Cape Haïtien and contains some substantial and well built commercial houses.

About nine leagues east of this place is the celebrated *Crête á Piérrot,* the place where the negro insurgents under the leadership of their celebrated General, Toussaint L'Overture, signally defeated the French under General LeClerc, broth-in-low to Napoleon I, who sent him to reduce the negroes again to slavery.

This fortification is considered second to that of Mole Saint Nicholas, the Gibraltar of Hayti.

Mole Saint Nicholas had once withstood a seige for ten years.

We stayed in Genaïves about ten days, after which we sailed for Port au Prince.

I shall not dwell any longer on the details of our trip through Hayti. But after visiting the principal towns in this Republic, we returned to Nassau, by way of Kingston, Jamaica, and embarking on board the Karnak, we made New York on the last of May, 1867.

M. Rochussen now proposed to visit Niagara Falls, Saratoga Springs, Kingston, Canada West, Montreal, and Quebec, where he intended to take passage on his return to Europe.

We accordingly left the Metropolitan Hotel, New York, and made Niagara Falls in due time, and, remaining here two weeks, we left for Hamilton, thence to Toronto, Kingston, Montreal, Ottawa City and Aylmer about nine miles north of the latter city.

Here M. Rochussen informed me that he had failed to receive his remittance in time, and said he had very urgent business in Quebec, and asked me if I could lend him a hundred pounds. I told him I had three hundred pounds that I could spare; he having told me he would return me my money in a fortnight.

He consented to my proposal and I handed him six £50 bills.

Next day he left for Ottawa City, leaving his effects and Madame Rochussen.

Three days after his departure, Madame received a telegraphic communication stating that M. Rochussen had met with a serious accident, and requesting her to repair to Quebec immediately. I was left to take care of their things, which consisted of five large trunks besides a number of sma [print not legible] ler ones.

After Madame Rochussen's departure, I had a strange presentiment that I would never see them again.

I waited at the British Hotel, where we had stopped, for three months *expecting* the return of my employer, but all in vain. Mr. John McCook, the clerk and business manager, for the proprietress, Mrs. McCormick, told me that M. Rochussen had absconded, and owed the Hotel $2000, and had borrowed £50 from himself.

His and my own things were seized, consequently, I lost all my clothing, consisting of four Turkish *costumes,* three full suits, of broadcloth, a dozen of linen and fine English flannel shirts, etc. etc., worth more than two hundred and fifty dollars.

I was almost penniless, with only one suit of clothes, and that a livery, with M. Rochussen's coat-of-arms on the buttons.

Having no trade, knowing no person to whom I could apply for help,—I was truly in a pitiful situation. But God who never forsakes us came to my relief.

During our stay at Aylmer, we had become acquainted with Rev. D. T. Johnston, a pastor of that parish, who loaned me ten dollars, and told me I had better go to Detroit, Michigan, or Buffalo, New York, where there were a great number of colored people; and where I could get into employment easier than to remain in Canada, where the cold was so intense.

I left Aylmer for Prescott, where I crossed the St. Lawrence to Ogdensburg, New York, thence to Rome, Watertown, Syracuse and Buffalo.

Here I took passage on the Concord for Detroit, Michigan, as a *deck hand.* The work was so hard for me that I only managed to make one *trip.* My will was good, but my strength failed. I informed the captain, who was a good man, of my former occupation, and he told me that he was not surprised at my giving out.

He paid me up promptly my $4.50, which was coming to me on reaching Detroit. I stayed here six months, during which time I became acquainted with Rev. Geo. Duffield, D.D., who recognized me, having seen me on board the Egitto, on our trip from Constantinople to Trieste, while I was in the service of Prince Mentchikoff.

This gentleman helped me a great deal by recommending me to the principal colored people of that city, some of whom gave me employment, to teach their children French.

At the end of six months, I had pretty well recuperated, and had some two hundred dollars in money and good suits of clothes. I then left for Toledo, Ohio, thence to Bellefontaine and Sandusky City, in the same state.

While in Sandusky City, I conceived the idea to go South, where I could be of great use to my benighted people in the capacity of a teacher.

I selected Charleston, South Carolina as the basis of my operation. Accordingly I left Sandusky City for Cleveland, Ohio, thence to Buffalo, Rochester, Albany, Troy, Poughkeepsie and New York City, and embarked for the port of my destination.

Having taken up my quarters at Mrs. Cobb's boarding house in Calhoune Street, I soon became acquainted with Wright, Langston, Randolph, Bozeman, Ransier, and a host of other less notable Northern colored men who came there for political purposes.

All the above named were very able men, but, with the exception of the last named, who was truly a very good and honest man, I have a very little opinion of their honesty.

I soon got into employment as a teacher, and taught here about a year.

I am proud to say that I have gained the esteem of numerous white friends in Charleston, among which are Messrs. General Simmons, Kanapaux, Dr. Ogier, Sim, De Saussure, Chazal, Cohen, and a host of others who have shown me a great deal of favor.

I left Charleston for Savannah, Georgia, in the commencement of 1870, and only remaining here three days I left for Thomasville, Thomas County Georgia.

While here I conceived the idea of writing my Biography or rather adventures. Several of my well-wishers to whom I communicated my idea said it was a very good thing.

The Editor of the "Thomasville Enterprise" gave me a most flattering notice in his paper, by which I gained many friends.

I accordingly set to work and wrote an essay to that effect consisting of about one hundred pages. When I completed that, I proposed to give lectures on "Africa and its resources." I made my dèbut in Thomasville, then at Bainbridge Albany, Americus, Macon, Griffin, and Atlanta. I soon got tired of that business which in fact did not yield me much profit, I left Atlanta, and got down to Forsyth in Monroe, where I took up a school sixteen miles from here in a village called Culloden.

I taught here six months and then retraced my steps to Thomasville where I had left my effects with a colored friend of mine, Solomon Harvey by name. To my no small disappointment he had left for Texas taking my goods with him.

After making arrangements as to the publication of my book, I started on a new plan, that of raising means by which to defray expenses of publication by *voluntary subscriptions.*

I have got a great many subscribers from Thomasville, Bainbridge, Quitman, Valdosta, Ga., Monticello, Madison, Tallahassee and Quincy Fla. From Quincy I returned to Bainbridge thence to Early county Georgia, always meeting with success and good treatment from the white and black people.

While in Georgia and Florida, I had heard from the black people that Alabama was a very dangerous State and filled with Ku-Klux that the freedmen there did not know what freedom was owing to the oppression of the whites under which they were situated.

I was advised not to go to that State my life, they said, would be in great danger. My own common sense dictated to me, of course, that it was not possible that such a state of affairs could exist in Alabama, besides that, there were good and bad in all countries.

I shall here say, however, that it was thought by the blacks and a good number of whites I travelled for the purpose of spying through the country. Blacks were sent at times to pick me, but I had nothing to tell them excepting that I travelled for my own amusement and gratification, at the same time, making a little something which I hoped would enable me to publish my Adventures.

Some said I was harmless and quiet, and others that I was a Yankee emissary and a scoundrel.

I crossed the Chattahooche into Henry county, Alabama, and to my great surprise, was received with respect and kindness. I shall truly say, that I have never had such a reception heretofore.

I shall never forget the kindness and attention paid to my humble self by that most intelligent and most gentlemanly Mr. M. Smith, of Columbia. When I left that place, after ten days stay, and was going to Abbeville, the county-seat, that kind man recommended me to Col. Oates, of that town:

COLUMBIA, ALA., July 21, 1871.

Colonel Oates:

The bearer, Nicholas Said, who is without a shadow of a doubt, a native African, and whose ostensible object in travelling through this country, is to obtain subscribers to his Autobiography, lectured here to-day.

And I am glad to say, gave entire satisfaction to his audience, which was composed of a goodly number of white and black people. He is, by far, the most intelligent, and the best educated man of the African race, with whom I have ever conversed, etc.

Any attention paid to Mr. Said will be thankfully received.

I am, Colonel,

Yours, most truly,

M. SMITH.

This letter did me an immense good in Abbeville, where I remained, and taught school until October of that year. I then went to Eufawla, Clayton, Troy. Montgomery, Selma, Greenville, Pineapple, Monroeville, Claiborne, Gainsville, and, finally to St. Stephens, Washington county, where I conceived the idea of *settling myself for life.*

On the 20th day of March, 1872, I found myself in St. Stephens, the county-seat of Washington county, Alabama, situated a few miles from the right bank of the Tombigbee river.

Here I felt an insurmountable desire to put an end to my peregrinations, that, is at least for a season; for I was perfectly exhausted, and as I had a notion to enlarge my Biography, and as the manuscript had become worn out, by constant handling; I had nothing better to do than to take a school somewhere, in order to accomplish my desired end.

Accordingly, on inquiry, I found that I could get one in the neighborhood of St. Stephens, and was suggested by Mr. ———, one of the Trustees, to see one Dr. W.H. Coleman, who, it was said, lived six miles above that place on the road to Bladon Springs, in Choctaw county, Alabama.

This gentleman was, it was said, one of the county supervisors, whose duty it was to examine teachers, as to their qualifications.

Consequently, having received a note from Mr. Bailey, which ran thus:

"*Dr. W.H. Coleman:*

"SIR: The bearer, Nicholas Said, desires a situation in our neighborhood as a teacher, please to examine him and oblige,

"Yours,

"Most respectfully,

"THOMAS BAILEY."

Armed with this document, I proceeded onward to Dr. Coleman's.

On entering the paling enclosure, I was informed that the Doctor was in the garden, and would be back in a few minutes.

Presently I saw him coming, and I asked him whether he was Dr. Coleman, and on being answered affirmatively, I presented the paper to him.

The Doctor appeared to be a man of about fifty years of age, with a kind and gentlemanly looking face and highly polished manners, and in stature something above the medium height.

His reception of me was quite flattering, for after my examination, I was asked whether I had been to breakfast; I told him I had not, whereupon "Bright," the servant girl, was called and instructed to furnish me with my breakfast.

This most kind and hospitable gentleman furthermore promised to *protect* me during my stay in his neighborhood; and I can truly say did more than he promised.

Shortly after I opened my school, the Doctor loaned me $5.00, thereby showing that he had confidence in my honesty. Through his instrumentality, my name has become popular through Washington and Choctaw counties.

I shall, so long as life lasts, remember him with unfailing gratitude, and shall render myself not unworthy of his confidence and good opinion of me.

The colored people in this section of the country should certainly be grateful to him for his unwearied zeal in causing a school to be established in their midst.

But alas! though painful to say, it is sadly true that my people here appreciate but slightly the benefits of education.

My honest and ardent desire is to render myself useful to my race wherever it may be. I have no aspirations for fame, nor anything of the sort. But I shall always prefer at all times to find myself in the midst of the most ignorant of my race, and endeavor to teach the rising generation the advantages of education.

Self-denial is now-a-days so rare, that it is thought only individuals of insane mind can speak of it. A person who tries to live only for others, and puts himself in the second place, is hooted at, and considered a fit inmate for the asylum.

The man who artfully extorts the earning of his fellow-man, and who seems to have no feeling for his daily wants, is, by a strange perversion, deemed the wise.

To me, it is impossible to conceive how a human being can be happy through any other channel, than to do as much good as possible to his fellow-man in this world.

81. **Malcolm X, "Malcolm X, United States 1964" from** *One Thousand Roads to Mecca: Ten Centuries of Travelers Writing about the Muslim Pilgrimage*

Michael Wolfe, ed., New York: Grove Press, 1997, pp. 486–503.

Malcolm X was born in Nebraska in 1925. While he was incarcerated from 1946 to 1952, he converted to the Nation of Islam, a religious, sociopolitical organization that preaches black nationalism. In 1964, Malcolm X disavowed the Nation of Islam and went on the Hajj to Mecca. During the Hajj, he converted to orthodox Sunni Islam. He was assassinated on February 21, 1965, in New York City. The following entry is Malcolm X's account of his Hajj experience. It illustrates how some African American Muslims relate to traditional Islamic rituals as empowering tools for personal and collective emancipation.

CAIRO AIRPORT. APRIL 1964 The literal meaning of Hajj in Arabic is to set out toward a definite objective. In Islamic law, it means to set out for [the] Ka'ba, the Sacred House, and to fulfill the pilgrimage rites. The Cairo airport was where scores of Hajj groups were becoming muhrim, pilgrims, upon entering the state of ihram, the assumption of a spiritual and physical state of consecration. Upon advice, I arranged to leave in Cairo all of my luggage and four cameras, one a movie camera. I had bought in Cairo a small valise, just big enough to carry one suit, shirt, a pair of underwear sets, and a pair of shoes into Arabia. Driving to the airport with our Hajj group, I began to get nervous, knowing that from there in, it was going to be watching others who knew what they were doing, and trying to do what they did.

Entering the state of ihram, we took off our clothes and put on two white towels. One, the izar, was folded around the loins. The other, the rida, was thrown over the neck and shoulders, leaving the right shoulder and arm bare. A pair of simple sandals, the na', left the anklebones bare. Over the izar waistwrapper, a money belt was worn, and a bag, something like a woman's big handbag, with a long strap, was for carrying the passport and other valuable papers, such as the letter I had from Dr. Shawarbi.*

Every one of the thousands at the airport, about to leave for Jidda, was dressed this way. You could be a king or a peasant, and no one would know. Some powerful personages, who were discreetly pointed out to me, had on the same thing I had on. Once thus dressed, we all had begun intermittently calling out "Labayk! Labayk!" ("Here I come, O Lord!") The airport sounded with the din of muhrim expressing their intention to perform the journey of the Hajj.

Planeloads of pilgrims were taking off every few minutes, but the airport was jammed with more, and their friends and relatives waiting to see them off. Those not going were asking others to pray for them at Mecca. We were on our plane, in the air, when I learned for the first time that with the crush, there was not supposed to have been space for me, but strings had been pulled, and someone had been put off because they didn't want to disappoint an American Muslim. I felt mingled emotions of regret that I had inconvenienced and discomfited whoever was bumped off the plane for me and, with that, an utter humility and gratefulness that I had been paid such an honor and respect.

Packed in the plane were white, black, brown, red, and yellow people, blue eyes and blond hair, and my kinky red hair-all together, brothers! All honoring the same God Allah, all in turn giving equal honor to each other.

From some in our group, the word was spreading from seat to seat that I was a Muslim from America. Faces turned, smiling toward me in greeting. A box lunch was passed out, and as we ate that, the word that a Muslim from America was aboard got up into the cockpit.

The captain of the plane came back to meet me. He was an Egyptian; his complexion was darker than mine; he could have walked in Harlem, and no one would have given him a second glance. He was delighted to meet an American Muslim. When he invited me to visit the cockpit, I jumped at the chance.

JIDDA The Jidda airport seemed even more crowded than Cairo's had been. Our party became another shuffling unit in the shifting mass with every race on Earth represented. Each party was making its way toward the long line waiting to go through customs. Before reaching customs, each Hajj party was assigned a mutawwif, who would be responsible for transferring that party from Jidda to Mecca. Some pilgrims cried, "Labayk!" Others, sometimes large groups, were chanting in unison a prayer that I will translate: "I submit to no one but thee, O Allah. I submit to no one but thee. I submit to thee because thou hast no partner. All praise and blessings come from thee, and thou art alone in thy kingdom." The essence of the prayer is the oneness of God.

Only officials were not wearing the ihram garb, or the white skullcaps, long, white, nightshirt-looking gown, and the little slippers of the mutawwif, those who guided each pilgrim party, and their helpers. In Arabic, an mmmm sound before a verb makes a verbal noun, so mutawwfmeant "the one who guides" the pilgrims on the tawaf, which is the circumambulation of the Kacba in Mecca.

I was nervous, shuffling in the center of our group in the line waiting to have our passports inspected. I had an apprehensive feeling. Look what I'm handing them. I'm in the Muslim world, right at the fountain. I'm handing them the American passport which signifies the exact opposite of what Islam stands for.

The judge in our group sensed my strain. He patted my shoulder. Love, humility, and true brotherhood was almost a physical feeling wherever I turned. Then our group reached the clerks who examined each passport and suitcase carefully and nodded to the pilgrim to move on.

I was so nervous that when I turned the key in my bag, and it didn't work, I broke open the bag, fearing that they might think I had something in the bag that I shouldn't have. Then the clerk saw that I was handing him an American passport. He held it, he looked at me and said something in Arabic. My friends around me began speaking rapid Arabic, gesturing and pointing, trying to intercede for me. The judge asked me in English for my letter from Dr. Shawarbi, and he thrust it at the clerk, who read it. He gave the letter back, protesting—I could tell that. An argument was going on, about me. I felt like a stupid fool, unable to say a word, I couldn't even understand what was being said. But, finally, sadly, the judge turned to me.

I had to go before the Mahgama Sharia, he explained. It was the Muslim high court which examined all possibly nonauthentic converts to the Islamic religion seeking to enter

Mecca. It was absolute that no non-Muslim could enter Mecca...No courts were held on Friday. I would have to wait until Saturday, at least.

An official beckoned a young Arab mutawwf's aide. In broken English, the official explained that I would be taken to a place right at the airport. My passport was kept at customs. I wanted to object, because it is a traveler's first law never to get separated from his passport, but I didn't. In my wrapped towels and sandals, I followed the aide in his skullcap, long white gown, and slippers. I guess we were quite a sight. People passing us were speaking all kinds of languages. I couldn't speak anybody's language. I was in bad shape.

Right outside the airport was a mosque, and above the airport was a huge, dormitory-like building, four tiers high. It was semidark, not long before dawn, and planes were regularly taking off and landing, their landing lights sweeping the runways or their wing and taillights blinking in the sky. Pilgrims from Ghana, Indonesia, Japan, and Russia, to mention some, were moving to and from the dormitory where I was being taken. I don't believe that motion picture cameras ever have filmed a human spectacle more colorful than my eyes took in. We reached the dormitory and began climbing, up to the fourth, top tier, passing members of every race on earth. Chinese, Indonesians, Afghanis. Many, not yet changed into the ihram garb, still wore their national dress. It was like pages out of the National Geographic magazine.

My guide, on the fourth tier, gestured me into a compartment that contained about fifteen people. Most lay curled up on their rugs asleep. I could tell that some were women, covered head and foot. An old Russian Muslim and his wife were not asleep. They stared frankly at me. Two Egyptian Muslims and a Persian roused and also stared as my guide moved us over into a corner. With gestures, he indicated that he would demonstrate to me the proper prayer ritual postures. Imagine, being a Muslim minister, a leader in Elijah Muhammad's Nation of Islam, and not knowing the prayer ritual.

I tried to do what he did. I knew I wasn't doing it right. I could feel the other Muslims' eyes on me. Western ankles won't do what Muslim ankles have done for a lifetime. Asians squat when they sit; Westerners sit upright in chairs. When my guide was down in a posture, I tried everything I could to get down as he was, but there I was, sticking up. After about an hour, my guide left, indicating that he would return later.

I never even thought about sleeping. Watched by the Muslims, I kept practicing prayer postures. I refused to let myself think how ridiculous I must have looked to them. After a while, though, I learned a little trick that would let me get down closer to the floor. But after two or three days, my ankle was going to swell.

As the sleeping Muslims woke up, when dawn had broken, they almost instantly became aware of me, and we watched each other while they went about their business. I began to see what an important role the rug played in the overall cultural life of the Muslims. Each individual had a small prayer rug, and each man and wife or large group had a larger communal rug. These Muslims prayed on their rugs there in the compartment. Then they spread a tablecloth over the rug and ate, so the rug became the dining room. Removing the dishes and cloth, they sat on the rug-a living room. Then they curl up and sleep on the rug-a bedroom. In that compartment, before I was to leave it, it dawned on me for the first time why the fence had paid such a high price for Oriental rugs when I had been a burglar in Boston. It was because so much intricate care was taken to weave fine rugs in countries where rugs were so culturally versatile. Later, in Mecca, I would see yet another use of the rug. 'When any kind of a dispute arose, someone who was respected highly and who was not involved would sit on a rug with the disputers around him, which made the rug a courtroom. In other instances it was a classroom.

One of the Egyptian Muslims, particularly, kept watching me out of the corner of his eye. I smiled at him. He got up and came over to me. "Hel-lo-" he said. It sounded like the Gettysburg Address. I beamed at him, "Hello!" I asked his name. "Name? Name?" He was trying hard, but he didn't get it. We tried some words on each other. I'd guess his English vocabulary spanned maybe twenty words. Just enough to frustrate me. I was trying to get him to comprehend anything. "Sky." I'd point. He'd smile. "Sky," I'd say again, gesturing for him to repeat it after me. He would. "Airplane...rug...foot...san dal...eyes..." Like that. Then an amazing thing happened. I was so glad I had some communication with a human being, I was just saying whatever came to mind. I said "Muhammad Ah Clay-" All of the Muslims listening lighted up like a Christmas tree. "You? You?" My friend was pointing at me. I shook my head, "No, no. Muhammad Ah Clay my friend-friend!" They half-understood me. Some of them didn't understand, and that's how it began to get around that I was Cassius Clay, world heavyweight champion. I was later to learn that apparently every man, woman, and child in the Muslim world had heard how Sonny Liston (who in the Muslim world had the image of a man-eating ogre) had been beaten in Goliath-David fashion by Cassius Clay, who then had told the world that his name was Muhammad Ah and his religion was Islam and Allah had given him his victory.

Establishing the rapport was the best thing that could have happened in the compartment. My being an American Muslim changed the attitudes from merely watching me to wanting to look out for me. Now, the others began smiling steadily. They came closer; they were frankly looking me up and down. Inspecting me. Very friendly. I was like a man from Mars.

The mutawwf's aide returned, indicating that I should go with him. He pointed from our tier down at the mosque, and I knew that he had come to take me to make the morning prayer, always before sunrise. I followed him down, and we passed pilgrims by the thousands, babbling languages, everything but English. I was angry with myself for not having taken the time to learn more of the orthodox prayer rituals before leaving America. In Elijah Muhammad's Nation of Islam, we hadn't prayed in Arabic. About a dozen or more years before, when I was in prison, a member of the orthodox Muslim movement in Boston, named Abdul Hamid, had visited me and had later sent me prayers in Arabic. At that time, I had learned those prayers phonetically. But I hadn't used them since.

I made up my mind to let the guide do everything first and I would watch him. It wasn't hard to get him to do things first. He wanted to anyway. Just outside the mosque there was a long trough with rows of faucets. Ablutions had to precede praying. I knew that. Even watching the mutawwf's helper, I didn't get it right. There's an exact way that an orthodox Muslim washes, and the exact way is very important.

I followed him into the mosque, just a step behind, watching. He did his prostration, his head to the ground. I did mine. "Bismillah ar-Rahman, ir-Rahman-" ("In the name of Allah, the Beneficent, the Merciful-") All Muslim prayers began that way. After that, I may not have been mumbling the right thing, but I was mumbling.

I don't mean to have any of this sound joking. It was far from a joke with me. No one who happened to be watching could tell that I wasn't saying what the others said.

LATER THE SAME DAY I kept standing at the tier railing observing the courtyard below, and I decided to explore a bit on my own. I went down to the first tier. I thought, then, that maybe I shouldn't get too far; someone might come for me. So I went back up to our compartment. In about forty-five minutes, I went back down. I went further this time, feeling my way. I saw a little restaurant in the courtyard. I went straight in there. It was jammed, and babbling with languages. Using gestures, I bought a whole roasted chicken and something like thick potato chips. I got back out in the courtyard, and I tore up that chicken, using my hands. Muslims were doing the same thing all around me. I saw men at least seventy years old bringing both legs up under them, until they made a human knot of themselves, eating with as much aplomb and satisfaction as though they had been in a fine restaurant with waiters all over the place. All ate as One, and slept as One. Everything about the pilgrimage atmosphere accented the Oneness of Man under One God.

I had just said my Sunset Prayer; I was lying on my cot in the fourth-tier compartment, feeling blue and alone when out of the darkness came a sudden light!

It was actually a sudden thought. On one of my venturings in the yard full of activity below, I had noticed four men, officials, seated at a table with a telephone. Now, I thought about seeing them there, and with telephone, my mind flashed to the connection that Dr. Shawarbi in New York had given me the telephone number of the son of the author of the book which had been given to me [in New York]. Omar Azzam lived right there in Jidda!

In a matter of a few minutes, I was downstairs and rushing to where I had seen the four officials. One of them spoke functional English. I excitedly showed him the letter from Dr. Shawarbi. He read it. Then he read it aloud to the other three officials. "A Muslim from America!" I could almost see it capture their imaginations and curiosity. They were very impressed. I asked the English-speaking one if he would please do me the favor of telephoning Dr. Omar Azzam at the number I had. He was glad to do it. He got someone on the phone and conversed in Arabic.

Dr. Omar Azzam came straight to the airport. With the four officials beaming, he wrung my hand in welcome, a young, tall, powerfully built man. I'd say he was six foot three. He had an extremely polished manner. In America, he would have been called a white man, but—it struck me, hard and instantly—from the way he acted, I had no feeling of him being a white man. "Why didn't you call before?" he demanded of me. He showed some identification to the four officials, and he used their phone. Speaking in Arabic, he was talking with some airport officials. "Come!" he said.

In something less than half an hour, he had gotten me released, my suitcase and passport had been retrieved from customs, and we were in Dr. Azzam's car, driving through the city of Jidda, with me dressed in the ihram towels and sandals. I was speechless at the man's attitude, and at my own physical feeling of no difference between us as human beings. I had heard for years of Muslim hospitality, but one couldn't quite imagine such warmth. I asked questions. Dr. Azzam was a Swiss-trained engineer. His field was city planning. The Saudi Arabian government had borrowed him from the United Nations to direct all of the reconstruction work being done on [the] Arabian holy places. And Dr. Azzam's sister was the wife of Prince Faysal's son. I was in a car with the brother-in-law of the son of the ruler of Arabia. Nor was that all that Allah had done. "My father will be so happy to meet you," said Dr. Azzam. The author who had sent me the book!

I asked questions about his father. Abd al-Rahman Azzam was known as Azzam Pasha, or Lord Azzam, until the Egyptian revolution, when President Nasser** eliminated all "Lord" and "Noble" titles. "He should be at my home when we get there," Dr. Azzam said. "He spends much time in New York with his United Nations work, and he has followed you with great interest."

I was speechless.

THE HIGH COURT I learned during dinner that the Hajj Committee Court had been notified about my case, and that in the morning I should be there. And I was.

The judge was Shaykh Muhammad Harkon. The court was empty except for me and a sister from India, formerly a Protestant, who had converted to Islam and was, like me, trying to make the Hajj. She was brown skinned, with a small face that was mostly covered. Judge Harkon was a kind, impressive man. We talked. He asked me some questions having to do with my sincerity. I answered him as truly as I could. He not only recognized me as a true Muslim, but he gave me two books, one in English, the other in Arabic. He recorded my name in the Holy Register of true Muslims, and we were ready to part. He told me, "I hope you will become a great preacher of Islam in America." I said that I shared that hope, and I would try to fulfill it.

The Azzam family were very elated that I was qualified and accepted to go to Mecca. I had lunch at the Jidda Palace [Hotel]. Then I slept again for several hours, until the telephone awakened me.

It was Muhammad Abd al-Azziz Magid, the Deputy Chief of Protocol for Prince Faysal. "A special car will be waiting to take you to Mecca, right after your dinner," he told me. He advised me to eat heartily, as the Hajj rituals require plenty of strength.

I was beyond astonishment by then.

Two young Arabs accompanied me to Mecca. A well-lighted, modern turnpike highway made the trip easy. Guards at intervals along the way took one look at the car, and the driver made a sign, and we were passed through, never even having to slow down. I was, all at once, thrilled, important, humble, and thankful.

Mecca, when we entered, seemed as ancient as time itself. Our car slowed through the winding streets, lined by shops on both sides and with buses, cars, and trucks, and tens of thousands of pilgrims from all over the earth were everywhere.

The car halted briefly at a place where a mutawwif was waiting for me. He wore the white skullcap and long nightshirt garb that I had seen at the airport. He was a short, dark-skinned Arab, named Muhammad. He spoke no English whatever.

We parked near the Great Mosque. We performed our ablution and entered. Pilgrims seemed to be on top of each other, there were so many, lying, sitting, sleeping, praying, walking.

My vocabulary cannot describe the new mosque that was being built around the Ka'ba. I was thrilled to realize that it was only one of the tremendous rebuilding tasks under the direction of young Dr. Azzam, who had just been my host. The Great Mosque of Mecca, when it is finished, will surpass the architectural beauty of India's Taj Mahal.

Carrying my sandals, I followed the mutawwif Then I saw the Ka'ba, a huge black stone house in the middle of the Great Mosque. It was being circumambulated by thousands upon thousands of praying pilgrims, both sexes, and every size, shape, color, and race in the world. I knew the prayer to be uttered when the pilgrim's eyes first perceive the Ka'ba. Translated, it is "O God, you are peace, and peace derives from you. So greet us, O Lord, with peace."

My feeling there in the House of God was a numbness. My mutawwf led me in the crowd of praying, chanting pilgrims, moving seven times around the Ka'ba. Some were bent and wizened with age; it was a sight that stamped itself on the brain. I saw incapacitated pilgrims being carried by others. Faces were enraptured in their faith. The seventh time around, I prayed two rakats, prostrating myself, my head on the floor. The first prostration, I prayed the Quran verse "Say he is God, the one and only"; the second prostration, "Say O you who are unbelievers, I worship not that which you worship...

As I prostrated, the mutawwf fended pilgrims off to keep me from being trampled. The mutawwfand I next drank water from the Well of Zamzam. Then we ran between the two hills, Safa and Marwa, where Hagar wandered over the same earth searching for water for her child, Ishmael.

THE PROCESSION TO ARAFAT Three separate times after that, I visited the Great Mosque and circumambulated the Ka'ba. The next day we set out after sunrise toward Mount Arafat, thousands of us, crying in unison: "Labayk! Labayk!" and "Allah Akbar!" Mecca is surrounded by the crudest-looking mountains I have ever seen; they seem to be made of the slag from a blast furnace. No vegetation is on them at all. Arriving about noon, we prayed and chanted from noon until sunset, and the asr (afternoon) and maghrib (sunset) special prayers were performed.

Finally, we lifted our hands in prayer and thanksgiving, repeating Allah's words: "There is no God but Allah. He has no partner. His are authority and praise. Good emanates from him, and he has power over all things."

Standing on Mount Arafat had concluded the essential rites of being a pilgrim to Mecca. No one who missed it could consider himself a pilgrim.

The ihram had ended. We cast the traditional seven stones at the devil. Some had their hair and beards cut. I decided that I was going to let my beard remain. I wondered what my wife, Betty, and our little daughters, were going to say when they saw me with a beard, when I got back to New York. New York seemed a million miles away. I hadn't seen a newspaper that I could read since I left New York. I had no idea what was happening there. A Negro rifle club that had been in existence for over twelve years in Harlem had been "discovered" by the police; it was being trumpeted that I was "behind it." Elijah Muhammad's Nation of Islam had a lawsuit going against me, to force me and my family to vacate the house in which we lived on Long Island.

The major press, radio, and television media in America had representatives in Cairo hunting all over, trying to locate me, to interview me about the furor in New York that I had allegedly caused-when I knew nothing about any of it.

LETTERS FROM MECCA I wrote to Dr. Shawarbi, whose belief in my sincerity had enabled me to get a passport to Mecca.

All through the night, I copied similar long letters for others who were very close to me. Among them was Elijah Muhammad's son Wallace Muhammad, who had expressed to me his conviction that the only possible salvation for the Nation of Islam would be its accepting and projecting a better understanding of orthodox Islam.

And I wrote to my loyal assistants at my newly formed Muslim Mosque, Inc., in Harlem, with a note appended, asking that my letter be duplicated and distributed to the press.

I knew that when my letter became public knowledge back in America, many would be astounded-loved ones, friends, and enemies alike. And no less astounded would be millions whom I did not knowwho had gained during my twelve years with Elijah Muhammad a "hate" image of Malcolm X.

Even I was myself astounded. But there was precedent in my life for this letter. My whole life had been a chronology of changes. Here is what I wrote... from my heart:

"Never have I witnessed such sincere hospitality and the overwhelming spirit of true brotherhood as is practiced by people of all colors and races here in this ancient Holy

Land, the home of Abraham, Muhammad, and all the other prophets of the Holy Scriptures. For the past week, I have been utterly speechless and spellbound by the graciousness I see displayed all around me by people of all colors.

"I have been blessed to visit the Holy City of Mecca. I have made my seven circuits around the Kacba, led by a young mutawwif named Muhammad. I drank water from the Well of Zamzam. I ran seven times back and forth between the hills of Mount Safa and Marwa. I have prayed in the ancient city of Mina, and I have prayed on Mount Arafat.

"There were tens of thousands of pilgrims, from all over the world. They were of all colors, from blue-eyed blonds to black-skinned Africans. But we were all participating in the same ritual, displaying a spirit of unity and brotherhood that my experiences in America had led me to believe never could exist between the white and the nonwhite.

"America needs to understand Islam, because this is the one religion that erases from its society the race problem. Throughout my travels in the Muslim world, I have met, talked to, and even eaten with people who in America would have been considered 'white'—but the 'white' attitude was removed from their minds by the religion of Islam. I have never before seen sincere and true brotherhood practiced by all colors together, irrespective of their color.

"You may be shocked by these words coming from me. But on this pilgrimage, what I have seen, and experienced, has forced me to rearrange much of my thought patterns previously held, and to toss aside some of my previous conclusions. This was not too difficult for me. Despite my firm convictions, I have always been a man who tries to face facts, and to accept the reality of life as new experience and new knowledge unfolds it. I have always kept an open mind, which is necessary to the flexibility that must go hand in hand with every form of intelligent search for truth.

"During the past eleven days here in the Muslim world, I have eaten from the same plate, drunk from the same glass, and slept in the same bed (or on the same rug)—while praying to the same God—with fellow Muslims, whose eyes were the bluest of blue, whose hair was the blondest of blond, and whose skin was the whitest of white. And in the words and in the actions and in the deeds of the 'white' Muslims, I felt the same sincerity that I felt among the black Africa Muslims of Nigeria, Sudan, and Ghana.

"We were truly all the same (brothers)—because their belief in one God had removed the 'white' from their minds, the 'white' from their behavior, and the 'white' from their attitude...

THE MUSLIM FROM AMERICA Prince Faysal, the absolute ruler of Arabia, had made me a guest of the state. Among the courtesies and privileges which this brought to me, especially—shamelessly—I relished the chauffeured car which toured me around in Mecca with the chauffeur-guide pointing out sights of particular significance. Some of the Holy City looked as ancient as time itself. Other parts of it resembled a modern Miami suburb. I cannot describe with what feelings I actually pressed my hands against the earth where the great prophets had trod four thousand years before.

"The Muslim from America" excited everywhere the most intense curiosity and interest. I was mistaken time and again for Cassius Clay. A local newspaper had printed a photograph of Cassius and me together at the United Nations. Through my chauffeur-guide-interpreter I was asked scores of questions about Cassius. Even children knew of him, and loved him there in the Muslim world. By popular demand, the cinemas throughout Africa and Asia had shown his fight. At that moment in young Cassius's career, he had captured the imagination and the support of the entire dark world.

My car took me to participate in special prayers at Mount Arafat, and at Mina. The roads offered the wildest drives that I had ever known: nightmare traffic, brakes squealing, skidding cars, and horns blowing. (I believe that all of the driving in the Holy Land is done in the name of Allah.) I had begun to learn the prayers in Arabic; now, my biggest prayer difficulty was physical. The unaccustomed prayer posture had caused my big toe to swell, and it pained me.

But the Muslim world's customs no longer seemed strange to me. My hands now readily plucked up food from a common dish shared with brother Muslims; I was drinking without hesitation from the same glass as others; I was washing from the same little pitcher of water; and sleeping with eight or ten others on a mat in the open. I remember one night at Muzdalifa with nothing but the sky overhead I lay awake amid sleeping Muslim brothers and I learned that pilgrims from every land—every color, and class, and rank; high officials and the beggar alike—all snored in the same language.

It was the largest Hajj in history, I was later told. Kasem Gulek, of the Turkish parliament, beaming with pride, informed me that from Turkey alone over six hundred buses—over fifty thousand Muslims—had made the pilgrimage. I told him that I dreamed to see the day when shiploads and planeloads of American Muslims would come to Mecca for the Hajj.

There was a color pattern in the huge crowds. Once I happened to notice this, I closely observed it thereafter. Being from America made me intensely sensitive to matters of color. I saw that people who looked alike drew together and most of the time stayed together. This was entirely voluntary; there being no other reason for it. But Africans were with Africans. Pakistanis were with Pakistanis. And so on. I tucked it into my mind that when I returned home I would tell Americans this observation; that where true brotherhood existed among all colors, where no one felt segregated, where there was no "superiority" complex, no "inferiority" complex—then voluntarily, naturally, people of the same kind felt drawn together by that which they had in common.

Constantly, wherever I went, I was asked questions about America's racial discrimination. Even with my background, I was astonished at the degree to which the major single image of America seemed to be discrimination.

In a hundred different conversations in the Holy Land with Muslims high and low, and from around the world—and, later, when I got to black Africa—I don't have to tell you never once did I bite my tongue or miss a single opportunity to tell the truth about the crimes, the evils, and the indignities that are suffered by the black man in America. Through my interpreter, I lost no opportunity to advertise the American black man's real plight. I preached it on the mountain at Arafat, I preached it in the busy lobby of the Jidda Palace Hotel. I would point at one after another—to bring it closer to home; "You...you...you—because of your dark skin, in America you, too, would be called 'Negro.' You could be bombed and shot and cattle-prodded and fire-hosed and beaten because of your complexions."

As some of the poorest pilgrims heard me preach, so did some of the Holy World's most important personages. I talked at length with the blueeyed, blond-haired Husayn Amini, Grand Mufti of Jerusalem. We were introduced on Mount Arafat by Kasem Gulek of the Turkish parliament. Both were learned men; both were especially well read on America. Kasem Gulek asked me why I had broken with Elijah Muhammad. I said that I preferred not to elaborate upon our differences, in the interests of preserving the American black man's unity. They both understood and accepted that.

I talked with the Mayor of Mecca, Shaykh Abdullah Eraif, who when he was a journalist had criticized the methods of the Mecca municipality and Prince Faysal made him the Mayor, to see if he could do any better. Everyone generally acknowledged that Shaykh Eraif was doing fine. A filmed feature The Muslim from America was made by Ahmed Horyallah and his partner, Essid Muhammad, of Tunis's television station. In America once, in Chicago, Ahmed Horyallah had interviewed Elijah Muhammad.

The lobby of the Jidda Palace Hotel offered me frequent sizable informal audiences of important men from many different countries who were curious to hear the "American Muslim." I met many Africans who had either spent some time in America or who had heard other Africans' testimony about America's treatment of the black man. I remember how before one large audience, one cabinet minister from black Africa (he knew more about worldwide current events than anyone else I've ever met) told of his occasionally traveling in the United States, North and South, deliberately not wearing his national dress. Just recalling the indignities he had met as a black man seemed to expose some raw nerve in this highly educated, dignified official. His eyes blazed in his passionate anger, his hands hacked the air: "Why is the American black man so complacent about being trampled upon? Why doesn't the American black man fight to be a human being?" . . .

Two American authors, best-sellers in the Holy Land, had helped to spread and intensify the concern for the American black man. James Baldwin's books, translated, had made a tremendous impact, as had the book Black Like Me, by John Griffin. If you're unfamiliar with that book, it tells how the white man Griffin blackened his skin and spent two months traveling as a Negro about America; then Griffin wrote of the experiences that he met. "A frightening experience!" I heard exclaimed many times by people in the Holy World who had read the popular book. But I never heard it without opening their thinking further: "Well, if it was a frightening experience for him as nothing but a make-believe Negro for sixty days—then you think about what real Negroes in America have gone through for four hundred years."

INTERVIEW WITH FAYSAL One honor that came to me, I had prayed for: His Eminence, Prince Faysal, invited me to a personal audience with him.

As I entered the room, tall, handsome Prince Faysal came from behind his desk. I never will forget the reflection I had at that instant, that here was one of the world's most important men, and yet with his dignity one saw clearly his sincere humility. He indicated for me a chair opposite from his. Our interpreter was the Deputy Chief of Protocol, Muhammad Abdal-Azziz Magid, an Egyptian-born Arab who looked like a Harlem Negro.

Prince Faysal impatiently gestured when I began stumbling for words trying to express my gratitude for the great honor he had paid me in making me a guest of the state. It was only Muslim hospitality to another Muslim, he explained, and I was an unusual Muslim from America. He asked me to understand above all that whatever he had done had been his pleasure, with no other motives whatever.

A gliding servant served a choice of two kinds of tea as Prince Faysal talked. His son, Muhammad Faysal, had "met" me on American television while attending a northern California university. Prince Faysal had read Egyptian writers' articles about the American "Black Muslims." "If what these writers say is true, the Black Muslims have the wrong Islam," he said. I explained my role of the previous twelve years, of helping to organize and to build the Nation of Islam. I said that my purpose for making the Hajj was to get an understanding of true Islam. "That is good," Prince Faysal said, pointing out that there was an abundance of English-translation literature about Islam—so that there was no excuse for ignorance, and no reason for sincere people to allow themselves to be misled.

* Dr. Mahmoud Youssef Shawarbi, Egyptian scholar, author, and UN adviser, helped Malcolm X with his pilgrim visa in New York.

** Nasser: Gamal Abdel Nasser (1918–70), first President of the Republic of Egypt (1956–70.)

82. **Imam W. Deen Mohammed, "How Islam Promotes Healthy Citizenship" from** *The Muslim Journal*

(5-9-03 to 5-16-03), originally transcribed October 5, 2002. Available online: http:// newafricaradio.com/articles/050903.html. Reprinted with permission of W.D. Mohammed.

Warith Deen Mohammed (for a biography, see the "Mohammed, W. D." entry in Volume 1) was born in 1933 to Clara and Elijah Muhammad. Elijah Muhammad was the head of the Nation of Islam, a religious, sociopolitical organization that preaches black nationalism. After his father's death in 1975, Warith Deen Mohammed assumed leadership of the Nation of Islam and reformed the group to bring it into line with orthodox Sunni Islam. The following entry is the transcript of a lecture Mohammed gave at the University of Wisconsin on October 5, 2002, on the relationship of Islam to citizenship. It emphasizes the role traditional Islamic identity plays in bringing African American Muslims in tune with mainstream American values.

Thank you and we thank G-d, the Lord and Cherisher of all the worlds. We witness that He is One. And we witness that Muhammed to whom the Qur'an was revealed over 14 centuries ago is His Servant and His Messenger and a Mercy to all the worlds, as G-d says in our Holy Book.

The way that Islam promotes healthy citizenship is very easy to address. It only takes a very few words, although I will give the topic more of our time. We know that what makes the society, the city or town bad for us is the people who are bad. Without bad people, towns are good.

So the simple answer to how Islam promotes healthy citizenship is by promoting healthy minded people. Christianity says, as I read in the Bible, "as a man thinks in his heart, so is he." It didn't say, "thinks in his head"; it says, "thinks in his heart." It connected the heart with the thinking.

This is what Islam wants for us, too, that we reflect on things. When I was a child in school, one thing they told me was that I would have to learn a lot of things by heart. One thing the school did for us was to learn a lot by memory, although they said, "learn it by heart."

That expression means "to make that learning very, very special and give it your concern, to value it and care about it." I was talking to someone very recently, who kept forgetting things that we were trying to remember. I said, "the reason you can't remember it is that you don't care enough about it. If you care enough about it, you will remember it; learn it by heart."

It has to be in the heart, too, not just in the mind. And when the heart and mind are working together, then you can get the best benefit from your brain or mind. But if they are not working together, then you won't get the best benefit from your brain. This is how Islam promotes healthy citizenship.

Islam wants us to reflect, and reflect means to do more than just think about it twice. It means to think about what it is worth to you and what you want it for. Think about what you are going to do with it. Think. Think. Think. Think. Think with the heart involved.

I once was told by a great scholar, Dr. Ibrahim Ezzid-din out of Egypt, that I speak more philosophy than religion. That angered me, because I thought it was just common sense. I tend to think in pictures and speak through pictures. There is a saying in the Qur'an, the Holy Book of the Muslims—which is for all people, just like the Bible is for all people: "By the Fig and the Olive and Mt. Sinai and this town made safe, secured, surely We have created the human in the best of molds."

There was a time when there were no public schools. Public schools came late in the history of nations, where you have to send your children to school. And if you don't, you are subject to be put in jail, taken to court and locked up for not permitting your children to get an education. Education is enforced for the society.

I believe that the reference I just gave from our Holy Book has in it the importance of education. It is addressing the stages in the mind, the intellect, the stages of how the mind develops. The first is given in a picture. And I need a picture in order to start talking.

So I see the fig and think about the fig. The Qur'an doesn't give any commentary on the fig; it leaves the commentary to the thinkers, the scholars. You think about the fig and it is bigger than the olive with many, many seeds. Whereas the olive has just one seed. The fig is easy to chew, even if it is dry.

If you bit into an olive and don't have any caution, you are going to break your dentals. Even a young person might hurt their teeth, if they bit down on that stone inside the olive that is hard.

It is not like the fig that you can chew through. The olive has only one seed, but you must be careful eating it. You can't rush and eat it, like you do the fig.

The fig has many seeds; it's like a burst of seeds. And think about the expression, "that's a figment of your imagination."

The olive is in the Bible and also in the Qur'an, but the Qur'an goes to the fig first. The fig is kind of put down in the Bible, and here the Qur'an is picking the fig back up.

It says: "By the Fig, by the Olive, by Mt. Sinai..." Mt. Sinai is the mountain where Moses went up on and G-d spoke to him there and gave him revelation on Mt. Sinai. Mt. Sinai is referring to ascending up or going higher up to G-d and getting communication from G-d and then coming back down.

The third in this reference is Mt. Sinai, and the fourth reference is "this town made safe." How do you make the town safe? You make it safe by respecting all the people.

All of us have imagination, but all of us don't have olives. All of us can think and have vivid imaginations. So you are to respect the common mind, and the fig is symbolic of the common mind. It is a metaphor representing the common mind.

You are to respect the common mind. And then you are to respect those who are looking for a single thought or single interest. They are focused on one thing. They are the educated people or those who become educated.

They focus on one thing and stay focused on that, until it becomes illuminated, like the oil. You can strike a match near it and get fire. These are people who focus on one thing so long, until it illuminates them. And then they get the insight or the knowledge and pass it on.

These are all stages. Then there is the town made safe; you have to develop in the town. You can go up on the mountain and get all of that good knowledge and good insight. But if you don't come back down and live with people, you will never know how to use it.

Where do we learn how to communicate with one another? It is by living with one another. We live with one another, then we know how to apply our knowledge. It takes this social interaction to show us how to apply knowledge, where to put it and how to use it. If we never have a chance to socialize or have social interaction, we will never truly become educated.

To have light and not put it to use is no education. I am sure when Moses came down from the mountain, he had a great light. But he had to come down and look at his people's circumstances and then look at how was he to use that light that G-d gave him on the mountain. And he wasn't selfish.

This is the same Moses who is in the Bible and Qur'an; he is for both of us. He didn't say he was going to do this by himself. The first thing he did was to look around and see what resources he had. He said, "OK, you doctors get together. You lawyers get together. You farmers get together. You musicians get together."

Moses started organizing people according to their skills and abilities, etc. Then he gave them what G-d gave him from the mountain, and he charged all of them with responsibility to use it and apply it and make their lives conform to it.

We can't do all of that, for it is too much for us. We are not Moses. But what we can do is respect everybody. Have respect for everybody. Islam begins with the promotion of good character. And good character is a respect for everything that deserves respect.

The reason why we don't have many people having this kind of serious thought about the great interest that we are trusted with, when we are trusted with the responsibility of citizenship, is because we don't have the perception of the country or the city that most religions, Judaism included, give us.

First of all, everything that we have was not ours to begin with. We came into the world owning nothing. The first people who came to this area—there was no Milwaukee here, no Wisconsin when the first people came here—did not make this land; they found land that could support their life.

So the gift is from G-d, originally. And that is what we have to remember, firstly. And under G-d, you are responsible for how you treat everything. You may dislike the government at times and may want to say, "Oh, I don't have any citizenship; my citizenship is not worth a plug nickel." You may feel like that, but remember everything is temporary, except G-d.

Bad circumstances are temporary, and G-d is not going to excuse you from your responsibility. You are going to have to answer to G-d one day. Don't look at the land just as government land and as private property. Look at it as land that G-d gave man. G-d gave man this land, and look at it as your possession. G-d gave it to all of us.

So this land we call Milwaukee was given to all of us, originally. We all had the right to it. Nobody had established a right to it, to exclude anybody else. In some primitive tribes and societies, the people respect that. They live with each other, but they don't put any claim on land or rivers.

If you use a boat, you are not even able to claim the boat. Some primitive tribes won't let you claim the boat, for it is only for traveling the river. And since the river doesn't belong to anyone special, then the boat can't belong to anybody in particular. The boat has to be for anyone who wants to get on it. If no one is riding on the boat and it is there beside the water, anybody can jump into that boat.

These are people who are still in touch with the first perception of these goods or things. The first perception is that we didn't do this; we didn't provide these things. They were here when we got here, so we should respect the Original Owner.

You should say, "This is my city," and mean it. "Milwaukee is my city." Mean that from your heart. As I have said, don't let your thinking be separated from the heart. G-d did not give this land to one person; it is for human beings. "My government has made a beautiful city here, and this is my city." Claim it!

Also under the Constitution of these United States we have "One Nation Under G-d." And it speaks of The Creator. "We hold these Truths to be self-evident. . . . That all men are created equal. . ." It is back to the common person and they are ". . . endowed with certain inalienable rights. . ." that can't be taken away. These are given to them by their Creator.

"Among these are life, liberty and the pursuit of happiness." Not even the government can take these away from a person. The right to life was not given by the government and cannot be taken away by the government. G-d created us to be free. The government didn't give us that, and the government shouldn't take it away.

G-d gave us the intelligence and the feet and the hands and the legs to go and get things we need to pursue happiness and to acquire wealth. And the government shouldn't take that away from us. Our government also says that we have rights that the government didn't give to us.

So don't say anymore that "this school that I attend is their school." I don't care if it is a private school or the biggest school in the state of Wisconsin. Don't say this is their school, no matter how bad you feel or how bad you are treated there.

Don't let them take you out of your rights. You need to be situated to be successful. If your psyche is not positive, you will not be able to perform as well. To have a positive psyche, you have to be positive. And be positive when it is right to be positive. You have a right to say: "Milwaukee is my town. This school I am going to is my school."

What do I mean? The wall is mine. The carpet is mine. Then treat it like it is yours. Respect it. Pick up paper when you see trash on the floor; don't wait for the janitor. I do that out in the public street. Some may call me a nut, but I am a healthy nut and a healthy citizen.

This is the way to have healthy citizenship. You have to think the way G-d wants us to think. And you have to know that great governments have respected the way G-d wants us to think. Then don't look at anything as belonging to the other person, without also looking at it as being your own.

Their life even belongs to them, but it also belongs to mankind, to humanity. If their life is in bad shape, that is your business, too, if they will let you help them out. Thank you.

83. "The Million Man March: Past, Present, and Future" from *The Final Call Newspaper*

November 4, 2003. Available online: http://www.finalcall.com/artman/publish/ printer_1099.shtml. Reprinted with permission of The Final Call.

Louis Farrakhan (for a biography, see the "Farrakhan, Louis" entry in Volume 1) was born in 1933 in New York. In the 1950s, he joined the Nation of Islam, a religious, sociopolitical organization that preaches black nationalism. He left the organization in 1977 due to ideological differences with the organization's leadership. In 1981, Farrakhan announced he had reconstituted the Nation of Islam along its original ideology. He is the head of the organization and founded The Final Call in 1979 as the Nation of Islam's newspaper. The following article is an interview, conducted by The Final Call, marking the ten year anniversary of the Million Man March, an African American protest march in Washington, DC, on October 16, 1995. It reflects the position of the Nation of Islam, in particular, its use of Islam as a tool against racism in the United States.

AN INTERVIEW WITH MINISTER LOUIS FARRAKHAN

[Editor's note: In an exclusive interview with The Final Call eight years after the overwhelming success of the Million Man March, the Honorable Minister Louis Farrakhan shares his reflections on maintaining unity, developing international relationships, enduring media and government attacks, and sacrificing to build a better world. This text originally appeared in Vol 23, No. 5, November 4, 2003]

In The Name of Allah, The Beneficent, The Merciful.

The Final Call (FC): What did Allah (God) allow you to see that sparked the call for the Million Man March?

The Honorable Minister Louis Farrakhan (MLF): I was shown in a vision-like experience that the President of the United States in early September of 1985 had met with his Joint Chiefs of Staff to plan a war. I was told that I should make it known and tell the world that I got this information from Elijah Muhammad from where he was at the time. He said he was on the Great Wheel.

As time went on, I learned that the government of the United States had planned a war with Libya and I recognized that that war was on two fronts: one dealing with the Libyan-Arab Jamahiriyyah; the second dealing with Black youth in the streets of America.

This insight caused me to go on a tour to stop the killing, and then another tour to speak to men only about the condition of the Black man in America. Out of that came the call for the Million Man March.

FC: How was the aim and purpose of the March directly linked to the insight that Allah (God) gave you? What did you hope the March would achieve?

MLF: During that time period, there was the arrival on the scene of crack cocaine; an increase in gang activity starting on the West Coast moving eastward with the Bloods and the Crips; and movies that portrayed our youth throughout the world, like "Colors" and "Menace to Society" that put Black men in particular, in a very ugly light. So that call for the Million Man March then led to efforts to organize for the success of it

FC: Please share your vision of the success of the March at that time, what you felt it produced then and since then?

MLF: We knew from the tremendous turnout of Black men that it was a great success; the unity that was present, the peace that was present. The commitment of those men to make life better for their wives and children, and to bring a greater amount of peace and security to our communities, that remained to be seen—whether we would follow through on that commitment.

There was great fear that these men would act in a way that would create the necessity of the National Guard, federal troops and others to intervene. So, government—city and federal—closed down on that day and the Million Man March became a major media event. This worldwide media attention put the nearly two million Black men who were present, and all of those who spoke, in the view of billions of people around the planet.

The way the March was characterized by the media caused me to be somewhat depressed and I went into solitude and quiet to ask Allah's (God's) guidance for what the next step should be.

FC: Can you elaborate on how the media portrayed the March?

MLF: First, they played down the numbers that were present. They mocked the value of the speech that I gave. Others tried to separate the success of the March from the man in whom Allah (God) had deposited the idea for the March.

I asked those men to join an organization of their choice that is working to better our condition. I also asked them to join a church, mosque, synagogue, or temple of their choice that would re-ignite spiritual values in our young men. As a result, organizations, churches and mosques grew with Black male participation.

So, in my solitude, I reflected on the actual fact that the President of the United States went to the Egyptian leadership and government asking them to send troops on the ground to attack Libya and promising to give them air cover, while CIA operatives in Libya would rise up internally against Muammar Gadhafi. As I looked at the geographical position of Egypt, seeing that it was east of Libya, and feeling that the government and the media propagation would try to say to the Muslim world that we, in the Nation of Islam were not true Muslims, I decided that I should go east in order to connect the Nation of Islam with our Muslim brothers and sisters throughout the world, and also to connect the struggle of Black people in America to the struggle of Black people and Indigenous people throughout the planet. As I reflected on my more-than-a-vision experience, it came to me that I should cement friendships with Africa, the Middle East and Asia.

FC: You are referring to your World Friendship Tours, after which you began another national tour to explain your motive, because of more negative media attention on your tours. Why did the media and the government continue to take a negative position?

MLF: There never has been a desire on the part of the government that the struggle of Black people in America should be linked to the struggle of our people in every part of the earth. Every leader that was international in scope and in reach became the target of the government—Paul Robeson, Marcus Garvey, W.E.B. DuBois, Martin Luther King Jr., Malcolm X, Kwame Ture and the Honorable Elijah Muhammad. Any Black leader who would try to connect us to our brothers and sisters in Africa and Asia were seen as a threat and became a target.

This is written in the prophecies of the Old Testament—that the enemy, Pharaoh, saw the Children of Israel multiplying and that they would try to unite with an enemy and come against them. So, they devised a plan, not only to cut the Children of Israel off inside the house of their torment, but to keep them from being in unity with anybody outside of Egypt that Egypt believed was its enemy.

If you look at our leaders historically, all of them were persecuted. I don't believe we have ever had a Black leader that was so widely accepted among the masses of people, as well as the leadership, in Africa, the Middle East, Asia, the Caribbean, Central America, as Allah (God) has blessed me to be accepted. Thus, this meant to the government that I was indeed a threat. The movement of us to link with our people around the world was also seen as a threat.

FC: What is it that we, as a people, are headed for, in relation to our enemy's plan, that would make the Million Man March and your World Friendship Tours impact that journey?

MLF: Everywhere we went in the world on behalf of our people we were received as a head of state. Both the leadership and the people saw the Black male in a different light than the savage condition that was being projected by Hollywood. The people of the world saw Black men now as a potential force politically that might impact and make positive change in the way the government formulated its policy toward Africa, the Middle East, the Caribbean, Central and South America and Asia. The Million Man March, in one day, helped to defeat all of the evil propaganda spread about Black men throughout the world.

FC: What benefits of your World Friendship Tours do we enjoy today? And how will we benefit in the future from cementing those friendships?

MLF: We are blessed to grow up in a country that is the world's leader. We are blessed to be some of the most well-educated Black persons anywhere to be found in the world. This education and talent can be used in a friendly relationship with Africa, the Middle East, the Caribbean and Asia to develop the wealth and resources of these nations. The friendship of us with our kith and kin around the world would cause both sides to benefit exponentially, based upon how well we develop these relationships.

FC: I want to get back to a point that you had made earlier in reference to the attack on youth. In 1997, you convened a Hip Hop Summit that brought peace to a feud between East and West Coast rappers. Now, we are facing a similar feud. What lessons did we learn in 1997 and perhaps have now forgotten?

MLF: The lesson learned by those who learned the lesson causes those who learned the lesson not to repeat the error or mistake that caused that split, which caused the loss of life of Biggie Smalls and Tupac Shakur and others.

As time moves on, a new generation arises that may not have experienced what the former generation of rappers experienced. So, the wisdom gained from the learning of that lesson has to be passed on to succeeding generations, otherwise the enemy will cause what was to become what is and to destroy the future of what could be. So, with God's help, we will work to diffuse this kind of thing again.

FC: In light of the worsening conditions in our communities, with Black men in particular, is there a need for another Million Man March, or do we miss the point in seeking to recreate what happened in 1995?

MLF: It's not necessary to have another March. The worsening conditions in our community is not necessarily directed toward those men who came to the Million Man March and are still working as mentors and in business, education, politics, and other areas to make the condition of our people better. As the condition of America and the world degenerates, it is we who are the weak or the poor or the ignorant who feel it worse.

Now we have to think, not in terms of what is good for an individual or a segment of the population or an organization or a sect of Christianity or Islam or Judaism, we have to think today of what is in the best interest of the whole of our people. The conditions that we are suffering force us to address the real issues that affect the life and well-being of the majority of our people. That is why the call for reparations and justice in dealing with the problems of Black people is so relevant now.

FC: Why was it significant that the men paid their own way to the March?

MLF: The Million Man March was held on a Monday. Most marches were always held on a weekend and most marches were paid for by philanthropic groups and organizations and labor unions, etc. So, the people who came did not necessarily have to make a great sacrifice to be there.

Our going to Washington was not to petition government, but to petition our God and Creator, that we may regain His favor and come into a position of power with Him that would allow us to correct our own condition.

I wanted to see if we, as men, in the spirit of atonement, reconciliation and responsibility, would accept the responsibility to be there on our own, to pay our own way, to stand in front of God and each other, after having made a sacrifice of that day of work, of school, that we were not going to go into any place of business or spend money on that day; that we were going to fast and pray and meet in our churches and meet in our mosques and in our homes to reconcile differences. It wasn't just the March itself, but it was the whole country of our people involved in a Holy Day of Atonement.

God showed us, on that day, His favor. I learned that the National Security Agency of the United States Government had recruited some of our young people to come to the March to create a problem. But the spirit of the brothers that were there was so strong that they could not. The favor of God was on us, so that those nearly two million men were present and there was not one arrest, and the crime in Washington, D.C. on that day was almost zero.

From the Million Man March to this day, the crime and murder rates have significantly decreased in the major cities of America, according to police reports. I believe that the Million Man March was a significant part of the reason for the decrease.

There was greater voter registration and voter participation by Black men since that time and an increase in economic enterprise and entrepreneurial spirit among Black men. So, there's great benefit that has come from it, but in order for us to truly be free, even greater sacrifice will have to be made by all of us.

FC: In your 2003 Holy Day of Atonement address, you outright declared that, "this government of the United States is our worst enemy." Why is it necessary to keep that at the forefront of our minds, in light of all the positive things that you just pointed out?

MLF: As long as the Children of Israel saw Pharaoh as a friend, they could not see Moses and Jehovah as their true friend. As they came into consciousness—by the wicked things that Pharaoh continued to do against them—that Pharaoh was indeed their enemy, then Moses and Jehovah's call to them to separate from Pharaoh to build a nation of their own became a reality.

As long as we see America and her wealth as something that we want, we will never leave Pharaoh. As God's hand touched the wealth of Pharaoh, it is now touching the wealth of America. As the Black man and woman become more awakened to the wicked machinations of government, the aim is the same today: We should never be free of their influence and power.

As Abraham Lincoln said, if there is to be a superior position, he would rather that superior position be assigned to the White race. That superior position must be protected by those who believe in White supremacy and they will do everything in their power to make sure that that position will always be throughout the generations.

So, our path is clear: We refuse to be inferior. We want to be exactly what Allah (God) has desired for us to be and we can't be that in their house. We either have to take over their house or go and build a house of our own.

FC: Let's focus on your critics and their attacks on your credibility. The Nation of Islam won a discrimination lawsuit brought by a woman in Boston against the Men's Only meeting held there, as part of the two-year organizing effort for the March. Why did you choose to put the men first? What didn't that sister, and others like her who criticized this aspect, understand about your motive?

MLF: Why, in the scriptures of the Bible and Holy Qur'an, did God create man first? I believe that we are in the genesis or the beginning or the birth of a new world order, so then man and woman have to be made new again. We started where God started—with men. If we can reform the man and make him a better man and a God-fearing man, then we have a chance, we believe, to build a better world.

Our talking to men may have been seen by some as a threat to women, but most Black women loved the idea of our trying to raise the level of consciousness of Black men. Many mothers brought their sons to the "men-only" meetings; many wives encouraged their husbands to come. When the women at home saw what the men committed themselves to do, they rejoiced. And, in fact, the Million Man March would never have been successful if it were not for the women who stood with us and helped to organize to make the March what it eventually became.

FC: Why was it important to conduct and publicize the complete audit of the Million Man March?

MLF: The enemy has always been able to point the finger of suspicion and/or guilt to Black leaders that they are enriching themselves at the expense of the people. Before the Million Man March took place, in my hotel room a very highly respected AME Bishop asked me two questions. One was about proselytizing Islam on that day where we had unprecedented Christian support. I told him that was not my purpose; that I would send these men to join mosques, synagogues, churches and temples. Secondly, he asked, what about the money? I said I would hire respected CPA firms, make a complete audit, and give to the world the results of that audit. I gave my word and I fulfilled my word.

A lot of the money that we saw in the hands of people we couldn't collect because the lines were so tight, there was no aisle to go through. But whatever we were blessed to get, within three months or so, we had the complete audit of every aspect of the Million Man March. The press was called; and, of course, they who were pointing this finger of suspicion at us, now when the audit was a reality, they wouldn't spread the news that the Minister had fulfilled his word.

This is the first march that we know of that was paid for completely by the people. We ended up with a loss, which the Nation of Islam paid. The Nation of Islam was the biggest contributor to the Million Man March, but poor people gave their nickels, dimes and dollars; some wealthy Black people gave money to make that March a success—and every nickel, every dime, every dollar was accounted for.

FC: You mentioned that there was unprecedented unity between Muslim and Christian communities and organizations. There are now leaders who have been taking credit for the March when they only participated but were not instrumental in organizing it. How can this play into the enemy's plan to break that unity and how can we avoid it?

MLF: The Minister was used by God to call the Million Man March. The Nation of Islam became the principle organizer, but all who participated can take credit because we didn't do it by ourselves. Every brother, every sister, all of the local organizing committees, there were countless hundreds of persons who helped to organize the success of this March. The Minister can only say with truth that Allah (God) inspired him with the idea. It was hundreds, maybe even thousands, that helped in the organization of the March that made it successful. So, all can claim it as theirs and that will never break our unity, except that any of us become vain.

I could never take credit for this great event. That's why on October 16, the eighth anniversary of the March, I asked the question from the scripture, *will a man rob God?* The scripture says not only in tithes and offerings, but man will rob God of the credit that He is due. If I ever tried to take credit for what God deserves the credit, He would be displeased with me, and I'm more interested in pleasing Him than pleasing ego or vanity.

So, all who participated, all who helped to organize, all that worked, are the organizers of the Million Man March. And in its success, all who worked can claim their part of its success.

FC: Since the initial days after the March, what do you see as a continuation of the enemy's effort to attack your credibility? The most recent example is the sniper murder case, where it was often repeated on the news that the suspect attended the Million Man March.

MLF: At the Million Man March, a group of brilliant young men and women, the Wellington Group, did a poll that determined that 80-85 percent of the men who were present claimed Christianity as their religion. Twelve percent said they were Muslims and the remaining percentage was other. When it was known that a Muslim made a call and 85 percent or so of those who answered that call were Christians, it was decided at another level that never again should a Muslim make a call and Christians respond.

As I went about the country again thanking the people for their support and encouraging the principles of the March, I found that, in the churches that were opened to me during the Men's Only Tour and in the pastors that I talked to, there was a new spirit. The 700 Club and other religious broadcasters were painting Louis Farrakhan as the anti-Christ.

Five years after the success of the Million Man March, we were able to go back to the Mall on Washington for the Million Family March. There were a little over 1.2 or 1.3 million people. Although less than the success of the Million Man March, it was a great success again and it showed the Minister's impact still with Christians, Muslims, Buddhists, Native Americans and Hebrews.

So, they were unsuccessful in destroying the beautiful unity created by the Million Man March, but there definitely was—and is—a great effort to erode that working together of Muslims and Christians for the benefit of our total community.

Now, to answer the other part of your question, John Allen Muhammad was definitely at the Million Man March. Of those two million men at the March, I don't know how many have had some run in with the law or have been institutionalized or are on probation, etc. But we are not responsible for the behavior of anyone that goes contrary to what we teach, any more than the Pope of Rome or the Archbishop of Canterbury or a religious leader who teaches moral law and values can be charged with the errant behavior of a parishioner or congregant who may violate their moral teachings. That is on the individual.

I don't know of Brother John Allan Muhammad's guilt in this, but he definitely was a member of the Nation of Islam. At the time of his arrest and being charged, he was not in good standing with the mosque. They're saying that the Minister taught him hatred and this is the reason why he did what he did. But he was also a member of the armed forces of the United States of America. Did they teach him hatred? We certainly didn't teach him how to shoot a rifle. He learned that from whomever his teachers were; we were not that.

These are all part of the ongoing effort to discredit the Minister and the Nation of Islam as terrorists, because we disagree with the government's position with respect to the war, which is our right to do. But to link us with terrorists and terrorism is a big, big stretch.

FC: There has been very little publicity overall about the Nation of Islam. Is that because the Nation is not doing anything worth mentioning in the public or because of some other motive to ignore the works of the Nation and separate the Nation from you?

MLF: The Honorable Elijah Muhammad said no matter how much they attacked him and the Nation of Islam under his leadership, they only helped the Nation to grow. So, the more they attacked me and the more I withstood that onslaught, the more thousands of people came out to, at least, hear a man that was being so vilified in the media. When they recognized that they were not hurting but helping me, they decided they wouldn't say anything except to continue to discredit. So, there is a conscious effort not to publicize anything that the Nation is doing of value.

But we are not a creature of the media, so we are not depending on the media publicizing us to make us successful. The media can if they will, and they don't have to if they don't wish to. Our work is the work of resurrection and reform of our people and we will continue that work, in the light of the media or out of the light of the media. Our success depends on us, our unity, and our willingness to submit to the will of Allah (God).

FC: What I just heard in your answer was that much of our strength, or all of our strength really, comes from seeing you properly and seeing you in response to what is done to you. What enables you to withstand these attacks?

MLF: We must remember that it is written that we would undergo these kinds of attacks. In the Bible and Holy Qur'an, God shows us through the life of His prophets and messengers that none of them came into the world to do their work without severe opposition against them. That was with Abraham, Noah, Lot, Moses, Jesus and Muhammad, peace be upon them all and all the prophets and messengers in between. That is our role today.

If we do what Allah (God) has asked us to do—to unite on the basis of truth, to reform our lives, to civilize ourselves and others, and to form a nation for His glory—and we are attacked by the government and maligned and evil spoken of, that is exactly why Jesus in his Sermon on the Mount said, "Blessed are ye when men shall revile you and persecute you and say all manner of evil against you falsely for My namesake."

Then, Jesus said when these kind of things happen, we should not be sad by it and walk around with our shoulders drooped and our head hung down; we should rejoice and be exceedingly glad, for great is our reward in heaven, for so did they, the prophets that were before us.

So, we are in a prophetic mode. We cannot escape what the prophets of God did not escape. If we bear it patiently and remain strong and united, Allah (God) says in the Qur'an that He loves those who are patient and steadfast under trial. We want to be those whom Allah (God) loves.

FC: Thank you.

84. **Khadijah Sharif-Drinkard, "Hijra from Harlem" from** *Living Islam Out Loud: American Muslim Women Speak*
Abdul-Ghafur, Saleemah (Ed.), Boston: Beacon Press, 2005, pp. 116–129. Reprinted with permission of Khadijah Sharif-Drinkard.

Khadijah Sharif-Drinkard was born in 1971 in Harlem, New York to Muslim parents. She received her B.A. from Columbia University in 1993 and her J.D. from Fordham University School of Law in 1997. The following is an autobiographical essay describing how Sharif-Drinkard grew up in Harlem and became a successful attorney and public servant in New York. Her story is representative of the position of middle and upper class, African American, second or third generation Muslims who form broader connections with other American Muslim populations.

I am among the strongest of faith. The Prophet Muhammad said, "Whosoever of you sees an evil action, let him change it with his hand; and if he is not able to do so, then with his tongue; and if he is not able to do so, then with his heart—and that is the weakest of faith."

I was born, the third of six children, to Muslim parents on November 19, 1971. My father was incarcerated, and my mother began her journey as a single parent, rearing her children in the housing projects of Harlem, New York. I learned early that I had to voice my opinion if I wanted to be heard. I was an innate activist and always found myself advocating on behalf of someone else and practicing my advocacy skills on my mother, whom I debated on almost every issue. I dreamed of becoming a lawyer since I was nine years old, and my life in Harlem was the training ground for my future.

I loved being a part of the Harlem community—a community mired in struggle. Despite the crackheads, prostitutes, and drug dealers, I loved my people and I had a burning desire to contribute to their advancement. My passion for Harlem stemmed from my appreciation and understanding of the historical events that took place there. I relished the fact that I was occupying a space that was once the home of such critical thinkers as Langston Hughes and James Baldwin. It was inspiring to live in a place where powerful activists like Marcus Garvey and Malcolm X led movements. It was because of people like Madam C.J. Walker and Adam Clayton Powell Jr. that our people no longer picked cotton but instead picked careers that had never been open to us before. My role models were Harriet Tubman, Sojourner Truth, Mary McCloud Bethune, Frederick Douglass, Shirley Chisolm, Barbara Jordan, and many others, especially my mother—Amidah Salahuddin, a true queen of Islam.

My mother, an activist with the NAACP in the 1960s who endured the brutal conditions of Jim Crow in the South, taught me the importance of standing up for what you believe in and taking action to effect change. While I took those lessons to heart, it was not until I read the autobiography of Shirley Chisolm that I knew I was destined for a career in public service. I was so moved by her grassroots approach to organizing that I was inspired to work on behalf of my peers. I realized that students were dropping out of school at an alarming rate, so I launched a campaign of stay-in-school rallies in the eighth grade at Adam Clayton Powell, Jr., junior High School in Harlem. Excited to put my newly learned skills to work, I began mobilizing my peers to take action. At first people made fun of me and called me a nerd, but after the movement gained momentum, I won the respect and admiration of my peers. No matter how strong-willed I was, I still found it difficult to be publicly ridiculed. What saved me was that I believed in what I was doing. I reminded myself that I was fighting for the rights of my ancestors, many of whom were slaves and were put to death if they expressed an interest in education. It was clear to me that I had the ability to reshape how my people saw education, and perhaps the biggest challenge for me at that time was to convey that African Americans who were smart were not acting "white."

I felt blessed to be a part of a new Harlem Renaissance, where young brothers and sisters were rededicating themselves to excellence in education. It was a time of great opportunity for me, and the fact that I was being raised on welfare did not dissuade me from pursuing my dreams. From as far back as I can remember, I loved learning and despised missing school. As I walked to high school at 6:30 A.M. for advanced placement courses, I passed drug users who cheered me on, asking me to stay in school and to make something of myself so that I could make them and the rest of Harlem proud. Some of them were adults; others were my age. They had often frightened me in the alleyway, but now they were my inspiration to achieve. I guess in some ways they were also my role models—meaning they showed me what not to do in order to be successful. They had inspired me so much that at least once a week I would stay up throughout the night and study until it was time to go to school, to make up for those who were not fulfilling their potential. By taking my academic goals seriously I knew that I could shape my own destiny.

I became a true activist in high school after reading the history of former slaves like Harriet Tubman. She was my favorite role model and the one I wanted to emulate the most. So when an opportunity arose that would allow me to be a youth advisor to David N. Dinkins, then the Manhattan Borough president, I thought about what she would do and stepped out there on faith. I was one of thousands of youths applying for one of the thirty-five seats on his youth advisory committee. Nevertheless, I submitted my application and later learned I had been accepted. It meant so much to me to be accepted because, as I suspected during the application process, if I was selected I would probably be the only Muslim on the committee. My notions were confirmed at our first meeting. The committee was largely made up of middle-class youths from the best high schools and prep schools in the borough, most of whom were unfamiliar with the issues facing young people in the hood. So, the way I saw it, I had a double mission—to educate them about issues affecting impoverished youth, and to give the Muslim American a human face. The latter task was no small feat considering that it was not commonplace to see positive images of Muslims in the mainstream. Nor were there Muslims in the upper echelons of politics. My entrée into the political field as an adolescent was in fact a stance on behalf of Muslim Americans. In addition, I was an African American Muslim, no longer in the Nation of Islam, and many of my colleagues did not know that African American Muslims existed outside of the Nation of Islam.

As a committee member at the age of fifteen, I was responsible for developing viable solutions to address some of the issues that plagued New York City youth—issues such as drug dependency, teenage pregnancy/parenthood, juvenile delinquency, and gang violence. The administration thought they could learn from young people how best to serve young people. Because we were so diverse in experience and thought, we disagreed on how to achieve our goals, and that is where I first learned about collaboration. It was no small task to allow a group of ninth through twelfth graders to govern themselves and produce results; yet we had many successes. One of my proudest moments on the committee was when I testified on the topic of education reform in front of the New York City Board of Education. My experience on the committee taught me how to work with people from different ethnicities and nationalities, distinct social and economic groups, and divergent political and religious beliefs. It was a crash course in inclusiveness and tolerance, and I've used those skills of governance throughout my life.

Throughout high school I remained involved in community service activities. I served as the president of my high school's chapter of ARISTA—the National Honor Society.

The mantra of the association was scholarship and service, and since my colleagues and I had the grades, our challenge was to ensure that we were of service. To that end, we led walk-a-thons and raised thousands of dollars for New York City's homeless population. We served food in soup kitchens around the city, and within our high school we volunteered as peer tutors to help our classmates with everything from calculus to physics. During my years at A. Philip Randolph Campus High School, I received a variety of awards and scholarships from many organizations and universities for academic and community service achievements. The one scholarship that I did not get was the Empire State Scholarship, which was awarded to individuals who scored above the 90th percentile on the Scholastic Aptitude Test.

In my senior year, I learned that the SAT scholarship distribution procedure had a disparate impact on women. Though women consistently have higher grade point averages than men, women tend to score lower than men on the SAT. In 1988, I joined with the American Civil Liberties Union and became the lead plaintiff in Sharif vs. the New York State Department of Education. After a grueling period of press conferences, interviews, and court dates, we were victorious, and the court ruled that the scholarships should have been distributed to seniors based on both their SAT scores and their GPA. In the end, I was awarded the Empire State Scholarship.

I decided to attend Columbia University, which was only nine blocks from my home in Harlem. I entered Columbia in August of 1989 as a bright-eyed and bushy-tailed seventeen-year-old ready to conquer the world. My mother and my siblings walked alongside me as I pushed my worldly possessions in a shopping cart up Broadway to the Columbia University dorms. My cart held items like my black-and-white television set with a wire coat hanger stuck in the hole where the antenna used to be, a suitcase with the few clothes that I had, a dictionary, a thesaurus, and of course, my Holy Qur'an. The latter would serve as my lifeline throughout college.

During my college tenure, serving as an activist was almost as important as my studies. I continued to work on behalf of those who were less fortunate. Because I did well academically and worked to effect change, the Muslim American Society named me Muslim Youth of the Year in 1990. 1 received this recognition because I had committed myself to serving all of humanity. It has always been my philosophy that Muslims should not just serve Muslims—they should be useful to society. I never focused my attention on becoming a Muslim activist; I focused my energies on being an activist, knowing that through my efforts I would inevitably serve Muslims.

The Youth of the Year award spurred me to work even harder. I joined the militant and outspoken Black Students' Organization (and I later served as its vice president). Somewhat frequently, I participated in protests against the university in an attempt to shed light on the lack of representation of people of color on the faculty and on the failure to create an African Studies Department (which was later established, in part, because of our demands). As active as I was on campus, I felt that my greatest contributions were made outside of the Victorian gates of Columbia University. On August 19, 1991, violence erupted in the Crown Heights section of Brooklyn following the death of Gavin Cato, a young Caribbean boy who was struck by a Hasidic driver as he rode his bike. In retaliation for his death, it was alleged, members of the Crown Heights community killed Yankel Rosenbaum, an Israeli student studying in the United States. For years Hasidim and West Indians had lived side-by-side in relative peace despite their distinct cultural and lifestyle differences, but all of that was about to change.

The violence was so intense that Mayor David N. Dinkins enlisted the help of community leaders and activists to serve as peacekeepers. I volunteered and was immediately deputized, which meant that I received a pass card which allowed me to identify myself as a temporary officer acting on behalf of the city and to travel freely throughout the embattled community. Mainly I calmed hysterical and angry citizens and asked them to return to their homes prior to dusk when the curfew went into effect. Some days later the violence ended but the community and the city were forever changed.

As difficult as that year was, it ended on a high note. In November 1991, Mayor Dinkins selected me and two other youths who served as peacekeepers during the Crown Heights riots to travel to South Africa and Italy as members of his delegation that included municipal officials, business executives, and education experts. I remembered the recurring dream in my head as I gazed out of my sixth floor bedroom window in the projects when I was a child. I prayed to Allah that He bless me to visit South Africa one day. At that time it seemed like an impossible dream, so far removed from my reality, since we had barely enough food to eat, made clothes from old curtains, and could hardly afford to buy items like toothpaste and deodorant. Nonetheless, I dreamed that I would return to the motherland one day, but I had no idea it would be as the guest of Nelson and Winnie Mandela.

The moment I stepped off of the plane Nelson Mandela greeted me in his usual charming and proper manner and said how happy he was that I had come home. He stated that I was so young to be a part of this historic delegation, and in return, I expressed how honored I was to be of service. It was an amazing feeling to return home where so many of my ancestors had accepted the religion of Islam. For me, the connection was more than the Afrocentricity that I shared with South Africans, it was also about the spiritual bond. When my foreparents were forced into slavery, they were compelled to relinquish their language, customs, mores, and religion. They tried to preserve the latter practicing Islam in secret; even so, many were forced to embrace Christianity as a faith. My return home as a Muslim was a reclamation of faith and an affirmation of my ancestry.

My task on the delegation was to serve on the education committee, where I would work with students who were a part of the African National Congress youth division on developing ideas around home-schooling and freedom schools. In addition, we presented more than ten thousand books and various school supplies to Black South African students from the City of New York. The delegation traveled to Johannesburg, Pretoria, Soweto, Cape Town, and more to speak directly with citizens about how they were affected under the apartheid regime. We attended pep rallies, protests, and vigils in an effort to speak out against the inequality, injustice, and lack of due process under the law for Blacks. I remember attending one rally in a remote location of the country where we marched into the streets chanting *Amadla-Nguwathu* (Power to the People). We danced the toyi-toyi (the South African national dance) from one shantytown to another. Being a human rights activist, I was concerned with the civil rights abuses taking place at home in Harlem, and I was equally concerned with the brutality that existed in South Africa. Apartheid was a modern form of slavery and disenfranchisement, and I was determined to leave my mark on what appeared to be the epicenter of the human rights struggle. To my surprise, however, my South African comrades left an indelible impression upon me. They endured physical abuse, mental torture, and constant humiliation. Although they were looking for answers from me, they were my inspiration

When I returned from my trip I was more grateful than ever for our apartment in Harlem. I was thankful to have hot running water most of the time, heat after October 15th, and a welfare system that provided food stamps, which lasted until the middle of the month. My friends back home in the motherland possessed none of these conveniences and still managed to go to school, lead movements, and excel in the face of insurmountable odds. I was humbled and incredibly appreciative to Allah for His favors upon me. I also knew that despite the fact that I was doing good work, I could do more. As a result, I promised myself that I would use the information and knowledge that I had gained to educate people back home about the true circumstances of the South African people. I so desperately wanted to make Harriet Tubman proud of me. I wanted her to know that her story had touched me and that I would show my appreciation for her struggle by struggling to help those who were disenfranchised.

I prayed to Allah to continue to use me as a vehicle for change. A few months after my return from South Africa, I learned of an opportunity to serve on another delegation abroad-this time in Russia. The United Nations and Legacy International were looking for twelve youth ambassadors from around the United States to travel to Russia to study the political, economic, social, cultural, and environmental issues affecting a regime that had recently become a democracy. After a grueling application process I learned that I had been selected. I was off on another mission that would forever change me.

The delegation arrived in Moscow in the summer of 1992. We lived in the countryside and in major cities like St. Petersburg, and what struck me the most was that the people of Russia were much like the citizens of South Africa. During my stay, I visited Chernobyl and learned about nuclear power, studied the Russian language, and became a student of their culture. I also studied their religious traditions, or the lack thereof, since during Communist rule the populace was prohibited from participating in religious worship. We visited at least two dozen churches that had just reopened after the fall of Communism and witnessed the destruction that had taken place. While it is no secret that many people were Christians in Russia prior to the rise of the Communist regime, I knew that there were Muslims there as well. I requested that we incorporate a visit to a mosque into our tour and curriculum. To my surprise our guides said that they were not aware of any. I was determined to visit a mosque, and so on the penultimate day of our journey I found a mosque in the city of St. Petersburg. It was indeed a relic, but a beautiful one that was undergoing a much-needed facelift. Nevertheless, you could see its beauty and history in each stone that was laid. I felt complete at that point because I had linked a piece of Russian history to my experience.

It meant a great deal for me to connect a piece of their history with my own life experiences. To see the evidence that Muslims had not only existed in Russia but had flourished there was amazing. I realized that Muslims penetrated every corner of the earth.

When I returned from Russia the youth ambassadors toured the United States, reporting on how this new democracy was being forged abroad. The trip was a rare opportunity to witness the embryonic stages of a democracy, and we eagerly presented our findings to community organizations and universities.

Two years later, I achieved my childhood dream and began my led studies at Fordham University School of Law. During my law school tenure I enjoyed my coursework as well as extracurricular activities such as serving as the National Parliamentarian for the National Black Law Students Association (NBLSA). Being affiliated with NBLSA provided me with the opportunity to travel round the country for regional meetings, participate in conferences, and preside over the annual national convention. I served in that capacity for just one year because I had my sights set on yet another delegation abroad-this time in China.

In 1995, I was informed that the United Nations was holding s Fourth World Conference on Women, and this time it would take place in Beijing. Although I was not a member of a nongovernmental organization, nor did I have any affiliation with the United Nations, I was determined to participate in this conference to represent the concerns of Muslim American women. As a result, I attended an orientation meeting at the United Nations for people who were traveling to China. At the meeting, I learned that because I had been a journalist for the Muslim Journal for the previous six years I would have special access as a member of the press corps. Not only would I be able to cover the conference, but I would be able to participate on the committees as a representative of the Muslim American Society. I was prepared in all respects, and thanks to the help of just a few generous individuals, I raised enough money to cover all of my expenses for the entire three weeks that I stayed in Beijing.

While in Beijing and in the remote location of Huairo, where most of the conference was held, I met the most amazing women from around the world, including many I was familiar with, like Winnie Mandela and the widow of Malcolm X, Dr. Betty Shabazz (we became friendly while serving together on the South African delegation). I participated in protests to end the trafficking of slave girls in Nepal and India, and I met with Muslim women from Iran who had been persecuted because they were scholars. I sat on the Document Committee for the Women of Color Caucus and assisted in drafting the Platform for Action, the document that was born from the conference detailing the international rights of women. I was moved by the stories of women struggling in every part of the world, and I was inspired to be a better woman because of it. Perhaps my greatest task there was to ensure that people knew that Islam had already bestowed God-given rights on women and that no document could recreate the rights that had already been provided to us by Allah. While I went there to share information, I certainly had no idea that I would spend as much time as I did propagating the religion of Islam in an effort to reveal the balance, justice, and freedom inherent to our way of life. Upon my return I shared the information with the Muslim American community as I traveled the country, lecturing about the conference and on the importance of African American Muslims having a stake in the process of going forward.

As I looked back on this experience over the years, it reminded me of being on a mini-hajj. When I went to Mecca in 2001 to complete my rites as a Muslim, I remembered that in China, like on hajj, there were people from all over the world coming together for one purpose. On hajj our goal was to bear witness to the Oneness of Allah (the Most High), and in China we were there to stand up for the rights of women.

The conference reminded me of how fortunate I am to practice Islam in America, where women could pursue education, serve as elected officials, walk freely in the streets or eat in restaurants without their husbands, and drive cars. It was there that I truly began to appreciate being an American Muslim. The countries with the worst records on women's rights were often led by Muslim governments. My participation in the conference and my trip to China gave me a better appreciation for the United States of America.

Two years later I graduated from law school, and many people, including myself, thought that I was headed for a career in public service. However, I took a job in a training program at MTV Networks that would teach me how to become an entertainment lawyer.

A year and three months after starting that program, I became the first lawyer hired at Nickelodeon as in-house counsel that had evaded the brutal clutches of law-firm life.

Despite my newfound interest in entertainment law, I still felt incomplete without participating in the political arena. As a result, I decided to work on the presidential campaign for Bill Bradley. While Senator Bradley's senior staff members wooed me to join the campaign full-time, I opted to stick with the Nickelodeon position and to volunteer my services instead. As a volunteer I campaigned in Vermont, worked the Iowa caucuses, and helped create a letter-writing campaign for Women in Support of Bill Bradley. My appetite for politics had been whetted again, and soon afterward I threw my hat into the ring and became the first Muslim to seek public office in the Township of Maplewood, New Jersey.

When I decided to run for the Township Committee (the equivalent of the city council), there were only ten weeks until the primary in June of 2002. Some well-intentioned people who were members of the Committee convinced me that I would be a good choice. I had never run for public office before, and I had only lived in my town for a year and a half. I had a lot to learn about Maplewood, and I had to know it before the debate against our opponents. My running mate and I walked the streets every night, knocking on the doors of residents to explain why we wanted them to vote for us. We held coffees in people's homes setting forth our agenda, answered questions about our solutions for decreasing property taxes, educational reform, and environmental issues, and attended every major public hearing that was held. In the end we lost by three hundred votes in the primary, but I received the highest number of votes in six districts, which meant that I won the second highest number of districts in the race. Ironically, the gentleman who won the least number of districts actually won the primary because his running mate carried him. I learned a lot about politics from working on campaigns and serving as an advisor to political officials, but I learned the most from actually running for office myself. It was perhaps one of the scariest things that I have ever done because I was putting the world on notice that I wanted my voice to be heard.

I was also curious to see how people would respond to me, since my name was clearly a Muslim name and we reside in a pretty uppity town despite its sprinkled diversity. What I found from that experience is that some people harbor prejudice, but most constituents are willing to hear your agenda and to see if you have viable solutions to their problems, and that is all one can ask. I am certain that one day I will run for public office again and that I will win.

My dream is to become the first Muslim president of the United States. I have had this goal since high school and believe that one day it will be a reality. As a Muslim president, I would strive to be a modern-day example of how Prophet Muhammad governed-respecting and valuing the contributions of all people. When I become president it will be a different world. Islam will no longer be seen as a threat to the West. The world will have a more in-depth understanding of the contributions of Islam and Muslims. We as Muslims will no longer allow others, who claim to practice our religion, to highjack our glorious way of life. Both Muslims and friends of our faith will have made monumental strides toward understanding our own roles in reshaping the world and our place in it. I believe that a Muslim president is needed to bring about balance, justice, and true freedom for all people.

I see running for office as a task that is as important as completing school and voting. Despite not winning a seat I am busier than ever. After the election many people called upon me to serve on a variety of boards. I could not accept all of the invitations that were extended to me, so I was extremely selective. Today I serve as a member of the Planning Board overseeing planning and development issues for the Township of Maplewood. In addition, I am currently an executive committee member of my neighborhood association, where my primary responsibility is handling the concerns of community residents. My involvement in community issues goes back to my roots when I served as the first female vice chairperson of the board of directors for The Valley, Inc.—the Harlem-based nonprofit organization where I was once a participant and a founding member of the women's empowerment group called the Circle of Sistahs. My faith and activism has allowed me to effect change carrying picket signs in the streets, making decisions in the boardroom, and coordinating book club discussions where we deal with hot topics around religion and race. I have found several methods as effective vehicles for change—the key is to be open and flexible to them all.

When I first became dedicated to public service I was inspired to make a change because I knew that we deserved better. I knew that my ancestors had struggled so much for the freedoms that I enjoyed, and I wanted to repay the debt. While today I feel similarly, I also know that being a mother of a young daughter has increased my desire to make this world a better place. Whenever I think about how exhausted I am after work as I head off to my next meeting after dinner, I remember that my little girl is counting on me to reshape our society so that she may have a better chance at succeeding than I had. Just when I feel that I need to quit a committee because I have to leave my house at dawn in order to attend a meeting, I am reminded that without sacrifice there is no progress. As I reflect back on all that I have accomplished, I believe that my greatest achievement was giving birth to Jalsa. It was through giving birth that I began to understand the true meaning of service. I pray that one day I can be her Harriet Tubman. I want to inspire her so that she understands and appreciates her power. If I can be as good a mother to Jalsa as my mother was to me, then we will have won. And that is the task currently at hand.

85. Halima Toure, "You Seem So Intelligent. Why Are You a Muslim?" from *Taking Back Islam: American Muslims Reclaim Their Faith*

Copyright Rodale Inc., Beliefnet, Inc., 2002. Reprinted with permission of Halima Toure. Halima Toure was born and raised in New York City. She is a professional writer and an African American woman who converted to Islam. The following entry illustrates her conversion process. For a description of Taking Back Islam: American Muslims Reclaim Their Faith, see the preface to Primary document 32.

A WOMAN WHO SEEMED TO "HAVE IT ALL" RECOUNTS HER SPIRITUAL VOYAGE TO ISLAM

A few years after I embraced Islam, a woman I worked for said to me, "You seem so intelligent. Why are you a Muslim?" I responded, "Because Islam appealed to my head as well as to my heart."

If anyone had told me a year before I became a Muslim that my head and heart would be open to Islam, my response would have been "You're out of your mind!" So how did I come to this point in my life?

On the outside, I had a good life. As a beneficiary of the civil rights movement, I became the first black editor at *Redbook* magazine in the mid-1960s. Then I freelanced for magazines and did research for television. I had a rich social and professional network. I believed, along with my friends and colleagues, that we could help make a positive change in America. It was the time of "Say it loud: I'm black and I'm proud." My Afro hairstyle and my support for the black arts movement expressed my black pride. The knowledge of Africa's great past awakened my African identity. My family was proud and supportive of my accomplishments. I'd made it.

On the inside, though, a creeping emptiness had begun to spread. I'd joined freedom rides, picket lines, and boycotts with the Congress of Racial Equality. I had volunteered with the National Urban League. But the bullets that killed John F. Kennedy, Robert Kennedy, Malcolm X, and Martin Luther King Jr. each killed a bit of my spirit and hope. Cynicism began to take root.

Meanwhile, I had drifted away from organized religion and settled on the middle ground of agnosticism. The death of a twenty-four-year-old relative left me angry and confused that God would take such a nice guy when so many bad people were creating mayhem. Neither my childhood beliefs nor my adult agnosticism could comfort or satisfy me

FINDING ANSWERS

The deep questions of life that periodically rise in us all began to surface: If I'd "made it," why did I feel so empty? Material goods, career, family, and friends alone did not fill my inner space. Is life just a free fall from birth to death? Is this all there is? Why am I here? I became hungry for meaning.

Then I met the man who would become my husband and the father of my child. He was a Muslim. He talked of our ancestors' African Islamic identity, along with his dream of a new future for people of African descent. He emphasized how our African past was linked to Islam in empires like Songhai and Mali and in renowned centers of learning like Timbuktu.

I read literature about the basic tenets of Islam. Several were similar to Christianity, although there were fundamental differences. The concept of unity (*tawhid*—the interconnectedness of all things) touched a deep chord in me. I saw how all parts of mind, body, spirit-connected to my total environment. This, for me, was profound.

At Friday services in the mosque, the imam, an African American who had studied Islam at al-Azhar University in Egypt, described Islam as a scientific way of life bound by God's spiritual, physical, and social laws. He believed it was just the medicine needed to uplift humanity, but especially for African-Americans suffering the after-effects of slavery.

I was impressed by the focus on family and by the bonds of brotherhood and sisterhood. Given the popular perception of the absentee African-American father, I was particularly impressed by seeing Muslim men talking to and laughing with young children, even holding infants. The women drew me into their circle and freely answered my questions.

I had met Betty Shabazz, the late widow of El-Hajj Malik ElShabazz (Malcolm X), when I was helping to edit a book about her husband. When she learned of my engagement, she extolled for me the benefits of being married to a Muslim man. In addition to their focus on family and responsibility, those men were sincere in practicing the faith and believed it was their duty to protect and support their wives and treat them with love and respect. She also pointed out that the ideal of Islam was free of racism and classism.

An *lid al-fitr* prayer service at the Islamic Center revealed the international character of Islam. In contrast to the racial separation of the United States on Sunday mornings, the colorful tapestry of humanity worshiping together impressed me as just what Allah intended. With the diversity was the unity—black, brown, yellow, and white prostrating themselves before their Creator, reciting the same prayers in the same tongue and intoning in unison, *"Allahu Akbar"* (God is greatest).

THE WORK BEGINS

On the evening that I sat in *hijab* (headscarf) on the carpet in front of the imam, ready to make my *shahada* (profession of faith), I was convinced that I needed Islam for me and not just to please my future husband. Before witnesses, I professed that there is no God but God (Allah), and that Muhammad is his prophet and messenger. Also, I professed belief in Allah's angels, in the Books of Allah, in Allah's prophets, and in life after death. Then the imam said, "You've taken the first step toward becoming a Muslim. Now the work begins."

That work is never-ending. It began with studying—learning what is *halal* (lawful) and *haram* (prohibited), and why. It continues with trying to incorporate its principles into all aspects of my world. I gave away the clothes of my old life, covered my hair, and made ankle- and wrist-length garments that both cover and conceal. The duty-free alcohol went down the toilet; the cigarettes went into the garbage. I scrutinized food labels to avoid *haram* ingredients. I learned the cleansing ritual before prayers, and I learned the prayers themselves. Gradually, I changed my work schedule in order to attend Friday services. The Islamic holy days replaced the holidays of my old tradition.

These outward changes were traumatic enough. My inward shifts, however, were, and continue to be, the most astonishing. For one, I was unaware of the extent of my arrogance and ignorance until I had to bow down to Allah in prayer. My credo had been, "I am the master of my fate! I am the captain of my soul!"

Yes, a measure of free will exists to make choices. What I came to understand, though, is that the great "I" played no part in providing the essentials of life that I took for granted: the air we breathe, the rain that nourishes our food plants, the sun that fuels life-sustaining processes. So shouldn't we humble ourselves to this powerful and generous creator? Could there be a more appropriate gesture of reverence?

Another big shift came five years after I embraced Islam. My father died suddenly of a massive stroke. I was grief stricken, but my behavior and attitude were different from what I had displayed ten years earlier when my young relative died. True, my father was older, but sixty-two is not so old. What was different was me.

What Muslims say on this occasion had real meaning: "We all come from Allah and to him we shall return." I could express my gratitude to Allah for long talks I'd had with my father over the previous year, evidence of a closeness we'd experienced that hadn't existed since I was a child. And despite my pain, I could be grateful that Allah took him swiftly.

Albert Einstein once said, "A problem cannot be solved on the same level of consciousness at which it was created." The hopelessness, cynicism, anxiety, rage, and despair that mark contemporary life-symptoms of an individual's and a society's loss of meaning-threatened to consume me. But on that day nearly thirty years ago, I opened a door to become something else, and I am still "becoming."

I could not comprehend how seeing life through the lens of an Islamic consciousness would change me. One friend was turned off by my zeal, screaming, "Give me a break!" Time and experience have since mellowed me.

My *hijab* and peaceful demeanor surprised another friend who saw me about eight years after my *shahada*. He remarked, "It suits you!"

Yes, it does suit me, and I have yet to feel empty again.

PART VI

MUSLIM ARTISTIC AND CULTURAL EXPRESSION IN AMERICA

This section gives a glimpse into the artistic productions of American Muslims. Music, literature, and comedy emerge as major fields of creativity, allowing hybridity and fusion between different genres from Muslim countries as well as the American context. They also illustrate the innovative characteristics of the new generations of American Islam across race and cultures, while at the same time bridging gaps with mainstream American popular culture and audiences.

86. **Sham-e-Ali al-Jamil, "Remembering Love," "Finding Home," and "Blessed Divine Woman" from** *Living Islam Out Loud: American Muslim Women Speak*

Excerpts from Abdul-Ghafur, Saleemah, ed., Living Islam Out Loud: American Muslim Women Speak, Boston: Beacon Press, 2005, pp. 53–54, 72–74, 181–183.

Sham-e-Ali Al-Jamil was born in Hyderabad, India and raised in the United Kingdom and the United States. She received her B.A. from Oberlin College and her J.D. from Northeastern University School of Law. Al-Jamil is a poet, writer, and lawyer. Her writing and poetry and appeared in Shattering the Stereotypes: Muslim Women Speak Out (2005). As a lawyer, she works on welfare rights for survivors of family and intimate-partner abuse.

"Remembering Love"

Don't ask me
whether I know
the Desi woman
married to the Black man
because we all don't know each other
and don't start
about when he converted,
we were both born
and raised Muslim.
What is wrong with converting anyway?
You question me
in hushed tones
about whether my parents
still speak to me,
feel entitled to ask
detailed questions
about my personal life.
Why would they stop
speaking to me? I respond.
See the speaker at the Desi wedding
praise the bride and groom
for preserving honor
by marrying within their
ethnic community,
then watch the hail of 300 people
applaud with delight.
The liberal intellectuals
clap alongside
the modest conservatives

in the name of purity.
Lots of talk about diversity in Islam,
but who is practicing?
Makes it easy to forget
the elderly man
in the city square
graying beard
and *tasbeh* in hand
staring at us
When asked,
What are you looking at?
he said, taken aback
with tears glistening,
You both look
so happy
and in love
I could not turn away.

"Finding Home"

In this room filled with
late night dreaming
your cries wake me
again.
Was it the fifth time you woke?
Was it really 5:00 AM.?
The scent of you,
fresh and safe
skin soft,
moonlight's caress on moving water.
The four-days-old of you,
bundled close against me.
Was it you inside me all along?
You within me?
When I learned
of your presence,
summer's gentleness
against my skin,
lavender lines that
revealed you,
the air gleamed bright
sky clear, open.
In my muscular nest
you nuzzled
swam in a concealed sea
urgently grew
beneath my heart.

You are here now,
in the last sigh of this night
drinking breast milk
near my heart,
close to me once more.
I curl around you fatigued
feeling some ancient story
coursing through me,
your warm breath
painting luminescent landscapes
against my skin,
fragile life in my care.
At this moment,
she swept over me
home did,
not the brick variety
or nation.
Though I searched for her
it was she who found me,
unsuspecting
we wept in the
serene yellow light
glowing sincere
exchanged stories
reconciled
She missed me.
Was this me?
Bearer of life,
birthing dreams
under the light of
the last stars shining
before daybreak
nourishing and protecting my
now sleeping infant
fluttering smiles of contentment
like sunlight,
my own belly full of
belonging
after finding myself.

"Blessed Divine Woman"

Hadrat Fatima Masumah,
your holy shrine
resides in the middle
of this city
like a heart

sustaining life,
sanctuary on saline earth,
clear blue solace.
Tonight,
rose water
moistens arid air,
strings of lights
shine like small
flowers glowing,
it is the anniversary
of your arrival to Qum,
You, whose presence
made this city
a holy place.
'Aalimah,
Learned Scholar,
I press my forehead gently
against the entrance
to your sanctuary,
smooth wooden door
cools my mind
as I humbly request
your permission
to enter.
In the sanctity
of this space,
pilgrims' supplications reflect
again and again against
intricate mirror work above,
prayers, gratitude and
tears blend
like scarlet blue
smears of color at dusk,
where our spirits
take rest
for a moment.
Of the million people
who visit your holy grave,
where wishes and hopes
grow like seedling trees,
where we weep
as we request
your intercession,
Gracious Healer,
we feel heard.
With my heart released
in this refuge,

next to other women
their children
grandmothers with *tasbeh*,
the smell of sweat and roses
whispers of prayer
I close my eyes, thankful
hold this memory of
ziyarat, close
a salve,
for wounded days.

87. "About the Tour—Allah Made Me Funny" from *allahmademefunny.com*

"Allah Made Me Funny: The Official Muslim Comedy Tour," accessed May 19, 2006. Available online: http://www.
allahmademefunny.com/about.html. Reprinted with permission of Preacher Moss and Allah Made Me Funny.

Preacher Moss and Azhar Usman founded Allah Made Me Funny: The Official Muslim Comedy Tour after September 11, 2001. Prior to the tour, Moss was a comedy writer for several actors from the television show "Saturday Night Live" and Usman received his J.D. from the University of Minnesota Law School. Allah Made Me Funny tours North America, performing at conventions, comedy clubs, schools and universities, and fund-raisers. It illustrates how a difficult time for Islam in America, such as the post–September 11th context, can be turned into a positive artistic moment helping to form a bridge with the dominant, non-Muslim society.

THE QUESTION has always been where can Muslims and non-Muslims go for social growth, and entertainment by us, for us, and about us? The answer? "Allah Made Me Funny: The Official Muslim Comedy Tour."

"The concept of this tour is to make a comprehensive effort to provide effective, significant, and appropriate comedy with an Islamic perspective, which is both mainstream and cross-cultural. The idea is to provide a venue whereby Muslims and non-Muslims can feel safe, relevant, and inclusive of an experience where humor is used to bridge gaps of bias, intolerance, and other social ills that are pre and post 9/11 relevant," says Preacher Moss, co-founder, and one of the featured comedians on the tour.

Preacher Moss and co-founder Azhar Usman have already made the international radar, as they will debut the tour in Toronto, Ontario from May 26 to 29, at Yuk Yuk's comedy club venue, during its first ever Muslim Comedy Festival.

"This project means people are coming out to not only be entertained, but also educated about the truths of Muslims and non-Muslims' existence in America following 9/11, but also preceding it. It involves the courage to step out of the shadows of silence, and fear and reach out and build bridges. We're building these bridges through humor, and understanding to make that journey a little easier for all of us," explains Moss.

Reflecting the diversity of the Islamic religion, as well as the diversity of this country, Azhar Usman, Preacher Moss, and Azeem Muhammad, a rising comedy star, have put down ego and pride to show the world a cooperation rarely seen in comedy. Through their commitment, they've brokered "a project built not on competition, but a coalition."

Says Moss, "We have a community tour designed to see not only the Muslim community grow, and be self-actualized, but to see the world community attain the same goals. This is done through dialogue, understanding...and humor as the glue that heals us all."

88. Michael Shapiro, "Sister Haero Interview" from *MuslimHipHop.com*

Published May 22, 2005. Available online: http://www.muslimhiphop.com/index.php? p=Stories/7._Sister_Haero_Interview. Reprinted with permission of Michael Shapiro and MuslimHipHop.com.

MuslimHipHop.com was founded in 2004 with the aim of providing Muslim artists with a place to post their music. In May 2005, the site shut down and was reopened in November 2005 with more professional quality content. The site promotes music that is specifically about Islam and does not integrate profanity, senseless violence, or sectarianism. MuslimHipHop.com hosts several styles of performance: hip-hop, pop, spoken stories, and traditional nashīd music, a spiritual, folk style of music from Islamic cultures.

One of the artists of MuslimHipHop.com is Sister Haero. She was born in Kurdistan in northern Iraq, but her family moved to California before her first birthday. Haero began writing and performing hip-hop when she was twenty years old. She pursues "halal [permissible] self-expression" in her art, including performing while wearing the ḥijāb. Her creation is representative of many young American Muslims who, defining themselves as both American and Muslim, strive to maintain Islamic principles within the framework of American culture. The following interview was conducted by Michael Shapiro of MuslimHipHop.com in 2005.

There are only a handful of female Muslim artists in the world today. These few, yet bold individuals are leading the way in halal self-expression. Giving young Muslims girls an alternative role model to Britney and Christina, it's incredibly refreshing to see a female artist being appreciated for her message, and not her sex appeal. Sporting hijab with a hip hop twist, Sister Haero proves that Muslim girls can be stylish, expressive and pious. Mashallah. MuslimHipHop.com took some time out with Haero to get the full story:

MUSLIMHIPHOP.COM: Where are you from originally? How did you get involved in hip hop?

SISTER HAERO: My parents are from Kurdistan in northern Iraq, and I've been in the States since I was 11-months-old, so this really is the only place I know as "home." I used to write poetry when I was real young, but I didn't start rhyming until I was almost 20...I saw Cannabis freestyling at a show and I turned to my brother and said "I wanna do that," and then next thing I know I'm writing spoken word pieces and rhymes, Alhamdulillah. From there I started to go to different spots to perform, and after some time organizations began inviting me to their events to host or perform. After a few years, I decided it was time to step up my game and record my music and spoken word, and I began freestyling, so that aspect brought more attention to me as an artist. Around the same time, I started getting into music. I began listening more to hip-hop and also joined the MSU (Muslim Student Union) on campus. I went to San Diego State University; and my disappointment with the current music of the time, and my new-found love of Islam, brought out a lot in me and I began to write about what I was feeling. I began writing stuff that was expressive, yet tasteful, at the same time. I actually had stopped listening to the radio because I was sick of hearing the same commercial songs over and over, and the music that was out wasn't challenging my mental state. The only time I listen to the radio now is if I'm around others who are listening to it...cause it really doesn't fulfill me at all. I'd rather just listen to the CD's I have.

MUSLIMHIPHOP.COM: What music has inspired you the most?

SISTER HAERO: Wow...I love a lot of artists: from Mos Def, J5, Common, De La, Pharcyde, The Roots, Pac...to Maxwell, Marvin Gaye, old school Jodeci, Brand Nubian, Digable Planets...the list goes on. I like listening to jazz as well...any particular artist? No. But most of the time I stick to the hip-hop. Every now-and-then, I'll listen to R&B, but I have to be in the mood for that. If I had to pick, I would rather listen to a hip-hop love song than an R&B love joint. That's just how I am. Some of my favorite songs are Pete Rock and CL Smoothe's "T.R.O.Y.", "Award Tour" by Tribe, and "Act II" by The Roots f/ Common.

MUSLIMHIPHOP.COM: What do you want your listeners to know about in your songs?

SISTER HAERO: Basically, I'm inspired to write about life, whether it's about politics, the ups-and-downs of relationships, the music industry and trying to make it in the game, to my family, society...what I see around me, what I experience, things I would like to achieve in life. Sometimes, I'll get on that "I'm tighter than you are tip," depending on the beat. A lot of times the beat dictates what I'm going to be writing about. I may have a topic that I want to touch upon, but if I don't have a beat that fits it, I won't write it. Usually, I'll hear a beat and then be like "ahhh, this is the hook...can you hear what it's sayin?" Because for me a lot of times the music is "talkin", so I write what I hear and just go with the flow of it all.

MUSLIMHIPHOP.COM: What is it like being a female Muslim artist? Do you get a lot of friction from Muslims?

SISTER HAERO: I love being a Muslimah artist, because so many people have stereotypes about Muslim women (we don't have fun, we're not allowed to state our opinions or showcase our talents, etc.), and I feel like I'm helping to break those stereotypes every time I step to the mic. And in regard to Muslims, mashallah, I've gotten a lot of support within the communities. Every now and then of course, I have to deal with more conservative people who prefer that I perform WITHOUT music. Alhamdulillah...though it's frustrating, I appreciate the fact that they've taken the step toward inviting sisters to their events to perform. I look at it as a small step toward progression, and Inshallah I'd like to be a part of that in any way possible.

MUSLIMHIPHOP.COM: What are your plans for the future musically?

SISTER HAERO: What ever Allah wills...there are benefits to getting a deal as well as remaining independent, but right now I'm just trying to stay focused on getting that message out there and giving dawah. Whatever comes, comes, and if it doesn't, I'ma stay doing my thing as long as Allah continues to bless me. I'm just blessed to be around not just talented people, but talented Muslims. And a lot of the people I'm working with are donating their time and services, so JAZAKALLAH KHAIR to all of them...y'all know who u are! Honestly, I would love to get to the point where I'm bringing in enough to pay back all these people who have helped me along the way, and who continue to help me. So if staying independent does that, coppin that record deal does that, then Inshallah it will manifest.

MUSLIMHIPHOP.COM: How is the Muslim artist scene when you lived in San Diego?

SISTER HAERO: (laughs)...That's a good one! I actually got frustrated and moved to L.A. so I could more actively pursue the music career, but San Diego seems to be growing. It's a more conservative city, and there just aren't as many venues or events to perform at or frequent. I still go back and do shows because I still have to show love to the place I came up in. But really, LA is a perfect fit for me. I don't know how long I'll be here, but I find myself sayin "I love LA" a few times a week. Despite not having my family around, I really feel like I'm at home.

MUSLIMHIPHOP.COM: Outside of music, what do you do?

SISTER HAERO: I currently work at an after school program in South Central L.A., so that keeps me pretty busy. If I'm not writing or working on a song or poem, I stay busy trying to schedule studio time and getting my hands on more beats. And of course, I go back to San Diego to visit my family. I just get out and about the city and meet up with good peoples...I'm a busy body. I don't like being at home unless I'm asleep or eating, otherwise I don't feel productive. I make it a thing to always "be somewhere." My mom (may Allah have Mercy on her soul) always said "you never like being at your own home," and she was oh so right! Even my cousin Suz (and roommate) knows when I'm bored and need to get out of the house. She'll just start laughing at me and call me out on it.

MUSLIMHIPHOP.COM: What projects are you working on?

SISTER HAERO: I am currently working on recording my album, doing shows whenever and wherever needed, and making as many contacts as possible. I always try to stay productive somehow. Inshallah, I'm doing a spoken word piece about police brutality for a documentary in San Diego, and Inshallah I'll be featured in an upcoming book about women in America. I've actually been featured in another book called "California 24/7" recently about being a Muslim female who raps, so Alhamdulillah I've been blessed to have good things come my way.

MUSLIMHIPHOP.COM: The Muslim Ummah has been struggling lately...how can we make change?

SISTER HAERO: Making dua. It can get frustrating, because we seem to be bringing ourselves down, but we have to stay positive. And also we have to support each other... that's very important, especially as Muslim artists. But really, the best thing is to make dua. We need more Muslim artists to get out there and actually PERFORM their work and showcase their talent. I don't know how many times I've heard a sister spit a poem or rap, and I'm like "you need to share that!" and I'll hear "I'm shy" or "I write just for me, not to do in front of others." But see, that's good and all, but we have to be an example for the many, many, MANY Muslim youth that are coming up and need someone that they can look up to. So even if it's on a "lower level" we've got to get out there and share our talents, our outlook on life and our perspectives.

MUSLIMHIPHOP.COM: How has your local Muslim community responded to your music?

SISTER HAERO: Mashallah, I've gotten a pretty good response. I think more Muslims are beginning to realize that we, as Muslim artists, are the ones they want their children to follow and support, so they are much more eager to support us.

MUSLIMHIPHOP.COM: How do you feel about Islam?

SISTER HAERO: I would be NOBODY, I would be NOWHERE without Islam.

MUSLIMHIPHOP.COM: What would you like to say to your fans?

SISTER HAERO: Jazakallah khair to everyone who has supported me and the other Muslim artists as well. It is a blessing to be able to do what we do, and Inshallah we're able to inspire others as well as make a positive impact within society as a whole. Stay strong, and make dua for us all, those who are oppressed all over the world, and remember our political prisoners like Imam Jamil. *throws fist in air* Dawud, Shaydia, and Aliya (my nephew and nieces) my biggest fans…there's no better feeling than to hear them sing my hooks. If they were the ONLY ones in the world who heard my music or who recited my lyrics, it would all be worth it! Jazakallah khair for blessing me with this interview. I appreciate all the support and hard work you all have put in.

89. **Waris and Wajid Syed, "Top 10 Muslim Hip-Hop Lyrics: The Five Elements of Hip-Hop Meet the Five Pillars of Islam" from** *Warbux Records*

Accessed May 31, 2007. Available online: http://www.beliefnet.com/story/153/ story_15303_1.html. Reprinted with permission of Shahed Amanullah and Warbux Records.

Waris and Wajid Syed are Kashmiri Muslims of Iraqi heritage. They founded Warbux Records as an independent hip-hop record company, intending to use hip-hop to challenge negative conceptions of Islam and Muslims. The following article is part of their project to connect the Five Pillars of Islam with the fundamentals of hip-hop music.

"Hip-hop music has been misconstrued," write Warbux founders Waris and Wajid Syed. "Commercial rap music has been mistaken as hip-hop music, and the mainstream media has exploited this ignorance. Hip-hop is a culture that consists of five elements… Therefore, we are bridging the five pillars of Islam with the five elements of hip-hop to create a platform to depict social and political inequity."

The Syed brothers compiled a Top 10 Muslim Hip-Hop lyrics list, first published on www.shobak.org and www.altmuslim.com. Beliefnet presents the list with their permission.

1. Artist: Eric B and Rakim

Album: Don't Sweat the Technique
Song: Don't Sweat the Technique
  Because of my culture, I'm a rip and destruct the
  Difficult styles that'll be for the technology
  Complete sights and new heights after I get deep
  You don't have to speak just seek

2. Artist: Nas

Album: I Am…
Song: Ghetto Prisoners
  A lot of rules, some locked in solitude
  Curse the day of they birth confused, who's to be praised?
  The mighty dollar—or almighty Allah

3. Artist: Common and Q-Tip

Album: Get on the Bus soundtrack
Song: The Remedy
  Q-Tip: To the human beings with taste, sight, touch, smell and sound
  Let's deem it profound!
  And prioritize this cause it was Allah's wish
  "Allah? I'm God."
  "No I don't believe that. That's a mystery."
  "If God is so good why does shit be happening to me?"

There's divinity within because we come from the divine
A force that's not seen
But you feel it every time

4. Artist: Mos Def

Album: Black on Both Sides
Song: Mathematics
Killin fields need blood to graze the cash cow
It's a number game, but shit don't add up somehow
Like I got, sixteen to thirty-two bars to rock it
but only 15% of profits, ever see my pockets like
sixty-nine billion in the last twenty years
spent on national defense but folks still live in fear like
nearly half of America's largest cities is one-quarter black

5. Artist: Common f/Cee-Lo

Album: One Day It'll All Make Sense
Song: G.O.D. (Gaining One's Definition)
Koran and the Bible, to me they all vital
And got truth within 'em, gotta read them boys
You just can't skim 'em, different branches of belief
But one root that stem 'em, but people of the venom try to trim 'em
And use religion as an emblem
When it should be a natural way of life
Who am I or they to say to whom you pray ain't right,
That's who got you doin right and got you this far,
Whether you say "in Jesus name" or "Al hum du'Allah"

6. Artist: Gangstarr f/Big Shug, Freddie Foxxx

Album: Moment of Truth
Song: The Militia
Guru: One of us, equals many of us
Disrespect one of us, you'll see plenty of us
Conflict, is what I predict,
You and your fellas is mad jealous, attempting to flare
We cleverly stalked ya, your fam'll miss ya, The war's on, that's why we formed
The Militia

7. Artist: The Root

Album: Things Fall Apart
Song: The Spark
Might act up, but I still can pass dawa
I'm usin' new ways to try to reach these better days
Instead of tryin' to take you under I just make you wonder
I still fast, make salaat, and pay zakat
I didn't make Hajj yet, but that's my next project
Livin' two lives, one of turn and one with true lies
Keeping up hope knowing he's answering to my du'as.

8. Artist: Public Enemy

Album: Fear Of A Black Planet
Song: Fight The Power
   People, people we are the same
   No we're not the same
   Cause we don't know the game
   What we need is awareness, we can't get careless
   You say what is this?
   My beloved lets get down to business
   Mental self defensive fitness

9. Artist: Wu-Tang Clan

Album: Wu-Tang Forever
Song: Triumph
   Inspectah Deck: I bomb atomically, Socrates' philosophies
   and hypothesis can't define how I be droppin these
   mockeries, lyrically perform armed robbery
   Flee with the lottery, possibly they spotted me
   Battle-scarred shogun, explosion when my pen hits
   tremendous, ultra-violet shine blind forensics

10. Artist: Jurassic 5

Album: Unified Rebelution 12
Song: Unified Rebelution
   Heaven does await us, put here to sedate us
   Make us in His image with his pilgramage
   Never perfect we're tripping, by a force unseen
   But we divulged its presence, so this rap goes back to the essence
   Lessons have been written from the end, but you're soon to see
   Kalil in community, rebels of rhythm unity

90. **Yusuf Islam, "I Have No Canons That Roar: How the Bosnian War Transformed My View of Music in Islamic Culture" adapted and updated from** *Taking Back Islam: American Muslims Reclaim Their Faith*

   Copyright Rodale Inc., Beliefnet, Inc., 2002. Updated February 2007 by Yusuf Islam.
   Yusuf Islam (for a biography, see the "Islam, Yusuf" entry in Volume 1) was born Steven Demetre Georgiou in England in 1948. During the 1970s, he was a successful musician going by the name Cat Stevens. In 1977, he converted to Islam, and he changed his name to Yusuf Islam in 1979. He is a prominent Muslim in Britain, supporting various charities and educational groups. He is also popular among American Muslims of all ages and as Cat Stevens retains a large U.S. fan base. In the following essay, Yusuf Islam has updated his 2002 essay on music in Islam to reflect his new perspective.

THE MUSICIAN FORMERLY KNOWN AS CAT STEVENS EXPLAINS HOW THE BOSNIAN WAR TRANSFORMED HIS VIEW OF MUSIC IN ISLAMIC CULTURE

The genocide in Bosnia at the end of the twentieth Century was a turning point for Muslims in Europe: it exposed people worldwide to the hitherto unknown treasure of Islamic

European culture and civilization which Bosnia represents. The T.V. pictures of blond haired, blue-eyed Muslims, chanting *'Allahu Akbar'* (God is Greatest) and reciting the verses of the Holy Qur'an amid the smoke and fury of the war, brought a whole new perspective to the concept and understanding of Islam for many who, like me, witnessed it. One of the outcomes of this terrible event was the re-evaluation of my position towards Music and its use in Islamic socio-political life. The issue—I realize now—is certainly not as cut and dried as it seemed when first presented to me back in 1977, following my embracing of Islam.

It's interesting to note now how my formative years as a Muslim were shaped by those I came into contact with. At that time the chief Imam in the London Central Mosque encouraged me to continue my profession of composing and recording; at no time was there ever an ultimatum for me to have to choose between music and Islam. Nevertheless, you didn't need a PhD to realise there were lots of things about the music industry which contravened the Islamic way of life.

Later on another event my doubts about the issue increased. I remember coming out of the Prophet's mosque (*peace and blessings be upon him*) in Madinah and meeting a fellow convert from America. This black brother asked me who I was and what I did for a living. I told him I was a singer; he let me know immediately his position, "O! You'll have to give up that—musical instruments are *haram* (forbidden)."

As a new Muslim, I decided to follow the safest course, which was to leave that which was doubtful or unclear. So I gave up singing and performing, to the alarm of many of my fans and fellow musicians, until I knew more. In the first interview I gave to a Muslim magazine back in 1980; when asked about my attitude to music I said, "I have suspended my activities in music for fear that they may divert me from the true path, but I will not be dogmatic in saying that I will never make music again. You can't say that without adding *Insha Allah*."

That was a parting of the ways, marking the line between my past and my future. Following that decision, most of my available time was spent bringing up a family with five children; establishing charities and working to serve educational needs of Muslim children in the West. I only wrote a couple of children's poems during the next ten years: "A is for Allah", was one of the results when I did manage to put pen to paper.

A giant leap in discernment regarding my understanding of culture and Islam came in 1992. The Bosnian War. It was the greatest violation of human rights and resulted in the most shameful and sordid crime against European Muslims ever seen—at least in my lifetime. During this time I remember receiving an urgent call from the head of one of the Islamic aid agencies working in Bosnia. The brother pleaded with me over the phone, "Do something for the children who are being killed here! Organize an international concert, use your talent." It was very emotional and I immediately felt inspired and began work writing a song called "Mother, Father, Sister, Brother". I had also half finished a poem called "The Little Ones" which I dedicated to the children of Sarajevo and Dunblane.

Something had changed with the event of the Bosnian War: Muslims were now shown the score. These indigenous Europeans were being killed simply because they were Muslim. In fact many of them had already adopted western cultural values: there were mixed marriages, some of them even shared a cigarette and a glass of beer with their neighbors, but that didn't help them—because they still had Muslim names.

Early in 1995, I was invited to a London Hotel to meet the new Bosnian Foreign Minister, Dr Irfan Ljubijankic. Dr. Irfan was one of the unsung heroes of the war; for most of the siege of Sarajevo he had worked tirelessly as a doctor in the basement of a makeshift hospital. With no proper light or heat; he helped attend to thousands of injured patients, many of whom had suffered blown-off limbs and shrapnel wounds. Now he was a Minister for the Bosnian Government, and I was truly honoured to meet him.

It seems Dr. Irfan was also eager to meet me: somehow, my former songs and recordings of the Seventies had made an impact on him during his early years as a student. During our meeting he played me a cassette of a song he had written entitled "I Have No Cannons That Roar". It was extremely moving. I remember him placing it in my hand and saying something like, "Please use it if you can for helping the cause". Not long after that, we heard the news: Dr. Irfan had been martyred, his helicopter shot down in a missile attack above Bihac. My heart dropped.

The Bosnian cause had been made to look all but lost. I realised that we required a confidence boost; our spirit had taken a beating and we needed to reassert our faith and identity. One of the things that lifted me greatly was listening to the cassettes coming out of Bosnia at that time; these were rich and highly motivating songs (*nasheeds*), inspiring the Bosnian army and nation with the religious spirit of sacrifice and selflessness. There was a new generation of singers and writers, blending the beautifully melodious sounds of the Balkans with the message of Islam.

Dr. Irfan's cassette recording was still in my possession. Soon it dawned on me: here was a magnificently potent tool; we simply had to use it. But what about the conventional Muslim ban on musical instruments? Many of these recordings had orchestration and instrumental backing; even if I personally refuse to touch them, how could I justify their use?

But looking again at the question of music in Islam, it became more clear that the issue was still highly debatable, particularly in circumstances of oppression and war. Without doubt in today's world, to have no cultural strategy or alternative would leave Muslims without any defence at all. Surely, I thought to myself, the use of certain musical instruments for the protection of the Islamic identity and culture of a nation is worthy of the same allowance as guns and rockets? It was, after all, the self-identification and culture of Bosnian Muslims and their Turkish influence (i.e. Islam), which had come under attack—not the Bosnian's military might.

A *hadith* (an incident or saying of the Prophet) may be worth quoting here. The Prophet was entering Makkah to perform his *'umrah* (small pilgrimage) with a group of unarmed Muslims; they were being closely watched by their adversaries and long-time persecutors, the Makkan polytheists. A Companion of the Prophet, 'Abdullah bin Rawahah, was walking in front of him reciting poetry against the disbelievers when 'Umar stopped him and said, "O Ibn Rawahah! In the presence of the Messenger of God and in the Holy sanctuary of Allah, you are reciting poetry?" The Prophet (pbuh) said, "Leave him o 'Umar. These couplets are more forceful than the showering of arrows upon them."

Looking again at this incident is revealing, because one of the closest similarities to singing and music in the Qur'an comes with its pronouncements on the subject of poetry. Towards the end of the Qur'anic Chapter entitled "The Poets", God Most High, says:

> As for the Poets, the deviants follow them.
> Hast thou not seen how they stray in every valley,
> And how they say that which they do not?
> Except such as believe and do good works, and remember Allah much,
> and vindicate themselves after they have been wronged...

We can see from this reference that poetry was generally disapproved of. It particularly alludes to the common ailment that many poets suffer: that is, their inability to emulate in their actions the noble words and excellence of their poetry. However, there are always exceptions to this general rule, as seen from the verse quoted.

In addition to the issue of poetry, drawings and art also provide an interesting parallel. From a juristic point of view, although in the collections of authentic *Ahadith* (sayings and traditions) the evidence against the creation of life-like images of animate beings is much stronger than the ban on musical instruments, scholars today are almost unanimous in accommodating [or at least remaining silent about] the use of pictures and illustrations in books and publications for educational purposes, while disputing the general use of photographs and TV for immoral or purely commercial purposes.

The foregoing only underlines the need to approach the issue of songs and music in a broader and more flexible context, without necessarily falling outside the rules of *Shari'ah* (Islamic Law) according to the needs of time and circumstance and choosing what is best for the good of the community—*Istihsan*.

"The war in Bosnia and Hertzegovina is not yet over, it has simply moved into a new phase", to quote the Head Mufti, Reis al 'Ulama, Mustafa Ceric. Today the danger facing Muslims in Bosnia and many other countries is not directly military, it is cultural: satellite TV, the Internet, CD's, fashion, advertising, the worship and adoration of personalities, film stars and so on. This doesn't necessarily only affect Muslims—everyone is adversely affected by the Media Moguls and their commercial empires. Many Christians and people of various denominations are also working to offset the negative impact on their beliefs and traditional values.

If we are to withstand the bombardment of music, art and philosophy based on morally unhealthy trends, we need to develop a unique and positive approach to the use of the media and its methodologies. Education—not simply entertainment—is still firmly the root of our media endeavours, for Muslims as well as non-Muslims, *insha Allah* (God willing).

The Prophet said, "The *halal* (lawful) is clear and the *haram* (unlawful) is clear." I humbly suggest, therefore, that if a person really cannot tell the difference between sex-driven, disco music and morally motivating devotional songs, which help people to improve their lives, then this may quite simply expose a lack of perceptiveness on their part. To stay away from the doubtful for them would be advisable, if not necessary, as it was for me at one time.

The Prophet Muhammad (pbuh) said, "There is no sin beyond *kufr* (disbelief)". Many people still have not had sufficient access to the message of peace and the universal belief in One God, which Islam holds uppermost. Music is not the most important issue for a person first learning about Islam.

After establishing one's faith in the One Supreme God of the universe and after accepting the Prophethood of Muhammad, as well as giving spiritual contentment, Islam also gives a person certain absolute directives on how, why, what, when and where, to do things in his or her daily life. Regarding a number of worldly matters, there is an area of flexibility and *fiqh* (juristic opinion). This is particularly true in the case of 'music', where the term itself covers a wide range of activities and has no direct Arabic equivalent.

It's true that I have gradually softened my objections to the use of music and songs over the years, and there are good reasons. Since the genocide against Bosnia in 1992, I learnt how important motivational songs are in keeping people's spirits high during times of great calamity. In many respects, the world today is passing through even more dangerous and calamitous phase than it was then. Therefore, the need to use music to calm people and bring back the message of peace and harmony is even more vital.

From the letters I've received over the years, it's clear that my songs have actually helped many people. Some even on the very verge of suicide have been influenced to see life in a positive light again; and God says, "Whoever save the life of one human being it is as if he has save the whole of humanity".

The positions that I took previously, I held fast to them, because I believed they were true. However, one only has to look at history, and not long ago, when we discover that the guitar itself was probably introduced to Europe through Spain by the Muslims. When you learn something like that, it forces you to revaluate how Islam has contributed—through its culture and art—the civilization we all enjoy today. True culture never really dies, it simply adapts to the suit the times and needs of society; I believe Muslims must do more to contribute to the global society—as much as they did in the past.

Today I personally stay away from political pronouncements, because that's what divides people. Islam is to do with accepting the One God of us all and the tremendous healing that fact brings. So today, I prefer to sing a song and that's perhaps the best thing I can do right now. To express myself in music is much easier than for me to stand up and give a lecture; because you can argue with a philosopher but you can't argue with a good song, and I think I've still got a few good songs.

After the Bosnian War I established Mountain of Light, a multi-media company. It was established with the intention of providing Muslims with a desperately needed cultural outlet in order to project a more moralistic form of musical art already sanctioned in the universal message of our *deen* (faith). We will watch its effect on people with interest, praying that it will open many hearts to the light of Islam and the harmony it brings to society and human civilization: And we pray to God Almighty for forgiveness for any mistakes made in connection with our work; may He pardon us and guide us to what is best—*Ameen.*

91. "Lipstick Jihad: An Interview with Azadeh Moaveni" from *MotherJones.com*

Published March 9, 2005. Available online: http://www.motherjones.com/news/qa/2005/03/moaveni.html. Reprinted with permission of MotherJones.com, copyright 2005, Foundation for National Progress.

Azadeh Moaveni grew up in San Jose, California. Her family moved to the United States from Iran in 1976. She studied politics at the University of California, Santa Cruz, and received a Fulbright scholarship for study in Egypt. After spending three years as a reporter in the Middle East, she wrote a memoir, Lipstick Jihad: A Memoir of Growing up Iranian in America and American in Iran (2005), dealing with her identity as an Iranian American. It demonstrates the conflicted identities of some second generation immigrant Muslims and how, in response to that conflict, they combine American values, Islamic principles, and elements of culture from their parents' home countries. The following is an interview with Moaveni conducted by Michael Lumsden, an editorial fellow with MotherJones.com. Interviewed By Michael Lumsden
An Iranian-American journalist discovers a complex, paradoxical Iran

Viewed from the outside, Iran seems an alien, forbidding place. What we know of its rulers—a clique of hard-core mullahs who run the country with a heavy hand—isn't encouraging; and what we know of its people…isn't very much at all. It's useful, then, to have a book like Azadeh Moaveni's *Lipstick Jihad: A Memoir of Growing up Iranian in America and American in Iran,* to show us that Iran is every bit as nuanced, as various, and as contradictory as we like to think the United States is.

Moaveni grew up in San Jose, Calif., her parents having left Iran in 1976, three years before the Islamic revolution unseated the Shah and established theocratic rule, and radical students took Americans hostage in the US embassy in Tehran. The unresolved tension she felt between her cultural identity as an Iranian and an American led her, after college, to go to Iran as a journalist.

For two years she wrote about Iran for *Time,* finding that beneath the surface of easy assumptions and cultural stereotypes lay a complex and varied reality. Her stay was bracketed, roughly, by the pro-democracy student demonstrations of 1999 and President Bush's "axis of evil" speech in 2001, after which the government clamped down hard on dissent—and on journalists: she felt compelled, after routine intimidation and occasional interrogations, to leave in fear for her safety.

Lipstick Jihad is the account of Moaveni's time in Iran, and of her quest to better understand her cultural identity. From her hotel room in Manhattan, where she began her book tour, she recently spoke by phone with MotherJones.com.

MotherJones.com: Given the tense history between the US and Iran, do you think it's more complicated being an Iranian-American that some other kind of hyphenated American?

Azadeh Moaveni: You have these two countries that have had this really fraught relationship for almost 25 years now. It's very charged. Being another hyphenated American, I imagine, is charged racially. But this is a political charge, you're in the shadow always of this relationship. The hostage taking, for America, was a uniquely traumatizing event, and we were so immediately linked to that. So there's a lot of baggage.

MJ.com: What are some of the biggest differences in your mind between American culture and Iranian culture?

AM: One big difference I've noticed is how class is experienced in both places. Even though America is so class-stratified, the idea that there is a national culture that transcends class is really present. In Iran, despite the revolution and its attempt to eliminate class as a category, there's now *political* class. That's different than social class, but it's still very much infused with the nuance that comes from a class-stratified place.

MJ.com: What are some ways that that manifests itself in Iran?

AM: The interesting thing is that you see the revolutionary elite becoming Western, because being privileged used to mean being Westernized in Iran. They came from a conservative background, made a lot of money off the revolution and were supposed to be political elites, but not westernized ones. But that association between the West and privilege lingered so persistently that even though they're still socially really bound to the revolution, token aspects of Western lifestyle are becoming part of what it means to be, paradoxically, revolutionary and anti-Western.

MJ.com: You also write about a distinctive kind of evasiveness in Iranian culture.

AM: Yes, I think this is the biggest difference between the US and Iran—how honesty is interpreted. American culture is incredibly forthright. There's this premium on telling it like it is and being frank. Iranian culture, and Farsi, the language, is really evasive; it has all these rituals and cues and formalities in how people deal with one another.

I think evasiveness took on a whole new meaning after the revolution. You suddenly had Islamic conservative values governing how society was run, which pushed a lot of things behind closed doors and under veils and chadors. Private behavior became much more weighted.

I write in the book about eroticization. It's not explicit, ever, but the emphasis on covering and the hidden and forbidden was sexualizing because everyone was very preoccupied with that. Nothing about how you conduct your private life is at all apparent from the way you look to everyone else. Evasiveness, privacy and eroticization all came together in the post-revolutionary culture.

MJ.com: The Western media paints a very dark picture of what life is like for women in Iran today. Is that accurate?

AM: I have a chapter on relationships and sexuality and how some women actually had their opportunities expanded by the revolution. I used to think that some traditional woman had more rights than secular women, but I've come to think about traditional women's current situation as more tragic than the way I wrote it in the book. The revolution was meant to be an emancipation for women. It ended up being a semi-emancipation, but promiscuity and drugs and all those things grew and festered after the revolution. So there was lost innocence and then young girls got nothing in its place. They didn't gain any freedom to actually explore themselves and they didn't get a chance to do anything with some of the new freedoms that come with education.

MJ.com: What kept Iranian girls and women from taking these new freedoms to the next step?

AM: I think society hadn't moved that far along. Suddenly you had all of these women going to college and becoming literate, which hadn't really happened before '79. But there weren't jobs for them. Also, traditional conservative Iranians weren't ready to see that next step. So our daughters get educated, but are we ready for them to go off and be independent and have jobs? No. There wasn't a parallel social evolution to match women's new freedoms.

MJ.com: Did living in Iran affect how you see yourself as a woman now?

AM: I'm always startled by how much I've internalized all of this stuff. I'll come back to the States and I'll see a woman in shorts, and I'll think, "Oh my God!" And then I'll stop and I'll think, "Why did you just have that thought?" It's an unreflexive internalization of these things. Of course it's very shallow, but it makes me realize why Iranian young people are so conflicted now, even after things opened up in '97. You're given all these messages all the time—that this is forbidden and you can't be with a guy on the street. Even if you don't really believe any of it on a conscious level, it seeps into how you think. I don't think young Iranians acknowledge that they've internalized any of that, but I think it's there. Even though young kids can be really hedonistic and rebellious in Iran, they'll come up with surprising ways of judging.

MJ.com: Has working in Iran changed you as a journalist?

AM: As a reporter you know not to take what people say at face value. But Iran really taught me that in a whole new way, because especially young people—when you ask them questions about how they feel about America or how they feel about the prospect of America pressuring this regime, you'll get the impression that they are incredibly pro-American. It wasn't until I really lived there that I saw a lot of it had to do with cultural associations and what America meant as a symbol of lifestyle freedom or as a way to get under the mullahs' skin. It was not so much about America but about being Iranian in Iran at that moment.

It made me much more inclined as a reporter to move away from *vox pops*. Do I talk to everyone all over a city or spend a day in a village understanding how big picture questions have changed one place? It made me value getting as micro as possible with big picture issues.

MJ.com: You came in for some intimidation in Iran. How does that compare to your experience in other Middle Eastern countries?

AM. Honestly, in most other places I worked I was never interrogated or followed or felt my reporting checked in an explicit way. I think that's probably reserved for, say, Egyptian journalists in Egypt or Lebanese journalists in Lebanon the way it was for me in Iran.

But as a reporter in those places, I was surprised by how much more closed off the debate was about political Islam. The debate in Iran was so startlingly open. These big issues about faith and Islam and the role it should play in politics is what everyone talks about Iran, and no one talked about it in any other Middle Eastern country, or they did so in very uninteresting and suppressed ways.

MJ.com: In the book, when you talk about Islamic politics, one of the expressions you use is "culture of lies." You also say you think that only secularism can safeguard basic human rights. Is that an absolute?

AM: My experience in Afghanistan recently informed my thinking about this. Having a legal system that incorporates both secular law and religious law at the same time, I think, is a way to bridge those who might want to have Islam involved in governing society and those who value the western notion of rights—the rights of the individual. If there's a way in which you can have secular approaches to different aspects of legal practices, I think it doesn't have to be *only* secular.

MJ.com: You mentioned western-style rights. What do you have in mind?

AM: I think this young generation in Iran wants Western-style rights. It's not "rights" in a very legalistic or human rightsy sense, but "rights" as in values—the right to individual choice in lifestyle, career choice, who you marry and who you don't. Rights as a way of not being bound by tradition or having to live a certain way.

MJ.com: Iraq's constitution looks likely to be grounded, to some degree, in Islamic law. Do you think in that case it'll be possible to retain the kinds of individual rights and freedoms you're talking about?

AM: In Iran, you have an elected government and the divine right by law and they're both trying to operate. You can have an elected parliament that makes laws, but if the judiciary is appointed by the Supreme Leader—who is a representative of God—then you're kind of at an impasse.

But Iraq won't have that top-down structure to deal with. I think it'll be a question of juries and due process and other elements of a secular legal system. You can have all of those in place with a system that's inspired by Islamic law, and if the system is trying to be reasonable and accountable, there's no reason why it has to be a disaster.

MJ.com: You say in the book that you didn't grow up as a devout Muslim. After living in several Middle Eastern countries, has your relationship to Islam changed?

AM: Between my experiences in Iran and Iraq, I learned how to become a secular Shiite, which I never knew was possible before. This idea that you are culturally a Shiite, yet you don't pray five times a day—in the Middle East I found this established tradition of never doubting for a second that you have Muslim identity, but that you're secular.

MJ.com: In Iran, too?

AM: Definitely in Iran. Iran is so secular. I'm so shocked by this. That you can have a secular middle class in an Islamic country, I think is just phenomenal. It's so rare in the rest of the region.

MJ.com: Why is that rare?

AM: In many other Middle Eastern countries, the government has made such a point of keeping Islam at arm's length. People have grown increasingly frustrated with their lives, with the economy and with the politics of the country. Islam becomes an appealing outlet. They've had a reason to become more religious, whereas in Iran, it was never taken away in the first place. In fact, it was imposed. So people are able to conclude whether they want to have a private relationship to their faith—which is actually what I mean when I say "secular" in Iran. It's this idea that everyone decides for ourselves, and the government doesn't decide for us, how much Islam there is in our lives.

MJ.com: Do you see Iran changing in our lifetime?

AM: Iranian young people want secular government. But they know this regime is around for a while, and the trick for them is to see how they can transform it from within. They are doing this in their everyday life, looking for small ways to press for more personal and political freedom.

I think Iran is the kind of place where it's difficult to predict what's going to trigger structural change. It's hard to also predict the role that civil disobedience or mass protests could play. Iranian young people are so modern and so secular, so connected to the world. It's hard to imagine that the culture won't change and then start putting pressure on the government to change. The horizon is 10, 20, 30 years, but I think it will happen.

MJ.com: How do you balance your disagreement with parts of the politics and policies of both countries?

AM: It's really tough, because in the U.S. you're so easily branded an apologist for the Islamic Republic or an accommodationist if you're not willing to say that everyone would welcome American tanks with flowers. But if you speak openly about what's going on in Washington and tell Iranians, "Look, America's really serious about your nuclear weapons," you're branded as being hawkish or you're speaking for America, when really you're just saying, "You gotta understand how the American government works."

MJ.com: What is the American media not reporting about the current standoff?

AM: There needs to be more attention paid to the spectrum of Iranian public opinion. I think Iranians are very conflicted about the bomb and whether the government should have it. They're very critical of the government's motives for wanting one. They're worried about the possibility of a Chernobyl. They're worried about whether this government is efficient enough to even run a huge nuclear power plant.

The Iranian government says, "We have the full support of the entire Iranian nation for our nuclear program." And then I see a lot of press coverage in the West that says, "Iranians back their regime over this." It's not terribly sexy to say, "Iranians are divided straight down the middle about something." But I think Iranians' ambivalence is going to be a huge factor.

MJ.com: Has the Iranian government cracked down on freedom of expression as the tension has mounted?

AM: The level of repressiveness has been semi-constant since Bush's "axis of evil" speech, which completely changed political culture in Iran and the extent to which you could have debate in newspapers and on weblogs about where the country should be going. It became really stifling then, and I think that's still the case.

MJ.com: Would you give some examples of how the government became more stifling? It almost seems like it was a self-fulfilling prophecy on Bush's part: His calling Iran "evil" pushed the clerics to become more repressive.

AM: If it's democracy you're trying to promote in Iran, if you have a fledgling trend of liberality and you suddenly make that regime feel like it's under attack, it's a no-brainer that it's going to crack down.

Before "axis of evil," you had reformist newspapers writing openly about Islam and punishment: does Islam justify stoning and lashings and these sorts of things? Afterwards, it had to go underground. Suddenly newspapers that had been extremely critical ran stories on runaway girls. You had to criticize obliquely through human-interest stories and pointing out how miserable people were in different walks of their life.

MJ.com: What lesson is there for Americans to learn from your experience as a journalist in Iran?

AM: That muckraking journalism is about agitating objectively, but that it's not driven by a political agenda, but rather a *rights-based* agenda. I would encourage people to think about media as a forum for politics.

In Iran, the way that that's approached is really sophisticated. If there's an objectively awful thing that's happening and you're writing about it in a way that communicates that, it's not seen as biased. That's how really rotten things in society can be changed. People should realize that it's not necessarily an insidious or regressive thing in the part of media.

MJ.com: How do you think the US media compares?

AM: I think there's this cult of objectivity in the U.S. about media. There are two sides to every story, but it's not always objective that one side has as much right to narrate a story. I think it's distorting to always impose that 50-50 impulse on everything you cover because otherwise you'll be branded as "liberal" or "having an agenda." Life is not 50-50.

Iranian society is really politicized, and your average person reads a bunch of newspapers—or at least used to, before the post–"axis of evil" government crackdowns—and thinks about these things. Reading the news is not a rarefied domain for only people who have two degrees. So even if the government would crack down on the press, people defended the press. Here, media is beleaguered. Even the mainstream media is being attacked, and most people don't seem to care!

92. Suheir Hammad, "In America" from *SuheirHammad.com*

Available online: http://www.suheirhammad.com/, accessed May 22, 2006.
Suheir Hammad was born in Amman Jordan in 1973 to Palestinian refugee parents. Her family moved to New York when she was five years old. As a poet, her work has been published in several different sources, and she has written a book of poetry, Born Palestinian, Born Black (1996) and a memoir called Drops of This Story (1996). She received several awards for her poetry, including the Morris Center for Healing Poetry Award (1996), The 2001 Emerging Artist Award (Asian/Pacific/American Studies Institute at New York University), and a TONY Award for her role in the Def Poetry Jam on Broadway (2003). The following is one of her poems.

In America

right now you are standing
on stolen land no matter

where you are reading this poem
i promise below you is stolen
land was Lakota was navajo
was creek was
and was and is and is and
this fact does not change
because you do not think
about it or you thought
the last Indian died before you were
born or you were born 1/15 Apache
this poem is not blaming you but
allowing you an opportunity to do
something start by saying something and
from where you are standing look north
south look west look east and see
the theft the occupation happening now
and do something start by
saying something

93. Daniel Abdal-Hayy Moore, "Man Among Us" from *Maulood* and "Ramadan Angels" from *Ramadan Sonnets*

Daniel Abdal-Hayy Moore, Philadelphia: Zilzal Press, 1995, pp. 49–51 and Philadelphia: The Ecstatic Exchange, 2005, pp. 70–72. Reprinted with permission of Daniel Abdal-Hayy Moore.

Daniel Abdal-Hayy Moore was born in 1940 in Oakland, California. He converted to Islam in 1970, taking the name Adbal-Hayy. He has written several books of poetry and has received the Ina Coolbrith Award for poetry and the James D. Phelan Award. He lives in Philadelphia with his family where he continues to write. The following poems are from his book Maulood (1996) and Ramadan Sonnets (1996).

"Man Among Us"

Muhammad whose genealogical tree went right straight back to Adam,
who said he was a prophet when Adam was between water and clay—
how can we properly praise him, surrounded as we are by madmen
who think they are sane and saviors, but who shrink from the light of day?
Muhammad, who at six was an orphan, and whose darkness was removed by angels,
who entered the valleys and date palms burst into fruit above him—
how can we possibly taste that quality of his wisdom
when oceans of plastic silence fill our ears with their deafening din?
Muhammad, who grew to be trustworthy, even his enemies trusted him,
who waited for three days on a corner to pay back a debt he owed someone—
how can such honor be followed, in a world so ethically stifled,
when the very foundations of trust have been laughed into mud and ruin?
Muhammad who stood on the mountaintop and saw the sky fill with angels
but distrusted such visions as raving and was afraid his mind had snapped—

how can we see such stillness in the pool of his heart so thunderstruck
when our own streets are hallucinations like savage animals trapped?
Muhammad who let the Truth lead him, and his moon-like light filled the tents
of the people whose hearts were empty but open as sky,
how can our people be touched by the stature of such a being
when most of them are full of sickness and most of them want to die?
Muhammad whose talk was like mountain streams clearly crossing rocks
and splashing into pools of clarity where we could finally see our light—
how can this thick time know him? The doorways are filled with ghosts,
the dumb are leading the eloquent, the leaders are fearful of insight!
Muhammad who went through the heavens on the back of the lightning-bolt mule
and whose gaze was steady and true face to face with the Face of the One—
how can mechanical thinking or the heart like a clock face in ice
begin to glimpse this other world with its other moon and sun?
Muhammad who led the armies with nothing but banners and trust
against mercantile idol-subscribers with the weapons and wealth of kings—
how can simplicity make sense to us, so overpowered by the magic
of High Technology's sorcery which clots up our senses with "things?"
Muhammad whose victory just humbled him more than he was before
so that thousands finally accepted the worship of Allah alone—
is it the same situation now as then for us, hard-hearted people asleep
who'd rather sit in a stupor and worship bits of wood or stone?
Muhammad whose Gate-Opening crashed the iceberg rock right open
to let us enter a world where actual events shed light,
how to sit or go through a doorway, drink water or lie down to sleep,
how to face absolute Oneness without losing balance from fright.
Muhammad, peace of Allah be upon you, Prophet and Messenger of Light,
the figure you made among people put love in their hearts for the Truth—
how can the graveyard society we live in possibly hear your heartbeat
when their drunken hearts drink darkness sold at the tyrant's corner booth?
O Prophet, O man among us, O light that goes ahead,
who gave out the last coin left to you when you lay on your first deathbed—
how can such stark reality reach into us when the air is so filled with lead
and such mention of life only bores the snoring multitudes of the dead?
O Light of the human touch in everything, Praiser and Praiseworthy in one,
we are naked before Allah at last, and we need your enlightening sun!
      1984

"Ramadan Angels"

Ramadan angels crisscross the sky
    just above the earth on
        watch for fasters who
lift up into other dimensions due to their
        turning away from
    created things to their Creator.
They are anonymous beings of light like

so many radiant molecules
doing their job in a well-oiled body
   acting at ease. But their
    body is the world, their
skin domains of transverse
   communication, inside and out,
distant and near, and they are the
blue angels of Arthur Rimbaud, heraldic angels with
   black wings of César Vallejo,
    angelic aurora borealis sprites of
Shelley shinnying up the
   purple shafts of night, and they are
supernatural warriors of India on plains of fiery clouds
riding fanatic horses steaming wide
   billows of green, and they are
recorders of breaths,
measurers of dewdrops,
conductors of vitality to
grass blades and beard-hair, they
congregate in geometric fluidity as
   vast as rock-crystals, as
    tightly packed as
air swiveling around inside air
like those Chinese ivory balls carved
almost infinitely
   one inside the other, or
one sphere outside the other, each
dimensional area totally
  inhabited by The
   Angelic!
No drop of water falls from
  faucet or
   sweating brow, no
corpuscle of blood
   circulates that is not
propelled and taken through its
paces by intentional consciousnesses
  sent on their errands by
   God!
And in Ramadan demons are chained up,
the Gates of The Garden are flung wide, and
angels scour territories of The Alive for
perfection in a dry throat, perfection in a
tight stomach, perfection in a
heart made lighter by the strong
recollection of its Source!
      13 Ramadan

94. **Marvin X, "For El Haji Rasaul Taifa" from** *Love and War: Poems by Marvin X*

Castro Valley, California: Black Bird Press, 1995, pp. 123–124. Reprinted with permission of Marvin X.

Marvin Jackson was born in 1944 in California. During the 1960s he converted to the Nation of Islam and the Black Muslims and changed his name to Marvin X. He received his B.A. and M.A. from San Francisco University. Marvin X helped found the "Black House" in Oakland, California and the Black Arts/West Theatre in San Francisco.

Oh, Taifa
Nationalist
ragin bull for a Black Nation
not perfect among men
but rare warrior of Allah
on haj to Mecca
forced to back of bus
by racist white Muslims
restrained killing them
by grace and mercy of Allah
Mr. T
organized Oaktown
for the get down
made peace among the brotherhood
rallying us when we wanted to fight
each other
Oh, Taifa
that dreadful day
nothing could save you
your diamonds gold real estate
women friends
nothing could prevail
Allah said come home
Surely we are Allah's
and to him we return
Salaam, my brother, my comrade.

95. **Majid Mohiuddin, "Ghazal—In Ecstacy," "Ghazal—In This Is a Sign," and "Ghazal—O Love" from** *An Audience of One*

Columbia, Missouri: Olive Media Services, 2001, pp. 15, 51, 59. Reprinted with permission of Majid Mohiuddin and Olive Media Services.

Majid Mohiuddin grew up outside Philadelphia in Cherry Hill, New Jersey. He began creative writing in high school, winning the New Jersey Governor's Award for Literary Arts (play writing) in 1993. He received his B.A. from Brown University and his M.D. from Brown University School of Medicine. The following three poems are from his first collection of poetry, An Audience of One (2001).

The term ghazal refers to a form of poetry composed of couplets that include a rhyme and refrain.

"Ghazal—In Ecstacy"

Reader! I ask you to please dance in ecstasy! Whirling round, all the Sufis dance in ecstasy...

Swirling from a single point to infinity, Constantly the galaxies dance in ecstasy.

What can a speck mean for the *Rabb al-Alamee n*? All the planets that Man sees dance in ecstasy.

What makes our bodies leap joyfully for the skies? Even dolphins on the seas dance in ecstasy.

Life's golden nectar comes from tiny pollen seeds, Signaling the Source, the bees dance in ecstasy.

Orange, red and yellow hues flicker in the Wind; Autumn leaves upon the trees dance in ecstasy.

The *Amir al-Mumineen* sends the battle cry! The flags of Persian armies dance in ecstasy.

The lovers eloped in fear through the pale of night—Sad eyes full of secrecies dance in ecstasy.

Forsake this world of traps and sensualities—Patiently waiting *houris* dance in ecstasy.

There's tension in the *ghazal,* freedom yet restraint—Shers love-drunk with mysteries dance in ecstasy.

This gliding Finger scribbles what Allah decrees—This carefree Pen can with ease, dance in ecstasy.

Recite what is written and contemplate the world; Shahzadah begs on both knees: Dance in ecstasy!

"Ghazal—In This Is a Sign"

When the clouds threaten a clear sky: in this is a Sign, When the thought of Him makes you cry: in this is a Sign.

When the twilight's wise haze descends before Maghrib time, When the sun has set from on high: in this is a Sign.

When will man truly feel how close Allah is to him? When you hear your own infant cry: in this is a Sign.

When will man remember his true state of helplessness? When your elders grow sick and die: in this is a Sign.

When you look at the mountains or the smallest of ants, When you muse how the birds can fly: in this is a Sign.

When you stare at the heavens and see millions of stars, When a lone streak goes shooting by: in this is a Sign.

Shahzadah like you, is amazed at the world's design,
When we wonder by asking "why?": in this is a Sign

"Ghazal—O Love"

Nature has left me amazed of love, O love—
How numerous are the ways of love, O love!

How does the Spider know how to spin a web?
The same instincts make me crazed of love, O love.
How do Pigeons fly blindly back to their roost?
I'm led to You through this maze of love, O love.
Like the sad Rosebud crying her morning dew,
Fleeting are our youthful days of love, O love.
When a Mare starts to stamp with pangs of birth,
She feels joy since her pain stays of love, O love.
When the Clouds burst forth leaving the earth refreshed,
All of the world weeps in praise of love, O love.
Like the stealth of a Tiger viewing her prey,
How silently I have prayed of love, O love.
In a sky full of stars, I can only see the Moon!
What more is there to say of love, O love?

96. Dawud Wharnsby, "Welcome to the I.C.E. (The I.N.S. Song)" from *Enter Into Peace*

2005. Available online: http://www.wharnsby.com/gallery2/d/734-7/W...e+INS+Song_. mp3. Reprinted with permission of Dawud Wharnsby, Enter Into Peace copyright 2005.

Dawud Wharnsby was born in Ontario, Canada, in 1972. He converted to Islam in 1993, changing his name from David to Dawud. He combines the folk song traditions of his Scottish and English ancestry with nashīd, a spiritual, folk style of music from Islamic cultures, a musical genre that is currently very popular among young Muslims. He has recorded several albums including "Blue Walls and the Big Sky" (1995) and "The Prophet's Hands" (2002). Wharnsby wrote the following song after being detained during a border crossing between the United States and Canada in 2001.

This is America, land of the free
where everyone is given equal opportunity (and scrutiny!).
A living dream, a land of plenty, milk and honey, neon lights,
but once you step inside these doors my friend you don't hold any old rights.
So go and sit down there and obediently wait your turn,
get familiar with your chair and watch your time and patience burn,
and welcome to the I.C.E. (I.N.S)
How long you'll be here, well it's all up to me, (Guess?)
'cause we're working in conjunction with Homeland Security,
so while you're in this country we'll decide if you are free.
Your name shows up here in our highlighted file, (see...it says "Yoosef"!)
says your ex-wife's cousin's husband lived in Baghdad for a while.
Says your uncle's neighbour's father's brother-in-law's nephew's twin
delivered groceries to man who looked a lot like Bin Laden.
Though that's as close as we can get, we're almost sure that you're a threat.
Everybody must be checked,
each beard and headscarf is suspect.
Welcome to the I.C.E. (I.N.S)
How long you'll be here, well it's all up to me,
'cause we're working in conjunction with Homeland Security,

so while you're in this country we'll decide if you are free.

Though we can't pronounce your name, let alone correctly spell it,

if there's a terrorist, fundo, suspect rat our nose is trained to smell it.

So don't ask why or try to lie.

When we say "jump" just ask "how high".

Don't underestimate our pomp, prestige our our power,

We're the highest paid government pawns at $25 bucks an hour.

Yes...this here is a modern day crusade.

You're either with us...or you're with the Moslems...er...ah...I mean the "terrorists".

We're gonna route you out, we're gonna smoke you out, we're gonna shine a light on ya!

So, "Bring em on!"

So you're old, withered, white haired, blind and you need a wheel chair,

so you're almost 8 months pregnant—well we don't really care.

Just get up! Faster! Face your luggage! Hands outstretched arms high!

We'll pat you down and feel you up and it's treason to ask why.

Just democratically comply.

And welcome to the I.C.E. (I.N.S)

How long you'll be here well it's all up to me,

'cause we're working in conjunction with Homeland Security,

so while you're in this country we'll decide if you are free.

In this land of the free your fate belongs to me.

In the name of freedom we'll destroy what it means to be free.

Yee-haw!

SELECTED BIBLIOGRAPHY

Abdo, Geneive. *Mecca and the Main Street: American Muslim Life After 9/11*. New York: Oxford University Press, 2006.

Abou El Fadl, Khaled. *The Great Theft: Wrestling Islam from the Extremists*. San Francisco: Harper, 2005.

Abraham, Nabeel, and Andrew Shryock. *Arab Detroit: from Margin to Mainstream*. Detroit: Wayne State University Press, 2000.

Abraham, Sameer Y., and Nabeel, Abraham, eds. *Arabs in the New World: Studies on Arab American Communities*. Detroit: Wayne State University Press, 1983.

Abu-Laban, Sharon McIrvin. "The Coexistence of Cohorts: Identity and Adaptation Among Arab-American Muslims." *Arab Studies Quarterly* 11, no. 2&3 (1989):45–63.

Abu-Laban, Sharon McIrvin, Regula Burckhardt Qureshi, and Earle H. Waugh, eds. *Muslim Families in North America*. Edmonton: The University of Alberta Press, 1991.

Ackerman, Spencer. "Religious Protection: Why American Muslims Haven't Turned to Terrorism." *The New Republic* 233 no. 24 (December 12, 2005).

American Muslim Council and Zogby International. "American Muslim Council/Zogby Poll Reveals." http://www.zogby.com/news/ReadNews.dbm?ID=255 (accessed online: August 28, 2000).

Aswad, Barbara C., and Barbara Bilgé, eds. *Family and Gender Among American Muslims: Issues Facing Middle Eastern Immigrants and their Descendants*. Philadelphia: Temple University Press, 1996.

Baker, Wayne, et al. "Preliminary Findings from the Detroit Arab American Study." http://www.isr.umich.edu/news/arab-amer/final-report.pdf (accessed online: 2004).

Bagby, Ihsan, Paul M. Perl, and Bryan T. Froehle. *The Mosque in America: A National Portrait*. Washington, DC: Council on American-Islamic Relations, 2001. Available at http://www.cair-net.org.

Bagby, Ihsan. *Report: A Portrait of Detroit Mosques*. Clinton Township: Institute for Social Policy and Understanding, 2004. pp. 1–65.

Barret, Paul M. *American Islam: the Struggle for the Soul of a Religion*. New York: Farrar, Straus and Giroux, 2007.

Ba-Yunus, Ilyas and M.M. Siddiqui. *A Report on the Muslim Population in the United States*. Richmond Hills: CAMRI, 1998.

Brittingham, Angela, and G. Patricia de la Cruz. "We the People of Arab Ancestry in the United States." Census 2000 special report, March 2005.

Bukhari, Zahid, John L. Esposito, et al., eds. *Muslims' Place in the American Public Sphere*. Walnut Creek, California: AltaMira Press, 2004.

Cainkar, Louise. "The Impact of 9/11 on Muslims and Arabs in the United States." In *The Maze of Fear: Security and Migration After September 11th*. Edited by John Tirman. New York: The New Press, 2004. pp. 215–39.

Cainkar, Louise. "No Longer Invisible: Arab and Muslim Exclusion After 9/11." *Middle East Report* 224, 2002 (Fall):22–30.

Cesari, Jocelyne. *When Islam and Democracy Meet: Muslims in Europe and in the United States.* New York: Palgrave, 2004. Reprint, 2006.

Dannin, Robert, "An Islamic Pedagogy of the Oppressed." In *Black Pilgrimage to Islam.* New York: Oxford University Press, 2002. pp. 237–60.

Dudziak, Mary L., ed. *September 11 in History: A Watershed Moment?* Durham, North Carolina: Duke University Press, 2003.

Elkholy, Abdo A. *The Arab Moslems in the United States: Religion and Assimilation.* New Haven: College and University Press, 1966.

Haddad, Yvonne Yazbeck. *Not Quite American? The Shaping of Arab and Muslim Identity in the United States.* Waco, Texas: Baylor University Press, 2004.

Haddad, Yvonne Yazbeck, ed. *The Muslims of America.* New York: Oxford University Press, 1991.

Haddad, Yvonne Yazbeck, ed. *Muslims in the West: from Sojourners to Citizens.* Oxford: Oxford University Press, 2002.

Haddad, Yvonne Yazbeck, and Adair T. Lummis, eds. *Islamic Values in the United States: A Comparative Study.* New York: Oxford University Press, 1987.

Haddad, Yvonne Yazbeck, and Jane Idleman Smith, eds. *Mission to America: Five Islamic Sectarian Communities in North America.* Gainesville, Florida: University Press of Florida, 1993.

Haddad, Yvonne Yazbeck, and Jane Idleman Smith, eds. *Muslim Communities in North America.* Albany, New York: State University of New York Press, 1994.

Haddad, Yvonne Yazbeck, and Jane Idleman Smith, eds. *Muslim Minorities in the West: Visible and Invisible.* Walnut Creek, California: AltaMira Press, 2002.

Haddad, Yvonne Yazbeck, and Jane Idleman Smith, eds. *Muslim Women in America: the Challenge of Islamic Identity Today.* New York: Oxford University Press, 2006.

Haddad, Yvonne Yazbeck, Jane Idleman Smith, and John L. Esposito, eds. *Religion and Immigration: Christian, Jewish, and Muslim Experiences in the United States.* Walnut Creek, California: AltaMira Press, 2003.

Haddad, Yvonne Yazbeck, and John L. Esposito, eds. *Muslims on the Americanization Path?* New York: Oxford University Press, 2000.

Hagopian, Elaine C., and Ann Paden. *The Arab Americans: Studies in Assimilation..* Wilmette: Medina University Press International, 1969.

Hasan, Asma Gull. *American Muslims: The New Generation.* New York and London: Continuum, 2000.

Jamal, Amaney. "The Political Participation and Engagement of Muslim Americans." *American Politics Research* 33, no. 4 (July 2005):521–44.

Jackson, Sherman, *Islam and the Black American: Looking Toward the Third Resurrection.* New York: Oxford University Press, 2005.

Leonard, Isaksen K. "State, Culture and Religion: Political Action and Representation among South Asians in North America." *Diaspora* 9(1), 2000:21–38.

Leonard, Karen. *Muslims in the United States: The State of Research.* New York: Russell Sage Foundation, 2003.

Leonard, Karen, "American Muslim Politics." *Ethnicities* 3(2), 2003:147–81.

Metcalf, Barbara Daly, ed. *Making Muslim Space in North America and Europe.* Berkeley: University of California Press, 1996.

Mohammad-Arif, Amina. *Salaam America: South Asian Muslims in New York.* London: Anthem Press, 2002.

"Muslim Americans: Middle Class and Mostly Mainstream." Washington, DC: Pew Research Center, 2007.

Naff, Alexa. *Becoming American: The Early Arab Immigrant Experience.* Carbondale: Southern Illinois University Press, 1985.

Nomani, Asra Q. *Standing Alone in Mecca: An American Woman's Struggle for the Soul of Islam.* San Francisco: Harper, 2005.

Nyang, Suleyman S. *Islam in the United States of America*. Chicago: ABC International Group, 1999.

Project MAPS: Muslims in the American Public Square/Zogby International. "American Muslim Poll" Nov/Dec 2001. www.projectmaps.com/pmreport.pdf.

Project MAPS: Muslims in the American Public Square/Zogby International. "American Muslim Poll 2004: Muslims in the American Public Square: Shifting Political Winds & Fallout from 9/11, Afghanistan, and Iraq." October 2004. www.projectmaps.com/AMP2004report.pdf

Safi, Omid, ed. *Progressive Muslims: On Justice, Gender and Pluralism*. London: One World Publications, 2005.

Smith, Jane I. *Islam in America*. New York: Columbia University Press, 1999.

Smith, Tom W. *Estimating The Muslim Population in the United States*. New York: The American Jewish Committee, 2001.

Suleiman, Michael W., ed. *Arabs in America: Building a New Future*. Philadelphia: Temple University Press, 1999.

Wadud, Amina. *Inside the Gender Jihad: Women's Reform in ISLAM*. Oxford: Oneworld Publications, 2006.

Wadud, Amina. *Qur'an and Woman: Rereading the Sacred Text from a Woman's Perspective*. New York: Oxford University Press, 1999.

Walbridge, Linda S. *Without Forgetting the Imam: Lebanese Shi'ism in an American Community*. Detroit: Wayne State University Press, 1997.

Westerlund, David, ed. *Sufism in Europe and North America*. New York: Routledge Curzon, 2004. Ch. 3, pp. 36–63.

Wolfe, Michael, ed. *Taking Back Islam: American Muslims Reclaim Their Faith*. Emmaus, Pennsylvania: Rodale Inc. & Belief Net, 2002.

X, Malcolm. *The End of White World Supremacy: Four Speeches*. New York: Arcade Publishers, 1989.

INDEX

Pages indicating entry titles are in **bold type.**

Manji, Irshad, 521

marriage, **397–400**; al-Hibri, Azizah on, 686, 687; Arab Americans, 174, 398; American Muslim attitudes about, 924–48; interfaith, 497, 686; *mut'a* (temporary marriage), 229, 234. *See also* family law; sexuality

martyrdom, **400–401**; Al Qaradawi on, 42–43; of the Prophet Muhammad's grandson, Husayn, 90, 115, 428

Marvin X, 1075

Maryamiyya Sufi Order, **402–4**

Mattson, Ingrid, **404–5**; "American Muslims' 'Special obligation'," 881–82; conversion to Islam, 163; "How Muslims Use Islamic Paradigms to Define Americans," 794–805; participation in mainstream American Associations, 635; President, Islamic Society of North America, 287, 342

Mauritania, 735, 766

Mawdudi, Maulana, **405–7**, 894, 1119

McCloud, Amina, 686

Mecca, **407–8**; and Danish cartoon crisis, 124, 662; dietery rules and, 186; first "House of God," 427; Five Percenters, 257; location of, 554, 780; pagans in, 360; pilgrimage to Mecca (hajj), 150, 160, 302, 332, 498–500, 736; prayer and, 258–59; Prophet Muhammad in, 289, 331, 412, 427, 434–35, 468–69; in the Quran, 529; in *The Satanic Verses,* 547

media, broadcast, 104–6

media coverage, **408–10**; portrayal of Muslims in, 950. *See also* internet

media, print, 511–12

medicine, **410–11**; abortion, 6; early practice of, 560; Islamic Wellness Institute (NYC), 32; Muslims practicing, 560; and permissibility of euthanasia, 178–79

Medina, **411–13**; "Constitution" of, 180; Hijra, 289–90; pre-Islamic, 289; Prophet Muhammad in, 81, 119, 407, 435, 499, 542; and the Quran, 529–30; religious conflicts in, 496

Mernissi, Fatima, 247, 487

Message International Magazine, 330, 393, 410, **413–14**, 511

Mevlevi Sufi Order, 546, 605

Middle East, U.S. foreign policy in, **414–21**

Milestones along the Road (Qutb), 172, 362, 374. *See also* Qutb, Sayyid

military service, **421–22**; African American Muslims and, 630; conversion to Islam of non-Muslims in U.S., 421; fatwas addressing, 43, 242, 256, 824–25, 824–27

Million Man March, 133, 161, 239; 353

Minaret magazine, 161

minorities, ethnic, 57, 137, 293. *See also* Fiqh of minorities

minorities, Jewish, 358

minorities, Muslim in non-Muslim U.S.: community and, 151; *Dār al-Islām* and *Dār al harb,* 172; and First Amendment, 156; interpretation of faith by, 562; legal questions about, 70, 374, 376, 650, 701; and PATRIOT Act, 912; portrayal in movies and television, 293

minorities, non-Muslim religious, 137; acceptance by Islam, 651; and First Amendment, 156; in Muslim lands, 313–14, 374, 496, 891

Moaveni, Azadehi, 90, 324, 1066–71

Mohammed, W.D., **422–26**; American Society of Muslims and, 94, 133; and Gulf War, 423; and Malcolm X, 423, 425

Mohiuddin, Majid, 1075–77

Mojahedin-e Khalk Organizaton (Mek): and activism, 324

monotheism, 227, 231, 327, 460, 496, 711, 990–93, 1004

Moore, Daniel Abdal-Hayy, 162, 501, 1072–74

Moorish Science Temple of America (MSTA), **426–27**; and African American Muslim identity, 303; and Noble Drew Ali, 13, 52–53, 471, 587; and prohibition of alcohol, 49

Mos Def, 162, 283

mosques, **427–32**; architecture in American, 429–30; art in, 430; authority of, 43; calligraphy in, 430; in Detroit, 428–29; gender issues in, 429; holiday celebrations in, 427–28, 432; in Houston, 414; Islamic Society of North America (ISNA), 83

mosques history, **432–34**

Muhammad (Prophet), **434–38**; ethics, 1000; hijra, 90, 331, 435; in Mecca, 289, 331, 412, 435, 468–69; in Medina, 81, 119, 407, 499, 542

Muhammad Speaks (newspaper), **438**; Malcolm X, 434

Muhammad, Elijah, **438–40**

ABOUT THE CONTRIBUTORS

Mohammad A. Abderrazzaq is a Ph.D. student at Boston University.

Fatina Abdrabboh is a graduate student at Harvard University.

Muneer I. Ahmad is a Professor at American University, Washington College of Law.

Azra Aksamija is a Ph.D. student at MIT.

Omar Ali is a Ph.D. student at Harvard University.

Blain Auer is a Ph.D. student at Harvard University.

Margot Badran is a Senior Fellow at the Prince Alwaleed Center for Muslim-Christian Understanding at Georgetown University.

Osman Balkan is a graduate student at Reed College.

Salima Bhimani is a Ph.D. student at University of Toronto.

Vincent F. Biondo III is an Assistant Professor of Western Religious Traditions at California State University, Fresno.

Levi Bjork is a Ph.D. student at the University of Wisconsin.

Jesse Bradford is a Ph.D. student at Harvard University.

Priya Chandra is an independent scholar, Boston.

Ali Chaudrey is an independent scholar, London, UK.

Louis Abdellatif Cristillo is a Research Assistant Professor in the Department of International and Transcultural Studies at Barnard College, Columbia University.

Alexis Debat is a Senior Fellow and Director of the Program on Terrorism and National Security at the Nixon Center, Washington, D.C.

Pete DeWan is a Ph.D. student at Harvard University.

Alireza Doostdar is a Ph.D. student at Harvard University.

Talal Eid, an imam, is Director of the Islamic Institute of Boston.

Sarah Eltantawi is a Ph.D. student at Harvard University.

Mohammad Fadel is an Assistant Professor in the Faculty of Law at the University of Toronto.

Fatimah Fanusie is a Ph.D. student at Howard University.

Yousra Y. Fazili is a graduate student at Harvard University.

Andrew Finkelman is a Ph.D. student at Tufts University.

Nathan Fonder is a Ph.D. student at Harvard University.

Supriya Gandhi is a Ph.D. student at Harvard University.

Shiraz Hajiani is a Ph.D. student at the University of Chicago.

Juliane Hammer is an Assistant Professor of Islamic Studies at the University of North Carolina, Charlotte.

John Hebden is a graduate student at Harvard University.

Jon Heit is a graduate student at Harvard University.

Marcia Hermansen is a Professor of Theology at Loyola University, Chicago.

Sally Howell is a Ph.D. student at the University of Michigan.

Aziz Huq is Associate Counsel at the Brennan Center for Justice, New York University School of Law.

Milia Islam is an independent scholar affiliated with the Islamic Society of North America.

Zahra N. Jamal is a Ph.D. student at Harvard University.

Christiaan James is a graduate student at Harvard University.

Rameen Moshref Javid is Executive Director of Afghan Communicator in New York City.

Murad Kalam is an independent scholar, Silver Spring, Maryland.

Saeed A. Khan is on the faculty at Wayne State University.

Shamael Khan is a graduate student at Harvard University.

Abigail Krasner is a Ph.D. student at Harvard University.

al-Husein N. Madhany is a Ph.D. student at the University of Chicago.

Dahlia Mahmoud is an independent scholar, Arlington Virginia.

Gwen McCarter is a graduate student at Harvard University.

Shabana Mir is an independent scholar, Washington, D.C.

Majid Mohiuddin is an independent scholar, Baltimore, Maryland.

Precious Rasheeda Muhammad is an independent scholar, Newport News, Virginia.

Adil Najam is an Associate Professor of International Negotiation and Diplomacy at the Fletcher School of Law and Diplomacy, Tufts University.

Henry Newman is a graduate student at Harvard University.

Martin Nguyen is a Ph.D. student at Harvard University.

Sara Omar is a Ph.D. student at Harvard University.

Erzen Oncel is a Ph.D. student at Boston University.

Hussein Rashid is a Ph.D. student at Harvard University.

Nadia Roumani is a Research Fellow at the University of Southern California, Center for Religion and Civic Culture.

Marc Sageman is the Principal at Sageman Consulting, LLC.

Nahed Samour was a Fulbright scholar at Harvard University, 2005–2006, and is a Ph.D. student at Humboldt University, Berlin.

Saif Shah Mohammed is a graduate student at Harvard University.

Sohail Shakeri is an Adjunct Lecturer at Saddleback College and National University in Southern California.

Joseph Shamis is a graduate student at Harvard University.

Maryam Sharrieff is a graduate student at Harvard University.

Nadia Shoeb is a graduate student at Georgetown University.

Nabilah Siddiquee is a graduate student at Harvard University.

Nate Spannaus is a Ph.D. student at Harvard University.

Aaron Spevack is a Ph.D. student at Boston University.

Abdur-Rahman Syed is a Ph.D. student at Boston University.

Licsi Aniko Szatmari is a Ph.D. student at Harvard University.

Liyakat Takim is an Associate Professor of Islamic Studies at the University of Denver.

Robert Tappan is at the University of Virginia.

Emily Tucker is a graduate student at Harvard University.

Deniz Turker is a Ph.D. student at MIT.

Nada Unus is a graduate student at Harvard University.

Ryan Weimer is a graduate student at Harvard University.

Danna M. Weiss is a graduate student at Harvard University.

Svend A. White is a graduate student in Islamic Studies at the University of Georgia, Athens.

William Wininger is a graduate student at Harvard University.

Ahmet Yukleyen is an Assistant Professor of Anthropology at the University of Mississippi.

Travis Zadeh is a graduate student at Harvard University.